MANAGEMENT SYSTEMS

The Wiley Series in

MANAGEMENT AND ADMINISTRATION

ELWOOD S. BUFFA, *Advisory Editor*
University of California, Los Angeles

MANAGEMENT SYSTEMS, SECOND EDITION
Peter P. Schoderbek

OPERATIONS MANAGEMENT: PROBLEMS AND MODELS, SECOND EDITION
Elwood S. Buffa

PROBABILITY FOR MANAGEMENT DECISIONS
William R. King

PRINCIPLES OF MANAGEMENT: A MODERN APPROACH, THIRD EDITION
Henry H. Albers

MODERN PRODUCTION MANAGEMENT, THIRD EDITION
Elwood S. Buffa

CASES IN OPERATIONS MANAGEMENT: A SYSTEMS APPROACH
James L. McKenney and Richard S. Rosenbloom

ORGANIZATIONS: STRUCTURE AND BEHAVIOR, VOLUME I, SECOND EDITION
Joseph A. Litterer

ORGANIZATIONS: SYSTEMS, CONTROL AND ADAPTATION, VOLUME II
Joseph A. Litterer

MANAGEMENT AND ORGANIZATIONAL BEHAVIOR: A MULTIDIMENSIONAL APPROACH
Billy J. Hodge and Herbert J. Johnson

MATHEMATICAL PROGRAMMING: AN INTRODUCTION TO THE DESIGN AND APPLICATION OF OPTIMAL DECISION MACHINES
Claude McMillan

DECISION MAKING THROUGH OPERATIONS RESEARCH
Robert J. Thierauf and Richard A. Grosse

QUALITY CONTROL FOR MANAGERS & ENGINEERS
Elwood G. Kirkpatrick

PRODUCTION SYSTEMS: PLANNING, ANALYSIS AND CONTROL
James L. Riggs

SIMULATION MODELING: A GUIDE TO USING SIMSCRIPT
Forrest P. Wyman

BASIC STATISTICS FOR BUSINESS AND ECONOMICS
Paul G. Hoel and Raymond J. Jessen

BUSINESS AND ADMINISTRATIVE POLICY
Richard H. Buskirk

Peter P. Schoderbek

with the editorial collaboration of
Charles G. Schoderbek

MANAGEMENT SYSTEMS

SECOND EDITION

John Wiley & Sons, Inc.
New York/London/Sydney/Toronto

Library of Congress Catalogue Card Number: 70-147237

ISBN 0-471-76226-1

Printed in the United States of America

10 9 8 7 6 5 4 3 2 1

Preface

Since the publication of the first edition of this book, we have received numerous comments from its users, explaining how they handled or experimented with the subject matter. We are, indeed, grateful for all of these helpful comments. We, too, have discovered through experience the pressing need for further conceptualization in the management-systems field. The present edition reflects our further efforts to describe systems from our viewpoint as well as the viewpoints of others.

Since the inception of the first edition, notable advances have been made in the field. The newer selections acquaint the reader with some of the salient progress that has taken place in systems thinking and implementation. Some of the prognostications made in the earlier selections already have been realized while others have not yet reached fruition. Some of the new selections articulate the subject or present important aspects that were not noted in previous selections.

The Table of Contents shows a rearrangement of some of the material for the purpose of clarity and order of presentation. We hope the success that the senior editor (P.P.S.) experienced in his classes with the new ordering will be duplicated elsewhere.

As in the first edition, we have tried to present more than one side of controversial matters. Because the focus of the book has been refined and the allocation of space is still an important consideration, articles of notable merit in the first edition has to be excluded from this second edition.

Part One, "Systems—A Viewpoint," deals with the theoretical constructs needed for viewing systems and with the postulates of a general systems theory; with cybernetics as a particularized approach to systems; and with measurement, models, and simulation as the conceptual and processual vehicles for an examination of systems.

The basic assumption underlying this part is that systems is a way of looking at sets of interrelated parts rather than an assortment of tools and techniques. Consequently the conceptual framework of systems, as enunciated in the introduction and as projected in the readings, should be readily applicable to many diverse fields.

Of the various particularized approaches to systems, the cybernetic approach probably comes closest to satisfying the postulates of general systems theory. Elsewhere other approaches are mentioned, such as industrial dynamics, which studies feedback behavior in social systems.

Systems imply the utilization of models—plans for relating the ideational to the empirical world. One of the fundamental problems associated with any model is that of quantification or measurement. To appreciate the difficulties encountered in the construction of models (a necessary enterprise for scientific problem solving), we should examine the nature and problems of measurement. These four sections—systems concepts, cybernetics, measurement, and models and simulation—constitute the theoretical framework for the systems viewpoint.

In Part Two, attention is focused on *information* and *information systems*. Here information is used in its semantic sense. In order to develop planning and control systems and to aid in decision making, we are explicitly concerned with *meaning*, not with channel capacity and the like. This conception of information underscores the notion that something of value is being communicated to some individual or individuals in the organizational structure. It is of value precisely because it is needed to reduce uncertainty or ignorance. Since individuals, for the purpose of making decisions, must resort to multiple information sources, some type of system that filters, condenses, stores, and transmits all of this information must be evolved. And because this information system is organized for the use of managers in the firm, it appropriately has been labeled *management information systems*.

This part is mainly concerned with the totality of management information systems, their design, implementation, and control, their impact on the organizational structure, their use for decision making, the integration of the firm's various information centers into a holistic system, and other sundry functions.

Part Three discusses the application of systems concepts and techniques that purport to satisfy systems criteria and constraints. The initial section, dealing with industrial dynamics, attempts to qualify both as a philosophy and as a technique—as a philosophy, since it satisfies the postulates of general systems theory as presented in Part One, and as a technique for problem solving, since it treats the organization as a system with interaction and feedback.

PERT and PERT/Cost-type techniques, which by now have captured a rather large following of both practitioners and academic personnel, must surely be included in any discussion of systems application, not only because of their universal application to certain types of problems but also because of their adherence to at least several of the underlying elements of systems. We admit that we have a pronounced predilection for these specialized systems techniques.

This part also deals with real-time systems, especially with the specific applications as embodied in the SAGE and the SABRE systems. These perhaps overworked examples still serve as hallmarks of the excellent material available from these sources.

Finally, there are some prognostications of the future—by us and by the contributors. An examination of the prologue to the future in the first edition reveals that the same oracles are still at work. Consequently we have included the previous prologue and affirm, confidently and unequivocally, that we expect *more of the same.*

Peter P. Schoderbek
Charles G. Schoderbek

Contents

Part Two: Management Information Systems

Part Three: Systems Applications

INTRODUCTION: SYSTEMS—A VIEWPOINT

Until several decades ago, science for the most part remained fractionalized, with each discipline staunchly maintaining its own separate identity as well as developing its own esoteric language. Research in each of the disciplines followed the proven methods of breaking the wholes into parts and then analyzing the relationships among the parts. Because of seemingly fundamental differences between the physical and the behavioral sciences, it was thought that few if any of the research results of the natural sciences were applicable to the other sciences, if indeed the linguistic obstacles of the various disciplines could ever be surmounted.

However, independent researchers in a number of different fields have become increasingly aware that many of the problems under investigation were not at all unique to their particular discipline, and that other researchers in totally unrelated fields (apparently) were also much concerned with the same problems. In time it was learned that possible solutions to problems in a particular discipline could be arrived at only from a different discipline. Thus arose the impetus for the interdisciplinary approach. In its short life span it has already merited encomiums from scholars such as Ackoff, who remarks:

> In the last two decades we have witnessed the emergence of the "system" as a key concept in scientific research. Systems, of course, have been studied for centuries, but something new has been added. . . . The tendency to study systems as an entity rather than as a conglomeration of parts is consistent with the tendency in contemporary science no longer to isolate phenomena in narrowly confined contexts, but rather to open interaction for examination and to examine larger and larger slices of nature. Under the banner of *systems research* (and its many synonyms) we have also witnessed a convergence of many more specialized contemporary scientific developments. . . . These research pursuits and many others are being interwoven into a cooperative research effort involving an ever-widening spectrum of scientific and engineering disciplines. We are participating in what is probably the most comprehensive effort to attain a synthesis of scientific knowledge yet made.[1]

Alongside the movement toward an interdisciplinary approach to complex problems there had been another, attempting to discover the fundamental principles that underlie the science of systems. The systems approach implies a departure from the traditional analytical solution so successful with simpler problems. Because of the increasing complexities of various tasks it was no longer possible to consider isolated solutions. Instead, a holistic approach or a gestalt approach was found to be more profitable. This is the underlying notion behind systems, a framework from which one looks at the entire problematic universe instead of segmented portions thereof. In this way one can better conceptualize and analyze the interrelationships existing between the various interacting components of the system.

It is at this point that a diversity of opinions prevails concerning further elaboration of systems. Various specialized frameworks of the systems approaches can be found in the literature. Among the more popular are the general systems theory, cybernetic systems, information theory, and operations research. Figure 1 illustrates a possible ordering of these various systems approaches.

Each of the following approaches is a way of constructing one's own conceptual model of systems; thus, one may view

[1] Quoted by Ludwig von Bertalanffy, "General System Theory—A Critical Review," *General Systems*, 7 (1962), 1–20.

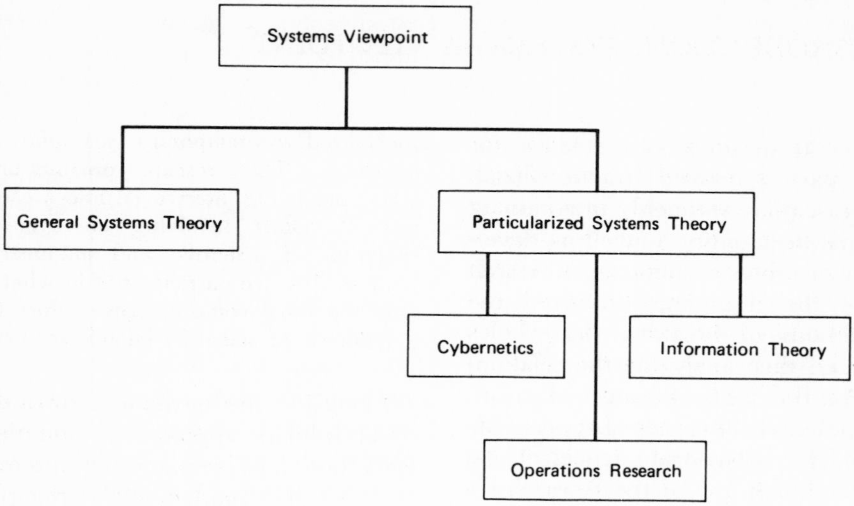

FIG. 1. Ordering of various systems approaches.

systems from a particularized systems approach such as cybernetics with its components of a selector, effector, and detector with some feedback mechanism between the parts. Likewise, one may utilize systems thinking within the framework of general systems theory. However, systems in general can also be subject to diverse interpretations. What constitutes a system? What are its characteristics? These are questions to which no definitive answer has yet been found. In attempting to derive generalizations valid for all systems theory, general systems theory must have recourse to the particularized systems enumerated above. An illustration of the generalizing process would be the law of growth derived from fields as varied as biology, crystallography, demography, and the like.

SYSTEMS CHARACTERISTICS

Of all the proponents of systems, C. West Churchman has given us perhaps one of the more logical expositions of the subject. He outlines five basic considerations concerning systems thinking.

1. Objectives of the total system and specifically the measure of performance of the system itself.
2. The systems environment.
3. The resources of the system.
4. The components of the system.
5. The management of the system.[2]

These five basic considerations are not meant to be all-inclusive, but even a cursory comparison with the basic system properties as outlined by other systems thinkers will reveal that most of these properties are included or implied in Churchman's delineation.

The above outline merits further consideration. Here a brief explanation will be given of each of the five points.

1. *Objectives.* By objectives of the system Churchman means those goals or ends toward which the system tends. Hence goal-seeking or teleology is a characteristic of systems. With mechanical systems the determination of objectives is not really difficult; with human systems, however, the task can be quite formidable. One must beware of the distinction (often a real one) between the *stated* objectives and the *real*

[2] See C. West Churchman, *The Systems Approach* (New York: Dalecort Press, 1968), Chapter 3.

objectives of the system. A student, to use Churchman's telling illustration, may give as his objective the attainment of knowledge while in fact his real objective may be the attainment of good scholastic grades. The test that Churchman proposes for distinguishing the real from the merely stated objective may be called the principle of primacy: will the system knowingly sacrifice other goals to obtain the stated objective? If the answer is yes, then the stated and real objectives are identical.

Objectives, however real, are in need of operationalization. Unless they are quantified in some manner, it will be impossible to measure the performance of the total system. In other words, one cannot state to what precise degree the system's objectives are being realized without having on hand some objective measure of the performance of the overall system.

Since objectives are realized only through the medium of activity, in evaluating objectives one should examine both the manifest and latent functions of any activity. Manifest functions are the intended and recognized consequences; latent functions are the unrecognized and unintended ones. Latent functions are unfortunately often overlooked in evaluating objectives.

2. *The Environment.* This constitutes all that is "outside" the system. This concept, though obvious on the surface, needs and does receive at Churchman's hands further clarification. Two features characterize the environment.

First, the environment includes all that lies outside the system's *control.* The system can do nothing, or relatively little, about the characteristics or behavior of the environment. Because of this the environment is considered to be "fixed" or the "given" to be incorporated into any system's problem. Second, the environment also includes all that *determines,* in part at least, the manner of the system's performance. Both features must be present simultaneously. The environment must be beyond the system's control and must also exert some determination on the system's performance. Implied here in the concept of environment are the notions of interrelation, interdependence, and interaction used so frequently by other proponents of systems. One can readily see that the concepts of inputs and outputs also have relevancy here, since the environment acts on the system and the system adapts to or reacts with the environment.

3. *The Resources.* These are all the means available to the system for the execution of the activities necessary for goal realization. Resources are inside the system; also unlike the environment, they include all the things that the system can *change* and use to its own advantage. The real resources of human systems are not only men, money, and equipment but also the opportunities (used or neglected) for the aggrandizement of the human and nonhuman resources of the system.

In a closed system all the resources are present at one time. Since no additional resources are available, the principle of *entropy,* which characterizes all closed systems, holds. In open systems, however, additional supplies of energy or resources can enter the system. Hence, the principle of entropy does not enter into the consideration of steady-state systems usually considered by business management.

4. *The Components.* By components Churchman means the missions, jobs, or activities the system must perform to realize its objectives. His concentration on functions rather than on structure or functional groups is well taken. Too often in formal organizations the traditional orientation is to the divisions, departments, and offices that appear in the accountant's ledger. By analyzing activities or missions, one can estimate the worth of the activity for the entire system. There appears to be no feasible way of estimating the worth of a department's performance for the total system.

The rationale behind this kind of thinking is the discovery of those components and activities whose measures of performance are in fact related to the measure of performance of the system's objectives. If all other elements are controlled for in an ideal case, then as the measure of performance of an activity increases, so should the measure of performance of the total system.

5. *The Management.* By systems management Churchman includes two basic functions: planning the system and controlling the system. Planning the system involves all the aspects of systems previously encountered, viz., its goals or objectives, its environment, its utilization of resources, and its components or activities.

Controlling the system involves both examination of the execution of the plans and planning for change. Managers must make sure that the plans as originally conceived and decided on are being executed; if not, then it must be discovered why not. This constitutes control in the most primary sense. In a secondary sense, control also concerns planning for change.

In any open system either substantial or partial, change is inevitable. Hence, in any ongoing system, plans must be subject to periodic review and reevaluation. Essential to all realistic planning, therefore, is the planning for a change of plans, since no manager or managers could possibly set down all the system objectives that are valid for all times and under all conditions; or could once and for all define the organizational environment so subject to constant change; or could permanently delineate all the relevant resources available to the organization; or could outline measures of performance that would never need improvement or updating.

Associated with the planning and control function of systems is the notion of information flow or *feedback,* so characteristic of cybernetic systems. Without adequate feedback the planning and control functions would be almost totally inadequate.

These five basic considerations of systems as proposed by Churchman seem to merit more consideration from students of systems. One needs no special course in logic to deduce from these basic premises other characteristics associated with systems, such as wholeness, order, and the like.

GENERAL SYSTEMS THEORY

When one delves into the literature on general systems, he is soon overwhelmed by the many and diverse characteristics that it seems to manifest. Obviously this is due to the many specialized systems that the systems theorists have investigated, whose traits are extrapolated to and predicated of general systems theory. Perhaps what one ought to search for first is some kind of synthesis of the underlying premises or assumptions of general systems theory; then and only then ought one to investigate the alleged characteristics of general systems, compiled from particularistic investigations. Such a synthesis was attempted by Kenneth Boulding, and the result is both informative and fascinating —informative because he does manage in a way to "get under" the system and see it at its grass roots; and fascinating because he does this detective work with good grace and humor.

According to Boulding, there are five basic premises that any general systems theorist would most probably subscribe to.[3] These premises could just as well have been labeled postulates (P), presuppositions, or value judgments. As such they are statements that one accepts without further proof, for no proof is needed or even, at times, possible. Whether they are all independent assumptions or whether some are corollaries themselves derived from one or more of the basic premises is left for the reader to decide. Even if the reader does not prefer to engage in the minute examination of the nature of each postulate, he will not fail to note that order is the order of the experiment.

P1. Order, regularity, and nonrandom-

[3] Kenneth Boulding, "General Systems As a Point of View," in Mihajlo D. Mesarovic (Ed.), *Views on General Systems Theory* (New York: John Wiley & Sons, 1964), pp. 25–38.

ness are preferable to lack of order or of regularity (= chaos) and to randomness.

The general systems theorist has a "rage for order." He will be fond of all those things that foster or manifest order.

P2. Orderliness in the empirical world makes the world good, interesting, and attractive to the systems theorist. "He loves regularity, his delight is in the law, and a law to him is a path through the jungle."

P3. There is order in the orderliness of the external or empirical world (order to the second degree)—a law about laws.

The general systems theorist is not only in search of order and law in the empirical world; he is in search of order in order, and of laws about laws.

P4. To establish order, quantification and mathematization are highly valuable aids.

Because these will enable the general systems theorist to pursue his unrelenting quest for order and law, he will use them "in season and out of season," always mindful that there may be (and are) empirical elements displaying order but still not amenable to quantification and mathematization.

P5. The search for order and law necessarily involves the quest for the empirical referents of this order and law.

The general systems man is not only a searcher of order in order and of laws about laws; he is in quest of the concrete and particularistic embodiments of the abstract order and formal law that he discovers.

The search for the empirical referents to abstract order and formal laws can begin from either one or the other of two starting points, the theoretical or empirical origins. The systems theorist can begin with some elegant mathematical relationship and then look around in the empirical world to see whether he can find something to match it, or he may begin with some carefully and patiently constructed empirical order in the world of experience and then look around in the abstract world of mathematics to discover some relationship that will help him to simplify it or to relate it to other laws with which he is conversant.

General systems theory then, like all of the true sciences, is grounded in a systematic search for law and order in the universe; unlike the other sciences, it tends to extend its search to a search for an order of order, a law of laws. It is for this reason that it can be called a *general* systems theory.

Having briefly considered some of the fundamental assumptions underlying general systems theory, one can then turn his attention to the many and varied characteristics that one or more systems theorists have attributed to general systems theory. Since GST has as yet no definitive body of doctrine (if it ever will),[4] one should be prepared to find little law or order in the characteristics of the systems theory that aims to search out order in order and to formulate a law of laws.

The following points do not comprise an all-inclusive list, nor do they constitute separate and distinct qualities. They do, however, reveal what theorists conceive as being the hallmarks of GST.[5]

1. INTERRELATIONSHIP AND INTERDEPENDENCE of objects, attributes, events, and the like. Every systems theory must take cognizance of the elements in the system, of the interrelationship existing between the various elements, and of the interdependence of the system components. Unrelated and independent elements can never constitute a system.

2. (W)HOLISM. The systems approach is not an analytical one, where the whole is broken down ("annihilating divisio") into its constituent parts and then each of

[4] The more general a science, the less content (body of doctrine) it will encompass. Mathematics owes its almost universal applicability to its amazingly contentless nature. Since GST aims to uncover the laws and order inherent in all systems, it ought to be the most contentless of all systems theories.

[5] Joseph A. Litterer, *Organizations: Systems, Control and Adaptation*, Vol. 2, 2nd ed. (New York: John Wiley & Sons, 1969), pp. 3–6.

the decomposed elements is studied in isolation; rather, it is a gestalt type of approach, attempting to view the whole with all its interrelated and interdependent parts in interaction. The system is not a reconstituted one (the whole is equal to the sum of its parts); it is an undivided one (the whole is greater than the sum of its parts).

3. GOAL-SEEKING. Systems embody interacting components. Interaction results in some final state or goal or an equilibrium position where the activities are conducive to goal attainment.

4. INPUTS AND OUTPUTS. All systems are dependent on some inputs for generating the activities that will ultimately result in goal attainment. All systems produce something (outputs) needed by other systems. In closed systems the inputs are determined once and for all; in open systems, additional inputs are admitted from the environment.

5. TRANSFORMATION. All systems are transformers of inputs into outputs. That which is received into the system is modified by the system so that the form of the output differs from that which was originally inputed.

6. ENTROPY. Adapted from the field of thermodynamics, entropy designates the state of a closed system where all the elements are in maximum disorder; the system is run down. For living systems, maximum entropy means death; for formal organizations, maximum entropy could mean a lack of all necessary information for running the system, or a maximum condition of disorganization.

7. REGULATION. This is a rather broad term and can mean many things to many men. If systems are sets of interrelated and interdependent components in interaction, then the interacting components must be regulated (Latin, regula = rule) in some fashion so that the systems objectives will ultimately be realized. In human organizations this implies the setting up of objectives and the determining of the activities that will result in goal fulfillment. This constitutes planning. Control implies that the original design for action will be adhered to and that all untoward deviations from the plan will be noted and corrected. *Feedback* is a requisite of all effective control. Some theorists distinguish further between adjustment, control, and learning.

8. HIERARCHY. Systems are generally complex wholes made up of smaller subsystems. The nesting of systems within other systems is what is meant by hierarchy.

9. DIFFERENTIATION. In complex systems, specialized units perform specialized systemic functions. This differentiation of functions by components is characteristic of all systems.

10. EQUIFINALITY. In open systems the same final state can be reached from several different starting points. (In living systems, death, the final state, can be arrived at from several initial starting positions.) One result can have different causes. Or to approach the subject from the opposite point of view, in open systems, an initial state can have various possible final states.

INFORMATION THEORY

In recent years the many claims regarding the importance of information theory and its applicability to the theory of business organizations have bordered on the extravagant. Since 1949, when the classic information theory was first formulated by Shannon and Weaver, the literature has grown by leaps and bounds. Already in 1953 F. L. Stumpers published a bibliography that contained some 800 entries, ranging from sophisticated analyses of radar systems and TV circuits to "crackpot speculations."[6] More recently the number of articles purporting to relate information theory to the business organization has noticeably increased.[7] This association of

[6] Anatol Rapoport, "The Promise and Pitfalls of Information Theory," *Behavioral Science,* I (1956), p. 303.

[7] See Norton M. Bedford and Mohamed Onsi,

information theory with business organizations undoubtedly arises from the frequent use of the word *information* in the business context. Here and there one speaks of management information system, accounting information, the information explosion, information for decision making, information control system, and so on. In most of these instances, the term *information* is equated with mere data acquisition, with the quality of data, its flow through the system, its functional characteristics, and the like. However, information theory as originally developed has little to do with these connotations. In classic theory, *information* is used in a very specialized sense: the amount of information contained in a particular message is a function of the number of messages that can be sent and the probability associated with each.

The basic insight that led Shannon and Weaver to develop a formal theory of communications was the realization that all the informational processes are essentially *selection* processes. When one seeks to obtain information of any sort, he must select from the available symbols (letters, words, and the like) in his vocabulary. In other words, the individual seeking information is faced with some kind of uncertainty. In the face of certainty (in a completely deterministic system, the probability is unity), no information can be conveyed to the individual. Thus, if one knows that in the English language the letter *q* is always followed by the letter *u*, then in the spelling of any specific English word in which the letter *q* appears, he will receive no information whatsoever when told that the next letter is a *u*. Likewise, if the reader can predict with certitude what his next sentence will say, he will not have acquired any information by its perusal. It is for this reason that information theory has been categorized as an extension of probability theory.

Information can be viewed as being related not only to a decrease in uncertainty but also to a decrease in ignorance.[8] Complete ignorance obviously precludes the transmission of any information. (If, for example, the previous sentence had by some strange connivance been printed in Arabic, most of the American readers would have derived no information therefrom.) To recapitulate, the amount of information conveyed can be measured by the resultant decrease in the uncertainty or the reduction in the ignorance. According to classical information theory, information is viewed as an entity that is neither true nor false, significant nor insignificant, reliable nor unreliable, accepted nor rejected. In no way is it related to semantics (meaning) or to effectiveness (results). It merely considers the *quantitative* aspects, the *how-much*ness of the uncertainty or ignorance reduction brought about by its communication.

In transmitting information there must be common agreement as to the language (symbols, phonemes, and the like) to be used. Specifically, both the sender and the receiver of information must agree on the set of symbols available in the language used. When the alternatives for selection are unknown, information is untransmissible. It is precisely this restriction that the alternatives for selection be known that makes possible the quantification of information. The larger the set of available alternatives for transmission, the greater the number of choices that can be made, the more uncertain the situation, and the more information that is needed to resolve the uncertainty. Thus one can see how information, selection, prediction, and uncertainty are all interrelated.

Information theory, it has been stated, can be regarded as an extension of probability theory. Since the receiver and the sender must both know the set of possible messages from which a particular one will be selected, a probability measure can be

"Measuring the Value of Information—An Information Theory Approach," *Management Services* (January-February, 1966), pp. 15–22.

[8] See T. F. Schouten, "Ignorance, Knowledge, and Information," in Colin Cherry (Ed.), *Information Theory* (New York: Academic Press, Inc., 1956), pp. 37–47.

assigned to each of the messages in the set. These assigned probabilities need not be equal, since in certain instances some messages will be more probable than others. For example, although in the English language there are twenty-six letters, not all have equal probabilities of occurrence. No great erudition is required to realize that the letter *z* will occur less frequently than the letter *e*. Consequently the probability of the former's occurrence will be less than that associated with the latter's. As a result, when *z* does appear, its informational content will be greater than when *e* occurs, since it does more to identify the word. In fact, it has been found that the letter *e* appears approximately 60 times more frequently than the letter *z*.[9]

To take account of differences in the *probability* of messages, a message is assigned a probability p when it is selected from a predetermined set of $1/p$ messages. The *amount of information* that must be transmitted for that message is then $\log_2 1/p$ or $-\log_2 p$. If all n messages have an equal probability of being chosen, then the probability of any of these is $p = 1/n$ and then $-\log_2 p = -\log_2 n$. If the probabilities assigned to n messages are $p_1, p_2, \ldots, p_n$, then the amounts of information associated with each message are $-\log_2 p_1$, $-\log_2 p_2, \ldots, -\log_2 p_n$.

Very seldom, however, is one concerned with a single message. Generally what is of interest is the capacity of the channel for generating messages and the average amount of information per message per channel. The average amount of such information from a particular source is generally given by the equation:

$$H = -(p_1\log_2 p_1 + p_2\log_2 p_2 + \ldots + p_n\log_2 p_n)$$

or more simply

$$\underset{i=1}{\overset{n}{H}} = \Sigma p_i(-\log_2 p_i)$$

[9] T. F. Schouten, p. 36. The frequency probabilities associated with letters in English messages are the feature of Edgar Allen Poe's classic story, "The Purloined Letter."

Since information theory is concerned with reducing the uncertainty associated with many possible outcomes, its focus on the *amount of information* is understandable and its prescinding from the semantics problem is justifiable.

One way to measure the amount of information in statements is to enumerate the number of possible outcomes that the statement eliminates. Thus, each time one of the alternatives is eliminated, one unit of information is communicated. When a small object like a coin is placed under one of 16 shells and the observer is asked to choose the shell under which the object is hidden, each time he chooses one shell, he eliminates one of the alternatives. Though this method could be used to advantage, it is not too practicable. It would be far more useful to be able to halve the number of alternatives each time, thus decreasing the number by a stated ratio instead of by absolute quantities. Reducing the alternatives from 16 to 15 would not be as dramatic as reducing the number to 8. Were halving the case, each time the number of alternatives is reduced, one unit of information would be gained. The unit of information that is generally used is the "bit," short for binary digit. A bit is the smallest amount of information possible, a single selection between two alternatives, as between ON or OFF, YES or NO, OPEN or CLOSED, 0 or 1. In fact, most computers use binary numbers for handling information, expressing the two alternatives as 0 and 1.

A central issue in information theory is, then, the number of bits required from among a predetermined set known to both the receiver and the source of information. One popular example is the game of Twenty Questions, in which the identity of a person is guessed through a series of questions, each of which is answered by a simple YES or NO. The first question, for instance, might be to decide whether the individual in question was a man or a woman. For these two alternatives one bit of information is all that is needed. If the selection process further required one to identify whether the person were either a man or a woman, living or dead, then for these four alternatives only two bits of information would be needed to make the selection. By the game's end the player would have acquired twenty bits of information.

Or suppose that there are four digits, 1, 2, 3, 4, all arranged in a column, and let us further suppose that the correct digit to be selected is the last one, 4. We ask the question, "Is the number chosen in the top half?" The response NO eliminates the numbers 1 and 2. With regard to the bottom half we again ask, "Is the number in the top half?" The answer NO eliminates the number 3 and enables one to identify the number 4 as the selected digit. So with four alternatives only two bits of information were required for positively identifying the correct item. In the same way only three bits of information would be needed to identify one item from among eight, four bits to identify one from sixteen, etc. For n alternatives the number of bits required would be $\log_2 n$.

> . . . Suppose that in front of me are eight letters, A through H, with a light over each. A distant sender has a switch for each letter, by which he can light the corresponding letter on my list. The sender presses his G button and my G light goes on. How many bits of information have been transmitted? The answer is three, since it requires three bits to select one signal from among eight. If our lists contained sixteen letters, the selection of one sign would represent four bits, and so on. If from sixteen signs the system could make 100 such four bit selections per minute, the system would be handling 400 bits per minute, or have an information rate of 400 bits per minute.[10]

In Figure 2 the relationship between the number of alternative choices and the number of bits is depicted.

[10] Alfred Kuhn, *The Study of Society: A Unified Approach* (Homewood, Ill.: Richard D. Irwin, Inc., and the Dorsey Press, Inc., 1963), p. 177.

Bits

1	2	3	4	5	6	7
2^1	2^2	2^3	2^4	2^5	2^6	2^7
(2)	(4)	(8)	(16)	(32)	(64)	(128)

Alternate Messages

FIG. 2. The Relationship Between the Number of Alternative Messages and the Number of Bits Needed to Move from Uncertainty to Certainty.

It should not be forgotten that information theory was initially developed for application in telecommunications, where it is both possible and feasible to compute the amount of information that can be transmitted over a wire or a radio band. For determining channel capacity it has indeed been of significant benefit. However, its utility when applied to other disciplines has been of doubtful value, and the not infrequent attempt to apply it to the business sector has been equally disappointing. In recent years some have endeavored to apply the formal theory to the fields of experimental psychology[11] and sociology,[12] decision making,[13] cybernetics, accounting,[14] and many other diverse situations.

> Results in the areas of the behavioral sciences and management have been rather meager, because the basic concepts of information theory are only analogous, not homologous, to those used in business. Besides, in the business and organization context, the problems are poorly conceptualized and confusedly defined. Unless the problem is known and accurately defined, it is impossible to establish information needs.[15]

[11] Colin Cherry, *On Human Communication* (New York: Science Editions, 1961).

[12] See Walter Buckley, *Sociology and Modern Systems Theory* (Englewood Cliffs, N.J.: Prentice-Hall, 1967).

[13] Russell L. Ackoff, "Toward A Behavioral Theory of Communication," *Management Science,* 4 (1957–1958), pp. 218–234.

[14] Norton M. Bedford and Mohamed Onsi, "Measuring the Value of Information—An Information Theory Approach," *Management Services* (January-February, 1966), pp. 15–22.

[15] Adrian M. McDonough, *Information Economics*

One of the underlying difficulties here seems to be the almost complete ignorance of the elements of the configuration available to the manager, that is, the set from which the messages describing the configuration from chaos are to be selected. Is this due to the multiplicity of channels encountered in the flow of management information or to the tendency of information to move "outside the channels" of communication? Thus it is no wonder that information theory to management information systems, and the like, has had only very restricted application. Rapoport succinctly summarizes this situation: "It is not hard to understand the disappointment with 'information theory' as a broad conceptual tool: the sound work is confined either to engineering or to rather trivial applications (rote learning, etc.); ambitious formulations remain vague."[16]

However, few accepted scientific concepts of today can boast of a noble and auspicious origin. The albeit modest results of information theory in settings other than engineering are therefore worthy of note. Rapoport duly notes:

> To many these results appear somewhat trivial. We do not agree. If information theory is to break out of its original habitat of bandwidths and modulations, a proper beginning must be made, which usually means a modest beginning. Experimental psychology had made this beginning possible. However, one must admit that the gap between this sort of experimentation and questions concerning the "flow of information" through human channels is enormous. So far no theory exists, to our knowledge, which attributes any sort of unambiguous measure to this "flow." . . . If there is such a thing as semantic information, it is based on an entirely different kind of "repertoire," which itself may be different for each recipient. . . . It is misleading in a crucial sense to view "information" as something that can be poured into an empty vessel, like a fluid or even like energy.[17]

and Management Systems (New York: McGraw-Hill Book Company, 1963), p. 48.

[16] Rapoport, p. 303.

[17] Rapoport, p. 306.

OPERATIONS RESEARCH AS A SYSTEMS APPROACH

If one were to single out the one technique that has aroused the most interest in the area of management during the last two decades, it would undoubtedly be that of operations research. Operations research (O.R.) has enjoyed a remarkable press with reputable and imaginative practitioners reporting from their richly diverse disciplines. Today a professional management meeting would hardly be considered complete unless it included at least one paper on the subject of operations research. A cursory examination of the talks given at recent seminars and symposia would reveal this fascination with that subject. Yet despite its almost total acceptance by management, a most perplexing feature is the disagreement as to the nature of the discipline. More often than not it is defined by its exponents in terms of its activities or with reference to the fields of application. An inkling of this somewhat confusing situation can be gotten by probing some of the pronouncements on the definitional aspect of the problem. Philip M. Morse of MIT, for instance, defined O.R. as

> . . . the application of the quantitative, theoretical, and experimental techniques of physical science to a new subject, operations. An operation is the pattern of activity of a group of men and machines doing an assigned, repetitive task.
>
> Horace C. Levinson has defined it as . . . an application of the method and spirit of scientific research to problems that arise in the general area of administration and organized activities. Its general purpose is to discover the most rational bases for action decisions.[18]

Other writers have been even more ambitious in their formulations. Stafford Beer defines operations research as

> the attack of modern science on complex problems arising in the direction and management

[18] Annesta R. Gardner, "What Is Operations Research?" *Dun's Review and Modern Industry* (December, 1955), p. 46.

of large systems of men, machines, materials, and money in industry, business, government and defense. Its distinctive approach is to develop a scientific model of the system, incorporating measurements of features such as chance and risk, with which to predict and compare the outcomes of alternative decisions, strategies or controls. Its purpose is to help management determine its policy and actions scientifically.[19]

Beer further elucidates the nature of the discipline:

Operational research, as has been seen, means doing science in the management sphere: the subject is not itself *a* science; it is a scientific profession. In turning now to the relevance of cybernetics, we encounter a science in its own right.[20]

Other equally notable scholars delineate the limits of O.R. in equally diffuse terms. The mathematician George Dantzig has this to say:

Operations research refers to the science of decision and its application. In its broad sense, the word *cybernetics,* the science of control, may be used in its stead.[21]

It comes as no great surprise to note that other writers have equated O.R. with the systems approach.

When one reexamines the ten previously enumerated assumptions underlying systems thinking, he would have to admit that despite its apparent affinity with the systems approach, operations research in the main provides basically a body of computational techniques. That the armamentarium of operations research methods, with its linear and dynamic programming, decision trees, queuing theory, transportation method, network analysis, and the use of simulation models, has been dramatically exploited in recent years there can be little doubt. These remain, however, but tools typically utilizing the computer.

The seemingly close identification of operations-research personnel with systems personnel probably stems from the fact that the former are frequently called on to deploy their skills in the design stage of a complex problem. They may be asked to construct models or modify existing ones or they may be involved in testing the effectiveness or boundaries of a system. In any event, operations-research personnel are generally called on first as trained observers to state the problem in explicit terms.

At the present stage of development, too little is known of operations-research principles that would provide the researcher with a blueprint for solving complex problems. One must admit, nevertheless, that the schematic representations of problems or the ingenious models employed could lead to better solutions. The decisions arrived at by the use of O.R. techniques can and do give optimal solutions according to formal theory, but they do not necessarily represent the way that the human operator behaves.[22] In the final analysis, the utility of a particular course of action must be determined subjectively by the human operator. It is precisely for this reason that the human element is retained in the system, since the operator's behavior cannot be incorporated into the system design. Even the contributions of formal organization theory purporting to describe the performance of the human operator are of little value to the systems designer, since the results tend to center about average

19 Stafford Beer, *Decision and Control* (John Wiley & Sons, Inc., 1966), p. 92.

20 Beer, p. 239.

21 George B. Dantzig, "Operations Research in the World of Today and Tomorrow," Office of Naval Research, January 1965; reprinted in *Operations Research Appreciation,* U.S. Army Management Engineering Training Agency, no date.

22 Beer lists three major limitations to classical decision theory: mathematical, methodological, and pragmatic. Regarding the mathematical limitation, he says that "it is mathematically impossible to optimize more than one variable of a situation at a time. That is to say, when a mathematical model has been set to maximize profit, or to minimize cost, that is *all* that it can do. If the management has other objectives than this, they have to be handled by other means." See Stafford Beer, *Decision and Control* (New York: John Wiley & Sons, 1966), p. 219.

performance and not performance of a given operator in a given situation. Since our understanding of the human component in systems is at present inadequate, it is necessary to resort to techniques that lie closer to the empirical world.

The techniques employed by the O.R. personnel are principally directed to operations management at the lower organizational levels. Of these techniques a favorite is simulation, concerned as it is with the construction of models of real-life situations. Although it has potential for assisting top management, it is in this very area that simulation has achieved but meager and mediocre results. For the most part, business problems are exceeding complex, and any worthwhile representation of the reality would require exceedingly complex models. In general, models can incorporate only a small segment of the important variables that need to be considered for problem solution. Consequently, the more complex the problem, the more difficult it will be to simulate realistically the business situation.

One must not forget that the utility of any model is rather stringently tied to the values assigned to the variables employed. The identification and valuation of these variables imply that these can be quantified. This may not always be the case. When dealing with the human equation, operational researchers may believe that it is better to quantify than not to quantify behavior. However, the businessman, with his own intuition based on previous experience, believes that he is on as safe a ground as the model builder. For unless the problem under investigation is well structured (and most of them are not), simulation is of little value. The value of simulation seems to diminish in proportion as it deals with behavioral variables. In this "no man's land" the manager, in the absence of scientific rigor, will base his judgment on his own observations, experience, and intuition.

What assumptions underlie the applications of operations research? Here, fortunately, there seems to be more general agreement. Probably the most fundamental element in O.R. is the need to quantify the business problem under study. Without quantification, operations research is unthinkable. Quantification itself implies that the problem is susceptible to rational treatment. There can be no question that the operations researcher is on unassailable ground when the problem he encounters is essentially quantitative and of a repetitive nature. Indeed, this is the one area most susceptible to O.R. applications. However, decisions that are more of a judgmental nature, less prone to recur with regularity, and more affected by environmental factors are not readily subject to quantification, and as long as decision making takes place within such an environment, decisions made are not prone to neat measurements. Likewise, at the upper levels of the organizational hierarchy, where decisions are typically unprogrammed and subjected to undetermined influences of competition; political overtones; changes in income tax structures; regulations by the SEC, FTC, and others; cold war consequences; labor-union maneuvering; irregular economic fluctuations, and so forth, the relevance of operational research for ensuing decisions still needs to be demonstrated.

When viewed in the light of the basic assumptions and characteristics of systems, operations research does not appear to conform too closely to the accepted pattern. It would be more realistic to view it as a technique rather than as a conceptual equivalent of systems.

The consideration of cybernetics and its relationship to systems and to operational research and the like will be taken up in a later chapter.

Part One

THE SYSTEMS CONCEPT

SECTION I

GENERAL SYSTEMS THEORY

In recent years theoretical model building has become a respectable and profitable undertaking in many a science. Not only have the mathematical and the physical sciences availed themselves of this analytical tool but particularly economics and the behavioral sciences, psychology and sociology, have increasingly turned to theoretical models for insightful analysis of data and utilitarian prognosis of trends. Past experience has too often only underscored the proposition that unless research is coupled with a theoretical framework it tends to lie fallow and produces nothing more than ephemeral results.

The general systems theory, as sketched by Kenneth Boulding in the first selection, is a skeleton of science that provides the framework or theoretical systemic structure by which the various disciplines can be oriented, integrated, and rendered mutually productive. As such, it lies midway between the highly abstract generalizations of mathematics and the lower level generalizations of specific disciplines. That the need for such a theory is acutely felt today is evidenced by the increasing difficulty in relevant communication between practitioners of related disciplines and the proliferation of interdisciplinary institutes.

Two possible approaches to the organization of general systems are proposed and illustrated. The first approach, that of general phenomena selectivity, is concerned both with the phenomena common to many disciplines and with the construction of theoretical models relevant to these phenomena. Population theory, interaction theory, growth theory, and information theory serve to illustrate this first approach.

The other approach to general systems theory is a more ambitious and difficult one. It involves the rearrangement of theoretical systems and logic constructs into an ordered hierarchy of complexity with levels of abstraction appropriate for each. Since the present state of knowledge varies considerably from science to science and within related fields of the same science, a multilevel approach, though somewhat unwieldy, seems to be the only viable avenue at present for realistic appraisal and productive research in scientific areas.

The nine levels of systematic analysis, arranged in order of increasing complexity, are summarized by Boulding as the levels of frameworks, clockworks, thermostat, cell, plant, animal, man, social organization, and transcendence. Unfortunately, adequate theoretical models have not yet advanced past the fourth level though it is only the last, the transcendental level, that will provide the framework on which basic principles of particular disciplines will be orderly and coherently organized. It is, hopefully, the general systems theory that will point the way to future scientific progress and to workable future goals.

It it is true that "nothing is so practical as a good theory," then a consideration of systemic and developmental models as key tools for diagnosis and prognosis is in order. However, such consideration necessitates the explicit formulation of concepts upon which models are built and the exposition of their underlying assumptions and limitations. Robert Chin's article takes up in sequential order an analysis of system models with their basic concepts of boundary, tension, equilibrium and feedback.

The concept of system utilized in this selection encompasses the components of organization, interaction, interdependency, and integration of parts.

Although open systems ("systems in contact with their environment and with input and output across system boundaries") are the type found in the extramental world, the utility of employing closed systems ("systems assumed to have little if any commerce across the boundary") must not be underestimated. Open systems are by their nature generally too complex for even simple analysis. By opening a closed system to new environmental variables, then closing it, we can observe and evaluate what really goes on.

An intersystem model consisting of two open systems joined to each other by conjunctive or disjunctive connectives is proposed by Chin as a workable tool for the agent of change since it retains all the advantages of system analysis and adds others of its own.

While systemic models have at times been associated with static analysis, developmental models designedly assume constant change and development over time. Fundamental to these models are the notions of direction or goal, states, forms of progression, forces, and potentiality, all of which are defined and illustrated in the text.

The practitioner and the social scientist generally view their fields quite differently. While the social scientist is primarily interested in learning *how* a system changes under varying conditions, the practitioner is principally set on understanding a system *in order to* change it. But to do so he must have some theory of change. Since such a theory incorporates elements from both systemic and developmental models in a framework specifically oriented to the processes facilitating change, it becomes increasingly evident that an adequate study of models is incumbent upon the practitioner.

Useful as they are, models have only limited applicability. Being abstractions of concrete events from the real world, their usefulness is in proportion to the goodness of fit between the model and the events abstracted.

Related to system theory is organizational theory. The final selection, by William Scott, presents an overview and appraisal of such a theory. To best accomplish his objectives the author has employed the historical approach, thus putting some of the concepts previously touched on in a somewhat different light, the better to relate and contrast them.

The classical theory of organization, dealing almost exclusively with the anatomy of formal organization, revolves around four pivotal concepts: the division of labor, scalar and functional processes, formal structure, and control span. Useful as these concepts are, they are of limited value for they ignore the interplay of personalities, informal groupings, interorganizational conflict, and the ever present decision-making processes.

The neoclassical theory has attempted to compensate for some of these deficiencies. Assuming as given the four basic elements of the formal organization as embedded in the classical theory, it has systematically incorporated the contributions of the behavioral sciences concerning informal organization, and it has also studied the impact of the informal group upon the formal structure. Typical of this "human relations movement" are the Hawthorne studies and many current works in industrial sociology. Like the classical theory, the neoclassical, though making use of relevant psychological and sociological findings, has also been found wanting.

Modern organizational theory is system theory. In his treatment of modern organizational theory, Scott details the various elements involved in system analysis. Although he singles out as systemic components the interdependency of parts, the linkage processes, and organizational goals, he nevertheless includes in his explanation both formal and informal organization, role theory, equilibrium and steady state, cybernetics, decision-making processes, and diverse organizational goals. Thus we see that modern organizational theory relates to the general systems theory advanced by Kenneth Boulding in the first selection in the present section, being an approximation to the level of social organization (the eighth level).

Does modern organizational theory have a future? A promising one? Scott believes that it does. Just as physics, economics, and sociology passed through an early macro stage in which schemes of broad extent were conceived, to be followed by a micro stage in which analysis dealt with parts of the organization, and then finally moved into another macro, holistic, systems period, so too will administrative science. The early classical theory of organization employed the macro approach, the neoclassical, the micro approach, whereas modern organizational theory is based on a holistic, a macro point of view. The latter's potential indeed appears great!

No consideration of systems would be complete without a look at the view projected by those who find systems theory unsatisfactory. Such a viewpoint is presented in the final selection by D. C. Phillips, who after examining various features of general systems theory, finds it wanting. The following five points are discussed.

Systems theorists, Phillips recounts, do not appreciate sufficiently the history of their theory. Systems theory really harkens back to Hegelian philosophy and integral in this organicist conception of the world was the theory of internal relations. This theory asserted that entities are altered by the various relationships into which they enter. However, modern philosophy, with its critical distinction between *defining* and *accompanying* characteristics, rejects the Hegelian theory of internal relations, since it would make all characteristics of an object *defining* characteristics. This is untenable. Many of the characteristics of an object are but accompanying characteristics. Furthermore, it cannot be proven that every characteristic *must be* a *defining* characteristic. Even when one prescinds from the truth or falsity of the theory of internal relations, the corollary to be drawn from it would demonstrate that all knowledge is impossible. For to understand an object, one would necessarily need to know all of its defining characteristics, since these make it precisely what it is. But since according to the theory every object is related to everything else in the world and all relationships are necessarily defining, one would need to know all the relationships with which the object enters into in the rest of the universe. This is not only ridiculous, it is impossible. Consequently, the theory of internal relations from which the corollary was logically inferred is untenable.

Other corollaries have been derived from the theory of internal relations: the whole is greater than the sum of its parts, the whole determines the nature of the parts, the parts cannot be understood in isolation from the whole, and the parts are interdependent. Some of these, however, may be supportable on other grounds.

Systems theories do not specify precisely what is meant by a *system*. Phillips certainly touches on a sensitive point here. Unfortunately, many advocates of systems propagate definitions that are extremely vague, obtuse, or tautological. The logical implications of these definitions are often never considered. The crucial problems of all systems center around how to conceive of systems in a clear and logically consistent way, how to define the system boundaries, and how to segregate the system under study from other systems without violating the basic premise of all systems thinking. Much additional deeper and serious thinking still remains to be done in systems theory.

The third point scored by Phillips is the vagueness of what is to be included in systems theory. The systems literature cited does show much confusion on the part of systems theorists. We ourselves admit to finding similar embarrassment in Bertalanffy's identification of seven bodies of systems theory. Not all of those mentioned are of the same level of abstraction or generalization nor of the same general type. It is hard to uncover any criterion by which these seven were included and all others excluded. Why is factor analysis, a very useful mathematical technique used to advantage by the behavioral and biological sciences, included along with general systems theory? Why should industrial dynamics or operations research not be included? In the introduction a first approximation of a classification of systems theory was attempted. There a distinction was made between systems theory, general systems theory, and some of the more specialized systems theories.

It was felt that at this early stage of systems development, general systems theory as currently advocated cannot yet be equated with the general discipline that draws its principles from all existing systems. Too little is still known of systems and of the particularized systems theories to warrant such a generalized systems theory.

Modern systems theory apparently developed out of the dissatisfaction experienced, especially by biologists, with the traditional mechanistic or analytical method of studying complex systems. At certain levels of complexity it was found that emergent properties appear that cannot be predicted from the study of the less complex levels. Phillips contends that this problem of emergence is not as insoluble as the advocates of general systems imagine. Every mechanistic explanation stipulates two conditions: a knowledge of the law or laws applicable to the system, and a knowledge of the initial systemic conditions. For the more complex systems encountered in biology, it may be extremely difficult to satisfy or realize these basic conditions. However, it has yet to be demonstrated that in principle these two tasks are impossible.

In dealing with the question of emergence, failure to consider the logical difficulty that the possession of an emergent property cannot possibly be deduced from premises that make no reference to the property lies at the heart of the problem. Because of this logical impossibility, not only does the mechanistic method fail to handle the problem satisfactorily but also, so must every other method.

The fifth point that Phillips makes can also serve as a conclusion to the article —general systems theory is not a scientific theory. One of the hallmarks of any scientific theory is its predictive ability. General systems theorists explain *post factum* what has happened; the predictions made before the event are too vague even to be refuted. This state of affairs was admitted by Bertalanffy himself in 1962. However, it is to be hoped that some progress has been made in the ensuing years.

1. GENERAL SYSTEMS THEORY—THE SKELETON OF SCIENCE

Kenneth E. Boulding *

General Systems Theory [1] is a name which has come into use to describe a level of theoretical model-building which lies somewhere between the highly generalized constructions of pure mathematics and the specific theories of the specialized disciplines. Mathematics attempts to organize highly general relationships into a coherent system, a system however which does not have any necessary connections with the "real" world around us. It studies all thinkable relationships abstracted from any concrete situation or body of empirical knowledge. It is not even confined to "quantitative" relationships narrowly defined—indeed, the development of a mathematics of quality and structure is already on the way, even though it is not as far advanced as the "classical" mathematics of quantity and number. Nevertheless because in a sense mathematics contains all theories it contains none; it is the language of theory, but it does not give us the content. At the other extreme we have the separate disciplines and sciences, with their separate bodies of theory. Each discipline corresponds to a certain segment of the empirical world, and each develops theories which have particular applicability to its own empirical segment. Physics, Chemistry, Biology, Psychology, Sociology, Economics and so on all carve out for themselves certain elements of the experience of man and develop theories and patterns of activity (research) which yield satisfaction in understanding, and which are appropriate to their special segments.

In recent years increasing need has been felt for a body of systematic theoretical constructs which will discuss the general relationships of the empirical world. This is the quest of General Systems Theory. It does not seek, of course, to establish a single, self-contained "general theory of practically everything" which will replace all the special theories of particular disciplines. Such a theory would be almost without content, for we always pay for generality by sacrificing content, and all we can say about practically everything is almost nothing. Somewhere however between the specific that has no meaning and the general that has no content there must be, for each purpose and at each level of abstraction, an optimum degree of generality. It is the contention of the General Systems Theorists that this optimum degree of generality in theory is not always reached by the particular sciences. The objectives of General Systems Theory then can be set out with varying degrees of ambition and confidence. At a low level of ambition but with a high degree of confidence it aims to point out similarities in the theoretical constructions of different disciplines, where these exist, and to develop theoretical models having applicability to at least two different fields of study. At a higher level of ambition, but with perhaps a lower degree of confidence it hopes to develop something like a "spectrum" of theories—a system of systems which may perform the function of a "gestalt" in theoretical construction. Such "gestalts" in special fields have been of great value in directing research towards the gaps which they reveal. Thus the periodic table of elements in chemistry directed research for many decades towards the discovery of unknown elements to fill gaps in the table until the table was com-

SOURCE: *Management Science* (April, 1956), pp. 197–208. Reprinted by permission of the Institute of Management Science.

* University of Colorado.

[1] The name and many of the ideas are to be credited to L. von Bertalanffy, who is not, however, to be held accountable for the ideas of the present author! For a general discussion of Bertalanffy's ideas see "General System Theory: A New Approach to Unity of Science," *Human Biology*, Dec., 1951, Vol. 23, pp. 302–361.

pletely filled. Similarly a "system of systems" might be of value in directing the attention of theorists towards gaps in theoretical models, and might even be of value in pointing towards methods of filling them.

The need for general systems theory is accentuated by the present sociological situation in science. Knowledge is not something which exists and grows in the abstract. It is a function of human organisms and of social organization. Knowledge, that is to say, is always what somebody knows: the most perfect transcript of knowledge in writing is not knowledge if nobody knows it. Knowledge however grows by the receipt of meaningful information—that is, by the intake of messages by a knower which are capable of reorganizing his knowledge. We will quietly duck the question as to what reorganizations constitute "growth" of knowledge by defining "semantic growth" of knowledge as those reorganizations which can profitably be talked about, in writing or speech, by the Right People. Science, that is to say, is what can be talked about profitably by scientists in their role as scientists. The crisis of science today arises because of the increasing difficulty of such profitable talk among scientists as a whole. Specialization has outrun Trade, communication between the disciples becomes increasingly difficult, and the Republic of Learning is breaking up into isolated subcultures with only tenuous lines of communication between them—a situation which threatens intellectual civil war. The reason for this breakup in the body of knowledge is that in the course of specialization the receptors of information themselves become specialized. Hence physicists only talk to physicists, economists to economists—worse still, nuclear physicists only talk to nuclear physicists and econometricians to econometricians. One wonders sometimes if science will not grind to a stop in an assemblage of walled-in hermits, each mumbling to himself words in a private language that only he can understand. In these days the arts may have beaten the sciences to this desert of mutual unintelligibility, but that may be merely because the swift intuitions of art reach the future faster than the plodding leg work of the scientist. The more science breaks into sub-groups, and the less communication is possible among the disciplines, however, the greater chance there is that the total growth of knowledge is being slowed down by the loss of relevant communications. The spread of specialized deafness means that someone who ought to know something that someone else knows isn't able to find it out for lack of generalized ears.

It is one of the main objectives of General Systems Theory to develop these generalized ears, and by developing a framework of general theory to enable one specialist to catch relevant communications from others. Thus the economist who realizes the strong formal similarity between utility theory in economics and field theory in physics [2] is probably in a better position to learn from the physicists than one who does not. Similarly a specialist who works with the growth concept—whether the crystallographer, the virologist, the cytologist, the physiologist, the psychologist, the sociologist or the economist—will be more sensitive to the contributions of other fields if he is aware of the many similarities of the growth process in widely different empirical fields.

There is not much doubt about the demand for general systems theory under one brand name or another. It is a little more embarrassing to inquire into the supply. Does any of it exist, and if so where? What is the chance of getting more of it, and if so, how? The situation might be described as promising and in ferment, though it is not wholly clear what is being promised or brewed. Something which might be called an "interdisciplinary movement" has been abroad for some time. The first signs of this are usually the development of hybrid disciplines. Thus physical chemistry emerged in the third quarter of the nineteenth century, social psychology in the second quarter of the twentieth. In the physical and biological sciences the list of hybrid disciplines is now quite long—biophysics, biochemistry, astrophysics are all well established. In the social sciences social anthropology is fairly well established, economic psychology and economic sociology are just beginning. There are signs, even, that Political Economy, which died in infancy some hundred years ago, may have a re-birth.

In recent years there has been an additional development of great interest in the form of

[2] See A. G. Pikler, Utility Theories in Field Physics and Mathematical Economics, *British Journal for the Philosophy of Science*, 1955, Vol. 5, pp. 47 and 303.

"multisexual" interdisciplines. The hybrid disciplines, as their hyphenated names indicate, come from two respectable and honest academic parents. The newer interdisciplines have a much more varied and occasionally even obscure ancestry, and result from the reorganization of material from many different fields of study. Cybernetics, for instance, comes out of electrical engineering, neurophysiology, physics, biology, with even a dash of economics. Information theory, which originated in communications engineering, has important applications in many fields stretching from biology to the social sciences. Organization theory comes out of economics, sociology, engineering, physiology, and Management Science itself is an equally multidisciplinary product.

On the more empirical and practical side the interdisciplinary movement is reflected in the development of interdepartmental institutes of many kinds. Some of these find their basis of unity in the empirical field which they study, such as institutes of industrial relations, of public administration, of international affairs, and so on. Others are organized around the application of a common methodology to many different fields and problems, such as the Survey Research Center and the Group Dynamics Center at the University of Michigan. Even more important than these visible developments, perhaps, though harder to perceive and identify, is a growing dissatisfaction in many departments, especially at the level of graduate study, with the existing traditional theoretical backgrounds for the empirical studies which form the major part of the output of Ph.D. theses. To take but a single example from the field with which I am most familiar. It is traditional for studies of labor relations, money and banking, and foreign investment to come out of departments of economics. Many of the needed theoretical models and frameworks in these fields, however, do not come out of "economic theory" as this is usually taught, but from sociology, social psychology, and cultural anthropology. Students in the department of economics however rarely get a chance to become acquainted with these theoretical models, which may be relevant to their studies, and they become impatient with economic theory, much of which may not be relevant.

It is clear that there is a good deal of interdisciplinary excitement abroad. If this excitement is to be productive, however, it must operate within a certain framework of coherence. It is all too easy for the interdisciplinary to degenerate into the undisciplined. If the interdisciplinary movement, therefore, is not to lose that sense of form and structure which is the "discipline" involved in the various separate disciplines, it should develop a structure of its own. This I conceive to be the great task of general systems theory. For the rest of this paper, therefore, I propose to look at some possible ways in which general systems theory might be structured.

Two possible approaches to the organization of general systems theory suggest themselves, which are to be thought of as complementary rather than competitive, or at least as two roads each of which is worth exploring. The first approach is to look over the empirical universe and to pick out certain general *phenomena* which are found in many different disciplines, and to seek to build up general theoretical models relevant to these phenomena. The second approach is to arrange the empirical fields in a hierarchy of complexity of organization of their basic "individual" or unit of behavior, and to try to develop a level of abstraction appropriate to each.

Some examples of the first approach will serve to clarify it, without pretending to be exhaustive. In almost all disciplines, for instance, we find examples of populations—aggregates of individuals conforming to a common definition, to which individuals are added (born) and subtracted (die) and in which the age of the individual is a relevant and identifiable variable. These populations exhibit dynamic movements of their own, which can frequently be described by fairly simple systems of difference equations. The populations of different species also exhibit dynamic interactions among themselves, as in the theory of Volterra. Models of population change and interaction cut across a great many different fields—ecological systems in biology, capital theory in economics which deals with populations of "goods," social ecology, and even certain problems of statistical mechanics. In all these fields population change, both in absolute numbers and in structure, can be discussed in terms of birth and survival functions relating numbers of births and of deaths in specific age groups to various aspects of the system. In all these fields the interaction of population can be discussed in terms of competitive, complementary, or parasitic relationships among populations of different species, whether the species consist of animals, commodities, social classes or molecules.

Another phenomenon of almost universal significance for all disciplines is that of the interaction of an "individual" of some kind with its environment. Every discipline studies some kind of "individual"—electron, atom, molecule, crystal, virus, cell, plant, animal, man, family, tribe, state, church, firm, corporation, university, and so on. Each of these individuals exhibits "behavior," action, or change, and this behavior is considered to be related in some way to the environment of the individual—that is, with other individuals with which it comes into contact or into some relationship. Each individual is thought of as consisting of a structure or complex of individuals of the order immediately below it—atoms are an arrangement of protons and electrons, molecules of atoms, cells of molecules, plants, animals and men of cells, social organizations of men. The "behavior" of each individual is "explained" by the structure and arrangement of the lower individuals of which it is composed, or by certain principles of equilibrium or homeostasis according to which certain "states" of the individual are "preferred." Behavior is described in terms of the restoration of these preferred states when they are disturbed by changes in the environment.

Another phenomenon of universal significance is growth. Growth theory is in a sense a subdivision of the theory of individual "behavior," growth being one important aspect of behavior. Nevertheless there are important differences between equilibrium theory and growth theory, which perhaps warrant giving growth theory a special category. There is hardly a science in which the growth phenomenon does not have some importance, and though there is a great difference in complexity between the growth of crystals, embryos, and societies, many of the principles and concepts which are important at the lower levels are also illuminating at higher levels. Some growth phenomena can be dealt with in terms of relatively simple population models, the solution of which yields growth curves of single variables. At the more complex levels structural problems become dominant and the complex interrelationships between growth and form are the focus of interest. All growth phenomena are sufficiently alike however to suggest that a general theory of growth is by no means an impossibility.[3]

Another aspect of the theory of the individual and also of interrelationships among individuals which might be singled out for special treatment is the theory of information and communication. The information concept as developed by Shannon has had interesting applications outside its original field of electrical engineering. It is not adequate, of course, to deal with problems involving the semantic level of communication. At the biological level however the information concept may serve to develop general notions of structuredness and abstract measures of organization which give us, as it were, a third basic dimension beyond mass and energy. Communication and information processes are found in a wide variety of empirical situations, and are unquestionably essential in the development of organization, both in the biological and the social world.

These various approaches to general systems through various aspects of the empirical world may lead ultimately to something like a general field theory of the dynamics of action and interaction. This, however, is a long way ahead.

A second possible approach to general systems theory is through the arrangement of theoretical systems and constructs in a hierarchy of complexity, roughly corresponding to the complexity of the "individuals" of the various empirical fields. This approach is more systematic than the first, leading towards a "system of systems." It may not replace the first entirely, however, as there may always be important theoretical concepts and constructs lying outside the systematic framework. I suggest below a possible arrangement of "levels" of theoretical discourse.

(i) The first level is that of the static structure. It might be called the level of *frameworks.* This is the geography and anatomy of the universe—the patterns of electrons around a nucleus, the pattern of atoms in a molecular formula, the arrangement of atoms in a crystal, the anatomy of the gene, the cell, the plant, the animal, the mapping of the earth, the solar system, the astronomical universe. The accurate description of these frameworks is the

[3] See "Towards a General Theory of Growth" by K. E. Boulding, *Canadian Journal of Economics and Political Science,* 19 Aug. 1953, 326–340.

beginning of organized theoretical knowledge in almost any field, for without accuracy in this description of static relationships no accurate functional or dynamic theory is possible. Thus the Copernican revolution was really the discovery of a new static framework for the solar system which permitted a simpler description of its dynamics.

(ii) The next level of systematic analysis is that of the simple dynamic system with predetermined, necessary motions. This might be called the level of *clockworks*. The solar system itself is of course the great clock of the universe from man's point of view, and the deliciously exact predictions of the astronomers are a testimony to the excellence of the clock which they study. Simple machines such as the lever and the pulley, even quite complicated machines like steam engines and dynamos fall mostly under this category. The greater part of the theoretical structure of physics, chemistry, and even of economics falls into this category. Two special cases might be noted. Simple equilibrium systems really fall into the dynamic category, as every equilibrium system must be considered as a limiting case of a dynamic system, and its stability cannot be determined except from the properties of its parent dynamic system. Stochastic dynamic systems leading to equilibria, for all their complexity, also fall into this group of systems; such is the modern view of the atom and even of the molecule, each position or part of the system being given with a certain degree of probability, the whole nevertheless exhibiting a determinate structure. Two types of analytical method are important here, which we may call, with the usage of the economists, comparative statics and true dynamics. In comparative statics we compare two equilibrium positions of the system under different values for the basic parameters. These equilibrium positions are usually expressed as the solution of a set of simultaneous equations. The method of comparative statics is to compare the solutions when the parameters of the equations are changed. Most simple mechanical problems are solved in this way. In true dynamics on the other hand we exhibit the system as a set of difference or differential equations, which are then solved in the form of an explicit function of each variable with time. Such a system may reach a position of stationary equilibrium, or it may not—there are plenty of examples of explosive dynamic systems, a very simple one being the growth of a sum at compound interest! Most physical and chemical reactions and most social systems do in fact exhibit a tendency to equilibrium—otherwise the world would have exploded or imploded long ago.

(iii) The next level is that of the control mechanism or cybernetic system, which might be nicknamed the level of the *thermostat*. This differs from the simple stable equilibrium system mainly in the fact that the transmission and interpretation of information is an essential part of the system. As a result of this the equilibrium position is not merely determined by the equations of the system, but the system will move to the maintenance of any *given* equilibrium, within limits. Thus the thermostat will maintain *any* temperature at which it can be set; the equilibrium temperature of the system is not determined solely by its equations. The trick here of course is that the essential variable of the dynamic system is the *difference* between an "observed" or "recorded" value of the maintained variable and its "ideal" value. If this difference is not zero the system moves so as to diminish it; thus the furnace sends up heat when the temperature as recorded is "too cold" and is turned off when the recorded temperature is "too hot." The homeostasis model, which is of such importance in physiology, is an example of a cybernetic mechanism, and such mechanisms exist through the whole empirical world of the biologist and the social scientist.

(iv) The fourth level is that of the "open system," or self-maintaining structure. This is the level at which life begins to differentiate itself from not-life: it might be called the level of the *cell*. Something like an open system exists, of course, even in physico-chemical equilibrium systems; atomic structures maintain themselves in the midst of a throughput of electrons, molecular structures maintain themselves in the midst of a throughput of atoms. Flames and rivers likewise are essentially open systems of a very simple kind. As we pass up the scale of complexity of organization towards living systems, however, the property of self-maintenance of structure in the midst of a throughput of material becomes of dominant importance. An atom or a molecule can presumably exist without throughput: the existence of even the simplest living organism is inconceivable without ingestion, excretion and metabolic exchange.

Closely connected with the property of self-maintenance is the property of self-reproduction. It may be, indeed, that self-reproduction is a more primitive or "lower level" system than the open system, and that the gene and the virus, for instance, may be able to reproduce themselves without being open systems. It is not perhaps an important question at what point in the scale of increasing complexity "life" begins. What is clear, however, is that by the time we have got to systems which both reproduce themselves and maintain themselves in the midst of a throughput of material and energy, we have something to which it would be hard to deny the title of "life."

(v) The fifth level might be called the genetic-societal level; it is typified by the *plant,* and it dominates the empirical world of the botanist. The outstanding characteristics of these systems are first, a division of labor among cells to form a cell-society with differentiated and mutually dependent parts (roots, leaves, seeds, etc.), and second, a sharp differentiation between the genotype and the phenotype, associated with the phenomenon of equifinal or "blueprinted" growth. At this level there are no highly specialized sense organs and information receptors are diffuse and incapable of much throughput of information—it is doubtful whether a tree can distinguish much more than light from dark, long days from short days, cold from hot.

(vi) As we move upward from the plant world towards the animal kingdom we gradually pass over into a new level, the "animal" level, characterized by increased mobility, teleological behavior, and self-awareness. Here we have the development of specialized information-receptors (eyes, ears, etc.) leading to an enormous increase in the intake of information; we have also a great development of nervous systems, leading ultimately to the brain, as an organizer of the information intake into a knowledge structure or "image." Increasingly as we ascend the scale of animal life, behavior is response not to a specific stimulus but to an "image" or knowledge structure or view of the environment as a whole. This image is of course determined ultimately by information received into the organism; the relation between the receipt of information and the building up of an image however is exceedingly complex. It is not a simple piling up or accumulation of information received, although this frequently happens, but a structuring of information into something essentially different from the information itself. After the image structure is well established most information received produces very little change in the image—it goes through the loose structure, as it were, without hitting it, much as a sub-atomic particle might go through an atom without hitting anything. Sometimes however the information is "captured" by the image and added to it, and sometimes the information hits some kind of a "nucleus" of the image and a reorganization takes place, with far reaching and radical changes in behavior in apparent response to what seems like a very small stimulus. The difficulties in the prediction of the behavior of these systems arises largely because of this intervention of the image between the stimulus and the response.

(vii) The next level is the "human" level, that is of the individual human being considered as a system. In addition to all, or nearly all, of the characteristics of animal systems man possesses self-consciousness, which is something different from mere awareness. His image, besides being much more complex than that even of the higher animals, has a self-reflexive quality—he not only knows, but knows that he knows. This property is probably bound up with the phenomenon of language and symbolism. It is the capacity for speech—the ability to produce, absorb, and interpret *symbols,* as opposed to mere signs like the warning cry of an animal—which most clearly marks man off from his humbler brethren. Man is distinguished from the animals also by a much more elaborate image of time and relationship; man is probably the only organization that knows that it dies, that contemplates in its behavior a whole life span, and more than a life span. Man exists not only in time and space but in history, and his behavior is profoundly affected by his view of the time process in which he stands.

(viii) Because of the vital importance for the individual man of symbolic images and behavior based on them it is not easy to separate clearly the level of the individual human organism from the next level, that of social organizations. In spite of the occasional stories of feral children raised by animals, man isolated from his fellows is practically unknown. So essential is the symbolic image in human behavior that one suspects that a truly isolated man would not be "human" in the usually accepted sense, though he would be potentially human. Nevertheless it is convenient for some purposes to distinguish the individual human as a system from the social systems which surround him, and in this sense social organizations may be said to constitute another level of organization. The unit of such systems is not perhaps the person—the individual human as such—but the "role"—that part of the person which is concerned with the organization or situation in question, and it is tempting to define social organizations, or almost any social system, as a set of roles tied together with channels of communication. The interrelations of the role and the person however can never be completely neglected—a square person in a round role may become a little rounder, but he also makes the role squarer, and the perception of a role is affected by the personalities of those who have occupied it in the past. At this level we must concern ourselves with the content and meaning of messages, the nature and dimensions of value systems, the transcription of images into a historical record, the subtle symbolizations of art, music, and poetry, and the complex gamut of human emotion. The empirical universe here is human life and society in all its complexity and richness.

(ix) To complete the structure of systems we should add a final turret for transcendental systems, even if we may be accused at this point of having built Babel to the clouds. There are however the ultimates and absolutes and the inescapable unknowables, and they also exhibit systematic structure and relationship. It will be a sad day for man when nobody is allowed to ask questions that do not have any answers.

One advantage of exhibiting a hierarchy of systems in this way is that it gives us some idea of the present gaps in both theoretical and empirical knowledge. Adequate theoretical models extend up to about the fourth level, and not much beyond. Empirical knowledge is deficient at practically all levels. Thus at the level of the static structure, fairly adequate descriptive models are available for geography, chemistry, geology, anatomy, and descriptive social science. Even at this simplest level, however, the problem of the adequate description of complex structures is still far from solved. The theory of indexing and cataloguing, for instance, is only in its infancy. Librarians are fairly good at cataloguing books, chemists have begun to catalogue structural formulae, and anthropologists have begun to catalogue culture traits. The cataloguing of events, ideas, theories, statistics, and empirical data has hardly begun. The very multiplication of records however as time goes on will force us into much more adequate cataloguing and reference systems than we now have. This is perhaps the major unsolved theoretical problem at the level of the static structure. In the empirical field there are still great areas where static structures are very imperfectly known, although knowledge is advancing rapidly, thanks to new probing devices such as the electron microscope. The anatomy of that part of the empirical world which lies between the large molecule and the cell however, is still obscure at many points. It is precisely this area however—which includes, for instance, the gene and the virus—that holds the secret of life, and until its anatomy is made clear the nature of the functional systems which are involved will inevitably be obscure.

The level of the "clockwork" is the level of "classical" natural science, especially physics and astronomy, and is probably the most completely developed level in the present state of knowledge, especially if we extend the concept to include the field theory and stochastic models of modern physics. Even here however there are important gaps, especially at the higher empirical levels. There is much yet to be known about the sheer mechanics of cells and nervous systems, of brains and of societies.

Beyond the second level adequate theoretical models get scarcer. The last few years have seen great developments at the third and fourth levels. The theory of control mechanisms ("thermostats") has established itself as the new discipline of cybernetics, and the theory of self-maintaining systems or "open systems" likewise has made rapid strides. We could hardly maintain however that much more than a beginning had been made in these fields. We know very little about the cybernetics of genes and genetic systems, for instance, and still less about the control mechanisms involved in the mental and social world. Similarly the processes of self-maintenance remain essentially mysterious at many points, and although the theoretical possibility of constructing a self-maintaining machine which would be a true open system has been suggested, we seem to be a long way from the actual construction of such a mechanical similitude of life.

Beyond the fourth level it may be doubted whether we have as yet even the rudiments of theoretical systems. The intricate machinery of growth by which the genetic complex organizes the matter around it is almost a complete mystery. Up to now, whatever the future may hold, only God can make a tree. In the face of living systems we are almost helpless; we can occasionally cooperate with systems which we do not understand: we cannot even begin to reproduce them. The ambiguous status of medicine, hovering as it does uneasily between magic and science, is a testimony to the state of systematic knowledge in this area. As we move up the scale the absence of the appropriate theoretical systems becomes ever more noticeable. We can hardly conceive ourselves constructing a system which would be in any recognizable sense "aware," much less self-conscious. Nevertheless as we move towards the human and societal level a curious thing happens: the fact that we have, as it were, an inside track, and that we ourselves *are* the systems which we are studying, enables us to utilize systems which we do not really understand. It is almost inconceivable that we should make a machine that would make a poem: nevertheless, poems *are* made by fools like us by processes which are largely hidden from us. The kind of knowledge and skill that we have at the symbolic level is very different from that which we have at lower levels—it is like, shall we say, the "knowhow" of the gene as compared with the knowhow of the biologist. Nevertheless it is a real kind of knowledge and it is the source of the creative achievements of man as artist, writer, architect, and composer.

Perhaps one of the most valuable uses of the above scheme is to prevent us from accepting as final a level of theoretical analysis which is below the level of the empirical world which we are investigating. Because, in a sense, each level incorporates all those below it, much valuable information and insights can be obtained by applying low-level systems to high-level subject matter. Thus most of the theoretical schemes of the social sciences are still at level (ii), just rising now to (iii), although the subject matter clearly involves level (viii). Economics, for instance, is still largely a "mechanics of utility and self-interest," in Jevons' masterly phrase. Its theoretical and mathematical base is drawn largely from the level of simple equilibrium theory and dynamic mechanisms. It has hardly begun to use concepts such as information which are appropriate at level (iii), and makes no use of higher level systems. Furthermore, with this crude apparatus it has achieved a modicum of success, in the sense that anybody trying to manipulate an economic system is almost certain to be better off if he knows some economics than if he doesn't. Nevertheless at some point progress in economics is going to depend on its ability to break out of these low-level systems, useful as they are as first approximations, and utilize systems which are more directly appropriate to its universe—when, of course, these systems are discovered. Many other examples could be given—the wholly inappropriate use in psychoanalytic theory, for instance, of the concept of energy, and the long inability of psychology to break loose from a sterile stimulus-response model.

Finally, the above scheme might serve as a mild word of warning even to Management Science. This new discipline represents an important breakaway from overly simple mechanical models in the theory of organization and control. Its emphasis on communication systems and organizational structure, on principles of homeostasis and growth, on decision processes under uncertainty, is carrying us far beyond the simple models of maximizing behavior of even ten years ago. This advance in the level of theoretical analysis is bound to lead to more powerful and fruitful systems. Nevertheless we must never quite forget that even these advances do not carry us much beyond the third and fourth levels, and that in dealing with human personalities and organizations we are dealing with systems in the empirical world far beyond our ability to formulate. We should not be wholly surprised, therefore, if our simpler systems, for all their importance and validity, occasionally let us down.

I chose the subtitle of my paper with some eye to its possible overtones of meaning. General Systems Theory is the skeleton of science in the sense that it aims to provide a framework or structure of systems on which to hang the flesh and blood of particular disciplines and particular subject matters in an orderly and coherent corpus of knowledge. It is also, however, something of a skeleton in a cupboard—the cupboard in this case being the unwillingness of science to admit the very low level of its successes in systematization, and its tendency to shut the door on problems and subject matters which do not fit easily into simple mechanical schemes. Science, for all its successes, still has a very long way to go. General Systems Theory may at times be an embarrassment in pointing out how very far we still have to go, and in deflating excessive philosophical claims for overly simple systems. It also may be helpful however in pointing out to some extent *where* we have to go. The skeleton must come out of the cupboard before its dry bones can live.

2. THE UTILITY OF SYSTEM MODELS AND DEVELOPMENTAL MODELS FOR PRACTITIONERS [1]

ROBERT CHIN [2]

All practitioners have ways of thinking about and figuring out situations of change. These ways are embodied in the concepts with which they apprehend the dynamics of the client-system they are working with, their relationship to it, and their processes of helping with its change. For example, the change-agent encounters resistance, defense mechanisms, readiness to change, adaptation, adjustment, maladjustment, integration, disintegration, growth, development, and maturation as well as deterioration. He uses concepts such as these to sort out the processes and mechanisms at work. And necessarily so. No practitioner can carry on thought processes without such concepts; indeed, no observations or diagnoses are ever made on "raw facts," because facts are really observations made within a set of concepts. But lurking behind concepts such as the ones stated above are assumptions about how the parts of the client-system fit together and how they change. For instance, "Let things alone, and natural laws (of economics, politics, personality, etc.) will work things out in the long run." "It is only human nature to resist change." "Every organization is always trying to improve its ways of working." Or, in more technical forms, we have assumptions such as: "The adjustment of the personality to its inner forces as well as adaptation to its environment is the sign of a healthy personality." "The coordination and integration of the departments of an organization is the task of the executive." "Conflict is an index of malintegration, or of change." "Inhibiting forces against growth must be removed."

It is clear that each of the above concepts conceals a different assumption about how events achieve stability and change, and how anyone can or cannot help change along. Can we make these assumptions explicit? Yes, we can and we must. The behavioral scientist does exactly this by constructing a simplified *model* of human events and of his tool concepts. By simplifying he can analyze his thoughts and concepts, and see in turn where the congruities and discrepancies occur between these and actual events. He becomes at once the observer, analyzer and modifier of the system [3] of concepts he is using.

The purpose of this paper is to present concepts relevant to, and the benefits to be gained from using, a "system" model and a "developmental" model in thinking about human events. These models provide "mind-holds" to the practitioner in his diagnosis. They are, therefore, of practical significance to him. This suggests one essential meaning of the oft-quoted and rarely explained phrase that "nothing is so practical as a good theory." We will try to show how the "system" and "developmental" approaches provide key tools for a diagnosis of persons, groups, organizations, and communities for purposes of change. In doing so, we shall state succinctly the central notions of each model, probably sacrificing some technical elegance and exactness in the process. We shall not overburden the reader with citations of the voluminous

[1] SOURCE: *The Planning of Change*, by Warren G. Bennis, Kenneth D. Benne, and Robert Chin, © 1961, Holt, Rinehart and Winston, Inc., New York. Pp. 201–214. Reprinted by permission.

[2] Boston University.

[3] "System" is used here as any organized and coherent body of knowledge. Later we shall use the term in a more specific meaning.

set of articles from which this paper is drawn.

We postulate that the same models can be used in diagnosing different sizes of the units of human interactions—the person, the group, the organization, and the community.

One further prefatory word. We need to keep in mind the difference between an "analytic" model and a model of concrete events or cases. For our purposes, *an analytic model* is a constructed simplification of some part of reality that retains only those features regarded as essential for relating similar processes whenever and wherever they occur. *A concrete model* is based on an analytic model, but uses more of the content of actual cases, though it is still a simplification designed to reveal the essential features of some range of cases. As Hagen [4] puts it: "An explicitly defined analytic model helps the theorist to recognize what factors are being taken into account and *what relationships among them are assumed* and hence to know the basis of his conclusions. The advantages are ones of both exclusion and inclusion. A model lessens the danger of overlooking the indirect effects of a change of a relationship" (our italics). We mention this distinction since we find a dual usage that has plagued behavioral scientists, for they themselves keep getting their feet entangled. We get mixed up in analyzing "the small group as a system" (analytic) and a school committee as a small group (concrete) or a national social system (analytic) and the American social system (concrete) or an organizational system (analytic) and the organization of a glue factory (concrete). In this paper, we will move back and forth between the analytic usage of "model" and the "model" of the concrete case, hopefully with awareness of when we are involved in a semantic shift.

THE "SYSTEM" MODEL

Psychologists, sociologists, anthropologists, economists, and political scientists have been "discovering" and using the system model. In so doing, they find intimations of an exhilarating "unity" of science, because the system models used by biological and physical scientists seem to be exactly similar. Thus, the system model is regarded by some system theorists as universally applicable to physical and social events, and to human relationships in small or large units.

[4] E. Hagen, chapter on "Theory of Social Change," unpublished manuscript.

The terms or concepts that are a part of the system model are "boundary," "stress or tension," "equilibrium," and "feedback." All these terms are related to "open system," "closed system," and "intersystem" models. We shall first define these concepts, illustrate their meaning, and then point out how they can be used by the change-agent as aids in observing, analyzing, or diagnosing—and perhaps intervening in—concrete situations.

The Major Terms

System. Laymen sometimes say, "you can't beat the system" (economic or political), or "he is a product of the system" (juvenile delinquent or Soviet citizen). But readers of social science writings will find the term used in a rather more specific way. It is used as an abbreviated term for a longer phrase that the reader is asked to supply. The "economic system" might be read as: "we treat price indices, employment figures, etc., as if they were closely interdependent with each other and we temporarily leave out unusual or external events, such as the discovery of a new gold mine." Or in talking about juvenile delinquency in "system" terms, the sociologists choose to treat the lower-class values, lack of job opportunities, ragged parental images, as interrelated with each other, in back-and-forth cause-and-effect fashion, as determinants of delinquent behavior. Or the industrial sociologist may regard the factory as a "social system," as people working together in relative isolation from the outside, in order to examine what goes on in interactions and interdependencies of the people, their positions, and other variables. In our descriptions and analyses of a particular concrete system, we can recognize the shadowy figure of some such analytic model of "system."

The analytic model of system demands that we treat the phenomena and the concepts for organizing the phenomena as if there existed organization, interaction, interdependency, and integration of parts and elements. System analysis assumes structure and stability within some arbitrarily sliced and frozen time period.

It is helpful to visualize a system [5] by drawing a large circle. We place elements, parts, variables, inside the circle as the components, and draw lines among the components. The lines may be thought of as rubber bands or springs, which stretch or contract as the forces increase or decrease. Outside the circle is the environment, where we place all other factors which impinge upon the system.

Boundary. In order to specify what is inside or outside the system, we need to define its "boundary" line. The boundary of a system may exist physically: a tightly corked vacuum bottle, the skin of a person, the number of people in a group, etc. But, in addition, we may delimit the system in a less tangible way, by placing our boundary according to what variables are being focused upon. We can construct a system consisting of the multiple roles of a person, or a system composed of varied roles among members in a small work group, or a system interrelating roles in a family. The components or variables used are roles, acts, expectations, communications, influence and power relationships, and so forth, and not necessarily persons.

The operational definition of *boundary* is: the line forming a closed circle around selected variables, where there is less interchange of energy (or communication, etc.) *across* the line of the circle than *within* the delimiting circle. The multiple systems of a community may have boundaries that do or do not coincide. For example, treating the power relationships may require a boundary line different from that for the system of interpersonal likes or dislikes in a community. In small groups we tend to draw the same boundary line for the multiple systems of power, communications, leadership, and so on, a major advantage for purposes of study.

In diagnosing we tentatively assign a boundary, examine what is happening inside the system and then readjust the boundary, if necessary. We examine explicitly whether or not the "relevant" factors are accounted for within the system, an immensely practical way of deciding upon relevance. Also, we are free to limit ruthlessly, and neglect some factors temporarily, thus reducing the number of considerations necessary to be kept in mind at one time. The variables left outside the system, in the "environment" of the system, can be introduced one or more at a time to see the effects, if any, on the interrelationship of the variables within the system.

Tension, Stress, Strain, and Conflict. Because the components within a system are different from each other, are not perfectly integrated, or are changing and reacting to change, or because outside disturbances occur, we need ways of dealing with these differences. The differences lead to varying degrees of tension within the system. *Examples:* males are not like females, foremen see things differently from workers and from executives, children in a family grow, a committee has to work with a new chairman, a change in the market condition requires a new sales response from a factory. To restate the above examples in conceptual terms: we find built-in differences, gaps of ignorance, misperceptions, or differential perceptions, internal changes in a component, reactive adjustments and defenses, and the requirements of system survival generating tensions. Tensions that are internal and arise out of the structural arrangements of the system may be called *stresses and strains* of the system. When tensions gang up and become more or less sharply opposed along the lines of two or more components, we have *conflict.*

A word of warning. The presence of tensions, stresses or strains, and conflict within the system often are reacted to by people in the system as if they were shameful and must be done away with. Tension reduction, relief of stress and strain, and conflict resolution become the working goals of practitioners but sometimes at the price of overlooking the possibility of increasing tensions and conflict in order to facilitate creativity, innovation, and social change. System analysts have been accused of being conservative and even reactionary in assuming that a social system always tends to reduce tension, resist innovation, abhor deviancy and change. It is obvious, however, that tension and conflict are "in" any system, and that no living system exists without tension. Whether these facts of life in a system are to be abhorred or welcomed is determined by attitudes or value judgments not derivable from system theory as such.

The identification of and analysis of how tensions operate in a system are by all odds

[5] A useful visual aid for "system" can be constructed by using paper clips (elements) and rubber bands (tensions) mounted on a peg board. Shifting of the position of a clip demonstrates the interdependency of all the clips' positions, and their shifting relationships.

the major utility of system analysis for practitioners of change. The dynamics of a living system are exposed for observation through utilizing the concepts of tension, stress and strain, and conflict. These tensions lead to activities of two kinds: those which do not affect the structure of the system (dynamics), and those which directly alter the structure itself (system change).

Equilibrium and "Steady State." A system is assumed to have a tendency to achieve a balance among the various forces operating within and upon it. Two terms have been used to denote two different ideas about balance. When the balance is thought of as a fixed point or level, it is called "equilibrium." "Steady state," on the other hand, is the term recently used to describe the balanced relationship of parts that is not dependent upon any fixed equilibrium point or level.

Our body temperature is the classic illustration of a fixed level (98.6° F.), while the functional relationship between work units in a factory, regardless of the level of production, represents a steady state. For the sake of simplicity, we shall henceforth stretch the term "equilibrium" to cover both types of balance, to include also the idea of "steady state."

There are many kinds of equilibria. A *stationary equilibrium* exists when there is a fixed point or level of balance to which the system returns after a disturbance. We rarely find such instances in human relationships. A *dynamic equilibrium* exists when the equilibrium shifts to a new position of balance after disturbance. Among examples of the latter, we can observe a *neutral* type of situation. *Example:* a ball on a flat plane. A small push moves it to a new position, and it again comes to rest. *Example:* a farming community. A new plow is introduced and is easily incorporated into its agricultural methods. A new level of agricultural production is placidly achieved. A *stable type of situation* exists where the forces that produced the initial equilibrium are so powerful that any new force must be extremely strong before any movement to a new position can be achieved. *Example:* a ball in the bottom of a goblet. *Example:* an organization encrusted with tradition or with clearly articulated and entrenched roles is not easily upset by minor events. An *unstable type of situation* is tense and precarious. A small disturbance produces large and rapid movements to a new position. *Example:* a ball balanced on the rims of two goblets placed side by side. *Example:* an organization with a precarious and tense balance between two modes of leadership style. A small disturbance can cause a large swing to one direction and a new position of equilibrium. *Example:* a community's balance of power between ethnic groups may be such that a "minor" disturbance can produce an upheaval and movement to a different balance of power.

A system in equilibrium reacts to outside impingements by: (1) resisting the influence of the disturbance, refusing to acknowledge its existence, or by building a protective wall against the intrusion, and by other defensive maneuvers. *Example:* A small group refuses to talk about a troublesome problem of unequal power distribution raised by a member. (2) By resisting the disturbance through bringing into operation the homeostatic forces that restore or re-create a balance. The small group talks about the troublesome problem of a member and convinces him that it is not "really" a problem. (3) By accommodating the disturbances through achieving a new equilibrium. Talking about the problem may result in a shift in power relationships among members of the group.

The concepts of equilibrium (and steady state) lead to some questions to guide a practitioner's diagnosis.

1. What are the conditions conducive to the achievement of an equilibrium in this case? Are there internal or external factors producing these forces? What is their quality and tempo?
2. Does the case of the client-system represent one of the typical situations of equilibrium? How does judgment on this point affect intervention strategy? If the practitioner feels the situation is tense and precarious, he should be more cautious in intervention than in a situation of stable type.
3. Can the practitioner identify the parts of the system that represent greatest readiness to change, and the greatest resistance to and defense against change? Can he understand the functions of any variable in relation to all other variables? Can he derive some sense of the direction in which the client system is moving, and separate those forces attempting to restore an old equilibrium and those pushing toward a new equilibrium state?

Feedback. Concrete systems are never closed off completely. They have inputs and outputs across the boundary; they are affected by and in turn affect the environment. While affecting the environment, a process we call output, systems gather information about how they are doing. Such information is then fed back into the system as input to guide and steer its operations. This process is called feedback. The "discovery" of feedback has led to radical inventions in the physical world in designing self-guiding and self-correcting instruments. It has also become a major concept in the behavioral sciences, and a central tool in the practitioner's social technology. *Example:* In reaching for a cigarette we pick up tactile and visual cues that are used to guide our arm and finger movements. *Example:* Our interpersonal communications are guided and corrected by our picking up of effect cues from the communicatees. *Example:* Improving the feedback process of a client system will allow for self-steering or corrective action to be taken by him or it. In fact, the single most important improvement the change-agent can help a client system to achieve is to increase its diagnostic sensitivity to the effects of its own actions upon others. Programs in sensitivity training attempt to increase or unblock the feedback processes of persons; a methodological skill with wider applicability and longer-lasting significance than solving the immediate problem at hand. In diagnosing a client system, the practitioner asks: What are its feedback procedures? How adequate are they? What blocks their effective use? Is it lack of skill in gathering data, or in coding and utilizing the information?

Open and Closed Systems

All living systems are open systems—systems in contact with their environment, with input and output across system boundaries. What then is the use of talking about a closed system? What *is* a closed system? It means that the system is temporarily assumed to have a leak-tight boundary—there is relatively little, if any, commerce across the boundary. We know that no such system can be found in reality, but it is sometimes essential to analyze a system as if it were closed so as to examine the operations of the system as affected "only by the conditions previously established by the environment and not changing at the time of analysis, plus the relationships among the internal elements of the system." The analyst then opens the system to a new impact from the environment, again closes the system, and observes and thinks out what would happen. It is, therefore, fruitless to debate the point; both open and closed system models are useful in diagnosis. Diagnosing the client as a system of variables, we have a way then of managing the complexity of "everything depends upon everything else" in an orderly way. Use of system analysis has these possibilities: (*a*) diagnosticians can avoid the error of simple cause-and-effect thinking; (*b*) they can justify what is included in observation and interpretation and what is temporarily excluded; (*c*) they can predict what will happen if no new or outside force is applied; (*d*) they are guided in categorizing what is relatively enduring and stable, or changing, in the situation; (*e*) they can distinguish between what is basic and what is merely symptomatic; (*f*) they can predict what will happen if they leave the events undisturbed and if they intervene; and (*g*) they are guided in selecting points of intervention.

Intersystem Model

We propose an extension of system analysis that looks to us to be useful for the problems confronting the change-agent. We urge the adoption of an intersystem model.

An intersystem model involves two open systems connected to each other.[6] The term we need to add here is *connectives.* Connectives represent the lines of relationships of the two systems. Connectives tie together parts (mechanics) or imbed in a web of tissue the separate organs (biology); connectives in an industrial establishment are the defined lines of communication, or the leadership hierarchy and authority for the branch plants; or they represent the social contract entered into by a therapist and patient; or mutual role expectations of consultant and client; or the affective ties between family members. These are conjunctive connectives. But we also have conflicts between labor and management, teenage gang wars, race conflicts, and negative emotional responses to strangers. These are disjunctive connectives.

[6] A visualization of an intersystem model would be two systems side by side, with separately identified links. Two rubber band-paper clip representatives can be connected with rubber bands of a different color representing the connectives.

Why elaborate the system model into an intersystem model? Cannot we get the same effect by talking about "sub-systems" of a larger system? In part we can. Labor-management conflicts, or interpersonal relations, or change-agent and client relationships can each be treated as a new system with sub-systems. But we may lose the critical fact of the autonomy of the components, or the direct interactional or transactual consequences for the separate components when we treat the sub-systems as merely parts of a larger system. The intersystem model exaggerates the virtues of autonomy and the limited nature of interdependence of the interactions between the two connected systems.

What are some of the positive advantages of using intersystem analysis? First, the external change-agent, or the change-agent built into an organization, as a helper with planned change does not completely become a part of the client-system. He must remain separate to some extent; he must create and maintain some distance between himself and the client, thus standing apart "in another system" from which he re-relates. This new system might be a referent group of fellow professionals, or a body of rational knowledge. But create one he does and must. Intersystem analysis of the change-agent's role leads to fruitful analysis of the connectives—their nature in the beginning, how they shift, and how they are cut off. Intersystem analysis also poses squarely an unexplored issue, namely the internal system of the change-agent, whether a single person, consultant group, or a nation. Helpers of change are prone at times not to see that their own systems as change-agents have boundaries, tensions, stresses and strains, equilibria, and feedback mechanisms which may be just as much parts of the problem as are similar aspects of the client-systems. Thus, relational issues are more available for diagnosis when we use an intersystem model.

More importantly, the intersystem model is applicable to problems of leadership, power, communication, and conflict in organizations, intergroup relations, and international relations. *Example:* Leadership in a work group with its liaison, negotiation, and representation functions is dependent upon connectives to another group and not solely upon the internal relationships within the work group. Negotiators, representatives, and leaders are parts of separate systems each with its own interdependence, tensions, stresses, and feedback, whether we are thinking of foreign ministers, Negro-white leaders, or student-faculty councils.

In brief, the intersystem model leads us to examine the interdependent dynamics of interaction both within and between the units. We object to the premature and unnecessary assumption that the units always form a single system. We can be misled into an utopian analysis of conflict, change-agent relations to client, and family relations if we neglect system differences. But an intersystem model provides a tool for diagnosis that retains the virtues of system analysis, adds the advantage of clarity, and furthers our diagnosis of the influence of various connectives, conjunctive and disjunctive, on the two systems. For change-agents, the essence of collaborative planning is contained in an intersystem model.

DEVELOPMENTAL MODELS

Practitioners have in general implicitly favored developmental models in thinking about human affairs, while social scientists have not paid as much attention to these as they have to system models. The "life sciences" of biology and psychology have not crystallized nor refined their common analytic model of the development of the organism, despite the heroic break-throughs of Darwin. Thus, we are forced to present only broad and rough categories of alternative positions in this paper.

Since there is no standard vocabulary for a developmental model, we shall present five categories of terms that we deem essential to such models: direction, states, forces, form of progression, and potentiality.

The Major Terms

Developmental Models. By developmental models, we mean those bodies of thought that center around growth and directional change. Developmental models assume change; they assume that there are noticeable differences between the states of a system at different times; that the succession of these states implies the system is heading somewhere; and that there are orderly processes which explain how the system gets from its present state to wherever it is going. In order to delimit the nature of change in developmental models we should perhaps add the idea of an increase in value accompanying the achievement of a new state. With this addition, developmental models focus on processes of growth and maturation. This addition might seem to rule out processes of decay, deterioration, and death from consideration. Logically, the developmental model should apply to either.

There are two kinds of "death" of concern to the practitioner. First, "death" or loss of some part or subvalue, as a constant concomitant of growth and development. Theories of life processes have used concepts such as catabolic (destructive) processes in biology, death instincts in Freud's psychology, or role loss upon promotion. On balance, the "loss" is made up by the "gains," and thus there is an increase in value. Second, "death" as planned changed for a group or organization—the dissolution of a committee or community organization that has "outlived its purpose and function," and the termination of a helping relationship with deliberateness and collaboration of participants is properly included as part of a developmental model.

Direction. Developmental models postulate that the system under scrutiny—a person, a small group, interpersonal interactions, an organization, a community or a society—is going "somewhere"; that the changes have some direction. The direction may be defined by (*a*) some *goal* or end state (developed, mature); (*b*) the *process* of becoming (developing, maturing) or (*c*) the degree of achievement *toward* some goal or end state (increased development, increase in maturity).

Change-agents find it necessary to believe that there is direction in change. *Example:* self-actualization or fulfillment is a need of the client-system. When strong directional tendencies are present, we modify our diagnosis and intervention accordingly. A rough analogy may be helpful here. A change-agent using a developmental model may be thought of as a husbandman tending a plant, watching and helping it to grow in its own natural direction of producing flowers. He feeds, waters, and weeds. Though at times he may be ruthless in pinching off excess buds, or even in using "grafts," in general he encourages the plant to reach its "goal" of producing beautiful flowers.

Identifiable State. As the system develops over time, the different states may be identified and differentiated from one another. Terms such as "stages," "levels," "phases," or "periods" are applied to these states. *Example:* psychosexual definition of oral, and anal stages, levels of evolution of species, or phases of group development.

No uniformity exists in the definition and operational identification of such successive states. But since change-agents do have to label the past, present, and future, they need some terms to describe successive states and to identify the turning points, transition areas, or critical events that characterize change. Here, system analysis is helpful in defining how parts are put together, along with the tensions and directions of the equilibrating processes. We have two polar types of the shifts of states: (*a*) small, nondiscernible steps or increments leading to a qualitative jump. (*Example:* black hair gradually turning gray, or a student evolving into a scholar); (*b*) a cataclysmic or critical event leading to a sudden change. (*Example:* a sickness resulting in gray hair overnight, or an inspirational lecture by a professor.) While the latter type seems more frequently to be externally induced, internal factors of the system can have the same consequence. In other words, the internal disequilibration of a balance may lead to a step-jump of the system to a new level. Personality stages, group stages, and societal phases are evolved and precipitated from internal and from external relations.

Form of Progression. Change-agents see in their models of development some form of progression or movement. Four such forms are typically assumed. First, it is often stated that once a stage is worked through, the client-system shows continued progression and normally never turns back. (Any recurrence of a previous state is viewed as an abnormality. Freudian stages are a good example: recurrence of a stage is viewed as regression, an abnormal event to be explained.) Teachers expect a steady growth of knowledge in students, either in a straight line (linear) or in an increasingly accelerating (curvilinear) form.

Second, it is assumed that change, growth, and development occur in a *spiral* form. *Example:* A small group might return to some previous "problem," such as its authority relations to the leader, but now might discuss the question at a "higher" level where irrational components are less dominant.

Third, another assumption more typically made is that the stages are really phases which occur and recur. There is an oscillation between various states, where no chronological priority is assigned to each state; there are cycles. *Example:* Phases of problem-solving or decision-making recur in different time periods as essential to progression. Cultures and societies go through phases of development in recurrent forms.

Fourth, still another assumption is that the form of progression is characterized by a branching out into *differentiated* forms and processes, each part increasing in its specialization, and at the same time acquiring its own autonomy and significance. *Example:* biological forms are differentiated into separate species. Organizations become more and more differentiated into special task and control structures.

Forces. First, forces or causal factors producing development and growth are most frequently seen by practitioners as "natural," as part of human nature, suggesting the role of genetics and other in-born characteristics. At best, environmental factors act as "triggers" or "releases," where the presence of some stimulus sets off the system's inherent growth forces. For example, it is sometimes thought that the teacher's job is to trigger off the natural curiosity of the child, and that growth of knowledge will ensue. Or the leadership of an organization should act to release the self-actualizing and creative forces present in its members.

Second, a smaller number of practitioners and social scientists think that the response to new situations and environmental forces is a coping response which gives rise to growth and development. Third, at this point, it may be useful to remind ourselves of the earlier discussion of the internal tensions of the system, still another cause of change. When stresses and strains of a system become too great, a disruption occurs and a set of forces is released to create new structures and achieve a new equilibrium.

Potentiality. Developmental models vary in their assumptions about potentialities of the system for development, growth, and change. That is, they vary in assumptions about the capabilities, overt or latent, that are built into the original or present state so that the necessary conditions for development may be typically present. Does the "seed"—and its genetic characteristics—represent potentialities? And are the supporting conditions of its environment available? Is the intelligence or emotional capability or skill-potential sufficient for development and change in a social and human process?

Change-agents typically assume a high degree of potentiality in the impetus toward development, and in the surrounding conditions that effectuate the potential.

Utility to Practitioners

The developmental model has tremendous advantages for the practitioner. It provides a set of expectations about the future of the client-system. By clarifying his thoughts and refining his observations about direction, states in the developmental process, forms of progression, and forces causing these events to occur over a period of time, the practitioner develops a time perspective which goes far beyond that of the mere here-and-now analysis of a system-model, which is bounded by time. By using a developmental model, he has a directional focus for his analysis and action and a temporal frame of reference. In addition, he is confronted with a number of questions to ask of himself and of his observations of the case: Do I assume an inherent end of the development? Do I impose a desired (by me) direction? How did I establish a collaboratively planned direction? What states in the development process may be expected? What form of progression do I foresee? What causes the development? His diagnoses and his interventions can become strategic rather than merely tactical.

THE CHANGE-AGENT AND MODELS

The primary concern of this paper has been to illustrate some of the major kinds of analytic models and conceptual schemes that have been devised by social scientists for the analysis of change and of changing human processes. But we need to keep in mind that the concern with diagnosis on the part of the social scientist is to achieve understanding, and to educe empirically researchable hypotheses amenable to his methods of study. The social scientist generally prefers not to change the system, but to study how it works and to predict what would happen if some new factor were introduced. So we find his attention focused on a "theory of change," of how the system achieves change. In contrast, the practitioner is concerned with diagnosis:

how to achieve understanding in order to engage in change. The practitioner, therefore, has some additional interests, he wants to know how to change the system, he needs a "theory of changing" the system.

A theory of changing requires the selection, or the construction, by theoretically minded practitioners, of thought-models appropriate to their intended purpose. This has to be done according to explicit criteria. A change-agent may demand of any model answers to certain questions. The responses he receives may not be complete or satisfactory since only piecemeal answers exist. At this period in the development of a theory of changing, we ask four questions as our guide lines for examining a conceptual model intended for the use of change-agents.

The first question is simply this: does the model account for the stability and continuity in the events studied at the same time that it accounts for changes in them? How do processes of change develop, given the interlocking factors in the situation that make for stability? Second, where does the model locate the "source" of change? What place among these sources do the deliberate and conscious efforts of the client-system and change-agent occupy? Third, what does the model assume about how goals and directions are determined? What or who sets the direction for movement of the processes of change? Fourth, does the model provide the change agent with levers or handles for affecting the direction, tempo, and quality of these processes of change?

A fifth question running through the other four is this: How does the model "place" the change-agent in the scheme of things? What is the shifting character of his relationship to the client-system, initially and at the termination of relationship, that affects his perceptions and actions? The question of relationship of change-agent to others needs to be part and parcel of the model since the existential relationships of the change-agent engaged in processes of planned change become "part of the problem" to be investigated.

The application of these five questions to the models of systems and models of development crystallizes some of the formation of ingredients for a change-agent model for changing. We can now summarize each model as follows:

"A "system" model emphasizes primarily the details of how stability is achieved, and only derivatively how change evolves out of the incompatibilities and conflicts in the system. A system model assumes that organization, interdependency, and integration exist among its parts and that change is a derived consequence of how well the parts of the system fit together, or how well the system fits in with other surounding and interacting systems. The source of change lies primarily in the structural stress and strain externally induced or internally created. The process of change is a process of tension reduction. The goals and direction are emergent from the structures or from imposed sources. Goals are often analyzed as set by "vested interests" of one part of the system. The confronting symptom of some trouble is a reflection of difficulties of adaptability (reaction to environment) or of the ability for adjustment (internal equilibration). The levers or handles available for manipulation are in the "inputs" to the system, especially the feedback mechanisms, and in the forces tending to restore a balance in the system. The change-agent is treated as separate from the client-system, the "target system."

The developmental model assumes constant change and development, and growth and decay of a system over time. Any existing stability is a snapshot of a living process—a stage that will give way to another stage. The supposition seems to be that it is "natural" that change should occur because change is rooted in the very nature of living organisms. The laws of the developmental process are not necessarily fixed, but some effects of the environment are presumably necessary to the developmental process. The direction of change is toward some goal, the fulfillment of its destiny, granting that no major blockage gets in the way. "Trouble" occurs when there is a gap between the system and its goal. Intervention is viewed as the removal of blockage by the change-agent, who then gets out of the way of the growth forces. Developmental models are not very sharply analyzed by the pure theorist nor formally stated, usually, as an analytic model. In fact, very frequently the model is used for studying the unique case rather than for deriving "laws of growth"; it is for descriptive purposes.

The third model—a model for "changing"—is a more recent creation. It incorporates some elements of analyses from system models, along with some ideas from the developmental model, in a framework, where direct attention is paid to the induced forces producing

Assumptions and Approaches of Three Analytic Models

Assumptions and Approaches to:	Models of Change: System Model	Developmental Model	Model for Changing
1. *Content*			
Stability	Structural integration	Phases, stages	Unfreezing parts
Change	Derived from structure	Constant and unique	Induced, controlled
2. *Causation*			
Source of change	Structural stress	Nature of organisms	Self and change-agent
Causal force	Tension reduction		Rational choice
3. *Goals*			
Direction	Emergent	Ontological	Deliberate selection
Set by	"Vested interests"		Collaborative process
4. *Intervention*			
Confronting symptoms	Stresses, strains, and tensions	Discrepancy between actuality and potentiality	Perceived need
Goal of intervening	Adjustment, adaptation	Removal of blockages	Improvement
5. *Change-Agent*			
Place	Outside the "target" system	Outside	Part of situation
Role	External diagnoser and actor	External diagnoser and actor	Participant in here and now

change. It studies stability in order to unfreeze and move some parts of the system. The direction to be taken is not fixed or "determined," but remains in large measure a matter of "choice" for the client-system. The change-agent is a specialist in the technical processes of facilitating change, a helper to the client-system. The models for changing are as yet incompletely conceptualized. The intersystem model may provide a way of examining how the change-agent's relationships, as part of the model, affect the processes of change.

We can summarize and contrast the three models with this chart. We have varying degrees of confidence in our categories, but, as the quip says, we construct these in order to achieve the laudable state of "paradigm lost." It is the readers' responsibility to help achieve this goal!

THE LIMITATIONS

It is obvious that we are proposing the use of systematically constructed and examined models of thought for the change-agent. The advantages are manifold and—we hope—apparent in our preceding discussion. Yet we must now point out some limitations and disutility of models.

Models are abstractions from the concreteness of events. Because of the high degree of selectivity of observations and focus, the "fit" between the model and the actual thought and diagnostic processes of the change-agent is not close. Furthermore, the thought and diagnostic processes of the change-agent are not fixed and rigid. And even worse, the "fit" between the diagnostic processes of the change-agent and the changing processes of the "actual" case, is not close. Abstract as the nature of a model is, as applied to the change-agent, students of the change-agent role may find the concepts of use. But change-agents' practices in diagnosing are not immediately affected by models' analyses.

Furthermore, there are modes of diagnosing by intervening, which do not fall neatly into models. The change-agent frequently tries out an activity in order to see what happens and to see what is involved in the change. If successful, he does not need to diagnose any further, but proceeds to engage in further actions with the client. If unsuccessful, however, he may need to examine what is going on in more detail.

The patch work required for a theory and model of changing requires the suspension of acceptance of such available models. For this paper has argued for some elements from both the system models and the developmental models to be included in the model for practitioners, with the use of a format of the intersystem model so as to include the change-agent and his relationships as part of the problem. But can the change-agent wait for such a synthesis and emerging construction? Our personal feeling is that the planning of change cannot wait, but must proceed with the available diagnostic tools. Here is an intellectual challenge to the scientist-scholar of planned change that could affect the professions of practice.

3. ORGANIZATION THEORY: AN OVERVIEW AND AN APPRAISAL[1]

WILLIAM G. SCOTT[2]

Man is intent on drawing himself into a web of collectivized patterns. "Modern man has learned to accommodate himself to a world increasingly organized. The trend toward ever more explicit and consciously drawn relationships is profound and sweeping; it is marked by depth no less than by extension."[3] This comment by Seidenberg nicely summarizes the pervasive influence of organization in many forms of human activity.

Some of the reasons for intense organizational activity are found in the fundamental transitions which revolutionized our society, changing it from a rural culture, to a culture based on technology, industry, and the city. From these changes, a way of life emerged characterized by the *proximity* and *dependency* of people on each other. Proximity and dependency, as conditions of social life, harbor the threats of human conflict, capricious anti-social behavior, instability of human relationships, and uncertainty about the nature of the social structure with its concomitant roles.

Of course, these threats to social integrity are present to some degree in all societies, ranging from the primitive to the modern. But, these threats become dangerous when the harmonious functioning of a society rests on the maintenance of a highly intricate, delicately balanced form of human collaboration. The civilization we have created depends on the preservation of a precarious balance. Hence, disrupting forces impinging on this shaky form of collaboration must be climinated or minimized.

Traditionally, organization is viewed as a vehicle for accomplishing goals and objectives. While this approach is useful, it tends to obscure the inner workings and internal purposes of organization itself. Another fruitful way of treating organization is as a mechanism having the ultimate purpose of offsetting those forces which undermine human collaboration. In this sense, organization tends to minimize conflict, and to lessen the significance of individual behavior which deviates from values that the organization has established as worthwhile. Further, organization increases stability in human relationships by reducing uncertainty regarding the nature of the system's structure and the human roles which are inherent to it. Corollary to this point, organization enhances the predictability of human action, because it limits the number of behavioral alternatives available to an individual. As Presthus points out:

> Organization is defined as a system of structural interpersonal relations . . . individuals are differentiated in terms of authority, status, and role with the result that personal interaction is prescribed. . . . Anticipated reactions tend to occur, while ambiguity and spontaneity are decreased.[4]

In addition to all of this, organization has built-in safeguards. Besides prescribing acceptable forms of behavior for those who elect to submit to it, organization is also able to counterbalance the influence of human action which transcends its established patterns.[5]

[1] SOURCE: *Journal of the Academy of Management,* Vol. 4, No. 1 (April, 1961), pp. 7–26. Reprinted by permission of *Journal of the Academy of Management.*

[2] University of Washington.

[3] Roderick Seidenberg, *Posthistoric Man* (Boston: Beacon Press, 1951), p. 1.

[4] Robert V. Presthus, "Toward a Theory of Organizational Behavior," *Administrative Science Quarterly* (June, 1958), p. 50.

[5] Regulation and predictability of human behavior are matters of degree varying with different organizations on something of a continuum. At one extreme are bureaucratic type organizations with tight bonds of regulation. At the other ex-

Few segments of society have engaged in organizing more intensively than business.[6] The reason is clear. Business depends on what organization offers. Business needs a system of relationships among functions; it needs stability, continuity, and predictability in its internal activities and external contacts. Business also appears to need harmonious relationships among the people and processes which make it up. Put another way, a business organization has to be free, relatively, from destructive tendencies which may be caused by divergent interests.

As a foundation for meeting these needs rests administrative science. A major element of this science is organization theory, which provides the grounds for management activities in a number of significant areas of business endeavor. Organization theory, however, is not a homogeneous science based on generally accepted principles. Various theories of organization have been, and are being evolved. For example, something called "modern organization theory" has recently emerged, raising the wrath of some traditionalists, but also capturing the imagination of a rather elite *avant-garde*.

The thesis of this paper is that modern organization theory, when stripped of its irrelevancies, redundancies, and "speech defects," is a logical and vital evolution in management thought. In order for this thesis to be supported, the reader must endure a review and appraisal of more traditional forms of organization theory which may seem elementary to him.

In any event, three theories of organization are having considerable influence on management thought and practice. They are arbitrarily labeled in this paper as the classical, the neo-classical, and the modern. Each of these is fairly distinct; but they are not unrelated. Also, these theories are on-going, being actively supported by several schools of management thought.

treme are voluntary associations and informal organizations with relatively loose bonds of regulation.

This point has an interesting sidelight. A bureaucracy with tight controls and a high degree of predictability of human action appears to be unable to distinguish between destructive and creative deviations from established values. Thus the only thing which is safeguarded is the *status quo*.

[6] The monolithic institutions of the military and government are other cases of organizational preoccupation.

THE CLASSICAL DOCTRINE

For lack of a better method of identification, it will be said that the classical doctrine deals almost exclusively with the *anatomy of formal organization*. This doctrine can be traced back to Frederick W. Taylor's interest in functional foremanship and planning staffs. But most students of management thought would agree that in the United States, the first systematic approach to organization, and the first comprehensive attempt to find organizational universals, is dated 1931 when Mooney and Reiley published *Onward Industry*.[7] Subsesequently, numerous books, following the classical vein, have appeared. Two of the more recent are Brech's, *Organization*[8] and Allen's, *Management and Organization*.[9]

Classical organization theory is built around four key pillars. They are the division of labor, the scalar and functional processes, structure, and span of control. Given these major elements just about all of classical organization theory can be derived.

(1) *The division of labor* is without doubt the cornerstone among the four elements.[10] From it the other elements flow as corollaries. For example, *scalar* and *functional* growth requires specialization and departmentalization of functions. Organization *structure* is naturally dependent upon the direction which specialization of activities travels in company development. Finally, *span of control* problems result from the number of specialized functions under the jurisdiction of a manager.

(2) *The scalar and functional processes* deal with the vertical and horizontal growth of

[7] James D. Mooney and Alan C. Reiley, *Onward Industry* (New York: Harper and Brothers, 1931). Later published by James D. Mooney under the title *Principles of Organization.*

[8] E. F. L. Brech, *Organization* (London: Longmans, Green and Company, 1957).

[9] Louis A. Allen, *Management and Organization* (New York: McGraw-Hill Book Company, 1958).

[10] Usually the division of labor is treated under a topical heading of departmentation, see for example: Harold Koontz and Cyril O'Donnell, *Principles of Management* (New York: McGraw-Hill Book Company, 1959), Chapter 7.

the organization, respectively.[11] The scalar process refers to the growth of the chain of command, the delegation of authority and responsibility, unity of command, and the obligation to report.

The division of the organization into specialized parts and the regrouping of the parts into compatible units are matters pertaining to the functional process. This process focuses on the horizontal evolution of the line and staff in a formal organization.

(3) *Structure* is the logical relationships of functions in an organization, arranged to accomplish the objectives of the company efficiently. Structure implies system and pattern. Classical organization theory usually works with two basic structures, the line and the staff. However, such activities as committee and liaison functions fall quite readily into the purview of structural considerations. Again, structure is the vehicle for introducing logical and consistent relationships among the diverse functions which comprise the organization.[12]

(4) *The span of control* concept relates to the number of subordinates a manager can effectively supervise. Graicunas has been credited with first elaborating the point that there are numerical limitations to the subordinates one man can control.[13] In a recent statement on the subject, Brech points out, "span" refers to ". . . the number of persons, themselves carrying managerial and supervisory responsibilities, for whom the senior manager retains his overembracing responsibility of direction and planning, co-ordination, motivation, and control." [14] Regardless of interpretation, span of control has significance, in part, for the shape of the organization which evolves through growth. Wide span yields a flat structure; short span results in a tall structure. Further, the span concept directs attention to the complexity of human and functional interrelationships in an organization.

[11] These processes are discussed at length in Ralph Currier Davis, *The Fundamentals of Top Management* (New York: Harper and Brothers, 1951), Chapter 7.

[12] For a discussion of structure see: William H. Newman, *Administrative Action* (Englewood Cliffs, New Jersey: Prentice-Hall, Incorporated, 1951), Chapter 16.

[13] V. A. Graicunas, "Relationships in Organization," *Papers on the Science of Administration* (New York: Columbia University, 1937).

[14] Brech, *op. cit.*, p. 78.

It would not be fair to say that the classical school is unaware of the day-to-day administrative problems of the organization. Paramount among these problems are those stemming from human interactions. But the interplay of individual personality, informal groups, interorganizational conflict, and the decision-making processes in the formal structure appears largely to be neglected by classical organization theory. Additionally, the classical theory overlooks the contributions of the behavioral sciences by failing to incorporate them in its doctrine in any systematic way. In summary, classical organization theory has relevant insights into the nature of organization, but the value of this theory is limited by its narrow concentration on the formal anatomy of organization.

NEOCLASSICAL THEORY OF ORGANIZATION

The neoclassical theory of organization embarked on the task of compensating for some of the deficiencies in classical doctrine. The neoclassical school is commonly identified with the human relations movement. Generally, the neoclassical approach takes the postulates of the classical school, regarding the pillars of organization as givens. But these postulates are regarded as modified by people, acting independently or within the context of the informal organization.

One of the main contributions of the neoclassical school is the introduction of behavioral sciences in an integrated fashion into the theory of organization. Through the use of these sciences, the human relationists demonstrate how the pillars of the classical doctrine are affected by the impact of human actions. Further, the neoclassical approach includes a systematic treatment of the informal organization, showing its influence on the formal structure.

Thus, the neoclassical approach to organization theory gives evidence of accepting classical doctrine, but superimposing on it modifications resulting from individual behavior, and the influence of the informal group. The inspiration of the neoclassical school were the Hawthorne studies.[15] Current examples of the neoclassical approach are

[15] See: F. J. Roethlisberger and William J. Dickson, *Management and the Worker* (Cambridge: Harvard University Press, 1939).

found in human relations books like Gardner and Moore, *Human Relations in Industry*,[16] and Davis, *Human Relations in Business*.[17] To a more limited extent, work in industrial sociology also reflects a neoclassical point of view.[18]

It would be useful to look briefly at some of the contributions made to organization theory by the neoclassicists. First to be considered are modifications of the pillars of classical doctrine; second is the informal organization.

Examples of the Neoclassical Approach to the Pillars of Formal Organization Theory

(1) The *division of labor* has been a long standing subject of comment in the field of human relations. Very early in the history of industrial psychology study was made of industrial fatigue and monotony caused by the specialization of the work.[19] Later, attention shifted to the isolation of the worker, and his feeling of anonymity resulting from insignificant jobs which contributed negligibly to the final product.[20]

Also, specialization influences the work of management. As an organization expands, the need concomitantly arises for managerial motivation and coordination of the activities of others. Both motivation and coordination in turn relate to executive leadership. Thus, in part, stemming from the growth of industrial specialization, the neoclassical school has developed a large body of theory relating to motivation, coordination, and leadership. Much of this theory is derived from the social sciences.

(2) Two aspects of the *scalar and functional* processes which have been treated with some degree of intensity by the neoclassical school are the delegation of authority and responsibility, and gaps in or overlapping of functional jurisdictions. The classical theory assumes something of perfection in the delegation and functionalization processes. The neoclassical school points out that human problems are caused by imperfections in the way these processes are handled.

For example, too much or insufficient delegation may render an executive incapable of action. The failure to delegate authority and responsibility equally may result in frustration for the delegatee. Overlapping of authorities often causes clashes in personality. Gaps in authority cause failures in getting jobs done, with one party blaming the other for shortcomings in performance.[21]

The neoclassical school says that the scalar and functional processes are theoretically valid, but tend to deteriorate in practice. The ways in which they break down are described, and some of the human causes are pointed out. In addition the neoclassicists make recommendations, suggesting various "human tools" which will facilitate the operation of these processes.

(3) *Structure* provides endless avenues of analysis for the neoclassical theory of organization. The theme is that human behavior disrupts the best laid organizational plans, and thwarts the cleanness of the logical relationships founded in the structure. The neoclassical critique of structure centers on frictions which appear internally among people performing different functions.

Line and staff relations is a problem area, much discussed, in this respect. Many companies seem to have difficulty keeping the line and staff working together harmoniously. Both Dalton[22] and Juran[23] have engaged in research to discover the causes of friction, and to suggest remedies.

Of course, line-staff relations represent only one of the many problems of structural frictions described by the neoclassicists. As often

[16] Burleigh B. Gardner and David G. Moore, *Human Relations in Industry* (Homewood, Illinois: Richard D. Irwin, 1955).

[17] Keith Davis, *Human Relations in Business* (New York: McGraw-Hill Book Company, 1957).

[18] For example see: Delbert C. Miller and William H. Form, *Industrial Sociology* (New York: Harper and Brothers, 1951).

[19] See: Hugo Munsterberg, *Psychology and Industrial Efficiency* (Boston: Houghton Mifflin Company, 1913).

[20] Probably the classic work is: Elton Mayo, *The Human Problems of an Industrial Civilization* (Cambridge: Harvard University, 1946, first printed 1933).

[21] For further discussion of the human relations implications of the scalar and functional processes see: Keith Davis, *op. cit.*, pp. 60–66.

[22] Melville Dalton, "Conflicts Between Staff and Line Managerial Officers," *American Sociological Review* (June, 1950), pp. 342–351.

[23] J. M. Juran, "Improving the Relationship Between Staff and Line," *Personnel* (May, 1956), pp. 515–524.

as not, the neoclassicists will offer prescriptions for the elimination of conflict in structure. Among the more important harmony-rendering formulae are participation, junior boards, bottom-up management, joint committees, recognition of human dignity, and "better" communication.

(4) An executive's *span of control* is a function of human determinants, and the reduction of span to a precise, universally applicable ratio is silly, according to the neoclassicists. Some of the determinants of span are individual differences in managerial abilities, the type of people and functions supervised, and the extent of communication effectiveness.

Coupled with the span of control question are the human implications of the type of structure which emerges. That is, is a tall structure with a short span or a flat structure with a wide span more conducive to good human relations than high morale? The answer is situational. Short span results in tight supervision; wide span requires a good deal of delegation with looser controls. Because of individual and organizational differences, sometimes one is better than the other. There is a tendency to favor the looser form of organization, however, for the reason that tall structures breed autocratic leadership, which is often pointed out as a cause of low morale.[24]

The Neoclassical View of the Informal Organization

Nothing more than the barest mention of the informal organization is given even in the most recent classical treatises on organization theory.[25] Systematic discussion of this form of organization has been left to the neoclassicists. The informal organization refers to people in group associations at work, but these associations are not specified in the "blueprint" of the formal organization. The informal organization means natural groupings of people in the work situation.

In a general way, the informal organization appears in response to the social need—the need of people to associate with others. However, for analytical purposes, this explanation is not particularly satisfying. Research has produced the following, more specific determinants underlying the appearance of informal organizations:

1. The *location* determinant simply states that in order to form into groups of any lasting nature, people have to have frequent face-to-face contact. Thus, the geography of physical location in a plant or office is an important factor in predicting who will be in what group.[26]
2. *Occupation* is a key factor determining the rise and composition of informal groups. There is a tendency for people performing similar jobs to group together.[27]
3. *Interests* are another determinant for informal group formation. Even though people might be in the same location, performing similar jobs, differences of interest among them explain why several small, instead of one large, informal organizations emerge.
4. *Special issues* often result in the formation of informal groups, but this determinant is set apart from the three previously mentioned. In this case, people who do not necessarily have similar interests, occupations, or locations may join together for a common cause. Once the issue is resolved, then the tendency is to revert to the more "natural" group forms.[28] Thus, special issues give rise to a rather impermanent informal association; groups based on the other three determinants tend to be more lasting.

When informal organizations come into being they assume certain characteristics. Since understanding these characteristics is important for management practice, they are noted below:

1. Informal organizations act as agencies of *social control.* They generate a culture based on certain norms of conduct which, in turn, demands conformity from group members. These standards may be at odds with the

[24] Gardner and Moore, *op. cit.*, pp. 237–243.

[25] For example: Brech, *op. cit.*, pp. 27–29; and Allen, *op. cit.*, pp. 61–62.

[26] See: Leon Festinger, Stanley Schachter, and Kurt Back, *Social Pressures in Informal Groups* (New York: Harper and Brothers, 1950), pp. 153–163.

[27] For example see: W. Fred Cottrell, *The Railroader* (Palo Alto: The Stanford University Press, 1940), Chapter 3.

[28] Except in cases where the existence of an organization is necessary for the continued maintenance of employee interest. Under these conditions the previously informal association may emerge as a formal group, such as a union.

values set by the formal organization. So an individual may very well find himself in a situation of conflicting demands.

2. The form of human interrelationships in the informal organization requires *techniques of analysis* different from those used to plot the relationships of people in a formal organization. The method used for determining the structure of the informal group is called sociometric analysis. Sociometry reveals the complex structure of interpersonal relations which is based on premises fundamentally unlike the logic of the formal organization.

3. Informal organizations have *status and communication* systems peculiar to themselves, not necessarily derived from the formal systems. For example, the grapevine is the subject of much neoclassical study.

4. Survival of the informal organization requires stable continuing relationships among the people in them. Thus, it has been observed that the informal organization *resists change*.[29] Considerable attention is given by the neoclassicists to overcoming informal resistance to change.

5. The last aspect of analysis which appears to be central to the neoclassical view of the informal organization is the study of the *informal leader*. Discussion revolves around who the informal leader is, how he assumes this role, what characteristics are peculiar to him, and how he can help the manager accomplish his objectives in the formal organization.[30]

This brief sketch of some of the major facets of informal organization theory has neglected, so far, one important topic treated by the neoclassical school. It is the way in which the formal and informal organizations interact.

A conventional way of looking at the interaction of the two is the "live and let live" point of view. Management should recognize that the informal organization exists, nothing can destroy it, and so the executive might just as well work with it. Working with the informal organization involves not threatening its existence unnecessarily, listening to opinions expressed for the group by the leader, allowing group participation in decision-making situations, and controlling the grapevine by prompt release of accurate information.[31]

While this approach is management centered, it is not unreasonable to expect that informal group standards and norms could make themselves felt on formal organizational policy. An honestly conceived effort by managers to establish a working relationship with the informal organization could result in an association where both formal and informal views would be reciprocally modified. The danger which at all costs should be avoided is that "working with the informal organization" does not degenerate into a shallow disguise for human manipulation.

Some neoclassical writing in organization theory, especially that coming from the management-oriented segment of this school, gives the impression that the formal and informal organizations are distinct, and at times, quite irreconcilable factors in a company. The interaction which takes place between the two is something akin to the interaction between the company and a labor union, or a government agency, or another company.

The concept of the social system is another approach to the interactional climate. While this concept can be properly classified as neoclassical, it borders on the modern theories of organization. The phrase "social system" means that an organization is a complex of mutually interdependent, but variable, factors.

These factors include individuals and their attitudes and motives, jobs, the physical work setting, the formal organization, and the informal organizations. These factors, and many others, are woven into an overall pattern of interdependency. From this point of view, the formal and informal organizations lose their distinctiveness, but find real meaning, in terms of human behavior, in the operation of the system as a whole. Thus, the study of organization turns away from descriptions of its component parts, and is refocused on the system of interrelationships among the parts.

One of the major contributions of the Haw-

[29] Probably the classic study of resistance to change is: Lester Coch and John R. P. French, Jr., "Overcoming Resistance to Change," in Schuyler Dean Hoslett (editor), *Human Factors in Management* (New York: Harper and Brothers, 1951), pp. 242-268.

[30] For example see: Robert Saltonstall, *Human Relations in Administration* (New York: McGraw-Hill Book Company, 1959), pp. 330–331; and Keith Davis, *op. cit.*, pp. 99–101.

[31] For an example of this approach see: John T. Doutt, "Management Must Manage the Informal Group, Too," *Advanced Management* (May 1959), pp. 26–28.

thorne studies was the integration of Pareto's idea of the social system into a meaningful method of analysis for the study of behavior in human organizations.[32] This concept is still vitally important. But unfortunately some work in the field of human relations undertaken by the neoclassicists has overlooked, or perhaps discounted, the significance of this consideration.[33]

The fundamental insight regarding the social system, developed and applied to the industrial scene by the Hawthorne researchers, did not find much extension in subsequent work in the neoclassical vein. Indeed, the neoclassical school after the Hawthorne studies generally seemed content to engage in descriptive generalizations, or particularized empirical research studies which did not have much meaning outside their own context.

The neoclassical school of organization theory has been called bankrupt. Criticisms range from, "human relations is a tool for cynical puppeteering of people," to "human relations is nothing more than a trifling body of empirical and descriptive information." There is a good deal of truth in both criticisms, but another appraisal of the neoclassical school of organization theory is offered here. The neoclassical approach has provided valuable contributions to lore of organization. But, like the classical theory, the neoclassical doctrine suffers from incompleteness, a shortsighted perspective, and lack of integration among the many facets of human behavior studied by it. Modern organization theory has made a move to cover the shortcomings of the current body of theoretical knowledge.

MODERN ORGANIZATION THEORY

The distinctive qualities of modern organization theory are its conceptual-analytical base, its reliance on empirical research data and, above all, its integrating nature. These qualities are framed in a philosophy which accepts the premise that the only meaningful way to study organization is to study it as a system. As Henderson put it, the study of a system must rely on a method of analysis, ". . . involving the simultaneous variations of mutually dependent variables."[34] Human systems, of course, contain a huge number of dependent variables which defy the most complex simultaneous equations to solve.

Nevertheless, system analysis has its own peculiar point of view which aims to study organization in the way Henderson suggests. It treats organization as a system of mutually dependent variables. As a result, modern organization theory, which accepts system analysis, shifts the conceptual level of organization study above the classical and neoclassical theories. Modern organization theory asks a range of interrelated questions which are not seriously considered by the two other theories.

Key among these questions are: (1) What are the strategic parts of the system? (2) What is the nature of their mutual dependency? (3) What are the main processes in the system which link the parts together, and facilitate their adjustments to each other? (4) What are the goals sought by systems?[35]

Modern organization theory is in no way a unified body of thought. Each writer and researcher has his special emphasis when he considers the system. Perhaps the most evident unifying thread in the study of systems is the effort to look at the organization in its totality. Representative books in this field are March and Simon, *Organizations*,[36] and Haire's anthology, *Modern Organization Theory*.[37]

Instead of attempting a review of different writers' contributions to modern organization theory, it will be more useful to discuss the various ingredients involved in system analysis. They are the parts, the interactions, the processes, and the goals of systems.

[32] See: Roethlisberger and Dickson, *op. cit.*, Chapter 24.

[33] A check of management human relations texts, the organization and human relations chapters of principles of management texts, and texts on conventional organization theory for management courses reveals little or no treatment of the concept of the social system.

[34] Lawrence J. Henderson, *Pareto's General Sociology* (Cambridge: Harvard University Press, 1935), p. 13.

[35] There is another question which cannot be treated in the scope of this paper. It asks, what research tools should be used for the study of the system?

[36] James G. March and Herbert A. Simon, *Organizations* (New York: John Wiley and Sons, 1958).

[37] Mason Haire (editor), *Modern Organization Theory* (New York: John Wiley and Sons, 1959).

The Parts of the System and Their Interdependency

The first basic part of the system is the *individual,* and the personality structure he brings to the organization. Elementary to an individual's personality are motives and attitudes which condition the range of expectancies he hopes to satisfy by participating in the system.

The second part of the system is the formal arrangement of functions, usually called the *formal organization.* The formal organization is the interrelated pattern of jobs which make up the structure of a system. Certain writers, like Argyris, see a fundamental conflict resulting from the demands made by the system, and the structure of the mature, normal personality. In any event, the individual has expectancies regarding the job he is to perform; and, conversely, the job makes demands on, or has expectancies relating to, the performance of the individual. Considerable attention has been given by writers in modern organization theory to incongruencies resulting from the interaction of organizational and individual demands.[38]

The third part in the organization system is the *informal organization.* Enough has been said already about the nature of this organization. But it must be noted that an interactional pattern exists between the individual and the informal group. This interactional arrangement can be conveniently discussed as the mutual modification of expectancies. The informal organization has demands which it makes on members in terms of anticipated forms of behavior, and the individual has expectancies of satisfaction he hopes to derive from association with people on the job. Both these sets of expectancies interact, resulting in the individual modifying his behavior to accord with the demands of the group, and the group, perhaps, modifying what it expects from an individual because of the impact of his personality on group norms.[39]

Much of what has been said about the various expectancy systems in an organization can also be treated using status and role concepts. Part of modern organization theory rests on research findings in social-psychology relative to reciprocal patterns of behavior stemming from role demands generated by both the formal and informal organizations, and role perceptions peculiar to the individual. Bakke's *fusion process* is largely concerned with the modification of role expectancies. The fusion process is a force, according to Bakke, which acts to weld divergent elements together for the preservation of organizational integrity.[40]

The fifth part of system analysis is the *physical setting* in which the job is performed. Although this element of the system may be implicit in what has been said already about the formal organization and its functions, it is well to separate it. In the physical surroundings of work, interactions are present in complex man-machine systems. The human "engineer" cannot approach the problems posed by such interrelationships in a purely technical, engineering fashion. As Haire says, these problems lie in the domain of the social theorist.[41] Attention must be centered on responses demanded from a logically ordered production function, often with the view of minimizing the error in the system. From this standpoint, work cannot be effectively organized unless the psychological, social, and physiological characteristics of people participating in the work environment are considered. Machines and processes should be designed to fit certain generally observed psychological and physiological properties of men, rather than hiring men to fit machines.

In summary, the parts of the system which appear to be of strategic importance are the individual, the formal structure, the informal organization, status and role patterns, and the physical environment of work. Again, these parts are woven into a configuration called the organizational system. The processes which link the parts are taken up next.

[38] See Chris Argyris, *Personality and Organization* (New York: Harper and Brothers, 1957), esp. Chapters 2, 3, 7.

[39] For a larger treatment of this subject see: George C. Homans, *The Human Group* (New York: Harcourt, Brace and Company, 1950), Chapter 5.

[40] E. Wight Bakke, "Concept of the Social Organization," in Mason Haire (editor), *Modern Organization Theory* (New York: John Wiley and Sons, 1959), pp. 60–61.

[41] Mason Haire, "Psychology and the Study of Business: Joint Behavioral Sciences," in *Social Science Research on Business: Product and Potential* (New York: Columbia University Press, 1959), pp. 53–59.

The Linking Processes

One can say, with a good deal of glibness, that all the parts mentioned above are interrelated. Although this observation is quite correct, it does not mean too much in terms of system theory unless some attempt is made to analyze the processes by which the interaction is achieved. Role theory is devoted to certain types of interactional processes. In addition, modern organization theorists point to three other linking activities which appear to be universal to human systems of organized behavior. These processes are communication, balance, and decision making.

(1) Communication is mentioned often in neoclassical theory, but the emphasis is on description of forms of communication activity, i.e., formal-informal, vertical-horizontal, line-staff. Communication, as a mechanism which links the segments of the system together, is overlooked by way of much considered analysis.

One aspect of modern organization theory is study of the communication network in the system. Communication is viewed as the method by which action is evoked from the parts of the system. Communication acts not only as stimuli resulting in action, but also as a control and coordination mechanism linking the decision centers in the system into a synchronized pattern. Deutsch points out that organizations are composed of parts which communicate with each other, receive messages from the outside world, and store information. Taken together, these communication functions of the parts comprise a configuration representing the total system.[42] More is to be said about communication later in the discussion of the cybernetic model.

(2) The concept of *balance* as a linking process involves a series of some rather complex ideas. Balance refers to an equilibrating mechanism whereby the various parts of the system are maintained in a harmoniously structured relationship to each other.

The necessity for the balance concept logically flows from the nature of systems themselves. It is impossible to conceive of an ordered relationship among the parts of a system without also introducing the idea of a stabilizing or an adapting mechanism.

Balance appears in two varieties—quasi-automatic and innovative. Both forms of balance act to insure system integrity in face of changing conditions, either internal or external to the system. The first form of balance, quasi-automatic, refers to what some think are "homeostatic" properties of systems. That is, systems seem to exhibit built-in propensities to maintain steady states.

If human organizations are open, self-maintaining systems, then control and regulatory processes are necessary. The issue hinges on the degree to which stabilizing processes in systems, when adapting to change, are automatic. March and Simon have an interesting answer to this problem, which in part is based on the type of change and the adjustment necessary to adapt to the change. Systems have programs of action which are put into effect when a change is perceived. If the change is relatively minor, and if the change comes within the purview of established programs of action, then it might be fairly confidently predicted that the adaptation made by the system will be quasi-automatic.[43]

The role of innovative, creative balancing efforts now needs to be examined. The need for innovation arises when adaptation to a change is outside the scope of existing programs designed for the purpose of keeping the system in balance. New programs have to be evolved in order for the system to maintain internal harmony.

New programs are created by trial and error search for feasible action alternatives to cope with a given change. But innovation is subject to the limitations and possibilities inherent in the quantity and variety of information present in a system at a particular time. New combinations of alternatives for innovative purposes depend on:

1. The possible range of output of the system, or the capacity of the system to supply information.
2. The range of available information in the memory of the system.
3. The operating rules (program) governing the analysis and flow of information within the system.
4. The ability of the system to "forget" pre-

[42] Karl W. Deutsch, "On Communication Models in the Social Sciences," *Public Opinion Quarterly*, 16 (1952), pp. 356–380.

[43] March and Simon, *op. cit.*, pp. 139–140.

viously learned solutions to change problems.[44] A system with too good a memory might narrow its behavioral choices to such an extent as to stifle innovation. In simpler language, old learned programs might be used to adapt the change, when newly innovated programs are necessary.[45]

Much of what has been said about communication and balance brings to mind a cybernetic model in which both these processes have vital roles. Cybernetics has to do with feedback and control of all kinds of systems. Its purpose is to maintain system stability in the face of change. Cybernetics cannot be studied without considering communication networks, information flow, and some kind of balancing process aimed at preserving the integrity of the system.

Cybernetics directs attention to key questions regarding the system. These questions are: How are communication centers connected, and how are they maintained? Corollary to this question: what is the structure of the feedback system? Next, what information is stored in the organization, and at what points? And as a corollary: how accessible is this information to decision-making centers? Third, how conscious is the organization of the operation of its own parts? That is, to what extent do the policy centers receive control information with sufficient frequency and relevancy to create a real awareness of the operation of the segments of the system? Finally, what are the learning (innovating) capabilities of the system? [46]

Answers to the questions posed by cybernetics are crucial to understanding both the balancing and communication processes in systems.[47] Although cybernetics has been applied largely to technical-engineering problems of automation, the model of feedback, control, and regulation in all systems has a good deal of generality. Cybernetics is a fruitful area which can be used to synthesize the processes of communication and balance.

(3) A wide spectrum of topics dealing with types of decisions in human systems makes up the core of analysis of another important process in organizations. Decision analysis is one of the major contributions of March and Simon in their book *Organizations*. The two major classes of decisions they discuss are decisions to produce and decisions to participate in the system.[48]

Decisions to produce are largely a result of an interaction between individual attitudes and the demands of the organization. Motivation analysis becomes central to studying the nature and results of the interaction. Individual decisions to participate in the organization reflect on such issues as the relationship between organizational rewards versus the demands made by the organization. Participation decisions also focus attention on the reasons why individuals remain in or leave organizations.

March and Simon treat decisions as internal variables in an organization which depend on jobs, individual expectations and motivations, and organizational structure. Marschak [49] looks on the decision process as an independent variable upon which the survival of the organization is based. In this case, the organization is viewed as having, inherent in its structure, the ability to maximize survival requisites through its established decision processes.

The Goals of Organization

Organization has three goals which may be either intermeshed or independent ends in themselves. They are growth, stability, and interaction. The last goal refers to organizations which exist primarily to provide a medium for association of its members with others. Interestingly enough these goals seem to apply to different forms of organization at varying levels of complexity, ranging from simple clockwork mechanisms to social systems.

[44] Mervyn L. Cadwallader, "The Cybernetic Analysis of Change in Complex Social Organization," *The American Journal of Sociology* (September, 1959), p. 156.

[45] It is conceivable for innovative behavior to be programmed into the system.

[46] These are questions adapted from Deutsch, *op. cit.*, 368–370.

[47] Answers to these questions would require a comprehensive volume. One of the best approaches currently available is Stafford Beer, *Cybernetics and Management* (New York: John Wiley and Sons, 1959).

[48] March and Simon, *op. cit.*, Chapters 3 and 4.

[49] Jacob Marschak, "Efficient and Viable Organizational Forms" in Mason Haire, editor, *Modern Organization Theory* (New York: John Wiley and Sons, 1959), pp. 307–320.

These similarities in organizational purposes have been observed by a number of people, and a field of thought and research called system theory has developed, dedicated to the task of discovering organizational universals. The dream of general system theory is to create a science of organizational universals, or if you will, a universal science using common organizational elements found in all systems as a starting point.

Modern organization theory is on the periphery of general system theory. Both general system theory and modern organization theory studies:

1. The parts (individuals) in aggregates, and the movement of individuals into and out of the system.
2. The interaction of individuals with the environment found in the system.
3. The interactions among individuals in the system.
4. General growth and stability problems of systems.[50]

Modern organization theory and general system theory are similar in that they look at organization as an integrated whole. They differ, however, in terms of their generality. General system theory is concerned with every level of system, whereas modern organizational theory focuses primarily on human organization.

The question might be asked, What can the science of administration gain by the study of system levels other than human? Before attempting an answer, note should be made of what these other levels are. Boulding presents a convenient method of classification:

1. The static structure—a level of framework, the anatomy of a system; for example, the structure of the universe.
2. The simple dynamic system—the level of clockworks, predetermined necessary motions.
3. The cybernetic system—the level of the thermostat. The system moves to maintain a given equilibrium through a process of self-regulation.
4. The open system—level of self-maintaining systems—moves toward and includes living organisms.
5. The genetic-societal system—level of cell society, characterized by a division of labor among cells.
6. Animal systems—level of mobility, evidence of goal-directed behavior.
7. Human systems—level of symbol interpretation and idea communication.
8. Social system—level of human organization.
9. Transcendental systems—level of ultimates and absolutes which exhibit systematic structure but are unknowable in essence.[51]

This approach to the study of systems by finding universals common at all levels of organization offers intriguing possibilities for administrative organization theory. A good deal of light could be thrown on social systems if structurally analogous elements could be found in the simpler types of systems. For example, cybernetic systems have characteristics which seem to be similar to feedback, regulation, and control phenomena in human organizations. Thus, certain facets of cybernetic models could be generalized to human organization. Considerable danger, however, lies in poorly founded analogies. Superficial similarities between simpler system forms and social systems are apparent everywhere. Instinctually based ant societies, for example, do not yield particularly instructive lessons for understanding rationally conceived human organizations. Thus, care should be taken that analogies used to bridge system levels are not mere devices for literary enrichment. For analogies to have usefulness and validity, they must exhibit inherent structural similarities or implicitly identical operational principles.[52]

Modern organization theory leads, as it has

[50] Kenneth E. Boulding, "General System Theory—The Skeleton of a Science," *Management Science* (April, 1956), pp. 200–202.

[51] *Ibid.*, pp. 202–205.

[52] Seidenberg, *op. cit.*, p. 136. The fruitful use of the type of analogies spoken of by Seidenberg is evident in the application of thermodynamic principles, particularly the entropy concept, to communication theory. See: Claude E. Shannon and Warren Weaver, *The Mathematical Theory of Communication* (Urbana: The University of Illinois Press, 1949). Further, the existence of a complete analogy between the operational behavior of thermodynamic systems, electrical communication systems, and biological systems has been noted by Y. S. Touloukian, *The Concept of Entropy in Communication, Living Organisms, and Thermodynamics*, Research Bulletin 130, Purdue Engineering Experiment Station.

been shown, almost inevitably into a discussion of general system theory. A science of organization universals has some strong advocates, particularly among biologists.[53] Organization theorists in administrative science cannot afford to overlook the contributions of general system theory. Indeed, modern organization concepts could offer a great deal to those working with general system theory. But the ideas dealt with in the general theory are exceedingly elusive.

Speaking of the concept of equilibrium as a unifying element in all systems, Easton says, "It (equilibrium) leaves the impression that we have a useful general theory when in fact, lacking measurability, it is a mere pretense for knowledge."[54] The inability to quantify and measure universal organization elements undermines the success of pragmatic tests to which general system theory might be put.

Organization Theory: Quo Vadis?

Most sciences have a vision of the universe to which they are applied, and administrative science is not an exception. This universe is composed of parts. One purpose of science is to synthesize the parts into an organized conception of its field of study. As a science matures, its theorems about the configuration of its universe change. The direction of change in three sciences, physics, economics, and sociology, is noted briefly for comparison with the development of an administrative view of human organization.

The first comprehensive and empirically verifiable outlook of the physical universe was presented by Newton in his *Principia*. Classical physics, founded on Newton's work, constitutes a grand scheme in which a wide range of physical phenomena could be organized and predicted. Newtonian physics may rightfully be regarded as "macro" in nature, because its system of organization was concerned largely with gross events of which the movement of celestial bodies, waves, energy forms, and strain are examples. For years classical physics was supreme, being applied continuously to smaller and smaller classes of phenomena in the physical universe. Physicists at one time adopted the view that everything in their realm could be discovered by simply subdividing problems. Physics thus moved into the "micro" order.

But in the nineteenth century a revolution took place motivated largely because events were being noted which could not be explained adequately by the conceptual framework supplied by the classical school. The consequences of this revolution are brilliantly described by Eddington:

> From the point of view of philosophy of science the conception associated with entropy must I think be ranked as the great contribution of the nineteenth century to scientific thought. It marked a reaction from the view that everything to which science need pay attention is discovered by microscopic dissection of objects. It provided an alternative standpoint in which the centre of interest is shifted from the entities reached by the customary analysis (atoms, electric potentials, etc.) to qualities possessed by the system as a whole, which cannot be split up and located—a little bit here, and a little bit there. . . .
>
> We often think that when we have completed our study of *one* we know all about *two*, because "two" is "one and one." We forget that we have still to make a study of "and." Secondary physics is the study of "and"—that is to say, of organization.[55]

Although modern physics often deals in minute quantities and oscillations, the conception of the physicist is on the "macro" scale. He is concerned with the "and," or the organization of the world in which the events occur. These developments did not invalidate classical physics as to its usefulness for explaining a certain range of phenomena. But classical physics is no longer the undisputed law of the universe. It is a special case.

Early economic theory, and Adam Smith's *Wealth of Nations* comes to mind, examined economic problems in the macro order. The

[53] For example see: Ludwig von Bertalanffy, *Problem of Life* (London: Watts and Company, 1952).

[54] David Easton, "Limits of the Equilibrium Model in Social Research," in *Profits and Problems of Homeostatic Models in the Behavioral Sciences*, Publication 1, Chicago Behavioral Sciences (1953), p. 39.

[55] Sir Arthur Eddington, *The Nature of the Physical World* (Ann Arbor: The University of Michigan Press, 1958), pp. 103–104.

Wealth of Nations is mainly concerned with matters of national income and welfare. Later, the economics of the firm, micro-economics, dominated the theoretical scene in this science. And, finally, with Keynes' *The General Theory of Employment Interest and Money,* a systematic approach to the economic universe was reintroduced on the macro level.

The first era of the developing science of sociology was occupied by the great social "system builders." Comte, the so-called father of sociology, had a macro view of society in that his chief works are devoted to social reorganization. Comte was concerned with the interrelationships among social, political, religious, and educational institutions. As sociology progressed, the science of society compressed. Emphasis shifted from the macro approach of the pioneers to detailed, empirical study of small social units. The compression of sociological analysis was accompanied by study of social pathology or disorganization.

In general, physics, economics, and sociology appear to have two things in common. First, they offered a macro point of view as their initial systematic comprehension of their area of study. Second, as the science developed, attention fragmented into analysis of the parts of the organization, rather than attending to the system as a whole. This is the micro phase.

In physics and economics, discontent was evidenced by some scientists at the continual atomization of the universe. The reaction to the micro approach was a new theory or theories dealing with the total system, on the macro level again. This third phase of scientific development seems to be more evident in physics and economics than in sociology.

The reason for the "macro-micro-macro" order of scientific progress lies, perhaps, in the hypothesis that usually the things which strike man first are of great magnitude. The scientist attempts to discover order in the vastness. But after macro laws or models of systems are postulated, variations appear which demand analysis, not so much in terms of the entire system, but more in terms of the specific parts which make it up. Then, intense study of the microcosm may result in new general laws, replacing the old models of organization. Or, the old and the new models may stand together, each explaining a different class of phenomena. Or, the old and the new concepts of organization may be welded to produce a single creative synthesis.

Now, what does all this have to do with the problem of organization in administrative science? Organization concepts seem to have gone through the same order of development in this field as in the three just mentioned. It is evident that the classical theory of organization, particularly as in the work of Mooney and Reiley, is concerned with the principles common to all organizations. It is a macro-organization view. The classical approach to organization, however, dealt with the gross anatomical parts and processes of the formal organization. Like classical physics, the classical theory of organization is a special case. Neither are especially well equipped to account for variation from their established framework.

Many variations in the classical administrative model result from human behavior. The only way these variations could be understood was by a microscopic examination of particularized, situational aspects of human behavior. The mission of the neoclassical school thus is "micro-analysis."

It was observed earlier, that somewhere along the line the concept of the social system, which is the key to understanding the Hawthorne studies, faded into the background. Maybe the idea is so obvious that it was lost to the view of researchers and writers in human relations. In any event, the press of research in the microcosmic universes of the informal organization, morale and productivity, leadership, participation, and the like forced the notion of the social system into limbo. Now, with the advent of modern organization theory, the social system has been resurrected.

Modern organization theory appears to be concerned with Eddington's "and." This school claims that its operational hypothesis is based on a macro point of view, that is, the study of organization as a whole. This nobility of purpose should not obscure, however, certain difficulties faced by this field as it is presently constituted. Modern organization theory raises two questions which should be explored further. First, would it not be more accurate to speak of modern organization theor*ies*? Second, just how much of modern organization theory is modern?

The first question can be answered with a

quick affirmative. Aside from the notion of the system, there are few, if any, other ideas of a unifying nature. Except for several important exceptions,[56] modern organization theorists tend to pursue their pet points of view,[57] suggesting they are part of system theory, but not troubling to show by what mystical means they arrive at this conclusion.

The irony of it all is that a field dealing with systems has, indeed, little system. Modern organization theory needs a framework, and it needs an integration of issues into a common conception of organization. Admittedly, this is a large order. But it is curious not to find serious analytical treatment of subjects like cybernetics or general system theory in Haire's *Modern Organizational Theory,* which claims to be a representative example of work in this field. Beer has ample evidence in his book *Cybernetics and Management* that cybernetics, if imaginatively approached, provides a valuable conceptual base for the study of systems.

The second question suggests an ambiguous answer. Modern organization theory is in part a product of the past; system analysis is not a new idea. Further, modern organization theory relies for supporting data on microcosmic research studies, generally drawn from the journals of the last ten years. The newness of modern organization theory, perhaps, is its effort to synthesize recent research contributions of many fields into a system theory characterized by a reoriented conception of organization.

One might ask, But what is the modern theorist reorienting? A clue is found in the almost snobbish disdain assumed by some authors of the neo-classical human relations school, and particularly, the classical school. Re-evaluation of the classical school of organization is overdue. However, this does not mean that its contributions to organization theory are irrelevant and should be overlooked in the rush to get on the "behavioral science bandwagon."

Haire announces that the papers appearing in *Modern Organization Theory* constitute, "the ragged leading edge of a wave of theoretical development."[58] Ragged, yes; but leading, no! The papers appearing in this book do not represent a theoretical breakthrough in the concept of organization. Haire's collection is an interesting potpourri with several contributions of considerable significance. But readers should beware that they will not find vastly new insights into organizational behavior in this book, if they have kept up with the literature of the social sciences, and have dabbled to some extent in the esoteria of biological theories of growth, information theory, and mathematical model building. For those who have not maintained the pace, *Modern Organization Theory* serves the admirable purpose of bringing them up-to-date on a rather diversified number of subjects.

Some work in modern organization theory is pioneering, making its appraisal difficult and future uncertain. While the direction of this endeavor is unclear, one thing is patently true. Human behavior in organizations, and indeed, organization itself, cannot be adequately understood within the ground rules of classical and neo-classical doctrines. Appreciation of human organization requires a *creative* synthesis of massive amounts of empirical data, a high order of deductive reasoning, imaginative research studies, and a taste for individual and social values. Accomplishment of all these objectives, and the inclusion of them into a framework of the concept of the system, appears to be the goal of modern organization theory. The vitality of administrative science rests on the advances modern theorists make along this line.

Modern organization theory, 1960 style, is an amorphous aggregation of synthesizers and restaters, with a few extending leadership on the frontier. For the sake of these few, it is well to admonish that pouring old wine into new bottles may make the spirits cloudy. Unfortunately, modern organization theory has almost succeeded in achieving the status of a fad. Popularization and exploitation contributed to the disrepute into which human relations has fallen. It would be a great waste if

[56] For example: E. Wight Bakke, *op. cit.*, pp. 18–75.

[57] There is a large selection including decision theory, individual-organization interaction, motivation, vitality, stability, growth, and graph theory, to mention a few.

[58] Mason Haire, "General Issues," in Mason Haire (editor), *Modern Organization Theory* (New York: John Wiley and Sons, 1959), p. 2.

modern organization theory yields to the same fate, particularly since both modern organization theory and human relations draw from the same promising source of inspiration—system analysis.

Modern organization theory needs tools of analysis and a conceptual framework uniquely its own, but it must also allow for the incorporation of relevant contributions of many fields. It may be that the framework will come from general system theory. New areas of research such as decision theory, information theory, and cybernetics also offer reasonable expectations of analytical and conceptual tools. Modern organization theory represents a frontier of research which has great significance for management. The potential is great, because it offers the opportunity for uniting what is valuable in classical theory with the social and natural sciences into a systematic and integrated conception of human organization.

4. SYSTEMS THEORY—A DISCREDITED PHILOSOPHY

D. C. PHILLIPS*

Modern systems theory appears to have developed as a result of dissatisfaction felt in certain quarters with the traditional method of studying complex systems. This traditional *analytic or mechanistic method* was to divide a system into discrete parts each of which was studied in isolation from the others. The whole system was then regarded as being the sum total of these isolated parts; according to this mechanistic view, it was the parts which determined the nature of the whole system. As an illustration a supporter of the mechanistic method might well choose the example of a watch. The features of the parts of the watch determine, so the argument runs, the features of the watch as a whole—for example, the accuracy and weight of the whole watch are determined by the precision and weight of the parts.

One of the founders of what is now known as general system theory was Ludwig von Bertalanffy. It is not surprising that he started his career as a biologist; for it is in biology, particularly, that an apparently good case can be made *against* the mechanistic or analytic method, and *for* the opposing *organismic* or *systems view*.[1] Consider, as an example of a complex biological system, the kangaroo. It could be argued by an organicist or system theorist that the features of the parts of this organism or system are determined by the characteristics of the whole organism—for example, the characteristics of the digestive tract of the kangaroo are determined by the nature of the whole kangaroo, his habitat, dietary habits, physiological features, heredity, evolutionary history, and so on.

But the organicist would not stop here. He would proceed to attack the mechanist's example by claiming that the treatment of a watch as an aggregate of parts is inadequate because it omits two essential features of the watch, namely, the order or interrelation of the parts, and the purpose that the watch was designed to fulfill. Any account of a watch that does not include these aspects is incomplete. Finally, apparently clinching his case, the organicist would argue that the theory which fails to describe a watch adequately, is utterly hopeless when faced with the task of describing a complex living system. This point is well illustrated by a passage written by Bertalanffy in 1933:

> Mechanism . . . provides us with no grasp of the specific characteristics of organisms, of the organization of organic processes among one another, of organic "wholeness," of the problem of the origin of organic "teleology," or of the historical character of organisms. . . . We must therefore try to establish a new standpoint which—as opposed to mechanism—takes account of organic wholeness, but . . . treats it in a manner which admits of scientific investigation.[2]

The new "standpoint" which Bertalanffy called for in order to do justice to "organic wholeness" was of course general system theory (GST). In a more recent work, *Problems of Life,* Bertalanffy called for the full and rigorous development of the organismic view, for he believed that organismic principles were applicable not only to the study of biological systems, but to *all* systems. Bertalanffy wrote:

SOURCE: *Abacus* (September, 1969), pp. 3–15. Reprinted by permission of Sydney University Press.

* Monash University, Victoria, Australia.

[1] These points are developed in more detail in D. C. Phillips, "Organicism in the Late Nineteenth and Early Twentieth Centuries," which is to be published in *The Journal of the History of Ideas.*

[2] Ludwig von Bertalanffy, *Modern Theories of Development,* transl. by J. H. Woodger, Harper Torchbooks, New York 1962, p. 46.

From the statements we have made, a stupendous perspective emerges, a vista towards a hitherto unsuspected unity of the conception of the world. Similar general principles have evolved everywhere, whether we are dealing with inanimate things, organisms, mental or social processes. What is the origin of these correspondences?

We answer this question by the *claim for a new realm of science, which we call General System Theory. It is a logico-mathematical field, the subject matter of which is the formulation and derivation of those principles which hold for systems in general. A "system" can be defined as a complex of elements standing in interaction. There are general principles holding for systems, irrespective of the nature of the component elements and of the relations or forces between them.*[3]

This call for the development of general system theory evidently was successful, for a considerable body of literature has developed in the field; an even greater mass of material has accumulated around the borders of the field—for example, William G. Scott has written that "Modern organization theory is on the periphery of general system theory."[4]

The foregoing brief discussion will serve as an introduction to general system theory. In the following pages five features of GST have been selected for examination, namely:

1. The failure of systems theorists to appreciate the history of their theory.
2. The failure to specify precisely what is meant by a "system."
3. The vagueness over what is to be included within systems theory.
4. The weakness of the charges brought against the analytic or mechanistic method.
5. The failure of GST as a scientific theory.

1. *The failure of systems theorists to appreciate the history of their theory.*

It is easy to find references, in recent writings on systems theory, to the work of Bertalanffy and to the shortcomings of the analytic method when applied to complex systems such as biological organisms. But it is rare to come across any more detailed account of the history of the central theses of GST.

One important insight into this history was revealed by Stafford Beer in a paper presented at the First Systems Symposium at Case Institute of Technology in 1960.[5] Beer commented that some of the ideas of the German philosopher Hegel (1770–1831) were relevant to systems theory, but he did not develop the point in any detail. The point *is* worth pursuing, however, for Hegelian ideas certainly are relevant to systems theory. Hegel held a form of organicism; he was an early but great systems theorist. But the interesting point is that his philosophy has long been discredited. The weaknesses of Hegelian thought are to some extent the weaknesses of GST.

Hegel is the most difficult, the most obscure, of all the major philosophers to read, but despite this (or because of it) he has been extremely influential. His philosophy dominated the English-speaking world of the late nineteenth and early twentieth centuries, and it is the Hegelian philosophy current at this time that will be referred to in what follows.

The Hegelians regarded the whole of reality as forming a *system,* the parts of which were *organically* or *internally* interrelated. Being a system, reality could not be studied successfully by dividing it into parts each of which was studied in isolation. For when a part was isolated from the whole system its nature changed—it was no longer a part of the whole, and it became an inaccurate guide as to the nature of the whole. It is apparent, therefore, that the Hegelian theory of organic or internal relations was directly opposed to the analytic or mechanistic method.[6]

The Hegelian theory of relations does not stand up to investigation. The theory is based upon the supposition that entities (such as the parts of a system) are altered by the relationships into which they enter. If A, B, and C are the interrelated parts of a system, then the natures of A, B, and C must be affected by

[3] Ludwig von Bertalanffy, *Problems of Life,* Harper Torchbooks, New York 1960, p. 199. (My emphasis)

[4] William G. Scott, "Organization Theory: An Overview and Appraisal," in Joseph A. Litterer (ed.), *Organizations: Structure and Behavior,* John Wiley, New York 1964, p. 23.

[5] Stafford Beer, "Below the Twilight Arch—A Mythology of Systems" in Donald P. Eckman (ed.), *Systems: Research and Design,* John Wiley, New York 1961.

[6] For further discussion *see* Phillips, "Organicism . . . ."

the interrelationships. Without this supposition, there would be no objection to isolating the parts of a system and studying them separately. The Oxford Hegelian philosopher, F. H. Bradley, writing in the late nineteenth century, gave a fairly clear account of the theory of internal relations.[7] He maintained that when entity A entered into a relationship with entity B or C it gained some property or quality or characteristic P as a result of this relationship. Without the relationship, and hence without the property P, Bradley argued, A would be different, it would be not-A. Any relation at all between A and any other entity necessarily determined some property of A, without which A would be different from what it is. This was the heart of the theory of internal relations: entities necessarily are altered by the relations into which they enter. Or as Bradley summed up the theory, "And the relation also must penetrate the inner being of its terms."[8] To mechanists, on the other hand, relations do not alter the entities that are related; as Hegel himself observed:

> And this constitutes the characteristic of Mechanism, which is, that whatever relation relates the terms is foreign to them and does not concern their nature; even if it involves the appearance of a One, it remains nothing else than a collocation, mixture, heap, or the like.[9]

The Hegelians' case has force so long as discussion centres around the "nature" of an entity, but much of the force is lost if the theory of internal relations is expressed in the terminology of the mid-twentieth century. The emphasis on the nature of entities is replaced by emphasis on the *defining and accompanying characteristics* affecting the usage of terms. Every entity has an indefinitely large number of characteristics, and those characteristics without which the entity would not be designated by a certain term are the characteristics that define the term. Accompanying characteristics are those characteristics that are not defining—their presence or absence makes no difference to the use of the term.[10]

Interpreted in this light, the Hegelians appear to have been maintaining that as a result of its relationship with any other entity B or C, entity A would have some characteristic P, and furthermore this characteristic would be one of the defining characteristics of A. Without A's relationship to entity B or C, this defining characteristic P would not exist, and thus in fact A would be not-A. Every relationship into which A entered, no matter what sort of a relationship it was, would determine a defining characteristic of A.

When phrased in terms of defining characteristics, the theory of internal relations can be seen to face serious difficulties. The main difficulty is that not all the characteristics of an entity are defining characteristics; many of the characteristics are accompanying characteristics. Thus, even if it is admitted that every relation which A enters into determines some characteristic of A, it is not *necessarily* the case that the characteristic determined by any one of these relations will be a defining characteristic of A. The characteristics determined by *some* of the relations will be defining characteristics, but some may not be.[11] It is possible, therefore, for A to enter into a relationship and yet remain unchanged.

A second difficulty in the theory of internal relations is that it makes the attaining of knowledge impossible. For to have knowledge of A, in the sense of knowing the defining features of A, all of A's relationships would have to be known; but since A is related to everything else in the whole of which it is a part, this whole must be known before A can be known. William James, who was a contemporary of Bradley, brilliantly parodied this particular feature of Hegelian thought:

> It costs nothing, not even a mental effort, to admit that the absolute totality of things may

[7] *See*, for example, F. H. Bradley, *Appearance and Reality*, Oxford University Press, 1962, pp. 513–19.

[8] Bradley, *Appearance and Reality*, p. 201.

[9] G. W. F. Hegel, *The Science of Logic*, transl. by Johnston and Struthers, Vol. II, Allen & Unwin, London 1929, p. 350. *See also* G. E. Moore, "External and Internal Relations" in his *Philosophical Studies*, Routledge and Kegan Paul, London 1960, especially p. 284.

[10] John Hospers, *An Introduction to Philosophical Analysis*, rev. edn, Routledge and Kegan Paul, London 1967, Ch. 1.

[11] This appears to have been the substance of G. E. Moore's attacks on internal relations around the turn of the century.

> be organized exactly after the pattern of one of these "through-and-through" abstractions. In fact, it is the pleasantest and freest of mental movements. Husband makes, and is made by, wife, through marriage; one makes other by being itself other; everything self-created through its opposite—you go round like a squirrel in a cage. . . . *What, in fact, is the logic of these abstract systems? It is, as we said above: if any Member, then the Whole System; if not the Whole System, then Nothing.*[12]

Or as Bertrand Russell said of Hegelianism more recently, "If all knowledge were knowledge of the universe as a whole, there would be no knowledge."[13]

The theory of internal relations had at least four corollaries that were recognized by Hegelian philosophers of the late nineteenth century (and, indeed, probably by everyone who accepted organismic ideas). They were:

> (i) the whole is more than the sum of the parts; (ii) the whole determines the nature of the parts; (iii) the parts cannot be understood if considered in isolation from the whole; (iv) the parts are dynamically interrelated or interdependent.

These ideas can be criticized on a number of grounds.[14] In the first place, being based upon the theory of internal relations, they become suspect as soon as this theory is rejected. The fourth idea, however, can be supported on other grounds, and removal of the support given by the theory of internal relations is not fatal to it—a mechanist, for example, can fully agree that the parts of certain systems are dynamically interrelated. Secondly, the first three ideas suffer from vagueness, or worse. The statement of the first idea, for instance, uses the term "sum," without making clear what precisely is meant. In mathematics there are three types of "sum"—arithmetic sum, algebraic sum, and vector sum; it is not a difficult matter to invent and stipulate a sense of "sum" in which the whole *is* greater than the sum of the parts. The second idea suggests that, because the parts are parts of the whole, the whole determines itself. As one critic wrote in 1903: "That this supposition is self-contradictory a very little reflection should be sufficient to show."[15] The third idea suggests that it cannot be predicted, from the fact that an entity has properties l, m, and n when it is isolated from certain other entities, what properties the entity will have when it comes into relationships with these other entities. This suggestion is unwarranted; the Hegelians and organicists have offered no evidence to show that this type of prediction is impossible. Furthermore, the weight of the evidence actually is against them here, for the physical sciences can provide numerous examples of successful prediction of the properties an entity can be expected to display when it is placed in novel conditions.[16]

Apart from Hegelian philosophy, there is one further aspect of the history of the ideas underlying general system theory that recent writers have ignored. This concerns developments within biological science in the late nineteenth century. Many of the points made by Bertalanffy in the decades since 1930 were given a prior statement in this earlier period. In the late nineteenth century, findings in embryology, cellular biology, and physiology, led a number of biologists to maintain that the mechanistic method was, in principle, inapplicable to biology.[17] The difficulty was that the biologists were unable to develop mechanistic theories to explain the new findings. (It can now be seen that their knowledge of biology, and of relevant related disciplines such as biochemistry, was not detailed enough to enable them to produce successful explanations.) Thus, writing in 1884, J. S. Haldane rejected the mechanistic approach; he produced this remarkably contemporary-sounding systems-type statement:

[12] William James, "Absolutism and Empiricism" in *Mind,* IX, 1884, pp. 282–3. (My emphasis)

[13] Bertrand Russell, *A History of Western Philosophy,* Allen & Unwin, London 1948, p. 772.

[14] A detailed discussion of the four ideas, and the criticisms that can be levelled against them, is given in Phillips, "Organicism . . . ."

[15] G. E. Moore, *Principia Ethica,* London 1960, p. 33.

[16] For example, it is possible to predict the properties materials will possess under abnormal conditions of temperature or pressure, or the characteristics a component will display when inserted into an electrical circuit.

[17] This led to a resurgence of vitalism in biology in the late nineteenth century, together with the development of organicism and the "theory" of creative evolution.

These parts (of the organism) stand to one another and to the surroundings, not in the relation of cause and effect, but in that of reciprocity. *The parts of an organism and its surroundings thus form a system,* any one of the parts of which constantly acts on the rest, but only does so, *qua* part of the system, in so far as they at the same time act on it.[18]

J. S. Haldane, together with his brother R. B., and Edmund Montgomery, were prominent organicists in the late nineteenth century; they were joined by many others in the twentieth century, including J. H. Woodger, C. Lloyd Morgan, E. R. Russell, W. E. Agar, and the statesman General Smuts.

In conclusion, it must be re-emphasized that the ideas that have been discussed in this account of the Hegelianism and organismic biology of the late nineteenth and early twentieth centuries are ideas that are often referred to by contemporary writers on systems theory. One could be excused for mistaking the following mid-twentieth-century argument from Bertalanffy, for example, for a sample of late nineteenth-century thought:

Every organism represents a *system,* by which term we mean a complex of elements in mutual interaction. From this obvious statement the limitations of the analytical and summative conceptions must follow. First, it is impossible to resolve the phenomena of life completely into elementary units; for each individual part and each individual event depends not only on conditions within itself, but also to a greater or lesser extent on the conditions within the *whole,* or within superordinate units of which it is a part. Hence the behaviour of an isolated part is, in general, different from its behaviour within the context of the whole. . . . Secondly, the actual whole shows properties that are absent from its isolated parts.[19]

2. *The failure to specify precisely what is meant by a "system."*

GST has as its function the formulation of the laws applicable to all systems, irrespective of what actually composes the elements of these systems. Although somewhat ambitious, the quest for GST is not necessarily Quixotic; all depends upon what is meant by the term "system." But it is here that the accounts given by systems theorists have been unsatisfactory.

Bertalanffy defined a system as a "complex of elements in mutual interaction." Anatol Rapoport stated that a "whole which functions as a whole by virtue of the interdependence of its parts is called a system . . . ."[20] And R. L. Ackoff wrote that initially "we can define a system broadly and crudely as any entity, conceptual or physical, which consists of interdependent parts."[21] These definitions show that no significant advance in thinking about the general concept of a system has taken place since the late nineteenth century; the Haldane brothers and the biologist Edmund Montgomery had ideas that ran parallel to those of mid-twentieth century systems theorists. It is instructive to examine the situation the men of the late nineteenth century found themselves in because of this notion of a system.

Edmund Montgomery had made a particular study of simpler animals; he reached the conclusion that in all animals the whole (or the system) "is here in all reality antecedent to its parts." The parts of an organism or system "are specialized and segregated from a pre-existing whole, and are in no way discrete and independent units joined together . . . ."[22] The Haldane brothers went further. J. S. Haldane wrote that the whole was not merely the organism, but the organism together with the environment; then with his brother he took another step forward; they suggested that it followed from the fact that an organism and its environment form a system, that the species "may itself be looked upon as a compound organism."[23] The Hegelian philosophers took the final step; all of reality (or the Absolute, as

[18] J. S. Haldane, "Life and Mechanism" in *Mind,* IX, 1884, p. 33.

[19] Ludwig von Bertalanffy, *Problems of Life,* pp. 11–12.

[20] Anatol Rapoport, "Foreword" in Walter Buckley (ed.), *Modern Systems Research for the Behavioral Scientist,* Chicago 1968, p. xvii.

[21] R. L. Ackoff, "Systems, Organizations, and Interdisciplinary Research" in Eckman (ed.), *Systems . . .,* pp. 27–8.

[22] Edmund Montgomery, "The Unity of the Organic Individual" in *Mind,* V, 1880, p. 326.

[23] R. B. and J. S. Haldane, "The Relation of Philosophy to Science" in Andrew Seth and R. B. Haldane (eds.), *Essays in Philosophical Criticism,* London 1883, p. 58.

they called it) was a whole, a system. In F. H. Bradley's words:

> The universe is one in this sense that its differences exist harmoniously within one whole, beyond which there is nothing. Hence the Absolute is, so far, an individual and a system. . . .[24]

It is apparent that the same reasoning underlies these various examples; the principles that led Montgomery to identify the whole as being the individual biological organism, led the Haldanes and the Hegelians to their respective views. An exactly similar situation exists for general system theorists. The concept of a system with which they operate does not give them any grounds for limiting their attention to anything but the universe as a whole. An example should make the point clear. Suppose a general system theorist is treating an army unit as a system. Now, if a system is a "complex of elements in interaction," it can be argued with some justice that an army unit is not an independent system as it is itself interrelated with many other "entities" to form a more embracing system. And once the general system theorist embarks on this road, as in fact he did when he defined a system as "elements in interaction," he seems committed to continuing his journey until he arrives at the end of the road and joins the Hegelians in contemplating the whole of reality! This difficulty has been recognized by at least one systems theorist; Stafford Beer, in his paper to the Symposium at Case Institute of Technology, stated that:

> . . . earlier it was contended that the boundaries of a system are subjective; and this is strongly supported at the philosophical level by the Hegelian axiom of internal relations—which of course makes it logically possible to equate every system with the universe itself. So the crucial scientific problem for systems research is this: how to separate a particular viable system for study from the rest of the universe without committing an annihilating *divisio* . . . these are problems of desperate urgency for every nontrivial systems study. . . .[25]

Beer was not exaggerating when he identified this problem as being of desperate urgency; and he also was right in raising the issue of triviality. It is indeed trivial to define a system in terms of interrelation of components; every entity in the universe enters into *some* relationships, and everything, therefore, can be regarded as a component of some sort of system.[26] The general system theorists' definition of a system, seen in this light, is not particularly informative. In effect the definition tells us that a system is that which can be composed of any things interrelated anyhow; for sheer profundity this bears comparison with William James' famous parody of the definition of evolution:

> Evolution is a change from a no-howish untalkaboutable all-alikeness to a some-howish and in general talkaboutable not-all-alikeness by continuous sticktogetherations and somethingelseifications.[27]

It might be thought that the general system theorists' problem of specifying what they mean by a system is susceptible of a simple solution. Cannot a theorist simply select out certain interrelated entities that happen to be of relevance to his particular investigation, and call this group of entities a system? This is proposed, for example, by A. D. Hall and R. E. Fagen, in the introductory chapter of *Systems Engineering*.[28] But this cure for the systems theorists' ills turns out to be far worse than the original disease, for it runs foul of some of

24 Bradley, *Appearance and Reality,* p. 127.

25 Stafford Beer, "Below the Twilight Arch," pp. 18–19. It is interesting to note that in a work on systems engineering Hall and Fagen raise the same problem in another form. They define the environment of a system as that which is in interrelation with the system, and this leads them to the problem of distinguishing when an object belongs to a system and when it belongs to the environment. They state: "The answer is by no means definite." A. D. Hall and R. E. Fagen, "Definition of System" in Buckley (ed.), *Modern Systems Research,* p. 83.

26 Hall and Fagen acknowledge this by stating "For any given set of objects it is impossible to say that no interrelationships exist . . .," "Definition of System," p. 82.

27 As quoted by Ralph Barton Perry, *The Thought and Character of William James,* Vol. I, London 1935, p. 482.

28 Hall and Fagen, "Definition of System," particularly p. 82.

the fundamental principles of GST. In the first place, the theorist can only select relevant entities if he has some principles of selection or criteria of relevance, and he can only have these for the particular problem under consideration if investigation has been under way and has made considerable headway. The investigation must have reached the stage where it is possible to say entities a, b, and c are relevant to the solution of the problem and entities d, e, and f are not relevant. Furthermore, this fairly advanced stage of investigation must have been reached without using systems methods, for what is under consideration here is what is necessary *before* a systems theorist can select or define his system. In fact, it is most likely that the mechanistic or analytic method that general system theorists claim is not applicable, has been the method used to achieve these important advances in the investigation.

The second objection to the simple cure that was proposed, is that in stipulating that the particular group of entities of interest to him form the relevant system, the general system theorist has not gone far enough. He also has to show that in isolating this system from the other entities with which it is normally interrelated, he has not introduced artifacts; or as Beer put it, the systems theorist has to show that he has not committed an "annihilating *divisio*." One of the main points made by GST is that the interrelationships between the parts of a system are of vital importance, and in isolating a system for study the theorist is *severing* some interrelationships—he is doing the very thing that his own creed tells him should not be done.

3. *The vagueness over what is to be included within systems theory.*

In Bertalanffy's early conception, GST had as its subject matter "the formulation and derivation of those principles which hold for systems in general."[29] In subsequent years, however, a puzzling situation developed. Some works on GST have put forward *classifications* of systems,[30] while others have contained discussions of concepts important in investigations of systems—wholeness, sum, emergence, open and closed systems, the entropy of systems, the principle of equifinality, and so on.[31] But the most puzzling feature emerges clearly in an essay by Bertalanffy published in 1962. Bertalanffy distinguished between systems theory in "the broad sense" and general system theory "in the narrower sense." He identified seven different bodies of theory as constituting systems theory in "the broad sense," namely: cybernetics, information theory, game theory, decision theory, topology, factor analysis, and finally, GST.[32]

The puzzle here is what these seven areas of systems theory have in common. Apart from the trivial fact that they all can have the word "system" applied to them, they seem to have little, if anything, in common. Certainly GST is different in kind from the other six areas of theory mentioned by Bertalanffy; if these six are regarded as second order studies, then GST is at an even greater level of abstraction and must be classified as a third-order study.[33] It follows that it is a serious confusion to group these second- and third-order studies together as if they were analogous or parallel studies. Furthermore, the opposition of GST to the mechanistic or analytic method, and its resemblances to Hegelianism and the biological organicism of the late nineteenth century, again mark it off as quite different from the other six areas of theory. If these basic tenets of GST were rejected, the other six bodies of theory identified by Bertalanffy apparently would be able to stand virtually unshaken by the calamity that had overtaken GST. Or to put the point another way, studies or theories of a lower order are always able to survive the demise of a theory of a higher order of abstraction, and so the six second-order systems studies could survive the death of the third-order study, GST. It is this third-order study that is the centre of interest for the present paper. The objections brought against GST do not

29 *See* footnote 3.

30 For example, Kenneth E. Boulding, "General Systems Theory—The Skeleton of Science" in Buckley (ed.), *Modern Systems Research.*

31 *See Modern Systems Research,* Parts II and III.

32 Bertalanffy, "General Systems Theory—A Critical Review" in *Modern Systems Research,* p. 13.

33 According to the usage adopted here, a first-order study would be a study of "particulars"—e.g., a particular feedback system; a second-order study would be at the next level of generality—e.g., a study of feedback systems in general; a third-order study would be even more general—e.g., a study of many different *types* of system (feedback, information, biological, and so on).

necessarily apply to these other areas of "systems theory in the broad sense."

4. *The weakness of the charges brought against the analytic or mechanistic method.*

The nature of the objections levelled by general system theorists against the traditional analytic or mechanistic method has already been outlined. This method is useful in many areas of science, they say, but it is not applicable to biology or any other area where complex systems are being studied. As Anatol Rapoport expressed it:

Biological processes are simply too complex to yield to the analytic method. . . . When we turn to attempts to subject human behavior to scientific analysis, the problem becomes even more severe. . . . It follows that understanding cannot be extended beyond the scope of physical science without introducing concepts which embody irreducible wholes in place of physically measurable variables.[34]

Or, in Bertalanffy's words:

Thus the problem of wholeness and organization sets a limit to the analytical and summative description and explanation.[35]

A further weakness of the analytic method, it has been claimed, is that it does not do justice to the hierarchical organization found in complex systems.[36] The particular fact which the analytic method cannot deal with is that

at certain stages of complexity in the interrelations of components, a "discontinuity" . . . or emergent level of organization with novel features, may develop.[37]

This is the well-known problem of emergence. Traditionally it has been illustrated by the following example: A molecule of the compound, water, consists of two atoms of hydrogen and one atom of oxygen in combination, hence the formula H_2O. If these hydrogen and oxygen atoms were studied in isolation from each other, and their properties determined, it could not be deduced from this information that if they were combined they would form the colourless, odourless and tasteless liquid we label with the name "water." The combination of the atoms, and the resultant production of a substance with unpredictable properties, is an example of the phenomenon of emergence.

These difficulties are not quite as difficult for the supporters of the mechanistic or analytic method to answer as general system theorists seem to imagine. In the first place, two conditions are necessary for the mechanistic explanation of any system: the law or laws applicable to the system have to be known, and the initial conditions have to be known.[38] Consider as an example a system consisting of a container full of water, into one corner of which some liquid dye has been introduced. With the passage of time the dye will diffuse throughout the container. For a satisfactory explanation of this particular phenomenon to be given, the law of diffusion has to be known, and so also does the set of initial conditions (the nature of the dye, its original temperature, and its original position in the container of water, etc.). The same two general conditions are necessary for the explanation of more complex systems, but here of course the discovery of the laws is more difficult, and there are so many factors involved that the statement of the initial conditions is an extremely complex task. General system theorists, however, have not shown that *in principle* either of these two difficult tasks is impossible; neither have they shown that there is any effective substitute for the piecemeal investigation of parts of the system—the method of investigation that is the core of the mechanistic method. By their own creed, systems theorists are bound to study the whole—which effectively is the whole of reality, and this is a method which in practice cannot be strictly followed. As Bertrand Russell pointed out, if knowledge is knowledge of the whole, then the attainment of knowledge becomes impossible.

Secondly, the question of emergence has

[34] Foreword in Buckley, *Modern Systems Research,* p. xvii.

[35] *Problems of Life,* p. 14.

[36] For an interesting discussion of hierarchical organization, and a novel vocabulary to facilitate discussion of this type of organization, *see* Arthur Koestler, *The Ghost in the Machine,* London 1967. In the book Koestler acknowledges his debt to Bertalanffy.

[37] Walter Buckley, Introduction to Part II in Buckley (ed.), *Modern Systems Research,* p. 37.

[38] Ernest Nagel, *The Structure of Science,* London 1961, pp. 438, 442–3.

often been mishandled because of failure to recognize a central point. The philosopher of science, Ernest Nagel, has written:

The logical point constituting the core of the doctrine of emergence is applicable to all areas of inquiry and is as relevant to the analysis of explanations within mechanics and physics generally as it is to discussions of the laws of other sciences.[39]

The logical point that Nagel refers to is that the conclusion of a valid deduction cannot contain an expression that does not appear in the premises; this indeed is the core of the issue, because scientific explanations can be put in the form of deductions. It follows from this logical point that the possession of an emergent property cannot be deduced from premises that do *not* contain reference to this property; it is logically impossible, for example, to deduce the production of a colourless, odourless and tasteless liquid (i.e. water), from premises that refer only to the properties of the gaseous substances hydrogen and oxygen. Thus, although the mechanistic method may fail to deal satisfactorily with emergent properties, no other method could do any better, for the stumbling block is a logical impossibility.

5. *The failure of GST as a scientific theory.*

Perhaps the most important feature of a scientific theory is its *predictive value*. With the aid of a theory it should be possible to make a prediction about some future observable event. Sir Karl Popper has explicated this predictive function of science in detail,[40] and he has argued that non-scientific theories (or pseudo-scientific theories) do not have predictive value. In one interesting passage, Popper wrote of his own youth when four theories aroused great interest—Einstein's theory of relativity, Marx's theory of history, Freud's psycho-analysis, and Alfred Adler's individual psychology. From Einstein's theory an improbable-looking prediction was made, and during an eclipse in 1919 Eddington made observations that could have refuted Einstein's theory; however, the theory stood the test and was corroborated. The case was quite different with the other three theories:

I found that those of my friends who were admirers of Marx, Freud, and Adler, were impressed by a number of points common to these theories, and especially by their apparent *explanatory power*. These theories appeared to be able to explain practically everything that happened within the fields to which they referred. . . . Once your eyes were thus opened you saw confirming instances everywhere: the world was full of verifications of the theory. What ever happened always confirmed it. . . . It was precisely this fact—that they always fitted, that they were always confirmed—which in the eyes of their admirers constituted the strongest argument in favour of these theories. It began to dawn on me that this apparent strength was in fact their weakness.[41]

In Popper's view, these theories were not scientific; they were not useful in making predictions, hence they never took a risk and they never faced even the possibility of refutation.

It is interesting to consider GST in the light of Popper's remarks. Like Marxism or Freudianism, GST is wise after the event—it is always possible for a general system theorist to explain in his own theoretical terms what has happened in a particular system he is investigating, but only *after* the "happening" has taken place. The theorist's predictions *before* the event usually are not predictions in the scientific sense at all—they are far too vague. (The exception would be when the theorist is investigating a system where precise laws have been discovered by the traditional mechanistic means, e.g., electronic circuits, mechanical systems, or certain physiological systems.)[42]

As an example of the weakness of systems theory with respect to predictive power—and hence its weakness as a scientific theory—consider the recent book, *The World Educational Crisis: A Systems Analysis*, by Philip H. Coombs, Director of the International Institute for Educational Planning, a division of

[39] *The Structure of Science*, pp. 372–3.

[40] Karl Popper, *The Logic of Scientific Discovery*, London 1965.

[41] Karl Popper, *Conjectures and Refutations*, 2nd edn., London 1965, pp. 34–5.

[42] Also included here would be predictions made by, for example, a cyberneticist or an informations expert. As was pointed out earlier, these areas of specialization are not subject to the serious criticisms that can be levelled against GST.

UNESCO.[43] Coombs studied the educational systems of many emerging and developed nations, his aim being to determine the effects on these systems of changes in various of their parts. He concentrated on such things as shortage of teachers, increases in costs, and increases in the number of pupils; the great changes in these items over the last few years constitutes the present world crisis in education. It is a marked feature of Coombs' book, however, that he is unable to make precise predictions. From the fact that a given educational system has had a threefold increase in incoming pupils in a very short period, for example, Coombs is unable to predict how the system will adjust to this serious alteration of input. It is a truism to say that some changes must occur; furthermore, it is possible to make a guess as to the likely changes, for the range of possibilities is a fairly limited one. But in order to make this sort of guess one does not have to be a systems theorist.

This weakness of GST seems to have been recognized by its keenest supporter. Perhaps it is well to end the paper where it began, with Bertalanffy. In a critical review of GST in 1962, he wrote:

> The decisive question is that of the explanatory and predictive value of the "new theories" attacking the host of problems around wholeness, teleology, etc. . . . *There is no question that new horizons have been opened up but the relations to empirical facts often remain tenuous.*[44]

[43] New York 1968.

[44] "General System Theory—A Critical Review" in Buckley (ed.), *Modern Systems Research,* p. 21.

BIBLIOGRAPHY

Ackoff, Russell L., "Systems, Organization, and Interdisciplinary Research," *General Systems,* **V**, 1960, 1–8.

———, *Scientific Method: Optimizing Applied Research Decisions,* John Wiley and Sons, 1962.

Ashby, W. Ross, "General Systems Theory as a New Discipline," *General Systems,* **III**, 1958, 1–6.

———, *Design for a Brain,* John Wiley and Sons, 1960.

Beer, Stafford, "Below the Twilight Arch: A Mythology of Systems," *General Systems,* **V**, 1960, 9–20.

Bertalanffy, Ludwig Von, "An Outline of General System Theory," *British Journal of the Philosophy of Science,* **I**, 1950, 139–164.

———, "General System Theory," *Main Currents in Modern Thought,* **II**, 1955, 75–83.

———, "A Biologist Looks at Human Nature," *Scientific Monthly,* **LXXXII**, 1956, 33–41.

———, "General System Theory—A Critical Review," *General Systems,* **VII**, 1962, 1–20.

———, *General System Theory,* George Braziller, Inc., 1969.

Boulding, Kenneth E., "Toward a General Theory of Growth," *General Systems,* **I**, 1956, 66–75.

———, "General Systems as a Point of View," in Mihajlo D. Mesarović (ed.), *Views on General Systems Theory,* John Wiley and Sons, 1964, 25–38.

Bross, Irwin, D. J., *Design for Decision,* The Macmillan Co., 1953.

Buck, R. C., "On the Logic of General Behavior Systems Theory," in Herbert Feigel and Michael Scriven, *Minnesota Studies in the Philosophy of Science,* Vol. 1, University of Minnesota Press, 1956.

Buckley, Walter (ed.), *Modern Systems Research for the Behavioral Scientist,* Aldine Publishing Company, 1968.

Churchman, C. West, *The Systems Approach,* Dalecort Press, 1968a.

———, *A Challenge to Reason,* McGraw-Hill Book Company, 1968b.

Eckman, Donald P. (ed.), *Systems: Research and Design,* John Wiley and Sons, 1961.

Hall, Arthur D., *A Methodology for Systems Engineering,* D. Van Nostrand, 1962.

———, and R. E. Fagen, "Definition of System," *General Systems,* **I**, 1956, 18–28.

Helmer, Olaf, "On the Epistemology of the Inexact Sciences," *Management Sciences,* **VI**, October, 1960.

Kuhn, Alfred, *The Study of Society: A Unified Approach,* Irwin & Dorsey, 1963.

Litterer, Joseph A. (ed.), *Organizations: Systems, Control and Adaptation,* Vol. 2, 2d ed., John Wiley and Sons, 1969.

Mesarović, Mihajlo D. (ed.), *Views on General Systems Theory,* John Wiley and Sons, 1964.

Miller, James, "Towards a General Theory for the Behavioral Sciences," *American Psychologist,* **X**, 1955, 513–531.

Rapoport, Anatol, "Mathematical Aspects of General Systems Theory," *General Systems,* **XI**, 1966, 3–11.

Sengupta, S. S., and Russell L. Ackoff, "Systems Theory from an Operations Research Point of View," *IEEE Transactions on Systems Science and Cybernetics,* November, 1965.

SECTION II

CYBERNETICS

For many years now automatic control systems, which have been largely confined to governors, servomechanisms, and the like, have had their greatest impact and application in the field of engineering. This is not a thing to be wondered at, for ever since the 1790's when James Watt invented his "governor"—the mechanical regulator for stabilizing the speed of rotation of the steam engine, the field of cybernetics has been almost wholly dominated by the mechanical engineer. Even today many of the guidance and control systems employed in missiles are based on fundamentally the same principles that were enunciated decades ago. While it is true that automatic control systems are being used more extensively year by year, still there is relatively little application of such systems outside the realm of mechanical devices. Until the recent contributions to cybernetics of such men as Norbert Wiener, W. Ross Ashby, and Stafford Beer (to name but a few), the all-important idea of feedback, so vital to a cybernetic system, has only with extreme difficulty been transferred to the political, economic, social, and managerial fields.

Historically cybernetics dates from the time of Plato who, in his *Republic,* used the term *kybernetike* (a Greek term meaning "the art of steersmanship") both in its literal sense of piloting a vessel and in the metaphorical sense of piloting the ship of state, i.e., the art of government. In time the metaphorical sense became the predominant one to be replaced by the literal mechanical sense, and it is only now that the meaning of the term has come full circle.

The various selections in this section will be concerned with the concise exposition of the field of cybernetics (often characterized as the science of communication and control) and with its application to several "orthodox" areas of investigation. It is not surprising that the social scientist as well as the industrial manager exhibit more than a passing interest in the science of cybernetics. Because of the tremendous technological advances of modern times, especially with regard to the high-speed electronic computer with its data processing potential, only now are the formal aspects of cybernetics being seriously applied to the man-to-machine and man-to-man systems.

One important characteristic of all control systems is feedback. Regardless of the particular type of control we are interested in, whether it be quality control, budgetary control, production control, inventory control, missile control, social control, etc., the idea of feedback permeates the entire control spectrum. Since control always implies the existence of some basic plan to be implemented or some standard to be applied and of some reliable means of measuring and correcting deviations from the plan or standard, feedback is essential if a steady state or equilibrium is to be achieved and maintained.

From the point of view of the business manager an understanding of feedback is vital and yet the appropriateness of this has often not been sufficiently recognized. An earlier section elucidated the role of the computer in providing timely, up-to-date feedback. And with the advent of the computer the behavior of even extremely complex systems can now be predicted.

Cybernetics is a new interdisciplinary science. As such it makes use of older concepts peculiar to several disciplines, concepts which have performed admirably in the service of the older sciences, and attempts to weave them into one general hybrid discipline centering around the information and control functions.

In the first selection, Charles Dechert outlines the history of the discipline from its early beginnings down to modern times, sketching rapidly the contributions of the mechanical engineers, mathematicians, and physiologists.

Every cybernetic system has three basic components, viz., a detector or sensor, a selector or decision-making element, and an effector. The detector is the component sensitive to the state of the particular quality to be controlled. The selector or control unit is the element capable of selecting from among several possible responses on the basis of information sensed by the detector or by the preset condition of the selector itself. Finally, the effector is that component that can bring about some change in the condition sensed by the detector. Consequently self-regulation demands that the three functions of perception, decision-making, and action be at least conceptually distinct.

It is however the control loop that characterizes any self-regulating system. Control necessarily involves the communication of information, here understood as any input data capable of influencing the behavior of another. Thus cybernetics is, in the words of Wiener, the "*control and communication* in the animal and the machine." Progress in communications and control theory has advanced so far that it is today one of the chief factors in the modern technological revolution.

In the popular imagination cybernetics and the digital computer have been wedded, and rightly so, for it is the computer that has made possible the automatic factory, and the myriad forms of automated activity that characterizes modern civilization.

In the man-machine system the machine is viewed as a projection of the human personality, subject normally to human control. In the simplest type of such a system the person serves both as the source of energy and the source of control. In more advanced types prime movers provide the energy while man provides the control. In still more advanced types the machine is more or less self-regulating and man controls the programming phase alone. As we advance up the hierarchy of systems we thus notice a gradual shift in the concept of control. The same is true as we move from the realm of machines controlling machines, men controlling machines, and men controlling men.

It is in the field of the social sciences that the author believes great possibilities exist for cybernetics. Many of the basic concepts of cybernetics are relevant to an understanding of social groups and social organizations. For years now political science, cultural anthropology, and social psychology have analyzed social groups as complex communications networks characterized by a multiplicity of feedback loops. However, much progress still remains to be made in the field of the behavioral sciences.

The brief reading excerpted from the excellent text by Klir and Valach enables one to locate cybernetics in the hierarchy of the sciences. In antiquity there was but one science, philosophy, encompassing all human knowledge, but as the fund of knowledge increased, the natural sciences (mathematics and astronomy) were distinguished from philosophy. These in the course of centuries underwent constant development and further refinement until today we have a proliferation of fundamental and specialized sciences. Of the fundamental sciences one can note the following: philosophy, mathematics, cybernetics, the natural sciences, the human sciences, and the engineering sciences. Philosophy still holds a very special place in the domain of the sciences, since its chief task continues to be the unification of all human knowledge dispersed in the individual sciences.

Each of the fundamental sciences can be divided and subdivided, with increasing specialization at the lower levels. This holds true of cybernetics too, a rather young science.

In any categorization of the sciences, it is well-nigh impossible not to have some overlapping. Cybernetics overlaps both mathematics and philosophy, as well as some specialized sciences. Its role with respect to linguistics is especially fascinating at the present time. In its relation to the other sciences one must carefully distinguish between the so-called-mass-energy viewpoint and the cybernetic viewpoint.

Churchman et al., in their reading, "Analysis of Organizations," are concerned with the application of cybernetic models (communication and control) to the industrial organization. The authors logically proceed with a discussion of the concepts of communications and control before attempting to integrate them.

Three types of knowledge are necessary to construct a communication model: (1) knowledge of a communication network that exists at a given level, (2) knowledge of existing control processes in the network, and (3) knowledge of how existing network and control processes change with time. With the above it is possible to construct a graphical model of the organization that would show the interconnection of the various parts. The resultant diagram would show the same type relationship as that of a physiologist's nervous system or an engineer's electrical circuit.

Organizations, however, exhibit another important characteristic, that of interdependency. The various elements of the organization must operate together to maintain or reach some goal. All organizations, departments, and the like are essentially goal-seeking (purposeful) units and as such direct their behavior to the attainment of some goal.

Given this goal-seeking attribute, negative feedback is required to reduce errors that may exist between the desired and the actual. From this simple negative feedback circuit, the authors go on to discuss second-order feedback systems that utilize a memory unit in which alternative actions can be considered whenever external conditions change. In the instance where information in the memory units can be recombined to produce new alternatives (third-order feedback systems), the organization is said to acquire a "consciousness" whereby it can change goals and direct its own growth.

A composite communication model is presented that ties together these concepts of communications and control in organizations.

Stafford Beer's 1958 paper presented to the Operational Research Society of London is an admirable example of clear thinking and of straightforward presentation. He attacks the problem very logically, first exposing for view the nature of cybernetics, then that of operations research, and finally tying both ends together.

Cybernetics is seen as the science whose object of study is control. It aims to study the nature of control *per se,* control common to many fields of investigation. Hence its interdisciplinary nature, hence its relevance to industrial, social, economic, mechanical, and biological systems.

Control is an essential attribute of a system which he then goes on to define in a relativistic way as "a collection of entities that can be understood as forming a coherent group." Relatedness is but the structural element of systems.

Every cybernetic system has three essential features. It is extremely complex, probabilistic, and self-regulating.

"Operational research," Beer affirms, "is the attack of modern science on problems of likelihood which arise in the management and control of men and machines, materials and money in their natural environment. Its special technique is to invent a strategy of control by measuring, comparing, and predicting probable behavior through a scientific model of a situation." Note that operations research is not considered to be a science; it is a method of science, a subset of the scientific method so appropriate for analysis of activity. As such it is nothing more or less than logical induction. The characteristic tool of operations research for dealing with problems of control is model construction.

Operations research and cybernetics have very much in common. They share the same general common concern for control, the same complexity and probabilistic nature, a common level of sophistication, reciprocity of method, and an interdisciplinary approach.

In Beer's view communication is nothing else than employing the language of the structure that makes the system what it is. The languages that can be used for this purpose are logic, mathematics, statistics, and metamathematics. Because cybernetics is interdisciplinary it must talk in the language of some science. The language of physiology so often employed is a language of identities, not merely of metaphors or analogies.

In summary, operational research is a body of methods which provide a powerful investigative tool. Cybernetics, on the other hand, is a body of knowledge enjoying the status of a science. The two are methodologically complementary; operations research is the natural technique in research of cybernetics, while the latter is the natural embodiment in science of the former.

5. THE DEVELOPMENT OF CYBERNETICS *

CHARLES R. DECHERT †

The term "cybernetics" derives from the Greek word *kybernetes* which means steersman. Plato uses it to describe the prudential aspect of the art of government.[1] Ampere in his *Essay on the Philosophy of Science* used the term *cybernétique* for the science of civil government.[2] The Latin term *gubernator* is derived from the Greek, and hence also our word governor. In English we use the term governor in at least two ways: first in the traditional sense of a public steersman or political decision-maker; second to refer to the self-adjusting valve mechanism on a steam engine which keeps the engine at a constant speed under varying conditions of load. In the steam engine governor, a valve linked to the engine's output shaft increases steam flow into the engine as the output speed decreases, raising the speed to the level desired, or reduces steam flow if the speed exceeds the pre-established level. Maxwell analyzed this control phenomenon mathematically in his paper on governors published in 1868.[3] What is essentially involved in steering behavior or control behavior of the type illustrated by the steam engine governor is a feedback loop through which the output of the system is linked to its input in such a way that variations in output from some pre-established or "programmed" norm result in compensatory behavior that tends to restore the system output to that norm.

An analogous process occurs in organisms subjected to internal or external changes that might disrupt metabolism. By the turn of this century physiologists such as Claude Bernard were fully aware of this process of "homeostasis" whereby an organism acts so as to restore its internal equilibrium. Cannon's *Wisdom of the Body* is a classical exposition of these phenomena in the autonomic processes of men. The self-regulatory aspect of neurophysiological phenomena was treated by such men as Sherrington in his work on reflexes, McCulloch in his analysis of neural networks, and Rosenblueth in his studies of psychomotor disorders. By the early 1940's physicists, electrical engineers, and mathematicians were all at work on servomechanisms, self-regulating systems that could be used for such military purposes as gun laying. A broad range of disciplines had been at work on analogous problems of self-regulation. Institutionally, the interdisciplinary study of self-regulation in the animal and the machine began at a meeting held in New York in 1942, sponsored by the Josiah Macy Foundation.

BEHAVIOR AND PURPOSE

One result was a paper on "Behavior, Purpose and Teleology" which serves as a watershed in which the breadth of the analogy was realized.[4] In 1943 *Philosophy of Science* published this article by Norbert Wiener, Arturo Rosenblueth and Julian Bigelow. The authors distinguish between the "functional analysis" of an entity and a "behavioristic approach." In the former ". . . the main goal is the intrinsic organization of the entity studied, its structure and its properties . . ." ". . . The behavioristic approach consists in the examination of the output of the object and of the relations of this output to the input." Wiener in his subsequent works largely restricted himself to ". . . the behavioristic method of study [which] omits the specific structure and intrinsic organization of the object." The authors assign the term "servomechanism" to designate machines with "intrinsic purposeful behavior." Purposeful behavior is directed at ". . . a final condition in which the behaving

SOURCE: *The American Behavioral Scientist* (June, 1965), pp. 15–20. Reprinted by permission of *The American Behavioral Scientist*.

* The original version of this paper was presented at a symposium on the Social Implications of Cybernetics held at Georgetown University, Washington, D.C., November, 1964.

† Catholic University.

object reaches a definite correlation in time or space with respect to another object or event." All purposeful behavior may be considered to require negative feedback, that is, ". . . the behavior of an object is controlled by the margin of error at which the object stands at a given time with reference to a relatively specific goal." The authors conclude on the note that "purposefulness [is] a concept necessary for the understanding of certain modes of behavior . . . ," and define teleology as "purpose controlled by feedback." The authors reject the concept of teleology as implying a "cause subsequent in time to a given effect."

In this model the key elements of self-regulation were reduced to a form amenable to mathematical analysis, and the knotty problem of consciousness so relevant to human behavior was bypassed. The novelty of this mode of conceptualizing purposive behavior lies in its implicit distinction between energy and information. " 'Control' is a special kind of relation between two machines or parts of machines, such that one part regulates the operation of the other. . . . The essential point is that the source of energy is dissociated from the source of instructions." [5] The transformation of relatively high energic inputs into goal-oriented outputs is subject to relatively low energies characterized by a formal content whose programmed interaction with these high energies produces the purposive transformation.

The principal characteristic of a self-regulating system is the presence of a control loop whereby system comportment may be modified on the basis of information inputs regarding performance and the comparison of performance with a criterion value. The control loop may be a "closed loop" existing within the boundaries of the system, or it may be an "open loop." In open loop feedback, part of the control information flow takes place outside the system boundary. The interaction of a self-regulating system with its external environment characteristically involves an open loop. Effector elements on the system boundary manipulate the environment to achieve certain objectives. Sensor elements (receptors) perceive environmental changes which are transmitted to a decision-making element that compares this percept with the objective and transmits new orders to the effector elements in terms of the difference between objective and achievement.

Basically, self-regulation requires a functional distinction between perception, decision-making, and action. This is normally achieved by a structural distinction between perceptor elements, control elements and effector elements in the system. Behaviorally, system may be defined as a "black box" characterized by a given set or range of inputs and outputs. Adequate knowledge of any system requires both structural-functional analysis and behavioral analysis. Where very large numbers of inputs and/or outputs are involved or where the system is composed of a large number of components, statistical techniques are required and behaviors are analyzed probabilistically. It is entirely possible, of course, that structurally diverse systems may effect identical transformations, and that structurally identical systems of a sufficient degree of complexity may produce very different outputs on the basis of identical inputs. The "sensitivity" of a system refers to the degree of departure of the output from a programmed norm that invokes an adjustive response. "Rapidity of response" refers to the speed with which a given system will correct behavior that does not correspond to the norm. "Stability" refers to the ability of a system to maintain a given behavioral posture over time. Normally there is a rather close formal relation between these aspects of systems behavior. The more sensitive a system, the less likely it is to be stable over a broad range of inputs and outputs. The more rapid the response of the system to an error signal, the more likely it is to overshoot the norm—to overadjust, and so invoke a counter-adjustment, to overadjust, and so forth. This behavior may lead to oscillation destructive of the entire system.

INFORMATION AND MESSAGES

It is clear at this point of our discussion that control involves the communication of information. In an operational sense, information is that which can or does influence the comportment of another. Information is conveyed as a message, that is, as a configuration of signal elements borne by a medium having actual or potential meaning for the recipient (destination). By the late 1920's communications engineers, concerned with the problems of interference (noise) and channel capacity, had begun to develop measures of information.[6] This work culminated in 1948 in a paper of

Shannon entitled, "The Mathematical Theory of Communication." [7] Shannon's study does not concern itself with meaning, that is, with the semantic aspects of communication but with the technical problems of the accuracy of transmission of various types of signals. Clearly, the purely technical problems of coding, transmitting, and decoding signal sequences are of critical importance in designing and understanding self-regulating systems. The actual comportment of such systems, however, is a function of the semantic content of these signal sequences. The "quantity of information" as a measure of the improbability of a signal sequence has no *necessary* relation to the amount of semantic information conveyed by a statement.[8]

In 1948 Wiener published *Cybernetics or Control and Communication in the Animal and the Machine* which formalized much of the thinking up to that time and suggested potentially fruitful areas for further inquiry. With the quantification of signal transmission and the formalization of control system theory a new and broadly applicable science of communications and control had become a reality. In its strict applications, communications and control theory has become a major factor in contemporary technology and lies at the base of the "second industrial revolution." In the "first industrial revolution" prime movers largely replaced human energy while men performed a control function. Under automation, process and production *control* is relegated to servomechanisms while the human operator programs, monitors, and maintains the automated system.

SCOPE OF CYBERNETICS

In the United States, scientists and engineers working in the theory and applications of self-regulation tend to avoid the term cybernetics which deals to a considerable degree with isomorphisms among various types of self-regulating systems. Since only a very limited range of systems and communications processes are presently amenable to mathematical formalization and manipulation, there has been a tendency to institutionalize fairly narrow disciplines concerned with limited formal or material applications of these concepts, such as computer engineering, bionics, and control systems engineering. In the Soviet Union, on the other hand, the term "cybernetics" is used quite broadly, ". . . not as the doctrine of Wiener, Shannon, Ashby, *et al.*, but as the general science of the control over complex systems, information, and communications. . . ." [9] Elsewhere in the Soviet literature we find cybernetics defined as ". . . the new science of purposeful and optimal control over complicated processes and operations which take place in living nature, in human society, and in industry." [10]

Cybernetics extends the circle of processes which can be controlled—this is its special property and merit. It can help control life activity in living nature, purposeful work of organized groups of people, and the influence of man on machines and mechanisms.

We shall divide cybernetics into three large subdivisions: theoretical cybernetics which includes mathematical and philosophical problems; the cybernetics of control systems and means which includes the problems of collecting, processing, and output of information, and also the means for electronic automation; finally, the field of the practical application of the methods and means of cybernetics in all fields of human activity.[11]

Many of the basic concepts of this science are relevant to an understanding of social groups. Norbert Wiener realized their applicability and suggested many insightful applications, but was concerned about potential abuses owing to the complexity of social processes and the limited applicability of existing methods of mathematical analysis. On the other hand, he also pointed out that the application of cybernetic concepts to society does not require that social relations be mathematicizable *in esse*, but only *in posse*—that is, the conceptual clarification of the formal aspects of social relations can make a positive contribution to the science of society.[12]

More recent definitions of cybernetics almost invariably include social organizations as one of the categories of system to which this science is relevant.[13] Indeed, Bigelow has generalized to the extent of calling cybernetics the effort to understand the behavior of complex systems.[14] He pointed out that cybernetics is essentially interdisciplinary and that a focus at the systems level, dependent upon mixed teams of professionals in a variety of sciences, brings one rapidly to the frontiers of knowledge in several areas. This is certainly true of the social sciences. The term "cybernetics" is used here in the more extended sense discussed above. It is entirely appropriate that this should be done, not only because of the traditional political and social connotation of the term governance, but because of the role played by the social and behavioral sciences in the explication and development of models of social control and decision-making. The first modern calculating machine was made by Charles Babbage, whose classic study (*On the Economy of Machinery and Manufactures*) was published in 1832 and anticipated by fifty years or more the beginnings of scientific management.[15] Organizational theory, political science, cultural anthropology and social psychology have for many years analyzed social groups as complex communications nets characterized by a multiplicity of feedback loops. Organizational decision-making was given a quantitative base, again at the time of World War II, by the development of the techniques of operations research. Von Neumann and Morgenstern succeeded in analyzing strategic optima in certain types of decision processes. In 1936 Leontief produced the first input-output matrix. Von Bertalanffy has pointed out analogies (isomorphisms) characterizing all systems, including social systems.[16]

ROLE OF COMPUTERS

Let us now examine certain aspects of the popular view of cybernetics. In one view, cybernetics is identified with the development and use of large digital computers. Computers are, of course, of fundamental importance to cybernetics, first because they embody so much communications and control technology, and second because they oblige us to sort out vague ideas and feelings from clearly formulated univocal ideas and relations if we wish to manipulate them by machine, and finally because once ideas are clarified the machine permits the rapid execution of long and detailed logical operations otherwise beyond human capability. In many cases these logical operations performed by machine permit a rationality in decision-making or precision of control hitherto unattainable. Until a few years ago it was impossible to compare very large numbers of decisional alternatives to find an optimum. Decision techniques and aids such as linear and dynamic programming, critical path analysis, large scale input-output matrices, network analysis, factor analysis, simulation, and so forth are largely dependent upon computers.

Computer technology, of course, lies at the base of the automatic factory, of sophisticated inventory control systems, and of the increasing automation of routine paper work. Fundamentally, any information handling operation that can be reduced to rule and rote is amenable to computer performance. Considered abstractly, this means that virtually every human job activity that does not require intellectual or artistic creativity or some human emotivity in its performance is potentially susceptible of automation. Under our existing institutional "rules of the game" the only limiting factor will be the cost of the machine as opposed to the cost of people.

It now seems increasingly likely that computer networks will be formed, first on a local, then a regional, and finally a national scale which will make unused computer capacity available, perhaps on a rental basis—and which as a unit will be capable of data processing tasks of hitherto inconceivable magnitude. Eventually each citizen may have access to computers and a vast complex of data storage centers on a rental-use basis. Computers might be used to handle such routine chores as tallying adding machine tapes, making out Christmas mailing lists and preparing income tax returns. At a more sophisticated level perhaps our citizen may use his machine to analyze interpersonal relations in his office sociometrically in order to optimize strategies for personal effectiveness. He may have access to a wide range of factual or bibliographic information; he may, perhaps, run machine searches of newspaper files or gather genealogical data. From a purely practical economic viewpoint there would be obvious benefits to American business to be gained from centralized insurance files, credit reports, accident reports, academic and job records, public opinion surveys, market surveys, and so forth. All of these would enhance predictability, and so also increase business' capacity for rational decision-making. The principal question that will arise in this process of increasing centralized information storage concerns the values in terms of which the information will be utilized in making decisions. Profit maximization? a politically imposed values-mix? or might new institutional forms permit more decentralized decision on the basis of widely varying criteria? In the not very distant future some hard public decisions must be made regarding who shall have access to what information and for what purposes, and perhaps as to what types of information may legitimately be collected and employed.

APPLICATIONS TO SOCIAL SYSTEMS

Let us return to our basic model of a self-regulating system, examine some of its fundamental operations a little more closely, and try to see wherein it is applicable to the study of social relations.

A system is an organized collection of interrelated elements characterized by a boundary and functional unity. The concept of system emphasizes the reality of complex relational networks and permits the analysis of mutual causal processes involving large numbers of interacting entities. Although systems of ideas and systems of symbols play a critical role in human society, we shall here treat of social systems as real composite entities in continuing self-regulated interaction with their environment(s). Social systems comprise every level of complexity from the family or primary work group through large scale formal organizations to the nation-state or even the whole human race conceived of as an interacting human community. Primary groups and ultimately all groups are composed of self-regulating persons as their components. Large social systems normally consist of functional groups as their component subsystems. The integrated activity of large social groupings is the product of effective internal communication and a willingness on the part of decision-makers in their component social subsystems and ultimately of their component persons to respond in a predictable and programmed manner to a defined range of perceptual inputs.

Fundamentally, a model of self-regulation requires a functional distinction between perception, decision-making, and action. This is normally achieved by a structural distinction between receptor elements, decision-making elements, and effector elements in the system. As social systems increase in size and complexity, these functions and the related communications functions tend to become concentrated in component social subsystems.[17]

If we apply these basic concepts in a very much simplified way to the political sphere they may help to systematize certain basic relations that are the traditional matter of political science, such as the constitution and the separation of powers.[18] Basically, a constitution is a program defining the nature (activities) and interrelations of the formal loci of political power. The outputs of the political system are enforceable laws defining the interrelations of persons and groups within the society. Demands on the political system are communicated by petition, by representatives of organized groups, by publicists, and other means including elections. Legislative decisions are made in the form of laws and resolutions. The executive puts the laws into effect and the judiciary serves a control function by comparing specific individual actions with the law that programs such action. Even judicial review in the United States is fundamentally a comparison of legislative action (output) with a constitutional norm.

Similarly in the conduct of foreign affairs, information on the international environment in the form of foreign intelligence is communicated to the foreign policy decision-makers—ultimately, in the United States, the President. The challenges of the environment are met by policy decisions allocating resources of the state to effector elements of the executive branch for the achievement of national objectives by various techniques: diplomacy, foreign assistance, propaganda, military action, and so forth.

If we apply the concepts of sensitivity and stability to political systems we see distinct analogies even at an elementary level. The founding fathers of the United States wanted the legislature (decision-maker) sensitive to public opinion, so they introduced a House of Representatives elected biennially on the basis of population. But they did not want the decision process too sensitive to public opinion, so they introduced a Senate elected on a different basis for a different term of office whose concurrence is necessary to legislation. In order to introduce further stability into the system they decoupled the legislative (decision-maker) from the executive (effector) branch and introduced an independent control element in the form of a Supreme Court. The inherent stability of the system has been proved over the past 175 years. It is interesting to note that most of the proposals for "reform" recommended by political scientists are directed at increasing the sensitivity of the system to public opinion.

Each entity in our experience, whether physical object or person or social group, exists in time and interrelates with others in time. In the temporal order what will occur cannot provide a real input into antecedent action—but as a foreseen possibility it may provide an imputed information input. If we conceive of the current state of a system as determined by its antecedent states, the future states of that system are a set of probabilities dependent on the possible future states of its environments, and for self-regulating systems upon their actions in the "now." Insofar as the self-regulating system can know not only its actual state and the state of its environment in the "now," but can project and "know" alternative trajectories that are possible as realizable in the future, to this extent the future can be an input into decisional processes. While recognizing and attempting to predict the future states of key variables over which there is no effective control, individual and social planning consists essentially in: a) projecting alternative trajectories as functions of direct action by the system and of the indirect effects of action by the system on its environment; and in b) choosing the set of actions which, on the basis of past experience or subjectively assigned probabilities, seems most likely to bring about a future state conceived of as desirable. It is perfectly clear that the actions undertaken to achieve a future state of the system may *determine* to a considerable degree that future state. Hence it follows that in the reality of human affairs means and ends can never be separated.

Social systems not only respond to an existing environmental challenge, but they may foresee such challenges and plan to forestall them or cope with them in the future. In brief men and societies are provident—they respond not only to perceptions of reality but to the extrapolation of reality into possible future states. Much social choice depends upon the image of the future deemed desirable by a society and it is for this reason that the abstract ideology or the utopia expressed in concrete terms plays a critical role in defining social purpose and hence in conditioning social decisions. The range of possible response to an existing challenge is normally quite limited, while the range of autonomous action becomes increasingly broad as increasingly long future time-spans are anticipated. As given future goals become increasingly clear, that is, concretely defined, social behavior may increasingly resemble that of a servomechanism in which guidance is reduced to control ". . . by the margin of error at which the object stands at a given time with reference to a relatively specific goal." Action may then become a routine problem of technical administration.

Action upon the environment is regulated by a continuing process of perception in which the perceived external reality is compared with an end state to be achieved. Now in this process it is clear that we are dealing with focused perceptions, that is, a set of sensory inputs to which attention adverts selected from the innumerable alternative sets to which the person or group might advert. In an evolutionary sense only reasonably adequate criteria of perceptual relevance permit survival of a given biological species. For men whose criteria of perceptual relevance are largely cultural, only cultures having reasonably adequate criteria of relevance can survive. Similarly the norms of behavior of the person, the criterion values on the basis of which action is undertaken, are crucially important to behavior and to survival. These too are largely a matter of culture. In the history of mankind certain patterns of value have proved to possess a higher survival value than others. Within the range of viable systems of value and perceptual relevance (ideologies) there have been diverse degrees of success as measured by the extent of their diffusion and survival. In man we are dealing with a broad range of potential criteria of action and the possibility of self-conscious choice among sets of alternative criteria. Hence in dealing with social systems in which men form the ultimate self-regulating components, we must deal with the problem of the adequacy of perception and of value to effective action within a natural and human environment. The analysis of men and societies as self-regulating systems brings us back to the perennial philosophic problems of the Good and the True.

MAN-MACHINE SYSTEMS

Let us now conceive of the individual's environmental system in terms of a man-machine relationship. The machine is essentially a projection of the personality, normally subject to direct or indirect human control, capable of converting a given input or set of inputs into an output or set of outputs having greater imputed utility.

In its simplest form this is the man-tool relation in which the person serves as both a source of energy and of control. In more sophisticated man-machine systems prime movers may provide energy and man the control. At a more advanced stage the machine is in whole or part self-regulating and human control is exercised only in the programming phase. As we move to "learning machines" the human control interface may be reduced to the direct or indirect construction of the machine (indirect construction might involve programming a machine to produce a machine) and the direct or indirect programming of the criterion values on the basis of which decisions affecting output will be made. There is also a man-machine interface at the output since, presumably, the machine serves some human value. The most sophisticated man-machine systems today are basically extenders of human perceptive, data processing, and motor capabilities.

In some sense complex organizations, especially economic organizations, are man-machine systems in which the components are both men and artifacts in programmed interaction to convert input values into output values having a higher (ascribed) value. Within such an organization both persons and things are subject to decisions and the output values may or may not directly serve the human component of the system itself.

As we move from the realm of machines controlling machines, to men controlling machines, and to men controlling men in society we subtly shift the meaning of the term "control." In machine controls the message either actuates some multiplying device such as a relay or by combining with energic inputs modifies their characteristics. In human control of a machine, the person observes directly, or indirectly through an instrument display, the comportment of the machine in its environment and manipulates control devices. Here our man-machine "interface" basically consists of displays and controls. Social control is the capacity (often based on control of material or financial resources) to manipulate the internal and/or external environments of other persons or groups so as to achieve a preconceived end. This normally involves selected changes in their information inputs designed to change in some way their perceptions or values so that they respond in the desired manner. It is largely concerned with "evoking" an "autonomous" response. Even the social effectiveness of negative sanctions in controlling behavior is contingent upon their being perceived and then evaluated more negatively than noncompliance. Basically, when dealing with objects as complex and autonomous as persons, control is reduced to presenting a challenge so structured that it evokes the desired response. Since social action normally involves a feedback loop, the socially controlled in some sense also control the controller; indeed this is the major characteristic of political decision-making in a democracy. Greniewsky points out: ". . . all control is communication. But on the other hand all communication is control. . . ."[19]

SYSTEM INTERFACES

A system interacts with its environment at the system boundary. Inputs move into the system across this boundary. Outputs move across this boundary into the system's environment. The area of contact between one system and another is termed an "interface." Operationally systems, and subsystems within systems, may be identified by the transactional processes that occur across their boundaries. For social groupings these transactional processes may involve the transfer of energy, material objects, men, money, and information.

The outputs of one social system are normally inputs for one or more other systems. These interrelations are amenable to analysis for economic sectors (and even for firms) by the use of input-output matrices. Quesnay in his *Tableau Economique* saw the national economy as an integrated system of monetary exchanges and exchanges of goods and services. The political system may be analyzed in terms of input demands and supports and an output of authoritative decisions that program the interrelations of persons and organized groups within the state. By extending our analysis to comprehend the five categories of exchange noted above, we are in a position to view the entire world as a (relatively) closed system of interrelated social components linked together by these transactional processes.

Communications and control technologies are already being extensively applied for purposes of social organization within the more advanced countries. The Soviet economy is now being organized on the basis of very extensive input-output matrices and computer programs designed to optimize resource utilization. These techniques may also help resolve the problem inherent in the limited use of market mechanisms to determine prices. By ascribing more or less arbitrary value to primary resource inputs (including the categories of human labor) all other prices in the economy can be made consistent. In the French indicative plan, a political decision, based on a consensus among all interested groups as to a future national mix of economic values, is reduced to an investment program that generates a high level of business confidence. The result has been an increasing tendency to reduce government to administration in terms of the technical achievement of concrete objectives. In the United States, the Social Security system has provided a means for national population control and is at the base of the new Internal Revenue Service computer system in which wage earners and salaried persons are posted on a biweekly or monthly basis. Given the increasing use of electronic data processing in our banks, plus the sophistication and widespread use of credit facilities, it is quite conceivable that all monetary transactions over say twenty dollars could be posted in a national accounting system (at least aggregate) through the use of cascaded computers. This would, of course, largely do away with the possibility of robbery—but above all would provide a rapid running account of interregional and intersectoral exchanges that would permit the use of indirect controls at strategic points to effect very rapid adjustments of the economy in terms of programmed goals such as full employment and planned rates of economic growth. Such a system would also permit more equitable taxation by doing away with unrecorded transfers.

I would suggest that cybernetics today possesses great relevance for the social scientist. First it has begun to provide conceptual tools of the greatest importance for the analysis of complex systems and their interrelations. It establishes a focus on the critical importance of control and communications relations, of individual and institutional modes of perception and values. Certainly this view of men and societies as complex self-regulating systems, interacting among themselves within complex environments should prove conducive to a more holistic approach to the social and behavioral sciences in all their multivariate complexity, and provides us with a more solid foundation for systematic scientific formalization than existed in a past in which "science" *par excellence* comprised the simplified model of a clockwork universe governed by the laws of classical mechanics. Second, the social scientist must examine closely the actual and potential relations of cybernetic modes of thought and technologies to social institutions. Cybernetics has profound implications both as an ideology and as regards ideology. This is already abundantly clear in the works of both the Russians and the Anglo-Americans. Cybernetic technologies lie at the root of the quantum shift in economic relations called automation and cybernation. Computer based "optimum" decisions based on cost-effectiveness analysis have begun to replace the interplay of interest in some key areas of political decision—specifically in U.S. military spending. These techniques are potentially applicable to the whole budget process.

Certainly the political sphere will be a major forum for the resolution of the problems of value and social philosophy that can no longer be ignored. Even in the absence of sophisticated competitive economic and social systems and competitive concepts of a good life, such as those of Russia and France, these decisions cannot long be postponed. What must now be demonstrated is the capacity of a democratic society to understand, confront, and resolve very complex problems of social organization in such a way as to retain traditional freedoms and consultative political institutions while moving into new patterns of economic and social relations in which we realize that our relation to the machine has become quasi-symbiotic.

REFERENCES

1. Plato, *Republic,* I, 346 B.C.
2. Ampere, A. M., *Essay on the Philosophy of Science* (1838).
3. Maxwell, J. C., *Proceedings of the Royal Society* (London), 1868, XVI, 270–83.
4. Josiah Macy Foundation Conference on Cerebral Inhibition, May, 1942. Rosenblueth, A., Wiener, N., and Bigelow, J., "Behavior, Purpose and Teleology," *Philos. Sci.,* 1943, 10, 18–24.
5. Guilbaud, G. T., *What Is Cybernetics?* New York: Grove Press, 1960, p. 11.
6. Nyquist, H., "Certain Factors Affecting Tele-

graph Speed," *Bell System Technical J.*, April, 1924, 324; "Certain Topics in Telegram Transmission Theory," *A.I.E.E. Transactions*, 47, April, 1928, 617; Hartley, R. V. L., "Transmission of Information," *Bell System Technical J.*, July, 1928, 535.

7. Shannon, C. E., and Weaver, W., *The Mathematical Theory of Communication.* Urbana: University of Illinois Press, 1949.
8. Bar-Hillel, Y., "An Examination of Information Theory," *Philos. Sci.*, 22, 1955.
9. Bershteyn, N. A., "New Lines of Development in Physiology and Their Relation to Cybernetics" in *Problems of Philosophy*, 1962, 8, 78–87 (JPRS; 17,117).
10. "Biological Aspects of Cybernetics," Moscow, 1962 (JPRS; 19,637, p. 17).
11. *Ibid.*, p. 19.
12. Wiener, N., *God and Golem, Inc.* Cambridge, Mass.: M.I.T. Press, 1964, p. 88.
13. *Encyclopedia of Science and Technology.* New York: McGraw-Hill, 1960. "Cybernetics: The science of control and communication in all of its various manifestations in machines, animals, and organizations."—"An interdisciplinary science."
14. Bigelow, J., Address at Founders' Dinner, American Society for Cybernetics, October 16, 1964, Washington, D.C.
15. Babbage, C., *On the Economy of Machinery and Manufactures.* London: 1832. For a very recent application of advanced analytic techniques to management see: Beer, S., *Cybernetics and Management.* New York: Wiley, 1959; "Toward the Cybernetic Factory" in Von Foerster and Zopf (eds.), *Principles of Self-Organization.* New York: Pergamon, 1962, p. 25.
16. Von Bertalanffy, L., "General Systems Theory," *General Systems*, vol. I (1956); "General Systems Theory: A Critical Review," *General Systems*, vol. VII (1962); Miller, J. G., "Toward a General Theory for the Behavioral Sciences," *Amer. Psychol.*, 10, 1955.
17. See Deutsch, K., *The Nerves of Government*, p. 258; Dechert, C., "A Pluralistic World Order," *Proceedings* of the American Catholic Philosophical Association, 1963, pp. 167–186.
18. See Easton, D., "An Approach to the Analysis of Political Systems," *World Politics*, 9, 1957, pp. 383–400; Dahl, R., *Modern Political Analysis.* Englewood Cliffs: Prentice-Hall, 1963.
19. Greniewsky, H., *Cybernetics without Mathematics.* New York: Pergamon, 1960, p. 52.

6. CYBERNETICS

Jiri Klir
Miroslav Valach

DEFINITION

Cybernetics is a science dealing, on the one hand, with the study of relatively closed systems from the viewpoint of their interchange of information with their environment; on the other hand with the study of the structures of these systems from the viewpoint of the information interchange between their elements.

A Survey of Science and the Place of Cybernetics

The task of science in a wider sense is the truthful cognition of the world.

In principle, science starts from the assumption that the world is indivisible in the sense that all phenomena in it are mutually dependent, even though their relations are not always sufficiently obvious. It is the aim of science to discover the corresponding relations and to prove them objectively.

If the world is indivisible, the process of cognition should also be indivisible, and thus there should exist only a single science. This, however, was possible only at a primitive stage of cognition, when the relations between individual phenomena were known only very superficially. At that time there really existed only a single science—philosophy—which encompassed all the knowledge of that time. As the amount of knowledge in philosophy gradually accumulated, an ever greater effort was needed to comprehend and elaborate it. An unavoidable result was the splitting of science into special branches, i.e., the introduction of the division of labour into science. Actually, this process cannot be considered as a division in the proper sense of the word, but as the process of distinguishing some new branches of science from philosophy, whose existence remained unaffected.

Natural science (at that time called physics) was separated from philosophy already in antiquity. At that time, the principal concerns of natural science were mathematics and astronomy.

A further division of science did not take place until the beginning of modern times (in the 15th and 16th centuries) when mathematics and physics were introduced as independent subjects, the latter being considered chiefly as mechanics (I. Newton). In the 18th century the scientific foundations were laid of chemistry (A. Lavoisier and M. V. Lomonosov) and partly of biology (K. Linné). Some special branches of physics also emerged, in particular mechanics and heat.

A great development of science took place in the 19th century, when the sciences concerned with inanimate nature became clearly separated from biology. Biology was put on a scientific footing, chiefly by the cell theory of J. Ev. Purkyně and the evolution theory of C. Darwin. Chemistry was divided into inorganic and organic chemistry, and a number of new branches appeared in mathematics and physics. The 19th century is also characterized by the evolution of the engineering sciences, especially mechanical engineering, and by the emergence of new human sciences (e.g., psychology, sociology, etc.).

Our century is marked by a still more rapid development of science. Fundamental scientific disciplines, such as mathematics and biology, are already subdivided into a great many special branches and new divisions are constantly appearing. In addition, some entirely new scientific disciplines emerged in the 20th century, such as astronautics, nuclear engineering, cybernetics, eugenics, semiotics,

SOURCE: *Cybernetic Modelling,* by Jiří Klír and Miroslav Valach, © 1967, Iliffe Books, Ltd., London. Pp. 69–79. Reprinted by permission.

bionics, sociometry, and others. Orientation in science is thus getting increasingly difficult, the more so because there is an absolute lack of literature dealing with the general classification of sciences or classification within the framework of individual special sciences.

Every scientific discipline studies the relations within the framework of a specific class of phenomena, which exhibit properties common from a given point of view and which form the subject of the scientific discipline under consideration. The precise statement of the subject of individual scientific disciplines is given by their definitions. The contents of a particular scientific discipline are considered to consist, on the one hand, of a well-ordered collection of all items of knowledge concerning its subject, and on the other hand of a set of methodical resources enabling us to obtain further knowledge.

However, philosophy has lost nothing of its importance even after the division of science into separate branches. Its main task consists in gathering, in a condensed form, all human knowledge dispersed in the individual sciences. Thereby it preserves a unified view of the world and thus creates a unified and consistent conception of the world.

Philosophy draws upon the findings of the other sciences and, based on them, it formulates hypotheses of the most general laws governing the evolution of nature and of human society. Conversely, philosophical hypotheses aid the individual sciences in choosing suitable methods of scientific research.

The tasks of philosophy also include the dividing of science into scientific disciplines. A correct division presupposes that, at a certain stage in the development of science, the corresponding system of scientific disciplines is complete and natural and thus forms a kind of "map" of our knowledge. In this sense, philosophy should exert its actual influence on this map, i.e., it should progressively adapt and supplement it.

Philosophy, as described, thus occupies a special position among the sciences. The other sciences can be divided roughly into mathematics, natural, human and engineering sciences. Within each of these classes we must distinguish fundamental from special sciences.

The fundamental natural sciences are physics, chemistry, and biology. The fundamental human sciences can be taken to include psychology, linguistics, sociology, history, political economics, etc. Among the engineering sciences let us mention, for instance, power engineering, chemical technology, communications engineering, and geodesy. The principal scientific disciplines comprise entire hierarchies of special sciences. Thus, for instance, physics is divided into mechanics, heat, optics, electricity, atomic physics, etc. In its turn, mechanics can be divided into the mechanics of solids, hydromechanics, and aeromechanics. The mechanics of solids is further subdivided into statics, kinematics, and dynamics.

A characteristic feature of mathematics (or the mathematical sciences) is that it encroaches to a considerable degree upon other scientific disciplines, particularly the natural and engineering sciences. It seems that a similar position will in the future be taken up by cybernetics, which cannot very well be included in any of the classes mentioned above. This is because cybernetics treats problems concerning forms of organization in any objects, no matter what branch of science they belong to.

Individual sciences will frequently be found to overlap to some extent. This is how interdisciplinary sciences, which actually belong simultaneously to two fundamental scientific disciplines, come into being. Among the best known let us quote, for instance, mathematical physics, physical chemistry, biophysics, and biochemistry. As will be seen in the next section, the emergence of cybernetics has also given rise to a whole series of new interdisciplinary sciences.

Special Branches in Cybernetics

Although cybernetics is still a very young science, certain tendencies to subdivide it are already appearing, particularly for two reasons:

1. Natural endeavours aiming at an efficient division of labour in cybernetics, called forth by the ever-growing number of new discoveries;
2. Overlapping with other scientific disciplines.

It is too soon yet to speak of a real "division of labour"; some typical trends are, however, already beginning to appear in the work of cyberneticists. It seems that in the future the following three main branches will be the first to become permanently established in cybernetics:

1. *Theoretical cybernetics,* in which so far three fundamental aspects manifest themselves most strongly.

(a) *The theory of systems transmitting information.*

(b) *The theory of systems which process information.*

(c) *The theory of control.*

2. *Experimental cybernetics,* directed chiefly towards cybernetic modelling as an aid to epistemology.

3. *Engineering cybernetics,* which treats the problems concerned with the design and construction of engineering cybernetic systems. For this field, cybernetic modelling is also of considerable importance, since many engineering cybernetic systems are produced as models of other systems, e.g., biological, psychological, mathematical, and other ones.

Where cybernetics overlaps with other scientific disciplines, new interdisciplinary sciences arise.

Of great importance is the overlapping of cybernetics and mathematics, especially in the sense that cybernetics abundantly utilizes already existing mathematical theories and instigates the foundation of new trends in mathematics. This fact sometimes leads to the impression that cybernetics is a mathematical discipline. This conclusion is incorrect, of course, since cybernetics utilizes, besides the apparatus of mathematics, other resources as well.

Cybernetics also overlaps to an important degree with biology. We shall later devote great attention to the resulting interdisciplinary science. The field simultaneously covered by cybernetics and biology is frequently termed *neurocybernetics.* We do not believe this name to be sufficiently expressive of the field covered, since cybernetic phenomena in living organisms need not always be of nervous origin. In our opinion, the name *biocybernetics* would far better serve our purpose, being analogous with the well-established terms biochemistry and biophysics. *Neurocybernetics* would then stand for one of the special branches of biocybernetics.

At the present, cybernetics is found to have many features in common with psychology, psychiatry and, possibly, pedagogy. According to present developments, very close relations may be expected to be set up in the near future between these fields on the one hand and cybernetics on the other, and a new independent interdisciplinary science will evidently emerge, the subject of which will be the study of psychological systems from the point of view of cybernetics. This new branch might very well be covered by the name *psychocybernetics.*

In many ways, cybernetics also encroaches upon the engineering sciences, especially by presenting a general theory for the design of the most diverse devices. The relation between cybernetics and engineering chiefly concerns the fields of data processing machines, automatic regulation, and communication engineering. The term *engineering cybernetics* has already become established for the interdisciplinary science between engineering in a wider sense and cybernetics. It seems likely that engineering cybernetics will have to be subdivided into narrower fields.

Engineering cybernetics is sometimes confused with bionics. In such cases we are concerned with an obvious mistake. *Bionics* is an interdisciplinary science between biology and engineering; its subject is the application of biological principles to engineering. The principles involved, e. g., the transformation of chemical into mechanical energy, photosynthesis, etc., need not concern cybernetics in all aspects. On the other hand, engineering cybernetics deals frequently with systems that are not inspired by biology.

An interesting relation is becoming established between cybernetics and linguistics. This relation leads to the emergence not only of a number of theoretical problems connected especially with information theory in its wider sense (the problem of the amount of information in language, the understanding of texts, etc.), but also of many practical problems (machine translation, abstracts, information language, etc.). Here we are concerned with very difficult problems, the majority of which have so far been only partially solved. The contents of this discipline, which is still being formed, would be very well expressed by the name *cybernetic linguistics.*

Cybernetics and one of the youngest scientific disciplines, *semiotics,* can also be observed to have many problems in common. This branch of science deals with arbitrary systems of signs used in human society.

Cybernetics is of considerable importance to economics and also to sociology. In this instance we are chiefly concerned with problems of the control of the national economy and with the control of society in a wider sense. Here the terms *cybernetic economy* and *cybernetic sociology* would be satisfactory.

Cybernetics also encroaches upon the most diverse branches of medicine. Here we are primarily concerned with new diagnostic methods, the design of artificial organs and limbs, problems of bioelectro-stimulation, etc. This field also includes problems concerning the pathology of mechanisms controlling the metabolism of cells. It seems that, in this connection, cybernetics can contribute considerably to the detailed exploration of the causes of one of the most fearsome diseases of our time—cancer—and that it is also capable of contributing to the discovery of effective preventive and curative methods for the suppression of this disease. The name *medical cybernetics* has come into use for the combination of cybernetics with medicine.

For the time being, a lesser influence is exerted by cybernetics upon chemistry, physics, jurisprudence, history, and fine arts.

Changes in Systems

Every system is defined on the one hand by its universe A, i.e., by the set of its elements, on the other hand by its characteristic R, i.e., by the set of relationships both between the elements of set A, and between these elements and the environment of the system.

Now let us consider a system $S_1 = \{A_1, R_1\}$, defined in some object from a certain point of view. From this system we can pass to another system $S_2 = \{A_2, R_2\}$, defined in the same object from the same point of view, by one of the three following procedures:

1. Change of universe.
2. Change of characteristic.
3. Change of both universe and characteristic.

Two types of changes must be distinguished, both in the universe and in the characteristic.

Changes of the first type concern only an increase or reduction in resolution level. These manifest themselves in the universe in that some elements of system S_1 are divided into several partial elements or, conversely, in that some elements of system S_1 are combined to form a single element. In the characteristic, a change of the first type manifests itself by an increase or reduction in the number of variables in the relationships r_{ij}.

It is easy to ascertain that changes of the first type lead to different systems within the framework of the same super-system.

The second type of change reveals itself in the universe by the introduction into the system S_2 of new elements which were not contained in System S_1 (i. e., which were not part of its elements) or, conversely, by the elimination of some of the elements of system S_1. In the characteristic this type of change shows by an exchange of some relationships $r_{ij} = 0$ for relationships $r_{ij} \neq 0$, or vice versa.

Any change of the second type necessarily leads always to a change of the super-system. Since we assumed, however, that the viewpoint remains the same, we shall only be concerned with changes within a certain class of super-systems.

The Cybernetic Viewpoint

The reader who has carefully read the foregoing explanation is certain to have noticed that a certain object may show different properties depending, on the one hand, on the viewpoint from which it is observed, on the other hand upon changes in the system mentioned in the preceding section.

The viewpoints from which an object is investigated can very roughly be divided into two classes. The first class contains quantitative viewpoints, from which we examine problems concerned with the magnitudes of masses and energies, their mutual effects and evolution in the system itself as well as between the system and its environment, etc. Such viewpoints find their widest field of application in the natural sciences. They will be called *mass-energy viewpoints*.

The second class comprises viewpoints from which problems are examined which are concerned with organization in its widest sense, its evolution within the system, transfer between elements of the system and between the system and its environment, etc. Since organization is the carrier of information, and it is the information aspect which chiefly interests us in organization, we are concerned in this class of viewpoints essentially with information problems. This class will be called *cybernetic viewpoints*.

Even though cybernetic viewpoints find their application in all the sciences, cybernetics emerged as a separate branch of science treating the information properties of various organizations without regard to their physical carrier. The title of cybernetics to the rank of an independent science follows from the extent and complexity of the problems involved and from the great importance of their solution to other sciences.

Quantitative problems of a mass-energy character cannot be entirely separated from problems of organization. When investigating metabolism, for instance, we will be concerned —according to our classification—with the examination of a living organism from a viewpoint of the first class. As a matter of course, problems of organization cannot be totally disregarded since the very existence of the living organism depends on a certain organization. It is important, however, that in the given case this organization is only presumed, but neither its static nor its evolutionary properties are subjects of our study. The application of the two classes of viewpoint to some of the sciences is indicated in Fig. 1.

Thus, cybernetics is interested only in such relations between the elements of a system which have an information content—considered, however, from the most varied aspects. Similarly, cybernetics concerns itself only with such effects of the environment on the system and the system on its environment, which also have an information content. Stimuli, responses, and relations between elements thus have, in physical cybernetic systems, always the character of signals. Inputs, outputs, and couplings between elements then constitute signal paths.

It should be noticed that the cybernetic viewpoint does not limit the universe of the system in any sense. Any universe can thus be part of a cybernetic system. Only its characteristic decides whether a system is cybernetic or not. In this sense we can now clearly state the definition of a cybernetic system:

Definition 4,1. *A* set $\{A, R\}$, where R is the set of informational or signal relationships r_{ij} $(i, j = 0, 1, \ldots, n)$ asserting themselves between the elements of the set $A = \{a_1, a_2, \ldots, a_n\}$ on the one hand and between these elements and the element a_0 (the environment) on the other hand, is a cybernetic system.

Some authors (e.g., Greniewski) use the name "information system" in place of "cybernetic system."

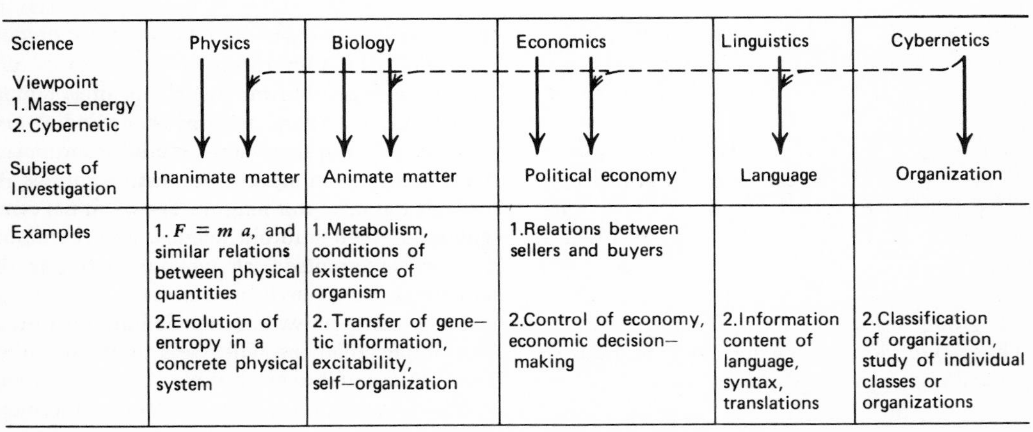

Science
Physics
Biology
Economics
Linguistics
Cybernetics
Viewpoint
1. Mass–energy
2. Cybernetic
Subject of Investigation
Inanimate matter
Animate matter
Political economy
Language
Organization
Examples
1. F = m a, and similar relations between physical quantities
2. Evolution of entropy in a concrete physical system
1. Metabolism, conditions of existence of organism
2. Transfer of genetic information, excitability, self–organization
1. Relations between sellers and buyers
2. Control of economy, economic decision–making
2. Information content of language, syntax, translations
2. Classification of organization, study of individual classes or organizations

FIG. 1. Illustration of the two basic viewpoints used in the investigation of systems.

7. ANALYSIS OF THE ORGANIZATION

C. West Churchman*
Russell L. Ackoff†
E. Leonard Arnoff‡

BASIC ASSUMPTIONS

During the late 1930's and the 1940's groups of physiologists, electrical engineers, mathematicians, and social scientists began to work on organizational problems. Many organizations, they found, had similar characteristics. For example, human beings seemed to suffer many faults in their nervous systems which were analogous to faults appearing in electric gun-control mechanisms. Diagrams (Fig. 1) which biologists and physiologists had drawn of the human nervous system even looked like electric circuit diagrams.

Groups of such scientists, working in Cambridge, Massachusetts, and elsewhere, soon saw the possibility of developing a generalized organization or control theory that would cut across scientific disciplines. Professor Norbert Wiener summarized the work of these mixed discipline groups in 1948. In his book *Cybernetics. Control and Communication in the Animal and the Machine,* he said that *communication* (or information transfer) and *control* were essential processes in the functioning of an organization. Professor Wiener used information as a general concept, meaning any sign or signal which the organization could employ for the direction of its activities. The information might be an electric impulse, a chemical reaction, or a written message; very generally, anything by which an organization could guide or control its operation.

Thus, the view of Cybernetics is that *a.* organizations composed of cells in an organism, *b.* organizations composed of machines in an automatic factory or electric communication network, and *c.* organizations of human beings in social groups all follow the essential processes of communication and control in their operation.[1]

One can often analyze industrial or military organizations, even though they are complex, in the same communication and control terms. Such analysis can be directed toward the construction of a *communication (or control) model*[1] of the organization.

SOME GENERAL COMMENTS ON THE COMMUNICATION MODEL

A communication model is not mathematical; it is not used for accurate predictions or calculations. It generally takes the form of a diagram. Such a diagram enables one to bring together, from various fields of research, knowledge about organizations. The diagram and other knowledge can be used to suggest points of attack upon organizational problems, to sort relevant information about an organization from the trivial, to suggest analogies and similarities among various kinds of organizations, and to suggest, for test, solutions to organizational problems.[1] These hints and guides are often sorely needed by Operations Researchers, particularly at the beginning of a new project.

Since communication models have this practical importance, we will stress their use rather than give a detailed discussion of their theoretical development. The chapter is therefore divided into three parts: 1. a simplified theoretical discussion of communication models; 2. a brief description of how to construct a

SOURCE: *Introduction to Operations Research,* John Wiley and Sons (1957), pp. 69–88. Reprinted by permission of John Wiley and Sons.

* University of California, Berkeley.
† University of Pennsylvania.
‡ Ernest and Ernest Co.

[1] K. W. Deutsch. "On Communication Models in the Social Sciences." *Public Opinion Quarterly* 16, (1952) pp. 356–380.

communication model in practice; and 3. a discussion of the ways one can use the communication model, once it has been constructed.

The communication model can be thought of as a glorified kind of fish net, spider's web, or network of nerves through which "information" passes or flows. The more formal material in later sections refers to a simple picture of this kind—in which various organizational characteristics are spoken of in terms of a communication network, of the information which passes through it, and of how both change with time.

CHARACTERISTICS OF COMMUNICATION MODELS

It is worth noting here, however, that a model is a miniature of, or compact representation of, an original. Usually models represent relevant points of interest in the original; these points can be combined so that the structure of the model and that of the original are similar. A set of rules may be included with a model to tell how it operates or how it can be manipulated.

The structure and points of interest used for a given model will change as the structure and points of interest in the original change. For example, if a road leading from one city to another is closed or abandoned, it may be eliminated from forthcoming editions of road maps of that area.

Development of a complete communication model follows similar lines. Knowledge of three kinds is required:

1. Knowledge of a communication network which exists at a given time (a collection of relevant points of interest and their connection).
2. Knowledge of existing control processes in the network (rules of operation of the network).
3. Knowledge of how existing network and control processes change with time.

For example, the physiologist may describe a nervous system and its evolution by a series of circles and interconnecting lines (as shown in Fig. 1). An increased complexity of organization of the nervous system will require increased or changing interconnection of the nerve centers (as shown in Fig. 2). Our development of the communication model will follow just this pattern.

THE COMMUNICATION MODEL DIAGRAM

An organization can be thought of as a group of elements (divisions in a company, operating units in a machine, people in a social group) which are in some way tied together through their communication with each other, i.e., through their letters, their phone calls, a flow of material, their division of labor, personal conversation, and the like.

If a diagram is drawn showing how communication takes place between various elements of an organization (e.g., if written material orders are traced within a manufacturing organization as they are sent from one department to another), and if the diagram also indicates communication between the organization and the outside world (e.g., if one maps the pathways through which sales orders are solicited by the company and also maps the pathways through which orders are sent back), a picture results which describes, at least in part, what the organization is doing.

The communication diagram will look—on paper—like a road map or circuit diagram similar to Fig. 1.

The first thing to be determined about an organization is the existing structure of the communication network. The communication diagram will show this.

INTERNAL PROCESSES IN THE ORGANIZATION: HOW IT IS CONTROLLED

Organizations—companies, groups of parts in a machine, the functional elements of the human body—operate together in a communication network, but they also exhibit another characteristic: the elements of an organization operate together to reach or maintain an external goal (or its goal-image within the organization).[2] For the purpose of discussing

[2] The definition of goal used by Wiener is the one meant here. Quoting from this paper: If we divide behavior into active and passive, then "Active behavior may be subdivided into two classes: purposeless (or random) and purposeful. The term purposeful is meant to denote that the act or be-

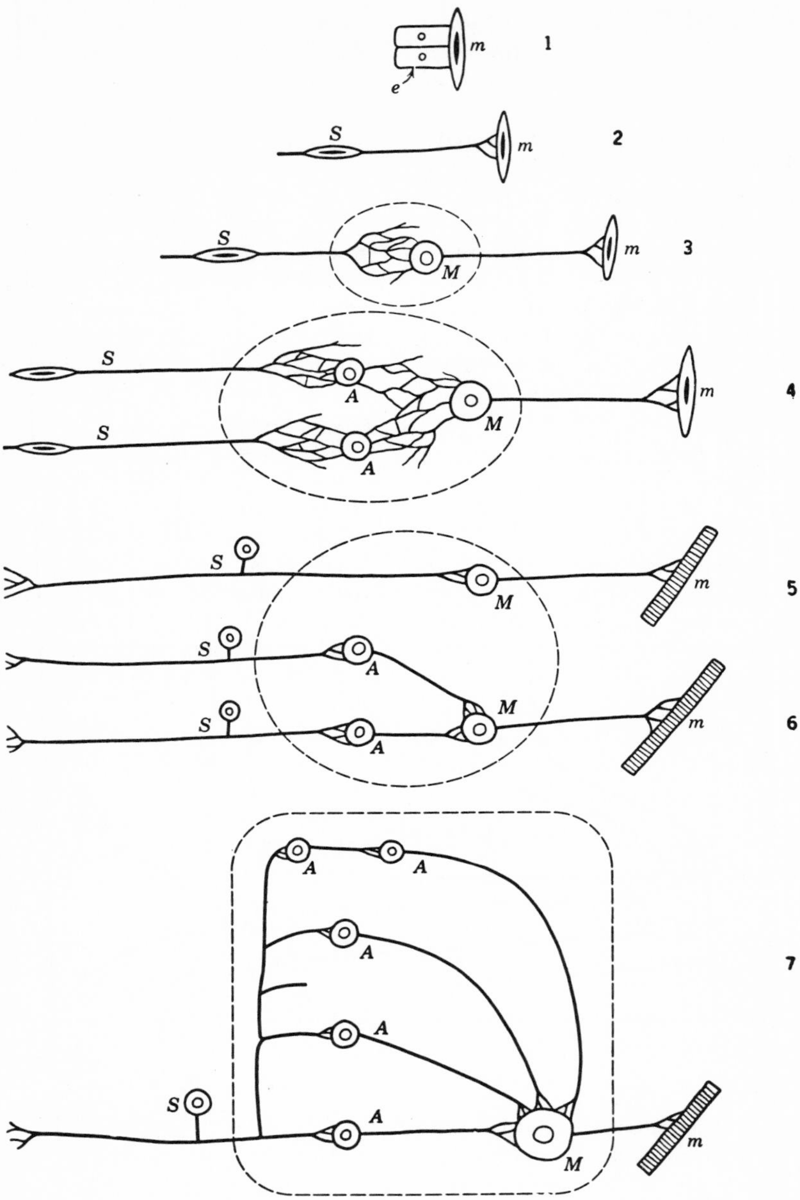

FIG. 1. The evolution of the nervous system. Diagrams of the central nervous system drawn by physiologists look similar to electric networks drawn by electrical engineers. In general, any organization may be described as such an interconnection of parts. S = sensory neurone; *A* = association neurone; *M* = motor neurone; *e* = epithelial cell; and *m* = muscle cell. The dotted lines indicate the boundaries of the nerve centers. (1) Sponge. (2) Sea anemone. (3) Simplest form in the earthworm. (4) Intercalation of association neurones in the earthworm. (5) Exceptional, simple, reflex arc in vertebrates. Possibly existing in the case of the knee jerk. (6) Usual type in vertebrates. The cell bodies of the sensory neurones are in the dorsal root ganglia, instead of in the receptor organs, except in the olfactory organ. (7) Addition of higher centers, consisting only of association neurones, some of which are inhibitory. They form, as it were, longer and longer parallel or alternative loops between the receptor and effector organs. These loops may be followed in Fig. 2. From Bayliss, W. M., *Principles of General Physiology*, Longmans, Green and Co., N.Y. 4th ed. 1927, p. 468.

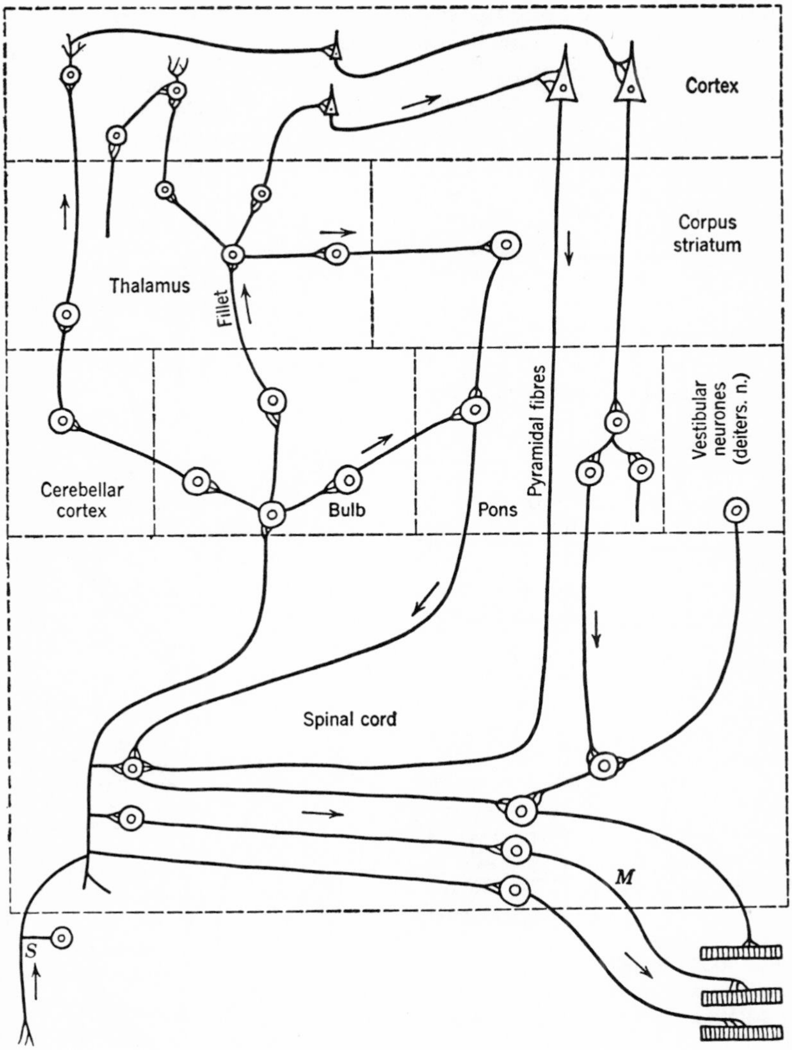

FIG. 2. Mammalian central nervous system, according to von Monakow and Mott. Shows the elaborate system of association neurones, arranged as parallel or alternative paths between the primary sensory neurones (S) and the final common paths (M). This is a further development of the diagrams shown in Fig. 1. Note the increased complexity of interconnection associated with the more refined nervous system. From Bayliss, *ibid*, p. 478.

communication models (in a simplified manner), a goal may be defined as the operating standard in use by the organization at a given time. A goal is a bench mark one aims for or tries to keep close to at a given time. For example, a shop foreman is given a production goal for the week; the accounting department will set up standard costs, etc. Such goals are fairly simple. The organization may also have more complex goals, or a whole set of simple and complex goals. The simplicity, or complexity, of the operating goal or set of goals —and the way they are used by the organization—permits one to rank organizations by their ability to handle information and "make up their own minds."

THE SIMPLE TRANSFORMATION UNIT

The elementary organization has its directions given to it continuously from an external source. It can find no goal of its own, so it must be told what to do all the time; it cannot be left alone. Such organizations correspond to simple units of mechanical or electric transformation (gear trains, amplifiers, etc.) that might be shown diagrammatically as in Fig. 3. The three fundamental processes in the link are (1) *reception;* (2) *conduction,* processing or transformation; and (3) *output transmission* (effector action). A simple industrial transformation takes place, for instance, when a sales order is transformed into an invoice.

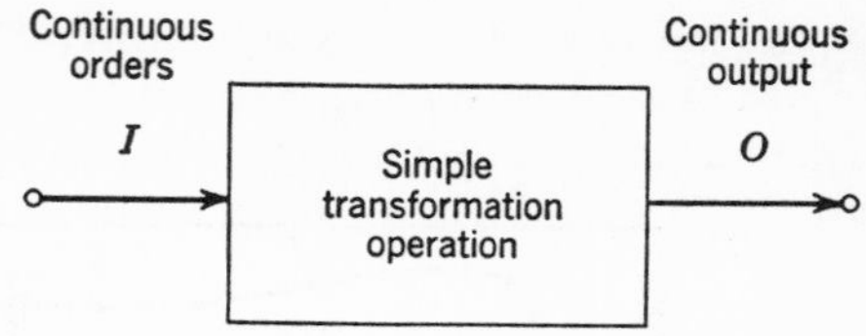

FIG. 3. A simple transformation unit. Continuous action is produced by a continuous series of orders. The unit has no goal of its own. An example: a gear train.

THE SIMPLE SORTING SYSTEM

Another elementary organization is the sorter, like a lemon grater or gravel sifter. A decision or sorting operation is built into the unit by its designer; the sorter also has to be fed continuously by an external operator. One input (say a load of gravel) can yield two or more different outputs (such as different sizes of gravel). A simple organization of this type might be diagrammed as in Fig. 4. It is similar to Fig. 3 but somewhat more complex. The most familiar sorting operation in business occurs in the mail room.

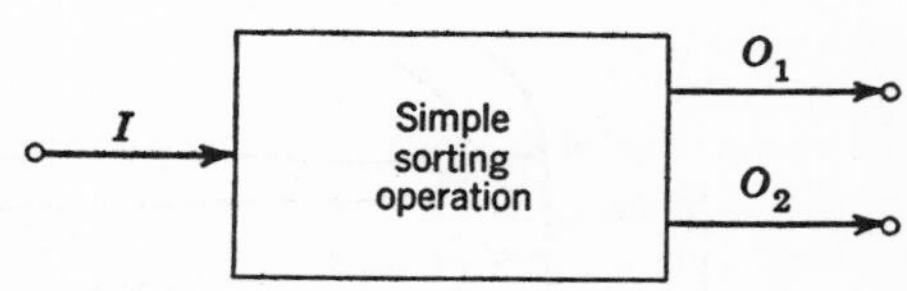

FIG. 4. A simple sorting unit. Two outputs are obtained from a single input. Rules for sorting (or decision) are built into the unit. The unit performs simple search and recognition operations common to more complicated processes.

Note that the sorting unit, in effect, makes a decision, the criteria for which are built into the unit. The gravel sorter must have built into it different sizes of mesh for sifting.

SIMPLE GOAL-MAINTAINING UNITS: CONTROL

The simplest type of organization which can, in some sense, control itself is characterized by its ability to monitor its own operation against an external goal. This type of unit

havior may be interpreted as directed to the attainment of a goal—i.e., to a final condition in which the behaving object reaches a definite correlation in time or space with respect to another object or event. Purposeless behavior then is that which is not interpreted as directed to a goal." The important restriction involved in this definition of goal is stated later in the paper: ". . . We have restricted the connotation of teleological behavior by applying this designation only to purposeful reactions which are controlled by the error of the reaction—i.e., by the difference between the state of the behaving object at any time and the final state interpreted as the purpose. Teleological behavior thus becomes synonymous with behavior controlled by negative feedback, and gains therefore in precision by a sufficiently restrained connotation."

Although this chapter will not discuss purposeful versus nonpurposeful behavior (or the philosophical issue of determinism versus free will), the subject was a fundamental one in the development of Cybernetics. (Understanding of this chapter may be aided by reading the original paper.) Rosenblueth, A., Wiener, N. and Bigelow, W., "Behavior, Purpose, and Teleology." *Philosophy of Science,* **10,** (1943) pp. 18–24.

is given one order and is left to carry that order out. An example of a purely mechanical goal-maintaining device is the governor of a steam engine (Fig. 5), which serves to regu-

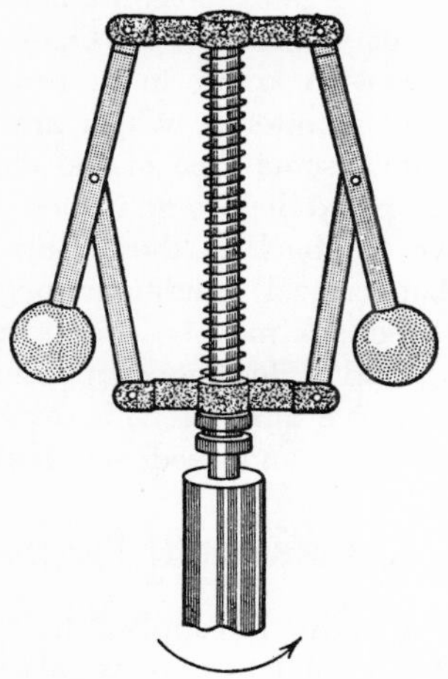

FIG. 5. A simple mechanical control unit, or governor, first treated by Clerk Maxwell. The governor seeks to maintain a steam-engine's velocity under changing load conditions.

late the engine's velocity under varying conditions of load. A desired velocity is set into the governor; the device seeks to maintain it.

In general, if an organization compares what it is doing with what its goal is, detects the error, if any, which exists between the two, and acts to reduce that error, then the organization *controls* its activities.

FEEDBACK NECESSARY FOR CONTROL

In order for an organization to determine if an error exists between what it is doing and what it intended to do to meet its goal, it must monitor its own activities: it must *feed back* a portion of its output for comparison with its input or standard. If the feedback tends to reduce error, rather than aggravate it, the feedback is called negative feedback—negative because it tends to oppose what the organization is doing.[3] The steam governor is a *negative feedback* device, and in business the constant comparison of operating costs against standard costs (in order to keep operating costs in line) is a form of negative feedback.

One can explain the term "keeping up with the Joneses" in terms of negative feedback. The "Joneses" are what the sociologist calls a "reference group." Those of us who have such a reference group or goal (to equal the financial or social position of the Joneses) would constantly monitor our own financial and social position, detect the error or difference between our own position and the Joneses', and try to reduce the error, if possible, by appropriate action.

The nature of negative feedback is explicit if one takes an example from electrical engineering. Figure 6 represents a simple feed-

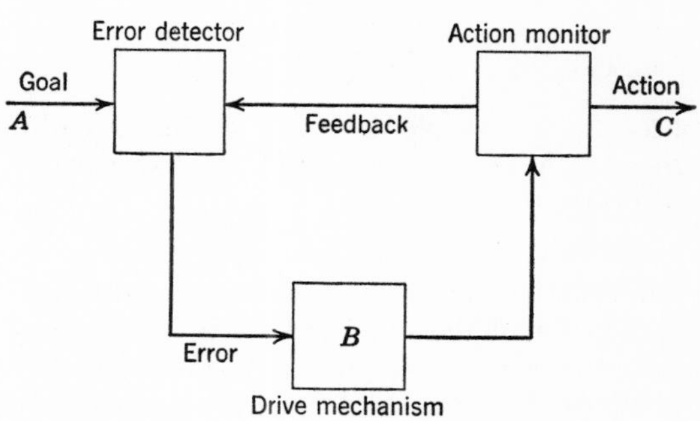

FIG. 6. The basic negative feedback circuit. The simplest organization which can control itself. Note the circularity of connection. A goal can be set at *A*, then the feedback circuit left to maintain that goal on its own. The steam governor works like this.

back circuit used in control devices called *servomechanisms*. Such devices can be used, for example, to actuate a radar antenna so that the position of the antenna matches the position set on a remotely located control box—in spite of wind resistance (load) at the antenna.

A certain position, or goal, can be set in the control box *A*, which in turn operates a motor or drive *B* to turn the antenna *C*. The actual position of the antenna, which may be different from the goal set because of, e.g., wind load, is fed back from *C* to *A*, and the error between the position of the antenna and the goal position set is detected at *A*. A signal in turn is sent to motor *B* to reduce the error.

Mathematically, the action of the circuit is

[3] Standard texts on electronic circuits and servomechanisms provide discussions of feedback characteristics.

described by the following relation (refer to Fig. 7)

$$E_2 = E_1 \left(\frac{K}{1 - (-b)K} \right)$$

where E_1 is the input or standard set into the unit, E_2 is the output of the unit, K is the

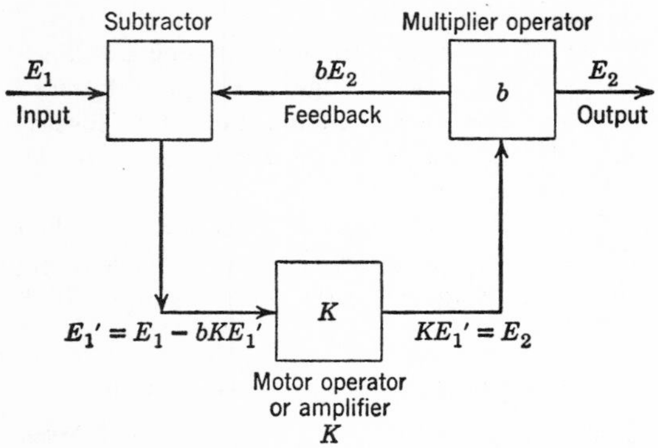

FIG. 7. The simple negative feedback circuit showing the mathematical relations which describe its operations.

amplification factor or mechanical transformation factor of the unit, and $(-b)$ is the fraction of the unit's output E_2, used as negative feedback for error correction. In general, the greater the negative feedback, the greater the error reduction or stabilization of the unit. The unit can be arranged so that, instead of negative feedback, *positive feedback* is obtained $(+b)$. Error would then be aggravated when it occurred, oscillations would occur in the circuit's operation, etc. *Critical points for oscillation, stabilization, and error reduction are of particular interest to the control engineer, and although further discussion of feedback characteristics is beyond the scope of this chapter, the serious user of communication models should familiarize himself with feedback literature, such as that given in the bibliography.*

Control systems are in a sense circular in their operation, as can be seen from the circuit in Fig. 6. The feedback circuit and drive mechanism constitute a loop (or circle) of action. Systems which operate with negative feedback to maintain or reach a goal are said to be "goal-directed," and because of the circularity of action required by feedback such systems have also been called "circular causal systems."

The communications diagram can be studied for the presence of such circular feedback loops. This tells something about feedback and control in the organizations studied—the second point of interest. The Operations Researchers want to know, in particular, which processes are monitored, which are not; they want to obtain some idea of the efficiency of feedback loops, to determine if there is positive or negative feedback in these loops, to learn under what critical conditions negative (or positive) feedback may be useful or harmful. Scheduling and order processing systems, for example, deserve analysis with respect to stability, time lags, and feedback checks.

THE SORTER WITH FEEDBACK

If feedback can be applied to simple mechanical transformation systems (like the steam-engine governor) it is also applicable to the simple sorter. The various sorted outputs are then compared with standards for these outputs to determine if the sorter is, in fact, operating properly. The consistency and stability of the sorting operation is thereby improved. Figure 8 would be a diagram of such

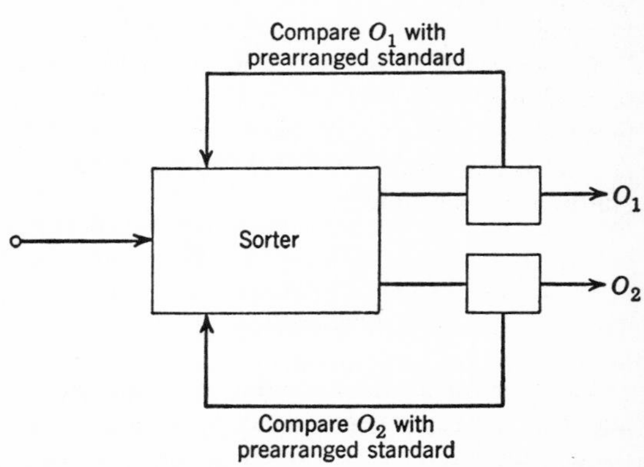

FIG. 8. The simple sorter with feedback applied. The output from the sorter is compared with the output desired (standard or goal) which has been built into the sorter mechanism.

a system. The industrial inspection system of quality control, which checks various finished products against standards, sorting good and bad products into different piles, is an example of this kind of feedback sorter.

COMBINATIONS OF TRANSFORMATION AND SORTER UNITS

To obtain a more complex organization that is more versatile, various combinations of transformation and sorting units (with or without feedback) can be combined. This is roughly what happens when various parts or divisions of an organization are brought together. The most useful combination for a given job is usually not obvious, however, since the number of changes one could make in a many-part organization is inconceivably large. Furthermore, the combination of various parts may have characteristics quite different from that of the parts themselves, particularly in industrial or human organizations. Professor Wiener, who was pressed by several of his social science friends to extend his mathematical theory of Cybernetics to the area of human organization, hesitated to do so because he realized that the rapidly changing conditions of social organizations, the necessity for short-run statistics, and the interaction of observers would make precise results difficult to obtain.

In other words, as stated on p. 191 of Wiener's book, in the social sciences

> we have to deal with short statistical runs, nor can we be sure that a considerable part of what we observe is not an artefact of our own creation. An investigation of the stock market is likely to upset the stock market. We are too much in tune with the objects of our investigation to be good probes. In short, whether our investigations in the social sciences be statistical or dynamic—and they should participate in the nature of both—they can never be good to more than a very few decimal places, and, in short, can never furnish us with a quantity of verifiable significant information which begins to compare with that which we have learned to expect in the natural sciences. We cannot afford to neglect them; neither should we build exaggerated expectations of their possibilities. There is much which we must leave, whether we like it or not, to the unscientific narrative method of the professional historian.

If the investigator is aware of these problems and he is looking only for fairly gross improvements in operations (as is often the case), some further discussion of complex organizations built up of the simple elements we have discussed may be helpful to the practical researcher.

THE AUTOMATIC GOAL-CHANGING UNIT

If an organization has several alternatives prepared for action, and also has the rules set up for applying one or the other of them *when external conditions change* (i.e., can *predict* the best alternative for changing conditions), it can control its own activities more effectively than can a simple feedback system. Such action requires a second-order feedback and implies that a reserve or memory of possible alternatives exists within the organization.

An example of this type of organization—which can switch its standards for different courses of action—is the telephone exchange. The immediate goal of the telephone exchange is to search and find a specific number dialed by a subscriber. There may be many such numbers dialed during the day; the exchange must be prepared to receive different numbers and take different courses of action automatically for each one. (Figure 9 shows a simplified diagram of such a system, which is in fact a complicated sorting operation.) Another goal-changing example of similar type is the cat that chases the rat—not by following the rat's position at a given moment, but by *leading* the rat's position based on the cat's memory of how other rats ran in the past.

If an organization can control itself, particularly if it can change its goals, we call it an *autonomous organization.* The autonomy of the automatic goal-changing organization lies in its memory and ability to recall. The better the memory and the faster the recall, the more autonomous the organization is likely to be.

The storing up of information, which allows the organization to prepare various alternatives for action, is a process of *learning*. Learning may result in a reconfiguration of the internal channels of the organization, or communication network. The learning organization's structure changes with time. For example, the circuits in a telephone exchange can be expanded to include the "numbers" of more subscribers by rewiring part of the telephone exchange.

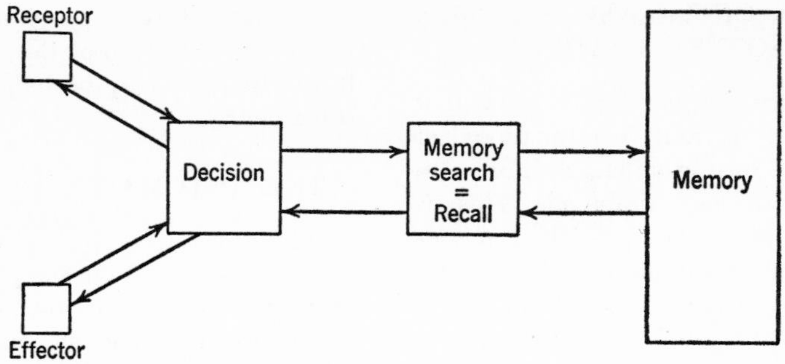

FIG. 9. Feedback circuit with memory device. By adding a memory and more complicated feedback loops, an organization can have more control over its own activities. In this case a series of alternatives for action is built into the system if external conditions (detected by the receptor) change. An example is the automatic switching of a telephone exchange.

Increased memory reserves generally require greater complexity of interconnection in the communication network. In terms of physiology, more memory means a greater interconnection of nerve cells. For a librarian, more memory means a greater cross referencing of index cards.

Thus, after we have found out what the existing communication and control processes in an "automatic" goal-changing organization are, we ask: How do these processes change with time? How do the inner channels of communication in the organization develop? Fall into disuse? Maintain themselves? Where is the memory of the organization located? What kind of information is put into the memory? By what manner is it stocked? What kind of information is taken out of the memory? What is the *content* of the memory; how does it change? Is the organization learning anything? Is it forgetting properly or improperly? What can it *predict* from its memory?

The operation of a system with a memory also means that certain messages have greater priority of transmission into and out of the memory than others. The possible courses of action have different priorities or *values* for application in different situations, and the researcher wants to know about these values to understand the action of the system. Again, reasoning in terms of the telephone exchange is useful. When ten telephone calls are received at once, the exchange must decide which to answer first.

THE REFLECTIVE GOAL-CHANGING UNIT

If an organization can collect information, store it in a memory, and then reflect upon or examine the contents of the memory for the purpose of formulating new courses of action, it will have reached a new level of autonomy. The mechanism that considers various goals and courses of action can be called the *consciousness* of the organization.[4] Reflective decision-making takes place in such third-order feedback systems. The action of the organization begins to approach what we would expect of an actual industrial or human organization. See Fig. 10.

To get a concrete picture of what consciousness is, imagine a person sitting back, relaxed in an overstuffed chair, speculating on what he will do next—on how he might improve his lot by completion of a certain type of research or sale of an invention, or on how his wife told him to put a new washer in the bathroom because the faucet leaks. He decides to please his wife rather than his pocketbook. He would then be using his reflective goal-changing circuits, or consciousness.

Conscious learning can be selective and take, from a wide range of external information sources, that information relevant to the organization's survival or other major goals. The consciousness may redirect the *attention* of the organization; make it *aware* of some happenings and unmindful of others. It can

[4] See in particular the writings by Deutsch on growth and learning.

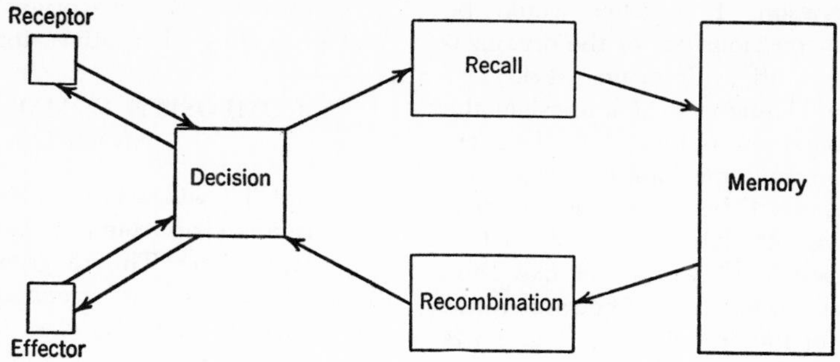

(a)

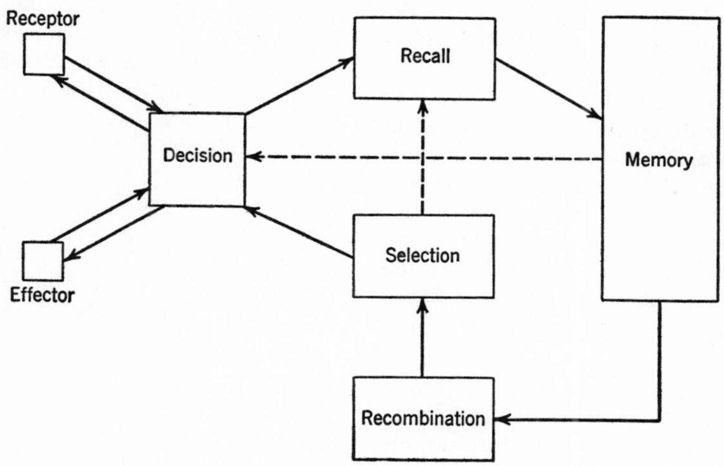

(b)

FIG. 10. (*a*) Additional memory refinements. If information in the memory can be recombined and new alternatives produced for action (by the machine or organization itself), the unit becomes more versatile and autonomous. This device makes simple predictions. (*b*) Additional memory refinements: development of a consciousness. If many memories can be combined, and if from the many combinations a few can be selected for further consideration, further recombination, etc., the unit will have reached a still higher level of versatility or autonomy. The dashed lines indicate comparisons of what is going on with what has happened in the past and what might occur in the future (second- and third- order predictions). In many organizations, these comparisons are poorly made.

initiate or cease courses of action, based on incoming information; *investigate* network conditions in the organization; *search* the organization's memory; and *pick up deviations* between various actions and the goals which direct them—to name but a few of the activities of this third-order control center.

By taking such actions, the organization with a consciousness can direct its own *growth.* The possibility of *recognizing* valuable information received by the organization, or valuable combinations of information in the memory, permits the organization to practice *innovation.* Such abilities are highly desirable for most organizations and so, as an industrial investigator, the Operations Researcher would be interested in the consciousness of the organization (what the executives do or do not do).

Reflective goal-changing is of interest in the field of electronic computers, too. For example, computers and mechanisms which repair themselves must be conscious of their internal circuit faults. The action of such a machine "consciousness" would be like this: The consciousness circuits would become aware that other parts of the organization (e.g., parts or tubes) had broken down or been superseded by a more efficient design. The consciousness circuits would then direct replacement of the broken or outmoded parts with new or improved ones. Such action lies in the realm of possibility for computers—but industrial organizations do it every day!

The consciousness could be expected to show all the faults, in its operation, that we might find in humans or in executive groups which run organizations: delusions, faulty direction, misinterpretation of messages, lack of awareness of new opportunities, poorly defined operating goals, and the rest. Such faults are the subject of the last half of this chapter. However, another example here may be illuminating.

Consider a computer which could repair itself. It would have consciousness circuits to direct the repairs. Now if the consciousness circuits themselves were faulty and directed indiscriminate repairs to be made on the properly working machine, disaster would result. Let a drunken repairman run through a local telephone exchange and randomly unsolder relay connections, and the result would be similar. It would become virtually impossible to find all the newly created faults. The unreliability of electronic components and circuits limits the application of "self-repair" or consciousness functions in computing machines today. Similarly, executives in industrial organizations can cause disaster if they get out of commission easily.

The O.R. team should make the most use of organizational knowledge brought together by Cybernetics in the analysis of complex organizations with a memory and a consciousness. One of the functions of O.R. with its mixed discipline teams is to increase an organization's memory—by bringing in a collection of knowledge different from that of the organization's routine—and to aid its consciousness (the executives) in developing and evaluating alternatives for action.

A COMPOSITE COMMUNICATION MODEL

Figure 11 will serve to tie together these various ideas on communication and control in organizations. The diagram was proposed by K. W. Deutsch as a general communication model which might be used to describe complex organizations.[5] For the sake of discussion, it might be considered as a block diagram of a radar input gun-control mechanism which contains a memory device.

Column I of Fig. 11 contains circuits which operate as a simple feedback system with a fixed goal. The circuits consist of a receptor and an effector, e.g., the radar equipment for spotting planes and the gun-positioning and firing mechanisms. When a plane is picked up by the receptor device, the gun-effector devices are directed to follow the plane, or goal, and to track the position of the plane as accurately as possible.

The addition of memory and goal-changing circuits, located in Column II, allows the gun control to predict where the plane will be—to anticipate the plane's position rather than follow its position slavishly—and thus increases the number of hits the device can secure. Column II circuits are essentially *automatic goal-changing circuits;* the rules for changing goals are designed into the device by the communications engineer. So the action of the gun-control device can be changed (by the device itself) depending upon the type of aircraft observed, weather conditions, the predicted quality of the pilot, etc.

Column III, the consciousness, contains *reflective goal-changing circuits.* These were sketched in so the reader can see the development of the whole system, from the simple receptor and effector circuits to the complicated feedback circuits a consciousness would require. The consciousness circuits are dashed, because they are not yet part of normal electronic computers.

Again, for the sake of comparison, *analogies with industrial organizations* have been in-

[5] Figure 11 is adapted from K. W. Deutsch. The Deutsch diagram may prove applicable to any level of social integration, including the individual.

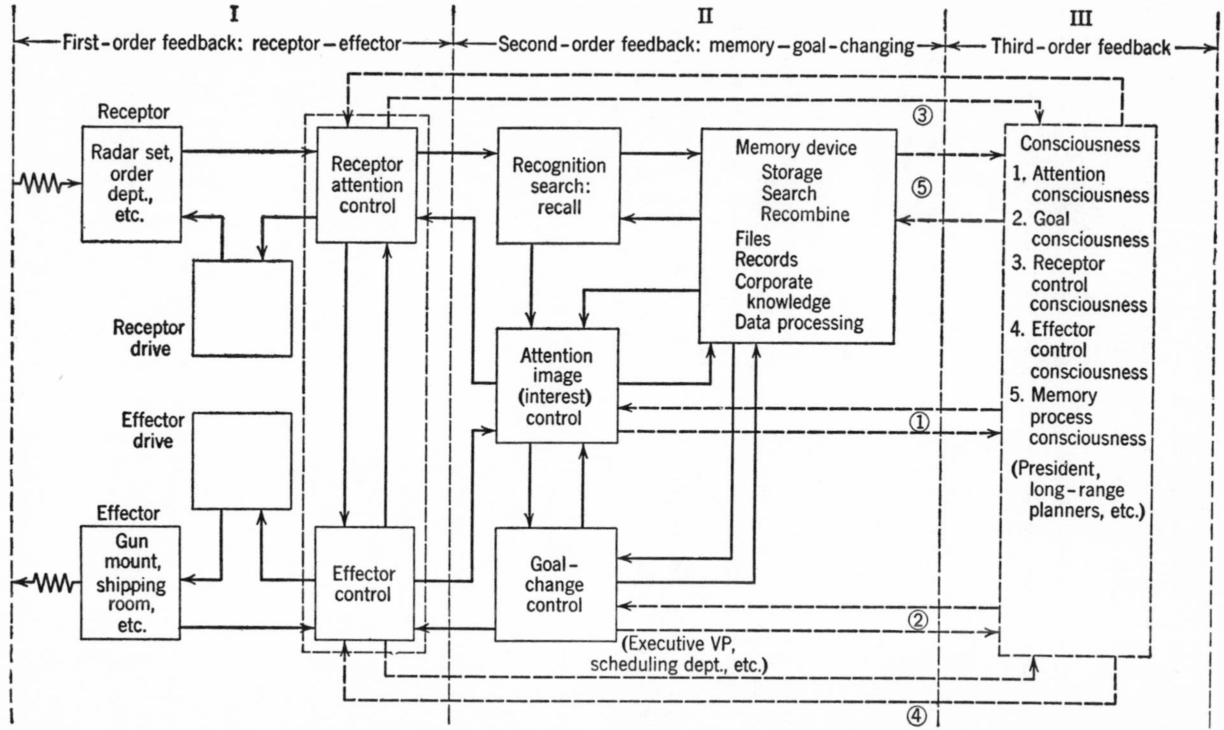

FIG. 11. Block diagram of a three-level feedback control system. Adapted from Deutsch, K. W. (Models of Communication and Education, Unpublished), Industrial Engineering Seminar 312, Columbia University, New York, March 13, 1951. For explanation of the figure, see text. Note that this diagram is a build-up of simpler units shown in Figs. 3 through 10.

cluded in Fig. 11. Column I corresponds to the production-line–order-department combination which receives orders and fills them in a routine manner. Column II represents the domain of staff personnel, the file department, the semi-automatic or tactical goal-changing responsibilities of the executive vice-president. Column III represents the long-range planning functions of the president or the board of directors in a normal organization.

The purpose of this description of some characteristics of internal communication and control in organizations has been to give an idea of the *elaboration* that one can make on the communication diagram in order to indicate some of the analogies that can be made by using the diagram. The arrangement of receptor, effector, and processing circuits in Fig. 11 is also a fairly standard method of drawing communication networks. The receptor and effector circuits are to the left in the diagram, the processing circuits to the right.

Before continuing, it may be helpful to summarize what we have to work with in a communication model.

SUMMARY OF COMMUNICATION MODEL CHARACTERISTICS

The communication model should provide:

1. A map of the communication network of the organization.
2. Knowledge of the goal-maintaining or goal-directing processes of control in organization.
3. In complex goal-directed organization, some knowledge of goal-changing processes. The processes of innovation, growth, learning, the functions of memory and consciousness, and the concept of autonomy occur here.

In each of these categories, the Operations Researchers will be interested in the kind or content of information transmitted and received.

So, the complete communication model consists of a series of network pictures similar to Fig. 11 (in which the inner channels of the organization will change with time), plus accumulated knowledge on the processes of communication and control taken from various disciplines. This knowledge can be co-ordinated by use of the diagram.

8. WHAT HAS CYBERNETICS TO DO WITH OPERATIONAL RESEARCH?

STAFFORD BEER *

Part 1 of this paper answers the question "What is cybernetics?" A brief historical review introduces a somewhat formal statement about the nature of systems and the way they are controlled. The unifying topic in the study of control in every context is an underlying identity of system: an example is taken from learning machines.

A comparably brief treatment of the question "What is operational research?" is given in Part 2. Operational research is thought to be the latest exemplification of scientific method rather than "a science." What is important about operational research is brought out through a description of an actual case study, and some of the activities which look like operational research but are not are mentioned. This leads to an attempted definition of operational research.

Part 3 tries to draw the answers to the first two questions together, and to show how operational research and cybernetics are related. It is possible to pursue each activity in its own right; but it is also possible to practise operational research with essentially cybernetic models, and to study cybernetics by operational research techniques. This thought is generalized into the idea that cybernetics is the science of which operational research is the method.

INTRODUCTION

"The Department of Operational Research and Cybernetics." This phrase is, I regret to say, rather a mouthful; and from what I hear some of my operational research colleagues find it too much to swallow. The last bit is not regarded as very respectable.

Now ten years ago operational research itself was not a particularly respectable activity. Today by contrast, the advertisement columns of the newspapers week by week attest to the fact that operational research is now highly respectable—and respected. It can only be a matter of time before cybernetics too achieves the status which it must have: I am quite confident of this.

Now you will gather that my mood is not very apologetic. In fact this address is meant to be polemical. That is why I have given it the aggressive title that I have; that is why I am wearing a bullet-proof waistcoat.

SOURCE: *Operational Research Quarterly* (March, 1959), pp. 1–21. Reprinted by permission of the *Operational Research Society*.

* International Publishing Corporation. Great Britain.

WHAT IS CYBERNETICS?

Cybernetics is the science of control; or, to expand it into Norbert Wiener's own words: [1] control and communication in the animal and the machine. Like most definitions, this one does not seem to say very much at first sight. To understand what cybernetics is about, one just must look at the origins of the work. As you probably know from Wiener's book, cybernetics originated in the work of a group of people representing a number of sciences. And the point I want to make, the first point, is that they did not get together to discuss the question of control in the first place. They had noted that the whole range of human thinking had been developing over the centuries into a pattern, a pattern represented today by a large number of subjects each generally discussed as if it were a valid object of study in its own right. Here was a pattern which represented the historical development of human thinking; could it be, however, that it might not represent the real world very accurately at all? Whole topics of enquiry might fall neatly between the stools of the established sciences.

The problem of control emerged from these early discussions as something which is common to every science. Soon it was discovered that the nature of this problem for scientists in every field was uniform in many respects. What I should like to call "the theory of organic control," which is applicable to mechanical and social systems as well as to biological, grew from this impetus. So the essence of cybernetics is to be interdisciplinary.

Now it is very easy at this stage to talk about uniting the body of thinking, to speak of the unity of science and the indivisibility of knowledge. I am as aware as anyone of the pitfalls of this kind of speech. One can quickly throw oneself open to a charge of being some kind of alchemist, of having naïve and probably egotistical views about the complexity and wonder of nature and the amount of insight into it that one brain can possibly acquire and comprehend. But if you look on this concept of the unity of science simply in terms of the dimension of control, which is the way the subject of cybernetics arose historically, such charges prove baseless. Cybernetics is not an attempt to comprehend the whole of science and knowledge in one glorious confusion, but rather an attempt to see whether the understanding of control problems so far acquired in many disparate sciences is being properly shared. Although a great deal is known about control in various departments of learning, little has been done about the nature of control *per se*. In attacking that problem, cybernetics must inevitably borrow the available information about its subject wherever that seems to be available; in this sense it is certainly a unifying influence on science at large.

Just as the concept of control appears in every science, any conclusions which can be reached about it must be applicable to many contexts. Very soon, Wiener and his associates realized that they were discussing something which was relevant to industrial, social and economic systems, as well as to the mechanical and biological ones. Now it is extremely difficult to talk scientifically about a topic which has so many utterly different origins, and also so many widely varied applications. For this reason, the essence of a developing science is that it has some formal technique for discussing the basic nature of its subject and of ridding itself of the trappings which make up the specific detail. Can we find a formal language in which to talk about problems of control wherever they arise?

I do not think there is any doubt about the answer: we can. In logic, in mathematics, in statistics, and in metamathematics, there are formal systems that we know how to manipulate. But in a general paper like this I must confine any formal analysis, not to some recondite algebra, but to a verbal version. Even in English, it is possible to discuss the nature of control formally, and without bringing in the details of many different sciences. But I must do this quickly, because it is rather a tiresome set of aphorisms that must be presented.

Control is the attribute of a system. A system is any collection of entities that can be understood as forming a coherent group. The fact of their being capable of being understood as a coherent group is precisely what differentiates a system from a meaningless collection or jumble of bits and pieces. Now that statement does not sound very important, but I think it is; because at once it reveals the relativity of this concept of a system. This means that we might have a series of numbers on the blackboard which to an uneducated man, or a savage, or indeed most of the general public, would appear to be a meaningless jumble of figures; but to a mathematician this would be at once recognizable as a binomial series.

Therefore the property of being a system is as much a property of the observing system, which is I, or you, or whatever we use for the purpose as extensions of ourselves, as of the observed system itself.

The structure of a system is its relatedness. A description of the way in which the system is interconnected *defines* its structure. The system and the structure are formal components of the analysis I wish to make, and are words which I shall henceforth use in this special way.

It seems to me that there are three main characteristics of a cybernetic system. The first is that it is extremely complex, to the point of indefinability. It may be that no real system is in principle indefinable; but many certainly are in practice, because (like the brain) they disintegrate once they are probed too closely. The reason for this characteristic of a cybernetic system is that the connectivity of its structure, of which I was speaking just now, is initially very great and changing continuously. Thus the brain, the economy, the industrial company; all these things are cybernetic systems under this first heading at the very least—the heading of extreme complexity.

May we note in passing that operational research itself often claims to deal with complex systems, and so it does. But when we talk about an operational research model we like to think, I suspect, that we are creating an isomorphic representation of our problem. If we use linear programming, for instance, to study a problem of the allocation of materials from five different sources to five different consumers, it may well be true that we can do this. But once we try and use it ouside the context in which the straightforward matrix of small order can be constructed, and turn to game-theoretic analysis of the entire operations of a company, we are in very great difficulty. This is more than a practical problem, it is a methodological one; because we can no longer determine in any sense that our model is an isomorphism. To be quite formal: we must end up with a homomorphic representation—by which I mean, of course, that there is a many-one relationship from every segment of the situation being described to each element of the matrix which is describing it. This is a very severe methodological limitation on the analysis by operational research techniques of extremely complex systems. Cybernetics tries to answer the problem by the use of Black Box theory. This is the theory which specifically begins by accepting the situation as indefinable in detail.

Now the second feature of a cybernetic system is its probabilism. Again, operational research deals with indeterminate systems. But we normally say this in the sense that *within* a rigid framework of related parts, most of the quantities which characterize the parts are not constants, they are distributed. For example, the relations which connect a queue to the machine which has to serve it are quite clear, distinct and unchanging. It is the waiting time and the service time that are the variables which lead us to call the system probabilistic. In cybernetics, however, the very structure of the system is indeterminate. The existence of connexion between entities which make up the system is itself problematic; the network of connectivity is itself defined by variables to which levels of probability can be assigned. If the levels fall below the threshold of statistical significance, then the system disintegrates and ceases to be recognizable as a system at all. If the level of threshold changes, the system itself changes, and is no longer describable as the system that it was.

The third major feature of cybernetic systems is the feature of self-regulation. How, after all, is a system to be controlled? In operational research, it is customary to design controls which can be operated within certain fiducial limits. This approach is a great advance over the less sophisticated notion that it is possible to have rigid error-free regulators. But consider the kind of system we have so far designated as cybernetic. It is to be so complex as to be indefinable; it is to be probabilistic not only in its operational parameters but in its very structure. It follows that no control at all designed to be imposed upon the system from outside could possibly work. A little reflection shows this must be the case, and that a regulator can only be designed in the sense that the system will operate it itself. Systems can in fact be designed as machines for self-regulation. Homeostasis is of course the example of this in biology and physiology; and thanks to Ross Ashby it is further exemplified in his kind of topological mathematics and ultrastable machines.

With these explanations, let me now try to finish my formal verbal statement. Control is the attribute of a system which tends to sustain the system's structure, to reinforce its cohesion. Control is the dynamics of the structure. To exert control in a new direction in a given system is to discover the language in which new structure may be discerned. To exert control in a recognized direction, on the other hand, is to facilitate the speaking of the language of a recognized structure. This is what communication means: the talkativeness of a structure within itself, the ease of association inside its relatedness. So to manage the system you must be able to talk to it, to talk inside it, as a competent conversationalist.

A system, and now I am speaking emphatically of any system, can be made responsive if it is talked to in the right language, the language of its own structure which makes it the system it is. By communication inside the system, it comes to be conditioned; this is to say that the probabilities which quantify the internal relatedness of the structure begin to change. Circumstances can be created in which the system becomes conditioned to suit the behaviour we require of it; circumstances in which, with perfect propriety, the system can be said to be learning and discriminating. As management of this kind goes on paths of facilitation inside the structure become established, certain languages become more fluent than others, and certain translations from one language to another become more readily available to the system itself. In this way the system comes to exhibit memory.

At this point we have arrived knee deep in the language of physiology, and I expect a lot of complaints about this. May I at once attempt to dispose of the problem about the free use of the languages of one science in the languages of another, a practice which is always so very unpopular. When, in cybernetics, we use machine language to talk about animals; when we use biological language to discuss machines; it is then that the trouble starts. We are breaking down inhibitions of language, we are breaking through habits of thought; we are accused of a facile rhetoric, and a mere glibness of tongue. What is the point of this polyglot language, and what is the validity of the comparison it implicitly makes?

Let us arbitrarily distinguish three levels of comparison. Firstly, there is the metaphor. Perhaps when we speak of memory and learning in machines, this is the level of comparison we intend. Now the validity of a metaphor is poetic; it can offer science no more help than its verbal facility. Secondly, there is the comparision of identity itself. Perhaps when we speak of a complicated logical gate made of electronic components as a neuron we mean that it is literally the same thing as a neuron in a nervous network. But the validity of the comparison of identity between things which are not one and the same is a mystical validity. Mysticism is not generally regarded as useful to science; it may offer insight, but the vision is cloudy. Thirdly, there is analogy. This comparison has a logical validity. If we choose to say that a machine has a neurosis, perhaps we mean that its behaviour is like the behaviour of a human neurotic. Such a comparison is useful in science although it is edged about with problems of the delineation of its application. Any argument which we do not particularly like can be said to be "pushing the analogy too far." Nonetheless, analogical thinking is extremely useful in operational research; and I think that many operational research men who object to cybernetic discussion do so because they imagine the thinking is analogical—by analogy with operational research!

Now I am extremely anxious to assert that the physiological language of cybernetics is neither metaphorical nor analogical. Despite the mystical connotations of the assertion, I contend that the comparisons of cybernetics are identities. If a mystic were to say that two things which are manifestly not the same are the same, we would say that he had perceived, or dimly understood, some kind of ultimate identity. I am claiming that in cybernetics we are trying to pinpoint that perception scientifically. And the identity we can pinpoint is the identity of structure—as I have already defined that word. Let us take an example.

We talk about learning in the animal and the machine. It is customary to take the example of a rat running a maze for the demonstration of animal learning: the maze has two outcomes and eventually the rat learns to go to the cheese rather than the electric shock. You have perhaps heard the story of the maze-running rat who said to his colleague: "I have that chap in the white coat conditioned. Every time I run to the end of the maze he gives me a piece of cheese." But let us take this maze-learning more seriously, and consider that the maze is so constructed that there is (on a basis of random running) an equal probability of getting a piece of cheese or an electric shock. Therefore the system begins in a state of even probability over these two outcomes. And as the experiment proceeds the rat begins to approach the cheese more often than the shock until after some considerable experience he almost invariably reaches the cheese. We call this process learning; and I refuse to be impressed by the kind of special significance which some people wish to give this word. They speak of learning as if it were a prerogative of animate things; in so doing they are being dragooned by a mere word. Our rat-maze system begins in a state of even probability over the two outcomes; ultimately it approaches a state of unit probability on the cheese outcome. I choose to label this behaviour "learning." Now if we do this experiment repeatedly, we find that the initial and final outcome of the experiment, designated 0.5/0.5 and 1.0/0, are connected through time by a curve which is reproducible —and what is more a curve to which statistical significance can be given.

Now there is the formal language and there

is the abstraction of the structure of the system of learning. It is expressed in mathematical terms as a stochastic process. Once that structure is understood, there is no reason why a machine should not be built, which is a probabilistic machine, to do the same thing. And indeed, as you no doubt know, this has been done. The result is an artefact of a learning rat, which will produce experimental learning (by a Monte Carlo procedure) and provide behavioral statistics which are indistinguishable to the animal physiologist from the real results. There is an example, an elementary one, of what a cybernetician would call a learning machine. The rat running a maze is a learning machine. The mathematical specification of this stochastic process is a learning machine. The mechanical artefact is a learning machine. This illustrates quite well the idea of the structural identity of all three things. There is neither metaphor nor analogy here: there is identity in a formal sense.

So that is the kind of process that cybernetics studies, that is how it analyses what is going on, that is the heuristic mechanism of cybernetics. The result of such studies is, inevitably, that we seek to build machines: and cyberneticians have built machines that learn. They have built machines which carry out many other functions normally attributed to animate systems by a similar process of reasoning. Let me now pick up three examples of actual machines which I choose to illustrate the three main features of cybernetic systems which I began by discussing. The feature of structural probabilism is exemplified in a small way by the learning machine already described. A learning machine is essentially a conditional probability mechanism. Secondly, there is the idea of self-regulation; this may be exemplified by Ashby's homeostat,[2] where the same process of finding the structural element that is common to all self-regulating systems is pursued. In this case, the discovery is of that formal structure which leads a system to fall into an equilibrial state when perturbed by unspecified causes. And thirdly, the idea of extreme complexity is very well illustrated by one of Gordon Pask's brilliant machines [3] which formally identifies the structural elements of a process of growth.

This is what I take cybernetics to be about, and this is what cyberneticians do. But please note that because of the definitions which I have already given about systems and their structure, and the account I have given of the formal languages by which they may be described, any collection of entities which is cohesive can be described as a machine. Thus whether cybernetics deals with animals, or hardware, any other kind of system, is irrelevant. It is always possible to journey into the problem of describing the behaviour of a complex, probabilistic, self-regulating system in this way. And therefore there is no necessity to characterize cybernetics by the building of machines in the metal. They may equally exist in the flesh. Above all, they may arise in economic and social relationships. If the description of a social system can be mapped into the formal structure of a learning machine, then that society is a machine for learning. There is no more to be said.

WHAT IS OPERATIONAL RESEARCH?

Having probed the nature of cybernetics, I would now like to probe the nature of operational research. I am really rather tired of the situation where, whenever anyone speaks on operational research, we have to make all these coy jokes about not really knowing what it is. What is our present approach to this question of the nature of operational research? I will tell you as I see it.

We say that this is a new and a young scientific endeavour, and that it would be very unwise to be dogmatic about it. Operational research is a sort of high-level activity; it involves studying things scientifically. Now this is a very estimable line to take. Consider how *mature* it is: one is not making any wild claims about what can be done, and what cannot be done. Consider how *safe* it is: the best of all worlds is ours to command. If someone says: "What about this operational research job, it just did not work," we may reply: "Oh, *that* was not really operational research." They may say: "Look at this wonderful job"; and we reply: "Yes—yes—*that* is operational research." Consider further how *comforting* this approach is: we sit in an esoteric coterie, hugging ourselves, and keeping warm together, which is a very superior sort of thing to do. Yes: our attitude is estimable: mature, safe, and comforting.

What price do we pay for this charming situation? We pay the price of utter confusion. There is today total confusion about the status, aims, and abilities of our work. Management has no idea of what we are trying to do, and is getting tired of trying to find out.

Recently I agreed to give a lecture on linear programming, and I was introduced by a senior and well-known industrialist who said: "Mr. Beer will give a lecture on linear programming, or as it is sometimes called, operational research." Management does not yet understand what operational research is about. Do our junior operational research people themselves? Most of the people at this meeting are fairly senior in operational research. I ask them what sort of future we can offer our staffs, what sort of professional status they will have in the years to come, in the brave new world? We, the Operational Research Society, have not managed to agree what operational research is, and have refused an authoritative definition to enquirers. Perhaps for this reason the Society is unable to give our staffs the professional distinction of the letters M.O.R.S. (or K.I.M.B.A.L. for that matter) to their names. And what about the national level? We have totally failed, as far as I can see, and despite some very distinguished senior men in our organization, in making anything like the right impact on the national problems to which operational research might offer a solution.

Now this is a very high price to pay for our present outlook, and I am boldly going to suggest that this outlook is simply cowardice masquerading as wisdom. For of course we know what operational research is. We have been doing it for years.

Let me quote. "Operational research may be regarded as a branch of philosophy, as an attitude of mind towards the relation of man and environment; and as a body of methods for the solution of problems which arise in that relationship." You will recognize that; it was our President speaking to the Operational Research Society.* Now I hope Professor Kendall will not think it an impertinence in me to say that I consider this is one of the best descriptions I have ever seen. It gives us an excellent start. Please notice that he did not say anything about queue theory, or search theory, or the inventory model. He gave us a description of a new man-oriented science. This is indeed what we are trying to do.

I would like to urge this point of view. Operational research is not *a* science, for it is not *about* anything; it *is* science.

Now the Newtonian universe has given place to several more sophisticated universes in succession. They are universes in which man has projected a greater maturity of his own intellect. In physics, the billiard-ball atoms have gone; in physiology, the reflex arcs have gone; in economics, the Robinson Crusoe economy has gone. We have replaced these elementary descriptions by those more advanced. In turn, operational research for me has replaced the "objectivity of science." It is the modern embodiment of "the scientific method." That phrase is one we use in the Society's constitution. But what is *the* scientific method? I gather that nobody ever seems able to define that either. For me, again, it can be nothing more or less than induction, which is part of logic.

This induction has three main principles which I should like briefly to review. Perhaps we can learn from the way these three principles are being recast, what is really happening in the attack of applied science. First, there is the old principle of the uniformity of nature—associated with John Stuart Mill. This principle insisted that nature is a connected whole, within which changes occur; it led to the notion of "physical laws." By today, the same notion has led us in our work to what I have always called the operational research of "organic wholes." You all have your names for this, but the idea is the same. It is not the job of operational research to investigate the fiddling details of industrial processes, nor the pin-pricking worries of management. The operational research job is to get the problem in perspective in its proper environment; in other words, we do not suboptimize. And the second lead that the principle of the uniformity of nature gave us was the notion that what is true this time will be true next time if the conditions are the same. That notion originally led to the whole of the nineteenth century idea of the laboratory experiments, controlled experiments. And to what has that outlook matured? It has matured straight into operational research, where we have rejected the laboratory investigation with its belief that variables can be altered one at a time. We have said: real life is not like this, we have statistical techniques and the design of experiments to help us in studying more natural patterns of variation. And so this thread un-

* Presidential Address on 23 October, 1958.

folds, until we find ourselves with the modern idea of active applied science—being precisely operational research.

Causation, the next principle of induction, is the most important exemplification of the principle of uniformity. Not only is there relatedness in the universe, there is causal relatedness. That lead, through the nineteenth century again, gave us "objectivity in science." It gave us nature as an inexorable machine, working out its answers deterministically—if only we could discover how. But the large clockwork toy has changed. The raw notion of cause has given place to the principle of indeterminacy. It was Sir Owen Wansbrough Jones whom I first heard in a broadcast talk comparing the problems of operational research with the problems of a physicist looking at the discoveries of Heisenberg. That was a useful idea, which I myself pursued in another paper.[4] We find it summed up again by Professor Kendall in his Presidential Address, when he said: "There is a broad movement against the nineteenth century attitude towards objectivity in science." We have learnt that the observer is part of the situation. In work study there is the spotlight effect. In the introduction of new ideas there is the Hawthorne effect. These are examples of a point made earlier tonight about the observer affecting the definition of the system he seeks to describe.

Finally, the third principle of induction: limited variety. This is the idea that properties go in sets; the idea that variety does not proliferate, as it could do in theory, by permutation and combination, but that attributes hang together in families. And for the Victorians that provided the argument from analogy. Already this evening we have had to dig ourselves out of the muddle which this testament has bequeathed. And already, I have tried to show how the concept of analogy in logic has grown and developed into the idea of structural identity. Today we have a new version of limited variety. We say: "Here is a stream of ingots coming from a melting shop, and the stream breaks up into six streams feeding six soaking pits." This model could equally well be a warehouse from which flows a stream of goods to six retail shops. Is this an analogy? No; these two things are identical in a formal sense. They are identified in a structure given by the statistics of queue theory.

In short: the universe has gone over from the motionless universe of Zeno, where nothing ever happens, to a Heracletian flux in which things are happening all the time. And the methods of science have gone from the stationary, one-variable-at-a-time kind of treatment to the treatment of operations conceived operationally—and what could that be but operational research? We no longer imagine ourselves to be using the three inductive principles to discover "what a thing is really like"; that is a pious hope belonging to the old conception. We use instead new versions of these three principles to say what makes an assembly of things tick. These new versions are essentially the operational research techniques; their object is to discover the strategy of the assembly. Thus I contend that operational research emerges as a subset of scientific methods appropriate to the analysis of *activity*, just as chemical methods of analysis from titration to spectroscopy are a subset appropriate to chemistry. And these sets of methods do not form a science—nor does operational research. And so I am saying let us do away with the idea of "*the* science of operational research"; and let us also do away with the idea "but we do not know what it is." There is really a wonderful ambivalence about these two statements anyway, is there not?

Let me now make these comments about the nature of operational research more specific by reference to a particular operational research job. I shall do this very briefly, because this is not intended as a specimen case history, but is put forward as revealing a number of important features of our work. This project identifies some of the things I take operational research to do, and which I would like to see incorporated in a definition.

The job arose in this way. What should the maximum demand for electricity be in a steelworks? Maximum demand is the greatest load of electricity you expect to call from the grid at any one time; you fix this level with your supplier in the summer, and say that you will not go beyond this figure at peak loading during the winter. The higher this figure is fixed the more safe you are, but the more expensive the contract is because the supplier has to cover himself against this load as a potential demand. The lower the figure is fixed, the less expensive the contract; but the greater risk is then run of exceeding it. Once the works comes up against its limit, it must either shed its load and thereby ruin its productivity, or must exceed its maximum demand and pay a severe fine for doing so.

We were told what the maximum demand figure operated the previous winter was; that it had in fact been exceeded more than once; and what the contractual terms and the excess levy had been. The question naturally was, what should the limit be set at now, having regard to the extra cost involved in diminishing the risk and the extra risk involved in diminishing the cost? This, you will agree, was very rightly conceived as an operational research job.

You will also agree that the main difficulty in operational research is the definition of the problem. The one we were given which I have outlined seems clear enough. But is it the real problem, or is it perhaps no more than the symptom of the real problem? We argued in this way. Electricity is a source of energy; but a steelworks has many sources of energy: coke-oven gas, blast furnace gas, steam, and oil, as well as electricity. And all these sources interact; because gas or oil can be burnt to make steam, and steam used to make electricity. Therefore, just as you can buy electricity from the national grid, you can sell electricity to the national grid (though for less money than you pay for buying it). Still further, gas can be stored in a gas holder; but if you have a contract to supply the local township with gas, the store must take that commitment into account. In fact, this is an exceedingly complex interacting system with many constraints.

It is now clear that to consider the original problem of maximum demand in a vacuum would be to suboptimize the larger problem. Effective operational research would study the whole energy system, and this is what we did. A large scale mathematical model of the system as a whole was constructed, and from a study of this a strategy for operating the whole energy system was evolved. This strategy had then to be expressed in terms which could be understood on the shop floor. There, one cannot discuss a strategy in set-theoretic terms; one must say: "If the reading on this meter has reached this point, then providing that reading on that meter has reached that point, pull this handle." The strategy, translated into these operational terms, was accepted by the management, explained to the operatives, and installed by the operational research team.

What was the answer to the original question? From the study just described, it was possible to evaluate the optimum level for maximum demand. Far from proposing to raise the previous level, and we had originally thought that we should have to do just that, it proved possible to *halve* it. The extra power to justify this had been obtained from degrees of freedom imported to the problem from the rest of the energy system. This recommendation was accepted, the strategy adopted, and the whole job was a success.

Several critical points about an operational research study emerge from this example. First, operational research involves an environment. In the case quoted, the issue is to decide what *is* the problem and what the environment. The answer was that the other energy systems had to be incorporated in the study of the first. It is always possible to bite off an arbitrary amount of a problem's environment, and to include it in the problem: the question is, how much? The first great characteristic of the operational research man is the ability to see this fact, to delineate his problem on that basis, to persuade the management that he is right, to find the method which will handle this organic structure; all this comes before the ability to solve the problem.

The important fact is that problems are simply not respecters of the official organization. A problem is first observed as a kind of outcrop; it appears in one cell of the business. There is a tendency to assume that the problem is completely contained in that cell: the cost office, a particular works department, a specific sales office. If it has ramifications elsewhere, then surely it is possible to make representations and to expect a little collaboration from "the other side." This is not the approach of operational research, which is essentially a problem-oriented activity. The real nature of the problem must be uncovered, and this requires a very general authority to investigate the state of affairs without being contained in the organizational locality where the outcrop first appeared. If operational research men cannot be trusted with this generalized authority, then either they are not fit people for the work or the management does not understand what sort of work it is.

The specimen study concerned a dynamic interacting state of affairs which must certainly be described as both complex and probabilistic. How did operational research seize hold of the problem? Its method was to construct a model; and my next point is to ask: how ubiquitous is the idea of a model in operational research? I have often tentatively proposed that no operational research job has ever been done without the use of a model, and since this has never provoked a counterexample I will now risk the statement that this is indeed a characteristic of the work. Should anyone seek to deny this, may I warn him in advance of my defence. He says of a given job: there was no model. I reply that a model of the situation must have existed in his brain before he could do the thinking required to solve the problem. A model is no more than a description into which the real situation can be mapped. If the mapping can be done inside the skull, so much the better. But if the situation is too complicated, then the brain cannot hold the structure and its owner must go on to paper with an elaborate scheme. But the idea is the same, I contend.

The final point to be brought out is the obvious one that mixed disciplines were playing their parts in the study quoted. This point must be made but need not be laboured; for no one has ever denied that the interdisciplinary attack is characteristic of operational research.

If this is the kind of approach which we would agree constitutes operational research, there are other kinds of activity which I feel we ought steadfastly to eliminate from that classification. In the first place, to plot a set of empirical results from the works, and to note that they form a normal distribution, and that therefore a specific probability can be allocated to the likelihood that values greater than a certain parameter of the variate will occur, is not in itself operational research. It is trivial. It may be perfectly good statistics to make this observation, but it is not operational research. To ensure that I am not misunderstood to say that industrial statistics is trivial, let me take the example further. Just look at some of the models for inventory control which have been published. They are not trivial statistics, they are very advanced. But should you come to *use* such models in the works, you find that you are speared and impaled on the assumptions implicit in the model. "Since this delay is likely to be exponentially distributed" has got into the script in small print; it seems innocuous enough. But should we plot the actual distribution as derived from an empirical study—why, it looks like the sunset silhouette of a file of camels walking down the Valley of the Kings. This is not to deny that academic model-building is useful; of course it is. But the *operational research* has hardly begun at the point when the proud author goes into print with his piece of mathematics.

The second class of cognate activity which I should like to segregate from operational research is what I classify as erudite fun-and-gamesmanship. Consider this example of model-building for the analysis of decision procedures.[5]

N is a sequence of decision rules applied to the decision situation d. We made this specific by applying a particular starred sequence to the decisions typified as d_i; and where u is the pay-off the outcome may be written:

$$u(N^*(d_i))$$

But other decision sequences are possible; let us designate another set N^1. The first sequence is preferable to the second if their difference is positive when this has been evaluated for all i. And so we get:

$$\sum_{i=1}^{n} \{u(N^*(d_i)) - u(N^1(d_i))\} > 0$$

which is called "the axiom of long-run success."

So far, so good. Say rather: so far and no farther. There is nothing much else we can do with this, but at least we have got a fine name. But I forget: there is another step after all. Put $\lim_{n\to\infty}$ in front of the expression, where (I quote) "the limit is assumed to exist." If I am going to take an infinite number of decisions I most certainly *expect* long-run success.

Let us have science, and mathematics; let us think deeply; let us be abstruse in our arguments where necessary. But let us relate operational research to operations and the possibility of improving them.

On the strength of this analysis, may I now attempt the definition of operational research for which I have been pleading. This one consists of two sentences including eight clauses:

(1) Operational research is the attack of modern science

(2) on problems of likelihood (accepting mischance)

(3) which arise in the management and control

(4) of men and machines, materials and money

(5) in their natural environment.

(6) Its special technique is to invent a strategy of control

(7) by measuring, comparing and predicting probable behaviour

(8) through a scientific model of a situation.

THE CONNEXION

The Shared Aspects. We have reviewed the nature of the science of cybernetics, and the nature of the modern scientific method that we call operational research. I have made no attempt as we went along to relate the two, but now is the time to show how much these topics have in common.

There is a shared general intention. Cybernetics studies control as its object; operational research is normally concerned with control problems. That is implied by clause 3 of my definition. Elsewhere [6] I have tried very hard to show that operational research jobs always involve control, and that therefore they must always involve a cybernetic model. Secondly, there is the shared nature of the problem; complex and probabilistic. The only difference between the two topics in this dimension is that cybernetics stands for the problem itself, and operational research stands for the approach made to it.

Thirdly, there is the shared level of sophistication. In cybernetics, this appears as the mapping of an inanimate system into the physiological model which makes it viable. In operational research the outlook is manifested in a refusal to isolate the system from its environment, together with the important idea that the observer himself is inextricably involved in the system.

Fourthly, there is the reciprocity of method between the two subjects of which I will say more in a moment. And fifthly, there is the shared organization: which is simply the interdisciplinary attack.

So there are all these points of contact, these shared characteristics. Therefore we may next ask: is cybernetics itself the same thing as operational research? The answer is: no, it cannot be. Would any operational research man really contend that his job in life is to build thinking machines? Does operational research really have the pure structure of control as the object of study? No again: it may involve the idea of control, but the object of study is (to put the point as precisely as possible) the improvement of an operation. Nevertheless, the relationships are there, and we must consider in what way they actually work.

Operational Research (cum Cybernetics). In the first place, there is the notion of characteristically operational research work which has a basically cybernetic model. In our Department, there are now some seventy people. More than fifty of these are scientists and technicians, working on twenty-seven different projects at the moment. No less than eighteen of these projects are in the area of production control (as we call it). This means the field of planning, progressing, programming, stockholding, the flow of material, and so on. All eighteen projects could be described as cybernetics, if we choose to define the object as the study of control itself. But if we concentrate on the mode of attack and the general intention to improve the state of affairs, no one here would dispute that we are doing operational research.

In being specific, I think there is no need to repeat to this audience an account of the servomechanistic model used years ago in our early work on production control in United Steel. There was an operational research attack, based on a definitely cybernetic model. Consider further, however, two more recent jobs in different works on the progressing of orders. A logical model of priority has been built which includes organic feedbacks from the plant and from the customer, so that the logic changes continuously as environmental events unfold. That is a cybernetic model. The job of quantifying the model, of transforming the logic into an arithmetic of priority numbers which can be handled as if they were natural numbers, and of installing this system to procure better deliveries, is a piece of thoroughgoing operational research. In the second works, the same problem has the different characteristic that it concerns jobbing engineering; a fact which results in a difficulty about commensurable facts. It is a typical operational research problem to find coherent measures for incommensurables, and to achieve the outcome of controlled production and accurate deliveries. But the model for this work is again entirely cybernetic. We are concerned with orders which *grow* from raw materials to completion—and growth is essentially an organic process in an organic world. It is also typified by a familiar sigmoid curve. This curve is our model, against which the growth of capital built into engineering products can be contrasted. Managerial decisions are based on fiducial control limits built on to the sigmoid curve. Finally, think of the concept, discussed elsewhere,[7] that the diversified management structure of a large industrial combine constitutes a learning machine for investing capital in stocks. There is no time to expand this point here; but I seek to implant the notion of a cybernetic machine having no hardware, no paperwork system, no automatic data processing; a machine whose operations can be studied solely by operational research.

The basis of these ideas about operational research in production control on a cybernetic model may be found in a paper entitled "The Cybernetic Analogue of Planning and Programming,"[8] which I wrote three years ago. I am very proud of this paper. The review in the *Operational Research Quarterly* was admirably succinct. It was: "Curious rather than important." Now curiosity is the essence of enquiring science; importance is the essence of conforming orthodoxy.

Cybernetics (cum Operational Research). Secondly, we come to the thought that in "doing cybernetics" the only methods available to the scientist are precisely those of operational research. I will give just one example of this, although the story of cybernetics is full of such illustrations. This one derives from a paper by Ross Ashby.[9]

Habituation in animals is the phenomenon whereby the response to any regularly repeated stimulus decreases. By analogy with neg-entropy it could be called neg-learning. Making a study of habituation is assuredly a job for the cybernetician: it is not an apparently operational research job. But Ashby's attack on it has many features of the operational research attack.

To begin with, he built a model of habituation, in terms of the special kind of topology he has derived from the French school known as Bourbaki. In studying this model, he came to the very surprising conclusion that habituation is a property of a wide class of general systems, and not uniquely a property of living ones as most people would suppose. Startling conclusions are typical of well-conceived operational research, and so is the result that the problem has been completely misapprehended. Moreover, Ashby finds that the habituating system is not independent of the observer: again a typical operational research result. The observer is muddled up with the system and cannot be detached. According to Ashby, to say "I tested this system for habituation, and I eventually found it to show a diminished response" is to verge on the tautologous.

As if this cybernetic study had not already revealed the operational research nature of its approach its author next proceeds to check his results by nothing other than a Monte Carlo simulation. He takes as his system a set of random numbers from Kendall and Babbington Smith, and by applying the rules of his model proceeds to show these numbers undergoing transformations in which habituation can be detected. This fittingly completes a beautiful example of the relationship I have been trying to demonstrate.

Conclusion. Now I must conclude, and I do so by answering the initial question: "What has cybernetics to do with operational research?" The answer will be given in two parts. First, as to subject matter, both topics are concerned in the main with control. This contention may be expressed in a Venn diagram (Figure 1) as follows:

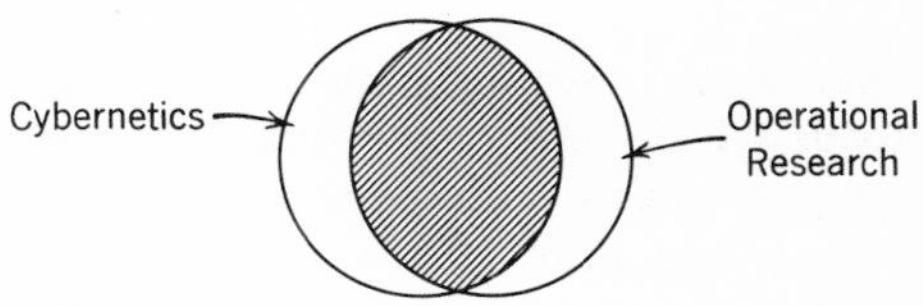

FIG. 1.

The overlapping area is where the subject matter is concerned with control. Secondly, as to methods, I cannot conceive an operational research technique which could not be applied in the field of cybernetics, and I think that most cybernetic studies must invoke operational research techniques. This conclusion is portrayed in another Venn diagram (Figure 2):

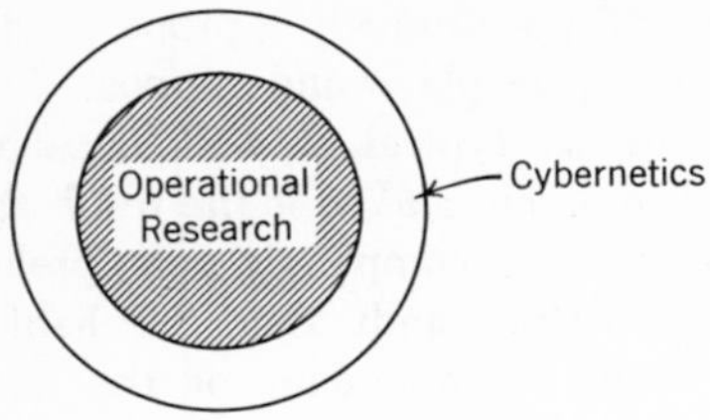

FIG. 2.

The unshaded portion of the diagram which belongs to cybernetics alone includes such methods as the dissection of the brain and the construction of electronic machinery.

It must be made clear that these oversimplified conclusions and the diagrams are offered simply as a résumé of these arguments. They are not meant to be logically demonstrable conclusions, as are the conclusions to be drawn from Venn diagrams in logic itself. I accept that they are arbitrary; by which is meant that a means of representing the existence of a dinosaurus or the relationship of church and state could doubtless be found and added to them. They are neither unique nor logically necessary: they are there to say what I mean.

Three years ago, I did try to educe the relationship between cybernetics and operational research in a formal way. This was done through the concept of causation which both subjects also share, and the method used was analysis by symbolic logic. I would like to quote from that part of the paper [10] which was written in ordinary English:

Operational research comprises a body of methods which cohere to provide a powerful tool of investigation. Cybernetics is a corpus of knowledge which might reasonably claim the status of a science. My contention is that the two are methodologically complementary; that the first is the natural technique in research of the second, and the second the natural embodiment in science of the first.

By definition, each is concerned to treat a complex and interconnected system or process as an organic whole. By methodology, each is concerned with models and analogies from every source. By science, neither is departmental. By philosophy, each attests to the indivisible unity of knowledge.

Three years and a good deal of research in both these fields later, I am more convinced than ever that cybernetics is indeed the science of which operational research is the method. Thus, as long as this profession treats "cybernetics" as a rather dirty word, and as long as the universities in the main ignore a new science which has the audacity not to fit into the hallowed academic structure; so long will operational research practitioners, their beards growing greyer and their eyes more wild, have to pretend that they do not really know what their subject is all about.

REFERENCES

1. Norbert Wiener, *Cybernetics*. John Wiley, New York (1948).
2. Ross Ashby, *Design for a Brain*. Chapman & Hall, London (1954).
3. Gordon Pask, "Physical Analogues to the Growth of a Concept," *Symposium on the Mechanization of Thought Processes*. H.M.S.O., London. (In press.)
4. Stafford Beer, "The Organization of Operational Research," *Research,* **9** (5) (1956).
5. William Morris, *The Rationalization of Industrial Decision Processes*. Ohio State University, Columbus, U.S.A. (1957).
6. Stafford Beer, *The Scope for Operational Research in Industry*. Institution of Production Engineers, London (1957).
7. Stafford Beer, "The Irrelevance of Automation," *Transactions of the Second International Congress on Cybernetics*. Namur, Belgium. (In press.)
8. Stafford Beer, "A Technical Consideration of the Cybernetic Analogue for Planning and Programming," *Process Control and Automation,* 3 (8), (9).
9. Ross Ashby, "The Mechanism of Habituation," *Symposium on the Mechanization of Thought Processes*. H.M.S.O., London. (In press.)
10. Stafford Beer, "Operational Research and Cybernetics," *Transactions of the First International Congress on Cybernetics*. Namur, Belgium (1959).

BIBLIOGRAPHY

Ashby, W. Ross, *Introduction to Cybernetics,* 3d ed., John Wiley and Sons, 1958.

Beer, Stafford, *Cybernetics and Management,* Science Editions, 1964.

Beer, Stafford, *Decision and Control,* John Wiley and Sons, 1966.

Bellman, R., "Control Theory," *Scientific American,* September, 1964.

Bruinsma, A. H., *Cybernetics,* Cleaver-Hume Press, 1956.

Churchman, C. West, and Russell L. Ackoff, "Purposive Behavior and Cybernetics," *Social Forces,* **XXIX**, 1950, 32–39.

Dechert, Charles (ed.), *The Social Impact of Cybernetics,* Simon and Schuster, 1967.

Eisenhart, C., "Cybernetics: A New Discipline," *Science,* April, 1949.

Evans, C. R., and A. B. J. Robertson (eds.), *Cybernetics,* University Park Press, 1968.

Fett, G. H., *Feedback Control Systems,* Prentice-Hall, Inc., 1954.

Foerster, Heinz von, *Cybernetics,* Charles Macy, 1953.

———, Margaret Mead, and Hans L. Teuber, *Cybernetics,* Transactions of Conferences, 5 vols., Josiah Macy, Jr. Foundation, 1949–1957.

George, F. H., *Automation, Cybernation and Society,* Leonard Hill, 1960.

———, *Cybernetics and Biology,* W. H. Freeman, 1965.

Gille, J. C., et al., *Feedback Control Systems,* McGraw-Hill Book Company, 1959.

Glushkov, V. M., *Introduction to Cybernetics,* Academic Press, 1966.

Greniewsky, H. K., *Cybernetics without Mathematics,* Pergamon Press, 1960.

Guilbaud, G. T., *What is Cybernetics?* Grove Press, 1960.

Kemeny, J. G., "Man Viewed as a Machine," *Scientific American,* April, 1955.

Klir, Jiri, and Miroslav Valach, *Cybernetic Modelling,* Iliffe Books, 1966.

Michael, D. N., *Cybernation: The Silent Conquest,* Center for the Study of Democratic Institutions, 1962.

Moray, Neville, *Cybernetics,* Hawthorn Books, 1963.

Smith, O. J. M., *Feedback Control Systems,* McGraw-Hill Book Co., 1958.

Theobald, R., "The Cybernated Era," *Vital Speeches,* August, 1964.

Taube, M., *Computers and Common Sense: The Myth of Thinking Machines,* Columbia University Press, 1961.

Tustin, Arnold, "Feedback," *Scientific American,* **187**, 1952, 48–54.

Wiener, N., *Cybernetics,* John Wiley and Sons, 1948.

SECTION III

MEASUREMENT

In the history of science there are two converging avenues along which flows the potential of progress: the avenue of ideas and the avenue of techniques. It is the confluence of these that has made possible the marvels of modern civilization.

Though ideas precede in time the appearance of any tool or technique (even these are born of previous concepts), it is the latter that can effect the implementation of the former. Ideas constitute, as it were, the threads with which the fabric of progress is spun, while the tools and techniques are the instruments employed in the spinning process.

Of all the basic techniques perhaps none is more fundamental than that of measurement. From the days of primitive man to our own space age, measurement has been a constant companion of progress. It is indeed a long way from the tally stick to the computer, from traditional Taylorism to scientific systems approach but the progress made along the way is attributable in part to refinements in measuring techniques. Recent years especially have witnessed increased interest in measurement philosophy and measurement standards. In the physical sciences units of length and of time have had to be redefined by the Bureau of Standards, so great was the need in this day and age for new standards. The behavioral scientists too have devoted much time and thought to measurement techniques applicable to as wide a field as possible.

Some of the confusion enveloping the field of measurement may be attributable either to the lack of fundamental probing for its basic assumptions and constitutive elements or to the identification of the measurement process with something else—with measure as a number or with definition. Measurement can perhaps be looked upon as an *operation*, a process involving an observer and some form of (measuring) apparatus, while measure is the *number* that emerges as a result of such an operation.[1] Operation(al)ism, popularized by P. W. Bridgman, identified the physical entity with the set of operations by which it was being measured, thus spreading even further the confusion already enveloping the concept of measurement by identifying definition with measurement.

In the selections that follow, chief consideration is given to the fundamentals of the measurement process since these seem most in need of critical examination. For too long they have lain shrouded in the dust of uncertainty and it is only in recent years that philosophers, scientists, and operation researchers have busied themselves clearing away the accumulated dust of the ages. Selections with a management approach have been preferred to mathematical treatises that may have appealed to the budding scientist or the frustrated mathematician.

At times it may be helpful to take a long and hard look at those things that we take for granted. This is exactly what Paul Kircher does in his selection when he singles out for critical examination the field of measurement and discusses its funda-

[1] Peter Caws, "Definition and Measurement in Physics," in C. West Churchman and Philburn Ratoosh (eds.), *Measurement: Definitions and Theories* (New York: John Wiley & Sons, 1959), p. 4.

mentals. This is especially appropriate since management is at present intent on upgrading its own admittedly inadequate measurement tools. Since measurement provides information and information provides a logical basis for decision making, the quality of decision making will ultimately be dependent upon the quality of measurement.

The measurement process can in no wise be viewed as a simple one. It can be broken down into a number of basic elements, the number depending upon the refinement of the analysis desired. Many standard analyses offer for consideration only a very few elements. Kircher here pinpoints seven distinct elements which he explains and relates to the world of business management. Each of these seven ingredients can involve considerable difficulty in the practical realm. These elements are: (1) definition of the objective, (2) determination of the factors relevant for attainment of the objective, (3) selection of the measurable key aspects of these factors, (4) choice of measuring method and unit, (5) application of the measuring unit, (6) analysis of the measurement, and (7) evaluation of the measurement's effectiveness.

The choice of a business executive to fill a vacancy well illustrates the difficulties attendant upon mensuration. What are exactly the objectives toward which a would-be executive is to work? What relevant factors ought to be considered in choosing such an executive? What quantifiable aspects of these factors are the important ones? What will be the unit of measurement? etc. It becomes immediately apparent that even at this late date much still remains to be done in this special area.

The operational researcher, R. W. Shephard, views measurement as an essential in ensuring confidence and maintaining objectivity in decision making. The basis for this view is the set of assumptions that concern the nature of operations research itself. Operational research, which is concerned with systems that include human beings, is essentially objective decision making and as such is oriented toward the improvement of confidence in these decisions. As was pointed out in an earlier selection by Stafford Beer, operations research is not a science but a technique, a method of science. Correct decisions can indeed be reached by methods other than operations research; the main difference between them and it is the degree of confidence that can be reposed in the results acquired by the various methods.

One of the problems that engages Shephard's attention is the measurement of the human factors involved in operations research. Since the degree of confidence in a decision reached by operations research methods depends upon all relevant factors being included and measured correctly, it follows that as much attention must be paid to measuring the psychological and sociological factors as to measuring the physical factors in the system under study. Unfortunately the measurement of these human factors is still at a rather primitive level, comparatively speaking, and a way to understand the problems involved would be to examine some of the problems of measurement in the physical sciences.

After commenting briefly on the traditional types of measurement scale and on basic and derived, direct and indirect measurement, he points out that the physical sciences need a form of measurement applicable to many diverse systems. Psycho-physical measurements, characterized by human variability, use a scale that generally represents the mean reaction of the population as a whole. This then serves as a norm. For at least some psycho-physical magnitudes ratio scales may be used.

Shephard concludes his article with a few observations concerning measurement in operational research.

C. West Churchman's selection looks at the problem of measurement from a decision-making viewpoint. He believes that the problems inherent in measurement are very difficult to solve, so much so that even now approximate solutions are unavailable. Yet somehow they must be solved if we do not want to pay the heavy penalties for our failure to do so.

Churchman arrives at his particular viewpoint in this way. Why is it considered better to measure than not to measure? Is it because measurement assigns numbers to objects? If so, why is the assignment of numbers better than non-assignment? Is it because it makes information precise? If so, then precise for what? Certainly not precise for precision's sake! Thus he is led to the function of measurement as the development of methods for generating a class of information applicable in a wide variety of contexts and problems. But there are many ways in which the objectives of measurement can be accomplished. Generally used are these two: the one that qualitatively assigns objects to classes, and the one that assigns numbers to objects. Which is better? This line of reasoning cannot but lead to the idea that measurement is essentially a decision-making activity to be evaluated by decision-making criteria.

From the functional point of view then there are at least four aspects of measurement that present decision-making problems: (1) language, (2) specification, (3) standardization, and (4) accuracy and control.

What language will the measurer use to express his results? The more precise the language the less generally will it be understood, yet the purpose of language is to communicate to as many potential users as possible. Thus the language of measurement is seen to involve a decision problem.

To what objects and in what environments will the measurements apply? Specification thus is seen to pertain to the scope of application of the measurements in terms of time, place, and items. It was seen that one of the aims of measurement is to develop information applicable to as many situations as possible, if possible, to all things at all times and all places. Yet the more general the information, the more useless it becomes to any specific context, also the more expensive to acquire. So here too there is a decision-making problem to be resolved.

How can measurements be used? Standardization is that aspect of measurement that allows us to use information in a wide variety of situations. The decision problem here springs from two rather conflicting needs: one wants to find a method of measurement such that a minimum amount of adjustment is required when times, places, and peoples change, and one wants to find a method for differentiating various aspects of the world we live in (precision). The greater the needed adjustment of the data to a standard, the less precise the information.

Accuracy concerns the degree to which a given measurement deviates from the "truth" while control provides the guarantee that the measurements can be used in a wide variety of contexts. The problem of accuracy is to develop measures that enable the user to evaluate in a meaningful way the information contained in the measurements. The problem concerning control lies in the amount and kind that should be had. Thus it is not economical to check every measurement against a standard nor is it economical to use measurements without any check.

The problems inherent in measurement are indeed formidable.

9. FUNDAMENTALS OF MEASUREMENT [1]

PAUL KIRCHER [2]

Measurement has always been an important factor in providing information to serve as the basis for solving business problems. But as business management has become more and more interested in using scientific tools to aid in making decisions, it has become increasingly evident that present methods of measurement in the business field frequently are inadequate.

For this reason the Management Sciences Research Project at UCLA (sponsored by the Office of Naval Research) has undertaken a research study of the general problem of measurement.

Preliminary analysis has shown that the fundamentals of measurement, as such, have never been clearly defined, even by scientists. Each discipline or science has developed its own techniques and methods, with few attempts at coordination with others. This is true in spite of the fact that it is difficult to evaluate the effectiveness of any system of measurement, or of any other logical activity, from criteria which are part of the system itself. If the system can be viewed from "outside," from a more fundamental point of view, it often is easier to correct mistakes and to obtain insights which lead to new and better methods.

There is a limit to this search for fundamentals, it must be admitted. One of the interesting aspects of modern mathematics is the discovery that as yet we cannot prove that the ultimate logical structure of mathematics is consistent. The most ambitious attempt to do this, by Hilbert, was shown by Godel to have the form of a proposition which could neither be proved nor disproved. It merely could be accepted, if one chose to do so.

[1] SOURCE: *Advanced Management* (October, 1955), pp. 5–8. Reprinted by permission of *Advanced Management*.

[2] University of California at Los Angeles.

There are many aspects of business logic which rest on indefinable terms or unprovable propositions. In the past these assumptions have been so numerous and so important that business has been characterized as an art. There have been few precepts of general significance—each problem the manager encountered was seen as being a brand new one, at least in some respects. As Vatter has said, "Business is an experiment."

Whereas, we can expect that much of this indefinability will continue, nevertheless there are many relationships which can be measured in business. Especially in situations where methods such as linear programming have proven useful, businessmen are coming to recognize that decision-making can be moved to a higher plane. In these situations, it can be seen that when certain objectives are clearly defined, and the factors of the situation are objectively measured, then decisions are already made. Scheduling the operations becomes mechanical—it can be done on an electronic computer.

As a simple example, suppose a manager makes the decision that he will choose the course which earns the highest profit. He has three courses open to him (such as shipping routes). If he can measure the profitability of each of the three routes, then the policy decision in effect makes the operating decision.

We are still a long way from being able to put policy-making on a scientific basis. Policies are always set in an atmosphere of much uncertainty. Indeed, a major difference between the human brain and the so-called "electronic computer brain" is that the former can operate with partial information. A computer must have a complete program, or it will stop or give inaccurate results.

However, policy-making can be improved with experience, since certain situations do tend to repeat themselves. But lessons can be learned only if the important factors in each situation are measured, so they can be compared and correlated with the results of the decisions.

THE STRUCTURE OF THE MEASUREMENT PROCESS

The major effort of the present research study is directed toward the attempt to establish the basic structure of the measurement process. It is hoped that by dividing the process into important elements, each of these may be studied with more precision, and the relationships between them can be seen more clearly.

As indicated in the paper presented by the author to the 1955 national meeting of the Operations Research Society of America,[3] the following elements of the measurement process have been identified:

1. Determination of the objective of the business entity, the purpose which is to be served in a particular situation.
2. Determination of the types of factors which might serve to attain the objective.
3. Selection of the key aspects of the factors, the aspects which are to be measured.
4. Choice of (a) a measuring method, (b) a measuring unit.
5. Application of the measuring unit to the object to be measured—the central action of measurement.
6. Analysis of the measurement—relating it to other measurements (other in time or in kind).
7. Evaluating the effectiveness of the measurement by determining the extent to which it assisted in the attainment of the objective.

Each of these needs investigation and is being studied in some detail. Since it is impossible to describe all the various considerations within the scope of a single article, an attempt will be made to indicate something of the direction and purpose of the research by relating each of the above elements to a few specific problems. Examples will be given from:

a. highly developed and effective systems, such as the measurement of length,
b. highly developed but less effective systems, such as accounting,
c. moderately developed systems, such as job evaluation, and
d. areas where systems hardly exist, as yet, such as selection and evaluation of executives.

[3] Held in Los Angeles, California, August 15–17, 1955.

The first and most obvious step is to define the objective. Obvious as it is, however, it is not always easy to do.

Executives have struggled with the problem of objectives ever since companies grew from the single proprietor stage. Now that social consequences are a major consideration, many executives spend a great deal of their time attempting to establish policies which exhibit business statesmanship, and which will lead to stability and continuation of earnings, as well as immediate gains.

Unless these problems are solved, it is not possible to develop the objectives in terms that will be susceptible of some sort of quantification. In other words, it is necessary to set the stage for measurement.

Without a clear understanding of the purposes which a to-be-hired executive is to serve, it is difficult to establish standards by which to select him, and later, to judge his performance.

DETERMINATION OF RELEVANT FACTORS

The second step is to determine which factors may be employed to attain the objective.

In physical problems this step is often clearly definable. When it is, the measurement process may become relatively easy, unless certain factors are physically inaccessible, or unless methods have not been sufficiently developed to handle the particular type of problem. For example, if the purpose is to provide a means of travel across a river at minimum cost, certain obvious alternatives are present—a bridge, a ferry, or a tunnel. (Of course, every such problem also presents an opportunity for the "genius" who can by-pass the problem, e.g., by finding a better route that does not go near the river, or by using helicopters.) Excepting the unusual solutions, the problem then becomes one of measuring the expected flow of traffic, measuring the cost of construction and operation of the various alternatives, and expressing the costs and capacities in comparable terms.

With a problem such as the selection of an executive the "factor" choice is considerably more difficult. In the first place, though the company organization chart may appear to offer a "slot" which is to be filled, it is not possible with present knowledge to describe the position in terms comparable to those which can be used to describe the quantity of traffic flow—such as the expected weights of the vehicles.

Even if it were possible to define the job narrowly, at the executive level the individual capabilities of the manager chosen will soon start reshaping the responsibilities and activities concerned.

Moreover, it is at least theoretically desirable that each vacancy should be the occasion for a re-examination of the company organization to see whether the position should be redefined, or perhaps even eliminated. Such considerations add considerably to the difficulty of the measurement problem.

SELECTION OF KEY ASPECTS

Once it has been determined what the purpose is, and the objects to be measured, it is necessary to select those aspects, which can and should be measured. These are the aspects which are themselves quantifiable, and are related in some way to the quantifiable aspects of the purpose or objective of the entity involved.

An example can be drawn from accounting. Various types of assets and liabilities are measured in order to obtain information concerning the revenue and expense flows, and the financial position of the firm. These are indicative of the degree of attainment of the profit-making objectives of the business.

The illustration from accounting is especially interesting since accountants have deliberately chosen to restrict their activities to those measurements which they believe can be made within a certain standard of accuracy. This means that certain other items, vital to the well-being of the firm, are resolutely omitted. For example, the company's investments in advertising its products, or in developing its executives, are not considered to be assets, but are written off in the period of expenditures, as a rule. Goodwill as such has almost disappeared from company statements.

In certain types of job evaluation, it is possible to quantify some of the key aspects. For example, a stenographer should be able to take shorthand at so many words per minute and type at a given rate, in order to perform the duties of a given job. Other important attributes, however, such as the ability to get along with others, are harder to quantify.

In choosing an executive the problem is much more difficult. There is little knowledge as to the particular abilities which are required for a manager to act successfully in a specific situation. Even where certain abilities have been ascertained as desirable, it is seldom that they can be expressed in terms which are quantifiable. They are seldom established on the basis of what the man can *do;* rather they are usually expressed in terms of what he *is*—e.g., sincere, capable, loyal, patient, trained, experienced, etc. These attributes are difficult to express quantitatively, and thus are difficult to relate to later performance, however measured.

CHOICE OF MEASURING METHOD AND UNIT

The act of choosing a measuring method and a measuring unit has been given considerable attention throughout history, but so far not much of the theoretical work is helpful to businessmen. Mathematics, "the Queen of the Sciences," is a logical process whose object, in the words of Comte, is "the indirect measurement of magnitudes," and "it constantly proposes to determine certain magnitudes from others by means of the precise relations existing between them."

Most of the theoretical mathematical work, however, has deliberately avoided the problems of application, especially to anything so "crass" as business problems. The essence of mathematics is deductive reasoning from explicitly stated assumptions. Only since World War II have many mathematicians discovered, much to the surprise of most of them, that business problems are difficult, challenging, and can be as intellectually interesting as the act of contemplating abstract "Number."

In recent years, however, activity in the application field has increased tremendously. In addition to increased activities in this field in many societies nationwide, three societies have been formed—"The Institute of Management Sciences," "The Operations Research Society of America," and the "Society for Industrial and Applied Mathematics," whose objectives express this interest.

DEVELOPMENT OF SCALES

Perhaps the most advanced work in the field of measurement of a type useful for choosing executives has been done by the applied psychologists. In their attempts to measure such things as intelligence, men like Thurstone have had to develop scales where zero could not be fixed, nor could absolute intervals be specified. In several works Stevens has shown how various types of scales are possible depending upon the type of manipulation which can be performed on the measurements—the nominal, ordinal, interval and ratio scales.

Further developments have been hampered, however, by lack of clear-cut definitions of the relationship between the concepts we call "qualitative" and those we call "quantitative." Following the mathematicians, most writers appear to treat "quantity" as referring to an abstraction which somehow has almost a physical significance of its own.

It would appear to be more useful to firmly establish the concept that quantities are measurements of qualities. For example, the quality "length" occurs in various physical objects. By choosing some standard unit, and determining the number of repetitions of the unit in the object, the length can be expressed as a quantity. Then, following Stevens, the manipulations of arithmetic—addition, etc.—can be attempted to see what type of scale is involved.

In this process of measurement the problem for the observer is to identify certain characteristics in the object to be measured, characteristics which appear similar to those in the measuring unit, and which also have some identifiable relationship to the purpose of the measurement. These characteristics should be invariant, in the sense that they can be identified and seen to persist. Basically, of course, every object and every event in the universe is unique, and it is constantly changing through time. To find invariant characteristics, then, requires the human process of abstraction.

In measuring an executive, for example, the objective desired may be the organization of a research program. It is necessary to determine which types of ability are required for this, then to find a means of measuring these types of ability in the alternative men available. Each type of ability must be defined in such a way that it can be seen as a distinct part of a complicated personality. It must also be comparable to a part of the complicated personalities of the other candidates.

We are far behind the physical sciences in our ability to accomplish this. So far behind, in fact, that many people consider any effort in this direction to be useless. However, it does appear to offer the best hope for eventual improvement over present intuitive methods, so research in this direction probably will continue.

The importance of invariance can be seen in the difficulties which arise when the measuring unit chosen has varying characteristics. The dollar, the measuring unit of accounting, is an example. Changes in purchasing power not only create difficulties of evaluation, but can lead to serious inequities. An appreciable part of the "income" taxed by our government in recent years is really the result of the diminished value of the dollar unit.

APPLICATION OF THE MEASURING UNIT

The simplest method of measurement is to identify the unit characteristics in the object to be measured, and then merely to count the recurrences. Almost equally simple are the cases where the unit can be directly compared, as in measurement of length or weight. More advanced measurements, such as in astronomy, require the construction of chains of relationships.

Most business measurements involve quantity of performance in given time periods, since business is a dynamic process. The time factor introduces many complications.

Another major factor in business measurements is the force of custom. Even when systems are demonstrably weak, the difficulties of retraining and reeducating the users of data, to say nothing of the problem of development of a better system, frequently operate to hinder improvements.

On the other hand, custom does offer some advantages. Most businessmen are familiar with the major elements of the accounting system, and so can interpret results even when these are not as precise as one might wish.

In newer fields, such as measurement of executive abilities, there are several systems in use. They exhibit few attributes in common. The result is that acceptance of the systems is correspondingly more difficult to achieve.

ANALYSIS OF THE MEASUREMENTS

The area of analysis of measurements in business has seen startling advances in recent years, and there is reason to hope that even greater improvements can be achieved. Primary interest has centered on attempts to relate various measurements into integrated systems that reflect the business operations. These attempts usually involve the construction of mathematical models of the operations.

Developments in linear programming, game theory, communication theory, etc., have shown that complicated situations can be resolved by the use of models if the relevant data can be obtained, and if the relationships are of certain types. While the use of some of these models requires advanced training in mathematics, others are simpler and yet very effective. Examples are the method for studying investment decisions (developed by Markowitz, see article by Weston and Beranek in the *Analysts Journal,* May, 1955) or for forecasting working capital needs (article by Rothschild and Kircher, *Journal of Accountancy,* September, 1955), or inventory control in production (Vazsonyi, *Management Science,* June, 1955).

One of the pioneers in the field of management improvement is General Electric. In a speech to the Controllers Institute, M. L. Hurni of General Electric's Management Consultation Services Division, gave a summary of the management problem which indicates how measurements are used and evaluated.

The examination of an operation, or a situation within an operation, as a problem in logic consists in doing fundamental research upon the operation itself. It is not providing quick isolated solutions to current problems as they arise on the basis of readily available means.

First, it consists of systematic examination of the environment in which the business exists for such things as the possible structure, range, and probability of specific demands upon the business, the recurrence or lack of recurrence of particular aspects of the environment, the drift in the environment from a given known position.

Such examination includes not only a qualitative examination of characteristics of this type, but also application to them of strict methods well known in other disciplines, for the purpose of determining units of measure through which such phenomena or characteristics may be increasingly quantified or expressed in numbers.

Second, it includes the systematic examination of the resources of the business for the purpose of determining quantitatively the identifying characteristics of such resources—for example, characteristics of performance, or probable malfunctioning, and the balances, limitations and restraints that may exist within the resources.

Lastly, it includes the development and testing of models of action that give a description of the relation between the environment and the resources and which will define needs for performance and contribution, the information which must be communicated to make such performance or contribution possible, units of measure of the resultant performance, and the statement of possible risks that will result from a range of probable courses of action.

In short, the purpose of the problem in logic is not the taking of specific action but the attainment of more complete understanding so that increasingly purposeful action may be taken with greater assurance.[4]

CONCLUSIONS

The material given in this article may serve to indicate that the problems of measurement in business are increasingly being investigated, and also that some progress is being achieved.

However, much more remains to be accomplished. The author would hesitate to present such limited results if it were not for the fact that this affords an opportunity to let people know of the research and to contribute criticisms and suggestions.

It does seem certain that progress in the directions indicated can be no more rapid than is permitted by our methods of measurement. This is a field in which business can carry on a great deal of basic research and discussion with some assurance that the payoff can be considerable.

[4] M. L. Hurni, "Planning, Managing and Measuring the Business," Part 6, *Future Horizons in Business Management,* Controllership Foundation, Inc., New York City, Jan., 1955.

10. WHY MEASURE?

C. West Churchman *

INTRODUCTION

"Measurement" is one of those terms which has attained a social prestige. Apparently—all other things being equal—it is better to measure than not to measure. Some people think that the social sciences do not—or cannot—measure; and one implication of the thought is "less power to them!"

Why should measuring have this preferential status? What is it that measuring accomplishes that nonmeasuring does not? These are the questions to be dealt with in this paper.

At the outset one can suggest a rather obvious answer to this question, namely, that measurement assigns numbers to objects. But this suggestion can scarcely be adequate to explain why measurement is to be preferred to nonmeasurement in some contexts. Why is number assignment a good idea? Whatever it is that number assignment accomplishes may give us a clue to the meaning of measurement. The contrast between quantitative and nonquantitative information seems to imply a contrast between "precise" and "vague" information. Precise information is information that enables one to distinguish objects and their properties to some arbitrarily assigned degree of refinement.

We are thus driven to a first formulation of the function of measurement which will suffice to define the problem area of this paper. There is no reason to be precise for precision's sake, of course. But the reason that precision is useful is that precise information can be used in a wide variety of problems. We know that we can measure the lengths of some objects very precisely. This means that, in the various situations where we want information about length, we can obtain the information we want. Sometimes we do not need to make a fine distinction between objects, and sometimes we do. But whatever our needs, length measurements can be found to satisfy them—within bounds, of course. Beyond the bounds there are still problems of length measurement which have not been solved—the very fine and the very far.

Suppose, then, we propose that the function of measurement is to develop a method for generating a class of information that will be useful in a wide variety of problems and situations. This proposal is very tentative. It needs defending in terms of the historical usage of the term "measurement" and the practice of measurement. It needs clarification, since "wide variety" may include time, place, persons, problem type, and many other properties of breadth and depth.

Instead of considering these important questions, I want to continue the theme with which I started. Suppose we acted as though we knew what the proposal meant to a sufficient extent to enable us to develop the problems entailed in such a functional definition.

We can begin by noting one rather striking consequence of the proposal. The objective of measurement can be accomplished in a number of ways, as this volume of papers clearly shows. The qualitative assignment of objects to classes and the assignment of numbers to objects are two means at the disposal of the measurer for generating broadly applicable information. But which means is better? The striking consequence of the proposal is that measurement is a decision making activity, and, as such, is to be evaluated by decision making criteria.

In this sense, i.e., measurement taken as a decision making activity designed to accomplish an objective, we have as yet no theory of measurement. We do not know why we do

SOURCE: *Measurement: Definitions and Theories*, John Wiley and Sons, pp. 83–94. Reprinted by permission of John Wiley and Sons, Inc., from *Measurement: Definitions and Theories*, © 1959. Edited by C. W. Churchman and P. Ratoosh.

* University of California, Berkeley.

what we do. We do not even know why we measure at all. It is costly to obtain measurements. Is the effort worth the cost?

I have no intention of developing a functional theory of measurement here. Instead, I want to reconsider some of the well-known aspects of measurement in the light of the tentative proposal given above. In each case, I want to ask what alternative decisions the measurer has, and to what extent he has guides which enable him to select the best alternative. The topics selected for discussion do not necessarily represent the best way of organizing measurement activities; I have selected them because they have each received considerable attention in the literature on measurement. In each case, it will be found that the measurer is caught between at least two desirable aims, and the more he attempts to emphasize one aim, the more he must sacrifice another—which is the typical problem setting of the decision maker.

The topics to be considered are: (1) the selection of a *language;* (2) *specification* of the items and their properties; (3) *standardization* of the information to permit adjustment to various times and places; and (4) *accuracy* and *control* of the measurement process.

Any "scheme" of measurement does violence both to reality and to the functional meaning since there are many methods of accomplishing a goal. I do not intend to imply, therefore, that these topics must occupy the attention of the measurer in this order. But it is safe to assume that every measurer must decide:

1. In what language he will express his results (*language*).
2. To what objects and in what environments his results will apply (*specification*).
3. How his results can be used (*standardization*).
4. How one can evaluate the use of the results (*accuracy* and *control*).

There is a distortion which I will have to introduce in order to discuss these topics. The method of deciding how to handle any one of the problems does eventually involve consideration of all the rest. But the main point here is to show that a true decision problem does occur in the case of each of the four topics, rather than to suggest how the decision problem is to be solved.

LANGUAGE

The measurer must develop a language which adequately communicates to another person what the user must do to utilize the information contained in the measurement. The emphasis here is on the language of communication.

One aim of the language of measurement is to communicate to as many potential users as possible since this will increase the scope of utilization. Another aim is to enable the user to employ the information when there is need for fine distinctions since this also will increase the scope of utilization. These two aims are apparently in conflict—the more common the language the more difficult it is to use the language for portraying fine distinctions.

One way out of a dilemma is to escape through the horns. This I think has been the solution proposed by advocates of "fundamental" measurements. Suppose there are some operations which can be described in unequivocal language so that virtually every intelligent person will understand what is meant, or can be trained to understand. Suppose, too, we can find a process by which other operations can be understood in terms of these more elementary ones, and that these operations permit greater and greater refinement. If this were so, then we could accomplish *both* a wide scope of communication and a great depth of utilization of measurement. One example of a simple operation might be the comparison of straight rods: by successive steps we go from the "simple" language of comparison to the more complicated language of measuring the distances between the planets. Another example of a "simple" operation is the preference comparison of commodities: we may try to go from the "simple" language of preferences to the more complicated language of utilities.

In recent years there has been considerable study of the various ways in which the process of going from the "simple" language and "simple" operations can take place. These studies have resulted in formalizations of measurement language which are undoubtedly important in the development of the theory of measurement. For example, the symbol "$<$" can be made to denote an operation of comparison of two objects (e.g., "shorter than," or "is preferred to"). Sometimes the comparisons obey some simple rules like transitivity ($a < b$ and $b < c$ implies $a < c$), which enable us to introduce into the language the concept of ordering. But we can only introduce the concept if the comparisons obey the rules; i.e., we cannot enrich the language unless certain rules are upheld. The measurer is faced with a decision making problem when the rules fail. He may look about for another comparison operation with which he is satisfied and for which the rules hold, or he may abandon the rule itself and look for other rules to enrich the language. In any case, it seems to be confusing to say, for example, that "transitivity" fails over the class of preference comparisons. Such statements hide the fact that the measurer may always select another meaning for "preference" (there are clearly very many possible meanings) rather than let the rule fail *if* this seems economically advisable.

The language of measurement may be enriched in many ways. In each case the measurer has to decide whether the formalization is advisable. An enrichment of the language often makes the measurements more useful as items of information. But additional rules must be satisfied, often at the expense of a great deal of research time.

The process of developing a measurement language which I have been discussing has the following character. A formal system is constructed which includes terms, and relations between the terms. Some of the terms and at least one of the relations are taken to be "primitive" in the formal sense: the terms and relations are not explicitly defined. These terms and relations are also taken to be semantically primitive: the things and the comparisons which they denote are supposed to be simple to understand or to perform. This method of constructing the language of measurement is neither the only one nor necessarily the best one available to the measurer. A language without semantic primitives has many obvious advantages, besides more realistically reflecting the actual operations of measurement (where nothing is simple to understand or to perform). But the techniques of developing such a language have not yet been explored. Further discussion of this point would take the present discussion too far from its central purpose.

Finally, the amount of complexity that one should permit in a measurement language is also a problem of considerable importance. The more complicated a language, no matter how it is developed, the fewer the number of people who will understand it. In some cases, this restriction on communications seems clearly desirable. In other cases, e.g., in inspection work, one tries to develop a language that will be widely understood although it may not be very precise.

In sum, the language of measurement does entail a decision problem. The more precise a language the less broadly is it understood. To put it otherwise—if one wanted to be cute about it—the clearer a language the more confusing it is to most people. Precise languages narrow the class of users but increase the degree of refinement that any user can attain. The proper balance between breadth and depth is the linguistic decision problem of measurement.

SPECIFICATION

The problem of the specification of measurement is the problem of deciding what objects are being described and under what circumstances. This is simply the problem of deciding on the scope of application of the measurements in terms of time, place, and individuated items. This is not a decision about how the application is to be made, which will be considered under another head.

A conflict of aims is clear in this instance as well. It would be very fine if we could develop information that could be used in connection with all our problems, i.e., on all things at all times and places. But the more general information becomes the more expensive it becomes to acquire, or, else, the more useless it becomes in any specific context.

Perhaps one illustration will suffice to clarify the issues. In the theory of detonation, we would like to measure the sensitivity of various compounds. It would be a nice thing if we could measure how sensitive a piece of mercury fulminate is wherever the piece may be, no matter what its size, and no matter what is happening to it. But we do not do this at all. The term "sensitive" applies only to compounds which have a specific kind of shape and which exist in a specific class of environments. We restrict the term to these items and environments because we feel it would be entirely too costly to try to extend the scope beyond them, relative to the gains made from the more extensive information. Generalizing:

each measurer is involved in the economic problems of balancing the "costs" of extending the application of measurement and the "returns."

STANDARDIZATION

We turn now to the aspect of measurement that enables us to utilize information in a wide variety of contexts. In searching for a suitable title under which this topic could be discussed, I could find no better one than "standards." Standards of measurement are designed to provide a basis for adjusting experience in widely different contexts. Although the term is usually used in a narrower sense than the one adopted here, the purpose of standards so exactly corresponds to the notion of "wide applicability" that the extension of meaning seems legitimate.

It is strange that in philosophical discussions of measurement, the problem of standards is often neglected. This may be because it is often assumed that the problem is trivial, or not nearly as important as setting up an adequate language. Yet even a casual inspection of the process of measurement shows how very intricate and delicate is the operation of standardizing measurement readings.

The necessity for standards of measurement is based, in part, on an almost obvious observation that not all human experience takes place at the same time or in the same circumstance. Even if there were but one mind in all the world, such a castaway would need to compare the experience of one moment and place with that of another moment and place. He would have to communicate with his own past. The devices that men have used to make these comparisons are many indeed. One of the most direct methods consists of reconstructing each experience into an experience of a given moment and a given time, i.e., the present experience is "adjusted" into the experience that would have taken place under some standard set of conditions. This is not the only way in which experiences of various moments can be communicated, but it is a very powerful device for communication. Robinson Crusoe cannot bring along his hut as he searches for a flagstone for his hearth. But he does need to compare an experience on the beach with a past experience in his hut. He does this (say) by the use of a piece of string. He argues that if the string length fits the flagstone, the flagstone will fit the hearth. What he is really saying is that each experience—of the hearth and the flagstone—can be adjusted to a comparison with the string under "standard" conditions.

The general purpose of standards can now be made clear. One wants to be able to assert that x has property y under conditions z at time t in such a manner that the information contained in the assertion can be used in a wide number of other conditions and times to enable many different kinds of people to make decisions. The assertion that company x had a net income of y dollars in the U.S.A. during 1919 means nothing at all unless there is some way in which this property can be compared with a net income in 1956, say, or in England. Hence, the need for a "standard" dollar. Even the standard dollar does not accomplish the desired result of transmitting meaningful information if the circumstances in which the company operated (e.g., postwar economy) were different from the circumstances of today (cold-war economy). We require richer standardization to enable us to make meaningful comparisons of such a company's activities.

The decision problem of standards arises because of two rather obvious needs. First of all, one wants to find a method of measurement such that a minimum amount of adjustment is required when times, places, and people change. This desire for simplification is so strong that many thinkers have believed that certain simple sensations have this very desirable property: reports about such sensations can be understood intelligibly by a wide number of people in a wide variety of circumstances. A witness of an accident can report which car was going faster, a laboratory technician can report the color of litmus paper, a stock clerk can report the number of items in a bin; in each case the report is supposed to be reliable, no matter how the surrounding conditions vary.

The other need that standards are supposed to supply is precision. This is the need to differentiate aspects of the world we live in. The planning of a large meeting only demands a rough notion of the size of the crowd, say, between 2000 and 3000, in order to select a meeting hall economically; but the planning of a dinner meeting requires much greater precision. The decisions about instrument readings, highly refined products, bridges, and the like, all demand extreme precision.

It requires little reflection to see that the aim of minimizing the effort to adjust data usually conflicts with the aim of precision. In effect, the "cost" of adjusting data rises as more precision is attained, just as the cost of the absence of precision goes up as we attempt to find "simpler" data. Experience has shown that it is possible to be naive with respect to precision in an attempt to be simple in procedures. All of the supposedly "simple" instances mentioned above—a report of a witness, of a laboratory technician, of a stock clerk—are not simple at all if the decision on which they are based has any importance. There are countless instances in which such reports have been shown to be faulty, and these instances have pointed to the need for "checking" the accuracy of the data. Such checks amount to setting up standards to which the data can be adjusted. For example, what is meant by saying that one car was seen to be speeding more rapidly than another? As a first approximation: the witness who saw this was "reliable." What does "reliable" mean? As a second approximation: had any other normal person been at the scene, he would have made the same report. What does "normal person" mean? As a third approximation: a person with an intelligence quotient in a certain range, with emotional factors below a certain level of intensity, with vision in a certain range, etc.

This "normal" is the standard of measurement for a "witness" report. It may be noted that defense attorneys often argue that the witness's report is *not* adjustable to this standard, e.g., that the witness is excitable, or known to exaggerate, etc. Usually, when the witness is shown to have a property significantly different from the standard, his report is rejected. In this case, we can say that the "adjustment" has been a rejection. This terminology will enable us to emphasize the economic gains that occur when "unreliable" reports can be adjusted to reliable ones, rather than rejected. If we knew, for example, that a witness was normal on all counts except an emotional instability of a certain type, then we might be able to adjust his report to the report that would have occurred if a completely normal person had been at the scene of the accident. We could do this if we could establish a law relating visual reports in various circumstances to the degree of a specific emotional disturbance. This kind of thing Bessel accomplished in his study of observer reaction times. It is not necessary to discard the readings of a "slow" observer if we can find a method of adjusting his readings, e.g., by adding a constant to each one.

Thus, we see three "levels" of standardization of data. The first tries to restrict itself to data reports that are virtually certain to remain invariant with time and place so that zero adjustment is required. This level minimizes the cost of adjustment, but the data themselves have little precision and, consequently, little value where refined distinctions are needed. The second level consists of rejecting data not collected under standard conditions. The method of adjustment is simple, but the waste of information may be considerable. The third level consists of adjusting data to standards by means of "laws" that enable one to say: *if* report R_1 was made at time t_1 in circumstance z_1 by a person having properties w_{11}, w_{12}, etc., then report R_0 would have been made at time t_0 in circumstance z_0 by a person having properties w_{01}, w_{02}, etc. The "standards" are specified in terms of circumstance, observer, and observer actions.

It seems natural enough to ask why reports should be adjusted to a standard report. If laws exist that enable one to adjust in the manner stated above, why not adjust directly from one circumstance to the problem context without going through the medium of a standard?

The reason for standardized data is easy enough to give. Without standards, one would have to report all the relevant information about the time, place, persons, etc., in addition to the data report itself. Otherwise, no one would know what values to assign to the variables in the laws that enable one to use the report in other circumstances. But once a standard has been given, then all data reports can be adjusted to the standard, and all that is needed is the data report itself. Thus, the standard conditions constitute a data processing device that simplifies the amount of reporting required. But the construction of an optimal standard is a very complicated problem, as anyone knows who has followed the literature on the selection of a standard of length. Indeed, the whole problem of standards has received a great deal of attention by various professional societies. But as far as I know, the philosophers of measurement, i.e., those interested in tying together the whole structure and function of measurement, have tended to ignore this work.

ACCURACY AND CONTROL

There are two other aspects of measurement—each fully as important as those just discussed. These are concerned with the accuracy of the measurements and with the control of the measuring process.

Accuracy is itself a measurement—the measurement of the degree to which a given measurement may deviate from the truth. No procedure can claim the name of measurement unless it includes methods of estimating accuracy.

"Deviation from the truth" must be defined in terms of the uses to which the measurement is put. This remark has the awkward consequence that accuracy is a highly relative term, the meaning of which depends on the individual decision maker. But measurements are pieces of information applicable in a wide variety of contexts and problems. This means that it must be possible to find accuracy measurements which are applicable in a wide variety of contexts and problems. It must be admitted that, at present, we tend to adopt a rather naive solution to the problem of measuring accuracy by using one overall figure such as the probable error or standard deviation of the mean. For example, in statistical literature, accuracy is sometimes defined in terms of a "confidence interval." In so far as this computed interval has any meaning, it tells us that a certain range of numbers constructed out of observations has a specific probability of including the "true" measurement. Each set of observations is the basis for forming a net to "catch" the truth, and the confidence interval tells us the probability of a successful catch. But it is almost always difficult to determine how the information supposedly contained in a confidence interval can be used; i.e., what difference would it make if the confidence interval were twice as large, or half as large? Most statisticians seem to prefer to negotiate this tricky question by urging the decision maker to set his own size of confidence interval. Since most decision makers honestly do not see the purpose of the interval in the first place, the interval is set "arbitrarily," i.e., pointlessly.

Now the problem of accuracy is to develop measures that enable the measurement user to evaluate the information contained in the measurements. It seems clear that to date we have overemphasized one aim and underemphasized another. We have tried to develop general measures of accuracy at the cost of their meaningfulness in specific contexts. The decision problem of accuracy, therefore, has not been adequately solved, except possibly for some industrial processes where there is repetition of data and cost functions can be obtained.

Control is the long-run aspect of accuracy. It provides the guarantee that measurements can be used in a wide variety of contexts. In other words, a control system for measurement provides optimal information about the legitimate use of measurements under varying circumstances. The economics of control are extremely difficult to work out. It is certainly not economical to check measurements at every feasible instant, nor is it economical to use measurements without any check. What the proper amount of control should be and what its structure should be are in general unsolved problems.

It may be noted that control is, in effect, the test of a good standard. If adjustments can satisfactorily be made to a standard in accordance with the criteria of control, then the standards have been sufficiently specified. If not, then either the laws of adjustment must be changed or, else, additional specifications must be added to the standard.

SCIENCE AND DECISION MAKING

Enough has been said to establish the point that measurement involves highly complicated—and as yet unsolved—decision problems. It is important, I think, to point out that I realize that many people feel that decision making models cannot be applied to scientific work. They arrive at the feeling in various ways. Some feel that formal decision models applied to scientific decisions would stifle the creative powers of the scientist. Others feel that the "costs" and "returns" of the scientific input and output are intangibles. These feelings may be right, but at least we owe it to ourselves as scientists to determine whether they are right, and this means a frank statement of our decision problems, which is what I have started to do in this paper. My argument is not with people who feel this way.

But others may feel that science is immortal, and what is not solved today will be solved sometime. Existing decision making models implicitly or explicitly assume a penalty for delays. Perhaps to an immortal mind no such penalty is relevant. Thus, we can investigate some aspects of our measurements now, and let the next generation solve some more. People with this attitude are serious opponents of the endeavor of this paper. However, they cannot be right. Science may be immortal and I hope it is—but this does not imply a zero penalty for delay. It is ridiculous (I feel) to think that science is a gradual accretion of bits of knowledge. Instead, we ought to think that, as time goes on, scientists will feel that the distance between what they know and what they could know is greater and greater. Hence, the penalties for wrong steps become magnified, not diminished, the longer the life of the institution. Therefore, the decision making problems of science are terribly important ones, and decision making models that penalize for delay, i.e., for overemphasis or underemphasis of some kind of activity, can be appropriately applied to science today.

SUMMARY

The decision making problems of any of the aspects of measurement are enormously difficult, and even an approximation to their solution still escapes us. Everything that has been said here about measurements is applicable to a broader class called "information" and "data." A rather significant portion of our resources is devoted to generating and processing data. However, it is apparent that no one knows how the data should be expressed (the decision problem of data *language* is now unsolved), what data are needed (the decision problem of data *specification* is unsolved), how the data are to be used in various contexts (the decision problem of *standardization* is unsolved), and how the data are to be evaluated (the decision problem of *accuracy* and control is unsolved).

11. AN APPRAISAL OF SOME OF THE PROBLEMS OF MEASUREMENT IN OPERATIONAL RESEARCH *

R. W. SHEPHARD †

Operational research is invariably concerned with the examination of systems which include human beings. Since the degree of confidence in a decision reached by operational research methods depends upon all relevant factors being included and measured correctly, it follows that as much attention must be paid by operational research workers to measurement in the fields of psychology and sociology, for example, as to measurement of physical quantities. Unless this is done, confidence will be reduced, and the whole purpose of operational research (which is to give confidence in decisions) defeated.

INTRODUCTION

There are advantages to be gained by surveying from time to time the progress operational research has made as a science; it is then possible logically to decide in which areas more emphasis should be given if advancement is to continue soundly in the future.

The choice of subject for this paper followed from taking stock in this manner. It was impossible not to be struck by the preoccupation there seems to be in operational research circles with methods (elegant or otherwise) for manipulating measurements, and, on the other hand, by the small amount of attention that appears to be given to the problems of making these measurements. There seem to be very few articles in operational research books or journals which even touch on the problem of how the factors under consideration are to be measured in practice.

This paper, therefore, expresses some personal opinions on this subject. The aim primarily has been to be provocative and to stimulate thought that may improve the situation.

SOURCE: *Operational Research Quarterly* (September, 1961), pp. 161–166. Reprinted by permission of the *Operational Research Society*.

* Based on a talk given to the Operational Research Society, London, on January 2, 1961.

† Ministry of Defence, Defence Operational Analysis Establishment, United Kingdom.

BACKGROUND

The following three statements provide the basis on which the rest of the paper is built:

(*a*) *Operational research is objective decision making.* Two comments must be made in this context. Firstly, operational research is not necessarily merely advisory, but is a scientific method by which decisions can be taken; it is only advisory if the people who use it are advisers. Secondly, since decision making is concerned essentially with future outcomes, the measurements that are necessary to keep operational research objective must often be essentially predictive in nature;

(*b*) *Operational research deals with systems.* These systems may be simple or complex, but in general they all contain human beings. To ignore these is to be guilty, often, of fatal sub-optimization;

(*c*) *Operational research is concerned with improving confidence in decisions.* A decision reached by operational research methods is not necessarily different from the decision that would be reached by other methods: a right decision is a right decision, irrespective of whether it is obtained by sticking a pin into a list of all the alternatives, or by a piece of operational research work. The basic difference is in the degree of confidence that can be placed on the correctness of the results.

It is worth while to digress for a moment on this question of confidence. In the physical sciences, facts from the real world are used as a basis on which to build hypotheses; predictions made from these hypotheses are in turn compared with other facts from the real world, and, if agreement is not complete, the hypothesis is rejected or modified. In operational research this approach is rarely possible: * an operational research model must be made and used for prediction before the "real life" situation occurs that enables a check to be made. Confidence in the model, therefore, often depends only on some intuitive assessment that it is realistic, backed up by confirmation that all relevant factors are included and measured correctly. Measurement is thus as essential in ensuring confidence as in maintaining objectivity—two of the most important requirements for any operational research study.

In this connection it is probably of value to stress the importance of following up a piece of operational research, and of checking upon the assumptions made and model used, in the light of subsequent knowledge. Only by this means can experience be gained and used to improve the quality of further research.

PROBLEMS OF MEASUREMENT

General

It has been pointed out that one of the main requirements for confidence in an operational research study is that all relevant factors should be included and measured; also that operational research is concerned essentially with systems that include human beings. It is clear, therefore, that it is important that as much attention should be given to measuring human factors (psychological and sociological) as to measuring physical factors in the system under examination.

Admittedly some progress has been made in this field; for example, quantitative methods of selection and training are becoming widely known, and the impact of ergonomics is beginning to be felt. But generally the measurement of human and subjective quantities is in a very elementary stage compared with physical measurement; factors such as goodwill, morale, motivation, and so on, tend to be treated as "imponderables" (that is, the operational research worker ignores them) or, alternatively, they are in effect given some arbitrary value (a 1 in 20 chance of running out of stock is assumed reasonable as far as goodwill is concerned) and no attempt is made to include them on the balance sheet. Neither of these approaches is logical, reasonable or conducive to confidence.

There is, of course, no doubt that measurement becomes more difficult the more subjective matters are included. It would seem of value, therefore, to examine some of the problems of measurement in the physical sciences in an effort to understand what is involved, and then to determine how far the experience obtained is likely to be transferable to other fields.

Measurement in the Physical Sciences

It is pertinent, in the first place, to mention briefly the manner in which scales of measurement are usually classified.[2] Measurement can be defined as the assignment of numerals to events or objects according to rules, and the distinction between the various types of scales —nominal, ordinal, interval and ratio—is essentially on the basis of the mathematical transformations that leave the scale form invariant. In turn, these determine which statistical measures are appropriate. Table 1 summarizes the distinctions in convenient form, and provides a background for subsequent discussion.

In the physical sciences measurements may also be classified according to whether they are basic (lb, ft, etc.) or derived (lb/ft^3, ft/sec). One very noticeable fact about the latter (secondary) quantities is that none is in present scientific use which does not satisfy the principle that its dimensional formula is composed of powers; that is, all are measured on ratio scales. The advantage is, of course, that the form of any mathematical expression in which these quantities are represented is independent of the precise units of measurement employed, and this flexibility has undoubtedly been responsible for the gradual elimination of measurements on scales weaker than the ratio scale.

It is also of interest to classify measurements according to the methods used to take them. These methods are either direct, as when an unknown length is measured by placing a foot rule immediately alongside, or indirect, as when a temperature, for instance, is measured in terms of the length of a column of mercury. The latter form of measurement generally im-

* See, in particular, the article by W. J. Strauss in the *Journal of the Operational Research Society of America*.[1]

Table 1. Types of Scales of Measurement

Scale	Basic Empirical Operations	Allowable Mathematical Transformation	Example	Statistics	Remarks
Nominal	Determination of equality	Any one to one substitution	Numbering types or classes	Mode χ^2 test	
Ordinal	Determination of $>$ or $<$	$x' = f(x)$ where $f(x)$ is any monotonic increasing function	Street numbers	Median Percentiles Rank order correlation	
Interval	Determination of equality of intervals	$x' = ax + b$ $a > 0$	Temperature (°C or °F) Potential energy	Mean, *s.d.*, *t*-test, *F*-test	Zero point by convention or for convenience
Ratio	Determination of equality of ratios	$x' = cx$ $c > 0$	Length Temperature (°K)	Geometric mean Harmonic mean	Actual zero point

NOTE: Each column is cumulative in the sense that any statement against a given scale not only applies to that scale but to all scales below it.

The third column shows the mathematical transformations that leave the scale form invariant.

plies that a quantitative relationship between the effect measured and the factor under examination is known; but this is not necessary. In fact it seems likely that in operational research indirect measurement will remain of extreme importance even if the connecting relationships are not known; the possibilities of measuring goodwill in terms of orders lost, or morale in terms of productivity are encouraging even though the causal connections are elusive.

One particular difficulty of measurement in the physical sciences is that, in general, it is desirable to have a form of measurement that can be applied to many different systems; only then can correlations between systems be expressed in a meaningful manner. Conversely, if measurements are to be applied to only one system they can be completely arbitrary; and this is the stage that has been reached in the majority of operational research problems—normally any system of measurement used is only invented for, and intended to apply to, the problem in hand. The desirability of eventually obtaining more universality is, however, obvious.

Psycho-physical and Subjective Measurement

It is now of interest to examine, against this background, the measurement of psycho-physical magnitudes, such as brightness, loudness, apparent length, and so on, and of other subjective magnitudes such as utility.

A noticeable difference between measurement in these fields and measurement in the field of the physical sciences is the intrusion of what may be called human variability; no two people react in exactly the same way to a given stimulus, and it is therefore obviously impossible to erect a single scale of values which can satisfactorily represent all their individual feelings. The most to be hoped for is that a scale can be chosen that will correspond to the mean reaction of the population as a whole. This scale can then be used as a basis on which to compare the effects of different stimuli, or as a "norm" against which individual idiosyncrasies may be measured.

Early work was carried out by Fechner who assumed that "just noticeable differences" corresponded to equal units of sensation; he was able to relate psychological magnitude, σ, to the magnitude of the stimulus, ϕ, by the well-known equation

$$\sigma = k \log \phi \qquad (1)$$

There is, however, some evidence that Fechner's assumption is not true for prothetic continua; that is, for magnitudes such as brightness or loudness in which excitement seems to be added to excitement as progress is made along the scale.[3] Just noticeable differences do not correspond to equal units of sensation in these continua, and, indeed, a relationship of the type

$$\sigma = k\phi^n \qquad (2)$$

will represent results at least as well, if not better, within the limits of experimental accuracy.

The implication is that a ratio scale (as distinct from the interval scale implied by Fechner's relationship) may be used for at least some psycho-physical magnitudes; since experience in the physical sciences has indicated the power of ratio scales there seems every advantage in pursuing this lead in the future.

A similar situation applies to the measurement of utility. There is an added difficulty here, of course; whereas the subjective response to, say, brightness can be tested out experimentally relatively easily, there is no method of asking for an estimate of the relative utility of £5 and £10 without mentioning the numbers 5 and 10, and this may well so bias the observer that his responses do not represent his real subjective feelings so much as a compromise between what he feels and what he thinks he ought to feel. The approach of von Neumann and Morgenstern is one attempt to overcome this problem; but the subject of an experiment on the lines they suggest is, in effect, asked not only to make assessments of utility but also of subjective probabilities, and the practical value is thus not really clear, in spite of the elegance of the approach. Other work, using more direct methods, has suggested that a ratio scale for utility may indeed be possible;[4] again, this would seem worth pursuing.

Other Aspects of Measurement in Operational Research

There are obviously many interesting implications of the above ideas, but these cannot be pursued here. In conclusion, however, it would seem pertinent to make the following three comments which refer particularly to measurement in operational research:

(a) The difficulty of combining measurements representing different aspects of a system (such as effectiveness and cost) into a single measure of overall value is well known, and is faced daily by operational research workers. The more aspects of a system that can be measured, the more difficult this combination is likely to be; and if all measurements use different types of scale, the problem will be aggravated still further. It is important not to lose sight of this when new scales are set up.

(b) Even if scales of measurement are available for all the aspects of a system in which an operational research worker is interested, there can still be an immense practical problem in obtaining data. The value of approximate methods, inequalities, taking limits, and so on, is therefore not likely to diminish in the future.

(c) There is a tendency in operational research always to examine a system in greater and greater detail, and this is often reflected in the scales of measurement that are set up. Great value has been obtained in the physical sciences, however, from building up overall measures of the system under examination; concepts of total energy, of conservation of mass, and of statistical mechanics, for example, are extremely powerful. Perhaps more use could be made of an analogous approach in operational research.

CONCLUSIONS

To sum up: Operational research is invariably concerned with the examination of systems which include human beings. Since the degree of confidence in a decision reached by operational research depends upon all relevant factors being included and measured correctly, it follows that as much attention must be paid by operational research workers to measurement in the fields of psychology and sociology, for example, as to measurement of physical qualities. Unless this is done, confidence will be reduced and the whole purpose of operational research (which is to give confidence in decisions) defeated.

REFERENCES

1. W. J. Strauss, "The nature and validity of operations-research studies, with emphasis on force composition," *JORSA*, 8, 675–693 (1960).
2. S. S. Stevens (ed.), *Handbook of experimental psychology*. John Wiley, New York.
3. S. S. Stevens, "On psychophysical law," *Psycho. Rev.*, **64**, 153–181 (1957).
4. C. W. Churchman and P. Ratoosh (eds.), *Measurement: definitions and theories*. John Wiley, New York.

BIBLIOGRAPHY

Anton, Hector R., "Some Aspects of Measurement and Accounting," *Journal of Accounting Research,* Spring, 1964.

Bedford and Onsi, "Measuring the Value of Information, An Information Theory Approach," *Management Services,* January-February, 1966.

Bello, Francis, "How to Cope with Information," *Fortune,* September, 1960.

Bergmann, G., and K. W. Spence, "The Logic of Psychological Measurement," *Psychologcial Review,* 1944.

Bonini, Charles P., Robert K. Jaedicke, and Harvey M. Wagner, *Management Control: New Directions in Basic Research,* Stanford University Graduate School of Business, 1964.

Chambers, R. J., "The Role of Information Systems in Decision Making," *Management Technology,* June, 1964.

Churchill, Neil S., and Myron Uretsky, "Management Accounting Tomorrow," *Management Accounting,* June, 1969.

Churchman, C. West, "A Materialist Theory of Measurement," in R. W. Sellers (ed.), *Philosophy for the Future,* The Macmillan Co., 1949.

———, and P. Ratoosh (eds.), *Measurment: Definitions and Theories,* John Wiley and Sons, 1959.

Didis, Stephen K., "Value Analysis of Information Systems," *Journal of Systems Management,* November, 1969.

Feltham, Gerald A., "The Value of Information," *The Accounting Review,* October, 1968.

Jaedicke, Robert K., Y. Ijiri, and O. Nielsen (eds.), *Research in Accounting Measurements,* American Accounting Association Collected Papers, 1966.

Joplin, H. Bruce, "The Accountant's Role in Management Information Systems," *The Journal of Accountancy,* March, 1966.

Kircher, Paul, "Fundamentals of Measurement," *Advanced Management,* **XX**, October, 1955.

Kochen, M., *Some Problems in Information Science,* Scarecrow Press, 1965.

Marschak, Jacob, "Problems in Information Economics," in Bonini, Jaedicke, and Wagner (eds.), *Management Controls,* McGraw-Hill Book Company, 1964.

———, "Economic Theory of Information," Working Paper No. 118, Western Management Science Institute, University of California, Los Angeles, May, 1967.

Mattessich, Richard, "Budgeting Models and System Simulation," *The Accounting Review,* July, 1961.

———, *Accounting and Analytical Methods,* Richard D. Irwin, Inc., 1964.

McDonough, Adrian M., *Information Economics and Management Systems,* McGraw-Hill Book Company, 1963.

Osgood, C. E., *Information Measurement,* Indiana University Press, 1965.

Quastler, H. (ed.), *Information Measurement,* Free Press of Glencoe, 1955.

Stern, Harry, "Information Systems in Management Science," *Management Science,* April, 1967.

Theil, Henri, *Economics and Information Theory,* Rand McNally and Company, 1969.

SECTION IV

MODELS AND SIMULATION

One of the features of any system may be said to be pattern maintenance. If a system is to remain what it is, for instance, an operable efficient communications system, it is evident that it must somehow manage to retain and renew the mechanisms and patterns integral to the system as a whole. Because every system is in some state of dynamic adaptation to its environment, here understood as everything outside the system boundaries, there will always be problems to be solved. And as long as the recurrent problems are of approximately the same nature, their solution presents no special difficulty, but when the problems are substantially different, new solutions may be called for. This is where the use of abstract system models proves advantageous.

No problem is ever solved without some kind of a model.[1] When the dependent and independent variables of significance for the solution of the problem are few and their interrelationships rather simple, a model of the situation as it exists in the mind of the problem solver may be all that is required in the way of explicit model construction. But when the number of significant variables becomes very large and their interrelationships complex, then the eventual problem solver may not be able to contain the model in his head and may be forced to use pencil and paper to elaborate his design. But in essence there is no difference, for in either case the model is but an abstract representation of what supposedly is the real world situation.

[1] Stafford Beer, "What Has Cybernetics to Do with Operational Research?" *Operational Research Quarterly*, March 1959.

The model generally used for the solution of systems problems is a mathematical one. Once the significant variables involved in the problem are identified, the problem is then posed in mathematical terms and solved by available mathematical techniques. There is, however, no simple way to do this. The identification of the variables that ought to be considered in the solution may be anything but easy, and the interrelationships of these variables extremely complex. A realistic model of the problem can involve knowledge and skills beyond the possession of the model builders. Take, for example, the problem of smog in urban areas.

A complete understanding of the problem involves knowledge of climate, the molecular behavior of gases, the chemistry of the automobile engine whose exhaust helps create smog, the number of automobiles, the geographic layout of the city, including the location of the homes, work places, and highway arteries, the availability of alternate means of transportation, the speed of traffic and the timing of traffic lights, the incomes of the population, the chemistry and biology of the lungs and blood stream, problems of microbes and virus growth under the chemical, light, and temperature conditions produced by smog —among many other problems.[2]

Once the components of the problem have been isolated and described in terms of mathematical symbols and the appropriate mathematical techniques employed

[2] Alfred Kuhn, *The Study of Society: A Unified Approach* (Homewood, Ill.: Richard D. Irwin and The Dorsey Press, 1963), p. 4f.

(here the electronic computer can be most efficiently used), there still remains the all-important step of translating the mathematical solution into the real-world solution. After all, the solution arrived at through logical reasoning was that applied to a mathematical model, not to the problems of the real world. As such it is an abstraction. The original process must therefore now be reversed. The mathematical symbols employed in the solution must be applied to the component variables and their interrelationships as they exist in the original problem. No matter how sophisticated the solution may appear, since it is based on a model which is itself but an abstraction of concrete events from the real world, its usefulness will be proportional to the goodness of fit between the model and the events abstracted. The bread-and-butter test of any model involves the use of data from the real world. Without this data mathematical model building would be just another pastime, another form of mathematical recreation. Without this data there could be no valid test of the model and hence no real scientific progress. Hard-headed data and speculative mathematical models must go hand in hand!

In the business world there has been an increased utilization of models in the form of simulation exercises (management games). These simulation exercises, currently used in many industrial, educational, and government organizations for the training and development of managers, are based on mathematical models of the business world which in many cases are highly realistic. Such models consisting of a group of cause and effect formulas enable one to determine the outcome of input decisions made by the participants. For complex games electronic computers are employed to rapidly process the results.

Most simulation exercises concentrate on general management principles such as decision making and planning; however, others are specifically oriented to developing particular skills and techniques. One of the chief benefits of these exercises is the overall orientation to the interacting dimensions of the company, i.e., the participants are made aware of the impact of their decisions on the whole company and not merely on their own functional entity. As with all models, some aspects of reality are omitted and, although in many cases such omissions do not impugn the utility of the model, in others the abstraction of reality makes it more of an analytical tool than a learning device. Simulation of not only business problems but of complex management and industrial engineering problems may someday provide a breakthrough in management education.

Irwin Bross's selection on models, though published in the 50's, still serves as a good introduction to the subject. After mentioning briefly the various linguistic uses of models, he treats of physical models, abstract (verbal) models, symbolic models, and, finally, of mathematical models, all the while exemplifying his treatment with down-to-earth illustrations. Models have various advantages, among which he lists their remarkable record of predictions in the past history of mankind, their use as a frame of reference on which to "hang the problem," their usefulness (even when a failure) for suggesting fruitful avenues of research, their simplification of the problem by employing only the significant attributes abstracted from the real world, their use of symbolic language for both manipulation of the model and for purposes of easy communication, and finally their economical approach to the costs of prediction. Among the disadvantages he notes the usual reversals of the coin: the tendency toward oversimplification, the limitations of the symbolic language used, etc. He also points out for special treatment the all-too-human tendency of model builders to reify their brain children, to look upon their models not as representations of the real world but as being identified with it. Scientific model building however, because it is not divorced from data, will always bring its creator, after his jaunt into the symbolic world, face-to-face with the stark world of reality. When his model does not fit the facts of the real world, it is the model that must give way, and not the other way around.

Models are neither true nor false; they are either useful or not useful for making predictions in certain situations. A knowledge of this will eliminate several apparent paradoxes that may otherwise prove a problem.

In his admirably lucid explanation of the role of the model Bross compares and contrasts the model with a work of art, with an artistic painting. In all of this he stresses the important relationship that should hold between real-world data and the hypothetical model and illustrates it with examples from the world of physics. The pendulum example is an especially happy one, for it also serves well to illustrate the nature of the statistical (probability) model.

In his selection, Karl Deutsch looks upon a model as "a structure of symbols and operating rules which is supposed to match a set of relevant points in an existing structure or process" and which can perform four more or less distinct functions (organizing, heuristic, predictive, and mensurative). The organizing function is the ability of a model to meaningfully order apparently unrelated data and to reveal previously unnoticed relationships; the heuristic function leads to discoveries of new facts and methods, even though these (predictions) cannot be verified by presently available techniques. The predictive function enables one to obtain predictions verifiable by physical operations. The predictive spectrum, however, admits of many degrees, from the yes-no at one end to the quantitative at the other end. The mensurative function becomes identical in a way with the predictive in its extreme quantitative dimension.

Evaluation of a model consists of examining its performance with regard to each of these four functions. To these considerations should be added three additional ones: originality, simplicity, and realism.

For truly scientific progress we need more than sophisticated mathematical models and techniques. The assumptions underlying these models must be relevant, not naive; the constants in the equations real, not arbitrary. Examples of pseudomodels in the social sciences are cited, notably Rashevsky's, Zipf's, and Richardson's. Mathematical disguises are no substitute for genuine intuitive insight.

Joel Kibbee's article illustrates management's use of models and deals exclusively with the type of simulation that management is currently concerned with—computer simulation.

After briefly noting the various usages of the term "simulation," he identifies it with what is sometimes known as "computer simulation," "analytic simulation," and "symbolic system simulation." Symbolic System Simulation (SSS), often represented by the now-famous Black Box with its many dials and meters, is illustrated by an example and a variety of its applications noted.

Nowadays simulation is extensively used as a training technique and the form generally used is that of the "business game." Since their inception many of these games have been devised, some for training purposes only, others for research and teaching, some simple, some rather complex. Among the more notable games are AMA Executive Decision Making Simulation, SMART for systems and procedures management, and STEPS for computer programmer management. Among the more complex and ambitious business games so far designed for research are the UCLA Game and the Carnegie Tech Management Game, both of which are described in the text. However, the AMA General Management Simulation (GMS) Game is the one singled out for most attention since this is the game used as the basis of the "Management in Action" course of the American Management Association. The objective of this particular game is training in general principles of organization theory, control, and human relations. As such it is designed to teach management principles and not business principles: stress is on management and human relations, not on costs and profits.

Human System Simulation (man *and* the Black Box) uses business games as a laboratory for research into management control principles and thus bears a striking resemblance to the type of sociological research now generally known as Small Group research. Instead of using human beings in the study of human behavior the AMA GMS uses computerized models of such behavior. Such models are useful, even though not all types of sociologically significant behavior can be programmed.

Kibbee then proposes for consideration a preliminary model for research on management control systems. His Black Box is made up of three smaller black boxes, one each for control, operations, and environment. The details needed for each will depend upon what is being researched. The management control subsystem is singled out for special study together with the experimental variables that are to be manipulated, viz., the organizational structure, the information flow network and the decision rules. Decision making is definitely not a unitary process. It can be broken down into operations decisions and into the more complicated procedural decisions.

The author concludes the discussion with a few considerations on modeling. He points out that simplicity in the details is absolutely essential if the model is ever to be successfully programmed and run on the computer, that complicated questions need not require complicated models, that randomized factors may not be required by a truly workable model, and that the basic time interval used is crucial to the study.

12. MODELS

IRWIN D. J. BROSS *

THE SYMBOLIC WORLD

. . . I want to devote some attention to the broad concept of a *model.* Models are vitally important in scientific work and, in my opinion, in any intellectual endeavor. An understanding of the nature and role of a model is prerequisite to clear thinking.

In ordinary language the word "model" is used in various ways. It covers such diverse subjects as the dolls with which little girls play and also the photogenic "dolls" who occupy the attention of mature men. I shall be concerned here with model in the sense of replica (as in a model airplane).

PHYSICAL MODELS

There are several kinds of model aircraft. Solid scale models resemble the actual planes in general appearance (shape, markings, etc.). The flying model aircraft not only resemble the originals in appearance but, to some extent, in *function* as well (i.e., they are capable of free flight). Some very elaborate models are essentially simplified versions of real aircraft; they have gasoline engines, operable controls, and may even have radio-control mechanisms which allow the plane to be directed from the ground.

A boy who is interested in aviation can learn about the subject from the construction and operation of such flying models. In much the same way a scientist who has constructed a model of some natural phenomenon may learn about this phenomenon from a study of his model.

The model aircraft is easier to study than a full-sized aircraft for various reasons. It is more convenient to handle and manipulate. It is also simpler than the original, and principles of operation may be more apparent. There is some danger of over-simplification, of course, and some characteristics of a real aircraft would be overlooked if all attention were focused on the model.

As a matter of fact, adult scientists use model aircraft to learn about the performance of full-sized aircraft. They build carefully scaled replicas and test these models in wind tunnels. This is a much more economical process than to build a full-sized airplane and then to test *it* in a wind tunnel (a mammoth wind tunnel is a fabulously expensive piece of equipment). This type of argument by analogy has proved quite successful and is used all the time by aircraft engineers.

I do want to emphasize that the aircraft engineers do not trust the method entirely, that they carefully test the full-sized aircraft as well as the model. In other words, it does not follow that one can *automatically* obtain useful information about the original phenomena from the study of a model. Whether a model will be useful or not will have to be learned from experience, by comparing the performances of the original phenomenon and the replica.

The model represents a process of abstraction. The real aircraft has many properties or attributes such as shape, weight, and so on. Only a few of these properties are duplicated in the model. The wind tunnel model, for example, duplicates only the shape. However, the aerodynamic performance depends largely on this one characteristic; the other properties are more or less irrelevant.

This is an example of an effective process of abstraction. It allows us to focus our attention on a much simpler phenomenon without much loss from the fact that many details have been neglected.

This particular type of abstraction, the construction of a physical model, is used in various branches of science, engineering, and industry.

SOURCE: *Design for Decision,* Macmillan Company, 1953, pp. 161–182. Reprinted by permission of the Macmillan Company from *Design for Decision,* by Irwin D. J. Bross, © 1953.

* Cornell University.

Models are used to design ocean liners, bridges, water supply systems, and all sorts of products from automobiles to stage scenery. Not all models involve a change in size. In aircraft construction, for example, a full-sized model of a part of a plane is sometimes constructed out of wood in order to insure that an absent-minded designer does not put components in places which cannot be reached for repairs. In this situation the relevant factor is size, and the mock-up (as it is commonly called) eliminates other factors such as weight, function, and so on.

ABSTRACT MODELS

In the scientific world physical models are occasionally used for instructional purposes. In a planetarium you will generally find a model —little spheres which revolve on wire arms around a big sphere—which presents a picture of the astronomer's conception of the solar system. This sort of model is often used to demonstrate a phenomenon such as an eclipse. A rather similar physical model is sometimes employed to explain the atom to the general public. The solar model and the atom model illustrate one striking and sometimes confusing characteristic of models; two very diverse phenomena can sometimes be represented by similar models.

The solar model which you can see in a planetarium has had a very interesting history. Nowadays we think of the sun as a giant globe with a large family of little spheres circling around it. We locate ourselves on the third little sphere (counting out from the sun), and this notion does not cause us any mental anguish. In earlier days the picture was quite different and the earth was regarded as the center of the system. Of course if we go back still further there are all sorts of fabulous models which involve giants, turtles, and sea serpents. The history of astronomy is the story of the evolution of a model.

Did you notice that in describing the solar model I was actually taking a further step in abstraction? I was going from a physical model to a *verbal* model. The little balls were replaced by their symbols, the words "little balls."

All of us are accustomed to using verbal models in our thinking processes and we do it intuitively. Verbal models have played an important role in science, especially in the preliminary exploration of a topic and presentation of results. Verbal models are subject to a variety of difficulties, some of which I have discussed earlier, and most scientific fields have advanced (or are trying to advance) to the next stage—symbolic models of a mathematical nature. Astronomy was one of the first subjects to make this transition to the symbolic model. It should be noted that *until* this stage was reached there was really no reason to prefer a model with the sun as a center to a model with the earth as a center.

SYMBOLIC MODELS

In a symbolic model the balls and wire arms of the physical model of the solar system are replaced by mathematical concepts. Geometrical points are substituted for the balls. The next problem is to replace the wire arms which hold the balls in place. Now the wire arms have fixed lengths, and these lengths can be stated numerically. If all of the little balls revolve in the same plane, only one additional number is needed to locate the geometrical point. This number would be the angle between the wire arm and a stationary arm which would serve as a reference point.

Hence two numbers—the radius (length of arm) and an angle—will fix the location of the geometrical point just as effectively as the wire arm fixes the location of the little sphere in the physical model. Actually the astronomer's model is much more complicated than the symbolic model which I have described, but the general principle of construction is the same.

Now suppose that the astronomer wants to use his model to predict eclipses. He will have to take observations to obtain specific numbers to use for the radius and angle. These empirically determined quantities are substituted in the mathematical model and, after various manipulations, the astronomer announces: "There will be an eclipse of the moon visible in the northeastern part of North America on such-and-such a date and at so-and-so time."

It is at this point that a comparison of alternative models can be made. If the predictions are borne out, the successful model can be used for future predictions. If, on the other hand, the eclipse does not occur at the specified time, the scientist must begin looking for another model.

The Ptolemaic astronomers set up a mathematical model of the solar system with the earth as a center. They first considered that the other astronomical bodies moved in circles. When this picture did not lead to adequate predictions the Ptolemaic astronomers decided the paths of the heavenly bodies were epicycles. If you would like to visualize an epicycle, imagine two gears, one large and standing still and the other small and rolling around the rim of the large one. An epicycle is the path of a tooth of the small gear.

This complication led to a little improvement in prediction, but the forecasts were still quite unsatisfactory so the model was complicated still further. This time the astronomers postulated that the paths of the heavenly bodies were epicycles *on* epicycles, literally a "gears within gears" situation.

If you think that this is getting too complicated consider the sad plight of the astronomers. *They* had to make the calculations which go along with this model of the solar system. Nonetheless it was many years before the simpler model with the sun at the center of the solar system was widely accepted.

There is a moral in this epicycle story. Scientists occasionally become attached to a model even though it does not give adequate prediction. They try to use the model by cutting off a piece here or adding a piece there. This patchwork can go on for many years, and the resulting crazy quilt may prevent the development of new and more efficient models. After all, when it takes a scientist ten years to master a complex model, he has a vested interest in it, and he sometimes is hostile to labor-saving devices which may deprive him of his job. "Epicyclitis" is a symptom of senility in a scientific field.

MATHEMATICAL MODELS

It might be puzzling to understand why the astronomers should go from a nice simple physical model with little spheres on wire arms to a symbolic model with all sorts of queer mathematical signs when, if sufficient care were taken in the construction of the physical model, it would be possible to use it directly in order to predict eclipses. The astronomer's choice is a matter of taste. From the astronomer's point of view it is the mathematical model which is the *simple* one and the physical model with balls and wire which is complex. Since the physical model is made out of metal it not only has attributes which are intended to simulate the solar system, but it also has a lot of attributes which depend on the materials used in its construction and the way in which it is made. Thus the wire arms can be geared to rotate at an appropriate speed but the mounting and drive arrangements of the model are attributes of the model and *not* attributes of the solar system which it is supposed to represent.

Even though great care is lavished on the construction of the physical model the predictions which would come out of it would depend on friction, vibration, and other characteristics of the *model*. Hence the prediction would be rendered inaccurate by the entrance of attributes other than the ones which were deliberately built into the model to simulate the solar system.

In a *mathematical* model, on the other hand, the material of the model itself—in this case the symbolic language—does not ordinarily contribute such extraneous and undesirable attributes. If we want friction in the mathematical model we can put it in symbolically, but otherwise this friction will not appear in the model and hence cannot disturb our predictions. In the physical model the process of abstraction tends to introduce new and irrelevant details, while in the mathematical model the process of abstraction does not.

In this sense, therefore, a mathematical model is simple whereas a physical model is complex. It may strike you as curious that I should say that Einstein is working with an extremely simple model in his theory of relativity, while a schoolboy is working with an extremely complex model when he builds an airplane. If you think it over carefully, however, you may see the justice of the statement.

Now and then a mathematical model gets beyond the resources of the mathematicians who construct it, so a physical model is substituted to obtain an answer. This is done in the Monte Carlo method, a device for solving mathematical problems by having one of the giant brain computers play gambling games with itself. However, such devices are used for computational convenience rather than conceptual simplicity.

The construction of symbolic models is an important part of the job of the scientist, and the great advances in science are those in which a useful new model is introduced. In physics the powerful model devised by Isaac Newton is one landmark, the relativity model of Einstein is another, and the quantum models are a third landmark. In chemistry the gas laws, the mass action laws, and the periodic table are all the end results of successful models of atomic and molecular processes. In biology the evolutionary model of Charles Darwin (a verbal model) has been developed into a mathematical model by R. A. Fisher and Sewell Wright. Another important biological model is the one which describes genetic inheritance. In medicine the models are mainly verbal, but they are of great importance. Harvey's model of the circulatory system, and the various models of the reaction of the human body to invading organisms have influenced the development of the modern treatment of diseases.

Effective verbal models which describe the transmission of disease have been useful in the eradication of many of the epidemic diseases which used to terrorize humanity. Efforts are currently in progress to translate these verbal models into mathematical ones (epidemic theory), but the earlier models have been so successful that a modern investigator is often hard put to find enough data to test his new mathematical models!

Currently, there is research under way which is attempting to devise mathematical models for sociological phenomena, such as the growth of cities, and for psychological phenomena. Norbert Wiener in *Cybernetics* [1] deals with the mathematical model associated with the operation of the human brain.

One of the key steps in the progress of a field of knowledge toward scientific maturity is the fabrication of models which enable successful prediction in that field. A tremendous amount of imagination and insight is needed for the creation of new models, but they are only half of the story. The mere creation of models is not enough; the models must survive exacting tests, they must meet the pragmatic criterion, they must work.

This brings us back to data. The test of the model involves data from the real world. Without adequate data the construction of models is a mathematical pastime. Purely speculative mathematical models may be as useless as purely speculative verbal models. For example, I might construct a very fancy mathematical model to describe the mechanism of transmission of some virus disease. No good diagnostic test may be known for the disease, and consequently the available data may be quite unreliable. If a doctor comes along with a quick, cheap, and effective skin test for this disease, it may then be possible to get adequate data to test my fancy model. Until this happens my model is just another mathematical game. After the development of the skin test, the model may turn out to be useful in the understanding and control of the disease or, as is more likely, it may turn out to be a complete waste of time.

Progress in science is based on this constant interplay between model and data. Sometimes there is a tremendous amount of observational data available but no satisfactory model, so that little progress is made. This was the situation in astronomy before the heliocentric model and it also has occurred repeatedly in the biological sciences. At other times there are elaborate models but little adequate data. Something resembling this situation occurred in economics where an elaborate mathematical theory was developed which did rather poorly when tested with actual data.

Occasionally a scientist not only works out the model but also obtains the data. Darwin and Galileo accomplished this feat. More often one man, such as Brahé, gathers good data and another man, such as Kepler, supplies the model. When this division of labor occurs it is rather pointless to say that the model-maker is a greater scientist than the data-grubber, for the advance depends on teamwork.

ADVANTAGES

Why should a model be used? The real answer to this question is that this procedure has been followed in the development of the most successful predicting systems so far produced, the predicting systems used in science. It is simply a matter of going along with a winner.

Some of the advantages of model-making might, however, deserve a separate statement. A big advantage of a model is that it provides a frame of reference for consideration of the problem. This is often an advantage even if the preliminary model does not lead to successful prediction. The model may suggest informational gaps which are not immediately apparent and consequently may suggest fruitful lines for action. When the model is tested the

[1] Wiener, N., *Cybernetics*, John Wiley & Sons, New York, 1948.

character of the failure may sometimes provide a clue to the deficiencies of the model. Some of the greatest scientific advances have been produced by *failure* of a model! Einstein's work was the outgrowth of the Michelson-Morley experiment in which the aether model led to unsuccessful prediction.

Another advantage of model-making is that it brings into the open the problem of abstraction. The real world is a very complex environment indeed. An ordinary apple, for example, has a great many properties—size, shape, color, chemical composition, taste, weight, ad infinitum. In making a decision about the apple, such as whether to eat it or not, only a few of these characteristics are considered. Some degree of abstraction is necessary for decision.

The model-maker must, therefore, decide which real world attributes will be incorporated in the model. He may decide that the size of the apple rather than shape is important to decision. He may, if he is setting up an inspection plan, concentrate on the number of worm holes. If he is interested in the velocity of a falling apple, on the other hand, he may include only the weight of the apple in his model.

By making this process of abstraction deliberate, the use of a model may bring such questions to light. Moreover, it may suggest preliminary experiments to determine which characteristics are relevant to the particular decision problem under consideration.

Once the problem is expressed in symbolic language there is the advantage of the manipulative facility of that language. The symbolic language also offers advantages in communication. It allows a concise statement of the problem which can be published. Moreover, it is more easily integrated with the other scientific work which is also in symbolic language.

Another advantage of mathematical models is that they often provide the *cheapest* way to accomplish prediction. Sometimes it is possible to reach the same results by the sheer mass of data—by a "brute force" attack on the problem—but the mathematical route is generally more economical.

One reason for this is that a newly-minted Ph.D. in mathematics can be hired (alas) for a salary which could not entice a good plumber. A Ph.D., a pencil, and some paper may be all the equipment necessary to handle the symbolic manipulations of the model. Only a very small proportion of the millions currently spent for research goes into model-making. Even when the scientists are well paid, most of the money goes into the process of collecting data.

DISADVANTAGES

The use of models also has some drawbacks. The model is subject to the usual dangers inherent in abstraction. A mathematically feasible model may require gross oversimplifications. There is no guarantee that an investment of time and effort in constructing the model will pay dividends in the form of satisfactory prediction. No process, however, can provide such a guarantee.

The symbolic language is also subject to limitations. It may be beyond the ability of a mathematician to manipulate the symbolic language so as to obtain useful results. In such cases it may be more efficient to use direct methods. In gambling-game problems, such as the game of solitaire, it may be easier to play a large number of solitaire games and determine the probabilities by the Direct System than to embark on a mathematical analysis of the probabilities.

There is another very grave danger in the use of models. After a scientist plays for a long time with a given model he may become attached to it, just as a child may become, in the course of time, very attached to a doll (which is also a model). A child may become so devoted to the doll that she insists that her doll is a real baby, and some scientists become so devoted to their model (especially if it is a brain child) that they will insist that this model *is* the real world.

The same sort of thing happens with verbal models, as the semanticists point out, when a word and its counterpart in the real world are regarded as the same thing. This identification in the world of words has led to unhappy results which are reflected in the real world. The behavior of individuals who are unable to distinguish between words and the real world may become so bizarre as to lead to the classification "insane."

Now things are not this bad at the scientific level largely because of the self-corrective features of the sequential process of model-making which provide a periodic return to the real world after each excursion into the symbolic world. The test of the model acknowledges, as it were, the supremacy of the real world. If the model fails to predict what will happen in the real world, it is the model that must give way. This is the standard of scientific sanity.

When this standard is not admitted, a conflict between a model's predictions and happenings in the real world will sometimes lead instead to the rejection of the real world. This course is the prelude to disaster. To guard against such disasters it is well to remember the following rule for working with models: A model is neither true nor false.

The standard for comparing models is utility, i.e., successful prediction. The evaluation of a model is therefore dependent on the situation in which it is to be used; it is not *intrinsic* (i.e., dependent only on the model itself). If this point is understood several apparent paradoxes in science disappear.

One such paradox is the simultaneous use of two contradictory models. An example of this paradox occurs in the field of physics in which a *wave* and a *photon model* for light are both accepted. Wave theories are used when *they* provide successful prediction, and in other situations the photon theory is employed. Hence the paradox arises only if the models are identified with the real world.

Another paradox is the occurrence of scientific revolutions which (unlike political revolutions) do not interrupt the orderly development of the area. If models are not identified with the real world, the revolution is merely the substitution of a refined model for a cruder earlier model. Most of the time the older theory continues to be useful in the original applications; it is only in extended applications that the newer theory gives better prediction. The older theory is often a special case of the new theory. This explains why, despite the revolutionary work of Einstein, the older Newtonian physics is still used. In designing a dam or bridge, for example, both models would lead to essentially the same predictions (or in other words, the predictions are indistinguishable at the practical level).

One class of scientific workers does not worry about the testing of its models. They are the mathematicians. Their only interest (as long as they are functioning as mathematicians) lies in symbolic derivations from the models. Their business is to provide models in which the symbolic implications are worked out—anyone who wants to use the model for real world predictions will have to test it first. Nevertheless, the mathematicians serve a useful purpose in society (though a pure mathematician would strenuously deny it) by providing the scientists with ready-worked models. Often the models created by mathematicians are not used for years, or even centuries, but the literature of mathematics is a sort of Sears-Roebuck catalogue of models which may be consulted whenever a special type of model is needed. Unfortunately it takes some mathematical sophistication in order to use this catalogue.

As long as the model is completely divorced from the real world the criterion of utility cannot be used. Instead the mathematicians employ an *intrinsic* standard, *consistency*. Various attempts have been made, all unsuccessful, to extend this standard to the real world. The only result which these attempts have accomplished is to confuse matters and cause an identification of models and the real world.

ROLE OF THE MODEL

The disadvantages inherent in the use of models can be avoided to a large extent by a judicious balancing of the two processes, model-making and data collection. The relationship between these two aspects of Scientific Method deserves careful consideration; it provides one of the main keys to scientific success, and it also involves several notions which can be carried over into our thinking about everyday problems. The relationship can be represented diagrammatically by Figure 1.

The model itself should be regarded as arbitrary; it represents an act of creation like a painting or a symphony. The model can be anything its creator desires it to be. In practice, of course, it is generally stimulated (and therefore affected) by data from the real world (which is labeled "Original data" in Figure 1). Artistic creations also use sensory data. Even in abstract canvases there is some influence from the original data (sensory experience). If the modern artist paints the portrait of a woman, it may not look like a human being to me. But presumably the dabs of paint have some relationship to the woman, though it may require an expert to understand this relationship. Similarly, a physicist's mathematical model of the atom may be far removed from any material substance; again only an expert can appreciate it.

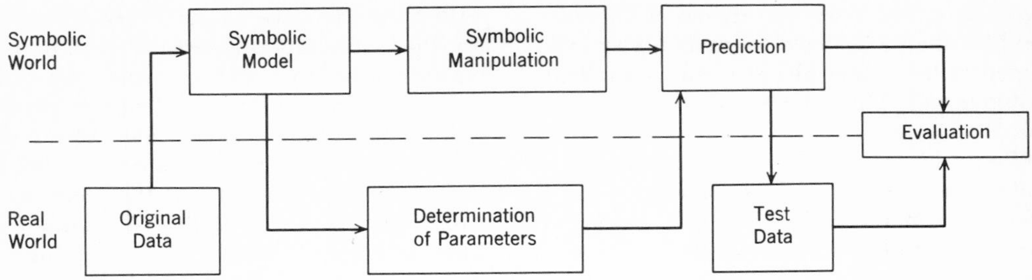

FIG. 1.

In many cases the symbolic representation used in the model is chosen because it was successfully used in previous models, because it seems plausible to the creator, or because it is convenient. However, some very useful models are based on assumptions which are not evident from common sense or—as in the quantum model—are actually repugnant to common sense.

I would not consider it very plausible to be seated at a desk in Los Angeles and then suddenly to find myself at a desk in Baltimore. It is even less sensible for this jump to have been accomplished in no time at all and without passing through any intermediate point in the process. Yet electrons jump around in this remarkable manner in the quantum theories of physics. Models which embody this curious behavior lead to successful prediction.

Scientists are generally pictured as coldly logical creatures with no disposition to embark on wild flights of fancy. But the geniuses of science have at least as much imagination as any other creative artist. In some respects the symbolic language of science allows greater freedom for expression than the printed word, musical notation, or oil paint.

There is one very important respect in which the scientist differs from the artist, however. The model itself may be arbitrary, but once it is constructed it must meet exacting and carefully specified tests before it is acclaimed as a masterpiece. In the artistic world the criteria for judging the finished product are vague and unsystematic.

There is a second respect in which science and art differ. In art the portrait is the end of the job; in science it is just the beginning. Once the model has been created there are two lines of development—one in the symbolic world and the other in the real world.

In the symbolic world the implications of the model are pursued by manipulations of the symbolic language. If I am interested in the behavior of a pendulum I can set up a mathematical model in which the bob of the pendulum is replaced by a geometrical point. The cord or arm of the pendulum is replaced by a symbol, L, which can be interpreted as the length of the cord. The Newtonian laws may be applied to this model and, by manipulations of the symbolic language, I may derive as a consequence of my model a relatively simple relation between the period (the length of time it takes to complete a full swing) and the length, L. All of this takes place in the symbolic language.

In the real world the numerical value for the length must be obtained. This quantity, L is often called a "parameter." The word "parameter" is merely mathematical jargon for a symbolic quantity, such as L, which may be associated with some measurable quantity in the real world. The process of measuring the length of the cord would therefore be called the "determination of the parameter." In most problems there will be more than one parameter involved.

The two paths from the model now join again when the numerical value from the real world is substituted in the formula (derived by symbolic manipulation) in order to obtain the period. The period is found, mathematically, to be proportional to the square root of the length, L. If my pendulum is 4 feet long it is easy to calculate that the period will be about 2.2 seconds. This statement is made as a prediction.

In order to test this prediction it is necessary to return once again to the real world. I set up my pendulum and time the swings. I find that the period as determined experimentally is about 2.2 seconds. Perhaps I go ahead and

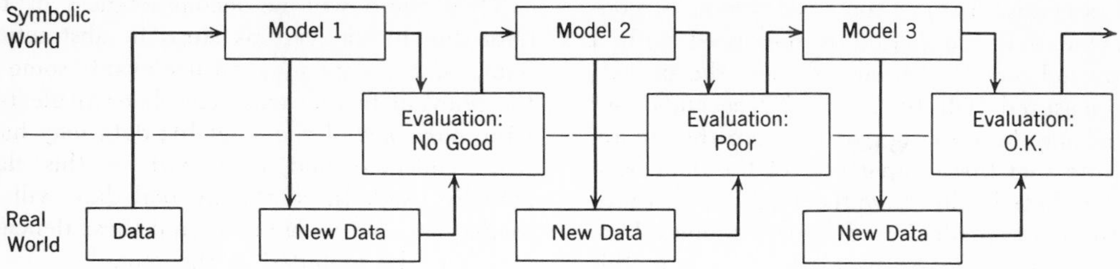

FIG. 2.

try a whole series of different lengths and the agreement between prediction and experiment seems to be good.

As a consequence of this agreement, I am encouraged to use my mathematical model for prediction purposes and also in the design of clocks or other equipment which utilizes a simple pendulum.

The reader may find it worth while to consider another example, such as the astronomical model of the solar system, and trace through the steps in Figure 1 in order to clarify his own ideas on the role of the model.

One striking characteristic of the relationship between the model and the data is the periodic return to the real world which is indicated in Figure 1. It should be noted that the original data used in the construction of the model may be quite useless for the determination of parameters or testing the model. Hence the return to the real world may not mean merely the collection of additional data, but it may require collection of data of a completely different *type* from the original data.

Now a reader who has forgotten his elementary physics may have wondered why I did not include the weight of the bob as well as the length of the cord in the model of the pendulum. An interesting feature of the mathematical model of the pendulum is that if this additional factor, weight, is included in the symbolic structure, it will cancel out in the manipulations. In other words, the model implies that the period of the pendulum does not depend on the weight of the bob, i.e., the weight is irrelevant in this particular problem. The same thing happens if other factors, such as the way in which the pendulum is set into motion, are included in the model. Thus the symbolic model has served the useful purpose of focusing our attention on the length of the cord. It has therefore suggested an efficient way of experimenting on the pendulum; the *model* has told us what *data* need to be collected.

The little story about the pendulum had a happy ending, for the model was satisfactory. However, few scientists are so fortunate or clever as to devise a useful model on the first attempt. If prediction from the first model turns out very badly the scientist will have to start over again. The way in which the predictions break down sometimes provides valuable information which can be used to construct a second model.

The role of the model as given by Figure 1 is therefore only a part of a larger sequential process. This sequential role is indicated by Figure 2.

The evolution of a successful model generally follows the above pattern. The first shots are often very wide of the mark, but by gradual stages the scientist zeroes in on his target. There is really no end to the sequence. Even after a model has years of successful usage (i.e., Newtonian models in physics), a situation may come along which will not be adequately predicted by the model. A new model must then be developed.

Some readers may find this viewpoint rather unpleasant because they would like this sequence to stop somewhere (i.e., at the truth). Nowhere in the scientific world has this stopping place been attained, although now and then the models have survived for many years. The attitude that the truth had been attained was often a barrier to progress.

A MODEL FOR DATA

The mathematical model for the solar system or for a pendulum can be used for prediction and then tested against actual data. In this test it is not expected that the data and prediction will agree *exactly*. In the pendulum example the predicted period of a 4-foot pendulum is

2.2 seconds. If a 4-foot pendulum is constructed and the period is measured with a stopwatch or other timing device, the periods so measured will be about 2.2 seconds, but there may be some departure from this figure.

Note that these departures of the data from the predicted value have received no allowance in the mathematical model for the pendulum. In order to *evaluate* the model, however, this behavior of the data must be taken into consideration. This may be done intuitively by an argument such as "the departures from the predicted value are very small and quite negligible for practical purposes." A more sophisticated approach is to set up a second model, a model to deal with the measurement data.

Such a model would be a *statistical* model; it would characterize the measurement process itself in mathematical terms. One parameter of this model might be interpreted as the *precision* or repeatability of the method of measurement and this might be estimated from new data collected for this purpose. Many scientific measurements are given in the following form: 2.22 ± 0.10 seconds. The number after the plus-and-minus sign relates to the precision of the measurement. Thus 2.22 might be the average period calculated from a series of measurements on the period of the pendulum. The 0.10 second might indicate that the average is only reliable to $\frac{1}{10}$ of a second. We would not be very surprised, therefore, if we had gotten 2.32 or 2.12 seconds as our average period. Consequently, there is no reason to feel that the data contradict our predicted value of 2.2 seconds. If, on the other hand, we had found the average period to be 3.22 ± 0.10 seconds, we would feel that something was wrong either with the model or with the data.

When we set about constructing a mathematical model which will describe data we immediately are confronted with the problem of including, in the mathematical formulation, the well-known inadequacies of data. Thus the inadequacies of the measuring instrument must appear in the model: it must include such things as sensory lapses of the human measuring instrument; various errors introduced by the inanimate instruments as microscopes, telescopes, or clocks; and, in biological work, where an animal is used in the measurement process, all sorts of additional sources of variation due to the animal.

Then there will be incompleteness of the data due to the various steps in abstraction. Some of the data may be irrelevant; some of the relevant factors may have been neglected. Also, only part of the available data may have been collected and only part of this data actually used. In short, any real data will be inadequate and incomplete, and these deficiencies must be included in the model.

It would be hopeless to try to catalogue all the things which might go sour in the process of collecting and utilizing the data, to analyze all of the factors which might operate to influence the experimental results. About all that is possible is to consider broad categories of deficiencies and to include these broad categories in the model.

Now how can these inadequacies, and the resulting uncertainties, be handled mathematically? As you might suspect, this is accomplished by the introduction of the concept of probability into the model. In fact, the notion of probability can be regarded as the distinguishing feature which sets statistical models apart from other mathematical models.

STATISTICAL MODELS

The role of a statistical model is in many respects quite similar to that of any other mathematical model. The diagrammatic representation is indicated in Figure 3. . . .

. . . Occasionally a simple model of this type can be applied to situations in everyday experience. Suppose that I am interested in the proportion of male babies in 10,000 records of live births. There are two outcomes possible when a baby is born (just as in a coin flip)—the baby can be a boy or a girl. I might therefore think of sex determination as analogous to the process of flipping a coin.

One distinction between the coin toss and sex determination is that while the mechanism for determining heads and tails on a coin is fairly well understood, the corresponding mechanism for fixing the sex of a baby is not well understood. Consequently it would be specious to argue that each sex was equally likely. There is, in fact, a large amount of data to show that this is not the case. Hence if a symbol, p, is used in the mathematical model to indicate the probability that a baby will be male, it may not be assumed that $p = \frac{1}{2}$.

Consequently, one of the things that will have to be done in order to use the model is to

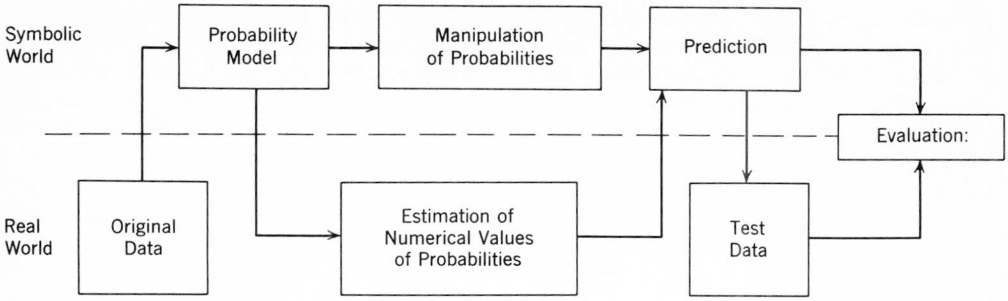

FIG. 3.

obtain data which will enable us to estimate the value of this parameter, p. Perhaps a number such as $p = 0.52$ will be determined from this excursion into the real world.

A second chain of reasoning stays in the symbolic world. Taking the probability as p that a live baby will be a boy, we must answer the question: What will happen in 10,000 births? I will not burden you with the manipulations of probabilities required to answer this question. The mathematics involved in calculating the probabilities for each of the 10,001 possible outcomes becomes too tedious, even for a statistician, and in practice a mathematical approximation which yields useful results with little effort is employed.

With the aid of this device, and substituting the value $p = 0.52$, we can obtain a prediction of the following form: The probability that there will be between 5,100 and 5,300 male births in the sample of 10,000 is equal to about 0.95. In other words, if I am convinced that the model is a good one and that my value of $p = 0.52$ is also reliable, I would be very confident that the actual data should show between 5,100 and 5,300 live male births.

This particular model has taken into consideration only one source of variability in the data on live birth—the variation due to sampling. Now in practice there are a number of other inadequacies of the data which might very well cause trouble. The reporting procedures may introduce difficulties. In a well-run department of vital statistics in the Western World the tabulation of births may be done rather carefully. On the other hand, if my 10,000 live births were reported by tribal chieftains in a colonial administrative district there might well be a tendency to forget female children.

The problem of *evaluation* of the statistical model is a tricky one. If I found 4,957 boys in the sample of 10,000, I could not say that this result was *impossible* insofar as my model was concerned. The model itself allows a very small chance of this sort of sample.

To a large extent the users of nonstatistical mathematical models can dodge the problem of evaluation by making the evaluation intuitive and simply stating that the agreement of prediction and data is either satisfactory or unsatisfactory. In statistical models one must come to grips with the problem. . . . A major part of a statistician's job lies in the no-man's-land between the symbolic world and the real world, and in particular he must evaluate the predictions of models relative to actual data.

SUMMARY

The key role played by models in scientific thinking is illustrated by several examples. The notion of a model for data is introduced and leads to the concept of a statistical model. The advantages and disadvantages of models are considered. Special stress is laid on the distinction between models of the real world and the real world itself.

13. THE EVALUATION OF MODELS

KARL W. DEUTSCH *

In recent years, increasing attention has been paid to both the use of symbols in the process of thinking, and to the problems that arise when symbols are combined into larger configurations or models—particularly when these models are then used as an aid in investigating or forecasting events that occur in the world outside the thinking system. One important use of such models is in describing the behavior of social organizations.

The organizations to be described may be informal groups, they may be political units or agencies of government, or they may be industrial or business organizations. Each of these organizations is composed of parts which communicate with each other by means of messages; it receives further messages from the outside world; it stores information derived from messages in certain facilities of memory; and all these functions together may involve a configuration of processes, and perhaps of message flow, that goes clearly beyond any single element within the system. Whenever we are discussing the past or future behavior of such an organization, we must use a model for it, and much of the effectiveness of our discussion may depend upon the degree of similarity or dissimilarity between the model and the thing supposedly modeled.

Investigation of such models, therefore, is more than a mere play upon some fine points in the theory of knowledge. We are using models, willingly or not, whenever we are trying to think systematically about anything at all. The results of our thinking in each case will depend upon what elements we put into our model, what rules and structure we imposed on those elements, and upon what actual use we made of the ensemble of possibilities which this particular model offered.

SOURCE: *The Public Opinion Quarterly* (Fall, 1952), pp. 356–367. Reprinted by permission of *The Public Opinion Quarterly*.

* Yale University.

In one sense the study of models, and the theory of organizations that could be derived from it, cuts across many of the traditional divisions between the natural and social sciences, as well as between the particular social sciences themselves. In all these fields, symbols are used to describe the accumulation and preservation of patterns from the past and their arrangement into more or less self-maintaining, self-destroying, or self-transforming systems. The resulting models are then used to describe further the impact of outside events upon such systems and the responses which each system makes to them. In this manner we use models in describing the behavior of a social group, or of a state, or of a nation, or of the memories and preferences that make up an individual personality. In a similar way, we use models in describing a system of logic, or in suggesting a theory of games, or in describing the behavior of an array of communications machinery.

SOME EARLIER WORK ON MODELS

By a model is meant a structure of symbols and operating rules which is supposed to match a set of relevant points in an existing structure or process. Models of this kind are indispensable for the understanding of more complex processes. The only alternative to their use would be an attempt to "grasp directly" the structure or process to be understood; that is to say, to match it completely point for point. This is manifestly impossible. We use maps or anatomical atlases precisely because we cannot carry complete countries or complete human bodies in our heads.

Each model implies a theory asserting a structural correspondence between the model and certain aspects of the thing supposed to be modeled. It also implies judgments of relevance; it suggests that the particular aspects to which it corresponds are in fact the important aspects of the thing for the purposes of the model makers or users. Furthermore, a model, if it is operational, implies predictions which can be verified by physical tests. A rough survey of major models used in human thinking in the course of history suggests that there has been a change in the character of the models that predominated in each period, and that it has been a gradual change from pictures to full-fledged models in the modern sense.

THE EVALUATION OF MODELS

We may think of models as serving, more or less imperfectly, four distinct functions: the organizing, the heuristic, the predictive, and the measuring (or mensurative).

By the *organizing* function is meant the ability of a model to order and relate disjointed data, and to show similarities or connections between them which had previously remained unperceived. To make isolated pieces of information fall suddenly into a meaningful pattern is to furnish an esthetic experience; Professor Paul Lazarsfeld once described it as the "Aha!-experience" familiar to psychologists.[1] Such organization may facilitate its storage in memory, and perhaps even more its recall.

If the new model organizes information about unfamiliar processes in terms of images borrowed from familiar events, we call it an explanation. The operational function of an explanation is that of a training or teaching device which facilitates the transfer of learned habits from a familiar to an unfamiliar environment. If it actually does help us to transfer some familiar behavior pattern to a new problem, we may feel that the explanation is "satisfactory," or even that it "satisfies our curiosity," at least for a time. Such an explanation might be subjectively satisfying without being predictive; it would satisfy some persons but not others, depending on each person's memories and habits, and since it yields no predictions that can be tested by physical operations, it would be rejected by some scientists as a "mere explanation" which would be operationally meaningless.[2]

Certainly, such "mere explanations" are models of a very low order. It seems, however, that explanations almost invariably imply some predictions; even if these predictions cannot be verified by techniques practicable at the present time, they may yet serve as *heuristic* devices leading to the discovery of new facts and new methods.[3]

The heuristic function of a model may be independent to a considerable degree from its orderliness or organizing power, as well as from its predictive and mensurative performance.

Little has to be said about the *predictive* function of a model, beyond the well known requirement of verifiability by physical operations. There are different kinds of prediction, however, which form something of a spectrum. At one extreme we find simple yes-or-no predictions; at higher degrees of specificity we get qualitative predictions of similarity or matching, where the result is predicted to be of this kind or of that kind, or of this particular delicate shade; and at the other extreme we find completely quantitative predictions which may give us elaborate time series which may answer the questions of when and how much.[4]

[1] Paul Lazarsfeld at a meeting of the Columbia University Seminar on Methods in the Social Sciences, March 12, 1951.

[2] Conant, James B., *On Understanding Science,* New Haven: Yale University Press, 1947; cf. also Bridgman, P. W., *The Logic of Modern Physics,* New York: Macmillan, 1927.

[3] For the concept of heuristics, see Polya, George, *How to Solve It,* Princeton: Princeton University Press, 1944.

[4] For the relationship of prediction to time series, cf. Wiener, Norbert, *Extrapolation, Interpolation, and Smoothing of Stationary Time Series,* Cambridge: Massachusetts Institute of Technology Press, 1949.

In the natural sciences a yes-or-no prediction might answer a question like this: Will this paper burn or not? A qualitative prediction might answer the question: Will it burn with a bright yellow flame? A quantitative prediction might answer the question: In how many seconds will it heat the contents of a test tube to 400° Fahrenheit?

In economics or politics, yes-or-no questions might be: Will the Jones Corporation build a new plant? Will the Blank party put on a political drive? Qualitative questions might be: Will the Jones Corporation build a large and modern plant? Will the Blank party put on a drive for clean government? Quantitative questions might be: How large a plant will they have built by what date? How many meetings, poster, radio appeals will the Blank party use before next November, and when will the drive reach its climax? It should be re-

At this extreme, models become related to measurement. If the model is related to the thing modeled by laws which are not clearly understood, the data it yields may serve as indicants. If it is connected to the thing modeled by processes clearly understood, we may call the data obtained with its help a *measure*—and measures again may range all the way from simple rank orderings, to full-fledged ratio scales.[5]

A dimension of evaluation corresponds to each of these four functions of a model. How great is a model's generality or organizing power? What is its fruitfulness or heuristic value? How important or strategic are the verifiable predictions which it yields? And how accurate are the operations of measurement that can be developed with its aid? If we collect the answers to these four questions under the heading of the "performance" of a model, we may then evaluate the model still further in terms of the three additional considerations of originality, simplicity and realism.

By the *originality* of a model, or of any other intellectual contribution, we mean its improbability. Any idea, scheme or model may be thought of as the product of the recombination of previously existing elements, and perhaps of a subsequent process of abstraction omitting some of the traces of its combinatorial origin. The greater the probability, or obviousness or triteness, of a model, the more frequent is this particular recombination in the ensemble of combinatorial possibilities at the immediately preceding stage. Originality or improbability is the reverse of this value.

A structure of symbols may be highly original but useless. Or a model may be original and perform well but require such a large share of the available means and efforts as to impair the pursuit of other work. Models are therefore evaluated for their *simplicity* or economy of means. But it turns out that the concept of simplicity is not completely simple. Francis Bacon declared in the controversy between Ptolemaic and Copernican Astronomy that, in the absence of conclusive data from observation, he would choose the simpler of the two hypotheses; he then duly chose the Ptolemaic system on the grounds that it required fewer readjustments of his everyday experience.[6] Clearly, all notions of simplicity involve some sort of minimization problem, but what is to be minimized? Is it the number of unverified assumptions or distinctions, as William of Occam seems to have taught? Or is it a number of calculating steps, as Copernicus suggested in praise of his system? Or is it the number of readjustments of acquired habits, as in Lord Chancellor Bacon's reasoning? If we could succeed in reducing the number of logical or calculating steps required in a model by introducing a large number of suitable fictions, have we simplified the model, or have we increased the complexity of its assumptions? Would we not have simplified it according to Copernicus, but made it more complex according to Occam?

Perhaps the concept of simplicity itself is operational, and could be considered to resemble the concept of efficiency in engineering and in economics. Efficiency in economics denotes the attainment of a given result with the greatest economy in the employment of those means which are shortest in supply at each particular time, place, or situation. Since such supply conditions are historical, simplicity, like efficiency, would then be a historical concept. (If there is merit in this approach, we might wonder about the effect of the availability of cheap calculating aids and electronic calculators on the traditional stress on elegance in mathematics.)

If simplicity is measured by the economy of means in critical supply, then claims to simplicity on behalf of rival models or theories can be evaluated more objectively. We might also be able to predict cross-cultural disagreements about standards of simplicity, as well as changes in accepted standards of simplicity over time. Some of these considerations of simplicity could also be applied to the evaluation of research programs as well as to the measurement of organizational behavior.

The last consideration for evaluating a model or a conceptual scheme is its *realism:* that is, the degree of reliance which we may place on its representing some approximation to physical reality. According to P. W. Bridg-

membered that the spectrum formed by these different kinds of questions might well be continuous.

[5] Cf. Stevens, S. S., "Mathematics, Measurement and Psychophysics" in Stevens, ed., *Handbook of Experimental Psychology,* New York: John Wiley, 1951, pp. 1–48.

[6] Frank, Phillip, *Modern Science and Its Philosophy,* Cambridge: Harvard University Press, 1949, pp. 209–10.

man, we may impute "physical reality" to a construct or model if it leads to predictions which are verified by at least two different, mutually independent physical operations. If we put this somewhat more formally, we may say that the statement "X is real" implies the prediction that "Predictions based on the assumption of X will be confirmed by $(2 + N)$ mutually independent physical operations, where N is any number larger than one." The larger N—the number of independent confirmatory operations—actually turns out to be, the greater the degree of reality, or content of reality, we may impute to X. If N approaches infinity, we may be justified in treating X as real, though by no means necessarily as exhaustive. This approach implies the assumption that every real object or process is in principle knowable but may be inexhaustible. It may seem farfetched to define the concept of reality as a prediction about a series of other predictions, but it is a definition that can be tested, and I believe, applied to the evaluation of models, or of statements about the inferred inner structure of organizations.

GENUINE VERSUS PSEUDO-MODELS

Mathematical models in the social sciences may lose much of their usefulness through starting from too naive assumptions, or through the introduction of pseudo-constants: that is, magnitudes represented as constants in the mathematical equations, but incapable of being checked by independent and impersonal operations.

An example of sophisticated mathematical techniques prevented from becoming useful by regrettably naive assumptions is found in Professor Nicholas Rashevsky's discussion of changing levels of activity in social groups and of the "interaction of nations," in his *Mathematical Theory of Human Relations.*[7] Professor Rashevsky assumes that members of the politically and economically "active population" differ from the "passive population" by hereditary constitution, and that the relative proportions of "active" and "passive" population then develop according to certain patterns of genetics and natural selection, depending largely on the numbers and density of total population. To what extent Professor Rashevsky's mathematical techniques could be applied to more realistic social and economic assumptions, and particularly to processes of social learning, in contrast to mere heredity, only the future can show.

A far more striking combination of relatively sophisticated mathematics with utter naïveté in social science can be found in the work of the late George Kingsley Zipf.[8] According to Zipf the size of communities in terms of their number of inhabitants should approximate a harmonic series for each country, if its cities were ranked in the decreasing order of size of population. The closeness of the actual distribution found to the theoretical harmonic series was then naively taken as an indicator of social stability. Thus, Zipf found that Austria between the two world wars had too large a capital city and too few cities of middle size, and that the aggregate series of cities in Germany and Austria after Austria's annexation by the Nazis approximated a harmonic series more closely than before. From this he concluded that the German annexations of Austria and the Sudetenland in 1938 had increased the stability of Germany and the social and economic balance of her "Lebensraum."[9] This "mathematical" conclusion completely overlooked the fact that before 1938 Germany had already been a food-deficit area, dependent on exports for part of her living, and that Austria as well as the Sudetenland had similarly been areas of food deficits, export dependence, and unemployment. What the Nazi annexations of 1938 had produced had been a merger of three deficits. The "greater Germany" of 1939 was more dependent on food imports and on export drives to pay for them than its component parts; the pooled threats of unemployment in all three territories were met by an armament drive, and food supplies and exports were sought by imperial expansion. What Professor Zipf has described as a harmonic series on paper, was in reality a situation of

[7] Rashevsky, N., *Mathematical Theory of Human Relations: An Approach to a Mathematical Biology of Social Phenomena,* Bloomington, Indiana: Principia Press, 1947, pp. 127–48 and esp. pp. 148–49.

[8] Zipf, George Kingsley, *National Unity and Disunity: The Nation as a Biosocial Organism,* Bloomington, Indiana: Principia Press, 1941; and *Human Behavior and the Principle of Least Effort,* Cambridge: Addison-Wesley, 1949.

[9] *National Unity and Disunity,* pp. 196–197 and figure 18.

extreme unbalance and disharmony, which led within a year to a violent explosion in the German invasion of Poland and the unfolding of the Second World War.

Perhaps it is too much to expect at this stage that individuals should undergo the highly specialized training of the advanced professional mathematician and at the same time, the at least equally intense training of the experienced social scientist. The difference in the intellectual techniques in these two fields should not obscure the fact that both approaches represent full-time intellectual jobs. The main task of the mathematician is perhaps to concentrate on the single-minded pursuit of long trains of symbolic operations. He may start out on these from any set of given initial conditions, without caring overmuch, as a rule, why just these conditions or assumptions and no others were selected.

Much of the training of the historian and social scientist is just the opposite. He must become familiar with a very wide range of social and economic situations at different places and times. The outcome of this part of his training is at best a sense of relevance, an experience in judging which factors in a situation must be taken into account and which ones may be neglected without much risk of error. To be sure, the social scientist can only benefit from analytic training. He does and should study economic, political and psychological theory, and to an increasing extent mathematics and symbolic logic. Yet all analytic work in the social sciences is primarily tied to judgments of relevance, to evaluating the realism of assumptions and the appropriateness of models. This ability is not easily acquired by mathematicians in their periods of rest between or after their more arduous professional labors. And the advice to younger social scientists to study more mathematics should be tempered with the insistence that they will have to judge the relevance of their models against their fund of factual knowledge as social scientists; no amount of mathematical knowledge or advice can take this task from their shoulders.

The most hopeful answer to this problem at the present time lies perhaps in the development of teamwork between men who are primarily social scientists but who have had enough analytical training to put their problems into a form where mathematicians can go to work on them, and mathematicians who have had enough of a solid training in the social sciences to understand what the social scientists need from them, and how to select lines of mathematical treatment which will lead more closely toward reality rather than away from it.

Another source of trouble with mathematical models in the social sciences stems from the tendency to put arbitrary constants or coefficients into equations so as to make their results fit a known series of numbers or their extrapolations. Thus, Lewis F. Richardson's "Generalized Foreign Politics" attempts to predict the armaments expenditures of two rival countries by equations which contain numerical coefficients for the "grievances" and the "submissiveness" of each country vis-à-vis the other.[10]

It is well known that any finite series of numbers can be fitted by more than one equation, and, on the other hand, that any result can be attained in an equation by introducing a sufficiently large number of arbitrary constants or coefficients. There is all the difference in the world between such arbitrary coefficients and a constant in physics, such as Planck's quantum constant h. Genuine constants in physics can be verified by impersonal physical operations of measurement, or by impersonally verifiable inferences from measurement. Such constants are the same for all physicists regardless of their sympathies or political beliefs, and they would be confirmed, in principle, by impersonal recording and measuring devices. The use of such operationally independent and verifiable concepts in models, such as in Bohr's model of the atom, is therefore quite legitimate. As long as social scientists cannot specify an impersonal set of operations for producing a numerical measure of "grievance" or "submissiveness," there will remain a grave suspicion that coefficients based on arbitrary estimates in such matters are

[10] Richardson, Lewis F., "Generalized Foreign Politics; A Study in Group Psychology," *British Journal of Psychology*, Monograph Supplement No. 23, London: Cambridge University Press, 1939; cf. also the summaries in Quincy Wright, *A Study of War*, Vol. II, appendix 42, pp. 1482–83; Kenneth J. Arrow, "Mathematical Models in the Social Sciences," in Daniel Lerner and Harold D. Lasswell, eds., *The Policy Sciences: Recent Developments in Scope and Method*, Palo Alto: Stanford University Press, 1951, p. 137.

somewhat akin to the "variable constants" familiar from the folklore of undergraduate humor.

To be sure, there may be cases where such mathematical pseudo-models may describe, however inadequately, some genuine intuitive insight of their author. It would be folly to suggest that only that is real which is measurable by present-day methods; the perception of *Gestalt* or the structural vision of a previously unrecognized configuration of phenomena all have their places among our sources of knowledge. In all such cases, however, it is the qualitative insights that are relevant, and not the mathematical disguises which they have prematurely donned.

14. MANAGEMENT CONTROL SIMULATION

JOEL M. KIBBEE *

INTRODUCTION

Simulation is one technique for the study of management control systems, whether of their design and evaluation or in the search for fundamental principles. That aspect of the general research approach with which we shall be concerned here is the simulation model. We shall begin with some comments on the type of simulation to be undertaken, shall describe certain "business games" which are related to such simulation, and conclude with a proposal for a preliminary model.

The term "simulation" has been applied to a variety of situations: a model of an airplane in a wind tunnel, a pilot in a Link Trainer, the simulated environment and inputs used in the SAGE System Training Program, research into the design of a bus terminal by the Port of New York Authority. Some authors have used the word "simulation" as a synonym for the Monte Carlo method. In its broadest sense any construction of a model, physical or symbolic, might be called simulation. Let us introduce the term "symbolic system simulation" for the type of experimentation to be discussed here. This has also been referred to as "analytic simulation," "computer simulation," and just "simulation."

SYMBOLIC SYSTEM SIMULATION

Symbolic System Simulation can be best illustrated by an example. Consider a retail store which handles one product, sells it daily to customers, and carries an inventory which may be replenished by orders placed at a factory. At the beginning of any day there is a particular quantity of stock on hand; during the day this is increased by deliveries from the factory and decreased by sales. When the stock is not sufficient to meet the customer demand there are stockouts, and the sales are less than the demand.

We may build a mathematical model of the above system: the inputs are the customer demand and the deliveries from the factory, the output is the number of sales, and the state of the system at the end of any day is the quantity of stock on hand. Suppose we are given the state of the system on day 1, i.e., the stock on hand, as well as the customer demand and the factory deliveries for each day for one month and that we want to know the total sales, the total stockouts, and the state of the system on day 30. If we knew that the inventory had always been sufficiently large to meet demand, and thus that there were no stockouts, the stock on hand on day 30 would be simply the stock on hand on day 1 plus the total deliveries minus the total demand. But in general there is no simple analytic expression relating the state of the system on day 30 to the state on day 1, nor for computing the total sales, and it is necessary to perform thirty computations, albeit simple ones, representing a day by day stepping through of the model.

Symbol System Simulation is thus characterized by the construction of a mathematical model of a real system—mathematical, meaning to include both logical and algebraic operations—and the "running" of it through a sequence of time intervals. Building mathematical models of real systems is a fairly common technique, and the behavior of such models is often investigated by analytic techniques. It becomes simulation, at least in our sense here, when the current state can be computed from the initial state only by stepping through all intermediate states.

Symbolic System Simulation is exemplified by such studies as United Air Lines Airport Model, the Port of New York Authority's Bus

SOURCE: *Management Control Systems,* John Wiley and Sons, 1960, pp. 300–320. Reprinted by permission of John Wiley & Sons, Inc., from *Management Control Systems,* edited by Donald G. Malcolm and Alan J. Rowe, © 1962.

* Systems Development Corporation.

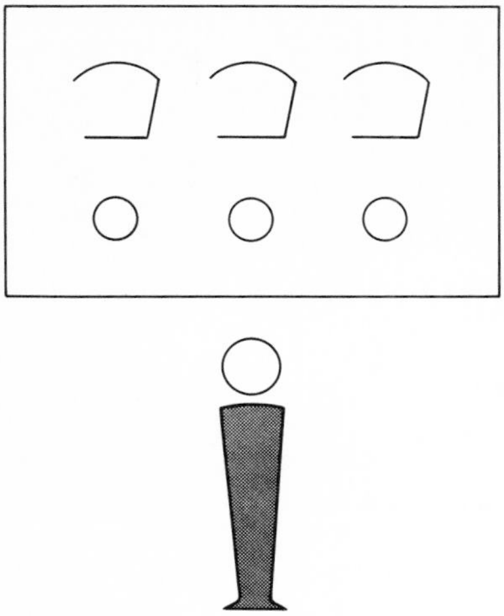

FIG. VI-C-1. A man and a model.

Terminal Model, and General Electric's Job Shop Scheduling Model. The mathematical model is nearly always programmed for a computer, the usual reason being that computations are generally too lengthy to be done by hand. However, worthwhile simulations have been performed without using a computer. Most real systems which one is likely to study will contain stochastic elements but stochastic elements are not necessarily a part of every simulation. In job shop scheduling if one begins with a known set of orders, rather than a sequence of random ones, there still may be difficult combinatorial problems, and such problems have been attacked through simulation.

Symbolic System Simulation has a variety of applications. As a research tool to search for optimal procedures, simulation of petroleum refineries has been particularly successful, and this is now a generally accepted technique. Other applications have been in such areas as production planning and control, distribution, transportation, and more recently in marketing and finance. It can be used as a management aid, helping a manager to select among several alternative decisions. When computers are placed "on-line" one can imagine operating decisions being quickly tried out, through simulation, before their implementation.

Symbolic System Simulation can be used in the design and evaluation of systems. It can be used for testing out a system before implementation, with the mildly paradoxical situation of modeling a "real" system before it exists. It can also be used as a research tool for discovering general principles of system design.

It is conceptually useful to think of a Symbolic System Simulation as a black box with certain dials and meters. For the moment let us place a man in front of the box. (Figure VI-C-1.) He sets the dials, the box purrs, and results appear on the meters. He observes the results, perhaps records them, sets the dials to new positions, and the cycle repeats. Normally the procedure would be carried out by a separate program within the computer, instead of by the man. This program would cause the model to be stepped through a sequence of time intervals, with relevant data being printed out, and then certain changes would be made in the parameters, and the model would again be stepped through a sequence of time intervals, etc.

Let us return to the man in front of the black box; perhaps a research worker is interested in studying the man's behavior. The human subject moves the dials, reads the meters, etc., and the research worker observes this through the usual one-way glass windows. For the research worker the model is no longer just the black box, it is the man and black box. When humans are included in the model we shall use the term "Human System Simulation." With several human subjects and several black boxes we have the type of simulation of the SAGE System Training Program, and also of the RAND Logistics Simulation Laboratory, though this is an oversimplified description: the black box is a bit more fuzzy, beginning to surround the man, and there are questions about simulating the environment.

Let us now assume that we construct some sort of mathematical model of the human subject himself. The model of the man is added to the other model inside of the black box, and the research worker is now twisting the dials on this new box attempting to learn something about the man-machine behavior without using a real man. Let us ignore for now the question as to whether we can usefully construct an adequate model to the man. What we have done is return to a Symbolic System Simulation. Most models used in Symbolic System Simulation do contain factors associated with human behavior. For example, in studying business problems one may introduce price-demand curves, as an aggregate model of customer behavior, instead of using human sub-

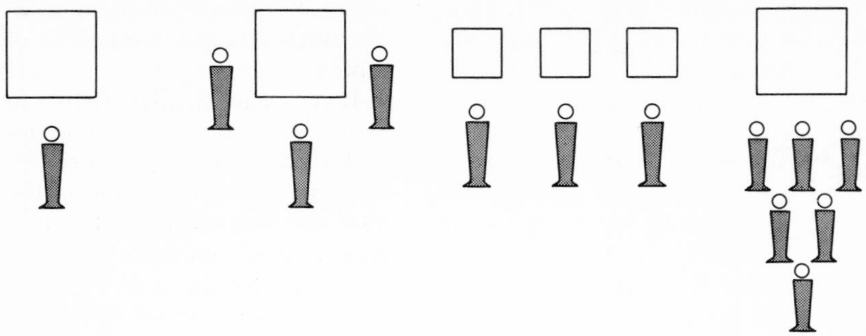

(a) (b) (c) (d)

FIG. VI-C-2. Various system simulation.

jects who, provided with the various prices, feed back to the model their decisions to buy or not.

Let us turn now to Figure V1-C-2. In (*a*) we have one man experimenting with a model. In (*b*) we have several men experimenting with the same model and in competitive interaction with one another. This is perhaps a model of several salesmen competing for a common customer. In (*c*) we also have a competitive situation, but without interaction between the men. This would be a case in which the men faced identical tasks and compared their performance. The first type of competition, characterized by interaction, is analogous to tennis; the second type is analogous to golf. Instead of one man, we might have a group of men, as in (*d*), each with their own dials to set, but working towards a common goal. And of course in (*b*) and (*c*) we could also replace each man by a team of men. In order to study management control systems one would be most interested in the situation represented by (*d*). To study a business management situation it would be necessary to include the concept of intercompany competition, but most likely one would do this through mathematical models within the box rather than by adding additional teams.

BUSINESS GAMES

Simulation has extensive use today as a training technique, and in particular there has been considerable publicity about its use in what are usually called "business games" or "management games," or, in order to avoid certain unfavorable misinterpretations of the word "game," are frequently called "simulation exercises." A business game involves humans using Symbolic System Simulation, in one of the forms illustrated in Figure VI-C-2; the model is of a business, or some part of a business, and the objective is training.

The first business game was introduced by the American Management Association, being initially demonstrated in December, 1956, in Los Angeles. This game is usually referred to as the AMA Game, though it would be more properly called the AMA Executive Decision Making Simulation, as AMA has since constructed, and has in use, several other games. UCLA, IBM, The Pillsbury Company, and many other organizations are using quite similar games. This particular set of games is characterized by several companies competing in a common market, each manufacturing and selling one product, and with decisions being concerned mainly with selling price, advertising, production level, and the purchase of capital equipment. However games, like automobiles, undergo frequent model changes, and a variety of other business elements such as credit, dividends, stocks, the ability to purchase information about the economy or one's competitors and to engage in market research are now fairly common. Games may be modeled after a complete business, or after some particular component such as production planning and control. They also may be specialized to a particular type of organization such as banking, public utilities, supermarkets, or the detergent industry. We have recently seen such specialized games as SMART, for systems and procedures management, and STEPS, for computer programmer management.

The pedagogical intent of the various games may differ greatly: practicing decising making, improving analytic ability, learning to learn from experience, gaining an appreciation for particular business problems. Of more importance to our present discussion is their use in exemplifying certain general management principles in the areas of organization theory, planning, communications, control, and human relations. It is possible that certain management principles could be evidenced by having the participants play football. Perhaps going out for the team should be a requisite in business administration colleges: as English leaders are developed on the playing fields of Eton, corporation presidents would be developed on the playing fields of Harvard Business School. There are, however, some fairly obvious advantages in providing a business model for business executives.

There are some important relationships between business games and Symbolic System Simulation. Executives playing a business game provide a ready-made laboratory for studying management problems, though very little work has so far been done along this line. Existing games can, at least, offer guidance to the research worker. Modeling techniques are quite similar whether one is interested in training or research. Furthermore, a few Symbolic System Simulations undertaken for problem-solving purposes have been models of a complete business organization, and certain business games now existing can serve as a preliminary step—one is tempted to speak of a model of a model.

Any business game could be used for some form of research; the obverse of the coin is that any simulation could be used for training. This has actually been done in several cases, such as in job shop scheduling, where, though the model was primarily designed to search for and evaluate decision rules, it can also provide training for operating production people. A simulation, used as a game, can serve as an orientation device. One can perhaps more easily evoke critical feedback by allowing someone to play with the model than by having him listen to an exposition about it.

USE OF SIMULATION FOR RESEARCH

In order to do research on management control systems one would want a simulation represented by item (*d*) in Figure VI-C-2. Until recently, most business games, while perhaps complex in concept, were at least simple in the playing details; optimum size teams were usually five or less. One could obviously have allowed ten people to work as a sort of executive committee—such large teams have been used—but this represented a type of cooperative decision making and the individuals did not each have detailed tasks to perform. If one is interested in a management system, as distinct from the behavior of one manager, then one must provide for quite a few tasks and quite a few decisions, so that an organization structure is a necessity, and so that information networks must be established, authority delegated, and so forth. In most organizations it is not a question of whether the chief executive wants to make all of the decisions, or whether he is capable of making the best decisions, but that it is impossible for him to make all of the decisions that have to be made.

There are games today which do have an increased complexity—complexity from the standpoint of the number of details that have to be considered by the participants rather than by the extent of the sophistication of any one element. We shall consider three of these games here: The TASK Manufacturing Corporation, a new game under development at UCLA; the Carnegie Tech Management Game, for which complete details have been published; and the AMA General Management Simulation, which will be discussed more fully below.

The new UCLA game is an extremely ambitious project. The model will comprise a great amount of detail, but also considerable flexibility. One type of flexibility is the possibility of having certain operations controlled by computerized decision rules or policies, or, instead, the possibility of breaking into the system, as it were, and allowing human beings to take various managerial roles. The model is being designed as a tool for both research and training. The model will certainly be able to accommodate quite a few human managers and as such can be used for studies on management control system problems. In addition, because of its modular structure, control system research can be performed completely within the computer through changes in interconnections between the modules, changes in decision rules, and so forth.

The Carnegie Tech Management Game was also an ambitious undertaking. It was designed to allow participants to exercise habits of thought and analysis rather than to give practice in rapid decision making. It is very complex and can accommodate, typically, a team of say nine participants, and each would be kept adequately busy. The model is patterned after the detergent industry, has extensive sub-models of the production, marketing, and financial functions, allows for introduction of new products and for removing them from the market if they prove unsuccessful. The model is designed so that it can accommodate either several teams acting as separate companies and competing in a common market, or one team, still in a competitive market, but with competitors programmed in the computer. Part of the research plan is to attempt to replicate—i.e., mathematically model—some of the decision processes of the participants. One would expect research results in the general area of management control systems as well as in other areas.

THE USE OF SIMULATION FOR TRAINING

The General Management Simulation, henceforth referred to as GMS, is currently being used as the basis of the fourth week—called "Management in Action"—of the four-week management course conducted by the American Management Association. This particular unit of the course was introduced in January, 1959, and since then has been given a little more often than once a month, with, on the average about sixty business executives participating. The unit is held at the AMA Academy at Saranac Lake, New York, and the IBM 650 installed there is utilized for the computations. GMS was expressly designed to exemplify certain general principles in the areas of organization theory, communications, control, and human relations. It was designed to teach management principles rather than business principles. Considerable design effort was directed, in fact, towards the de-emphasis of such things as the relationship between price and demand, and other quantitative factors. The task is one of running a business represented by the mathematical model within the computer, but the emphasis is not on the task as such, not on the profit attained, but on the management problems associated with the task, and on the human interrelations that result.

The simulation takes place in quarters, with decisions being made at the beginning of quarters, and operating reports, prepared by the computer, distributed at the end of quarters. A history of the company is provided to the participants before they arrive at the Academy, together with the most current quarterly reports. A typical history states how the company started—in a Circleville, Ohio, garage in 1935—and how it grew, expanded to new areas, improved its products, and so forth. Today the hypothetical company manufactures and markets a "Gopher" and a "Midgit," and may develop additional products. Some reality is given to these products with regard to their general nature, but they are not identified with any particular industry.

The model is somewhat intermediate in size between the first generation aggregated games and the more complex UCLA and Carnegie Tech games. The simulated company has plants, sales regions, and a home office. It markets several products, some of which may be developed during the play through a research and development program. There are the usual problems of production scheduling, marketing policies (i.e., pricing, advertising, the number of salesmen to employ and what to pay them), purchasing, shipping, finance, and so forth. Altogether there are about seventy decisions which can be made for each quarter.

USE OF THE GMS IN ORGANIZATIONAL TRAINING

The accounting system has been specially designed to allow for a flexibility in the management organization structure. An average costing system of inventory evaluation is used, and all manufacturing costs, raw material costs, and corporate overhead costs find their way out to the sales regions so that individual profit and loss statements can be prepared for any product or any region. As such it permits a company to organize by product line, or by geographic location, or by function, or by any combination.

The GMS requires about fifteen participants to adequately operate one company—the complexity of the model and the pace of the decision periods were designed for about this level of participation. Many companies can be in operation simultaneously, each facing similar problems. There is no interaction between them. On the average, one year is simulated in a couple of hours, many "years" of operations taking place during the week. A method of job rotation has been introduced and each participant gets the opportunity to fill various positions.

It would be pleasant to discourse at length on the various non-computer aspects of the week at AMA; however, from the standpoint of training, the mathematical model (which was the author's primary responsibility when with the American Management Association) is of somewhat minor importance. The model without its environment is like an outboard motor without a boat. Briefings, planning sessions, critiques, and so forth are all of considerable importance, and the manner in which they are being handled is most impressive. There are also many projects or incidents completely unassociated with the profit and loss aspects of the model. The emphasis is always on humans, not on mathematics.

In order to allow additional feedback on less quantifiable aspects of performance, an "observer" role has been created. The physical setup includes one-way glass observation booths with earphones connected to microphones in the various company offices. In addition to verbal reporting at critique sessions, the observers could influence the profit and loss directly by feeding their judgments to the computer, based on the observation of non-quantifiable elements of company performance such as stated personnel policy, which in turn can directly affect, within the computer, such items as worker or salesman effectiveness.

The GMS model seems well suited to its needs. Discussions in critique sessions, which are usually not directed by the staff, center more often around management problems and management principles than around pricing or production policies. GMS is being used solely as an aid in management training. It does provide an example of the type of laboratory that one could use for studying management control systems. A footnote to this is that GMS has been used in the AMA Systems and Procedures Course, where the participants operate the company for a few years, then engage in a project session where procedures and controls are designed, and are then implemented in an additional few years of company operations.

Most business games are run in a somewhat similar manner. The participants represent new management taking over a going concern. The first problems they face are ones of organization, planning, and setting of policies. They have to decide on particular organization structure, assign individuals to specific positions, and designate the lines of authority. This is not just a question of drawing an organization chart—there are decisions to be made and individuals have to be designated to make them. There is a need for coordination, for controls, for communications. It is gratifying that in most games disorganization leads to poor performance, even to chaos. The pedagogical objective is to give practice in the application of organization principles, not to try to demonstrate the efficiency of a particular organizational scheme.

The organization chart that does emerge will usually be of some conventional hierarchical form. There will usually be a president and vice presidents, sales manager and plant manager, manager of research and development, of personnel and purchasing, controller, and so forth. One of the principles soon apparent is that the particular organization established must be suited to the task to be performed, and not merely something that looks good when drawn up by the company's art department. There is not much use in having a manager of research and development if the model does not include research and development. This is not a failing in the model, but a reinforcement of the realization that people organize to do something, not just to be organized. Thus an executive leaves his real-life company, replete with traditions, and its own way of doing things, and is faced with a new real-life-like situation. It is an exercise in the design of a management control system.

We should note again that the majority of games being used do not require very large teams and are not as useful for demonstrating organization principles as the second generation games discussed. All games do, however, produce a variety of problems in coordination and control, an example being the conflict between sales and production. There are problems of pricing, of scheduling, etc. There is a need to coordinate the hiring and training of manpower with company long-range objectives. There is the ever-present problem of cash flow. In every decision that is made there is a need for coordination and control.

Most games produce a large quantity of information in the form of reports and there are questions as to who gets what reports. In the newer games the information content can be as perplexing as in real life, and thus can be used to exercise the participants' system design abilities. Furthermore the games are dynamic, with new situations arising, perhaps the introduction of new products; and from time to time—just as in real life—management may decide to reorganize, or to overhaul the system.

We have then, in present-day business games, laboratories which could be used for research into management control principles. A great amount of data has been generated; however, nearly all games are being used almost exclusively for training purposes, and no research has been published. This situation will no doubt be altered for the Carnegie Tech and UCLA games.

MANAGEMENT CONTROL SYSTEM SIMULATION

Using business games as a laboratory for research into management control principles would be an example of what has previously been called Human System Simulation. This is also related to the type of work that has been done, or is being done, by such people as Bavelas, Guetzkow, Christie, Ackoff, and others through the observation of small task performing groups. In such work the groups are usually small, the tasks simple, and the experimental conditions well controlled—even here experimental design is a severe challenge. Controlled experimentation using business games with ten to twenty participants poses formidable problems. The amount of data to be collected and analyzed is in itself staggering.

The advantages and disadvantages of using human beings in the study of human behavior have often been discussed. An alternate approach is the construction of a completely computerized model. Experimenting with numbers inside a computer rather than human subjects inside a room offers many inducements, such as ease of control, reproducibility of results, and above all, the immense increase in speed. In the AMA GMS, a typical decision cycle would be about thirty minutes, with about twenty minutes spent on making decisions, and about ten minutes spent on processing them. Of this ten minutes only about two minutes are devoted to internal processing within the computer, the total ten minutes representing the interval from collection of decisions to distribution of reports. Thus, even with the comparatively slow speed of an IBM 650, the computer could run through several simulated years of operations while the humans are planning their decisions for just one quarter.

The primary challenge to a Symbolic System Simulation is the inclusion into the computer of certain aspects of human behavior. However, to study organization, communications, and control problems, one is not interested in individual behavior in its idiosyncratic sense, but in over-all sociological behavior. Certain individual characteristics can be included—e.g., the rate at which decisions can be made—and one might even develop managerial types, analogous to social types; but one would ignore the particular image—syndromes, neurotic or otherwise—and the myriad of interpersonal relationships which we know greatly affect real-life situations. It is hoped that there are fundamental management principles which are independent, except in unusual circumstances, of the particular personalities involved.

The social sciences offer a sufficient number of abstractions and generalizations that have been drawn in spite of the variety of the individual man. The search for general principles to guide the design of management control systems is too important to be put aside simply because of the difficulty of computerizing those aspects of the system that arise from human behavior. Furthermore, as machines continue their invasion into the field of decision making, the value of such an approach will increase.

A PRELIMINARY MODEL

As a first approach to the design of a Symbolic System Simulation to be used for research on management control systems it is helpful to make some arbitrary separations within the over-all model. We begin (see Figure VI-C-3) by assuming that within the total black box there are three smaller black boxes, which we shall label "control," "operations," and "environment." Each of these is a subsystem of the total system.

The operations subsystem is essentially a physical mechanism for performing a task. It could consist of business, military, or government organizations. As an example, let us think of a manufacturing organization. The operations subsystem would represent the flow of material, men, and money, which we might generalize here by the single term "material flow." The task is to take raw material, capital equipment, men, and money and to produce products and distribute them to the customers. It would be something similar to the UCLA, Carnegie Tech and AMA second generation game models already discussed.

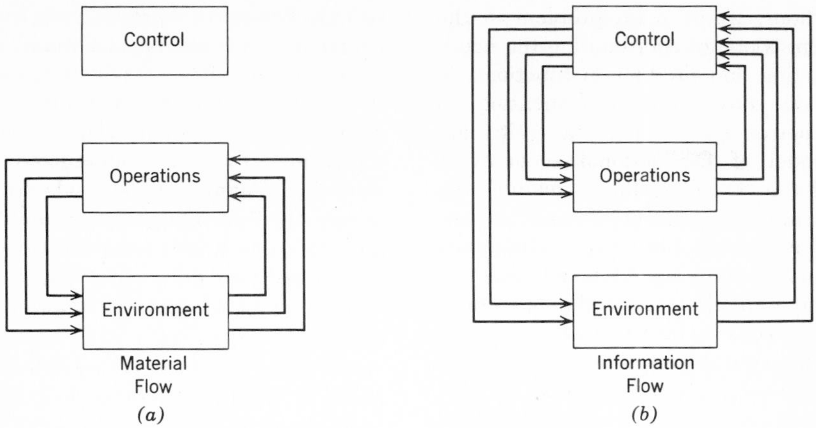

FIG. VI-C-3. Separation within the total model.

The control subsystem is the management control function, being made up primarily of decision making and information flow. We shall describe this subsystem in more detail in the next section. The environment represents those items external to the manufacturing company, such as the vendors of raw material, the customers, and the competitors, as well as the government, the over-all economy, the sources of funds, and so forth.

In Figure VI-C-3, we show first of all the separation of the over-all model into its three subsystems. We have further separated the material flow and the information flow. In item (*a*) we see the material—using the term in a very general sense to include such non-material items as financial credit and purchasing by consumers as well as such obvious items as raw material and labor supply—originating within the environment, being processed by the operations subsystem, and returned as products, as well, perhaps, as several less obvious items, to the environment. In item (*b*) we see information originating in the environment, such as raw material costs and general economic indices, together with information originating in the operations, such as stock reports and production costs; these are communicated to the management control subsystem, which in turn uses this information to arrive at certain decisions such as level of production, as well as certain information which may be thought of as being supplied to the environment, such as the sales price, which are communicated to the operations subsystem.

Before examining the inside structure of the various boxes shown in Figure VI-C-3 it is necessary to point out that in any model there can be various levels of detail, or of aggregation. As an example, consider customer demand. For certain questions it is adequate to provide, as input, random customer demands generated within the computer. In other cases one might wish to tie the demand to the company policies through somewhat aggregated functions, such as a price-demand curve, an advertising-demand curve, and so forth; this is essentially the method used in the AMA's General Management Simulation. In certain competitive-type business games an individual company's demands are dependent on the behavior of the other competing companies. In the UCLA TASK Manufacturing Company, detailed models—such as the "customer image" —have been constructed. If one is mainly interested in marketing problems then perhaps one has need for more details in the models of customers and competitors. If one is interested in inventory control, a simple aggregated demand function should prove adequate. The most desirable procedure is a modular one, where at the outset certain aggregated submodels are used, but when the need arises, they can be replaced by more detailed models.

In looking at management control systems, at least in those aspects which are mainly associated with the internal flow of information, and with internal controls, one would want the control subsystem to be quite detailed, the operations subsystem only moderately detailed, and the environment least detailed. This suggestion is predicated on certain types of research questions. If the main problem in the control system is one of coordinating the needs of the marketing and production functions, in such things as setting and implementing an inventory control policy, then a quite aggregated model of the national economy is adequate. If the control system is mainly concerned with pricing, long-range capital investment, or research and development, the model of the national economy would have to be more detailed. The same is true of the operations subsystem. It needs to be sufficiently complex to provide the control subsystem with realistic control problems, but it need not be so detailed as would be necessary, for instance, if one were studying job shop scheduling problems.

In a preliminary model the environment would provide merely some over-all economic factor which, coupled with a set of curves for price, advertising, and perhaps research and development, would yield a customer demand for each product. A price-demand curve implies both the behavior of the consumers and the existence of competitors; the curve can also change with time, representing, for example, price changes on the part of the competitors. The environment would also supply such items as the cost of raw material, the size of the labor market, etc.

An adequate operations subsystem might be that shown in Figure VI-C-4. This represents a manufacturing organization which produces and markets several products. In the particular model there would be one plant, and several sales regions. The products would require several raw materials, some of them shared by more than one product. The vendors would be represented by a very aggregated model (not shown in Figure VI-C-4) which would give merely the cost of the raw material, the maximum possible supply, and the time from placing an order to delivery of the material. This delivery time would be represented by a probability distribution.

The plant would have a raw material warehouse, a finished goods warehouse, and possibly, depending on the production mechanism used, one or more in-process warehouses. There is considerable variety in the type of production process that could be modeled. A simple scheme would have several production lines, each capable of handling only one product at a time, and each with its own flow rates, and so forth. Including a limited capacity, and production set-up time, the management control system would be faced with production scheduling problem. The plant would also have a work force, but perhaps only one class of workers. However, for costing purposes there could be provision for both direct and indirect labor costs, as well as supervision and management costs. Again we have an analogy here with several business games; on the other hand,

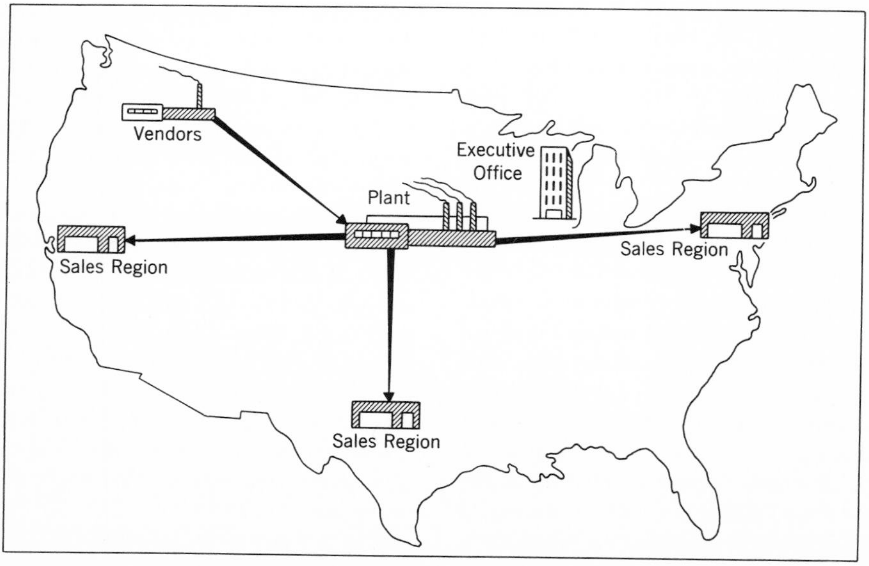

FIG. VI-C-4. An operations subsystem.

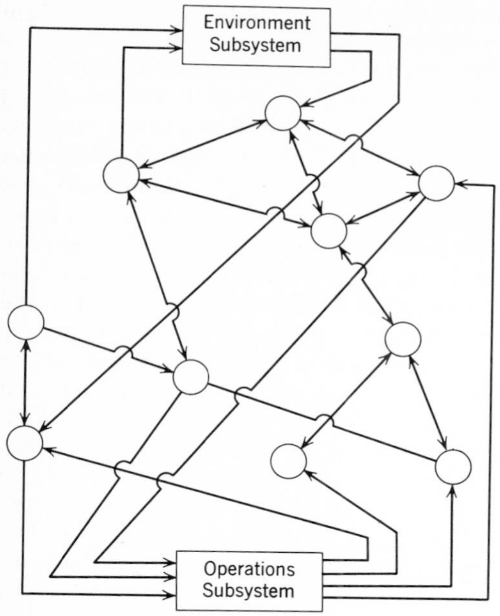

FIG. VI-C-5. The management control subsystem and a typical information flow.

the new UCLA game permits a distinct image for each individual worker, not only his capabilities, but also his desires.

Finished goods would be shipped directly from the finished goods warehouse at the plant to the warehouses in the sales regions. One would provide for perhaps a normal and expedited method of shipment; otherwise the transportation aspects of the model would be kept simple. Even the most simple model engenders adequate problems for the control system, there being the fundamental problem of inventory control as affected by warehouse costs, expected demand, and so forth.

In the sales regions one would have a certain number of salesmen, perhaps problems about the level of compensation, together with the usual marketing questions of price and advertising. There could be both local and national advertising; there could be local or national pricing. These are the types of problems that the management control system would face—there is not only a question of what price to set, which of course is very much tied to the environment model, but also the question of who is to set the price, when, on what basis, and how it is to be implemented.

THE MANAGEMENT CONTROL SUBSYSTEM

In Figure VI-C-5 we take a look inside the management control subsystem. The operations and environment subsystems are shown as black boxes, the remaining structure in the figure represents the inside of the box previously shown as the control subsystem. At the outset it is necessary to distinguish between the experimental variables, which represent those inputs provided by the staff research worker, and those inputs which are outputs from the other subsystems. The variables which are to be manipulated are primarily the organizational structure, the information flow network, and the decision rules. Figure VI-C-5 illustrates one possible information network with a particular set of rules. The management control subsystem takes information from the other subsystems, such as customer demands, stock status, and costs, and by means of decision rules provides the operations subsystem with such information as a production schedule, shipping orders, and sales price.

Within the other subsystems, there are also parameters which can be varied, such as costs, general economic condition, etc. The experimental plan is to study a particular management control system, observe its effect on over-all system performance, of which there are many measures in addition to the most common one of profit and loss, and to also test the sensitivity of the management control system to variations in the parameters within the other subsystems. One can then experiment with some other management control system. The schematic plan shown in Figure VI-C-5 is then merely one experimental setup. The model would allow complete flexibility in the choice of an information network.

For want of a better word, the circles shown in Figure VI-C-5 will be called "nodes." A node is any point at which information is received, processed, and transmitted. A node may be a man, a machine, or it could be a group of men acting as a committee. Although many straightforward data-processing tasks are now performed by computers, it is helpful in discussing this model to take an anthropomorphic view and assume that each node represents one human being.

From the internal structure of the model, as it would be programmed on a computer, there is a great similarity between what might be called data processing on the one hand and decision making on the other. We may, at least in this preliminary model, think of a decision maker as a man who takes certain information, such as customer demands and stock on hand, and, by the use of a decision rule, arrives at what might be called new information—such as the production level—it is information to the person who is informed of the decision. Structurally this is the same as a clerk or a computer adding up a column of numbers and arriving at a total. There are, of course, some important differences between decision making and data processing; two of these, as pointed out by Roger Sisson, are the difficulty of formulating the decision rules and the search for optimum ones. But if one is provided with a set of decision rules, then, within the model, the node acts like a data processor. This is obviously true for such decision rules as an inventory reordering rule; it becomes more questionable as one looks at what might be called higher order decisions.

DECISION MAKING AND INFORMATION FLOW

In a preliminary model one might provide the management control subsystem with only those decisions which are necessary for the operations subsystem directly, such as how many units of raw material to purchase, what production level to set, and so forth. One might call these, "operations decisions." At the next higher level of complication one might allow the management control system to make decisions affecting its own operations directly, such as the decision rule at one node changing the decision rule at another node, or automatically changing the information flow network: we might call these, "procedural decisions." As one examines the types of decisions made in the real world it is obvious that the operations decisions are only a small subset of all possible ones.

If one is interested in the decision maker *qua* decision maker a great amount of research and effort would have to go into the attempt to model him. However, certain questions about the management control system might be investigated with even a quite simplified model of the decision-making process. For this preliminary model let us assume that only operations decisions will be made by the management control subsystem.

Each node will have a certain amount of internal structure. A node will have several tasks to perform, be they simple data processing or decision making. Each of these tasks will take time and certain queuing problems will arise. In addition there will be various random tasks facing each node. The node will be able to communicate with other nodes, receiving and sending information, either in the form of reports, or as specific requests. In any particular scheme the nodes will take on the names of typical blocks in the organizational structure, as the plant manager, the president, the shipping clerk, the controller, the regional sales manager. The experimental scheme will consist in the assignment of tasks—just where do shipping orders originate and how are they implemented: perhaps the regional sales manager, based on his information as to stock status and past sales, sends an order directly to the shipping clerk, who immediately fills the order; perhaps the orders have to be cleared through a materials manager; perhaps the market research manager first supplies the regional manager with a sales forecast, or vice versa. The myriad problems of coordination, planning, and control are fairly obvious.

Associated with every information channel there would be time delays, costs, and random noise. There would be a choice of sending a report by a slower and cheaper medium, or a faster but more costly medium. The number of messages sent on a particular channel could be counted. As mentioned previously, the computer plays two roles: one part of the program is the model itself; another part monitors the operations and prints out that information which the staff wishes to analyze.

SOME MODELING CONSIDERATIONS

It should be noted that the simplified picture of the management control subsystem is a generalized one. In computer terminology it is somewhat analogous to a program compiler. Given a particular management organization—real or hypothetical—with its decision rules and information pattern, one manipulates the various parameters so as to achieve the applicable model.

Simplicity is not a too-well-defined word: an algebraic expression might be simple to look at, but complex to solve, and vice versa. A simulation model may be conceptually complex, but, as most people who have worked in the field continually stress, simplicity in the details is essential. Computers work fast, but not instantaneously. In designing models one is constantly faced with the problem: what to leave in and what to leave out. If the model is ever to be successfully programmed and run on a computer it is essential that it be kept simple. Fortunately, quite complicated behavior can result from the interaction of many simple elements.

There is no *a priori* reason to assume that complicated questions can only be answered using a complicated model, as is evidenced by much research that has been done in the physical sciences. There are a variety of techniques for combining initial simplicity with flexibility for expansion. For example, one can program for a polynomial function but begin by using only the linear terms, later, as part of sensitivity studies, introducing quadratic and higher order terms. A business game that used a linear price-demand curve exhibited quite real behavior. Thus one need not be delayed because of difficulties, such as the precise shape of a demand curve, in representing reality. One might expect to find certain management control principles which are independent of the shape of a particular curve; one might also be able to at least demonstrate those situations in which more precise knowledge is necessary.

Similar remarks can be made about random factors. While some stochastic elements are certainly essential, this does not mean that every factor in the model need be randomized. In one business game all random effects were eliminated, but, as one participant said, "Sales still seem damn random to me." Jigsaw puzzles can be tough even when one has all of the pieces at the outset. Since computer capacity and speed are always limited one should only introduce random factors when there is a clear understanding of their relationship to the activity being studied.

Symbolic System Simulation always requires the use of some basic time interval. The choice of that time interval presents problems: if it is small it might require too much computer time to cover an adequate total period and if it is large it might mask certain of the factors in which one is interested. Consider a manufacturing organization: Does one want to use simulated hours, days, weeks, months, or years? The answer of course depends on the questions to be asked. The same model cannot be used for all problems. In the preliminary model discussed here it seems fruitful to allow the operations subsystem to run in days—that is, all sales for a particular day are aggregated—and to allow the management control system, by means of a clock arrangement attached to each node, to proceed in minutes. In this latter case it does not mean that one would cycle through several hundred minutes each day, but that task times would be given in minutes, and that the clock would then indicate whether a particular node was free for its next task.

If the operations subsystem is carried forward in days then it is obvious that certain types of problems cannot be examined with this model, problems relating to long-range planning, to capital investment, to financing. The preliminary model would then be used to examine day-to-day type problems associated mainly with the flow of material through the system. One would use a different model, in which certain quantities were now aggregated, to examine the behavior of the control system under conditions of new product introduction, long-range economic factors, and so forth. One could use one over-all model in which, through parameter changes, certain components would be aggregated or not, though this is conceptually similar to having two models. A somewhat different approach would be to allow for two types of time intervals, a short and a long, and to use the short one to perform a sort of sampling experiment for the latter. That is, the model would proceed in detail for one month, then extrapolate the results for the remainder of the year. The next year conditions may have changed—perhaps a new product has been introduced—and again a month of operations is sampled. In the approach first mentioned, one has to supply the program with separate functions, those for short time intervals and those for long; in the second approach the computer, through simulation, arrives at its own functions for the larger time interval run.

CONCLUSION

Management control problems can be studied by means of simulation, either of the Human System type, which is similar to doing research on executives playing business games, or of the Symbolic System type, for which a preliminary model has been discussed here.

The Symbolic model presents many design problems, but it does avoid the complications inherent in experimentation with human subjects, and, above all, it offers the speed of modern computers.

Some scientific advances are made by starting with a particular hypothesis and designing an experiment to test it, but this is not the only approach. The existence of an adequate simulation model will help formulate the problems to be investigated, and the modeling process itself can lead to new insights. We can best conclude with a quotation from an article by Chapman, Kennedy, Newell, and Biel in the April, 1959, issue of *Management Science:* "A scientific investigation is not the cold-blooded, straight-forward, logical process that texts proclaim. It's an adventure. Sheer scientific excitement arises from the unexpected event, from the obvious assumption that's very wrong, from the hunch that pans out, from the sudden insight, and from the invention that covers the unanticipated procedural gap. The fact is that as organizations took form before our eyes, their struggle determined ours."

BIBLIOGRAPHY

Alberts, W. E., and D. G. Malcolm, *Report of the Second System Simulation Symposium,* American Institute of Industrial Engineers, February, 1959.

Arrow, Kenneth J., "Mathematical Models in the Social Sciences," *General Systems,* I, 1956, 29–47.

Bonini, Charles P., *Simulation of Information and Decision Systems in the Firm,* Prentice-Hall, Inc., 1963.

Buffa, Elwood S., *Operations Management,* John Wiley and Sons, 1968.

Buzzell, R. D., *Mathematical Models and Marketing Management,* Division of Research, Graduate School of Business Administration, Harvard University, 1964.

Charnes, A., and W. Cooper, *Management Models and Industrial Applications of Linear Programming,* John Wiley and Sons, 1961.

Chestnut, H., "Modelling and Simulation," *Electrical Engineering,* **81**, No. 8, 1962.

Chorafas, D. N., *Systems and Simulation,* Academic Press, 1965.

Churchman, C. West, Russell L. Ackoff, and E. L. Arnoff, *Introduction to Operations Research,* John Wiley and Sons, 1957.

———, and P. Ratoosh (eds.), *Measurement: Definitions and Theories,* John Wiley and Sons, 1959.

———, and Verhulst, *Management Sciences, Models and Techniques,* Pergamon Press, Inc., 1960.

Cyert, Richard M., and James G. March, *A Behavioral Theory of the Firm,* Prentice-Hall, Inc., 1963.

Emshoff, James R., and Roger L. Sisson, *Design and Use of Computer Simulation Models,* The Macmillan Co., 1970.

Forrester, J. W., *Industrial Dynamics,* John Wiley and Sons, 1961.

Goode, Harry H., and R. E. Machol, *System Engineering—An Introduction to the Design of Large Scale Systems,* McGraw-Hill Book Company, 1957.

Hare, Van Court, *Systems Analysis: A Diagnostic Approach,* Harcourt, Brace & World, Inc., 1967.

Hoggatt, Austin C., and Frederick E. Balderston (eds.), *Symposium on Simulation Models: Methodology and Applications to the Behavioral Sciences,* South-Western Publishing Co., 1963.

Hopeman, Richard J., *Systems Analysis and Operations Management,* Merrill Publishing Co., 1969.

Kibbee, Joel M., *Management Control Simulation,* Systems Development Corporation Report, SP-110, July, 1959.

Langhoff, Peter (ed.), *Models, Measurement and Marketing,* Prentice-Hall, Inc., 1965.

Malcolm, Donald G., "Systems Simulation—A Fundamental Tool for Industrial Engineering," *Journal of Industrial Engineering,* May-June, 1958.

———, A. J. Rowe, and L. F. McConnell (eds.), *Management Control Systems,* John Wiley and Sons, 1960.

McMillan, Claude, and Richard F. Gonzalez, *Systems Analysis—A Computer Approach to Decision Models,* Richard D. Irwin, Inc., 1968.

Morris, William T., "On the Art of Modeling," *Management Science,* August, 1967.

Naylor, Thomas H., et al., *Computer Simulation Techniques,* John Wiley and Sons, 1966.

Rosenblueth, Arturo, "The Role of Models in Science," *Philosophy Science,* **17**, 1950.

Rowe, Alan J., *Modeling Considerations in Computer Simulation of Management Control Systems,* SP-156, Systems Development Corporation, March, 1960.

Simon, Herbert A., *Models of Man,* John Wiley and Sons, 1957.

Tocher, K. D., *The Art of Simulation,* English Universities Press, 1963.

Part Two

MANAGEMENT INFORMATION SYSTEMS

SECTION I

INFORMATION TECHNOLOGY

Space-age technology has decidedly invaded the managerial field. Through the utilization of high-speed computers with their seemingly unlimited capabilities for instantaneous processing of vast amounts of data, the operating manager has been substantially aided in his decision-making process. The simple increase, however, in the quantity of data generated does not necessarily lead to more informed decisions. In fact, the very redundancy of inputs, and in some cases of outputs also, has led many a manager down the path of confusion. Some companies apparently operate under the erroneous assumption that the more data available to the manager, the better must be the decision reached. Even the continuous updating of information and the graphical and visual display of relevant data will not of themselves lead to better decisions. What is needed is an understanding of the type of information actually required by the decision maker at his own particular organizational level. It should be fairly obvious that even now information must still be carefully filtered at the various organizational levels just as was the case a decade or so ago when computers were first coming into use in the business world.

While increasing amounts of information can considerably aid middle managers in making decisions, the top echelon must still rely on intuitive judgment. This is not to gainsay the value of computers as well as the newer mathematical and statistical techniques now available for processing the mountains of data pertinent to scientific decision making. Electronic computers do enable top management to focus more attention on the data, but they have not rendered obsolete the time-honored managerial intuitive know-how. The reason, of course, is that the high level decisions are less susceptible to automation than are those made at lower managerial levels. Often the type of data collected and analyzed by the computer is of little value to top management precisely because these decisions do not rely solely or even mainly on the fund of computer-generated data but rather are based on historical data in the budgetary sense—for example, long-range planning as to products, competition, customers, service areas, and the like.

One can readily understand how the premise ("the more data the better the decision") may have come into vogue. Since the use of costly computers, which is currently the fad, must somehow be justified, there is a tendency to have them generate as much data as possible, irrespective of the utility or cost of the output. What underlies this faulty premise is the confusion as to what constitutes information.

In the past, information was identified with data, facts, news, and similar phenomena. This all-inclusive identification is definitely no longer serviceable in the computer age. Consequently, the distinction between data and information is a necessary prerequisite to any intelligible discussion of information technology or management information systems.

In the literature, various distinctions have been proposed but in the last analysis they all harken back to the original etymology of the terms used. Data, which is a term derived from the Latin verb, *do, dare,* meaning *to give,* is most fittingly applied to the *unstructured, uninformed* facts so copiously *given out* (spewed forth) by the computer. Information, however, is data that has form, structure, or organization. Derived from the Latin verb *informo, informare,* meaning *to give form to,* the term information etymologically connotes an imposition of organization on some indeterminate mass or substratum—the imparting of form that gives life and meaning to otherwise lifeless or irrelevant matter. It is most fittingly applied to all data that has been oriented to the user through some form of organization.

Two principal but related categories of distinctions can be repeatedly discovered in the available literature. One defines information as selected data for the decrease of ignorance or for the reduction in the amount or range of uncertainty surrounding a decision.[1] This distinction is a functional one. The prime function of informed data is to enable the decision maker to make an informed decision, one solidly based on *certain knowledge*. Whatever contributes to the diminution of ignorance or of uncertainty surrounding an impending decision merits the label of information. Information, therefore, ranges in value from a position in which it eliminates completely all ignorance and uncertainty surrounding a decision to a position in which it contributes absolutely nothing to the diminution of existing ignorance and uncertainty. From this standpoint it is rather obvious, therefore, that simply increasing the amount of data or facts does not of itself insure the generation of information.

The amount of information necessary for a particular individual in a decision-making situation will therefore be proportional to the amount of uncertainty initially surrounding the problem. The greater the uncertainty, the greater will be the amount of information necessary to reduce it. One can also view this topic from a probabilistic viewpoint. If the decision maker is practically certain as to which alternative he will decide on, then this choice would have a probability close to unity, while the other choices would approximate a zero probability. In many instances the assigning of some probability to particular choices or alternatives is necessary for the validity and utility of the information. For example, in a simulation model in which one of the factors is sales, some weighting would definitely be necessary for ascertaining the changes in demand.

A second distinction popular among current writers restricts the label of information to *evaluated data*. Here the orientation is not so much directed to the function of informed data as to the explicit and specific circumstances surrounding the user. Accordingly the term data is used to refer to materials that have not been evaluated for their worth in regard to a specified individual in a particular situation. Information refers to inferentially intended material evaluated for a particular problem, for a specified individual, at a specific time, and for the explicit purpose of achieving a definite goal.[2] Thus what constitutes information for one individual in a specific instance may not do so for another or even for the same individual at a different time or for a different problem. Information useful for one manager may well turn out to be totally devoid of value for another. Not only is the particular organizational level important but also the intended functional area. A production manager, for example, is typically unconcerned with sales analysis by product, territory, customer, and the like, while the one in charge of inventory control is little concerned with the conventional accounting reports that affect him only indirectly. To recapitulate, in the definition here being considered, information concerns *selected data*—data selected with respect to problem, user, time, and place.

All information must consequently be viewed as being imbued with merely relative value. Much of the so-called information utilized in management systems today enjoys a "sacred definiteness" that in reality is subject to wide ranges of both human and institutional errors. Valueless data has

[1] See Frederick A. Ekeblad, *The Statistical Method in Business* (New York: John Wiley & Sons, Inc., 1962), p. 37; also T. F. Schouten, "Ignorance, Knowledge, and Information," in Colin Cherry (ed.), *Information Theory* (New York: Academic Press, Inc., 1956), 37–47.

[2] Norton Bedford and Mohamed Onsi in "Measuring the Value of Information—An Information Theory Approach," *Management Services* (January-February, 1966), pp. 15–22, distinguish thus between data and information. Information is likewise distinguished from knowledge, which they regard as "evaluated data for general future use" in contradistinction to information, which is "evaluated data for a specific use." See also Adrian McDonough, *Information Economics and Management Systems* (New York: McGraw-Hill Book Co., 1963), Chapter 5.

in many instances been accepted as information simply because of an emotional investment on the part of the practitioners who have traditionally treated such data in their routine operations. Understanding and caution are therefore called for if the computer is not to add to the confusion already compounded.

It will be noticed that both of the above distinctions between information and data are predicated upon qualities extrinsic to the material under consideration. There is thus no intrinsic or objective distinction; all important is the external user, his present knowledge and degree of certainty, the particular problem with which he is faced, the specific situation that he finds himself in at the time, and the like. The subjective nature of information should therefore not be forgotten in the ensuing readings. Too often the computer is humanized to a degree in which it alone seems to carry the moral guilt for management's plight. Nothing could be less true. The computer-generated output is indifferent to information. The human user himself will decide.

Information theory's contribution to management information systems is of limited and dubious value.[3] Fundamentally its focus is on the capacity of information channels (as typified in the telegraph and telephone systems) to handle messages with the smallest probability of error. It is totally indifferent to the semantic significance of the communicated message. While it is undoubtedly true that the manager is interested in the computer's increasing capacity to handle company data without significant error, he is interested primarily in the semantic content of the data produced or derived. The application of information theory to management has, unfortunately, always been accompanied by a notable loss in precision and effectiveness.

[3] See Albert E. Hickey, Jr., "The Systems Approach: Can Engineers Use the Scientific Method?" *Transactions on Engineering Management* (June, 1960), pp. 76ff; also Wayne Boutell, *Computer-Oriented Business Systems* (Englewood Cliffs, N.J.: Prentice-Hall, Inc., 1968), Chapter 5.

In the first reading Russell Ackoff reveals the basic fallacies that underlay management's misinformation system. He demonstrates that managers suffer from a surfeit of irrelevant data rather than from a lack of relevant information; that because the manager does not know what he really needs for decision making, he plays it safe and asks for "everything"; that even were he supplied with all requisite information, the manager still could hardly be expected to exploit this information because of deficiencies and limitations in training, experience, and judgment; that only when organizational structure and performance measurement are taken into account will increased communication between managers result in improved organizational performance; and that lack of knowledge concerning the workings of the information system constitutes a sizeable handicap in evaluating and controlling the system.

Because managers suffer from an overabundance of irrelevant data, Ackoff proposes two processes to avert this condition: filtration and condensation. Filtration involves evaluation of data as to relevancy, while condensation involves curtailment of redundancy in the mass of otherwise relevant information. However, as Rappaport points out,[4] there must be some agreement on the useful limits to both processes. Indiscriminate filtration and overcondensation can lead to the other extreme, paucity of the information necessary for sound decision making. Overcondensation, though probably less frequent and more serious than overabundance of data, is difficult to set objective limits to, since the degree of uncertainty surrounding the decision maker is a subjective phenomenon unknown to others or since the quantity and quality of information needed by a particular decision maker in a specialized setting and working on a definite problem are generally unknown to the nondecision maker.

[4] Alfred Rappaport, "Management Misinformation Systems—Another Perspective," *Management Science,* 15 (December, 1968), pp. B-133 to 136.

The filtration process is no less problematic. Who should decide what is to be filtered out? If this filtering is done at the lower organizational levels, then the limited perspective of the men carrying out the evaluation is open to question; if done at the higher levels, then no relief from the overload is experienced. Somewhere in between overabundance and underabundance (overcondensation and overfiltration) lies the golden mean to be discovered by the top managers themselves.

The second and third points scored by Ackoff are reinforced in the reading by Churchman, viz., that managers generally do not even know what information they need for sound decision making, and even if they had the requisite information, no improvement in decision making would result therefrom. Churchman's experimental results lend support to these propositions. Managers do not make correct decision not because they lack sufficient information, not because they lack the necessary analysis, and not because they lack improved modes of communication. His negative conclusions lead him to believe that the researcher still does not know enough about how the manager decides where to direct his attention.

Rappaport questions Ackoff's assertion that improved communication between managers does not necessarily improve organizational performance. The example cited by Ackoff does not support this generalized proposition. It merely shows that communication among departments with conflicting measures of performance does not ameliorate organizational performance. One realizes, of course, that illustrations neither prove nor disprove a proposition.

Hardly anyone would argue against the preferability of the manager's knowing how a system works to his simply knowing how to use it. The crucial question arises: just how much knowledge of the system is necessary for a manager to have in order to be able to evaluate and control it rather than be controlled by it?

In the final section of his article, Ackoff suggests several procedures for designing a management information system.

In the third reading, Daniel points out that one of the consequences of the information explosion made possible by the electronic computer is the impact on organizational structure. After World War II, changes in organizational structure in the United States were precipitated by the tremendous growth, diversification, and international character of many corporations. However, the intimate linkage of information requirements with organizational structure has not always been acknowledged. Reorganization was not always followed up by a revamping of the information system. This failure may have been due to a basic misunderstanding of the nature of information required by managerial decision makers.

The type of information needed by managers must be related to their planning and control functions. The planning function is concerned with the setting up of realistic goals or objectives, with the formulation of alternative strategies for realizing the objectives, and with the determination of a particular choice of action from among the many alternatives possible. For this purpose, environmental information relating to population composition, labor force, transportation, price levels, and foreign trade is necessary; information concerning one's competitors in the field must be systematically gathered; and necessary quantitative and nonquantitative internal information must be amassed. The control function of the manager is concerned with measuring performance, with isolating variances that develop, and with necessary replanning. Quite different in nature is the information suited for the control role of the manager.

Johnson and Derman, in the final reading, take up where Daniel left off. It is the top executives who come in for special attention. Because of the differences in the need for facts at various levels, the management information system has rarely been designed to satisfy the requirements of upper management. Top-management planners need of a type of information different from that of lower and even middle management. Upper managers need to be informed of the threats, opportunities, risks, future resource requirements, economic and technological sources, investment-payoff criteria, and techniques for evaluation. A total management information system that would collect, process, and convert this type of data into information suitable for goal setting, and strategy determination by top management would indeed be expensive. However, when weighed against the cost of maintaining the present inadequate information system and the value of such information in terms of one's competitive advantage, the investment may well be justified.

An interesting array of information sources for both middle and top management is presented in this selection. If these diverse classes of information were incorporated into the present data base, the operational capabilities of the computer system would certainly be upgraded and the gap between organizational failure and success would be surprisingly narrowed.

15. MANAGEMENT MISINFORMATION SYSTEMS

Russell E. Ackoff*

Five assumptions commonly made by designers of management information systems are identified. It is argued that these are not justified in many (if not most) cases and hence lead to major deficiencies in the resulting systems. These assumptions are: (1) the critical deficiency under which most managers operate is the lack of relevant information, (2) the manager needs the information he wants, (3) if a manager has the information he needs his decision making will improve, (4) better communication between managers improves organizational performance, and (5) a manager does not have to understand how his information system works, only how to use it. To overcome these assumptions and the deficiencies which result from them, a management information system should be imbedded in a management control system. A procedure for designing such a system is proposed and an example is given of the type of control system which it produces.

The growing preoccupation of operations researchers and management scientists with Management Information Systems (MIS's) is apparent. In fact, for some the design of such systems has almost become synonymous with operations research or management science. Enthusiasm for such systems is understandable: it involves the researcher in a romantic relationship with the most glamorous instrument of our time, the computer. Such enthusiasm is understandable but, nevertheless, some of the excesses to which it has led are not excusable.

Contrary to the impression produced by the growing literature, few computerized management information systems have been put into operation. Of those I've seen that have been implemented, most have not matched expectations and some have been outright failures. I believe that these near- and far-misses could have been avoided if certain false (and usually implicit) assumptions on which many such systems have been erected had not been made.

There seem to be five common and erroneous assumptions underlying the design of most MIS's, each of which I will consider. After doing so I will outline an MIS design procedure which avoids these assumptions.

SOURCE: From *Management Science* (December, 1967), pp. 147–156. Reprinted by permission of the Institute of Management Science.

* University of Pennsylvania.

GIVE THEM MORE

Most MIS's are designed on the assumption that the critical deficiency under which most managers operate is the *lack of relevant information*. I do not deny that most managers lack a good deal of information that they should have, but I do deny that this is the most important informational deficiency from which they suffer. It seems to me that they suffer more from an *over abundance of irrelevant information*.

This is not a play on words. The consequences of changing the emphasis of an MIS from supplying relevant information to eliminating irrelevant information is considerable. If one is preoccupied with supplying relevant information, attention is almost exclusively given to the generation, storage, and retrieval of information: hence emphasis is placed on constructing data banks, coding, indexing, updating files, access languages, and so on. The ideal which has emerged from this orientation is an infinite pool of data into which a manager can reach to pull out any information he wants. If, on the other hand, one sees the manager's information problem primarily, but not exclusively, as one that arises out of an overabundance of irrelevant information, most of which was not asked for, then the two most important functions of an information system become *filtration* (or evaluation) and *condensation*. The literature on MIS's seldom refers to these functions let alone considers how to carry them out.

My experience indicates that most managers receive more data (if not information) than they can possibly absorb even if they spend all of their time trying to do so. Hence they already suffer from an information overload. They must spend a great deal of time separating the relevant from the irrelevant and searching for the kernels in the relevant documents. For example, I have found that I receive an average of forty-three hours of unsolicited reading material each week. The solicited material is usually half again this amount.

I have seen a daily stock status report that consists of approximately six hundred pages of computer print-out. The report is circulated daily across managers' desks. I've also seen requests for major capital expenditures that come in book size, several of which are distributed to managers each week. It is not uncommon for many managers to receive an average of one journal a day or more. One could go on and on.

Unless the information overload to which managers are subjected is reduced, any additional information made available by an MIS cannot be expected to be used effectively.

Even relevant documents have too much redundancy. Most documents can be considerably condensed without loss of content. My point here is best made, perhaps, by describing briefly an experiment that a few of my colleagues and I conducted on the OR literature several years ago. By using a panel of well-known experts we identified four OR articles that all members of the panel considered to be "above average," and four articles that were considered to be "below average." The authors of the eight articles were asked to prepare "objective" examinations (duration thirty minutes) plus answers for graduate students who were to be assigned the articles for reading. (The authors were not informed about the experiment.) Then several experienced writers were asked to reduce each article to ⅔ and ⅓ of its original length only by eliminating words. They also prepared a brief abstract of each article. Those who did the condensing did not see the examinations to be given to the students.

A group of graduate students who had not previously read the articles were then selected. Each one was given four articles randomly selected, each of which was in one of its four versions: 100%, 67%, 33%, or abstract. Each version of each article was read by two students. All were given the same examinations. The average scores on the examinations were then compared.

For the above-average articles there was no significant difference between average test scores for the 100%, 67%, and 33% versions, but there was a significant decrease in average test scores for those who had read only the abstract. For the below-average articles there was no difference in average test scores among those who had read the 100%, 67%, and 33% versions, but there was a significant *increase* in average test scores of those who had read only the abstract.

The sample used was obviously too small for general conclusions but the results strongly indicate the extent to which even good writing can be condensed without loss of information. I refrain from drawing the obvious conclusion about bad writing.

It seems clear that condensation as well as filtration, performed mechanically or otherwise, should be an essential part of an MIS, and that such a system should be capable of handling much, if not all, of the unsolicited as well as solicited information that a manager receives.

THE MANAGER NEEDS THE INFORMATION THAT HE WANTS

Most MIS designers "determine" what information is needed by asking managers what information they would like to have. This is based on the assumption that managers know what information they need and want it.

For a manager to know what information he needs he must be aware of each type of decision he should make (as well as does) and he must have an adequate model of each. These conditions are seldom satisfied. Most managers have some conception of at least some of the types of decisions they must make. Their conceptions, however, are likely to be deficient in a very critical way, a way that follows from an important principle of scientific economy: the less we understand a phenomenon, the more variables we require to explain it. Hence, the manager who does not understand the phenomenon he controls plays it "safe" and, with respect to information, wants "everything." The MIS designer, who has even less understanding of the relevant phenomenon than the manager, tries to provide even more than everything. He thereby increases what is already an overload of irrelevant information.

For example, market researchers in a major oil company once asked their marketing managers what variables they thought were relevant in estimating the sales volume of future service stations. Almost seventy variables were identified. The market researchers then added about half again this many variables and performed a large multiple linear regression analysis of sales of existing stations against these variables and found about thirty-five to be statistically significant. A forecasting equation was based on this analysis. An OR team subsequently constructed a model based on only one of these variables, traffic flow, which predicted sales better than the thirty-five variable regression equation. The team went on to *explain* sales at service stations in terms of the customers' perception of the amount of time lost by stopping for service. The relevance of all but a few of the variables used by the market researchers could be explained by their effect on such perception.

The moral is simple: one cannot specify what information is required for decision making until an explanatory model of the decision process and the system involved has been constructed and tested. Information systems are subsystems of control systems. They cannot be designed adequately without taking control in account. Furthermore, whatever else regression analyses can yield, they cannot yield understanding and explanation of phenomena. They describe and, at best, predict.

GIVE A MANAGER THE INFORMATION HE NEEDS AND HIS DECISION MAKING WILL IMPROVE

It is frequently assumed that if a manager is provided with the information he needs, he will then have no problem in using it effectively. The history of OR stands to the contrary. For example, give most managers an initial tableau of a typical "real" mathematical programming, sequencing, or network problem and see how close they come to an optimal solution. If their experience and judgment have any value they may not do badly, but they will seldom do very well. In most management problems there are too many possibilities to expect experience, judgment, or intuition to provide good guesses, even with perfect information.

Furthermore, when several probabilities are involved in a problem the unguided mind of even a manager has difficulty in aggregating them in a valid way. We all know many simple problems in probability in which untutored intuition usually does very badly (e.g., What are the correct odds that 2 of 25 people selected at random will have their birthdays on the same day of the year?). For example, very few of the results obtained by queuing theory, when arrivals and service are probabilistic, are obvious to managers; nor are the results of risk analysis where the managers' own subjective estimates of probabilities are used.

The moral: it is necessary to determine how well managers can use needed information. When, because of the complexity of the decision process, they can't use it well, they should be provided with either decision rules or performance feed-back so that they can identify and learn from their mistakes. More on this point later.

MORE COMMUNICATION MEANS BETTER PERFORMANCE

One characteristic of most MIS's which I have seen is that they provide managers with better current information about what other managers and their departments and divisions are doing. Underlying this provision is the belief that better interdepartmental communication enables managers to coordinate their decisions more effectively and hence improves the organization's overall performance. Not only is this not necessarily so, but it seldom is so. One would hardly expect two competing companies to become more cooperative because the information each acquires about the other is improved. This analogy is not as far fetched as one might first suppose. For example, consider the following very much simplified version of a situation I once ran into. The simplification of the case does not affect any of its essential characteristics.

A department store has two "line" operations: buying and selling. Each function is performed by a separate department. The Purchasing Department primarily controls one variable: how much of each item is bought. The Merchandising Department controls the price at which it is sold. Typically, the measure of performance applied to the Purchasing Department was the turnover rate of inventory. The measure applied to the Merchandising Department was gross sales; this department sought to maximize the number of items sold times their price.

Now by examining a single item let us consider what happens in this system. The merchandising manager, using his knowledge of competition and consumption, set a price which he judged would maximize gross sales. In doing so he utilized price-demand curves for each type of item. For each price the curves show the expected sales and values on an upper and lower confidence band as well. (See Figure 1.) When instructing the Pur-

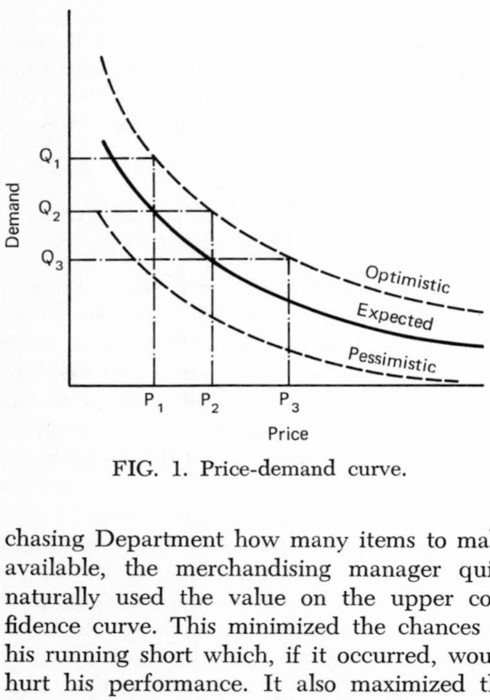

FIG. 1. Price-demand curve.

chasing Department how many items to make available, the merchandising manager quite naturally used the value on the upper confidence curve. This minimized the chances of his running short which, if it occurred, would hurt his performance. It also maximized the chances of being over-stocked but this was not his concern, only the purchasing manager's. Say, therefore, that the merchandising manager initially selected price P_1 and requested that amount Q_1 be made available by the Purchasing Department.

In this company the purchasing manager also had access to the price-demand curves. He knew the merchandising manager always ordered optimistically. Therefore, using the same curve he read over from Q_1 to the upper limit and down to the expected value from which he obtained Q_2, the quantity he actually intended to make available. He did not intend to pay for the merchandising manager's optimism. If merchandising ran out of stock, it was not his worry. Now the merchandising manager was informed about what the purchasing manager had done so he adjusted his price to P_2. The purchasing manager in turn was told that the merchandising manager had made this readjustment so he planned to make only Q_3 available. If this process—made possible only by perfect communication between departments—had been allowed to continue, nothing would have been bought and nothing would have been sold. This outcome was avoided by prohibiting communication between the two departments and forcing each to guess what the other was doing.

I have obviously caricatured the situation in order to make the point clear: when organizational units have inappropriate measures of performance which put them in conflict with each other, as is often the case, communication between them may hurt organizational performance, not help it. Organizational structure and performance measurement must be taken into account before opening the flood gates and permitting the free flow of information between parts of the organization. (A more rigorous discussion of organizational structure and the relationship of communication to it can be found in [1].)

A MANAGER DOES NOT HAVE TO UNDERSTAND HOW AN INFORMATION SYSTEM WORKS, ONLY HOW TO USE IT

Most MIS designers seek to make their systems as innocuous and unobtrusive as possible to managers lest they become frightened. The designers try to provide managers with very easy access to the system and assure them that they need to know nothing more about it. The designers usually succeed in keeping managers ignorant in this regard. This leaves managers unable to evaluate the MIS as a whole. It often makes them afraid to even try to do so lest they display their ignorance publicly. In failing to evaluate their MIS, managers delegate much of the control of the organization to the system's designers and operators who may have many virtues, but managerial competence is seldom among them.

Let me cite a case in point. A Chairman of

a Board of a medium-size company asked for help on the following problem. One of his larger (decentralized) divisions had installed a computerized production-inventory control and manufacturing-manager information system about a year earlier. It had acquired about $2,000,000 worth of equipment to do so. The Board Chairman had just received a request from the Division for permission to replace the original equipment with newly announced equipment which would cost several times the original amount. An extensive "justification" for so doing was provided with the request. The Chairman wanted to know whether the request was really justified. He admitted to complete incompetence in this connection.

A meeting was arranged at the Division at which I was subjected to an extended and detailed briefing. The system was large but relatively simple. At the heart of it was a reorder point for each item and a maximum allowable stock level. Reorder quantities took lead-time as well as the allowable maximum into account. The computer kept track of stock, ordered items when required and generated numerous reports on both the state of the system it controlled and its own "actions."

When the briefing was over I was asked if I had any questions. I did. First I asked if, when the system had been installed, there had been many parts whose stock level exceeded the maximum amount possible under the new system. I was told there were many. I asked for a list of about thirty and for some graph paper. Both were provided. With the help of the system designer and volumes of old daily reports I began to plot the stock level of the first listed item over time. When this item reached the maximum "allowable" stock level, it had been reordered. The system designer was surprised and said that by sheer "luck" I had found one of the few errors made by the system. Continued plotting showed that because of repeated premature reordering the item had never gone much below the maximum stock level. Clearly the program was confusing the maximum allowable stock level and the reorder point. This turned out to be the case in more than half of the items on the list.

Next I asked if they had many paired parts, ones that were only used with each other; for example, matched nuts and bolts. They had many. A list was produced and we began checking the previous day's withdrawals. For more than half of the pairs the differences in the numbers recorded as withdrawn were very large. No explanation was provided.

Before the day was out it was possible to show by some quick and dirty calculations that the new computerized system was costing the company almost $150,000 per month more than the hand system which it had replaced, most of this in excess inventories.

The recommendation was that the system be redesigned as quickly as possible and that the new equipment not be authorized for the time being.

The questions asked of the system had been obvious and simple ones. Managers should have been able to ask them but—and this is the point—they felt themselves incompetent to do so. They would not have allowed a hand-operated system to get so far out of their control.

No MIS should ever be installed unless the managers for whom it is intended are trained to evaluate and hence control it rather than be controlled by it.

A SUGGESTED PROCEDURE FOR DESIGNING AN MIS

The erroneous assumptions I have tried to reveal in the preceding discussion can, I believe, be avoided by an appropriate design procedure. One is briefly outlined here.

1. Analysis of the Decision System

Each (or at least each important) type of managerial decision required by the organization under study should be identified and the relationships between them should be determined and flow-charted. Note that this is *not* necessarily the same thing as determining what decisions *are* made. For example, in one company I found that make-or-buy decisions concerning parts were made only at the time when a part was introduced into stock and was never subsequently reviewed. For some items this decision had gone unreviewed for as many as twenty years. Obviously, such decisions should be made more often; in some cases, every time an order is placed in order to take account of current shop loading, underused shifts, delivery times from suppliers, and so on.

Decision-flow analyses are usually self-justifying. They often reveal important decisions that are being made by default (e.g., the make-buy decision referred to above), and they disclose interdependent decisions that are being made independently. Decision-flow charts frequently suggest changes in managerial responsibility, organizational structure, and measure of performance which can correct the types of deficiencies cited.

Decision analyses can be conducted with varying degrees of detail, that is, they may be anywhere from coarse to fine grained. How much detail one should become involved with depends on the amount of time and resources that are available for the analysis. Although practical considerations frequently restrict initial analyses to a particular organizational function, it is preferable to perform a coarse analysis of all of an organization's managerial functions rather than a fine analysis of one or a subset of functions. It is easier to introduce finer information into an integrated information system than it is to combine fine subsystems into one integrated system.

2. *An Analysis of Information Requirements*

Managerial decisions can be classified into three types:

(a) Decisions for which adequate models are available or can be constructed and from which optimal (or near optimal) solutions can be derived. In such cases the decision process itself should be incorporated into the information system thereby converting it (at least partially) to a control system. A decision model identifies what information is required and hence what information is relevant.

(b) Decisions for which adequate models can be constructed but from which optimal solutions cannot be extracted. Here some kind of heuristic or search procedure should be provided even if it consists of no more than computerized trial and error. A simulation of the model will, as a minimum, permit comparison of proposed alternative solutions. Here too the model specifies what information is required.

(c) Decisions for which adequate models cannot be constructed. Research is required here to determine what information is relevant. If decision making cannot be delayed for the completion of such research or the decision's effect is not large enough to justify the cost of research, then judgment must be used to "guess" what information is relevant. It may be possible to make explicit the implicit model used by the decision maker and treat it as a model of type (b).

In each of these three types of situation it is necessary to provide feedback by comparing actual decision outcomes with those predicted by the model or decision maker. Each decision that is made, along with its predicted outcome, should be an essential input to a management control system. I shall return to this point below.

3. *Aggregation of Decisions*

Decisions with the same or largely overlapping informational requirements should be grouped together as a single manager's task. This will reduce the information a manager requires to do his job and is likely to increase his understanding of it. This may require a reorganization of the system. Even if such a reorganization cannot be implemented completely what can be done is likely to improve performance significantly and reduce the information loaded on managers.

4. *Design of Information Processing*

Now the procedure for collecting, storing, retrieving, and treating information can be designed. Since there is a voluminous literature on this subject I shall leave it at this except for one point. Such a system must not only be able to answer questions addressed to it; it should also be able to answer questions that have not been asked by reporting any deviations from expectations. An extensive exception-reporting system is required.

5. *Design of Control of the Control System*

It must be assumed that the system that is being designed will be deficient in many and significant ways. Therefore it is necessary to identify the ways in which it may be deficient, to design procedures for detecting its deficiencies, and for correcting the system so as to remove or reduce them. Hence the system should be designed to be flexible and adaptive. This is little more than a platitude, but it has a not-so-obvious implication. No completely computerized system can be as flexible and adaptive as can a man-machine system. This is illustrated by a concluding example of a system that is being developed and is partially in operation. (See Figure 2.)

The company involved has its market divided into approximately two hundred marketing areas. A model for each has been constructed as is "in" the computer. On the basis of competitive intelligence supplied to the service marketing manager by marketing researchers and information specialists he and his staff make policy decisions for each area each month. Their tentative decisions are fed into the computer which yields a forecast of expected performance. Changes are made until the expectations match what is desired. In this way they arrive at "final" decisions. At the end of the month the computer compares the actual performance of each area with what was predicted. If a deviation exceeds what could be expected by chance, the company's OR Group then seeks the reason for the deviation, performing as much research as is required to find it. If the cause is found to be permanent, the computerized model is adjusted appropriately. The result is an adaptive man-machine system whose precision and generality is continuously increasing with use.

Finally it should be noted that in carrying out the design steps enumerated above, three groups should collaborate: information systems specialists, operations researchers, *and managers*. The participation of managers in the design of a system that is to serve them, assures their ability to evaluate its performance by comparing its output with what was predicted. Managers who are not willing to invest some of their time in this process are not likely to use a management control system well, and their system, in turn, is likely to abuse them.

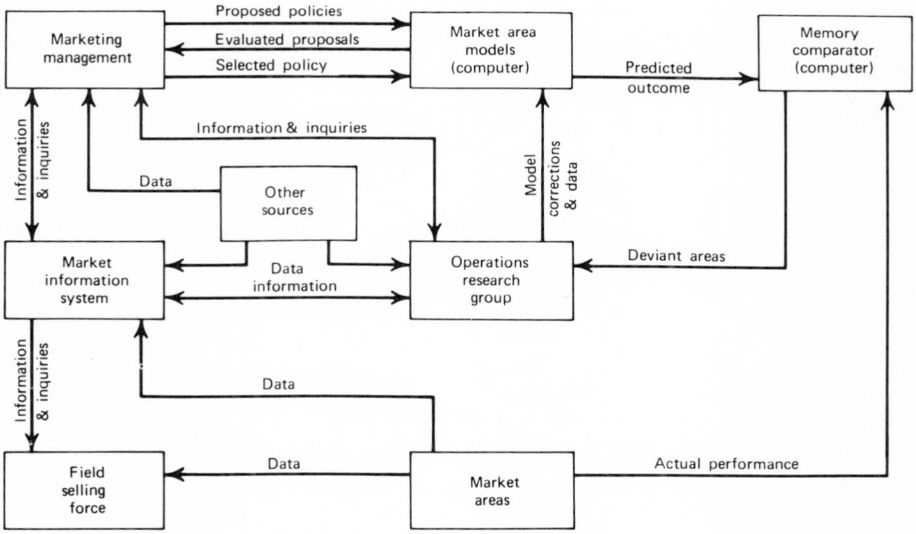

FIG. 2. Simplified diagram of a market-area control system.

REFERENCE

1. Sengupta, S. S., and Ackoff, R. L., "Systems Theory from an Operations Research Point of View," *IEEE Transactions on Systems Science and Cybernetics,* Vol. 1 (Nov. 1965), pp. 9–13.

16. MANAGEMENT INFORMATION CRISIS

D. Ronald Daniel *

In late 1960 a large defense contractor became concerned over a major project that was slipping badly. After 15 months costs were running far above the estimate and the job was behind schedule. A top-level executive, assigned as program manager to salvage the project, found he had no way of pinpointing what parts of the system were causing the trouble, why costs were so high, and which subcontractors were not performing.

Recently an American electronics company revamped its organization structure. To compete more aggressively in international markets, management appointed "area managers" with operating responsibility—e.g., in Latin America, Western Europe, and the Far East. After nine months it was apparent that the new plan was not coming up to expectations. On checking with three newly created area managers, the company president heard each say, in effect:

- "In half of the countries in my area the political situation is in flux, and I can't anticipate what's going to happen next."
- "I'm still trying to find out whether our operating costs in Austria are reasonable."
- "I don't know where in South America we're making a profit."

A small but highly successful consumer products company recently followed the lead of its larger competitors by establishing product-manager positions. Although outstanding men were placed in the new jobs, an air of general confusion soon developed, and the product managers began to show signs of frustration. After much study it became apparent that an important cause of the trouble was that no one had determined what kind of information the product managers would need in order to perform their new functions.

In retrospect it is obvious that these three companies were plagued by a common problem: inadequate management information. The data were inadequate, not in the sense of there not being enough, but in terms of relevancy for setting objectives, for shaping alternative strategies, for making decisions, and for measuring results against planned goals.

ASSESSING THE GAP

In each company the origin of the problem lay in the gap between a static information system and a changing organization structure. This difficulty is not new or uncommon. There is hardly a major company in the United States whose plan of organization has not been changed and rechanged since World War II. And with revised structures have come new jobs, new responsibilities, new decision-making authorities, and reshaped reporting relationships. All of these factors combine to create new demands for information—information that is usually missing in existing systems. As a result, many leading companies are suffering a major information crisis—often without fully realizing it.

Far-Reaching Trends

Some idea of the scope of this problem can be gained by reviewing the intensity of the three major causes of recent organization changes in American business:

Growth. Since 1945 the Gross National Product has risen 135%. In specific industries the growth rate has been even greater. Plastic production, for example, tripled between 1948 and 1958; electronics sales nearly quadrupled in the decade from 1950 to 1960. Many individual companies have shown even more startling growth. This growth, in turn, has fostered organizational change:

SOURCE: *Harvard Business Review* (September–October, 1961), pp. 111–121. Reprinted by permission of *Harvard Business Review*.

* McKinsey & Company, Inc.

• Divisions have been created and decentralization has been encouraged.

• Greater precision in defining line-staff relationships has been necessitated.

• Organization structures that were once adequate for $50-million businesses have proved unworkable for $500-million enterprises.

Diversification. Merger and acquisition have accounted for the growth of many large organizations. For these companies, the task of finding, evaluating, and consummating diversification deals—and assimilating newly acquired products and businesses—has required continuous organizational adjustment. Some corporations have diversified by developing new product lines to satisfy shifting market requirements; some have used other means. But always the effect has been the same: different organization structures for parts of or perhaps for the entire enterprise.

International Operations. There has been a threefold increase in the value of United States investments abroad since World War II. Major companies that once regarded foreign markets as minor sources of incremental profits, or as markets for surplus production, now look overseas for the bulk of their future profits and growth. They are setting up manufacturing and research as well as marketing organizations in foreign countries. Consequently, we are growing used to seeing a company's "export department" evolve into the "international division," and national companies grow into world-wide enterprises.[1] All this calls for extensive modifications of organization structure.

The impact of any one of the above factors alone would be sufficient to create great change in an enterprise, but consider that in many cases at least two, and sometimes all three, have been at work. It is easy to see why so many company organization structures do become unstable and how this creates a management information problem large enough to hamper some firms and nearly paralyze others.

Linking Systems and Needs

Organization structure and information requirements are inextricably linked. In order to translate a statement of his duties into action, an executive must receive and use information. Information in this case is not just the accounting system and the forms and reports it produces. It includes *all* the data and intelligence —financial and nonfinancial—that are really needed to plan, operate, and control a particular enterprise. This embraces external information such as economic and political factors and data on competitive activity.

When viewed in this light, the impact of organization structure on needs for management information becomes apparent. The trouble is that in most companies it is virtually taken for granted that the information necessary for performance of a manager's duties flows naturally to the job. To a certain extent this is so. For example, internally generated information—especially accounting information—does tend to flow easily to the job or can be made to do so. Also, in companies doing business in only one industry and having a small, closely knit management group much vital interdepartmental and general information is conveyed by frequent face-to-face contact and coordination among executives. Economic and competitive information from outside is similarly transmitted, the bulk of it coming into the concern informally. Further, through trade contacts, general reading, and occasional special studies, executives toss bits of information into the common pool and draw from it as well.

The point is, however, that while such an informal system can work well for small and medium-size companies in simple and relatively static industries, it becomes inadequate when companies grow larger and especially when they spread over several industries, areas, and countries. At this point, most large companies have found that information has to be conveyed in a formal manner and less and less through direct observation.

Unfortunately, management often loses sight of the seemingly obvious and simple relationship between organization structure and information needs. Companies very seldom follow up on reorganizations with penetrating reappraisals of their information systems, and managers given new responsibilities and decision-making authority often do not receive all the information they require.

[1] See Gilbert H. Clee and Alfred di Scipio, "Creating a *World* Enterprise," *HBR,* November–December 1959, p. 77.

Causes of Confusion

The cornerstone for building a compact, useful management information system is the determination of each executive's information needs. This requires a clear grasp of the individual's role in the organization—his responsibilities, his authorities, and his relationships with other executives. The task is then to—

- Design a network of procedures that will process raw data in such a way as to generate the information required for management use.
- Implement such procedures in actual practice.

Such action steps, while demanding and time-consuming, have proved to be far less difficult than the creative and conceptual first step of defining information requirements. Seldom is the open approach of asking an executive what information he requires successful. For one thing, he may find it difficult to be articulate because the organization structure of his company is not clearly defined.

Further, and more important, there is a widespread tendency among operating executives to think of information exclusively in terms of their companies' accounting systems and the reports thus generated. This way of thinking can be a serious deterrent because:

1. Many conventional accounting reports cause confusion in the minds of nonfinancially trained executives. Take, for example, the profit-and-loss statement, with its arbitrary treatment of inventories, depreciation, allocated overhead expenses, and the like, or the statistical sales report, which is often a 40-page, untitled, machine-prepared tabulation of sales to individual customers. Such reports have made an indelible impression on managers' thinking, coloring their understanding and expectations of reports in general.

2. By its very nature traditional accounting fails to highlight many important aspects of business operations. Accounting systems often are designed primarily to meet SEC, Internal Revenue, and other statutory requirements—requirements that, more often than not, fail to correspond to management's information needs. Accounting describes the past in dollars, usually without discriminating between the critical and noncritical elements of a business—the elements that control competitive success in a particular industry and the elements that do not.

3. Accounting reports generally describe what has happened inside a company. Just consider what this approach omits:

- Information about the future.
- Data expressed in nonfinancial terms—e.g., share of market, productivity, quality levels, adequacy of customer service, and so on.
- Information dealing with external conditions as they might bear on a particular company's operations.

Yet all of these items are essential to the intelligent managing of a business.

PLANNING NEEDS DEFINED

The key to the development of a dynamic and usable system of management information is to move beyond the limits of classical accounting reports and to conceive of information as it relates to two vital elements of the management process—planning and control. In the pages to follow I shall focus largely on the planning aspect.

We hear more and more these days about new techniques for inventory, cost, and other types of control, but information systems for business planning still represent a relatively unexplored horizon.

Planning, as used in this article, means: setting objectives, formulating strategy, and deciding among alternative investments or courses of action. This definition can be applied to an entire company, an integrated division, or a single operating department.

As Exhibit I shows, the information required to do planning of this kind is of three basic types:

1. *Environmental information.* Describes the social, political, and economic aspects of the climate in which a business operates or may operate in the future.
2. *Competitive information.* Explains the past performance, programs, and plans of competing companies.
3. *Internal information.* Indicates a company's own strengths and weaknesses.

Now let us consider each of these categories in some detail.

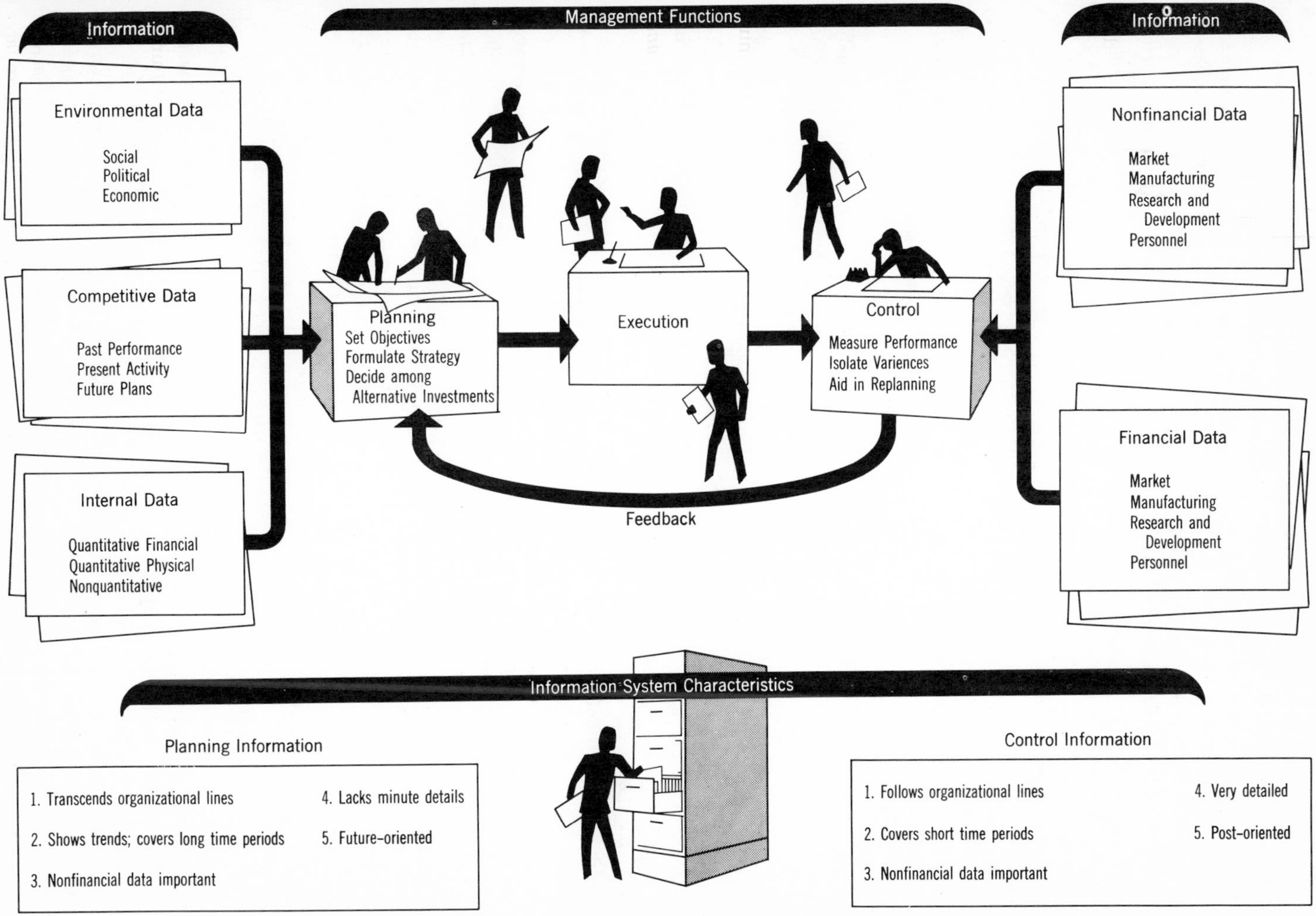
Information
Environmental Data
Social
Political
Economic
Competitive Data
Past Performance
Present Activity
Future Plans
Internal Data
Quantitative Financial
Quantitative Physical
Nonquantitative
Management Functions
Planning
Set Objectives
Formulate Strategy
Decide among
Alternative Investments
Execution
Control
Measure Performance
Isolate Variences
Aid in Replanning
Feedback
Information
Nonfinancial Data
Market
Manufacturing
Research and
Development
Personnel
Financial Data
Market
Manufacturing
Research and
Development
Personnel
Information System Characteristics
Planning Information
1. Transcends organizational lines
2. Shows trends; covers long time periods
3. Nonfinancial data important
4. Lacks minute details
5. Future-oriented
Control Information
1. Follows organizational lines
2. Covers short time periods
3. Nonfinancial data important
4. Very detailed
5. Post-oriented

EXHIBIT I. Anatomy of Management Information.

Environmental Information

The environmental data category is one of the least formalized and hence least used parts of a management information system in most companies. Specific examples of the data included in this category are:

- Population—current levels, growth trends, age distribution, geographical distribution, effect on unemployment.
- Price levels—retail, wholesale, commodities, government regulation.
- Transportation—availability, costs, competition, regulation.
- Foreign trade—balance of payments, exchange rates, convertibility.
- Labor force—skills, availability, wages, turnover, unions.

To this list a company operating internationally would add another item—systematic collection and interpretation, on a country-by-country basis, of information on political and economic conditions in the foreign areas where business is being done. Here is an example of what can be accomplished:

> A well-established international corporation with a highly sophisticated management makes a three-pronged effort to get data on local political and economic conditions. (a) There is a small but highly competent and well-paid four-man staff at corporate headquarters which travels extensively and publishes, using its own observations plus a variety of other sources, a weekly commentary on world events as they relate to the company. (b) This corporation has trained all its country managers to be keen observers of their local scene and to report their interpretive comments to headquarters regularly. (c) There is a little-talked-about group of "intelligence agents" who are not on the company's official payroll but are nevertheless paid for the information they pass along.

Certainly, not every organization has to go to these ends to keep itself informed of the situation in which it operates. However, those organizations that ignore environmental data or that leave its collection to the informal devices of individual executives are inviting trouble. Those companies that are knowledgeable concerning their environment are almost always in tune with the times and ahead of their competition. To illustrate:

> 1. Good intelligence on the sociological changes taking place in the United States led several heavy manufacturing companies to enter the "leisure time" field with a great deal of success.
>
> 2. Insight into the possible impact of foreign labor costs on parts of the electronics industry caused some U.S. corporations to acquire their own manufacturing facilities abroad. As a result, the firms were able not only to protect their domestic markets but also to open up profitable operations overseas.
>
> 3. Knowledge of trends in age distribution in the United States added to an awareness of the rate of change of scientific learning provides ample proof for some firms of the desirability of being in the educational publishing field for the next decade.

To be of real use, environmental data must indicate trends; population figures, balance-of-payment data, or political shifts are of little significance when shown for one period because they don't help management make *analytical* interpretations.

The collection and transmission of good environmental data are often problematical. Even in the United States some kinds of information are not readily available and must be pieced together from several sources or acquired *sub rosa* from officially inaccessible sources. Transmitting environmental data, particularly political information, is so awkward that sometimes the data collector must sit down personally with those who need to know the information.

In sum, environmental data are an aspect of planning information that requires more attention and warrants formalization, especially in large geographically dispersed companies. The emergence of the corporate economics department [2] is one development that could lead to better results in this area, but it is my impression that so far the progress of these units has been uneven.

Competitive Information

Data on competition comprise the second category of planning information. There are three important types to consider:

[2] Clark S. Teitsworth, "Growing Role of the Company Economist," *HBR*, January–February 1959, p. 97.

1. *Past performance*. This includes information on the profitability, return on investment, share of market, and so forth of competing companies. Such information is primarily useful in identifying one's competitors. It also is one benchmark when setting company objectives.

2. *Present activity*. This category covers new product introductions, management changes, price strategy, and so on—all current developments. Good intelligence on such matters can materially influence a company's planning; for example, it may lead to accelerating research programs, modifying advertising strategy, or switching distribution channels. The implication here is not that a company's plans should always be defensive and prompted by a competitor's moves but simply that anything important a competitor does should be recognized and factored into the planning process.

3. *Future plans*. This includes information on acquisition intentions, facility plans, and research and development efforts.

Competitive information, like environmental data, is an infrequently formalized part of a company's total information system. And so there seldom is a concerted effort to collect this kind of material, to process it, and to report it to management regularly. But some interesting exceptions to this general lack of concern exist:

Oil companies have long employed "scouts" in their land departments. These men report on acreage purchases, drilling results, and other competitive activity that may be pertinent to the future actions of their own company.

Business machine companies have "competitive equipment evaluation personnel" who continually assess the technical features of competitors' hardware.

Retail organizations employ "comparison shoppers" who appraise the prices and quality of merchandise in competitive stores.

Commercial intelligence departments are appearing more and more on corporate organization charts. An excerpt from the charter of one such group states its basic responsibility thus:

To seek out, collect, evaluate, and report information covering the past performance and future plans of competitors in such a manner that the information will have potential utility in strategic and operational planning of the corporation. This means that in addition to reporting factual information, emphasis should be on determining the implications of such information for the corporation.

Internal Information

The third and final basic category of planning information is made up of internal data. As they relate to the total planning process, internal data are aimed at identifying a company's strengths and weaknesses—the characteristics that, when viewed in the perspective of the general business environment and in the light of competitive activity, should help management to shape its future plans. It is useful to think of internal data as being of three types:

1. *Quantitative-financial*—e.g., sales, costs, and cost behavior relative to volume changes.
2. *Quantitative-physical*—e.g., share of market, productivity, delivery performance, and manpower resources.
3. *Nonquantitative*—e.g., community standing and labor relations.

In reporting internal data, a company's information system must be discriminating and selective. It should focus on "success factors." In most industries there are usually three to six factors that determine success; these key jobs must be done exceedingly well for a company to be successful. Here are some examples from several major industries:

- In the automobile industry, styling, an efficient dealer organization, and tight control of manufacturing costs are paramount.
- In food processing, new product development, good distribution, and effective advertising are the major success factors.
- In life insurance, the development of agency management personnel, effective control of clerical personnel, and innovation in creating new types of policies spell the difference.

The companies which have achieved the greatest advances in information analysis have consistently been those which have developed systems that have (a) been selective and (b) focused on the company's strengths and weaknesses with respect to its acknowledged success factors. By doing this, the managements have generated the kind of information that is most useful in capitalizing on strengths and correcting weaknesses. To illustrate:

An oil company devised a system of regularly reporting its "finding" costs—those costs incurred in exploring for new reserves of oil divided by the number of barrels of oil found. When this ratio trended upward beyond an established point, it was a signal to the company's management to consider the acquisition of other oil companies (together with their proved reserves) as a less expensive alternative to finding oil through its own exploratory efforts.

In the minds of most executives the accounting system exists primarily to meet the company's internal data needs; yet this is often an unreasonable and unfulfilled expectation. Accounting reports rarely focus on success factors that are nonfinancial in nature. Moreover, accounting practices with respect to allocation of expenses, transfer prices, and the like, often tend to obscure rather than clarify the underlying strengths and weaknesses of a company. This inadequacy should not be surprising since the *raison d'être* of many accounting systems is not to facilitate planning but rather to ensure the fulfillment of management's responsibility to the stockholders, the government, and other groups.

TAILORING THE REQUIREMENTS

If a company is to have a comprehensive, integrated system of information to support its planning process, it will need a set of management reports that regularly covers the three basic categories of planning data—i.e., environmental, competitive, and internal. The amount of data required in each area will naturally vary from company to company and will depend on such factors as the nature of the industry, the size and operating territory of the company, and the acceptance by management of planning as an essential function. However, it is important in every case for management to *formalize* and *regularize* the collection, transmission, processing, the presentation of planning information; the data are too vital to be ignored or taken care of by occasional "special studies." It is no accident that many of the most successful companies in this country are characterized by well-developed planning information systems.

What is gained if such an approach is taken? What difference does it make in operations? We do not need to conjecture to answer these questions; we can turn to concrete company experience. For instance, Exhibit II illustrates how the information used by the marketing department of an oil company changed as a result of a thorough study of the information needed to formulate effective plans. In this instance, the study indicated an increase in the data required by the vice president and his staff. (However, this result is not inevitable; it holds only for this particular situation. In other circumstances reviews of this kind have led to significant *cutbacks* in information.)

Several points should be noted in examining Exhibit II:

1. The information shown is not all for the *personal* use of the vice president, although much of it is generated and used in his field.
2. For simplicity, most of the information listed in the exhibit was presented to company executives in graphic form.
3. The exhibit highlights only the reports used for retail gasoline marketing; omitted are fuel oil marketing, commercial and industrial marketing, and other topics which the new reporting system also covered.

Many companies have found that the most effective approach to determining requirements for planning information, whether it be for one executive or an entire company, is to relate the three types of planning data described earlier to the steps in the planning process—i.e., setting objectives, developing strategy, and deciding among alternative investments. Thus, one asks himself questions like these:

- What political data are needed to set reasonable objectives for this company?
- What sociological and economic data about the areas in which this company operates are needed to formulate new product strategy?
- What competitive intelligence is necessary to develop share-of-market objectives?
- What internal cost information is needed to choose between alternative facility locations?

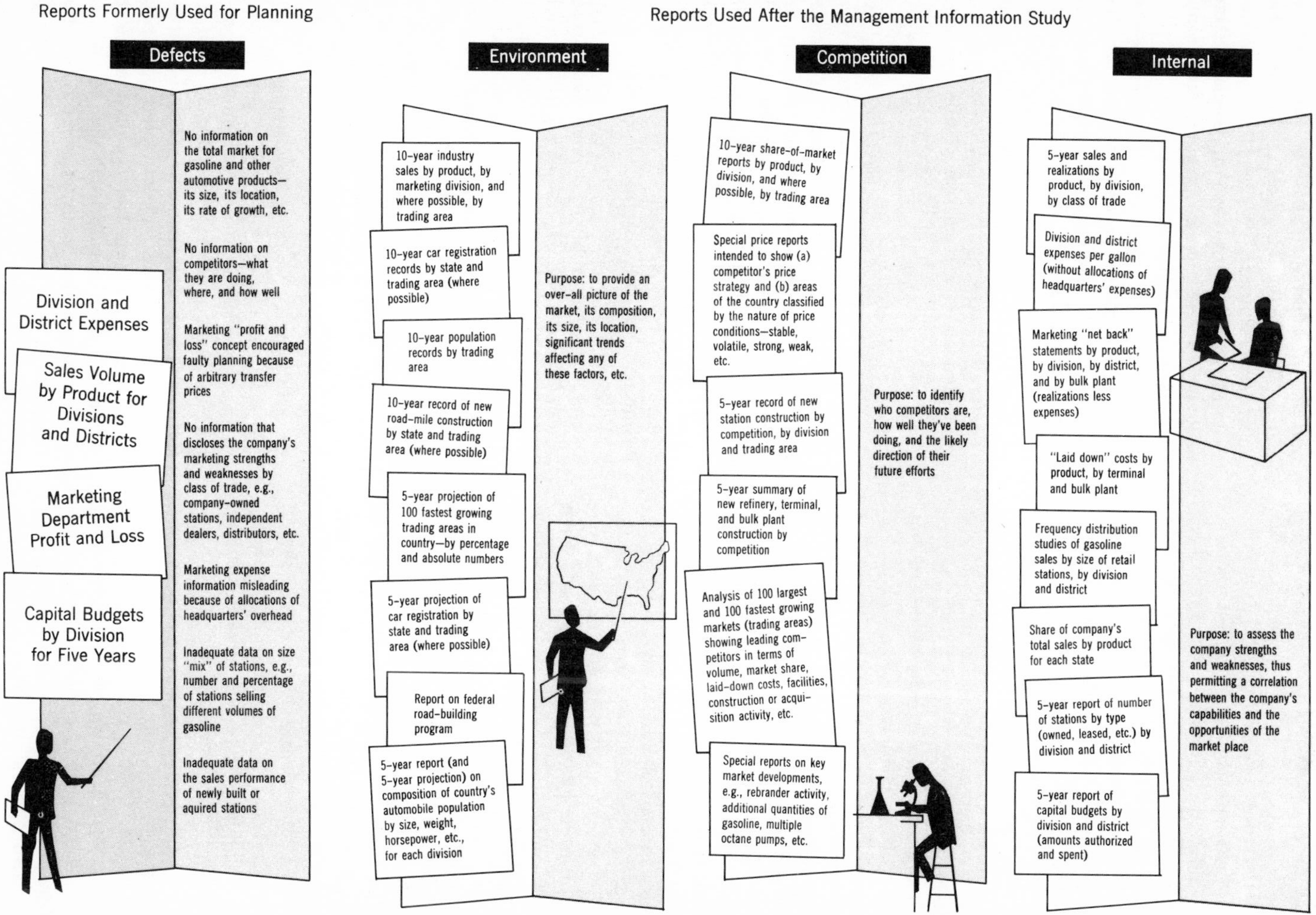

Reports Formerly Used for Planning
Defects
Division and District Expenses
Sales Volume by Product for Divisions and Districts
Marketing Department Profit and Loss
Capital Budgets by Division for Five Years
No information on the total market for gasoline and other automotive products—its size, its location, its rate of growth, etc.
No information on competitors—what they are doing, where, and how well
Marketing "profit and loss" concept encouraged faulty planning because of arbitrary transfer prices
No information that discloses the company's marketing strengths and weaknesses by class of trade, e.g., company-owned stations, independent dealers, distributors, etc.
Marketing expense information misleading because of allocations of headquarters' overhead
Inadequate data on size "mix" of stations, e.g., number and percentage of stations selling different volumes of gasoline
Inadequate data on the sales performance of newly built or aquired stations
Reports Used After the Management Information Study
Environment
10-year industry sales by product, by marketing division, and where possible, by trading area
10-year car registration records by state and trading area (where possible)
10-year population records by trading area
10-year record of new road-mile construction by state and trading area (where possible)
5-year projection of 100 fastest growing trading areas in country—by percentage and absolute numbers
5-year projection of car registration by state and trading area (where possible)
Report on federal road-building program
5-year report (and 5-year projection) on composition of country's automobile population by size, weight, horsepower, etc., for each division
Purpose: to provide an over-all picture of the market, its composition, its size, its location, significant trends affecting any of these factors, etc.
Competition
10-year share-of-market reports by product, by division, and where possible, by trading area
Special price reports intended to show (a) competitor's price strategy and (b) areas of the country classified by the nature of price conditions—stable, volatile, strong, weak, etc.
5-year record of new station construction by competition, by division and trading area
5-year summary of new refinery, terminal, and bulk plant construction by competition
Analysis of 100 largest and 100 fastest growing markets (trading areas) showing leading competitors in terms of volume, market share, laid-down costs, facilities, construction or acquisition activity, etc.
Special reports on key market developments, e.g., rebrander activity, additional quantities of gasoline, multiple octane pumps, etc.
Purpose: to identify who competitors are, how well they've been doing, and the likely direction of their future efforts
Internal
5-year sales and realizations by product, by division, by class of trade
Division and district expenses per gallon (without allocations of headquarters' expenses)
Marketing "net back" statements by product, by division, by district, and by bulk plant (realizations less expenses)
"Laid down" costs by product, by terminal and bulk plant
Frequency distribution studies of gasoline sales by size of retail stations, by division and district
Share of company's total sales by product for each state
5-year report of number of stations by type (owned, leased, etc.) by division and district
5-year report of capital budgets by division and district (amounts authorized and spent)
Purpose: to assess the company strengths and weaknesses, thus permitting a correlation between the company's capabilities and the opportunities of the market place

EXHIBIT II. Comparative Analysis of Marketing Planning Information.

Contrast with Control

In Exhibit I I have listed the five principal characteristics of planning data compared with the characteristics of control data. Note that in all but one case (nonfinancial information) they are different. It is most important to keep these differences in mind, lest the "fuel" for the planning system be confused with the "fuel" for the control system, and vice versa. Hence, I should like to emphasize the contrasts here:

1. *Coverage.* Good planning information is not compartmentalized by functions. Indeed, it seeks to transcend the divisions that exist in a company and to provide the basis on which *integrated* plans can be made. In contrast, control information hews closely to organizational lines so that it can be used to measure performance and help in holding specific managers more accountable.
2. *Length of time.* Planning information covers fairly long periods of time—months and years rather than days and weeks—and deals with trends. Thus, although it should be regularly prepared, it is not developed as frequently as control information.
3. *Degree of detail.* Excessive detail is the quicksand of intelligent planning. Unlike control, where precision and minute care do have a place, planning (and particularly long-range planning) focuses on the major outlines of the situation ahead. In the words of two authorities, L. Eugene Root and George A. Steiner, "The further out in time the planning, the less certain one can be about the precision of numbers. As a basic principle in planning it is understood that, in the longer range, details merge into trends and patterns." [3]
4. *Orientation.* Planning information should provide insights into the future. Control information shows past results and the reasons for them.

FUTURE DEVELOPMENTS

The heightened interest of management in its information crisis is already unmistakable. Dean Stanley F. Teele of the Harvard Business School, writing on the process of change in the years ahead, states, "I think the capacity to manage knowledge will be still more important to the manager. . . . The manager will need to increase his skill in deciding what knowledge he needs." [4]

Ralph Cordiner of General Electric Company in his book, *New Frontiers for Professional Managers,* writes:

> It is an immense problem to organize and communicate the information required to operate a large, decentralized organization. . . .
> What is required . . . is a . . . penetrating and orderly study of the business in its entirety to discover what specific information is needed at each particular position in view of the decisions to be made there. . . .[5]

Invariably, increasing attention of leaders in education and industry precedes and prepares the way for frontal attacks on business problems. In many organizations the initial reaction to the management information problem is first evidened by a concern over "the flood of paper work." Eventually, the problem itself is recognized—i.e., the need to define concisely the information required for intelligent planning and control of a business.

Following this awakening interest in business information problems, we are likely to see the acceleration of two developments already in view: (a) improved techniques relating to the creation and operation of total information systems, and (b) new organizational approaches to resolving information problems.

Improved Techniques

While the crisis in management information has been growing, tools that may be useful in its solution have been under development. For example, the evolution of electronic data-processing systems, the development of supporting communications networks, and the formulation of rigorous mathematical solutions to business problems have provided potentially valuable tools to help management attack its information problems. Specifically, progress on three fronts is an encouraging indication that this kind of approach will prove increasingly fruitful:

[3] "The Lockheed Aircraft Corporation Master Plan," in *Long-Range Planning for Management,* edited by David W. Ewing (New York, Harper & Brothers, 1958), p. 151.

[4] "Your Job and Mine," *The Harvard Business School Bulletin,* August 1960, p. 8.

[5] New York, McGraw-Hill Book Company, Inc., 1956, p. 102.

1. Managements of most companies are far more conversant with both the capabilities and the limitations of computer systems than they were five years ago. This growing understanding has done much to separate fact from fancy. One key result should be the increasing application of electronic data-processing concepts to the more critical, less routine problems of business.

2. Computer manufacturers and communications companies are learning the worth of their products. They show signs of recognizing that it is not hardware but an information system which is extremely valuable in helping to solve management's problems.

3. Significant improvements have been made in the techniques of harnessing computers. Advances in automatic programing and developments in creating a common business language are gratifying evidence that the gap is being narrowed between the technical potential of the hardware and management's ability to exploit it.

Organizational Moves

The development of new organizational approaches is less obvious. Earlier in this article I noted that: (a) progress in the systematic collection and reporting of information dealing with a company's environment or with its competitive situation has been slow, and (b) traditional accounting reports are often inadequate in providing the data needed for business planning. These conditions may result from a very basic cause; namely, that most organization structures do not pin down the responsibility for management information systems and tie it to specific executive positions. Controllers and other financial officers usually have been assigned responsibility for *accounting* information—but this, of course, does not meet the total need.

Nowhere has the absence of one person having specific and *total* responsibility for management information systems had a more telling effect than in defense contractor companies. In such organizations the usual information problems have been compounded by the rapid rate of technological advance and its attendant effect upon product obsolescence, and also by the requirement for "concurrency," which means that a single product or product complex is developed, tested, produced, and installed simultaneously. Under these conditions, some companies have been nearly paralyzed by too much of the wrong information.

Having recognized this problem, several corporations have attacked it by creating full-time management information departments. These groups are responsible for:

1. Identifying the information needs for all levels of management for both planning and control purposes. As prerequisites to this responsibility it is necessary to (a) define the authority and duties of each manager and (b) determine the factors that really contribute to competitive success in the particular business in question.

2. Developing the necessary systems to fulfill these information needs.

3. Operating the data-processing equipment necessary to generate the information which is required.

To some extent these departments, reporting high in the corporate structure, have impinged on responsibilities traditionally assigned to the accounting organization since they are concerned with financial as well as nonfinancial information. But to me this overlapping is inevitable, particularly in companies where the financial function operates under a narrow perspective and a preoccupation with accountancy. The age of the information specialist is nearing, and its arrival is inextricably tied in with the emergence of some of the newer tools of our management sciences. This notion is not far removed from the concept of Harold J. Leavitt and Thomas L. Whisler, who foresee the evolution of information technology and the creation of a "programing elite." [6]

CONCLUSION

The day when management information departments are as common as controller's departments is still years away. But this should not rule out concerted efforts to improve a company's information system. In fact, I would expect many broad-gauged controller's organizations to assume the initiative in their companies for such programs.

To this end, the nine questions listed in Exhibit III are for the executive to ask himself as a guide to assessing the improvement potential

[6] "Management in the 1980's," *HBR,* November–December 1958, p. 41.

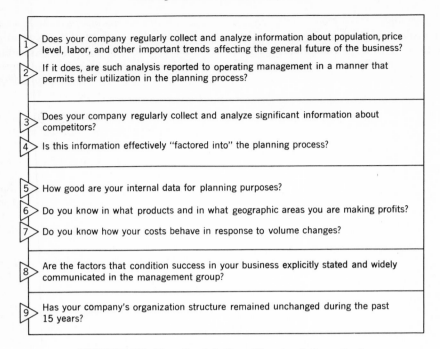

1. Does your company regularly collect and analyze information about population, price level, labor, and other important trends affecting the general future of the business?
2. If it does, are such analysis reported to operating management in a manner that permits their utilization in the planning process?

3. Does your company regularly collect and analyze significant information about competitors?
4. Is this information effectively "factored into" the planning process?

5. How good are your internal data for planning purposes?
6. Do you know in what products and in what geographic areas you are making profits?
7. Do you know how your costs behave in response to volume changes?

8. Are the factors that condition success in your business explicitly stated and widely communicated in the management group?

9. Has your company's organization structure remained unchanged during the past 15 years?

EXHIBIT III. How Good Is Your Planning Information?

in his organization's planning information. If the answers to these questions tend to be negative, the chances are strong that changes are in order.

The impact of the information crisis on the executive will be significant. To an increasing extent, a manager's effectiveness will hinge on the quality and completeness of the facts that flow to him and on his skill in using them. With technology changing at a rapid rate, with the time dimension becoming increasingly critical, and with organizations becoming larger, more diversified in product lines, and more dispersed geographically, it is inevitable that executives will rely more and more on formally presented information in managing their businesses.

What is more, some organizations are concluding that the easiest and most effective way to influence executive action is to control the flow of information into managerial positions. This notion holds that the discipline of information can be a potent factor in determining just what an executive can and cannot do—what decisions he can make, what plans he can draw up, what corrective steps he can take.

To the extent that this is true, information systems may be increasingly used to mold and shape executive behavior. Better data handling might well become a substitute for much of the laborious shuffling and reshuffling of positions and lines of authority that now goes on. Most reorganizations seek to alter the way certain managers or groups of managers operate. But simply drawing new organization charts and rewriting job descriptions seldom ensure the implementation of new concepts and relationships. The timing, content, and format of the information provided to management, however, *can* be a strong influence in bringing about such purposeful change.

Thus, developments in management information systems will affect the executive in two ways. Not only will the new concepts influence what he is able to do, but they will to a great extent control how well he is able to do it.

17. MANAGERIAL ACCEPTANCE OF SCIENTIFIC RECOMMENDATIONS

C. WEST CHURCHMAN*

An exploration of the subtle relationship between information and decisions.

Those who have thought and written about management often refer to management "know-how" as an essential ingredient of success. By know-how they apparently mean the ability of the manager to understand what is going on in his environment. It is the chief concern of the management scientist to translate these vague stipulations about management knowledge into precise and verifiable assertions about how decisions are made and how decisions ought to be made.

One of the central problems of management science is the understanding of the role of information in decision making. The reason this problem is so difficult is that we have failed to pay enough attention to the very subtle concept of the *use of information*. The much maligned, classical economic man was supposed to act in accordance with his self-interest, given complete information. But what does "given" mean in this context? What the economist meant was that the information was automatically fed into the rational decision process, and the correct answer was thereby derived. If the manager of a firm can be adequately represented as a computer, this concept of "given" may be adequate for then we merely mean by "given" information the inputs to a computer program.

SOURCE: *California Management Review* (Fall, 1964), pp. 31–38. Reprinted by permission of the Regents of the University of California.

* C. West Churchman, University of California, Berkeley.

However, when we consider real managers in their real environments, the concept of "given" is not clear at all. Let us picture a manager busily at work making a number of decisions. Suppose by some lucky chance that sufficient information is "available" for him to make a perfect decision in each case. We need some operational definition of "available," and the one that comes most readily to mind is that information is "available" if it is stored in the form of retrievable symbols in the environment of the manager. More precisely, a piece of information is available to a manager if he can retrieve it at virtually zero cost (e.g., by asking someone, or looking it up, or retrieving it from computer memory). Even this more precise meaning of "available" leaves much to be desired, but the definition will suffice for the purpose of stating the problem of this article, which is: There is sufficient evidence to show that a manager may have perfect information "available" to him and yet not make the correct decision. What is the explanation of this phenomenon? Why don't managers act on the information stored in their environments?

Before proceeding to discuss this problem in depth, something more needs to be said about the concept of a "right choice," i.e., about knowledge of the correct action. A man may choose the right action by accident, so to speak, when in his clumsy way he stumbles upon the correct way to act. Thus, an archer who hits the bull's-eye does not necessarily know how to shoot. What makes the expert archer is the ability to adjust his method of controlling the arrow so that, no matter what the motion of his target, within limits he can perform successfully. Hence, knowledge about a decision consists of choosing the correct action even though the conditions change. Knowledge is a sensitivity to changes in one's environment.

INVENTORY CONTROL

The point can be illustrated very well by referring to inventory control within industry. Most companies do reasonably well with their inventories during periods of stable demand. This is because the managers responsible for controlling inventory learn from experience that ordering too large or too small quantities is bad policy, and they have also learned to prepare for normal shifts in demand in terms of buffer stocks. But we would not say that the management has knowledge of the control of inventory unless it had developed a method of adjusting to large shifts in demand or in costs.

Hence, when an operations research team comes in and tries to develop models, it often finds that its recommendations do not deviate very far from the current practice of the management. This does not imply, however, that the work of the operations research team has been wasted. On the contrary, once a model is developed, the parameters of the model can be adjusted to take care of variations in the environment, such as the upswing or downswing of demand, the costs of carrying inventory, placing orders, or shortages. Thus, the great advantage of modeling industrial operations is that the manager is then in an excellent position to adjust for changes. In other words, according to the definition of "knowledge" introduced above, the manager is provided with awareness of the right action rather than mere display of the right action.

The point cannot be overemphasized. Often in companies we find that men with years of experience have arrived at methods of managing operations which cannot be matched by analysis. For example, a vice-president of sales of a large company would forecast sales of the company's products based on reports received from the field, economic data, and other types of information, coupled with his own judgment. He seemed to have an uncanny way of coming up with accurate estimates that we could not duplicate by any statistical methods known to us. In this case the company could be said to have arrived at the correct action, but again I doubt if we would want to say that the company had *knowledge* of forecasting. If the vice-president were to leave, the environment would be changed, and the company would have no obvious way to adapt to the change. Thus, our statistical methods, though perhaps slightly inferior to those of the vice-president under current conditions, constituted something more like knowledge than the vice-president's intuitively based decisions.

A MATTER OF ABILITY

In the discussion above, it is clear that I have been describing knowledge as a matter of ability. It is the ability of a decision-maker to adjust his decisions to changes in the situations that confront him. We could go on to describe deeper forms of knowledge. For example, we might want to consider the way in which knowledge of decision-making in one area assists decision-making in another area or the way in which knowledge of decision-making can be refined, so that finer and finer distinctions can be made between types of decisions. I think these deliberations would lead us to a consideration of "understanding" as opposed to mere knowledge, because understanding is essentially the process by which the decision-maker knows why his method of decision-making is correct. To know "why" is to go beyond the present situation to a larger world, to understand why the decisions in the present situation are justified by considerations of the larger world. Essentially, understanding represents the highway from knowledge to wisdom; wisdom is the highest form of understanding.

Assuming that enough has been said about knowledge, let us return to the problem stated at the outset. We have pictured a man in an environment where sufficient information is "available" to provide him with knowledge of how to make decisions. Why doesn't knowledge occur?

One ready answer is that the information is too costly to obtain. Indeed, we have hidden in the definition of "available" the very difficult concept of "cost of information", and we could devote many pages to discussing this concept as is done, for example, in the work of Marschak and Radner (1) on the theory of teams.

Instead, in order to put the problem of this article into sharp relief, we will assume for the moment that we are talking about a manager who can retrieve information readily at no cost. Why does this manager fail to use the information so readily available to him?

USE OF INFORMATION

The obvious answer is that he does not know how to transform the available information into a knowledge of action. In other words, he does not have a program built into his mind that will transform the inputs into correct outputs. Thus, operations researchers have suggested to the manager the wisdom of using personnel who do know how to do just exactly this: They know how to take the information available and calculate a decision system which, in effect, provides the manager with the knowledge of how to behave. We generally refer to this type of activity as analysis. Hence, the suggestion is that the missing gap for many managers is the lack of someone or some device capable of performing the necessary analysis.

Unfortunately, we have overwhelming evidence that available information plus analysis does not lead to knowledge. A management science team can properly analyze a situation and present recommendations to the manager, but no change occurs. The situation is so familiar to those of us who try to practice management science that I hardly need to describe the cases. Some of my graduate students undertook to write to the authors of cases reported in *Operations Research* over the first six years of its publication to determine to what extent the recommendations of the studies had been carried out by management. In no case was there sufficient evidence that the recommendations had been accepted.

At the University of California, Professor Ratoosh and I have been conducting some experiments in which we have been able to establish in controlled situations that analysis plus available information does not lead to knowledge. In our experiments, five subjects run a small firm. The instructions given to the subjects provide complete "available" information about the firm's operations. That is, it is possible to analyze the information so that the managers of our laboratory firm can adopt the right action. Furthermore, by analysis it is possible to generate a model which will provide the managers with a method of making decisions, even though demands and costs and other factors change. In other words, the model can provide the managers with a *knowledge* of how to act. In some of our groups we have placed a person who has gone through the analysis beforehand. He is then given the task of persuading the rest of the management team. Therefore, in our laboratory we have constructed a situation in which there is available information plus analysis. The result has almost uniformly been one in which knowledge does not occur. The managers do not accept the recommendations and are far from gaining any knowledge from the analysis (2).

Of course, one could say that the difficulty is that the available information is in one location (the instructions given to the subjects), the analysis is in a second (in the head of one person), and the decision-making is in a third. One might feel that if all three of these components could be combined into one unit, the problem could be solved.

This suggestion is a reasonable one and brings us back to the original definition of "available" information for the purpose of revising it somewhat. The original definition made "available" a very passive kind of thing and ignored the very important concept of transmittal of information. How is the information to be retrieved? If the channels of retrieval are obscured by linguistic ambiguities and other noises, the information may not be "available," no matter how precisely it is stored.

CONCEPT OF COMMUNICATION

The concept we seem to require is "communication." Communication is a device for taking several minds and making them act more like one mind.

Thus, many people have suggested that the missing variable in the equation is proper communication, that available information *plus* analysis *plus* communication leads to knowledge. They say that if only operations researchers could learn to talk in a language the managers can understand, there would be no further difficulties in implementing operations research recommendations. Thus, articles on the implementation of recommendations speak over and over again about the need for better communication between the scientist and the manager. These articles point to the fact that the scientist talks in a semi-formal language (mathematics) and the manager talks in his own management terms, which are not exactly those of normal discourse. The problem, say these articles, is to make the proper translation.

MODE OF COMMUNICATION

Of course, to prove the invalidity of the new formula (information + analysis + communication leads to knowledge) is very difficult because there are so many modes of communication. However, in our experiments we have found no adequate mode. We have presented the solution in simple graphical form, in simple arithmetical form, in ordinary discourse, as well as in the form of more complicated mathematical expressions. We can find no evidence that the mode of communication makes any difference. We have presented the solution in pieces and in a total report, and again, we have found no difference. I am aware of the fact that the sociological literature, and especially the work of Hovland (3), has dealt at length with the importance of mode of communication with respect to persuasion, but we have not been able to translate these findings into our own work.

Of course, I am not saying that the mode of communication has no effect whatsoever. It is not very difficult, even in our experiments, to prepare messages which are so incomprehensible that they have no effect whatsoever, except to annoy the managers. What I am saying is that the formula will not do. More precisely, the prescription for "better" communication ends up by being no more than a restatement of the problem: to find some set of activities so that with complete information "available," the manager will come to know the correct action. It is the attempt to find such a set of activities that makes the problem very difficult because by now we have exhausted all the obvious possibilities.

The next suggestion is one with which I am sure most managers and scientists are familiar. One must bear in mind the distinction between the personal goals of the manager and the organizational goals. Even if the corporate goals are explicit and clear, the manager's own personal ambitions may be at variance at times with the interests of the corporation. Therefore, if the scientist generates a method of making decisions that best serves the corporate aims, he may encounter resistance because the recommendations do not fit into the manager's personal goals. In other words, it is possible that a manager who really wanted to accomplish the organizational goals would come to know the correct action.

For example, it is a well-known fact that managers feel threatened by modern techniques of analysis. They have reason to believe that analysis, with the help of high-speed computers, may take over their roles. In order to preserve their status, they resist the recommendations that analysis provides. At this point one usually distinguishes between a perceived threat and a real threat. The perceived threat is one that may be incorrect; for example, it may happen that sophisticated analysis strengthens rather than weakens the manager's role. The task of the researcher in this case is one of clarifying the situation for the manager, though how this is to be done is often very obscure. A real threat is one that does, in fact, threaten the manager's role, making it either obsolete or less important.

REACTION TO CHANGE

A more general way to describe the problem is as follows. When a change is suggested to a manager, he reacts in ways that are typical to his own personality. Part of him will resist the suggestion, and often the resistance is so strong that he will reject the suggestion altogether. Nevertheless, the persons responsible for making the suggestion may learn enough about the manager's personality so that they know what to say to him to break down his resistance. Thus, they recognize that there is a part of the manager's personality that will adjust to change. On the other hand, there may be a part that remains invariant, no matter what the environment. Indeed, psychological literature leads us to believe that most men display invariant characteristics over most of their lives: they rarely change from an extrovert to an introvert or from a thinking type to a feeling type, for example.

These reflections imply that the missing ingredient in the process of implementation is the understanding of the manager. Any research team that fails to study the manager and his personality may very well fail to bring about a recommended change. Furthermore, any research team that believes it can implement a recommendation by the same process, regardless of who is managing, is simply naïve.

Because he often lacks a methodology of understanding people, the researcher may give up any attempt to implement broad changes of policy. Instead, he may be satisfied to work in areas where the status and role of the manager remain invariant no matter what is changed. A manager may not feel threatened if the equipment in his shop is redesigned or if physical sequences of actions are changed. But if someone asks whether his shop should manufacture the items it does, in the quantities it customarily makes, he cannot help but regard this question as one that is directed to his own role. If he is a reflective type, he may enjoy the question; if he is an anxious type, he may not. Even if he enjoys the question, he may believe that a solution arrived at by analysis stifles his imagination. His personality may be such that he must act instinctively and creatively or not act at all.

COALITIONS IN MANAGEMENT

Perhaps the most important invariances of personality occur in the formation of coalitions in organizations. These are the so-called political aspects of management in firms. A coalition may arise because the members of the coalition recognize certain common economic advantages. But it is well known that coalitions also come about because of the personalities of their members; some mix of attitude, trait, and opinion creates a loyalty that is hard to dissolve. The loyalty is strengthened by opposition. Thus, various obscure and complicated coalition frameworks occur among managers; they are obscure because no one ever writes down their bylaws and articles of confederation or ever announces them publicly. Indeed, most managers are not clearly aware of them. For a further discussion of this point, see Cyert and March (4).

These coalitions of managers are like the "invisible colleges" of scientists; see, for example, Derek Price (5). They are the sources the manager consults; they are the basis of the language he uses; they provide the criteria of what is important and what is unimportant. They are made up of persons, books, journals, and other communication devices in the manager's environment.

Thus, in the context of managerial politics, the researcher is apt to find that his recommendations are viewed from the point of view of their effect on a coalition and not from the point of view of the whole organization. Since the researcher usually doesn't know who belongs to what coalition, and is far from understanding what holds the coalition together, he cannot determine how to overcome coalition biases. He finds himself in a confusing welter of contradictory reactions of managers.

A SCARCE COMMODITY

The most significant outputs of the hidden managerial coalition are the importance of issues and the ways in which important issues should be considered. Managers control a very scarce commodity: their own time and attention. Their most conscious problem is one of determining to what they should pay attention. A researcher who claims he can save them a few thousands or millions of dollars may immediately lose their attention, because the managers believe that a new market or a threat to the corporation's existence are far more demanding of their attention than cost savings, especially if the method of analysis is alien to them.

In other words, one aspect of the formula suggested earlier was quite faulty. It may be true that information + analysis ideally leads to knowledge, but analysis takes up a significant portion of the manager's time and energy. One measure of the *cost of analysis* for him is the distance of the analytic method from his typical way of thinking about problems. His typical way of thinking comes from his coalition. A very striking example of a manager's reaction to "scientism," i.e., alien thinking, is to be found in a recent article by Lilienthal (6).

Thus, to discover what a manager thinks is important and how he believes he should think about important issues, one must determine to whom he listens, and to determine to whom he listens one must understand the coalitions to which he belongs. Some of these coalitions are external to the company; they are the other members of the managerial community whom the manager respects. These large coalitions of managers in specific industries account for the managerial styles and fads. If these coalitions come to believe that science and especially mathematics and computers are important, managers will pay attention to scientists. If not, they won't pay attention, no matter how elegant the recommendations the scientists make.

PROBLEM OF ATTENTION

I have purposefully been vague about the meaning of a coalition, in order to emphasize a point. But the definition is really quite simple: A manager's coalition is the group of people who influence what the manager attends to. I do not say that they are the group that influences what he does, because this is too narrow a concept. The manager of a competing firm may hire an operations research group. If this influences another manager to learn about operations research, the first manager belongs to the second's coalition.

There is little doubt that, in the experiments we have run at the University of California at Berkeley, the problem is one of attention. The subjects quickly form one or more coalitions and then become much too busy to want to attend to the recommendations that are made to them, even though these recommendations are correct. The analysis offered may be foreign to the way in which they have taught themselves to think about their task. In some mysterious way, the subjects agree that the way they are organized, "not going into the red," and various other secondary aspects of the task are the most important.

If we are to learn more about the implementation of recommendations, we must learn more about how people decide where to direct their attention. It is for this reason that at Systems Development Corporation, Herbert Eisenberg, Martin Shubik, and I have started a few very simple experiments on deliberation and its role in decision-making. Deliberation is the process by which the mind in reaching a decision scans various aspects of the problem. In our experiments, we present one subject with alternative points of view to which he may pay attention, and other subjects try to influence him towards one viewpoint or another. We are attempting to learn more about the way in which managers come to pay attention to issues.

This essay is a mystery novel, with the added frustration that the culprit remains unidentified even at the end. Perhaps the advantage of such a devilish novel is that it may suggest a better plot for the next one to be written. With this in mind, let me end by introducing some broad philosophical generalities, not supported by the "available" evidence but nonetheless helpful in future research.

We started by looking for the ingredients that a research staff would seek to supply in order to bring about a recommended change: available information, analysis, and communication. We argued in the end that none of these ingredients matters at all unless the manager pays attention to the problem and that paying attention is an obscure process of the managerial mind, little understood by management scientists.

AN OBSCURE CONCEPT

The obscurity we face in this regard is simply the obscurity of the concept of decision-making itself. We do not yet understand how to describe a human decision. The descriptions usually offered reflect the psychological traits of the describers. A thinking type believes that the mathematical theories of games and of optimization will provide all the concepts necessary to define a decision clearly, as well as a correct decision. He is arrogant enough to label his efforts "decision theory," without any uneasy pang of conscience. The feeling type asserts that a decision is essentially a unique expression of human values and that the meaning of a decision cannot be captured by generalized mathematical expressions. An intuitive type believes that decisions are insights, quick flashes of understanding how to solve a problem. They frequently assert that the manager leaps to his conclusion without benefit of, or even need for, analysis. Finally, there are those who assume that the whole business of decision-making is contained in available information: what decision is made depends solely on what facts are known.

A MANAGER'S WORLD

Philosophy attempts to take one step back from the issues that divide scientists into intellectual camps. All the points of view mentioned above are valid. They amount to saying that decision-making can be conceptualized in many ways. What seems to be common to these ways of describing decisions is the concept of focus (7). A specific decision is the focus of a mathematical model, of a general value structure, of insightful behavior, of masses of data. The focusing that leads to decision-making takes the manager's whole world and displays a subarea where he must seek a solution. Within this subarea the coalitions that influence this behavior lead him to confine his attention to certain aspects. Eventually, he is led to one alternative, to the choice.

The rational mind of the scientist would like to remove all irrationality from this focusing of attention of the manager. The trouble is that, in order to do this, we scientists must understand the world of the manager—not a piece of it but the whole world. If we only understand a piece of the manager's world, we have no justification for asserting that he should pay attention to the piece that we present to him.

Thus, in order to recommend important changes to a manager, we must understand the process by which this whole world becomes focused on certain issues and aspects of his environment. Any decision is a snapshot of the universe of the manager. An optimal decision is a snapshot of a rational universe.

REFERENCES

1. Roy Radner and J. Marschak, *Economic Theory of Teams*, 1964.
2. Philburn Ratoosh and C. W. Churchman, "Innovation in Group Behavior," Working Paper No. 10, Center for Research in Management Science, University of California, Berkeley, January 1960; "Report on Further Implementation Experiments," Working Paper No. 26, *loc. cit.*, March, 1961.
3. Carl I. Hovland, Irving L. Janis, and Harold H. Keeley, *Communication and Persuasion* (New Haven: Yale University Press, 1954); Carl I. Hovland, et al., *The Order of Presentation in Persuasion* (New Haven: Yale University Press, 1957).
4. Richard M. Cyert and James G. March, *Behavioral Theory of the Firm* (Englewood Cliffs: Prentice-Hall, Inc., 1963).
5. Derek J. de Solla Price, *Science since Babylon* (New Haven: Yale University Press, 1961).
6. D. E. Lilienthal, "Skeptical Look as 'Scientific Experts'," *New York Times*, September 29, 1963.
7. Thomas A. Cowan, address delivered at the American Association for the Advancement of Science meetings in Denver, December, 1961.

18. HOW INTELLIGENT IS YOUR "MIS?"

ROBERT L. JOHNSON* AND IRWIN H. DERMAN†

Business organizations provide for the accomplishment of corporate objectives through the delegation of accountability and authority. The organizational hierarchy represents a network for the flow of communications without which such delegation and reporting activities would be impossible. Except for such institutions as the press and schools, few organizations have been formed with the objective of producing and utilizing information. Few businesses, in fact, consider themselves in the information business, yet none could long exist without information and effective distribution channels.

"TOTALITY OF INFORMATION" CONCEPT

Since most organizational activity is centered around the acquisition, production, or transfer of information in various forms, employees are the targets of a conglomeration of data, information, and intelligence. Decisions are communicated by passing information to those with the delegated authority and responsibility for performance. Standards are established against which product quality, cost, and completion time are measured; evaluation procedures are developed for checking performance against the standards. The entire operation is continually monitored by a reporting system that communicates performance information to the manager, who uses a control system to feed back instructions to correct or prevent deviations from planned performance.

Within the operational framework, the words, "data," "information," and "intelligence" do not represent the same entity. The distinction lies more in usage than in format. Data represent facts catalogued according to a retrieval scheme, maintained either by computer or manually, and, as elements of knowledge at the statistical level, are passive. Information, on the other hand, represents data to which the need to satisfy a requirement has been added. In other words, information consists of data combined with direction. In contrast to data, information pertinent to the understanding of a situation or to forming the basis for action is active and has a limited useful life expectancy. Finally, in the business communications hierarchy there is intelligence resulting from the analysis of organized information that provides the decision maker with a preferred course of action after having evaluated available alternatives.

Businessmen are subjected to a barrage of data—organized and random—that impinge on their conscious as well as their subconscious minds. These data may be meaningless or pertinent at either level, and only a small amount relates generally to work interests or specifically to work projects. That which is relevant comes from a variety of sources, not exclusively through a formalized information transfer structure. From the entire universe of data, a finite amount is applicable to a specific decision. Because a decision maker never has all the data needed to guarantee the correctness of an action, decisions ultimately must be based on imperfect intelligence made up of a combination of data, experience, opinions, and intuition.

Information as a Resource

A resource is an entity that has present or potential utility. Until recently, information was neither recognized nor appreciated as a corporate resource valuable to management when used to effect the operation of an organization. Without information, day-to-day

SOURCE: *Business Horizons* (February, 1970). Reprinted by permission of Foundation for School of Business at Indiana University.

* Arcata National Corp.

† Stanford Research Institute.

or long-range organizational functions cannot be carried out. The executive commands a higher salary than the janitor because he has learned to use information more profitably for the organization; the more scarce the possessors of knowledge on a given subject, the more valuable is the master of that information.

Information has many of the characteristics of material resources. It can be produced, stored, and distributed; it is perishable to the extent that it has no utility beyond the time it is needed; yet it is not consumable in the sense that it can be used up. As for its worth, the less a decision maker knows about a problem and its possible solutions, the higher the cost he must pay for potentially useful information. The greater the potential value of information, the larger the investment management must be willing to make for its acquisition.

Information Resource Management

Since information has value as a resource, it must be treated like other valuable resources. Because of the costs associated with procurement, transfer, storage, and conversion, information should receive consideration similar to that given such corporate resources as materials and facilities. To estimate the worth of a piece of information, its cost-value factors must be carefully examined, including the cost of acquisition and conservation, and the cost of not having it available when needed. In the latter case, the cost of raw data depends on the cost consequences of making a decision without that data.

The cost of the procurement of information on an *ad hoc* basis is high and sometimes intolerable. Nevertheless, most information needed for top management decision making is procured in this manner, since the formal management information system rarely is responsive to the special needs of the corporate executive. When gathering data, he must either search for, find, and exploit an external source or assign the task to a staff information specialist. Consequently, the search for, and isolation of, required data from the available universe and the conversion to information and intelligence results in the consumption of another valuable resource—time.

In short, an information system designed for the orderly and systematic procurement, transfer, storage, and conversion of data will reduce time, effort, and cost, and increase the utility of information. The cost of developing and implementing such a system must be weighed against the cost of searching for, finding, and handling data on an *ad hoc* basis or, worse, the consequences of making a decision without pertinent information.

IMPACT ON TOP MANAGEMENT

Executive Awareness

The executive often feels he is deluged with data, but rarely feels he is receiving enough information. To replace intuition and opinion, he sifts a mass of data to satisfy his information needs; nevertheless, he must often intuitively evaluate the risks of a poor decision in the absence of perfect information about the probable consequences of his actions.

All modern corporations have some form of information system that is supposed to reduce the cost of decision making and lower the probability of making poor decisions because relevant information is lacking. These systems have been designed to provide information to support corporate studies. Typically, however, they lack the essential elements of an intelligence system required to support top management marketing and investment decision making and so imperil the very survival of the corporation. Even detailed information about company resources and activities is of limited value to top management for planning corporate response to major technological, political, or economic shifts. A class of facts relating to the environment in which the corporation operates is what is really required by top management.

Today's top executives are aware of this knowledge gap in decision making. Information systems have proved their worth in supporting operating level activities by assuring a steady flow of tools, materials, and information essential for production and distribution of goods. Existing data processing systems also do a reasonable job of helping top managers get a general indication of corporate efficiency from accounting summary reports, from which financial and market reports can be extrapolated. The top executive must know that these information systems, efficient and useful as they may be to the functional managers, are not much help in making those decisions on which corporate prosperity or even survival depend.

The Problem

Too much of the executive's time is spent searching for the technical, economic, and political intelligence needed to make policy and strategy decisions. Existing information systems, generally, cannot tell him the potential impact of industry, government, and corporate threats and opportunities; he lacks, therefore, the essential elements of intelligence required for evaluating the risks and rewards associated with various options. An executive cannot obtain, remember, or retrieve all available facts pertinent to a strategic situation.

Because of the differences in the needs for facts at various levels, the corporate information system has rarely been designed to satisfy upper management requirements. Appeals by top management for more pertinent information usually bring the same data—a summary of what has happened or what is happening—not what is likely to happen "if," or how the firm can exploit an opportunity or cope with a threat, or what cost or profit may result from a future action.

To perform their tasks, top management planners need intelligence on threats, opportunities, risks, and information about future resource requirements and sources (both economic and technological), investment-payoff criteria, and techniques for evaluation of alternatives. A complete system designed to collect data, process them into information, and convert them to intelligence suitable for goal setting and strategy determination would indeed be costly. Weighed against the value of such intelligence in terms of competitive advantage, however, the investment may well be warranted. If the cost of getting and processing the information top management now uses is considered, the investment may be even more justified.

Unfortunately, few executives are aware of how much it is costing them to get strategic intelligence. They do not consider the cost of consultants, corporate staff planners, and economic analysts; business periodical and services subscriptions; and the expenditure of their own time in searching for and processing information in the same way they might calculate the costs and benefits from the operational support of management information systems.

Information Economics

The value of information to a business is a function of timeliness and the hierarchical position of the user in the organizational structure. With regard to production work, the value of an instruction, job order, or job sheet is the profit obtained from the sale of a product. If the sale is forfeited because of mistiming or incomplete information, the cost to the firm is more than just the worker's wages; it is also the lost profit from the potential sale. It is obvious that the potential loss will exceed the cost of having provided the worker with necessary information. Therefore, management willingly commits the required funds to establish a system to provide job-related data to the operating level personnel.

People in resource management, on the other hand, have different requirements for data than do production workers. It is more difficult, for example, to justify economically such long lead time activities as an information system where the purpose is to facilitate resource management data acquisition, processing, and reporting. These systems generally begin with the limited objective of developing an operational management data base and a reporting system to account for the expenditure of time and materials. Where time is especially valuable, as in managing high cost, potentially automatic processes, the extension of the system to real time monitoring, might even be justified.

Sharing of repetitive resource and program management information can justify a high investment in a computer-based information processing system, relieving the manager of *ad hoc* data collection and processing. A computer system has an obvious advantage—its ability to "remember" facts useful to a number of management problem solvers. Inventory management, for example, may be systematized to monitor stock levels to optimize the time and effort of production control, purchasing, and stock control personnel. With a computer monitoring out-of-control conditions, the inventory manager is free to devote more time to research, creative planning, managing, and communication, the work he is best qualified to perform. Having the computer provide the manager with exception reports removes him from the normal crisis management loop to which he now devotes much of his day-to-day activity.

The computer, then, can make planners out of managers instead of forcing them to "plan on the fly." The computer, with its ability to remember rules and recall stored transaction data, introduces elements of predictability, reliability, and capability that go far towards establishing a true management environment. Since the computer is not under pressure to do "more important things," there is little danger that priorities could develop that would result in the postponement of decisions vital to production efficiency.

Limited Utility of Operating Activity Data

A look at the business oriented activities performed by computers shows that day-to-day applications predominate. Payroll, accounts receivable, accounts payable, inventory control, and tax processing—all activities that involve simple manipulations of data—comprise the major portion of business data processing. This is because of the ease in identifying potential cost savings that result from automating such operating activities. Since computers can handle simple, repetitive tasks, the overwhelming majority of past design activity has been directed toward installing operating level information systems.

Although the survival of the firm is rarely threatened by operating level decisions, the financial consequences of a poor decision can easily exceed the cost of reducing the probability of making such a decision. With the development of computer programs to systematize operating procedures, it was expected that the data base would provide information pertinent to long-range business activities. Planning was to be facilitated by the use of modeling techniques and simulation routines that operate on the data to identify preferable courses of action. The computer capability to recall, manipulate, and integrate large masses of data was supposed to ease the problem of handling data required for top management activity.

What has happened, though, is that top management has found operating data no more than vaguely useful for executive decision making. Therefore, those companies that went the computer/data base route have discovered information systems have had little effect on middle and upper management activities.

If the information system is not providing sufficient data to allow management to carry out planning activities, what kinds of information are lacking? It is difficult, at best, to make a definitive list of information required to run a company. First, industry considerations are important in determining the kinds of information needed to carry out all kinds of activity. Next, such factors as the size of the company, its market share, objectives, interest in acquisitions, and growth pace strongly influence the establishment of a comprehensive information base. In general, certain classes of information can be identified as potentially useful to a manager during a study or planning activity.

Fact-Opinion Dichotomy

Executives are paid for their knowledge, the relative use made of that knowledge, and their decision-making guts. Knowledge, in this case, consists of some combination of factual information, insight, and opinion. Even though some decisions must be made on the basis of insight and intuition in the face of data contradicting such judgments, the executive should have the integrity to examine pertinent facts when they are available. In other words, he must be aware of the dichotomy of fact and opinion. The information system should provide for this dichotomy by separating fact from opinion, and making the collected mass available to the manager in the form of information or intelligence.

An intelligence system for top management then can provide both data and opportunities to use those data in testing probable consequences by use of simulation prior to actual decision making. Such simulations can provide a feedback of more information to improve the odds of making a good decision.

TYPES AND SOURCES OF INFORMATION

Some kinds of information are not now included in corporate information system data bases. Although such information is available in some form, it is the ability to retrieve a fact within a specified time frame that is crucial. A key piece of information needed to make the optimum decision, but not available at the right time or not known to be in existence, may make the difference between success and failure. Certain information classes, if included in the corporate data base, will upgrade operational capabilities of computer systems into true corporate-wide information systems.

Middle Management Information Sources

Although it is the function of a company library to maintain a complete file of *general business publications* like the *Wall Street Journal, Forbes, Business Week,* and *Fortune,* imagine a situation in which the index of these publications is stored in the corporate data base. When a manager needs information relevant to a particular topic, he would use a computer terminal to communicate his request for citations to a retrieval program that would scan all indexes to produce a list of pertinent articles. A simple approach to the scanning problem would be the use of a KWIC (Key Word in Context) program to scan the indexes. Information retrieval would then be reduced to a document retrieval problem. The importance of this step lies more in focusing the power of the computer on the speed-of-retrieval problem than in the replacement of the manual search of a card file.

Trade association publications constitute a source of information relevant to particular industries. Besides maintaining an index of available material in the computer, it would be well to monitor selected association publications and data releases for industry wide information that could be included in the company data base as support material.

Because of the difficulty of obtaining proprietary information about competitors, a structured data format for *competitive information* would be hard to specify and maintain. Certainly there are sources of information on such matters as competitor sales, long-range plans, research activities, and plant location announcements that have a direct effect upon company plans. Although most information would be of a qualitative nature, some form of structure, including retrieval codes, could be imposed, and the data base could be designed to accommodate such qualitative information.

The *federal government* publishes a wealth of statistics on a wide range of subjects. Although most of this is unrelated to the interests of a particular company, general categories of material, besides specific industry-oriented publications, can be invaluable in supporting planning activities. For example, reports of pending legislation can be used to determine the effect of laws on the conduct of business on a nationwide basis. The same would be true, of course, for state and local communities passing legislation directly affecting manufacturing, distribution, or sale of company products. For example, federal legislation on truth-in-packaging is of immediate interest to product planning and manufacturing activities.

A general class of information published by the Bureau of Labor Statistics is also useful. Information such as salary surveys in selected areas would be of interest to personnel managers for salary comparisons or to planning managers for new facility location determinations.

Consumer purchasing behavior is, after all, the final determinant of company success. Even companies not selling consumer products are affected by the percentage of the consumer dollar remaining after purchases of necessities and conveniences, leisure services, and savings. It is in the long-range interest of a company to monitor closely shifts in consumer preferences, not only to protect future profitability in existing product lines, but also to guide potential development of related or diverse products and services. In addition to reports of trends that can be found in magazines and newspapers, the federal government is a potential source of long-range information; a government staff, headed by the Special Assistant for Consumer Affairs, could be a valuable source of consumer related facts.

Closely related to consumer expenditure statistics is the information on the *gross national product* published by the government. Many companies look to this information to help establish trends for consumer and industrial purchases. Research has attempted to relate the trends of certain key indicators to company sales. By isolating leading and lagging indicators in the components of GNP, a firm would be able to predict sales based on the over-all activity of the economy. GNP information could supplement the data normally contained in the company data base to assist management in the conduct of predictive studies and economic simulations.

With the federal government sponsoring so much *research,* it is reasonable to assume that discoveries will be made outside a company's R&D activity that will affect the future course of the firm. In the medical field, for example, research is conducted not only at the National Institute of Health but also in universities and private laboratories. The results of these projects will shape the activities of companies directly and indirectly allied to the health field. Although such results may be "far out," some kind of project directory with supporting descriptive information should be available to planning managers who must predict future health developments. The same is true in other fields of commercial interest in which there is government supported R&D.

Predictions are being made constantly, with varying degrees of supporting material, that can be used to plot the course of future company activities. Even qualitative information gleaned from these reports and included in a supportive section of the data base would be of assistance to company planners. What effect will a coming election have on the business and consumer climate for the following period? What are the weather predictions by the U.S. Weather Bureau for the coming year? What is the extent and duration being forecast for a flu epidemic that may hit the United States? (How many employees will probably miss work and how long will they be out?) These are examples of questions that have a direct bearing on every business.

Top Management Information Sources

What has been examined is a class of information, not normally formalized for inclusion in a company data base, that should be useful to management—especially middle managers—in planning beyond day-to-day company activities. Were such information to be included in a company information base with ready access provided to middle managers, there would be a marked improvement in the coverage and completeness of studies performed at the middle management level.

Yet this is not the whole story. An existing data base stands in relation to operating personnel as the preceding information stands to middle management in fulfilling its missions. That does not complete the evaluation of information for the firm as a whole. There is a class of activities, performed primarily by top management, that must also be considered. Here, the act of management must be viewed more nearly as an art. Consequently, it is significantly more difficult to isolate the data needed by top managers to carry out their roles successfully. Whereas middle managers have a more clearly defined set of information requirements, top management needs are seen as a series of dimensions to the art of management. Several kinds of activities are representative of top management interests.

Threats to the firm encompass such areas as the political climate of the firm in relation to governmental agencies and consumers. There are also the internal problems such as organizational structure, labor constraints, and individual executive power plays, as well as external threats—competitive action, substitute product development, and natural disasters, for instance. Where possible, the data base should contain information pertinent to all forms of threat to organizational integrity.

Risks include such areas as resource allocation, setting priorities for undertaking new projects, research and development decisions, new product development and integration, and investment decision making.

Top management must be aware of *future resource cost.* This calls for knowledge of developments in the money market; keeping a satisfactory debt-to-equity ratio, given the varying conditions of the investment community and awareness of general stock market trends as well as the effects of particular actions on the company stock in order to protect stockholders' interests.

Future resource technology is a top management interest. Product development of competitive firms must be monitored, and the effects of developing technology must be projected to ensure that current products and production processes are not made obsolete by competitive action. This includes a continuing need to evaluate the cycle time from development to implementation of a process, product, or service.

Top management must take the lead in *concept developments*—determining the nature of the firm and its policy. Where is the expertise of the firm and how can it be best exploited?

What are the *goals* of the business? Is the effort of the firm to be directed toward maintaining the highest return on investment, the highest return on sales, the highest earnings per share? What are the short-term goals and the long-term goals, assuming they differ?

Strategy determination is required. Given the goals of the firm, what steps must be taken to implement them? In the short run? In the long run? In the growth area alone, a range of strategies might be followed. Growth could come from existing product lines; diversification into complementary lines or unrelated services; product and facilities acquisition in either complementary or competing industries; acquisition of an entire subsidiary; the sale of the firm to another company; or liquidation, if the assets are deemed more valuable than the going concern.

Company Posture

A company is more than a production and distribution entity. In the complex society of today, a company must have a posture on public issues. It must be able to react to consumer pressures, be aware of pending legislation as it may affect the firm, be prepared to handle the problems of minority employment, and know the dimensions of the government interface.

The preceding list is neither exhaustive nor set out in any order of priority. Items were selected to point out the areas of concern for top management decision making. In each of these areas, some combination of experience and available information must be used to arrive at the optimum answer for the firm. Although operating daily activities can be carried out by operating personnel using a maximum of data and a minimum of "creative art," the opposite is true of the kinds of decisions made by top management. Even though it is more difficult to isolate those items of information that top management must have, the requirement that they be available when needed is critical. *A lack of information at the operating level may cost the firm some money or time. A lack of information at the top management level may cost the firm its entire existence.*

SUMMARY

Information technology, associating the power of the computer and advanced techniques for management planning and control, has significantly improved the practice of management in the past fifteen years. The phrase "management information system" is widely understood in business and government organizations. Many corporations are installing computer-based systems to support operating managers with the information needed for effective planning and control of resources and programs; some provide varying levels of opportunity for the manager to interact with the computer.

Current operating systems provide for status and performance accounting, with a variety of detail from a high level of summarization and consolidation to a mass of operational level data. Because such data have been recognized as a corporate resource, management generally is aware of its value and the wisdom of investing in systems for its economical production and distribution.

Top management, and middle management to a lesser degree, has not yet reaped similar benefits from the information revolution. The bulk of knowledge relevant to major corporate decisions is still a personal resource; decisions with life-or-death impact on the corporation are often made more on the basis of intuition and guts than on valid information. The cost of collecting and processing the information currently used is high, especially in the use of executive time. The "typical" management information system with its operation-oriented data base is of low utility in major decision-making situations, since the character of data needed for internal operations differs significantly from that used in policy making and strategic planning.

Top management is aware of its need for strategic information and is frustrated by the failure of existing systems to satisfy that need. It is apt to be unaware of the low investment required, relative to the cost of maintaining present intelligence gathering methods, to develop a strategic intelligence capability as a logical extension of an existing or planned system. Corporate management must first recognize the utility of a strategic intelligence system, then consider the options for development of such a system appropriate to the corporate and industry environments. It must consider the investment and payoff implications of the viable options; then, with that imperfect information plus its intuition and guts, the investment decision can be made. Implementation of a strategic intelligence system should prove of significantly greater value to top management than current management information systems to middle management.

BIBLIOGRAPHY

Anthony, Robert N., John Dearden, and Richard F. Vancil, *Management Control Systems: Cases and Readings,* Richard D. Irwin, Inc., 1965.

Donald A. G., *Management, Information and Systems,* Pergamon Press, Inc., 1967.

Emery, James C., *Organizational Planning and Control Systems,* The Macmillan Co., 1969.

Firmin, Peter A., "The Potential of Accounting as a Management Information System," *Management International Review,* **II**, 1966.

Freed, Roy N., "Get the Computer System You Want," *Harvard Business Review,* November-December, 1969.

Glams, Thomas B., B. Grad, D. Holstein, W. E. Meyers, and R. N. Smith, *Management Systems,* Holt, Rinehart & Winston, Inc., 1969.

Holmes, Robert W., "Information Systems for Senior Management," *Financial Executive,* April, 1969.

"How the Computer is Changing Management Organizations," *Business Management,* July, 1967.

Kefalas, Asterios, *Scanning the Business Environment,* Unpublished PhD dissertation, University of Iowa, 1971.

Meier, Robert C., William Newell, and Harold L. Pazer, *Simulation in Business and Economics,* Prentice-Hall, Inc., 1969.

Prince, Thomas R., *Information Systems for Management Planning and Control,* Richard D. Irwin, Inc., 1970.

Roscoe, Perry E., *Developing Computer Based Information Systems,* John Wiley and Sons, 1967.

Sanders, Donald H., *Computers in Business,* McGraw-Hill Book Company, 1968.

Schellenberger, Robert, *Managerial Analysis,* Richard D. Irwin, Inc., 1969.

Simon, Herbert A., *The New Science of Management Decision,* Harper & Row Publishers, 1960.

———, "Information Can be Managed," *Think,* May-June, 1967.

Uhl, K. P., and B. Schoner, *Marketing Research—Information Systems and Decision-Making,* John Wiley and Sons, 1969.

SECTION II

INFORMATION TECHNOLOGY AND ITS IMPACT

The cumulative and permanent effects of the new technology on middle management still remain to be seen. Some have already prophesied the eventual elimination of middle management as such, or, hedging a bit, predict a significant reduction of functions to the extent that existing organizational roles will no longer be meaningful. At any rate, since more and more of the work customarily assigned to the middle management level can readily be programmed and covered by somewhat standardized procedures, the overall job structure will be noticeably altered.

Along with this change, the trend toward bigger and bigger middle management will likewise cease. At the present time middle managers are but small cogs in a gigantic bureaucratic system. Like other middle echelon specialists, they operate along rather narrow functional lines. Regardless of their qualifications, their role is segmented, specialized, and impersonal. These swollen middle layers of management, sometimes unfavorably referred to as "management by bureaucracy" or "management by bureaucracy specialists," are destined to shrink appreciably within the very near future.

The introductory reading by Simon provides some elementary insights into the role of automation and its impact on man and the manager in particular. The production of symbols is seen as being on par with the tool-building activity that characterized the Industrial Revolution of a bygone century. The products that flowed from the factory are no more real or important than the symbols that mark our present highly automated age. Automation introduced nonhuman machinery as both a complement and a supplement to human resources in information processing. Of the information-processing machines so far introduced, the electronic digital computer is perhaps the most significant. It is not limited to storing symbols (as paper and pencil are) nor to copying symbols (as in printing) nor to transmitting symbols (as in radio, TV, telegraphy, and telephony). It can manipulate symbols much as human beings do. It is this capability of the computer that enables it to solve problems, make decisions, and translate information from one language to another. From this flows as a consequence its effectiveness in processing human information that has so visibly affected the educational and work sectors of our present generation.

Physical production is becoming less important than symbol production for managers, who must learn to live symbiotically with information-processing machines. The latter will take up a larger role in the day-to-day operations of the firm and factory. As a result, the functions of the former will be modified, and more of the manager's time and effort will be devoted to the designing and planning of tasks rather than to the control and supervision of the man-machine systems. The repercussions of these shifts in emphasis should be felt in the training and education of managers and executives. These will now need to know a great deal more than formerly, but what they need to know most is how to continue to acquire new knowledge and revise the old. The day is gone when managers can be taught all that they will need to know.

Leavitt and Whisler, in the second reading, are of the opinion that centralization of management will be made easier by the new technology. The line of demarcation between top management and middle management will be more sharply drawn as time goes on, and on the whole middle managers will be downgraded, since more and more of their routine functions will be programmable. However, not all middle management jobs will be affected in the same way by the new technological explosion. At least two classes of middle jobs will move upwards, toward a state of deprogrammedness. One of these will be that of the programmers, who are themselves the high priests of the new information technology. The other will be that of the research and development engineers, whose innovative abilities will become increasingly important to top management.

As for top management, the newer and more efficient information-processing techniques will free them from the more mundane executive details so that they can extend their abilities to encompass newer and broader tasks. They will not only be freer to think but now they will be forced to do so. Since change will be the ethos of the times, we can expect a heavy turnover in top managers, who quickly burn themselves out as far as innovative ideas are concerned.

With the advent of management systems departments in numerous organizations, many of the predictions of Leavitt and Whisler have already taken shape. Production problems have become increasingly routinized; simulation has proved an invaluable managerial device; tools such as PERT and similar planning and control techniques have been developed; programmers and operation researchers have been assigned important top-level roles; innovation and creativity have become increasingly vital; and the modern trend of employing more and more mathematicians has shown no signs of letting up.

To date, many companies have reorganized in an attempt to meet the changing and challenging technology of the twentieth century. One large company created a management-systems department, one section of which employs 54 mathematical and programming technicians, seventeen of whom are Ph.D.'s.

Although some organizations have created new systems departments, not all writers concur with the view that middle management is adversely affected by the new information technology. Burlingame, in the third reading, contends that "all managers are deeply involved in problems where judgment and human values are the important elements." And more specifically, "they are concerned with situations where the decisions cannot be anticipated, the information needs predicted, or the decision elements quantified." Far from eliminating middle management, the new technology, in Burlingame's view, will provide middle management with the tools it needs to do a better job. Instead of rendering managerial ability obsolescent, it will put a high premium on native ability for exercising initiative and for shouldering judgment responsibilities. "This effect," he believes, "should far outweigh in importance any tendency of computers to eliminate jobs where the nature of decisions is mechanical, especially when it is remembered that the growth in the complexity of business is increasing the need for effective managers."

To be realistic, both of the above positions seem valid. While on one hand information technology has revolutionized some managerial functions, on the other hand, it has not depersonalized the functions of the middle managers. Progressive management is not so naive as to assume that all personal needs will be adequately satisfied off the job. On the contrary, if anything, organizations have increased their efforts to cater to the personal and social needs of their managers as well as those of their rank-and-file. This practice, however, is in no way at variance with the demands of the new technology. Experienced managers are still the backbone of the organization and will conceivably continue to be so in the future. There is no doubt that managers have been upgraded; more information has been placed at their disposal to aid them in their decision-making function. But even so, a gradual and perceptible shift is taking place and a new breed of manager is emerging.

Three readings attempt to critically appraise the various predictions made concerning the future of middle managers. The study by Schaul was made in the first half of the 1960s, while that by Reif was done in the latter half of the same decade. Together, their findings either reinforce one another or throw additional light on an aspect of the problem by introducing a necessary distinction.

Schaul interviewed some fifty middle managers and a dozen or so top managers in eight companies, and he discusses his results in terms of change in middle managers' functions and scope, decision-making authority, and status. As could be expected, change differentials were encountered in the various categories investigated.

Regarding the functions of the middle manager (planning, organizing, staffing, directing, and controlling), less and less time was being devoted to the control function as a result of EDP and much more to the planning function. In general, none of these functions have been eliminated, nor has any specialist group arisen to appropriate any one of them. What has actually happened is that only the amount of time devoted to each has been adjusted.

The scope of the middle manager's job has been appreciably expanded. Many new activities have been assigned, while the traditional functions have become increasingly complex. The predicted reduction in the decision-making authority granted to middle managers has not been borne out by this study. The EDP system had no significant influence on their authority. What was experienced was a change in authority coincident with the increase or decrease in the number of assigned activities.

Far from being progressively eliminated, middle managers saw an increase in their number. Also, instead of the predicted lowering of status, an enhanced status was reported.

Reif's case study of three firms was meant to be representative of three major business classifications as well as of varying firm size. Furthermore, the three firms selected had utilized the computer for different lengths of time.[1]

Computers were observed to bring about a centralization of decision making in the management hierarchy: fewer decisions were being made at the lower levels and more at the higher levels, while less important decisions were left to the decentralized managers. Line-staff relationships were being redrawn, with the staff groups appropriating more decision-making authority.

Changes in the informal communication network resulted from the introduction of the computer; changes in the formal aspect had not yet been incorporated into the organizational structure.

The implications of the computer for middle management are more in line with the dire predictions reported above. However, Reif does not discriminate between the various functions reported on separately by Schaul. In both studies the control function seems to be severely restricted by EDP, since this function is most easily programmable. The susceptibility to replacement by the computer, Reif found, is tied to the type of routine decisions for which middle managers are held responsible. The difference in the findings in the two studies, when clearly evident, may be a function of the sampling procedures used. In Reif's case study a utility company, a bank, and a large manufacturing company alone were utilized.

In an article published at about the same time, Blumenthal[2] examined the role of advanced business systems from a pragmatic standpoint. He was not so much concerned with the computer-manager symbiosis. Computers, he found, were definitely here to stay and so were the managers. As a result of the interaction process, middle management was on the decline, not so much functionally but simply in terms of numbers. The immediate effect of the impact of

[1] In 1964 Lee studied the impact of EDP on patterns of business organization in three carefully selected firms, the same three types later reported on by Reif, viz, a public utility, a bank, and a manufacturing firm. He found that in the utility and banking firms the effect of the computer on decision making was relatively small, that an increase in the managerial personnel as a whole resulted from the introduction of EDP, and that the status of managerial jobs was generally upgraded by the elimination of clerical work and the concentration on decision making. See Hak Chong Lee, *The Impact of Electronic Data Processing Upon the Patterns of Business Organization and Administration,* School of Business, State University of New York at Albany, 1965.

[2] S. C. Blumenthal, "Breaking the Chain of Command," *Business Automation* (November, 1963), pp. 20–27.

the new information system on the structure was the diminution of the clerical staff and of their managers.[3] A return to centralization was fostered by the concentration at the top of the limited pool of executives and technicians capable of dealing with the new technology.

Departmentalization was also coming to an end because more and more dimensions of the organization could effectively be coordinated into one integrated data stream based on common sources of raw data. More and more of the top management positions were being filled with professionals able to wed the realities and subtleties of management planning and control to information systems.

In his article entitled "Emerging EDP Patterns," Charles Hofer not only provides the reader with up-to-date EDP scorecards of the armchair predictors and the pavement-pounding researchers but also presents the results of his own investigation in this area. His study population consisted of two manufacturing firms, one with sales in excess of $200 million and the other with sales of approximately $8 million. While many of the studies cited in this report examined the effects of computers in but one or more functional areas, Hofer's study embraced a wide spectrum of functional areas such as marketing, finance, general management, employee relations, manufacturing, and engineering at all levels of the organization. His methodology consisted of extensive interviews with nearly eighty managers, as well as a thorough examination of supplemental company data.

Hofer's findings can be summarized according to the following five categories: EDP's effect on formal structure, on decision making, on operational planning, on budgeting, and on measurement. The three managerial levels scrutinized were those of the general managers, top functional managers, and operational managers.

As for the area of organizational structure, Hofer found no changes wrought by the computer at either the general or top functional management levels. However, where the activities involved called for the processing of a large volume of data, the operational level was affected. In this regard, some tasks were abrogated, others enhanced, and others just modified. But the principal effects were most noticeable where large data volume processing occurred.

The structure of the top levels of the organization was not visibly affected, since the specific tasks performed at these levels were also not significantly influenced by the computer. The computer does not assist managers in managing people or in understanding a subordinate's job.

As for decision making, no direct effects were observed at the general management level. However, some de facto delegation did take place at the top functional level. This delegation for the analysis and evaluation of certain classes of decisions generally involved those decisions most amenable to systems and procedures treatment. As expected, at the operational level a substantial number of decisions involving production were programmed.

Again, the general management level was not affected by any changes in the area of operation planning. This may have been attributable to the fact that these managers do not get involved in the day-to-day operational planning that goes on, except for monitoring activities. Top functional managers were provided with more useful information for improving existing systems, while the more accurate information given the operational managers did assist them in improving their planning operations.

With respect to the effects of EDP on budgeting, two changes were observed.

[3] Job reduction consequent upon the introduction of EDP is treated more extensively in Andrew J. Grimes and Roger C. Vergin, *The Impact of the Computer: A Management View,* Business Report No. 5 (Minneapolis: School of Business Administration, University of Minnesota, April, 1963), pp. 5–6, and also in Roger C. Vergin and Andrew J. Grimes, "Management Myths and EDP," *California Management Review,* 7 (Fall, 1964), pp. 59–70.

The first, occurring at the top functional level, pertained to the rapidity with which budgets could be altered to meet changing circumstances. The other related increased accuracy to a more refined cost breakdown at the operational level.

In the area of measurement, however, the impact of the computer was felt at all levels of the organization. General management was able to request additional back-up information in many areas of uncertainty. In other instances the computer allowed for in-depth penetration of problem areas by providing data hitherto unavailable. Top functional managers as well as operational managers benefited in the area of measurement by more quantitative reporting and by more objective evaluation of subordinates, replacing many qualitative subjective judgments.

Hofer's general predictions for the future are not as universal as one might expect. This is due to the nature of the diverse processes involved, the levels of the organization, the way change is implemented, and a host of other environmental variables.

19. THE IMPACT OF NEW INFORMATION-PROCESSING TECHNOLOGY ON MANAGERS

HERBERT A. SIMON*

The term "automation" is so widely current, and has become, as a result, so vague that it does not require or admit precise definition. Two or three hundred years ago—after two thousand years of relative stability—the techniques and technical equipment that man used to meet his needs, began to undergo continuous, accelerating change and improvement. These changes, starting on a large scale in Western Europe and America, are still in the process of diffusing to other parts of the world.

Even today, in many hundreds of thousands of villages around the world, these great trends are known to the peasants only as vague rumors, borne to them by an off-course airplane, a truck bumping over a rutted trail, or, too often, a band of marauding soldiers. These peasants—a majority of the world's population—would feel quite at home with the tools and artifacts used by a Greek farmer at the time of Alexander the Great (and he with theirs).

In the Western world, however, with its expanding boundaries, it is change that has become commonplace. In the Western child's vocabulary, "olden times" does not mean classical Greece, Medieval knighthood, or even frontiersmen and Indians. It means the world of his parents. For Western man, the Industrial Revolution holds more significance than any political revolution (unless, as in Russia, he confuses the two).

At the heart of the increases in productivity that mark the Industrial Revolution is a great burst of tool-building activity. After having been satisfied for thousands of years with his domestic cattle, draft animals, and crops, and with his hand implements of stone, bronze, and iron, he discovered fire for the second time—this time as a source of energy many times more powerful than his own.

With mechanical energy came mechanization—the devising of tools for applying that energy to the processes of production. The human worker remained an essential part of the system of production, but his main function became that of guiding nonhuman forces rather than applying his own. In very recent years, in speaking of "automation" rather than "mechanization," we mean to note the fact that man's tool-building ingenuity has not limited itself to capturing and harnessing mechanical energy, but has now extended also to the processes of guiding and controlling that energy. Automation, to paraphrase Clausewitz, is a continuation of the Industrial Revolution by other means.

From the earliest times, the productive resource in human economies has always been man-with-tool. In pre-industrial societies, the tool may be inconspicuous—a stone blade held in the fist—but it is always there, and essentially there. Fly over India at 15,000 feet, and see how slightly man has scratched the earth's surface. Man's green crops and earthen huts need no camouflage to merge into the landscape. Fly lower, and man becomes visible. However superficially, he has changed the natural environment to facilitate growing his food, moving about, and sheltering himself. Land your plane and walk into the village, and you see that man almost never lives in a natural environment, but always in an environment of his fellow men and his own artifacts and implements.

Man's economy, his whole culture, even in peasant societies, is less accurately viewed as an interaction of man with nature than as a *man-tool system,* a system that increasingly shields man from a direct, naked confrontation

SOURCE: *Commercial Letter* (October, 1966), pp. 1–7. Reprinted by permission of the Canadian Imperial Bank and the University of Toronto.

* Carnegie-Mellon University.

with nature. With the Industrial Revolution and mechanization, the man-tool system becomes a man-machine system; and by the time we reach the contemporary stage of automation, the intermingling, in the productive process, of man and his tools is almost complete.

Viewing from this perspective, we are less struck by the differences between peasant and industrial cultures than by their similarities. Both the peasant economy and the modern industrial economy are man-tool systems. In both, man lives and works surrounded by his own artifacts. When westernization reaches his village, it poses no particular problem for the peasant to learn to live in a man-made environment; he has been living in one all his life. It may pose a real problem to learn to live in a *different* environment than the one to which he has become accustomed, and an even more difficult problem to adjust to massive changes in that environment each generation. Thus it is important to distinguish between the "artificiality" of an automated economy, which presents no essential novelty at all, and its changeability, which does, in fact, represent something new under the sun. I will have occasion to return to this distinction at later points in my talks.

TECHNOLOGICAL CHANGE AND JOB CONTENT

Before I turn to the particular effects of automation upon the shape of the industrial firm, I should like to call attention to the subtle and indirect ways in which advances in technology sometimes alter the processes of production. Since these indirect consequences are often more important than the direct impact, we must keep our eyes open for them. An illustration will make the point.

We do not usually think of the physician's profession as one that is highly mechanized—capital-intensive in the economist's language. Perhaps, classifying it as a service occupation, we do not regard its productivity as having been much affected by technological change. But let us take a closer look.

At the turn of the century, the most-used skill of a Canadian or American physician was the skill of driving a horse. That is how he spent ninety per cent of his working time, driving from farm to farm. The invention of the automobile and the construction of a system of farm roads probably multiplied the productivity of the rural doctor by a factor of at least two, and perhaps four or five. More recently, the invention and widespread use of antibiotics caused a second large leap in medical productivity. Not only is the pneumonia patient far more likely to recover than he was in 1900, but while he is doing so, he takes only five or ten per cent as much of the physician's time. (That is why we in the United States have only very recently become aware of the failure of the number of physicians to keep pace with the growth of our population and affluence.)

The medical profession may at present be on the brink of an automation and mechanization that will be far more visible and direct than this earlier one. I refer not only to the increasingly elaborate equipment employed in diagnosis and treatment, to the point where it becomes difficult to be sure whether one is in a hospital or a factory, but to the imminence of effective automated techniques for diagnosis, and the already developed methods for monitoring automatically the condition of post-operative patients. It is not clear whether this newer automation will bring about productivity increases any more dramatic than those produced in less direct ways by the earlier ones I have described.

When we turn our attention to corporate automation, we must be on the alert for comparably indirect effects. Thus, to use a hypothetical example, selling will become a very different and more efficient occupation when video-telephone communication replaces air travel. (So, I might add, will lecturing.)

THINKING AS A FACTOR OF PRODUCTION

We can still accept the classical list of factors of production—land, labor, and capital. But the content of several of the items, notably labor and capital, has greatly changed. As "capital" became "power-driven machinery," "labor" became "thinking." What a modern worker—whether blue collar or white—rents out when he accepts employment is his brain, its sensors—eyes and ears—and its effectors—mouth and hands. It is seldom, and increasingly seldom, of importance what shoulder and leg muscles are thrown into the bargain.

It was traditional to conceptualize a factory

in terms of flows of energy and materials. Raw materials were received; power was applied to them through machines; the finished product came out at the other end, to be shipped to customers. Workmen controlled the process, and contributed to those parts of it that demanded the kind of flexibility and dexterity that is best provided by the coordination of hand with eye.

But often there isn't a physical product, except in the sense that books and advertising flyers are physical products. Many businesses produce services, not goods. And even where there is a tangible product, the physical and energy flows are paralleled by an equally indispensable flow of words and symbols: the words and symbols that represent the organization's decisions, that transmit its information, that constitute its accounts and records. A factory that takes wheat and manufactures flour also takes in vast quantities of words and transforms them into other words. Most of the working force, and an increasing proportion of the machines in any corporation are engaged, not directly in the manufacture of a physical product, but in the manufacture of words.

Often, in our old-fashioned physiocratic way, we regard the physical product as "real," while we regard the words as some kind of epiphenomenon, perhaps indispensable, but certainly regrettable. Most of our ways of referring to them are pejorative: "red tape," "bureaucracy," "paperwork," "overhead." (Prefix the adjective "unnecessary" to each term, and we have all the makings of an efficiency expert's report or a legislative investigation.)

Of course it is an illusion to suppose that the words are any less real than the things, or that any human endeavor, substantial or slight, can go on without a vast production of symbols. We use the term "thinking," or more commonly now, the term "information processing," as a name for the whole collection of processes involved in manufacturing finished words from symbolic raw materials. Thus, a corporation is, among other things, a vast information-processing system, and its production machinery consists largely of information-processing machines.

Until recently, almost the only information-processing machines available for symbol production were human brains. For a long time there have been minor exceptions—steam engine governors and thermostats, for example—but these were few and inconsequential. Taking account of the manufacture of both symbols and physical products, the human brain has been by far the most important factor of production in the modern economy. About three-quarters of the total cost of doing business goes to the payment of labor, with only about one-quarter to the rental and replacement of machines.

What is most novel about automation—as contrasted with the earlier phases of mechanization—is the extent to which it introduces non-human machinery to complement and supplement human resources in information processing. Again, I must qualify the claims of novelty, lest I be convicted of gross historical inaccuracy. Many thousands of years ago, man discovered that his thinking was much impeded by his exceedingly small short-term memory—he could only hold on to a half-dozen things at a time in his thoughts. Moreover, the reliability of his long-term memory was mediocre. The difficulty in short-term memory slowed him down in doing sums, while the inaccuracy of long-term memory made him forget how many bushels of corn his neighbor owed him. Then he discovered that he could store symbols outside his own brain by recording them in physical form—by writing. The brain still had to do all the active information processing, but it could supplement its insufficient memories with the papyrus and clay tablet.

Much more recently, only five hundred years ago, man found a way in which he could manufacture cheaply an indefinite number of copies of the contents of a memory: printing. In this instance, the mechanization encompassed only the simplest—copying—of the basic information processes, leaving the more complicated transformations to human brains. Still more recently, a century ago, man discovered a way of communicating copies of symbols, by telegraph, radio, and telephone, in a moment over vast distances. Still, this new invention was only a means for distant copying, not for the transformation of information.

A more accurate way, then, of saying what is novel, is to observe that automation represents the first large-scale mechanized *active* information processing that goes beyond simple recording, copying, and transmission of copies. The inventions of writing and of printing have always been regarded as among the most significant and consequential human discoveries. From the importance that has been attached to the mechanization of these simplest aspects of information processing, we obtain a scale that helps us assess the prospective significance of the invention, about twenty years ago, of quite general-purpose, information-processing machinery.

Public discussion of automation has focused mainly on the blue collar worker. We see that automation has even greater import for the symbol factory than for the factory that produces physical products. In the petroleum and chemical industries, we are already very close to the automatic factory for physical production. But we need to pay even more attention to the prospects of using the modern electronic digital computer to equip automatic information processing factories. To evaluate this prospect, we must understand the nature of the computer.

THE ELECTRONIC DIGITAL COMPUTER

I have referred to the modern computer as a general-purpose information-processing machine. The term "general-purpose" is meant to imply that a computer is capable of carrying out all of the basic kinds of information processes that are carried out by the human brain. It is not limited to storing symbols, as paper and pencil is; nor to copying symbols, as is printing; nor to transmitting symbols, as is telegraph and radio. In addition to these, it can carry out the other processes that are essential if a system is to think—that is, to make decisions, recognize patterns, solve problems, translate information from one language or encoding to another, and so on. The main additional capability that appears essential for thinking is the ability to match two symbols, to determine whether they are the same or different, and to make subsequent processing conditional on the outcome of the matching process.

How do we know this? How do we know what information processing takes place when a human being thinks, or what processes a machine would need to accomplish thinking? First, it should be said that we don't know completely, or with certainty. What we do know is that computers have been programmed to perform a wide range of tasks that require thinking when performed by human beings. With respect to some of these programs, we know that the paths they follow in seeking problem solutions or in making decisions parallel very closely the paths followed by human subjects performing the same tasks when we study them in the laboratory.[1]

We have found this out by asking people to think aloud while solving problems of various kinds in the laboratory, and by recording their verbalizations. We then compared their tape-recorded verbal protocols with the step-by-step output of a computer that had been programmed to solve problems of the same kinds, the programs having been constructed to use the same processes we thought people used. When a close match was achieved between the computer output and the human protocol, we could conclude that we had explained at least some of the main features of the human thinking. The computer program most certainly contained a *sufficient* set of processes for problem solving—or it would not solve the problems or parallel the human verbalization. And since the computer programs contained only basic processes of the sorts mentioned earlier, we could know that these processes, appropriately organized, are sufficiently powerful to permit a system processing them to solve problems like some solved by people.

Thus, there exists today a theory of human thinking relating to at least several tasks of real-life complexity; and, moreover, a theory that passes some rather severe tests of its sufficiency to explain the phenomena. It is a sufficiently powerful theory so that computer programs based on it can perform non-trivial thinking tasks; and it is sufficiently powerful so that some of the programs use information-processing methods in performing these tasks very similar to the processes used by people.

This development of the past decade, which continues to unfold rapidly, has two quite distinct implications. In our fascination with either of them, we must not ignore the other.

[1] Readers who wish a closer acquaintance with the research on computer simulation of human thinking that is the basis for these assertions will find a fuller description in E. Feigenbaum and J. Feldman (eds.) *Computers and Thought,* McGraw-Hill, New York, 1963. There is a briefer discussion in the last half of my book, *The Shape of Automation,* Harper and Row, New York, 1965.

First, it opens up the prospect, already mentioned, of complementing and supplementing human labor with machinery in our symbol factories. But, second, it also opens up the prospect of greatly enhancing the effectiveness of the human information-processing in those factories. Since the latter prospect is less obvious than the former, I should like to examine it in a little more detail.

THE IMPROVEMENT OF HUMAN THINKING

Human thinking, we have seen, is an important—the most important—economic resource. For some people, under some conditions, thinking is also fun. When we talk about increasing the effectiveness of human thinking, we must not forget its dual character; and we might well be willing to forego greater efficiency of thought if we could only improve thought by dehumanizing it. I mention this caveat at the outset so that we will not lose sight of it in the course of this discussion. I will anticipate my own personal conclusion to the extent of saying that I believe we can improve human thinking without making it less fun.

Volumes on improving thinking are staple items on the shelf of how-to books. Evidently, lots of people want to improve their thinking. Experience in improving other kinds of things carries one important lesson for anyone who wants to improve his thinking: to improve something, more than superficially, you must understand it. If your automobile uses too much gas, burns oil, or doesn't run at all, you are unlikely to remedy matters much unless you know something about the mechanics of an automobile, and how its parts operate. If you are suffering from chronic digestive ills, you are unlikely to find a cure except at the hands of someone who understands the anatomy and physiology of the human digestive system.

In the past, the improvement of human thinking has foundered on the rock of understanding. We could tell when a human being had been thinking effectively because he produced an output—a solved problem, a design, a decision. We could measure the relative effectiveness of different thinkers by noting the speed with which they could solve problems, or the difficulties of the problems they could handle. But we didn't know *why* one was more effective than another, or precisely what to do to improve either.

I am exaggerating our ignorance, of course. For a long time we have had processes called "teaching," "learning," and "education" which seem sometimes to improve the quality of thinking. But we haven't quite understood why or when they work. They have been a sovereign remedy, like blood-letting was for an eighteenth century physician, that we could apply when we didn't know what else to do.

The most widely accepted theory of the educational process was largely an information-inventory theory. Clearly, most kinds of thinking required information; improvements in the amounts and quality of relevant information should improve the thinking. Hence to educate was to fill the information granaries against the day of knowledge drought. An educated brain was a library shelved centrally for handy access.

There were competing theories of education, particularly after printing raised the question of whether book knowledge was not better left in well-indexed books. Some thought that the task of education was not simply to store the raw materials for information processing, but to improve the processes themselves. "Mental discipline" was one of the forms this doctrine took. Empirical evidence later showed that courses in Latin or logic did not necessarily produce straight thinking, and this finding was extrapolated into skepticism about the possibility of teaching people how to think better.

Skepticism, or at least pessimism, is quite unjustified today. We are beginning to get precise information as to how, for example, a high school student processes information to solve a word problem in his algebra class. We understand why one student, given a description of a physically impossible situation, will proceed to set up his equations as though nothing were wrong; while another, with precisely the same information, will discover the physical incongruity. Understanding this, we can design remedial treatment for the first student.

While the range of human thinking tasks for which this kind of analysis has been carried out in detail is still very small, it includes not only tasks at the level of school courses, but also certain tasks taken from the work of middle-level business executives and professional engineers. I am not referring to situations where executive decision making has been automated by substituting for it complex mathematical models, and then using computers to solve the resulting arithmetic problems. This has been done too, on a large scale, but it has nothing to do, directly, with human thinking. Humans do not do high-speed arithmetic as a computer does when it is planning production for a refinery by solving a linear programming problem. People use quite different methods, not requiring high-speed calculation, when they have to plan production without computer assistance.

But a computer's processing is not limited to high-speed arithmetic. (This is just another talent it has, in addition to those possessed by people.) It is, as I said earlier, a general-purpose information-processor; and the programs that are interesting for an understanding of human thinking are those that do not require high-speed arithmetic. To have a name for them, let's call them "heuristic programs," and —those requiring rapid calculation—"operations research" programs. A number of operations research programs have been written to carry out the factory scheduling task known as assembly-line balancing. But Tonge wrote a heuristic assembly-line balancing program that, instead of doing complex arithmetic, simulates closely the processes that were used by a human industrial engineer, experienced in performing that scheduling task.

Similarly, all electrical manufacturers now possess programs for *designing* (not just evaluating the designs of) many kinds of motors, generators, and transformers—programs that resemble closely the design processes formerly used by professional engineers. These are not highly "creative" design activities, but they are activities that had until recently been thought to require the thinking of a college-educated engineer.

Finally, Clarkson has written a program that simulated remarkably closely the decision-making behavior of a bank trust officer whose job it was to buy stocks and bonds for trust funds. The program predicted, with a high degree of accuracy, what specific stocks and bonds he would buy for a trust with specified assets and goals, and how many shares of each.[2] Other programs have been written more recently to simulate the pricing behavior of a department store buyer.

Some of the computer programs I have mentioned were aimed at improving the human performance by automating it; the others simply at understanding it. It is the latter goal with which we are concerned here. The programs are part of the growing body of evidence about the nature of human thought processes, evidence that is leading us to a deep understanding of these processes, and that will lead us from understanding to their improvement.

THE INFORMATION-PROCESSING FACTORY

I think we can now begin to put the pieces of the puzzle together. I do not mean by this that we can expect to attain a perfectly clear, detailed picture. But I believe we can see some ways for thinking clearly and productively about the future, a frame for viewing it.

1. Physical production is becoming a less important aspect of management than the production of symbols. The significant factory is the information-processing factory.

2. The information-processing factory is becoming a man-machine system involving a close symbiosis between human thinkers and information-processing machines—especially digital computers.

3. As computers become cheaper and more plentiful, and as we learn to program them to behave more flexibly, they will be able to assume a larger part of the task of day-to-day operation of the information-processing factory.

4. The division of labor between men and computers will be gradually modified as a function of the relative availabilities and capabilities of the two. In the short-run and middle-run, we may expect the executive's task to become more and more a designing and planning task. That is, he will have less to do with the actual running of the system on an hour-to-hour basis, and more and more with improving the system itself by modifying and redesigning it.

5. We may expect our understanding of human thinking, and our ability to improve it, to advance nearly as rapidly as our understanding of computers. Hence, technological progress in the manufacture of information will

[2] Clarkson's program is described in Feigenbaum and Feldman, op. cit., pages 347–371.

result from improvements in both the human and machine processing.

If you want a more concrete picture of what the information-processing factory will look like a few years hence, you will probably not be too badly misled if you examine two analogous situations that can be observed in our economy today. There are already nearly-automated factories for manufacturing physical products in the chemical industry, and there are already nearly-automated electronic data processing departments in insurance companies, banks, and large corporations generally.

When you visit either of these kinds of establishments—the automatic factory or the computerized office—you are struck first by the fact that the human workers are outside the direct work stream. The chemicals are produced untouched by human hands, as are the documents in the modern computer installation. The humans, in fact, can go away, at least for short intervals of time, without disrupting the work. They seem to be little concerned with doing the "work," much concerned with detecting unusual situations, performing preventive and corrective maintenance, and considering how the system can be altered for its improvement. They are, in fact, performing the kinds of functions that we may expect executives in the future to perform in the larger organizations to which these components belong.

It is worth noting that these nearly-automated establishments do not at all resemble the stereotype of the assembly line, with the human worker locked to the machine and forced to its work pace. If the assembly line was a thoroughly bad human environment, as many think, we need not worry that it has any similarity to the automated factory. On the contrary, the kinds of automation we have been discussing appear to permit an "interface" between man and machine that is much more adaptive to the needs and nature of each than the linkages that bound man to his tools in the past.

THE EDUCATION OF THE EXECUTIVE

We have pictured the executive as a designer and maintainer of man-machine systems that process information. We have argued that he and other human beings can expect to understand their own thought processes much more fully than they have understood them in the past. If these propositions are correct, they carry clear implications for the education of executives. One major stem of that education will be devoted to the improvement of thinking and decision-making. Another stem will be concerned with the theory and technique of designing information-processing systems.

In trying to spell out the curriculum at the next level of detail, matters become much more conjectural. It is easiest to make some statements about what it will *not* be. In the light of our analysis, and taking account of the rapid change in our society, specific factual content will become a less important part of it. We will not fill the granary with current institutional knowledge of marketing, production, and finance, because most of that knowledge is almost sure to spoil before the drought comes when we want to use it. I do not mean that people do not need to know anything in order to think and make good decisions. They need to know a great deal, but what they need to know changes, and cannot be taught —because it is not known—a decade before use. What people most need to know is how to continue to acquire new knowledge and revise old knowledge throughout their careers.

It turns out, then, that learning how to think and learn, and learning how to design an information-processing system are not really separate and distinct topics. They are parts of the same topic. A human thinker is an organization of memories combined with a system of basic information processes that uses those memories, together with new information, to solve problems. But that is a definition of a business organization, too, whose components —men and computers—are, in turn, systems of the same general sort. This is the kind of system—at the level of the individual, and at the level of the organization—that we must understand if we are to continue our technical progress.

CONCLUSION

I have tried to indicate what seem to me some of the main implications of the contemporary trends in automation for business and for management in the future. My remarks have been less a sketch of the future than a suggestion of a framework for thinking about it. I have had little to say about the implications of these trends for the wider society in which organizations operate; and I should like to devote my second lecture to those broader implications.

The impact of automation and computers is felt not only individually but also collectively —not only by an individual business but also by the whole economy. The effects on productivity, consumption, unemployment, technology, and other factors have broad implications which cut across the whole economic, social, and political spectrum of a Nation.

20. MANAGEMENT IN THE 1980's

HAROLD J. LEAVITT * AND THOMAS L. WHISLER †

Over the last decade a new technology has begun to take hold in American business, one so new that its significance is still difficult to evaluate. While many aspects of this technology are uncertain, it seems clear that it will move into the managerial scene rapidly, with definite and far-reaching impact on managerial organization. In this article we would like to speculate about these effects, especially as they apply to medium-size and large business firms of the future.

The new technology does not yet have a single established name. We shall call it *information technology*. It is composed of several related parts. One includes techniques for processing large amounts of information rapidly, and it is epitomized by the high-speed computer. A second part centers around the application of statistical and mathematical methods to decision-making problems; it is represented by techniques like mathematical programing, and by methodologies like operations research. A third part is in the offing, though its applications have not yet emerged very clearly; it consists of the simulation of higher-order thinking through computer programs.

Information technology is likely to have its greatest impact on middle and top management. In many instances it will lead to opposite conclusions from those dictated by the currently popular philosophy of "participative" management. Broadly, our prognostications are along the following lines:

1. Information technology should move the boundary between planning and performance upward. Just as planning was taken from the hourly worker and given to the industrial engineer, we now expect it to be taken from a number of middle managers and given to as yet largely nonexistent specialists: "operations researchers," perhaps, or "organizational analysts." Jobs at today's middle-management level will become highly structured. Much more of the work will be programed, i.e., covered by sets of operating rules governing the day-to-day decisions that are made.

2. Correlatively, we predict that large industrial organizations will recentralize, that top managers will take on an even larger proportion of the innovating, planning, and other "creative" functions than they have now.

3. A radical reorganization of middle-management levels should occur, with *certain classes* of middle-management jobs moving downward in status and compensation (because they will require less autonomy and skill), while other classes move upward into the top-management group.

4. We suggest, too, that the line separating the top from the middle of the organization will be drawn more clearly and impenetrably than ever, much like the line drawn in the last few decades between hourly workers and first-line supervisors.

THE NEW TECHNOLOGY

Information technology has diverse roots—with contributions from such disparate groups as sociologists and electrical engineers. Working independently, people from many disciplines have been worrying about problems that have turned out to be closely related and cross-fertilizing. Cases in point are the engineers' development of servomechanisms and the related developments of general cybernetics and information theory. These ideas from the "hard" sciences all had a direct bearing on problems of processing information—in particular, the development of techniques for conceptualizing and measuring information.

SOURCE: *Harvard Business Review* (November-December, 1958), pp. 41–48.

* Stanford University.
† The University of Chicago.

Related ideas have also emerged from other disciplines. The mathematical economist came along with game theory, a means of ordering and permitting analysis of strategies and tactics in purely competitive "think-" type games. Operations research fits in here, too; OR people made use of evolving mathematical concepts, or devised their own, for solving multivariate problems without necessarily worrying about the particular context of the variables. And from social psychology ideas about communication structures in groups began to emerge, followed by ideas about thinking and general problem-solving processes.

All of these developments, and many others from even more diverse sources, have in common a concern about the systematic manipulation of information in individuals, groups, or machines. The relationships among the ideas are not yet clear, nor has the wheat been adequately separated from the chaff. It is hard to tell who started what, what preceded what, and which is method and which theory. But, characteristically, application has not, and probably will not in the future, wait on completion of basic research.

Distinctive Features

We call information technology "new" because one did not see much use of it until World War II, and it did not become clearly visible in industry until a decade later. It is new, also in that it can be differentiated from at least two earlier industrial technologies:

1. In the first two decades of this century, Frederick W. Taylor's *scientific management* constituted a new and influential technology—one that took a large part in shaping the design of industrial organizations.

2. Largely after World War II a second distinct technology, *participative management*, seriously overtook—and even partially displaced—scientific management. Notions about decentralization, morale, and human relations modified and sometimes reversed earlier applications of scientific management. Individual incentives, for example, were treated first as simple applications of Taylorism, but they have more recently been revised in the light of "participative" ideas.

The scientific and participative varieties both survived. One reason is that scientific management concentrated on the hourly worker, while participative management has generally aimed one level higher, at middle managers, so they have not conflicted. But what will happen now? The new information technology has direct implications for middle management as well as top management.

Current Picture

The inroads made by this technology are already apparent, so that our predictions are more extrapolations than derivations.[1] But the significance of the new trends has been obscured by the wave of interest in participative management and decentralization. Information technology seems now to show itself mostly in the periphery of management. Its applications appear to be independent of central organizational issues like communication and creativity. We have tended until now to use little pieces of the new technology to generate information, or to lay down limits for subtasks that can then be used within the old structural framework.

Some of this sparing use of information technology may be due to the fact that those of us with a large commitment to participative management have cause to resist the central implications of the new techniques. But the implications are becoming harder to deny. Many business decisions once made judgmentally now can be made better by following some simple routines devised by a staff man whose company experience is slight, whose position on the organization chart is still unclear, and whose skill (if any) in human relations was picked up on the playground. For example:

We have heard recently of an electric utility which is considering a move to take away from generating-station managers virtually all responsibility for deciding when to use standby generating capacity. A typical decision facing such managers develops on hot summer afternoons. In anticipation of heavy home air-conditioning demand at the close of working hours, the manager may put on extra capacity in late afternoon. This results in additional costs, such as overtime premiums. In this

[1] Two examples of current developments are discussed in "Putting Arma Back on Its Feet," *Business Week*, February 1, 1958, p. 84; and "Two-Way Overhaul Rebuilds Raytheon," *Business Week*, February 22, 1958, p. 91.

particular geographical area, rapidly moving cold fronts are frequent. Should such a front arrive after the commitment to added capacity is made, losses are substantial. If the front fails to arrive and capacity has not been added, power must be purchased from an adjacent system at penalty rates—again resulting in losses.

Such decisions may soon be made centrally by individuals whose technical skills are in mathematics and computer programing, with absolutely no experience in generating stations.

Rapid Spread

We believe that information technology will spread rapidly. One important reason for expecting fast changes in current practices is that information technology will make centralization much easier. By permitting more information to be organized more simply and processed more rapidly it will, in effect, extend the thinking range of individuals. It will allow the top level of management intelligently to categorize, digest, and act on a wider range of problems. Moreover, by quantifying more information it will extend top management's control over the decision processes of subordinates.

If centralization becomes easier to implement, managers will probably revert to it. Decentralization has, after all, been largely negatively motivated. Top managers have backed into it because they have been unable to keep up with size and technology. They could not design and maintain the huge and complex communication systems that their large, centralized organizations needed. Information technology should make recentralization possible. It may also obviate other major reasons for decentralization. For example, speed and flexibility will be possible despite large size, and top executives will be less dependent on subordinates because there will be fewer "experience" and "judgment" areas in which the junior men have more working knowledge. In addition, more efficient information-processing techniques can be expected to shorten radically the feedback loop that tests the accuracy of original observations and decisions.

Some of the psychological reasons for decentralization may remain as compelling as ever. For instance, decentralized organizations probably provide a good training ground for the top manager. They make better use of the whole man; they encourage more active cooperation. But though interest in these advantages should be very great indeed, it will be counterbalanced by interest in the possibilities of effective top-management control over the work done by the middle echelons. Here an analogy to Taylorism seems appropriate:

> In perspective, and discounting the countertrends instigated by participative management, the upshot of Taylorism seems to have been the separating of the hourly worker from the rest of the organization, and the acceptance by both management and the worker of the idea that the worker need not plan and create. Whether it is psychologically or socially justifiable or not, his creativity and ingenuity are left largely to be acted out off the job in his home or his community. One reason, then, that we expect top acceptance of information technology is its implicit promise to allow the top to control the middle just as Taylorism allowed the middle to control the bottom.

There are other reasons for expecting fast changes. Information technology promises to allow fewer people to do more work. The more it can reduce the number of middle managers, the more top managers will be willing to try it.

We have not yet mentioned what may well be the most compelling reason of all: the pressure on management to cope with increasingly complicated engineering, logistics, and marketing problems. The temporal distance between the discovery of new knowledge and its practical application has been shrinking rapidly, perhaps at a geometric rate. The pressure to reorganize in order to deal with the complicating, speeding world should become very great in the next decade. Improvisations and "adjustments" within present organizational frameworks are likely to prove quite inadequate; radical rethinking of organizational ideas is to be expected.

Revolutionary Effects

Speculating a little more, one can imagine some radical effects of an accelerating development of information technology—effects warranting the adjective "revolutionary."

Within the organization, for example, many middle-management jobs may change in a manner reminiscent of (but faster than) the transition from shoemaker to stitcher, from old-time craftsman to today's hourly worker. As we have drawn an organizational class line between the hourly worker and the foreman, we may expect a new line to be drawn heavily, though jaggedly, between "top management" and "middle management," with some vice presidents and many ambitious suburban junior executives falling on the lower side.

In one respect, the picture we might paint for the 1980's bears a strong resemblance to the organizations of certain other societies—e.g., to the family-dominated organizations of Italy and other parts of Europe, and even to a small number of such firms in our own country. There will be many fewer middle managers, and most of those who remain are likely to be routine technicians rather than thinkers. This similarity will be superficial, of course, for the changes we forecast here will be generated from quite different origins.

What organizational and social problems are likely to come up as by-products of such changes? One can imagine major psychological problems arising from the depersonalization of relationships within management and the greater distance between people at different levels. Major resistances should be expected in the process of converting relatively autonomous and unprogramed middle-management jobs to highly routinized programs.

These problems may be of the same order as some of those that were influential in the development of American unions and in focusing middle management's interest on techniques for overcoming the hourly workers' resistance to change. This time it will be the top executive who is directly concerned, and the problems of resistance to change will occur among those middle managers who are programed out of their autonomy, perhaps out of their current status in the company, and possibly even out of their jobs.

On a broader social scale one can conceive of large problems outside the firm, that affect many institutions ancillary to industry. Thus:

- What about education for management? How do we educate people for routinized middle-management jobs, especially if the path from those jobs up to top management gets much rockier?
- To what extent do business schools stop training specialists and start training generalists to move directly into top management?
- To what extent do schools start training new kinds of specialists?
- What happens to the traditional apprentice system of training within managerial ranks?
- What will happen to American class structure? Do we end up with a new kind of managerial elite? Will technical knowledge be the major criterion for membership?
- Will technical knowledge become obsolete so fast that managers themselves will become obsolete within the time span of their industrial careers?

MIDDLE-MANAGEMENT CHANGES

Some jobs in industrial organizations are more programed than others. The job that has been subjected to micromotion analysis, for instance, has been highly programed; rules about what is to be done, in what order, and by what processes, are all specified.

Characteristically, the jobs of today's hourly workers tend to be highly programed—an effect of Taylorism. Conversely, the jobs shown at the tops of organization charts are often largely unprogramed. They are "think" jobs—hard to define and describe operationally. Jobs that appear in the big middle area of the organization chart tend to be programed in part, with some specific rules to be followed, but with varying amounts of room for judgment and autonomy.[2] One major effect of information technology is likely to be intensive programing of many jobs now held by middle managers and the concomitant "deprograming" of others.

As organizations have proliferated in size and specialization, the problem of control and integration of supervisory and staff levels has become increasingly worrisome. The best answer until now has been participative management. But information technology promises better answers. It promises to eliminate the risk of less than adequate decisions arising from garbled communications, from misconceptions of goals, and from unsatisfactory measurement of partial contributions on the part of dozens of line and staff specialists.

Good illustrations of this programing process are not common in middle management, but they do exist, mostly on the production side

[2] See Robert N. McMurry, "The Case for Benevolent Autocracy," *HBR*, January–February 1958, p. 82.

of the business. For example, the programmers have had some successes in displacing the judgment and experience of production schedulers (although the scheduler is still likely to be there to act out the routines) and in displacing the weekly scheduling meetings of production, sales, and supply people. Programs are also being worked out in increasing numbers to yield decisions about product mixes, warehousing, capital budgeting, and so forth.[3]

Predicting the Impact

We have noted that not all middle-management jobs will be affected alike by the new technology. What kinds of jobs will become more routinized, and what kinds less? What factors will make the difference?

The impact of change is likely to be determined by three criteria:

1. *Ease of measurement*—It is easier, at this stage, to apply the new techniques to jobs in and around production than in, say, labor relations, one reason being that quantitative measurement is easier in the former realms.
2. *Economic pressure*—Jobs that call for big money decisions will tend to get earlier investments in exploratory programing than others.
3. *The acceptability of programing by the present jobholder*—For some classes of jobs and of people, the advent of impersonal rules may offer protection or relief from frustration. We recently heard, for example, of efforts to program a maintenance foreman's decisions by providing rules for allocating priorities in maintenance and emergency repairs. The foreman supported this fully. He was a harried and much blamed man, and programing promised relief.

Such factors should accelerate the use of programing in certain areas. So should the great interest and activity in the new techniques now apparent in academic and research settings. New journals are appearing, and new societies are springing up, like the Operations Research Society of America (established in 1946), and the Institute of Management Sciences (established in 1954), both of which publish journals.

The number of mathematicians and economic analysts who are being taken into industry is impressive, as is the development within industry, often on the personal staffs of top management, of individuals or groups with new labels like "operations researchers," "organization analysts," or simply "special assistants for planning." These new people are a cue to the emergence of information technology. Just as programing the operations of hourly workers created the industrial engineer, so should information technology, as planning is withdrawn from middle levels, create new planners with new names at the top level.

So much for work becoming more routinized. At least two classes of middle jobs should move *upward* toward *de*programedness:

1. The programmers themselves, the new information engineers, should move up. They should appear increasingly in staff roles close to the top.
2. We would also expect jobs in research and development to go in that direction, for innovation and creativity will become increasingly important to top management as the rate of obsolescence of things and of information increases. Application of new techniques to scanning and analyzing the business environment is bound to increase the range and number of possibilities for profitable production. Competition between firms should center more and more around their capacities to innovate.

Thus, in effect, we think that the horizontal slice of the current organization chart that we call middle management will break in two, with the larger portion shrinking and sinking into a more highly programed state and the smaller portion proliferating and rising to a level where more creative thinking is needed. There seem to be signs that such a split is already occurring. The growth of literature on the organization of research activities in industry is one indication.[4] Many social scientists and industrial research managers, as well as some general managers, are worrying more and more about problems of creativity and

[3] See the journals, *Operations Research* and *Management Science*.

[4] Much of the work in this area is still unpublished. However, for some examples, see Herbert A. Shepard, "Superiors and Subordinates in Research," *Journal of Business of the University of Chicago*, October 1956, p. 261; and also Donald C. Pelz, "Some Social Factors Related to Performance in a Research Organization," *Administrative Science Quarterly*, December 1956, p. 310.

authority in industrial research organizations. Even some highly conservative company presidents have been forced to break time-honored policies (such as the one relating salary and status to organizational rank) in dealing with their researchers.

Individual Problems

As the programing idea grows, some old human relations problems may be redefined. Redefinition will not necessarily solve the problems, but it may obviate some and give new priorities to others.

Thus, the issue of morale versus productivity that now worries us may pale as programing moves in. The morale of programed personnel may be of less central concern because less (or at least a different sort of) productivity will be demanded of them. The execution of controllable routine acts does not require great enthusiasm by the actors.

Another current issue may also take a new form: the debate about the social advantages or disadvantages of "conformity." The stereotype of the conforming junior executive, more interested in being well liked than in working, should become far less significant in a highly depersonalized, highly programed, and more machine-like middle-management world. Of course, the pressures to conform will in one sense become more intense, for the individual will be required to stay within the limits of the routines that are set for him. But the constant behavioral pressure to be a "good guy," to get along, will have less reason for existence.

As for individualism, our suspicion is that the average middle manager will have to satisfy his personal needs and aspirations off the job, largely as we have forced the hourly worker to do. In this case, the Park Forest of the future may be an even more interesting phenomenon than it is now.

CHANGES AT THE TOP

If the new technology tends to split middle management—thin it, simplify it, program it, and separate a large part of it more rigorously from the top—what compensatory changes might one expect within the top group?

This is a much harder question to answer. We can guess that the top will focus even more intensively on "horizon" problems, on problems of innovation and change. We can forecast, too, that in dealing with such problems the top will continue for a while to fly by the seat of its pants, that it will remain largely unprogramed.

But even this is quite uncertain. Current research on the machine simulation of higher mental processes suggests that we will be able to program much of the top job before too many decades have passed. There is good authority for the prediction that within ten years a digital computer will be the world's chess champion, and that another will discover and prove an important new mathematical theorem; and that in the somewhat more distant future "the way is open to deal scientifically with ill-structured problems—to make the computer coextensive with the human mind." [5]

Meanwhile, we expect top management to become more abstract, more search-and-research-oriented and correspondingly less directly involved in the making of routine decisions. Allen Newell recently suggested to one of the authors that the wave of top-management game playing may be one manifestation of such change. Top management of the 1980's may indeed spend a good deal of money and time playing games, trying to simulate its own behavior in hypothetical future environments.

Room for Innovators

As the work of the middle manager is programed, the top manager should be freed more than ever from internal detail. But the top will not only be released to think; it will be *forced* to think. We doubt that many large companies in the 1980's will be able to survive for even a decade without major changes in products, methods, or internal organization. The rate of obsolescence and the atmosphere of continuous change which now characterize industries like chemicals and pharmaceuticals should spread rapidly to other industries, pressuring them toward rapid technical and organizational change.

These ideas lead one to expect that researchers, or people like researchers, will sit closer to the top floor of American companies in larger numbers; and that highly creative people will

[5] See Herbert A. Simon and Allen Newell, "Heuristic Problem Solving: The Next Advance in Operations Research," *Operations Research,* January–February, 1958, p. 9.

be more sought after and more highly valued than at present. But since researchers may be as interested in technical problems and professional affiliations as in progress up the organizational ladder, we might expect more impersonal, problem-oriented behavior at the top, with less emphasis on loyalty to the firm and more on relatively rational concern with solving difficult problems.

Again, top staff people may follow their problems from firm to firm much more closely than they do now, so that ideas about executive turnover and compensation may change along with ideas about tying people down with pension plans. Higher turnover at this level may prove advantageous to companies, for innovators can burn out fast. We may see more brain picking of the kind which is now supposedly characteristic of Madison Avenue. At this creating and innovating level, all the current work on organization and communication in research groups may find its payoff.

Besides innovators and creators, new top-management bodies will need programmers who will focus on the internal organization itself. These will be the operations researchers, mathematical programmers, computer experts, and the like. It is not clear where these kinds of people are being located on organization charts today, but our guess is that the programmer will find a place close to the top. He will probably remain relatively free to innovate and to carry out his own applied research on what and how to program (although he may eventually settle into using some stable repertory of techniques as has the industrial engineer).

Innovators and programmers will need to be supplemented by "committors." Committors are people who take on the role of approving or vetoing decisions. They will commit the organization's resources to a particular course of action—the course chosen from some alternatives provided by innovators and programmers. The current notion that managers ought to be "coordinators" should flower in the 1980's, but at the top rather than the middle; and the people to be coordinated will be top staff groups.

Tight Little Oligarchy

We surmise that the "groupthink" which is frightening some people today will be a commonplace in top management of the future. For while the innovators and the programmers may maintain or even increase their autonomy, and while the committor may be more independent than ever of lower-line levels, the interdependence of the top-staff oligarchy should increase with the increasing complexity of their tasks. The committor may be forced increasingly to have the top men operate as a committee, which would mean that the precise individual locus of decision may become even more obscure than it is today. The small-group psychologists, the researchers on creativity, the clinicians—all should find a surfeit of work at that level.

Our references to a small oligarchy at the top may be misleading. There is no reason to believe that the absolute numbers of creative research people or programmers will shrink; if anything, the reverse will be true. It is the *head men* in these areas who will probably operate as a little oligarchy, with subgroups and sub-subgroups of researchers and programmers reporting to them. But the optimal structural shape of these unprogramed groups will not necessarily be pyramidal. It is more likely to be shifting and somewhat amorphous, while the operating, programed portions of the structure ought to be more clearly pyramidal than ever.

The organization chart of the future may look something like a football balanced upon the point of a church bell. Within the football (the top staff organization), problems of coordination, individual autonomy, group decision making, and so on should arise more intensely than ever. We expect they will be dealt with quite independently of the bell portion of the company, with distinctly different methods of remuneration, control, and communication.

CHANGES IN PRACTICES

With the emergence of information technology, radical changes in certain administrative practices may also be expected. Without attempting to present the logic for the statements, we list a few changes that we foresee:

With the organization of management into corps (supervisors, programmers, creators, committors), multiple entry points into the organization will become increasingly common.

Multiple sources of potential managers will develop, with training institutions outside the firm specializing along the lines of the new organizational structure.

Apprenticeship as a basis for training managers will be used less and less since movement up through the line will become increasingly unlikely.

Top-management training will be taken over increasingly by universities, with on-the-job training done through jobs like that of assistant to a senior executive.

Appraisal of higher management performance will be handled through some devices little used at present, such as evaluation by peers.

Appraisal of the new middle managers will become much more precise than present rating techniques make possible, with the development of new methods attaching specific values to input-output parameters.

Individual compensation for top staff groups will be more strongly influenced by market forces than ever before, given the increased mobility of all kinds of managers.

With the new organizational structure new kinds of compensation practices—such as team bonuses—will appear.

Immediate Measures

If the probability seems high that some of our predictions are correct, what can businessmen do to prepare for them? A number of steps are inexpensive and relatively easy. Managers can, for example, explore these areas:

1. They can locate and work up closer liaison with appropriate research organizations, academic and otherwise, just as many companies have profited from similar relationships in connection with the physical sciences.
2. They can re-examine their own organizations for lost information technologists. Many companies undoubtedly have such people, but not all of the top executives seem to know it.
3. They can make an early study and reassessment of some of the organizationally fuzzy groups in their own companies. Operations research departments, departments of organization, statistical analysis sections, perhaps even personnel departments, and other "odd-ball" staff groups often contain people whose knowledge and ideas in this realm have not been recognized. Such people provide a potential nucleus for serious major efforts to plan for the inroads of information technology.

Perhaps the biggest step managers need to take is an internal, psychological one. In view of the fact that information technology will challenge many long-established practices and doctrines, we will need to rethink some of the attitudes and values which we have taken for granted. In particular, we may have to reappraise our traditional notions about the worth of the individual as opposed to the organization, and about the mobility rights of young men on the make. This kind of inquiry may be painfully difficult, but will be increasingly necessary.

21. INFORMATION TECHNOLOGY AND DECENTRALIZATION

JOHN F. BURLINGAME *

Are the middle manager and the decentralized organization doomed to extinction as the result of advances in information technology—or destined to take an even greater role in business?

What kinds of management problems are most likely to lend themselves to solution by the new data-handling techniques?

In what ways can data technology be used to simplify business complexities and distribute decision-making responsibility more widely?

What must the manager do to ensure that the new techniques are used to further the ends of the company and society?

Recent progress in information technology has been so rapid that various observers have predicted the elimination of middle managers and the reversal of the trend of the last decade toward decentralization in business. Computers and the associated technologies, the argument runs, will make better decisions of the type now made by middle managers and will make them faster. Companies will find it possible to process and structure relevant information in such a comprehensive fashion and so quickly that decentralized responsibilities will be withdrawn and noncomputer decision making limited to a top-level elite in the organization. Apparently the manager's work in the future will be depersonalized and personal satisfaction will have to be found in activities pursued outside working hours.

If so, technological progress will have resolved some of business's most vexing problems. No longer will there be any need to sort out and evaluate the many human, social, and economic considerations hitherto important in operating and organizing a business. Rather, all there will be left to do is to climb on and ride the one band wagon harmonious with previously determined future events.

SOURCE: *Harvard Business Review* (November-December, 1961), pp. 121–126. © 1961 by the President and Fellows of Harvard College.

* General Electric Co.

I believe it can be shown, however, that these conclusions are both dubious in themselves and unreliable as a basis for organizational action. Indeed, if we couple our experience in decentralized organizations with a realistic evaluation of the nature and extent of the future impact of information technology in such organizations, we can establish a very reasonable basis for concluding that decentralization and the middle manager are much more likely to *grow* and *flourish* than to wither and die in the decades ahead.

TYPES OF DECISIONS

For the purposes of our discussion, the concept of decentralization can be simply stated. Decision-making responsibility is assigned at the lowest point in the organization where the needed skills and competence, on the one hand, and the needed information, on the other hand, can reasonably be brought together. A great improvement is believed to result in any firm when the creative talents of responsible individuals are encouraged to develop in a climate of individual responsibility, authority, and dignity—a climate that is made possible by the decentralization of decision making.

This view of decentralization is fundamentally different from the mere application of traditional centralized managerial control concepts to smaller and more dispersed units of people. Confusion over this difference may well be a fundamental factor responsible for the earlier mentioned viewpoints predicting future trends away from decentralized organizations.

In assessing the future impact of information technology on decentralized business, some attention must be paid to the subject of decision making. The philosophy within which decisions are made distinguishes the organization which is centralized from the one which is not. The aspects of decision making that are important are (a) the way decisions are classified and (b) the way responsibility for them is assigned:

In any decision system we can identify two classes of decisions—those which can be predetermined by a rigorously defined selection process and those which cannot. The former are generally decisions concerning measurable and objective physical phenomena. The latter involve human beings and intangible, subjective human values; the balancing of social, moral, and economic values; and the assessment of situations in which information needs cannot be adequately anticipated or adequately filled.

In a centralized organization, the attempt is made to retain in as small a group as possible the responsibility for the latter type decisions and to delegate only the former. But in a decentralized organization, no attempt is made to separate the types of decisions in assigning responsibility; instead, the attempt is to relate all decisions to work purpose. Responsibility is assigned where the skills and competences, on the one hand, and the needed information, on the other, can reasonably be brought together.

Thus, in a centralized organization, the decision structure tends to be one where the decisions at the top are original and sensitive to human and social considerations; decisions at the bottom are more likely to be routine and insensitive to such considerations. By contrast, in a decentralized organization, no such division exists. Rather, all types of decisions are made throughout the organization at all levels. Only the breadth and complexity of impact tends to decrease from top to lower echelons in the organization.

Sources of Confusion

It should be noted that the use of the word *decision* to describe both of these classes of action is unfortunate and has caused much confusion in assessing the contribution of information technology to decision making. Trouble has also been caused by the term *computer decision making,* which has been applied in a glamorizing fashion to describe the application of computers to the more routine tasks. Although the terminology is new, the concept and its application substantially predate the high-speed electronic computer. For instance, the clock thermostat which turns on the furnace at 6:30 A.M. because the house temperature is below that preset for daytime operations is a mechanical "decision maker" in the same sense as the computer is when it computes and prints a bill for a customer. So is the regulating system for traffic lights which modifies the signal sequencing depending on volume of traffic, time of day, and day of week (and sometimes it factors in holidays, as well).

We now have many mechanical devices that carry out predetermined processes and actions. The additional advantage the high-speed electronic computer brings is its ability to handle a large number of variables in a complex process at high speed. Calling the action *computer decision making,* however, implies that a computer decides a man's salary because it prints out his monthly check. Such a description is, at the very least, misleading.

POTENTIAL AND LIMITATIONS

Information technology embraces the various techniques and disciplines (applied mathematics, simulation, electronic data processing, and so on) which can be and have been applied to the development of data in business. This technology has mushroomed in the past ten years with most of the practical application confined thus far to electronic data processing. However, enough theoretical and first-stage application work has been done in such areas as business simulation and computer duplication of human logical processes to envision that, ultimately, information technology will have a major impact on business. Yet, while the future impact will be great, there are factors in the growth of the technology and the evolution of business which will limit the nature and extent of the impact.

Effect of Industry Changes

One such factor is the expected increase in the complexity of business in the next few decades. When information technology was in its early development stage, a $1 billion sales volume point was a commonly accepted dividing line between the really large business and the "all-other" category. But when the technology eventually reaches a point of reasonable maturity, $10 billion or more in sales should represent such a dividing line.

In association with such a growth in sales we can expect an increase in complexity arising from such factors as increased product variety, additional manufacturing locations, foreign expansions, and the need for additional and diversified labor, which usually attend a significant volume increase. Simultaneously, the complexities arising from the changing role of industry in society—its relations with government, labor, and other segments of the economy—will undoubtedly also increase as they have during the past decade, and will require a host of new, different, difficult decisions.

When we view the impact of the advancing information technology on business, therefore, it would be naive to predict the outcome without taking into account the increased size and more diverse nature of the industrial world. Will the simplifications possible from applications of the new science outpace, keep abreast of, or fall behind trends making business more complicated? At the same time we need to be specific about the impact of data technology. To what extent do the kinds of situations to which it is amenable represent the total range of situations that must be handled in industry?

Most Likely Applications

The status of some current work in the computer application field might help in making an assessment. The prediction has been made, on the basis of this work, that a computer will be the world's chess champion within the next decade. What is significant here, as far as impact on business is concerned, is that it will take roughly a decade for enough progress to be made to handle a problem which has no unknowns—even where the rules of play are completely defined, where the scope of action is limited, where the relationships between the elements are explicit, where there is but a single, defined objective, where the value system is determined and unambiguous, and where the problem is precisely the same now as it was 100 years ago and as it will be 100 years from now.

Suppose that we look at chess as a complicated variation of ticktacktoe—the complication arising from increases in the number and kinds of relationships, but with no reduction in definition. Then we have a reasonable basis for speculating that, during the next two decades, data technology will have the greatest impact on those facets of business where the complication is due primarily to the number and kinds of explicitly known relationships. It is highly likely, for example, that an electronic computer program will be the basis for scheduling production, ordering material, and allocating output in the case of some products which historically have had highly predictable patterns of demand.

The Human Element

Such programs, however, will contain as one of their elements the limits within which scheduling, ordering, and allocating are to be computer-determined. When these limits are exceeded, as happens when the data inputs indicate environmental changes, the expansion of established patterns, or factors requiring human value consideration, then the program will shut the computer down awaiting human instruction. For example:

A large industrial company is developing an automated information system designed to permit its salesmen (located throughout the United States) to determine immediately the availability of thousands of products and, if an order is placed, when and from where an item will be shipped. This system, using the latest techniques and equipment, will keep continuous records of all products and update them each time an order is placed, a shipment made, or a product manufactured. When an order is placed, the system—in accordance with the rules of its design—will automatically process it, selecting the warehouses best able to fill it.

The first step in the automatic processing of an order in this system is to check the credit status of the customer. If the order, together with the unpaid balance, is less than the customer's credit limit, the complete order process is carried out and the proper warehouse is automatically instructed when and how to make the shipment. But if the credit limit is exceeded, this information is printed out and the system holds up processing of the order until it receives further instruction.

This company considers the decision involved in selecting a course of action when a customer's order exceeds his credit limit to have enough important intangible considerations so that human judgment should be exercised in each case and so that the disposition should be made humanly, not mechanically.

Similarly, when the business situation is one where the market is being developed, the product is new, and the distribution channels include perhaps a variety of foreign markets (all with volatile characteristics), then the information-handling techniques, while providing a factual base, will still fall very short of the requirements for taking action. The final assessment of the risk and the decision to act must be made by a manager integrating the factual information with the less well-defined elements in the situation.

Since in a great number of businesses this last kind of situation predominates, and since the number of such situations increases with the growth in complexity, we can anticipate that the major long-term impact of the new technology will be to improve the basis of human decision making rather than to make decision making routine and mechanical.

Now let us proceed to the next part of our problem. If we couple experience with decentralization and the application of information technology with likely trends in business and data technology, what conclusions can be drawn about the probable results of their interaction over the next few decades?

GREATER DECENTRALIZATION

Counter to many arguments, the anticipated advances in information technology, in my opinion, can *strengthen* decentralization in those businesses that have adopted it and will encourage *more* managements to experiment and to operate in accordance with the decentralization philosophy.

A great many businessmen are repelled by the idea that most people in industry can be used only to execute, within narrowly defined limits, the orders of an elite group who alone can exercise judgment, imagination, creativity, and intuition. They feel that this concept shuts the door on a major resource—the creative and imaginative talents and the growth potential of large numbers of people. On the other hand, these same businessmen recognize the need to guide the use of creativity and imagination so that the sum total will not be dissipated inefficiently, but will be applied in a disciplined fashion to achieve the selected goals of the organization.

This is where information becomes vital. Employees have to have the pertinent facts if they are to see clearly the interrelationships between their contribution and the contribution of others, and to act, on their own initiative, in a manner which will serve the best interests of all. The advancing data technology can make remarkable contributions to meeting this need. *This, in fact, may be its most significant feature.*

But to succeed in this way, information technology needs constantly to be guided away from its Babel-like preoccupation with designing superhuman intellects to make superhuman decisions, and brought back to its primary business purpose: contributing to the simplification of business complexities. Because this is a more difficult purpose to achieve, and because it means more focus on steady, day-by-day accomplishment and less on intoxicating expectations, shifting the emphasis to simplification will not be an easy task.

Pattern Identification

Today advanced techniques and large computers are coupled in a great assault on complex systems. Systems are analyzed microscopically and synthesized; over-all performance is predicted by considering the behavior of each element. This approach is fine as far as it goes, but often just does not go far enough.

What is needed, and what information technology *can* produce, if properly guided by the businessman, is the next step: simplification through pattern identification. This step can provide the kind of information which permits individuals to act responsibly on their own initiative. It also can make it possible to sort out those things which can best be done humanly from those best done mechanically, in order to obtain most effective use of both human and machine resources. Thus:

One of the products of a manufacturing business was an instrument device. Some 85,000 units of 400 different models were manufactured annually with no apparent stable patterns of market preference for any particular model. Each model was manufactured to order, and shipment averaged about six weeks from the date the order was placed. All of the paper work involved in processing the order was originally handled manually, but, with the advent of electronic computing equipment, it was no trick to convert to machines.

However, those responsible for the conversion in this instance were not satisfied simply to mechanize an existing complex human routine. They felt that before a major investment was made in mechanizing the paper flow, an effort should be made to determine whether or not there were fundamental patterns in this operation which ought to be taken into account.

Although there was no apparent stable pattern of demand on a model basis, they found from an analysis of the major components (which, when assembled, made up the models) that there were significantly greater requirements for some components than for others, and that a high degree of stability existed in this pattern. They determined, by a process of regrouping and redefining components, that of the 1,800,000 components of 280 different varieties required annually, some 99% could be classed under only 84 types.

With this new understanding, they were able to change the basic concept of the business from one where each model was fabricated to order to one where 84 types of components were manufactured in more or less continuous production, 196 being stocked in inventory. Final assembly alone was accomplished subsequent to the receipt of an order. The average delivery cycle went from six weeks to four days. More important, from the point of view of this discussion, an information structure was developed showing how families of models were related through the identical components in their composition. The resulting simplification made possible better and faster decisions and permitted further delegation of decision making to lower organizational echelons.

Prior to the work described, realistic forecasting on a model-by-model basis was just about impossible with or without a computer. Decisions on advance ordering were difficult to make and, because of the lack of pertinent information, were made relatively high in the organization. Subsequent to the simplification work, and with the business process organized around component types rather than end-product models, forecasts by family were all that were needed. Not only were these forecasts much easier to make and inherently much more accurate, but they permitted the responsibility for advance ordering to be placed at a lower organizational echelon, one nearer the level of actual manufacture since the information could now be made available for decisions at this level.

The contribution of information technology was increased manifold in this case by a recognition of the responsibility, not only to find a way to carry out complex operations more quickly, but also to find a way to simplify an operation so that a more efficient total system could be developed, one in which both the human and the machine resources could be most effectively utilized.

Dispelling Illusions

Insisting on simplification as the desirable end result is a task which must fall to businessmen. The danger of a parochial viewpoint is great, and one detects a strong tendency on the part of some to consider the complicated model as itself the "goal" and a kind of monument to their technical skills. In some instances the lack of widespread knowledge about the technology and its associated jargon is even used as a sort of witch doctor's cloak behind which to hide a growing empire, supposedly capable, ultimately, of making many of the businessman's decisions.

Businessmen, along with the technical experts, have a responsibility to ensure the technology's being used in a manner to further the ends of the company. Defining the business purposes to which the technology should be applied is essential to discharging this responsibility and cannot be left to the technologist alone.

Help for Middle Managers

How will information technology fortify the role of the middle manager in a decentralized business? As stated earlier, a characteristic of such a firm is a decision structure where the breadth of impact of the decision, rather than the judgment content, varies in the organization. Both upper-level managers and managers at the first level are deeply involved in problems where judgment and human values are the important elements. They are concerned with situations where the decisions cannot be anticipated, the information needs predicted, or the decision elements quantified. And this is equally true of many functional specialists reporting to these managers.

The stock in trade of these managers is their ability, as leaders, to obtain balanced results through the work of other people. To perform adequately here requires the ability to synthesize information, intuition, judgment, and values into courses of action and decisions which will produce the balanced results. It is reasonable to anticipate that the new technology will, over the next few decades, make a major contribution by providing such men with powerful tools to accomplish their work better. Their ability to exercise initiative and judgment responsibly should be strengthened. This effect should far outweigh in importance any tendency of computers to eliminate jobs where the nature of decisions is mechanical, especially when it is remembered that the growth in the complexity of business is increasing the need for effective managers.

IMPACT IN CENTRALIZED FIRM

I have been discussing the situation of the company with a philosophy of decentralization. But what about the firm with the opposite concept of operations?

There are two paths along which centralized businesses are likely to move as a result of the impact of information technology. Thus:

If the managers are committed to their philosophy and if the purpose for which the technology is employed is limited to the mechanization and improved efficiency of the operation as it exists, then the likely evolution will be along those lines predicted by a number of writers. Under these conditions, organizational reconsolidations will be encouraged and the ability of the few who have nonroutine, decision-making responsibility to make better decisions will be enhanced. Many currently in middle management will be replaced. Because men in this group were needed for their knowledge of complex but now obsolete routines, relocation will be difficult for them.

On the other hand, some businesses have adopted the centralized decision-making philosophy because of the difficulties involved in achieving a harmonious unifying of individual creativity and initiative. Here the technology can be used as a tool for simplification rather than simply mechanization, and will provide a basis for the adoption of a decentralized approach as a more desirable and more effective way.

CONCLUSION

It seems hardly conceivable that the social forces which are present today and which will be important in the future could permit the separation of society into two classes—one, an elite corps of thinkers (top managers, technologists, or some combination of the two), and the second, all other human beings.

It is a simple matter to conclude, as some writers have, that information technology has the potential to force the entire organization —from the middle manager on down—to satisfy personal needs and aspirations off the job. However, with a rapidly increasing percentage of our population acquiring advanced education, it is difficult to believe that the members of this group who go into business will be satisfied with spending their daily working hours, comprising a great part of their lifetime, in pursuits devoid of intellectual satisfaction. It is more than likely that they will attempt to curtail the freedom to act of businessmen or any other group that tries to force such a condition on them.

Since at least one sound, well-conceived concept—decentralization—provides an economically and socially acceptable alternative, it appears that the nub of the situation is not in the technology but in the wisdom with which managers apply it. Businessmen should have had enough experience with the Technocrats, on the one hand, and the self-seeking, public-be-damned Robber Barons, on the other, to realize that continued progress and growth lie in the best match of economic efficiency and social responsibility. This need is met by decentralization, coupled with an advancing information technology.

If, during the next decade or two, we do not see a continued trend in the direction of business decentralization, we must look for the failure, not in any unalterable laws of technological advance, but in the decisions of businessmen.

22. WHAT'S REALLY AHEAD FOR MIDDLE MANAGEMENT?

DONALD R. SHAUL*

During the past few years, thousands of hard-working middle managers have looked on with rising uneasiness while theoreticians of all hues have been cheerfully debating what effects the inexorable spread of electronic data processing will have on their future. Has the death knell sounded for middle management? A good many authorities have intimated as much, forecasting that, with the widespread reorganization necessitated by EDP, a vast number of middle-management jobs will either vanish altogether or become so structured that for all practical purposes their incumbents will become mere supervisors, denuded of their decision-making powers and stripped of their status.

Moreover, say these prophets of doom, much of the innovating and planning now being done by middle managers will be taken away from them by top management. The planning of work activities will become programed. The middle managers who remain will be highly specialized, adept at systems analysis, operations research, model building, and advanced EDP techniques. For the most part, their control function will be taken over by the computer itself.

The proponents of this school of thought have not had it all their own way, however. At the opposite extreme there are some authorities who maintain that, as a result of EDP, either more middle managers will be needed than ever or, at worst, that there will be a minimal change in the demand for them. These writers say that middle managers will have to be more able, that their decisions will become more important and far-reaching, and that their status will be enhanced. Between these two opposing viewpoints are the inevitable fence-straddlers, who have hypothesized that either side may be right in the long run.

There has been argument also over what effect the new technology will have on the locus of authority and decision making in the enterprise. One group believes that EDP must lead to the centralization of authority as well as of activities, and that the EDP elite will eventually make most of the decisions. Another holds that EDP should be used to assist individual managers at all levels to make better decisions and hence should remain decentralized.

Nearly all those who have written on the subject agree, though, on one thing: EDP will relieve middle managers of a vast amount of detailed administrative work, since all decisions that do not require the exercise of individual judgment will be made by the system.[1]

How do these varying speculations square with actual experience? With the aim of throwing some light on this question, I recently interviewed 53 middle managers and 14 top managers in eight companies, all of which had had at least two years' operating experience with an EDP system. The companies studied included representatives of both manufacturing and service industries—aircraft, petroleum, electronics (solely government work), radio and TV, banking, life insurance, finance, and telephone. All the managers interviewed had had several years' service with their companies.[2]

SOURCE: *Personnel* (November-December 1964), pp. 8–16. Reprinted by permission of American Management Association, Inc.

* California State College, Fullerton.

[1] For relevant references, see the selected bibliography at the end of this article.

[2] For the purposes of this study, the term "middle manager" included any manager above the level

The interviews, which were conducted with the aid of a written questionnaire, focused on the effects of EDP on these aspects of the middle manager's job: (1) the nature and scope of his functions; (2) his decision-making authority; and (3) his status. Before I go on to discuss my findings in detail, I may perhaps summarize their general tenor by saying that the prophesied demise of the middle manager, like the reported death of Mark Twain, seems to have been greatly exaggerated.

CHANGES IN MANAGEMENT FUNCTIONS

To assess what effect EDP had had on the nature of the middle manager's job, I took as my yardstick the traditional executive functions —planning, organizing, staffing, directing, and controlling. Let's see now what changes, if any, my interviewees reported under each of these heads:

Planning. Sixty per cent of the managers interviewed said they work longer on planning activities now than they did before the EDP system was installed. This, they said, was due in the main to three reasons: (1) the increased volume and reliability of the data received; (2) the speed-up in the flow of information; and (3) the demands of their superiors for more detailed analyses, as well as for greater output from the system. All these pressures are compelling managers to plan more intensively and make more decisions than they used to before EDP came on the scene.

Some typical comments on this score:

> Things are moving much faster today. Our decisions must be made more quickly and yet our plans have to take into account the increased complexity of interrelationships involved in the information system.

> The computer is performing calculations that formerly were impossible, and I now use this information in formulating my plans.

> Just being an integral part of an information circuit forces us to plan more carefully as well as to make decisions more quickly.

of first-line supervisor and below the level of division manager or the equivalent. The term "EDP" was defined as a system that (1) makes an original entry or records data in an electronically or mechanically usable form, (2) communicates and processes these data automatically, and (3) integrates or coordinates all related data processing activities and procedures to provide swift and orderly information for managerial planning and control.

Organizing. EDP seems to have had little effect on this function. Nearly all the managers reported that there had been practically no change in their organizing activities.

Staffing. Somewhat more change was noted here. EDP requires higher-caliber managers to fill the same positions now, my respondents said. Hence, additional time is needed to train people for them. Nearly everyone agreed that all managers should be familiar with the capabilities and limitations of their own company's EDP system.

Directing. A high percentage of the managers I talked with agreed that they now have to spend more time on directing the work of their departments. Several reasons were advanced for this change: (1) When a department is an integral part of an information circuit, the manager must have a thorough knowledge of its operations; (2) more complex relationships with interdependent departments have arisen because of the overriding influence of the EDP system; (3) there is more information to digest and use; (4) the addition of new activities has enlarged the manager's span of control; and (5) the increased reliance on EDP now makes it necessary for the manager to spend more time with his subordinates to insure that they are aware of the relationships involved in the new system, as well as what it can—and cannot—do.

As a result, the installation of an EDP system tends to expand the middle manager's personal contacts with his subordinate managers. As a rule, though, his contacts with his superiors at the top echelons are no more frequent than they used to be. Apparently, having discovered the wealth of information the computer can provide, top managers are now demanding more analytical studies, most of them in greater depth, than of old. They often ask, my respondents said, for information that has not hitherto been available, and demand to be supplied immediately with facts that actually take considerable time to extract from the tape files. Such requests usually entail more frequent consultations between the top-level middle manager and his subordinates, but do not require him to see his own boss more often than before.

Controlling. Approximately two-thirds of my interviewees agreed with the prediction that the computer will reduce the time managers need to spend on controlling. However, they rejected the notion that the middle-management ranks will be thinned as a result. In fact, they said, the computer has made it possible for managers to devote more time to their other (and previously neglected) functions. In general, the respondents felt that as more sophisticated techniques of computer usage were developed they would spend even less time controlling, because fewer exceptions requiring action would be brought to them for decisions. Thus, they would have more time for considering opportunities, because they would no longer be so preoccupied with solving problems. In any event, they said, human judgment would always have to make the final appraisal of the exceptions reported by computers. Moreover, they pointed out, the fact that computers were now helping in their control function did not relieve them of responsibility for the performance of their departments.

There was no evidence in these conversations substantiating the gloomy predictions that (1) the position of middle managers will become highly structured; (2) they will become mere specialists in computer techniques and operations; and (3) their job will take on the characteristics of straight leadership and supervision. It is true that the repetitive types of decisions, involving such matters as control of inventories, optimum shipping routes, product mix, credit checks, and maintaining quality-control standards, have been programmed into the computer; but this accomplishment now permits managers to spend more time on important decisions—the decisions involving risk and uncertainty.

In fact, it appears that middle managers are being forced to go on making full use of their experience and judgment by the nature of the EDP system itself. In the first place, the increased volume of information forthcoming from the computer necessitates evaluation by experienced personnel if it is to be effectively used. Second, decisions are becoming increasingly complex because of the interdependency of relationships within the information system.

The effects of decisions on interdependent departments now have to be carefully weighed before action is taken. Managers are finding it increasingly necessary to confer with their peers on mutual problems—problems that involve the new information system as well as the departments themselves. As a result, *coordination*—the very essence of management—has become more vital than ever before to successful managerial performance.

In short, the experience of the managers I interviewed has not borne out the prediction that EDP would bring about basic changes in the nature of the middle-management job. No executive functions have been eliminated nor has the advent of the computer led to the creation of "functional" managers—one group for planning, another for organizing, and a third for control, for example. There has been a shift, though, in the amount of time middle managers spend on their individual functions. They now do less controlling and more planning, staffing, and directing. More time is available for motivating, leading, and training—functions the computer cannot handle—as well as for weighing new opportunities, and devising better work methods and better ways to provide service to customers or other departments.

CHANGES IN SCOPE

Far from contracting the scope of the middle manager's job, EDP is expanding it, my respondents reported. A number of the managers I interviewed said that, on balance, more activities had been assigned to them since the system was installed. Many entirely new activities had been added, because the computer had made it possible to develop new services. Moreover, managers are now expected to make more thorough evaluations and to make more planning decisions because of the increased volume of information available to them.

Because middle managers are receiving more information—and more accurate information—faster than before, the expectation is that the quality of their decisions will improve. In some of the companies studied, an improvement in decision making has been noted, but this is not likely to become widespread for a long time to come. It will be many years before the EDP system will be available to middle managers seeking optimum solutions to simulation problems involving the use of different variables. The high investment in programmed information, the heavy volume of work handled by the computers, and the higher priority of top management and staff work all preclude the use of the system at lower levels at the present time.

My respondents agreed with the prediction that EDP would increase the visibility and speed of business decisions and make it possible to "see" more in a shorter planning period. They also confirmed that a continuous and rapid feedback permits faster adjustment to new conditions. Plans can now be made for longer periods ahead; alternatively, more accurate forecasts are possible for the short run. Either way, the result is that middle managers are developing an increasing awareness of their responsibility to engage in planning decisions at their level, and they are making more planning decisions, not fewer, as some experts have prophesied.

Busy top managers, in fact, are finding the EDP system is an important aid in delegating decision making to their subordinates. From my interviewees' comments it seems evident that they will continue to do so.

BROADER AND FASTER

Actually, then, EDP has made the middle manager's job more complex. Now, the manager must not only have some knowledge of the capabilities and limitations of the system itself; he must also be constantly coordinating his activities with those of other departments. Moreover, he is expected to react faster, make decisions more quickly (and take more facts into account in making them), and make more elaborate plans.

Almost half the middle managers I interviewed thought that EDP had definitely helped them to make better decisions. The rest said that they had not noticed any change. So far as planning was concerned, it was generally agreed that the system now enables detailed forecasts to be made for considerably longer periods ahead. On the other hand, because more accurate information is now available much faster than before, many operational activities do not have to be planned so far in advance.

Among the top managers interviewed, there was unanimous agreement that EDP itself does not create positions whose incumbents perform both line and staff functions; it has no effect on the number of middle managers rotated between line and staff positions; and it is not used to concentrate authority in top managers. However, this group was divided about the effect EDP had on rotating line and staff positions. Some felt that staff personnel would make the transition more easily because they had had the opportunity to familiarize themselves with all the ramifications of the information system, whereas line managers had a restricted viewpoint—the nature of their jobs and the vastly increased demands on their time did not permit them to become so familiar with the system's over-all operations. Other top managers took the view, however, that line managers are being kept sufficiently well informed of the operations and interrelations of the EDP system to make the transfer to a staff position without difficulty.

CHANGES IN AUTHORITY

There has been a slight drift away from rigid enforcement of the rules governing middle managers' decision-making authority, my study shows. The computer has aided in this change by being instrumental in providing better controls. As superior managers gain confidence in their subordinates they sometimes grant approval, *ex post facto,* for actions taken during their absence. For example, one division manager now gives tacit consent to certain of his subordinates to exceed expenditure limits while he is away. On his return, he approves the transactions. But, in general, there has not been any change in the number of rules imposed upon middle managers.

Changes in the authority delegated to middle managers coincide with the increase or decrease in the number of activities assigned to departments, according to my respondents. The considerable reduction in the decision-making authority granted to middle managers predicted by some experts has not taken place. Apparently, the EDP system itself has had no significant influence upon the decision-making authority of middle managers.

In fact, half the managers studied are now using more of their experience and judgment in rendering decisions, while the rest are using at least as much as before. A number of reasons were offered in explanation of the greater demands on experience and judgment. There are more information now and many new classifications to analyze; the manager must understand the EDP system and all interrelated activities to perform his job properly; new ways to use the information provided by the system are constantly being sought; decisions must be made faster and more often; and problems now have to be probed more deeply.

There was general agreement that middle managers are not sharing their decisions with top managers or staff specialists, nor are they being denied the opportunity to continue making decisions on subjects under their control. While corporate policies are being improved and better information is available to all levels of management much more quickly, the operating decisions continue to be made at the lowest level at which sound judgment, based on the available facts, can be brought to bear on the problem.

CHANGES IN STATUS

My respondents were also unanimously of the opinion that, contrary to many predictions, the status of middle managers had not been lowered since EDP came on the scene. In fact, they pointed to a number of reasons substantiating the belief that, rather, the middle manager's status has been raised: (1) His job is more complex; (2) he has a greatly increased volume of information to analyze in greater depth; (3) he is using more experience and judgment; and (4) EDP has either added to his activities or replaced some with more responsible functions.

Several of the top managers interviewed made these points:

> The middle manager's job is more complex today because he has more controls to adhere to daily—quality, budget, cost. In effect, a manager today must have at least a working knowledge of the EDP system and is handling a job that a superintendent was handling before.

> Middle-manager jobs are more complex because there are more things going on in our department and they are more elaborate than they used to be. We do more of the total procedure now, instead of a simple part of it. Timing is much more important and reactions must be faster. What used to be one department is now three departments.

> The administration of the system will require managers to have a thorough knowledge of its operations, so that they can be placed in spots where they can coordinate activities that are not related to each other in their daily operations, yet, being an integral part of the information system, must be supervised so that no action is taken that would be detrimental to broad company goals. A production line can have only one person making decisions that affect the administrative processes.

From the above findings it should be evident that while EDP has undoubtedly eliminated a vast amount of monotonous, detailed administrative work, there has been no accompanying reduction in the need for middle managers. Indeed, some of the companies studied are now finding it necessary to establish new criteria for determining the salaries of middle managers instead of compensating them on the basis of the number of subordinates assigned to them. Where there have been reductions in the number of workers, these have usually been compensated for by new activities being assigned to existing departments, or by the creation of new departments. Thus, the centralization of *activities* has not been accompanied by the elimination of managerial positions. On the contrary, the reorganization necessitated by the installation of EDP, and the new types of activities, coupled with the expansion of existing operations, all of which the system has made possible, have resulted in the addition of over 50 middle-management positions in the companies studied.

Moreover, in many of these companies the top managers are finding that they require more specialists. Several told me that the volume of data now being received may well require additional managerial personnel with the requisite experience to interpret it properly. One manager said he thought that in his company several supervisors and a few lower-echelon middle managers would eventually be eliminated; but he also visualized that the upper-echelon middle managers would require experienced staff personnel of their own.

All in all, then, instead of middle managers' facing a drastic reduction in their decision-making power and a lowering of their status, my survey indicates that this vital component of the management hierarchy is recognized as being more important than ever. Certainly, overall, no serious threat to middle managers seems to be posed by EDP. Their real menace is still the traditional causes of business failure, whether stemming from poor performance within the enterprise, from technological changes such as automation, or from external forces over which the company has little or no control.

23. COMPUTER TECHNOLOGY AND MANAGEMENT ORGANIZATION

WILLIAM E. REIF*

The impact of computers and information technology on the organization has been described in the following words:

> This increasing rate of technological change seems to create some fundamental problems for management. In part, these are problems concerning the process by which management puts the technology to work. And in part they concern the way in which the technological innovations themselves affect the very process of management.[1]

The management process referred to above, functions within the framework of formal and informal relationships which constitute the structure of organization. This study has attempted to shed some light on the types and extent of changes in the structure of organization which result from the implementation of computer systems in business firms.

THE LEVEL OF DECISION MAKING

The results of the study indicate that computers have the effect of centralizing decision making within the management hierarchy. This conclusion is based on an analysis of four determinants which were observed to have an effect upon the level of decision making. They are: standardization, greater centralized control, functional integration, and the availability to top management of timely information about company operations. The research findings point out that: (1) fewer decisions are being made at lower levels in the management hierarchy; (2) less important decisions are being made by decentralized managers; and (3) there is greater control of local operations by high level executives.

While the general trend is in the direction of greater centralization, the firm, in trying to grant decision-making prerogatives to the most qualified individuals, also appears to be concentrating certain decisional responsibilities at designated managerial levels—line and staff—throughout the organization. The ability of the computer to process and disseminate information required for company-wide planning and control decisions to virtually anyone in the organization has enabled the firm to become highly discriminate in designating whom it wants to make the decisions.

LINE-STAFF RELATIONSHIPS

Line-staff relationships are being redefined. Staff groups are becoming more powerful and are making more decisions which directly affect the internal affairs of operating departments. To be sure, this shift in the balance of power from line to staff is not in most cases officially sanctioned by the organization. Staff does not as yet possess formal authority but is playing a more prominent role in the informal aspects of the decision-making process.

The computer staff offers a good example of the changing line-staff relationship. Computer specialists usually do not have formal authority to define the objectives and information requirements of computer systems. Informally, however, they exercise considerable influence over company activities which have been computerized or which are in the process of being converted to computer processing.

SOURCE: William E. Reif, *Computer Technology and Management Organization* (Iowa City: Bureau of Business and Economic Research of the University of Iowa, 1968).

* Arizona State University.

[1] John Diebold, *Beyond Automation* (New York: McGraw-Hill Book Company, 1964), p. 18.

THE COMMUNICATIONS NETWORK

The results of this study indicate that the adaptation of the firm to computer systems has resulted in few revisions in the formal channels of communication which supply management with the information necessary for planning, coordinating, and controlling organizational activities. This statement in no way negates the conclusion expressed in the preceding chapter that the computer is responsible for initiating observed changes in the communications network, especially the formation and expansion of lateral flows of information throughout the management hierarchy. It only serves to emphasize the point that present changes have been restricted primarily to the informal network of communications and as yet have not been incorporated into the formal structure of organization.

IMPLICATIONS FOR FUTURE CHANGES

What will be the future impact of the computer upon the structure of organization? Herbert Simon feels there will be little need to change the hierarchical structure of organization:

> [The] automation of decision making, irrespective of how far it goes and in what direction it proceeds, is unlikely to obliterate the basically hierarchical structure of organization. . . .[2] It may, by bringing about a more explicit formal description of the entire system, make the relations among parts clear and more explicit, [however]. . . .[3] The organizations of the future . . . will be hierarchies, no matter what the exact division of labor between men and machines.[4]

The conclusions from this study tend to confirm Simon's forecast. It is quite possible that as electronic computers increase management's knowledge of the firm's operating environment, increase the accuracy of information, and increase the speed with which it is obtainable, the process of management will undergo certain revisions. And, as advanced simulation techniques permit the objective evaluation of alternative courses of action, business operations will be managed more rationally than in the past. Rapid changes in information technology, however, need not appreciably change the present structure of organization.

Although the hierarchical structure of organization will most likely remain intact, present line-staff relationships may change. As staff groups become more dominant and exercise greater control over line operations, the organization will probably conform by changing to a functional-type structure. In doing so, the firm will officially recognize the right of designated staff groups to operate in a line capacity and accordingly will delegate functional authority to them. This would amount to little more than formalizing the relationship which exists in many firms at the present time.

The firm may also experience a reduction in the total number of departmental units within the organization. This will be the result of consolidating several presently autonomous units into one department or management system and of eliminating the duplication of staff effort at decentralized management levels. The impetus behind increased functional integration is information technology which allows management to cope with increasingly complex problems and geographically dispersed operations while using fewer people and a more centralized organization.

This type of change might be forthcoming in The Community Bank. Following The Community Bank's conversion to an on-line system, the personnel requirements will be greatly reduced, and the organization may conceivably consist of the president, the vice presidents, the data processing department, and the window tellers. The tellers would be responsible for feeding information about customer accounts into the system and for retrieving information requested by customers from random access computer files. Information for installment loan, trust, and real estate decisions also would be processed and stored by the computer and would be immediately accessible upon request. Many firms which had previously set up departments on the basis of recordkeeping activities will probably experience similar changes as the computer takes over the bulk of clerical operations.

[2] Herbert Simon, *The New Science of Management Decision* (New York: Harper & Row, Publishers, 1960), p. 42.
[3] *Ibid.*, p. 40.
[4] *Ibid.*, p. 43.

The elimination of decentralized staff departments reflects the capability of a central staff group, with the aid of the computer, to execute more efficiently activities once performed by local units.

The Computer and Middle Management

The management group which will be most affected by the organization's increasing reliance on the computer is middle management. The middle manager has traditionally been responsible for routine administrative and control decisions. As more of these functions become programmed, the middle manager will be left with the task of implementing the decisions and supervising the work force. As automation continues to reduce the number of employees required to perform the work, and as closed-loop computer feedback systems practically eliminate the need for human intervention, there appears to be little left around which to build a job description. Although few will argue that computer technology is not capable of producing the above situation, the desirability of such action is open to question. And, if management decides that the anticipated payoff in increased operational effectiveness does not compensate for the perceived disadvantages associated with a drastic reduction in middle-management positions, the described changes may be postponed indefinitely.

Even in those instances when management elects to lessen the full impact of information technology, it is anticipated that the ranks of middle management will be thinned out to some extent as the computer partially replaces the need for human decision makers, assumes the major share of record-keeping and reporting activities, reduces the number of managers required to supervise the work force, and eliminates the need for various decentralized line and staff departments.

The findings of this study reveal that the types of routine decisions for which middle managers largely are responsible have a great deal to do with their susceptibility to replacement by the computer. The retention or replacement of decisional responsibilities also seems to be contingent on the functional area to which the manager is assigned. As pointed out in the preceding chapter, the potential elimination of jobs in production is much greater than in marketing, where the availability of computer-processed information has been responsible for actually expanding the ranks of middle management. So the incident of change is not uniform throughout the organization but depends on a number of factors influencing the decision-making process.

IMPLICATIONS FOR MANAGEMENT

This study indicates that management thus far has been content to let the informal organization absorb the major impact of computerization. Either management assumes that the informal organization can adequately compensate for any required changes in formal structural relationships; or it is reluctant to make changes which are not compatible with the existing—in most cases line-staff—structure of organization. For example, management demonstrates an unwillingness to grant systems analysts the functional authority to make decisions regarding the planning, implementation, and control of computer systems. At the same time management has felt the need to create centralized computer staff groups and has given the computer specialists unofficial support in their dealings with line managers. Without the status derived from the high-level staff position and without the informal backing of top management, the computer staff could not in many instances effectively perform its prescribed function for the organization.

As the organization continues to experience change, the informal organization probably will be unable to counteract effectively the lack of formal direction and control. Top management will be forced eventually to redefine formal authority relationships, to rewrite the job descriptions of staff and operating managers, and to take a more positive approach to defining horizontal channels of communication. A logical structure of organization does not hold a manager directly responsible for the performance of a task which is no longer under his immediate control; yet this predicament was observed in the studied firms. Certain changes in the management framework appear to be imperative if the firm is to maintain harmony between information technology and the structure of organization.

SUGGESTIONS FOR FUTURE RESEARCH

Is the line-staff structure outmoded and a relic of the first industrial revolution? Will organizations in the future conform more nearly to information flows rather than to scalar authority relationships? Before these questions can be answered with any degree of certainty, and before more consideration is given to the characteristics of future organizations, the present impact of the computer upon the firm must be thoroughly studied and analyzed; for herein lies the basis for research concerning the optimum structure of organization.

The immediate problem is to determine what changes are currently taking place in business organizations. If valid conclusions are to be drawn in this regard, more empirical research must be conducted. This study has based its conclusions on findings from three case studies. Whether the results from these firms are representative of changes occurring in all firms is not certain.

Additional research will be needed to keep abreast of the organizational changes required to meet the demands of more advanced technologies. There is a need for research in regard to the type of managerial structure which will permit management to utilize most profitably information technology supporting totally integrated information systems.

More attention must be paid to the impact of information technology on the manager and his future role in the organization. The manager is still the key variable in the formula for organizational success. And, if managers are to successfully adapt to changes in the organizational environment, they must become more knowledgeable about the potential capabilities of the computer and more adept in using information technology to further the goals of the organization.

24. EMERGING EDP PATTERN

CHARLES W. HOFER*

FOREWORD

Does the computer have greater impact on organizational processes and delegation of authority than on the characteristics of formal structure? Is its impact greater at the operational level or at the top functional level? The author's answers to questions like these have wide applicability for companies both large and small in many industries.

It is commonplace that there has been a great increase in management's understanding of how to apply the computer to a wide variety of tasks, ranging in complexity from simple, routine accounting applications to large simulations of entire industries.

But there has been little knowledge about the overall impact the computer has had on the organizational structures and processes of the companies—both large and small—using EDP.

The purpose of this Special Report is to present the findings of a recent study I conducted in this area, which I feel make some needed additions to our knowledge. But first let me comment that there have been many speculations, opinions, and previous research studies devoted to the effects of the computer on organizations. Each has differed to such a degree, however, that no clear-cut pattern of the total impact of this technology on the organizational structures and processes of businesses has heretofore emerged.

For example, the *predictions* of such observers of the business scene as Harold J. Leavitt, Thomas L. Whisler, Melvin Anshen, John F. Burlingame, and John Dearden differ substantially, as indicated in the ruled insert on page 18.

Likewise, the accompanying *findings* of researchers such as Ida Russakoff Hoos, Donald Shaul, Hak Chong Lee, and Rodney H. Brady differ, although each of their independent studies supports one of the sets of predictions.

Research Focus

In search of a clearer understanding of how the use of the computer and related technology has made an impact on industrial companies, I conducted a study of two manufacturing organizations. One was an independent division of a large multiproduct corporation whose total divisional sales exceeded $200 million. The other was a small company with sales of about $8 million. Both organizations were considered to be leaders in their respective industries in the application of computer techniques to management problems.

For example, both utilized nonconversational systems in a batch-processing operation in which the major files were updated daily. Both also had electronic data-collection devices which gathered and transmitted input data from remote locations. In addition, the larger organization utilized a corporate time-shared computer for some engineering and managerial applications.

Unlike previous researchers who had focused their efforts on one or two components of the companies they studied (usually the accounting and/or production scheduling and inventory control activities), I examined the effects of the computer in every type of organizational *component*—such as marketing, finance, engineering, manufacturing, employee relations, general management, and so on—and at every *level* in the hierarchy (from the president's office to the production floor).

Over a period of two years in the two or-

SOURCE: *Harvard Business Review* (March-April, 1970), pp. 16–170.

* Visiting Lecturer at Singapore Institute of Management.

ganizations, I interviewed nearly 80 managers, with each set of interviews covering from one to six hours although no single interview took longer than two hours. To supplement and confirm the data obtained from my interviews, I also (a) studied organizational charts, statistics, and job descriptions; (b) analyzed budgeting, operational planning, and measurement and evaluation procedures; (c) constructed detailed decision matrices; and (d) examined computer and noncomputer company reports, all covering a period of 12 years in each organization.

Obviously, however, I could not possibly examine the effects of the computer on all organizational characteristics and processes. Consequently, I focused my attention first on the more important characteristics of formal structure, such as

(a) The method of task specialization.
(b) The method of coordination.
(c) The span of control.
(d) The size of organizational components.

Then I examined such important organizational procedures as

(a) The various operational planning processes.
(b) The budgeting process.
(c) The measurement and evaluation process.

Synopsis of Findings

With but a few exceptions, my research—which is summarized in Tables 1 and 2—shows that the effects of the computer were the same in both companies even though the one organization was nearly 25 times larger than the other, both in dollar sales and in total employees, and even though the larger one had a rate of growth of less than 2% in dollar sales for the period covered by the study while the other had a compounded growth rate of over 10%. In both companies, the effects of the computer varied according to the organizational characteristic or process examined, the hierarchy level involved, and the nature of the principal tasks of the organizational component involved.

For example, on the one hand, the computer had no effect on the methods of coordination at the general management level or in components whose principal tasks did not involve the processing of large amounts of quantitative data. On the other hand, it did affect both the measurement and evaluation process at the general management level, and the methods of coordination in components whose principal tasks did involve the processing of large amounts of quantitative data.

In general, the research findings showed that the effects of the computer were:

- Greater on organizational processes and delegation of authority than on the characteristics of formal structure.
- Greater at the operations level than at the top functional level, and greater at both of these levels than at the general management level.
- Greater on the organizational components whose principal tasks involved the processing of large amounts of quantitative data than on components whose tasks did not.

Effects on Formal Structure

Although I examined all of the changes (over 200) in formal structure which had occurred in both organizations during the 12-year period covered by the study, I found no instances in which the computer had caused changes in structure at either the general management level or at the top functional level in those components whose principal tasks did not involve the processing of substantial amounts of quantitative data.

(In one instance, a computer report served as a catalyst for a change from a functional grouping to a product grouping at the top functional level, but the computer did not influence the nature of the change.)

There were limited changes at the top functional level in components whose principal tasks involved the processing of quantitative data and at the operations level in components whose principal tasks did not. In the former case, the majority of the changes were related to changes in structure which occurred at the operations level. For example:

- In the larger company, a 30% reduction in the number of personnel in the general accounting and cost accounting sections permitted the consolidation of these two components, with the consequent elimination of a managerial position.
- In the smaller company, the responsibility

Table 1. Summary of Computer Impact in a Large, Multidivision Manufacturing Corporation

Level in Hierarchy	Methods of Specialization	Methods of Coordination	Span of Control	Size of Components	Decision Making and Delegation of Authority	Operational Planning	Budgeting	Measurement and Evaluation
General management	No change	No change	No change	No change	No change	No change	No change	Managers able to ask for more detailed back-up statistics on problems
Top functional: Components that do not process large amounts of quantitative data	No change	No change	No change	No change	De facto delegation of some decisions or some aspects of the decision making process to subordinates	Managers devoted more time to examining ways to improve systems and procedures at the operations level	Managers able to change budgets quickly as projects changed in nature or scope	Quantitative measures of the performance of operations level personnel and components improved in both content and accuracy
Top functional: Components that process large amounts of quantitative data	Creation of position of information systems manager	Some components transferred in hierarchy to improve implementation of computer technology	No change	Some role positions reduced in number because of decrease in size of components at operations level	Additional time allocated to other activities, such as operational planning			
Operations: Components that do not process large amounts of quantitative data	No change	No change	No change	Size of components per dollar sales decreased slightly (about 10%) because of increased efficiency of remaining personnel	Better decisions because of more accurate information	Managers better able to direct attention to areas where efforts would be most productive	Accuracy of manager's budgets increased because of more accurate information on indirect costs and greater detail on direct costs	Quantitative measures of the performance of employees, distributors, suppliers, etc. improved in both content and accuracy

Level in Hierarchy	Methods of Specialization	Methods of Coordination	Span of Control	Size of Components	Decision Making and Delegation of Authority	Operational Planning	Budgeting	Measurement and Evaluation
Operations: Components that process large amounts of quantitative data	Creation of roles related to data processing such as programmers and systems analysts Elimination of some clerical role positions Some roles upgraded	Coordination activities increased in frequency, become more formalized Some components transferred as a result of systems changes	No change	Size of components per dollar sales decreased substantially (30% to 50%) because of elimination of clerical personnel	Some decisions programmed into computer	No change		

Table 2. Summary of Computer Impact in a Small Manufacturing Company

Level in Hierarchy	Methods of Specialization	Methods of Coordination	Span of Control	Size of Components	Decision Making and Delegation of Authority	Operational Planning	Budgeting	Measurement and Evaluation
General management	No change	No change	No change	No change	No change	No change	No change	Managers able to ask for more detailed back-up statistics on problems
Top functional: Components that do not process large amounts of quantitative data	No change	No change	No change	No change	De facto delegation of some decisions or some aspects of the decision-making process to subordinates	Managers devoted more time to examining ways to improve systems and procedures at the operations level	No change	Quantitative measures of the performance of operations level personnel and components improved in both content and accuracy
Top functional: Components that process large amounts of quantitative data	Creation of position of data processing manager	Some components transferred in hierarchy to improve implementation of computer technology	No change	No change	Additional time allocated to other activities, such as operational planning		No change	
Operations: Components that do not process large amounts of quantitative data	No change	No change	No change	Size of components per dollar sales decreased moderately (about 20%) because of improved methods	Better decisions because of more accurate information	Managers better able to direct attention to areas where efforts would be most productive	No change	Quantitative measures of the performance of employees, distributors, suppliers, etc., improved in both content and accuracy
Operations: Components that process large amounts of quantitative data	Creation of roles related to data processing, such as programmers and systems analysts Some roles upgraded	Coordination activities increased in frequency, become more formalized	No change	Size of components per dollar sales decreased substantially (about 40%) because new activities performed with existing personnel	Some decisions programmed into computer	No change	No change	

for the purchasing component was transferred to the manager of finance, who was also in charge of data processing, when the system and procedures in that area were automated.

The major changes in formal structure brought about by the computer occurred at the operations level in components whose principal tasks involved processing large amounts of quantitative data. Here, new roles were created, while old roles were modified or eliminated. In addition, the coordination mechanisms became more frequent and formal, and organizational components were transferred or combined as a result of new systems and new procedures. Finally, there were substantial decreases in the total number of personnel per total dollar sales at this level, even after taking into consideration the additions of computer-related personnel. For example:

- In the larger company, as the result of the development of a computerized production scheduling system, there was a threefold increase in the number of formal meetings between market forecasting personnel and production scheduling personnel to discuss major changes in production schedules.
- In both companies, after data-manipulation activities had been programmed into the computer, the tasks performed by cost accountants were upgraded.
- In the larger company, because of increased efficiency resulting from the use of computer models in design work, the number of product design engineers decreased about 10%.
- In the smaller company, the automation of accounting records resulted in a 40% decrease in the number of accounting personnel per $1 million of sales.

Why not more changes? Since the effects of the computer on formal structure which I found were far less than many business observers had predicted, I attempted to ascertain why this was the case and also to learn whether further changes in structure were anticipated in the future. In general, the interview responses were to the effect that the computer had not affected formal structure at the general management level or in those components which did not process large amounts of quantitative data because it did not basically alter either the tasks performed by these components or the way in which those tasks were performed. The interviews also predicted that this would continue to be true in the future.

Typical of these kinds of interview responses was this observation by a corporate staff specialist on organizational design and development:

> I do not expect the computer to have much effect on our approach to managing and organizing at the general management level in the near future.
>
> Most of the information in a business is recorded inside people's heads. All the computer contains is a series of abstractions, and usually financial ones at that, which may serve to alert the general manager to a situation in which he should become involved. When he actually does get involved, it is necessary for the manager to go far beyond these abstractions by talking with the people involved to get at the underlying factors affecting results.

A sales manager offered this explanation as to why there are not more changes in his area:

> There is not much potential for changes in structure in the sales section due to the computer. The way we organize depends on our sales volume, the size and location of our customers, the number and nature of our channels of distribution, the number and diversity of our product lines, and so on, and these factors are not affected by the computer.

An engineering manager viewed the computer's impact in this way:

> I do not expect major changes in the organizational structure of the engineering section in the near future due to the increased use of the computer, although I do feel that the computer will increase the productivity of our present personnel.
>
> The reason for this is the fact that in the engineering section organizational structure is based on the physical characteristics of the products we produce, the nature of the production process, and the level of new product development and cost reduction activities rather than on the ways we process data.

Finally, this comment was given by a manufacturing manager:

Table 3. Effects of Computers on Organizational Structures and Processes*

A. The Observers' Predictions

Harold J. Leavitt and Thomas L. Whisler[a]

- Jobs at today's middle management levels will become highly structured.
- Top managers will take on an even larger portion of the innovating, planning, and other "creative" functions.
- The programmers and R&D personnel will move upward into the top management group.
- Large industrial organizations will recentralize.

Melvin Anshen[b]

- The new technology will not erode or destroy middle management jobs. Instead it will present opportunities for expanding management capacity and performance in areas that have suffered from scant attention.
- The tasks of middle managers will more closely resemble those of top management.
- Computer personnel will not assume top management responsibilities or become the fundamental source for top management personnel.
- The trend toward decentralization of decision making will be slowed down.

John F. Burlingame[c]

- If the company's philosophy is one of centralization, then the likely evolution will be along the lines predicted by Leavitt, Whisler, and others.
- If a company's activities are centralized because of difficulties involved in achieving a harmonious unifying of individual creativity and initiative, then the computer will provide a basis for the adoption of a decentralized approach as a more desirable and more effective way.
- If the company's philosophy is one of decentralization, then the technology should strengthen the existing decentralization of operations. Middle management should grow and flourish rather than wither and die.

John Dearden[d]

- The computer will have no impact on the organization of top and divisional management, relatively little impact on the ability of the top manager to control profit centers, and limited impact on management levels below the divisional manager even though there may be some centralization of data processing and logistics systems.
- With the exception of certain routine operating control problems in such areas as logistics, production scheduling, and inventory control, it will not be practicable to operate a real-time information system; and, even if it were, such a system would not solve any of top management's real problems.

* Here are some of the predictions and research findings concerning EDP's impact on manufacturing companies.

[a] "Management in the 1980's," HBR November-December 1958, p. 41.

[b] "The Manager and the Black Box," HBR November-December 1960, p. 85.

[c] "Information Technology and Decentralization," HBR November-December 1961, p. 121.

[d] "Can Management Information Be Automated?" HBR March-April 1964, p. 128; "Myth of Real-Time Management Information," HBR May-June 1966, p. 123; and "Computers: No Impact on Divisional Control," HBR January-February 1967, p. 99.

First, let me say that I could supervise more people than I do now. However, the computer really could not increase the number of men I could supervise. I must evaluate the man as well as the job he does, and the computer could not help there.

In addition, the real limitation I have is understanding the nature of the tasks performed by each man well enough to evaluate him. The computer does not help too much there, either.

In the case of my subordinates, the computer has given them better measures, so they could probably supervise a few extra employees. But I prefer them to spend their time improving their supervision of the employees who currently report to them.

Moreover, the computer has not given them that much more time, because they spend only a small portion of their time in evaluating employees. Most of their time is spent in trying to improve operations by training personnel or by improving methods, and the computer does not help there.

Effects on Decision Making

My study revealed no direct effects of the computer on decision making or delegation of authority at the general management level. At the top functional level, however, there

Table 3 (*Continued*)

B. The Researchers' Findings

Ida Russakoff Hoose[e]

- Computer applications have led to drastic changes at the middle management level (supervisory to executive junior grade). Many jobs have been either combined or eliminated.
- EDP has systematized and standardized formal information flow and also has seemed to dam up the upward and downward flow of information through both formal and informal channels.
- As more and more operations are programmed, the power and status of new computer personnel have been expanded, while the functions of other departments have been undercut, and the authority of their managers truncated.
- EDP stimulates two distinct kinds of recentralization—one type referring to the integration of specific functions, the other involving regrouping of entire units of the operation and causing sweeping changes of the external structure as well.

Donald Shaul[f]

- While EDP has undoubtedly eliminated a vast amount of monotonous, detailed administrative work, there has been no accompanying reduction in the need for middle managers. Actually, EDP has made the middle manager's job more complex.
- The centralization of *activities* has not been accompanied by an elimination of managerial positions. On the contrary, EDP and the new activities have resulted in the addition of over 50 middle management positions in the companies studied.

Hak Chong Lee[g]

- The nature and magnitude of the EDP impact is basically governed by the computer technology and the management attitude toward the use of the technology.
- Drastic changes (centralization of the decision-making process and reduction in the number of middle management jobs) have not occurred to date in the companies studied during the early period of industrial experience with EDP.

Rodney H. Brady[h]

- Top management does not seem to use the computer directly for decision making.
- The use of the computer by middle management permits top management to:
  - (a) Make some decisions at an earlier date.
  - (b) Gain time in which to consider some decisions.
  - (c) Consider more thorough analysis of some situations.
  - (d) Review several courses of action on many problems.
  - (e) Examine analyses of the impact that recommended courses of action will have on the problem or opportunity identified.
  - (f) Obtain additional information from middle managers concerning problems, opportunities, and promising alternatives before making decisions.

[e] "When the Computer Takes Over the Office," HBR November-December 1960, p. 102.
[f] "What's Really Ahead for Middle Management?" *Personnel*, November-December 1964, p. 8.
[g] *The Impact of Electronic Data Processing Upon Patterns of Business Organization and Administration* (Albany, New York, State University of New York at Albany, 1965).
[h] "Computers in Top-Management Decision Making," HBR July-August 1967, p. 67.

was considerable de facto delegation to subordinates of the analysis and evaluation phases of certain classes of decisions.

The major reason for this appeared to be the fact that the executives involved felt that the improved systems and procedures enabled their subordinates to handle these tasks on their own. One financial manager put it this way:

> The computer has enabled me to become less involved in day-to-day activities because the system design is such that many tasks that used to occupy my time are now handled routinely by my subordinates. This is possible because the parameters are spelled out in such a way that I know my subordinates can do the job.
>
> For example, I used to have to worry about our overdue accounts receivable. Now we have a report which indicates accounts receivable for each customer by billing date. We send a copy of this report to each of our customers every month. This eliminates a lot of calls we used to have to make.
>
> In addition, my subordinates can now follow up on the routine cases so that I only have to handle the exceptional ones.

At the operations level, managers in components that did not process large amounts of quantitative data felt they were able to make better decisions as a result of more accurate data. In the components that did process large amounts of quantitative data, a substantial number of decisions were programmed into the computer. These were usually associated with activities such as production scheduling, machine loading, determination of inventory levels, and so on.

Effects on Operational Planning

The majority of the general managers I interviewed did not become heavily involved with operational planning. Their participation was usually limited to keeping tabs on the activities of their subordinates. The use of the computer did not change this. Thus one general manager commented:

> I do not get deeply involved in the day-to-day operations of the departments reporting to me. In the first place, I do not have the time, and, besides, that is not my job; it's the job of the department general manager. Rather, I just monitor the departments' activities to make sure the managers are doing their jobs.
>
> In a sense, I'm really not evaluating plans; I'm evaluating people and the way they think, and to do this I must talk with them. A set of statistics cannot tell me how a man thinks.

At the top functional level, however, the computer enabled managers to devote more time to examining ways to improve existing systems and procedures, and it had given them better information to do this. For example, one manufacturing manager described this incident:

> We have three or four peak demands for our punch presses each year. In the past, after each peak period, trained personnel were either laid off or moved to other jobs. Last year, I noted that we were using a lot of overtime and part-time labor to produce these parts during one of the periods of peak demand, so I asked our information systems people to explode our requirements for these parts for the past several years.
>
> "Their figures showed that the total demand was large enough to keep all regular employees busy all year. It did not take me much longer to calculate that it would cost us substantially less to keep those men on full time and build up inventories than to lay them off and then have to work overtime and part-time.
>
> Without the computer, however, it would not have been possible for me to do this because we would not have had the information stored anywhere. Even if it had been, it would probably have been prohibitively expensive to try to pull it out and process it.

At the operations level, the increased accuracy of computer-prepared reports enabled managers to improve their planning and to direct their attention to areas where their efforts would be most profitable. For example, in the large company, computer reports on tool usage, dollars of expense on tooling, and dollars of maintenance by machine have enabled the engineers to plan replacement, repair, and maintenance work more accurately and profitably than ever before.

Effects on Budgeting

Inasmuch as my study only tangentially examined the effects of the computer on the budgeting process, I observed only two types of changes. At the *top functional* level, managers were able to change their budgets far more rapidly when the circumstances on which they were based were also changed.

Thus one engineering manager developed a program for use on a time-shared computer which contained his yearly expense budget broken down by project. Whenever a project had to be changed, he used the program to generate several "alternative" budgets for discussion purposes. When agreement was reached on the changes to be made, he then revised the original program to incorporate the new inputs.

At the *operations* level, utilization of the computer resulted in an increase in the accuracy of the manager's budgets. This occurred because the computer permitted direct costs to be broken down in greater detail than was previously economically feasible. The computer also permitted the development of detailed reports on indirect costs at this level for the first time. The result was better decision making by the managers involved. Typical was the comment of one supervisor who remarked that he was now able to do his job on the basis of facts rather than on intuition or guesswork.

Effects on Measurement

One of the few areas in which the computer directly affected the activities of the general manager was that of measurement and evaluation. The major result was that these men were able to request more detailed back-up statistics on many problems than previously. In addition, one general manager said that he used the additional information in running his business:

> The availability of almost any sort of information I want makes it possible for me to know where to apply pressure, and/or how I ought to organize activities. For example, before the computer, I had little idea of our costs or profits for our smallest business in the XYZ market on a current basis because these data were buried in other statistics on our major markets. The development of such information has permitted me to examine the problems in a given area more closely and to evaluate the managers involved on the basis of facts.

At both the top functional level and the operations level, the computer changed the measures managers use to evaluate the performance of their subordinates. Here is a typical comment:

> In some cases the computer has affected the way I, and other managers like me, evaluate our subordinates. The ideal measure has not changed, of course, but the actual measure has. For example, we have always felt that the best way to measure the performance of our manufacturers' representatives was by the share of market our distributors got.
>
> However, since we had no way to estimate total sales for their territories, we used other, less desirable measures. Thus, in the past, if a distributor sent in a large order or if his personal contact with us was good, we felt he was doing well.
>
> After we got the computer, we started generating reports of quarterly and annual sales by distributor. This revealed that for several distributors the big order did not repeat or that the good contact was a substitute for good sales. These reports have enabled us to upgrade the performance of both our manufacturers' representatives and our distributors, even though we still are not able to measure market share.

A manufacturing manager offered this comment on performance evaluation:

> Previously, I used to have to judge performance on the basis of output. Now I have reports which indicate both machine and labor efficiency for the section as a whole, as well as for each machine and each employee. They have helped me to identify areas where efficiency could be improved. I suspect, however, that these reports are of even greater value to my subordinates than they are to me.
>
> For example, the other day one of them told me about a situation in which our labor efficiency report helped him to increase productivity. We had started making parts using a nonstandard material, and he was worried about productivity. But, when he went through the shop, everyone looked busy enough, so he felt pleased.
>
> The next day, however, the labor efficiency report indicated that one employee's productivity had been extremely low. A quick check revealed that the worker did not know how to machine the new material. A little on-the-spot training solved that problem.
>
> The point is that without the report the situation would probably have gone unnoticed, since it was a short run. As a consequence, we would have suffered decreased productivity.

Generality of Study Results

The fact that my research covers only two somewhat similar companies is not as limiting as it might initially seem to be. The results are applicable to many companies in many industries.

I say this because the independent studies described previously (and others like them) tend to support my own research findings. As I mentioned earlier, all of these studies appear to be contradictory when taken individually. However, when one views each as a piece of a larger pattern, rather than as the entire pattern, and then compares each piece with the corresponding portion of my findings, the fit is good indeed.

For example, Hoos's observations of the impact of the computer on the structure and processes of government agencies, banks and insurance companies, and manufacturers of industrial and consumer products dealt primarily with organizational components at the operations level whose principal tasks involved the processing of large amounts of quantitative data.

When her findings (see the ruled insert on page 18) are compared with mine (see *Exhibit I* and *Exhibit II*) at the same level for the same types of components, the similarity is unmistakable even though the characteristics of the organizations involved are different.

Similar comparisons of my findings with those of Shaul, Lee, Brady, and others yield the same results. In fact, I found *no* study whose findings are in disagreement with mine when compared in this manner.

Since these studies covered a wide variety of businesses and industries, it would seem that my findings possess substantial generality. Because of limitations in the data available, however, it is not possible to develop a detailed classification system of the types of companies to which the figures would apply.

Future Changes

As we have seen, the computer's impact on organizational structure and processes has varied according to the characteristics of the process, the level of the organization, and the nature of the task of the component involved. Will the pattern and magnitude of the effects observed so far remain the same in the future?

It depends. In my opinion, companies which are just starting to use the computer will experience changes such as those described in this Special Report. However, I feel this pattern will change in the future for the two manufacturing companies I studied, as well as for others like them. More specifically, I predict that in such companies this pattern will emerge by 1975:

- The computer will not have any significant effects on any of the major characteristics of formal structure—methods of specialization, coordination, span of control, and so forth—at either the general management or the top functional level.
- The effects on formal structure at the operations level will be similar to those observed here, but the magnitude of these changes will be substantially less than those that have occurred to date.
- For certain important operating decisions, general management will delegate the analysis and evaluation phases of the decision-making process to top functional management. As better information becomes available, and as top management becomes convinced that functional managers can do the job, top management may also delegate the responsibility for the final choice.
- Top functional managers will become even less involved in routine, day-to-day decision making. Instead, they will concentrate their time on the important operating decisions delegated to them (for which they will probably begin to use simulation models), and on improvement of system design.
- At the operations level, managers will increasingly be able to focus their attention on those areas with the greatest payback. Fewer decisions will be programmed into the computer than in the past, but the caliber of decision making will increase as information is processed and summarized in more pertinent ways.
- At the general management level, the introduction of financial and other complex simulation models will permit the development of variable budgets. The latter will in turn permit better evaluation of the performance of the general manager involved. Such models should also be useful to general management in the investment planning process.
- There will be continued improvement in the quantitative measures available to evaluate performance at both the functional and operations levels. In a real sense, the computer will make the concepts of both management-by-exception and management-by-objectives operational at these levels.
- In general, the computer is going to affect management decision making and processes—such as operational planning, and measurement and evaluation—substantially more than it will affect the various characteristics of formal structure. This will hold for all levels in the hierarchy and for all types of organizational components.

Conclusion

The computer has brought a number of changes in the structure and processes of businesses. These changes have been less than some would have liked and more than others have wanted. If the same effort and original thinking had been applied to existing operations as was applied to the development of computer systems, some of the changes probably could have been made without the computer. In other cases, the speed and accuracy of the computer were absolutely essential in bringing about the changes.

Further changes will occur in the future. These will primarily involve increases in management efficiency and effectiveness, especially at the top functional level. They will be more subtle and more complex than those changes which have occurred to date and will be more difficult to justify economically, since they will not be accompanied by such substantial decreases in the total number of clerical personnel at the operations level as in the past.

To accomplish these changes will require advances in our knowledge of organizational relationships and business processes, as well as advances in computer hardware and software. Such advances can be aided by management support and training, but they cannot be halted. Kenneth Boulding described the reasons in another context:

> There is probably no way back. The growth of knowledge [computer systems] is one of the most irreversible forces known to mankind. It takes a catastrophe of very large dimensions to diminish the total stock of knowledge in the possession of man. Even in the rise and fall of great civilizations surprisingly little has been permanently lost, and much that was lost for a short time was easily regained. Hence there is no hope for ignorance or for morality [management] based on it. Once we have tasted the fruit of the tree of knowledge, as the Biblical story illustrates so well, Eden is closed to us.[1]

The computer is a tool. Tomorrow's manager will use it in the same manner that today's manager uses a slide rule, or an adding machine, or a telephone.

[1] *The Meaning of the 20th Century: The Great Transition* (New York: Harper and Row, 1964), p. 23.

BIBLIOGRAPHY

American Foundation on Automation and Employment, Inc., *Automation and the Middle Manager,* American Foundation on Automation and Employment, Inc., 1966.

Anshen, Melvin, and G. L. Bach, *Management and Corporations: 1985,* McGraw-Hill Book Company, 1960.

Boore, William F., and Jerry R. Murphy, *The Computer Sampler: Management Perspectives on the Computer,* McGraw-Hill Book Company, 1968.

Computer Systems—Their Contribution and Challenge to Management, McKinsey & Co., Inc., February, 1963.

Elliott, J. D., "EDP—Its Impact on Jobs, Procedures, and People," *The Journal of Industrial Engineering,* September-October, 1958.

Emery, James C., "The Impact of Information Technology on Organization," *Proceedings of the 24th Annual Meeting,* Academy of Management, December, 1964.

Fransica, J. R., "Electronic Data Processing and Its Significant Impact on Management," *National Underwriter,* January, 1962.

Gallagher, James D., *Management Information Systems and the Computer,* American Management Association, Inc., 1962.

Greenberger, Martin (ed.), *Computers and the World of the Future,* MIT Press, 1962.

Haverstroh, Chadwich J., "The Impact of Electronic Data Processing on Administrative Organizations," *National Tax Journal,* September, 1961.

Jackson, Robert, "Computers and Middle Management," *Journal of Systems Management,* April, 1970.

Kleinschrod, Walter A., "Computers and Middle Management," *Administrative Management,* May, 1969.

Korbin, C. L., "Computer: Its Impact on Management," *Iron Age,* March 8, 1962.

Krout, A. J., "How EDP is Affecting Workers and Organizations," *Personnel,* July, 1962.

Lee, Hak Chong, *The Impact of Electronic Data Processing Upon Patterns of Business Organization and Administration,* New York School of Business, State University of New York at Albany, 1965.

———, "The Organizational Impact of the Computer," *Management Services,* May-June, 1967.

Mann, Floyd C., and K. Williams, "Observations on the Dynamics of a Change to Electronic Data Processing Equipment," *Administrative Science Quarterly,* September, 1960.

Melitz, Peter W., "Impact of Electronic Data Processing on Managers," *Advanced Management,* April, 1961.

"Middle Management and Technological Change," *Management Review,* October, 1963.

Myers, Charles A. (ed.), *The Impact of Computers on Management,* MIT Press, 1967.

Schwitter, Joseph P., "Computer Effect Upon Management Jobs," *Journal of the Academy of Management,* September, 1965.

Simon, Herbert A., *The Shape of Automation for Men and Management,* Harper & Row Publishers, 1965.

Stilian, Gabriel M., "Impact of Automation on the Manufacturing Executive's Job," *Management Review,* March, 1958.

Vergin, Roger, "Computer Induced Organization Changes," Michigan State University, *Business Topics,* Summer, 1967.

Weber, Edward, "Change in Managerial Manpower with Mechanization of Data Processing," *The Journal of Business,* April, 1959.

Whisler, Thomas L., *Executives and Their Jobs: The Changing Organizational Structure,* Graduate School of Business, University of Chicago, Selected Papers, Number 9.

———, *Information Technology and Organizational Change,* Wadsworth Publishing Co., Inc., 1970.

———, "The Manager and the Computer," *The Journal of Accountancy,* **CXXII**, January, 1965.

SECTION III

COMPUTERS AND THE ORGANIZATIONAL SETTING

No single tool has had as great an impact on business operations as the computer. Its almost blanket acceptance by the business world has raised it to a pinnacle and turned it into an awesome deity that has mesmerized many a neophyte in its spotless temples. To assert that computers have revolutionized business is but to acknowledge a fact of life. In our day they are engaged "shoulder to shoulder" with management personnel in the making of decisions. There is hardly a company nowadays that has not in some way or other been affected by the presence of the computer or data processor.

When speaking of computers we are referring to the electronic devices for the processing, transfer, and storage of data. Computers are capable of performing arithmetical operations at fantastic speeds, and it was for this reason that they were first used, thus reducing data-processing costs. In those instances where they were properly employed they were generally successful. Because of the computer's large memory-storage capacity and because of its ability to make logical comparisons and thus render routine decisions, it has great potential in the business world, where it is inundated with enormous waves of analyzable data. The computer can present management with greater speed and accuracy in the processing of such data, with more timely reporting, and with the predicted results of choosing alternative courses of action.

In spite of the obvious advantages of computers, they somehow have not lived up to their expectations. It is interesting to note here that some authorities attribute this failure to management and not to any inherent defects or shortcomings of the hardware. As with other novel techniques that have invaded the managerial field, computers too have often been looked on as a panacea for all of management's problems, and when they have not been proven such, their failure was duly noted. While some companies have been able to justify the use of computers on the basis of clerical savings alone, others, lacking imagination and initiative in utilizing them in the areas where they possess their greatest potential, have found it hard to justify their continued use. Some believe that present-day data-processing systems are grinding out far more data than any manager can possibly assimilate. Others have seen the organizational structure as the villain blocking the proper utilization of the computer for information technology. Because of the similarity to punched-card accounting equipment, the responsibility for the data-processing equipment was often "logically" assigned to the assistant controller, who typically lacked the creative ability to optimize the computer's potential and who further lacked authority, status, and the entrepreneur's viewpoint of the company as a whole.

Another possible factor to be considered in connection with business's failure to utilize the computer's full potential may be the opposition exhibited by middle management, the familiar line-staff conflict. Their lack of participation in the initial planning stages may be due to an apparent threat (as they see it) to their traditional authority on the part of the computer personnel, "the high priests of the new cult."

In the McKinsey & Company's survey of 27 large corporations, it was found that only one-third of the companies had achieved outstanding success with their computer systems.[1] In the companies considered successful, the greatest single cause of this success was attributed to top management's assessment of computer potential. Top management indicated a positive attitude toward the computer and as such gave continuing direction and guidance. In the less successful companies, top management viewed the computer as a glorified accounting machine that could best be left to the care of specialists.

Brabb and Hutchins are much concerned

[1] John Garrity, "Top Management and Computer Profits," *Harvard Business Review,* July-August, 1963, pp. 6–8.

with the place of the electronic computer in the organizational structure. In the first reading they remind the reader of the surprisingly rapid adoption of the computer by industry since its initial introduction in 1954. Yet despite its eager acceptance, for some the computer has been a bitter disappointment. Generally the blame is laid on the men who use and sell computers. Specifically, failure has been attributed to inadequate organizational planning and to the lack of clear delineation of authority and responsibility. Because of the serious nature of these charges, the authors are intent on examining the various facets of the problem. They discuss four at length: (1) the internal organization of the computer department; (2) the location of the data-processing department in the corporation; (3) the status of the computer personnel; and (4) the impact of the computer on middle management and on other departments.

History, of course, has had something to do with the internal organization of computer departments. Originally computers were introduced in order to reduce clerical costs, and were put under the charge of the controller and used for routine accounting. No wonder computers failed at times to turn in a profit. However, they did enable the personnel to acquire valuable computer experience and to get an inkling of its real potential. Since then a different view, fortunately, has prevailed. The computer is no longer looked upon as a mere clerical replacement but as the core element in an effective information system. As such it should not be viewed as the exclusive property of one department, but should be made to contribute to the common good of the entire company.

Because of this change in outlook, computer departments are generally and most naturally taken up with tasks such as systems analysis, computer programming, and computer operation. Each of these functions is sufficiently specialized to be best carried out by specialized groups. But with the assigning of functions goes the shouldering of responsibility. Neuschel believes that breaking up the responsibility and spreading it out over all the departments involved is conducive to little good. No one is really being held responsible. Nor should a department head be invested with the charge of a specific function, unless in actual practice he does have such a function. Otherwise special difficulties could easily arise. Work priority could become a divisive issue and the head could be asked to perform services normally outside his role. In principle, then, the computer personnel should be held accountable to top management. In this way interdepartmental objectives can more systematically be integrated and their implementation assured.

Computer programming and computer operation are two distinct functions to be performed by distinct groups. Because of their rather specialized knowledge and experience, the programmers should be in position to advise when certain work, such as exception routines, ought not to be programmed into the system and when valuable computer time could be saved by revising existing programs. Such revision, some believe, can best be left to a special set of programmers, and for sound reasons. In any event, the management of computer programming should be distinct from that of operations. Computer operations typically involve an input unit and a console operating unit.

Brabb and Hutchins believe that it is better to teach a programmer something about accounting and the like than to teach an accountant something about programming. The latter approach tends to isolate departments and to encourage work duplication.

The second point discussed is the physical and sociological location of the data-processing department in the corporation. The physical location should be determined by the nature of the information required. Whether there should be centralized or decentralized facilities, though the former are normally more economical, will have to be decided by the geographical scope of the business and the bulk of its operations. Because of the changes effected by the computer in the clerical section, these groups may have to be physically relocated or centralized for better operation.

Furthermore, top executives should see to it that the data-processing department is not located either physically or sociologically in a major department of the business, for this would eventually turn that major department into a servicing unit for other departments or necessitate similarly expensive facilities in other major departments. Besides, the surrender of authority by department heads to the head of the major department with EDP would certainly be resented. It is best if the EDP group is constituted an independent major department that reports to a "neutral" executive who himself is not a direct user of the equipment. This department would accept input data from all other departments and produce all required information, but it alone would be responsible for the intermediate processing.

The location of the computer is emphasized in the two-part reading by Schoderbek and Babcock. This recent study of organizational location of the computer underscores the changes that have taken place within the past few years. In more and more companies computer activities have been relocated from their original accounting location to an independent department. One of the more significant findings of this study was that 95 per cent of the EDP managers believed that EDP should be independent of all operational departments, in spite of the fact that only about half of them were so organized at the time. It was also found that companies with an independent EDP department had fewer problems than did those in which this function was located within the financial or accounting department.

The status of the EDP personnel must be clearly defined by top management. The systems analysts, programmers, and the rest should be given both the authority and the responsibility to execute their respective tasks. This may necessitate extensive changes in the organizational structure if a piecemeal approach to EDP is to be avoided. For a realistic total systems approach, the data-processing director should be an independent member of the top management team. That this may give rise to intensely felt human problems elsewhere can easily be understood, but these problems must be faced and solved satisfactorily by top management.

How these problems have been solved can be seen from the Schoderbek and Babcock reading and from other research reports current in the literature.[2] The 1969 study by Schoderbek and Babcock revealed that 70 per cent of the EDP departments were at the upper-management level, compared to 48 per cent as previously reported. This increase in reporting to upper management may have been due to the belief that at this high level computer activities that cut across departmental boundaries would produce less friction and more efficiency. (The study did attest to the greater success of computer systems located at higher levels of management.) Also, the enhancing of status of the EDP function has been a frequent phenomenon. More and more companies have assigned

[2] The results of the study by Robert Reichenbach and Charles Tasso, *Organizing for Data Processing*, Research Study No. 92, American Management Association, New York, 1968, differ considerably from those of the 1965 study by Margaret V. Higginson, *Managing with EDP: A Look at the Art*, Research Study No. 71, American Management Association, New York, 1965. In the latter study employing a rather large sample (340 companies), 70 per cent of the companies surveyed showed EDP managers reporting to financial executives, while only 30 per cent of the EDP managers reported to nonfinancial executives. In the former study, responsibility for the computer complex was lodged in the financial or accounting departments in only six of the sixteen study companies. A trend was noted there for the creation of an independent EDP capability reporting to a top officer in the corporation. The differences in the two studies may be attributed to the grossly different size sample employed as well as to the different size of the companies studied.

high-level executive-vice-presidential status to this function.

As for the fourth and final point, the specific impact of the computer on middle management, the authors acknowledge that the question is not yet settled. They admit that the computer has made a substantial impact on all of business management, but just how it will affect middle management they do not know. We have already considered this particular point, when we saw that some believe that the computer will take over many lower and middle management functions and will consequently cause these groups to diminish both in number and in function. The top management staff, on the other hand, will grow in size and handle more of the decision making. Other authors, however, see very little change. Anschen and Bach, for instance, believe that the management situation in 1985 "will not be startingly different than what it is today." When all is said and done, the limiting factor of computer application to the problems of management may well be not engineering know-how but the willingness to use and the art of applying the computer to these problems.

Since the publication of the article by Brabb and Hutchins, much research has been conducted on the impact of the computer on middle management.[3] In the reading by Schoderbek and Babcock, it was found that managers were taking a more active role not only in the purchasing of new and expensive EDP equipment but also in new computer applications. This increase in participation can be attributed, at least in part, to the better education of modern-day managers in computer concepts and techniques. However management still is far from optimizing the advantages inherent in EDP. The trend of computerization, although definitely away from the financial and accounting applications, leans heavily toward the past, since accounting programs still account for most of the computer time used.[4] The results of the Schoderbek and Babcock study show no statistically significant differences from that of Dean conducted a year before.[5]

Robert McFarland, a psychologist, treats an aspect of the computer problem that has hardly been touched on in the literature. In "Electronic Power Grab" he poses an unusual question, "Is it possible for an individual or for several individuals working in collusion by computer facilities manipulation to take over control of a firm with regard to the key operating and policy decisions without the company executives and stockholders being aware of it?" However, before tackling the issue directly, he first reviews other aspects that have a bearing on the problem.

One of the perennially perplexing tasks of management has been how to keep from being overwhelmed by floods of irrelevant, useless, and perhaps unreliable reports. At present this problem is even more acute. For the earlier man-made machines (engines and generators), there were clearly set limits to the amount of abuse and misuse they would tolerate before breaking down, but for the computer there are, unfortunately, no such limits. Asked a stupid question, it will not break down, but will grind out answers in kind for the fool. And the fool will unquestionably proceed to act on the given oracle. Hence today, with so much information being processed by com-

[3] Besides the research reported in the footnotes, reference should also be made to the studies conducted by Booz, Allen, and Hamilton in 1966 and replicated in 1968. These are cited in James W. Taylor and Neal J. Dean, "Managing to Manage the Computer," *Harvard Business Review,* September-October, 1966, and in Neal J. Dean, "The Computer Comes of Age," *Harvard Business Review,* January-February, 1968.

[4] "What One Survey Shows About Computer Use," *Business Management,* September, 1966, p. 24. This survey of 153 companies in central Illinois revealed that nearly half the firms had some sort of EDP equipment, but that most of this was used for the conventional business applications (accounting).

[5] Neal J. Dean, "The Computer Comes of Age," *Harvard Business Review,* January-February, 1968, p. 89.

puters, there is an even greater need to check the output for relevance, utility, reliability, and validity.

Another problem arises with the need to increase EDP capitalization and the computer-operating staff. The supervisor, typically a person with an accounting background who was originally responsible for computer applications in the firm, continues to favor the accounting-oriented applications and either sidetracks or delays other worthwhile computer projects. And when newer computer facilities are to be acquired, a power struggle is apt to ensue at the top management level as to who should control the computer.

A third problem, involving effective computer use by several operating divisions, arises when lower-echelon groups control the computer facilities. Unless top management is actively involved in the problem, the middle-management group controlling the computer staff will assign too low a priority for interdivisional applications.

In view of all this, McFarland subscribes to the opinion voiced by Philip Thurston and by John Garrity in the McKinsey report, that top management must direct, manage, and lead and must not abdicate control to the computer personnel or to much lower echelon managers.

The McKinsey report proposed an examination of conscience for the chief executive, the items of which McFarland reproduces. His aim is not to endorse the technique but simply to stress the chief executive's part in the control system. Since executives are human, methodologies developed in other behavioral-science fields would appear applicable also to them. So rather than formulate answers to the five soul-searching questions in the McKinsey report, top-level managers would find more useful methodologies concerned with identifying the relevant controllable variables in a given company situation.

The final portion of the reading deals with the concept of effective "computermanship" in terms of "how to steal a company without anyone ever catching on." In explaining the method, the author breaks it down to three fundamental techniques.

The first of these concerns how one goes about eliminating potential competition. McFarland presumes, of course and rightly too, that the individual interested in effective "computermanship" is bright, capable, and aggressive and is willing to master enough computer technology and other allied activities in order to forge ahead. With those potential competitors 40 years old or more, one should ostensibly agree that the old tried ways are the best and that these newfangled ideas, besides being ineffective, are costly in terms of money and effort. One could also reinforce the competitor's fears that these ideas are far too technical and besides, not worthwhile. The months and years spent in mastering the new technology would be wasted, for in that time the field would have advanced so far that one would still be hopelessly behind.

The other two techniques are concerned with one's competitors, who are presumably also young, energetic, and aggressive, and willing to master the necessary computer technology. With this group different techniques will undoubtedly be necessary. Since these men will also be maneuvering for power, the all-important detail to be attended to is: Am I now ready for the power play, for the coup d'etat, for the showdown?

If the answer is in the negative, then technique No. 2 concerning how one goes about slowing down or delaying the showdown should go into effect. If one is on the computer staff, a wise move would be to discourage, as much as possible, other company divisions from getting involved with the computer. If, however, they unfortunately are already involved, one could repeatedly slow down their programs by making relevant suggestions, thus engaging them in endless rewriting and debugging of programs. One could also discourage the use of the larger computer installation by encouraging them to get their own smaller computers, never once letting on that such things as Shared Time and Data Phone transmission ever existed.

If the answer is in the affirmative, then technique No. 3 concerning how one goes about forcing a showdown should be employed. Of course, one should be reasonably sure that he will win the upper hand. The evident thing to do is to insist that if one were given complete managerial responsibility, he could make the computer installation a profitable enterprise by employing systems approaches and other operational-research techniques. One must be sure that the chief executive to whom the claim is made actually manages these company operations; otherwise, those who do will not fail to withhold the support so necessary for validating one's claims.

Other noninterpersonal ploys could also be used. Organizing information flow so that the actual decision-making functions bypass the operating managers and pass over to the computer is one that is illustrated with two true-to-life examples. Also, the deliberate withholding of technical or analytical skills by an elite group as a form of job insurance is another way. The main point that McFarland makes here is that the aspiring electronic power-grabber, by identifying the relevant controllable variables as suggested by control systems theory, could innocuously program the data along with the mass of traditional input data and by occasionally checking the key data would be able to establish a reputation as a remarkably accurate forecaster, or, better, could covertly make use of this valuable information for his own private advantage.

25. ELECTRONIC COMPUTERS AND MANAGEMENT ORGANIZATION

GEORGE J. BRABB * AND EARL B. HUTCHINS †

Electronic data processing has made significant contributions to improved operations in many businesses since the first introduction of a commercially produced large-scale computer in 1954. By fall of 1957, over 450 electronic digital computer systems were actively processing business data in industry and government.[1] By March of 1961, nearly 5,000 electronic data-processing systems (including 540 in government) had been delivered and an additional 6,500 were on order.[2] Machines in current use are produced by twenty different manufacturers and include about forty models varying widely in size, capacity, and speed. Computers are effecting an "information handling revolution" and now handle a major share of the recording and reporting of most routine business transactions of major industrial firms. In addition, they have made possible the application of many new managerial skills.

The revolution now in progress, like all revolutions, is not progressing smoothly and without problems. There have been reports of disappointment and disillusionment and even, in some instances, of withdrawal of computers. The situations have more often been attributable to those who use and those who sell rather than to the equipment itself.

The reasons and combinations of reasons for these negative results are numerous. Many such failures can be attributed, however, primarily to inadequate organizational planning, including lack of a clear delineation of authority and responsibility.[3]

The importance of appropriate and effective organization and direction of the data-processing function is further emphasized by the dramatic change from viewing the computer as a "clerical replacement" in existing data-processing systems to viewing the computer as providing the cornerstone for an effective management-information system. The original need and commonly envisioned purpose of a business-data processor was to reduce or curb the growth of large clerical forces required to handle the burgeoning paperwork burden. It soon became evident, however, that the proper role of business-data processing should be to process from source generation all basic business data and to produce selected information as required to operate the business. To successfully exploit the potential capability of the enormously powerful and versatile equipment presently available in "automated information factories," a competent personnel force is required to design, program, and operate the complete information system. The placement of this force in the corporate structure, its own internal organization, and the support extended to its activities by top management will obviously determine how successfully it accomplishes its objectives. The National Industrial Conference Board's report covering a study of the experiences of 124 companies concluded that the deterrents to data-processing progress include "poor planning, weak organization, and lack of internal support." [4]

This paper will be devoted to a consideration of the four facets of the subject which deserve particular attention:

- Internal organization of the computer department.
- Location of the data-processing department in the corporation.
- Status of computer personnel management.
- Impact of the computer on the organiza-

SOURCE: *California Management Review* (Fall, 1963), pp. 33–42.

* University of Montana.
† General Electric Company.

tion of other departments of the company with particular reference to its effects on middle management personnel.[5]

We will attempt to determine the major outline of an effective organizational structuring of the data-processing function, based on interpretations of experience and understanding of the problems as these have been reported through formal studies, by management consultants, and by individuals engaged in data-processing work. A brief initial section will examine the current organizational status as background for this task.

There is, of course, no necessarily optimum organization of the electronic data-processing (EDP) function or best single definition and scope of EDP functional responsibilities. Also, other factors important to the success or failure of an EDP installation are recognized but will not be specifically discussed in this paper. A suggested list of such factors would include selection of the proper equipment, correct economic decisions on computer applications, and competence of the various EDP staff groups.

Throughout this paper reference is to a general purpose rather than a special purpose computer. Scientific and engineering applications, while not specifically discussed, could comprise part of the working load of the centralized computer.

The subjects of location in the corporate structure and effective internal organization of the data-processing function are discussed from the standpoint of a major manufacturing organization. The computer has made substantial contributions to the handling of business data for many other types of businesses, such as insurance companies, banks, utilities, and major retail establishments, but manufacturing firms generally present more diversified potential applications for computers, offer a relatively similar organizational pattern as a common framework for discussing optimum structuring, and comprise the largest sector of the civilian economy.

FIRST INTEREST

The first interest of industrial firms in conducting a computer feasibility study and acquiring an electronic data processor usually has been to reduce clerical costs. Consequently, two results are common: operation of the computer is placed within the controller's department and accounting routines, normally little changed from the manner in which they were previously performed, are the first jobs placed on the computer. Following the payroll and a few other accounting activities, machine applications are developed for inventory control, production scheduling, sales and market analysis, and personnel analysis. The machines may also be used in the solution of scientific, engineering, and operations-research problems.

Generally the routine handling of "programmed" work has been successfully accomplished, but limited progress has been made toward "integrated" and "automated" processing of total business data. Also, returns to date have not been in terms of financial gain, but rather in computer experience and in awakening to a clearer understanding of the potential of computers as the foundation of a total business information system.

With two to six years of EDP experience behind them, most large manufacturing companies are looking for the answers to some important questions. Have the original computer acquisition objectives been met; if not, are they still valid? What are the opportunities ahead for improving the business, and how can the data-processing function help to realize these? How can computer capabilities be more fully and profitably exploited? Should we develop an integrated business information system and, if so, how is this done?

Several administrative questions are being asked at this point. Who should operate and control the scheduling of the computer(s)? Who should be responsible for developing new applications, and what should be the criteria for their implementation? What should be the relationship among the groups directly associated with the computer and between the computer operation and its "customers," the operating departments?

The primary administrative responsibility of the manager of data processing can be defined as the organization of the EDP department to more effectively contribute to the over-all objectives of the company. He must possess a command of current data-processing technology sufficient to realize top management expectations from electronic data processing. He, therefore, has the important continuing responsibilities of evaluating the efficiency and progress of the department and of the specific employees, as well as of managers in operating components of the department.

The most natural and conventional subdivisions of the functional work associated with the computer department are:

- Systems analysis.
- Computer programming.
- Computer operation.

"Systems analysis is an orderly study of the detailed procedure for collecting, organizing, and evaluating information within an organization, with the objectives of improving control of the operations of the organization." [6] When used to describe a work function this term usually is understood to include also "systems design," which is the creative phase of devising a new system.

Programming, as applied to computers, is the technique for completely specifying to the data-processing equipment all the possible operations which might occur in the solution of a problem.[7]

Computer operations pertain to the actual day-to-day functioning of the centralized data-processing equipment, i.e., machine scheduling, operation, and maintenance. This component usually provides key-punching service, machine processing of established and developmental application programs, and preparation of output in usable form.

Each of the three computer department functions is of sufficient complexity and magnitude to warrant separate specialization and management. Some companies have believed that the ideal organization has a single group of employees providing all three functions for computer applications. However, "this has generally been found to be impractical. The functions are therefore carried out by specialized units. . . ." [8]

The reasons offered by proponents of separate sections within the EDP department, as opposed to combining at least two of the functions are:

1. Each operation is a distinctly different kind of work and requires different knowledge and skill.

2. Performance of each major function by a separate staff helps to avoid compromises in the new system or in machine-programming or operation.[9]

The study and analysis of business information requirements are vital steps in bringing a potential machine application into reality. The systems analysis group designs a system or set of procedures and thus tends to establish specifications for the auxiliary equipment required to implement the system. This group recommends, or decides in cooperation with the components having operating responsibility, the new methods and procedures to establish, the files to set up or eliminate, the equipment to obtain or discard, and the organizational changes to make. This group also reviews the economic aspects of proposed changes.

Neuschel [10] has covered the subject of where in the organizational structure the responsibility for interdepartmental systems and procedures should be placed. He points out (p. 48) three alternatives: assignment of the responsibility to all departments; assignment to the head of a major function, typically the comptroller; retention of the responsibility by top management.

His primary conclusions are:

1. When responsibility for interdepartmental procedures is broken up and distributed among all departments, accountability for completeness of the program is wholly lost. No position can be held responsible for observing needs or crystallizing objectives. Nor can there be any assurance that the most promising opportunities are being exploited . . . (p. 56).

2. It may be stated as a general principle, therefore, that responsibility for investigation, analysis, and recommendation regarding interdepartmental procedures should not be assigned to a functional executive unless, in actual practice as well as in the minds of the other division heads, he operates in the capacity of "chief of staff" on this kind of work for the principal executive (pp. 60–61).

3. In principle, staff personnel engaged in interdepartmental procedures studies should report to the chief executive of a relatively self-contained operating unit—that is, either to the president, executive or administrative vice-president, or general manager of a company . . . (p. 62).

In addition, the common result of procedures developed within each department (1 above) is that the resulting systems become data-processing "islands" because they are usually only loosely connected to adjacent areas. The work tends to be viewed out of perspective with the organization as a whole; as a result, integration and over-all economy are seldom obtained.

TWO PROBLEMS

Two of the main problems which arise when consolidated systems analysis is assigned to a particular functional department (2 above) are that the priority of work usually becomes a major issue and the manager of the department is asked to provide many services which are outside the normal scope of his particular function. Finally, systems integration cutting across departmental lines must have the direct support of top management if the objectives desired are to be achieved.

The computer-programming function poses fewer controversial alternatives as to its optimum organization. Only a few companies believe that once the system has been designed its complete implementation should be the function of a single staff.[11] The argument is that employees with equipment knowledge are best qualified to develop the program of machine instructions and that the intimate knowledge of machine operations will reveal the best refinements for programming. They further reason that the manager of the computer operation should be responsible not only for meeting the due dates of a new application but also for the quality and efficiency of the programming, which has a close relationship to best utilization of the computer.

Experienced programmers often can make significant contributions also to the design of an application through recognition that there is a definite point at which it becomes uneconomical and unwise to include work within the computer system. For example, the cost of programming and operating many exception routines usually makes it more economical to process these phases of the work manually.

Revisions to existing EDP programs are an important part of the programming function. Virtually every company which has used electronic computers for several years has programs which, if revised, would release valuable machine time, speed up overall processing time, and permit a greater input-output flexibility for the particular application.

A Controllers Institute research study advocates a separate program-revision group in preference to programmers handling both new and revised programs. Reasons for this preference center around the freedom to do a more thorough job; to reduce "set-up" time and conflicts with deadlines on new work; and to take advantage of the "natural" divisions in personality, technical ability, and new work versus improvement work preferences of programmers.[12] The programming activity should, however, be managed separately from the computer-operation functions. Reasons for this are the importance and complexity of the work, difficulty of recruitment and training, and the volume of work in installations of the size considered in this paper. In actual practice, separate management of the programming group is the most commonly used organizational arrangement.

Occasional variations in the normal structuring of the computer-operation section include separate management of the input function, operation of a separate punched card department, and use of an "open shop" computer center.

The "typical (and ultimate) EDP organization" [13] usually consists of an input manager in addition to a programming manager and an operations manager. The usual input unit would consist of key punch supervisors and operators and a control section responsible for proofing, batching, and other activities necessary to input and output operations. The operations unit would have the usual console and machine operators, tape handlers, and perhaps a supporting punched card operation. A separate input unit can develop conflicts with the computer operating unit.

Companies usually have not merged conventional punched card departments with the EDP operation if EDP utilizes large-scale computers.[14] This tends to support the viewpoint that both types of data-processing equipment have particular areas in which they can best serve. (In companies using small or medium scale computers, operations commonly have been combined with those of the conventional tabulating department.)

The final alternative approach to computer operations is to provide data-processing hardware and limited technical assistance but generally to expect using components to provide their own systems design, programming, and operators. This technique has been successfully tried in engineering departments using smaller computers but should not be regarded as an acceptable alternative for operation of a large-scale, multiple-usage computer. The National Industrial Conference Board found this to be a costly method in comparison with the conventional approach of providing a full line of technical assistance.[15] More important, it tends to delay the development of an integrated information system since it encourages departmental isolation and duplication of processing activities among departments.

Current developments in computer-programming languages have led some persons to believe that it is easier to teach the subject-matter expert (accountant, economist, etc.) how to program than to teach the programmer something about the subject matter (accounting, economics, etc.). Even if this approach were completely feasible, which it is not,[16] the basic point remains, this approach cannot be expected to lead to the development of an integrated information system for the organization. Rather, it tends to encourage departmental isolation and duplication of processing activity.

The location of the data-processing function must correspond to the dynamics of the operations for which information is desired. The information requirements are important determinants of both the locations and organization of data-processing facilities. Thus, the question of centralized versus decentralized computer facilities will have to be answered within the operational and geographical scope of the particular business. Operations that are concentrated at only one location pose less problem as to physical location, but still contain problems concerning organizational location and relationships. Normally, centralized processing of all operations offers some economies of scale through the use of larger-scale equipment. Alternatively, problems of communication and scheduling may offset some of these advantages. Finally, a variety of operations usually can be handled more economically on a centralized large-scale computer. Actually, the use of electronics has tended to force many companies toward centralization of data processing, although decentralization is taking place in manufacturing, engineering, and marketing operations.

Geographically dispersed operations present problems of both physical location and organizational structure. A centralized processing unit is valuable for dealing with numerous, undispersed operations and is probably mandatory for highly centralized management control. On the other hand, divisional data-processing facilities may often be justified by the nature and volume of divisional activity and degree of local autonomy. Current developments in telecommunications equipment at least make centralized processing easier to accomplish. Centralization of data processing, however, does not preclude stages or phases of data processing at the divisional level.

LOCATING EDP

In addition to the more vital issue of where to locate the EDP function, it should be noted that another type of organizational impact is often associated with successful computer applications. Because of extensive change in the procedures of clerical sections which prepare and receive machine-processed data, these groups are or should often be transferred or centralized for more logical or economical operation. There is in such instances a twofold need. First, it must be determined to what extent consolidation of work units or (perhaps) more fundamental changes will be needed. Second, the likelihood that these organization changes or shifts in responsibility will, in fact, be made must be evaluated.[17]

The degree of success of an EDP installation depends to a large extent upon the understanding and cooperation received from top management and from the key individuals throughout the company who are affected by the new methods of electronic data processing. Good work by the EDP group in the technical aspects is not enough. Positive participation by top management is essential to successful cooperation between two or more components with diverse interests.

As pointed out in the National Industrial Conference Board study,

> Failures arose from such conditions as poor systems, inaccurate source information, and lack of adequate top-management support. Companies have also found that the more advanced the equipment and its proposed use, the more serious internal obstacles become.[18]

Top management should be periodically satisfied in at least five areas concerning the data-processing function: objectives, applications, hardware, organization, and economics.[19]

If for no other reason, executive management must act in accordance with the recognition that data processing is one of the largest single indirect costs of business operation. Members of top management cannot in the long run divorce themselves from direct participation in decisions pertaining to expenditures of time and money on the scale required by the typical

EDP system. The cost of failure or inefficiency can be substantial because of the investments involved. Top management must also recognize that poor execution can often prevent a good decision from being fully effective.

Milton Stone states the case as follows:

> The time would seem to have arrived for management to pay some attention to the management of its data-processing tools, to measure performance, to judge results.
>
> Far from exercising control over the more ambitious systems, management treats this complex, hard-to-understand child of technology with the kid gloves and indecision of the modern parent. In many organizations, lack of understanding by top management allows the data-processing activity to determine its own objectives, set its own standards, and measure its own performance against those standards.[20]

In its broadest scope, the job of administrative organization is to marshall and use the limited resources of business to achieve specific objectives. Organization defines the lines of authority and the responsibility of individuals and coordinates individual efforts for harmonious attainment of the predetermined objectives.[21] These points of predetermined objectives, definite authority and responsibility, and harmonious relationship are the principal missing ingredients in much of present administration of the data-processing function.

With the possible exception of a limited introductory period, the alternative of placing the computer installation within a major department is not satisfactory for a complete manufacturing business. As soon as other major departments require a large amount of EDP work, a decision must be made to adopt one of the two alternatives: operation as a servicing unit or installation of similar "captive" facilities in each major department. A major objection to the second alternative is that an equivalent amount of money spent to operate multiple data-processing centers will not buy as much computing ability as will a single installation. More important, the computer applications become "islands" of data processing instead of being integrated into a complete business information system.

There are several operating variations of the service center which is located within a major department. These variations include having a charter which stresses its interdepartmental nature, having each department do its own developmental work, including machine programming, and reserving particular shifts for each department.

Such a service center is not intended to interfere with existing departmental structures; however, as reported in the Controllers Institute research study,

> When a center is responsible to another major departmental user, many department heads feel they have lost some of their former authority and responsibility. This reaction can become fairly strong . . . the broader the scope of the application, the greater the reluctance appears to be to turn over a major part of a function to a machine center supervised by another department. This reluctance does not appear to be as great when the EDP group reports to a "general" or "neutral" executive who himself is not a direct user of the equipment.[22]

Typically, computers have been the administrative responsibility of a company's financial group. While this can be an appropriate organizational location, there are conditions under which this arrangement impedes rather than facilitates effective exploitation of the computer's potential. These conditions usually involve the personality, interest, and company status of the controller or financial officer and the nature of the applications chosen for computer processing. When the controller is accounting-oriented, rather than general management-oriented, experience to date indicates that chances are good that the computer will not be used to its best advantage.[23] Also, if feasible applications include many engineering problems or manufacturing activities in addition to accounting work, there is a strong possibility that a computer system including those activities will be slow to develop.

THIRD ALTERNATIVE

The third alternative, establishing the EDP component as an independent major department whose responsibility is to process data from source acquisition to final report form appears to be most likely to lead to the development of an efficient, integrated data-processing system. The EDP department accepts input data as approved by each department and produces all required information. The originating department has responsibility for approving and initiating the source data and, within limits, prescribing the final data, but the intermediate processing is not its concern. It should be emphasized that only the programmed data-processing activities and not the important decision-making or control responsibilities are assumed by the EDP servicing center.

Much of EDP's value lies in its capacity for consolidating separate information files and for preparing interrelated series of operations without manual intervention. Management of the EDP facility should be assigned authority to effectively exploit the information potential of basic raw data. This does not imply that EDP would usurp the primary responsibilities of the other major departments. Rather, the EDP facility would operate as a production center serving all traditional major functions of the business.

Responsibility of the director of data processing should in general include the following:

1. Planning, supervision, and control of the electronic data-processing program.
2. Continuous study of interdepartmental systems and procedures.
3. Determination of acceptability of new machine applications.
4. Continuous review of current applications, including appropriateness, degree of integration, usefulness, etc.
5. Appraisal and evaluation of new EDP equipment.
6. Conducting a formal program to teach managers how to use data-processing advantageously.
7. Development of competent staffs for systems analysis, machine programming, and machine operation.
8. Establishment of processing priorities.
9. Prescribing of forms and methods for input procedures.
10. Limited authority over the form, content, and scheduling of records and reports output.

Vesting authority in the director of data processing to decide matters which closely affect departments over which he has no line authority naturally leads to occasional conflicts which must be solved by persuasion or appeal to higher authority. In actual experience, the most sensitive areas involving questions of authority are the following:

- Systems definitions.
- The dates for input data to be available.
- Priorities for various applications.
- Acceptance and servicing of new applications.

To attain maximum effectiveness of the EDP installation, the organizational role of the data-processing operation must be defined by top management. The entire organization must be made aware of management's interest and involvement. It must be made to understand the desirability for a computer operation involving systems analysts who will have a voice in the internal operations of individual departments. Finally, the central data-processing group must feel it has both the authority and the responsibility to execute the tasks before it.

In order to put computer capabilities to work more rapidly, the piecemeal approach to EDP should be abandoned in favor of the more efficient total systems development. A management-control system must be "designed" complete with all specifications necessary to make required decisions. Necessarily, "the constraints of the existing organization must be ignored." [24] Operating executives at the highest management levels must be induced to cooperate fully in making the changes necessary to accomplish these goals. That such cooperation is not extended to an executive of lower rank or to the manager of a "computing" operating department is not surprising. These considerations dictate that the director of data processing be an independent member of the top management team.

Since first recognition that digital computers could be successfully used for processing business data, there has been a continuously mounting tide of conjectural discussion and speculation as to the computer's ultimate effect on managerial responsibilities and business organization. There is no disagreement on the inevitability of very extensive and substantial impact on the role of all business management. Rather, most controversy centers around the technical capacity of computers to duplicate and surpass human activities including thinking, the degree to which decision-making can be assumed by the computer, and the extent to which present managerial functions will be taken over by computers.

Predictions of the impact of computers on business management have consistently emphasized the same two basic points: computers being programmed to make middle-management level decisions, and necessary organizational changes.

Without going into the arguments of whether computers can be designed to think creatively and hence to perform virtually all managerial functions including policy determination, we can safely assert that currently available computer technology greatly exceeds the present usual role of computers in business decision-making and problem-solving.

Daniel's assessment is:

> To date, largely because of the routineness of most applications, this impact on organizational structure has not been felt, except in a few companies which have made substantial innovations. These efforts usually involve establishment of a separate business information department which assumes responsibility for the paperwork processing activities of the major functional departments.[25]

Recent advances in information technology lead to emphasis on quantification and the explicit definition of assumptions and judgments involved in specific decision processes. In addition, the use of computers improves information technology because more data can be considered, a greater range of alternatives can be explored, and a more comprehensive evaluation of a given decision's impact is possible.

These developments would seem to indicate that the staff of top management can be expected to increase sharply as these new decision-making processes become more important. There may well be fewer lower and middle management jobs handling the routine technically-oriented operating decisions which can be handled best by the computer. Human beings will be needed, however, to control the machines, handle the non-routine problems, and supervise employees. The pressures on top managers will undoubtedly increase. The advances in information technology now under way will tend to integrate decision-making and move it higher in the organization. At the same time, it will provide additional information which will make possible a detailed check on the success of individual management decisions.[26]

Although there is no positive way to forecast accurately the overall future effect of computer-based information systems on business management, it appears reasonable to conclude that the extent and speed of advances in information technology will be determined by personal and economic rather than technical considerations. Some of the content of management jobs will change, information available for decision-making will be greatly increased, and the computer will become a vital tool in the overall improvement of management abilities.

We can agree with Postley that "it seems likely that the art of applying digital computers to problems, and not the art of engineering the machines to do the jobs assigned to them, will (continue to) be the limiting factor in digital computer use." [27]

Most people, including business managers, resist changes which they believe will deeply affect their established responsibilities, duties, and routines. Intensely human problems arise. The apparent loss of prestige and authority by operating executives is probably the major cause of management difficulties in the transition to the computer as a business information system.

UNCEASING CHALLENGE

In spite of the unceasing challenge to the status quo in the years ahead, extension of the role of the computer in business management will be at the most only "dynamically evolutionary" because of inherent institutional and individual inertia. Irrespective of the pressure exerted by rapid technological advancement, it would be unrealistic to expect rapid and radical changes in organizational structure and functions of managers.

Dean Simon, who is one of the optimistic prognosticators of the eventual capabilities of computers, has stated:

> The conclusion I draw—is that the automation of decision making, irrespective of how far it goes and in what directions it proceeds, is unlikely to obliterate the basically hierarchial structure of organizations. The decision making process will still call for departmentalization and subdepartmentalization of responsibilities.[28]

A symposium discussion on this topic concluded that the management situation in 1985 "will not be startlingly different from what we see today." [29]

The most critically necessary element for

more rapid development of integrated information systems is the increased interest of top management. Top management has generally failed to devote sufficient attention to data processing, particularly the development of information systems. Marion Harper, Jr., expresses this need aptly in stating that "to manage a business well is to manage its future; and to manage the future is to manage information." [30]

One of the keys to successful computer innovation and improvement therefore becomes that of reorienting the thinking of those most closely involved in order to overcome human resistance. As Arnold Keller has so succinctly observed, "It seems to me that we have a much greater need for 'integrated management' than we do for integrated data processing." [31] Or, as Blank has written of the proposition, "What all this probably implies is that, in addition to needing management-oriented systems personnel, there is a real need for systems-oriented management personnel." [32]

REFERENCES

1. Peggy Courtney, ed., *Business Electronics Reference Guide* (Controllership Foundation, Inc., New York, 1958), pp. 273–274.
2. "Computer Census," *Data Processing,* April 1961, p. 32. These data on number of computer systems delivered are also supported by the John Diebold and Associates computer census at the end of 1960 as reported in their *Automated Data Processing Newsletter* of January 23, 1961.
3. See Richard F. Neuschel, *Management by Systems* (McGraw-Hill Book Company, Inc., New York, 1960), p. 40; James D. Gallagher, "Organization of the Data Processing Function," Chapter II-B, *Management Control Systems,* Donald G. Malcolm and Alan J. Rowe, eds. (John Wiley and Sons, New York, 1960); and Carl G. Baumes, *Administration of Electronic Data Processing,* Studies in Business Policy, No. 98 (The National Industrial Conference Board, New York, 1961).
4. Baumes, *Administration of EDP,* p. 4.
5. Adapted from D. Ronald Daniel, "Measure Your EDP Progress: A '5,000-Mile Checkup' for Computer Installation," *The Management Review,* March, 1961, pp. 75ff.
6. Robert H. Gregory and Richard L. Van Horn, *Automatic Data Processing Systems—Principles and Procedures* (Wadsworth Publishing Co., Belmont, Calif., 1960), p. 378.
7. John A. Postley, *Computers and People* (McGraw-Hill Book Company, Inc., New York, 1960), p. 24.
8. Baumes, *Administration of EDP,* p. 57.
9. *Ibid.* See also Daniel, "Measure Your EDP Progress," esp. p. 76.
10. Neuschel, *Management by Systems.*
11. Baumes, *Administration of EDP,* p. 59.
12. J. Gibbons Conway and D. Watts, *Business Experience and Electronic Computers, a Synthesis of What Has Been Learned from Electronic Data Processing Installations* (Controllers Institute Research Foundation, Inc., New York, 1959), p. 80.
13. Conway, *et al., Business Experience,* p. 80.
14. Baumes, *Administration of EDP,* p. 59.
15. *Ibid.*
16. For two expositions which indicate that programming languages still have a way to go before they reach their full potential, see "The Rand Symposium: 1962," *Datamation,* October, 1962, pp. 25–32, and Harry N. Cantrell, "Where Are Compiler Languages Going?" *Datamation,* August, 1962, pp. 25–28. That programmers are still much in demand and considered to be, in part, "born" rather than "made," is maintained by Olaf Engelsen in "A Pressing Problem: Trained Programming Personnel," *Data Processing Digest,* October, 1962, pp. 17–20.
17. Neuschel, *Management by Systems,* p. 269.
18. Baumes, *Administration of EDP,* p. 8. See also Neuschel, *Management by Systems,* p. 23. John S. Sinclair in the foreword to the National Industrial Conference Board study suggests possible reasons for the neglect in direction and guidance. "First of all, management may be so impressed with the great power and versatility of electronic computers that they may be led to think it possible to achieve savings despite weak planning, lack of sound organization, and the inertia or resistance of their employees. For another thing, many managements are not aware of the degree of coordination and integration that is needed to make electronic data-processing really pay off."
19. Daniel, "Measure Your EDP Progress," p. 23.
20. Milton M. Stone, "Data Processing and the Management Information System," *Data Processing Today: A Progress Report,* Albert Newgarden, ed. (American Management Association, New York, 1960).
21. William P. Leonard, "The Management Audit," Chapter 5, p. 94. See also, Edward McSweeney, "How to Organize Your Business for More Effective Management." Section 3, pp. 116–117; *J. K. Lasser's Business Management Handbook,* Sydney Perau, ed., 2nd ed. (McGraw-Hill Book Company, New York, 1960).

22. Conway, *et al., Business Experience,* pp. 146–147.
23. Daniel, "Measure Your EDP Progress," p. 76.
24. D. G. Malcolm and A. J. Rowe, "An Approach to Computer-Based Management Control Systems," *California Management Review,* Spring, 1961, as summarized in *Data Processing Digest,* August, 1961, p. 18. See also, Virgil Blank, "The Management Concept in Electronic Systems," *The Journal of Accountancy,* January, 1961, p. 59, and "Editorial," *Data Processing,* May, 1961, p. 50.
25. Daniel, "Measure Your EDP Progress," p. 76; see also, Baumes, *Administration of EDP.*
26. George P. Shultz and Thomas L. Whisler, eds., *Management Organization and the Computer* (The Free Press of Glencoe, Illinois, 1960), pp. 18–19.
27. Postley, *Computers and People,* p. 19.
28. Herbert A. Simon, *The New Science of Management Decision* (Harper and Brothers, New York, 1960), p. 42. Simon's comments on another occasion are summarized in Melvin Anshen and George Bach, eds., *Management and Corporations, 1985* (McGraw-Hill Book Company, New York, 1960), p. 207.
29. Anshen and Bach, *Management, 1985,* pp. 207–208. See also Anshen, "The Manager and the Black Box," *Harvard Business Review,* November–December, 1960.
30. Marion Harper, Jr., "Business Needs an Intelligence Director," *Management and Business Automation,* March, 1961, p. 20; see also, Wallace, *Management Influence on the Design of Data Processing Systems, A Case Study* (Harvard Business School, Division of Research, Cambridge, Mass., 1961).
31. "Effects of Business Automation in the Sixties," Round Table, Part 2, *Management and Business Automation,* February, 1961, p. 28.
32. Blank, "Management Concept," p. 66.

26. THE PROPER PLACEMENT OF COMPUTERS AND MANAGEMENT INVOLVEMENT IN EDP

PETER P. SCHODERBEK* AND JAMES D. BABCOCK†

The business computer has not yet reached its full profit-making potential. The most significant determinant of success is the organizational climate. The research studies of the authors have indicated that EDP departments are moving away from the accounting department, becoming independent, and progressing upward in the managerial hierarchy. At present, independent computer systems positioned at higher corporate levels are among the more successful departments. The early and continuous participation of top management is essential to the success of an EDP system, and the study indicates that managers are indeed taking a more active role. Operating managers now originate over half of the new applications in half of the companies surveyed. The study also indicates that the trend in computerization is away from financial and accounting applications. The greatest increases were noted in the areas of marketing operations and research, development, and engineering.

Although many business-operated computers are not utilized to their full capabilities, their profit-making potential remains great. Having a computer does not automatically guarantee success since it is only one of the many requisites for the operation of a successful electronic data processing installation. One of the significant, if not the main, determinants is the organizational climate within which it must function. Some writers feel strongly about this:

> Nothing is more significant to the success of EDP operations than a strong, well-defined organization. . . . The organizational strength of the EDP group will be the single most important limitation on the extent to which EDP is effectively applied to the information processing needs of a company. The strong organization will successfully produce the sound application definitions, computer system design, effective operating procedures, and control-oriented programs which are essential to well-managed operations.[1]

> Perhaps top management's prime interest in the EDP installation program is getting it properly organized so that it has a reasonable chance for success.[2]

Failure to recognize the important organizational considerations can directly impair the efficiency and effectiveness of the computer's function. "Somewhere, somehow management must carve out a place in its organization chart for a major responsibility which has to do with the entire process of information gathering."[3] Where the responsibility for guiding and directing this function should lie is a matter of controversy. The two major arrangements mentioned most frequently are:

1. Locate the activity within the accounting or financial department.

SOURCE: Peter P. Schoderbek and James D. Babcock, "The Proper Placement of Computers," *Business Horizons* (October, 1969), pp. 35–42; also, "At Last—Management More Active in EDP," *Business Horizons* (December, 1969), pp. 53–58. Reprinted by permission of Foundation for School of Business, Indiana University.

* University of Iowa.

† University of Iowa.

[1] Michael R. Moore, "A Management Audit of the EDP Center," *Management Accounting* (March, 1968), p. 25.

[2] Richard G. Canning, *Installing Electronic Data Processing Systems* (New York: John Wiley & Sons, Inc., 1957), p. 11.

[3] Robert Beyer, "Management Services—Time for Decision," *Journal of Accountancy* (March, 1965), p. 48.

2. Establish an independent electronic data processing section.

EDP IN THE ACCOUNTING DEPARTMENT

When the computer was first introduced, the plausible course of action was to give the responsibility for computer systems to the controller or accounting department. This was done for a number of reasons:

1. The first interest in using computers arose among people in this area.
2. This is the traditional location of the punched card data processing equipment.
3. Many of the most easily mechanized data processing applications occur in the accounting areas.
4. The functions of the controller cut across all areas of the organization.[4]
5. The data flow is well-established and information needs are well known.[5]

One of the advantages of this location is that typically the controller is already experienced in the operation of management information systems and is also well qualified to become the manager of an electronic data processing system. Joplin notes some of these qualifications:

> The accountant, because of his experience with the only existing information system, has certain qualifications which should be considered when choosing the manager of information systems. Because of the length and nature of his association with top management, he is presumed to have their confidence, an important attribute in systems development. He has the knowledge of management's needs for information and the extent to which management relies upon such information for decision making. He is aware of the problems and limitations involved in supplying information for decision making.[6]

Another advantage of the accounting position would be a smoother transition to fully integrated computer systems. Since many accounting functions have already been mechanized by punched card applications, these can be easily converted without drastic changes in system and procedures.[7]

Locating the EDP system in the accounting department also has a number of disadvantages associated with it. The tendency of the accountant to place higher priority on his own work than on that of other user departments or of the company as a whole is scored big. Withington states that:

> The financial and accounting applications will always receive favored treatment, and there may be a reluctance to start employing the computer in an operational or decision-making role which is foreign to personnel familiar only with accounting work. . . . It is difficult for the computer activity to provide important services for departments other than the one in which it is located, for however well intentioned they may be, the personnel dealing with the computer system's operation and the development of its future applications are naturally going to be most responsive to those who control their promotions and salary reviews. As a result, most or all of the organization's available resources for computer applications development will be channeled into the "parent" accounting department.[8]

Another drawback to this organizational set-up is the accountant's limited knowledge of new methods and techniques for handling information.[9] Often he will tend to slight these new approaches and concentrate more upon his functional area. Since he is usually judged on his performance in the accounting area rather than on his knowledge of computer techniques, any deficiencies in EDP may be rationalized by claiming insufficient time to accomplish both objectives.

[4] E. Wainright Martin, *Electronic Data Processing* (rev. ed.; Homewood, Ill.: Richard D. Irwin, Inc., 1965), p. 484.
[5] Bruce Joplin, "Can the Accountant Manage EDP?" *Management Accounting* (November, 1967), p. 3.
[6] "Can the Accountant Manage EDP?" p. 7.
[7] William E. Reif, *Computer Technology and Management Organization* (Iowa City, Ia.: Bureau of Business and Economic Research, 1968), p. 33.
[8] Frederic G. Withington, *The Use of Computers in Business Organizations* (Reading, Mass.: Addison-Wesley Publishing Co., 1966), pp. 159–61.
[9] Philip H. Thurston, "Who Should Control Information Systems?" *Harvard Business Review* (November-December, 1962), pp. 137–38.

EDP AS AN INDEPENDENT FUNCTION

An alternative to the above and one which finds acceptance in many companies is the operation of EDP as a separate activity reporting to one of the members of top management. The main advantage of this alignment is its neutrality and independence from pressures of particular groups in the organization.[10] Decisions will be made in the interest of the entire company rather than that of the department controlling the computer. The needs of the various departments will presumably be objectively evaluated, and service will be extended on the basis of priorities set by top management. Some departments will no doubt receive higher priorities for their applications, but this decision will be based on organizational requirements.

A second advantage is that the staff already has detailed knowledge of EDP equipment and techniques. They know how to utilize available information, how to derive information from new data, how best to secure data not in the system, and how to do all this at the lowest possible cost.[11]

A third benefit is that the computer department tends to take a broader view of systems problems. Operating managers too often take a narrower point of view and regard systems problems as separated by departmental lines. The staff does not confine its planning to existing organizational structures but looks at the firm in terms of over-all flow of information.

This arrangement is, however, not without its shortcomings. One likely disadvantage is that operating managers may view the actions of this department as an intrusion into their area, especially if the computer personnel try to by-pass management. Thurston notes this condition:

> Operating people resist planning in which they have no part; they resist the efforts of specialists to seek information or to install systems changes; and they delay accepting responsibility for new operating systems installed by specialists.[12]

Another possible disadvantage is the EDP staff's limited knowledge of the functional areas or departments of the company. The data processing personnel may have some difficulty in assembling the information necessary for systems decisions and in recognizing the changes needed to improve the operation. However, much of this can be alleviated by placing people knowledgeable in specific areas (accounting, production, and inventory control) into the EDP activity.

ANALYSIS OF LOCATION

Although the EDP function has traditionally been within the controller's domain, the decline of the accountant's control of the computer function has been such that his department no longer enjoys the dominant position it once held.

Were the computer to process only accounting work, there would be little reason to challenge the placement of this function within the accounting department.[13] However, increasing experience and greater confidence in the use of computers has provided a growing recognition of the computer's full potential. More and more companies are shifting to new and more sophisticated applications, and the percentage of computer time spent on routine accounting jobs is steadily decreasing.

Booz, Allen and Hamilton, in a 1966 study, determined that in many companies the finance and accounting applications comprised slightly less than half the computer effort. The 1968 study by the same firm indicated a continuance in the trend away from these applications. In three to five years, finance and accounting applications are estimated to decrease to only 29 per cent of the total computer effort as against the 44 per cent of the present time. Some of the results of these studies are presented in Table 1.

At least four facts play a major role in determining success in computer systems and

[10] Rudolph Borchardt, "Computer Systems: How Now Their Effects on the Organization?" *Systems and Procedures Journal* (May-June, 1967), p. 29.

[11] C. I. Keelan, "Your Data Processing Organization 15 Years From Now," *Office* (June, 1959), p. 140.

[12] "Who Should Control Information Systems?" p. 137.

[13] Winford H. Guin, "EDP Systems in Organizational Structure," *Management Accounting* (October, 1966), p. 45.

Table 1. Major Computer Installations[a]

Application	Per Cent, 1966	Per Cent, 1968	Per Cent, 1972[b]
Finance and accounting	47	44	29
Production	16	19	24
Marketing	12	13	15
Distribution	11	10	12
Research, development, and engineering	8	11	13
Planning and control	6	3	7

[a] SOURCES: James W. Taylor and Neal J. Dean, "Managing to Manage the Computer," *Harvard Business Review* (September-October, 1966), p. 102; and Neal J. Dean, "The Computer Comes of Age," *Harvard Business Review* (January-February, 1968), p. 89.
[b] Estimated.

which have significant bearing on the location of responsibility. These factors are:[14]

1. Understanding of the objectives of an operation and knowledge of the existing operating patterns, coupled with ability to relate the information system to operating needs.
2. Ability and organizational position to work with operating people to effect change.
3. Competence in the designing of information systems.
4. Motivation to make systems change.

Because of the varying nature of the above factors, each company must decide for itself which organizational form can best fulfill these conditions for success. Placement of the EDP function will depend to a large extent upon the basic company philosophy and the capabilities of certain key personnel.[15] The obvious or presently convenient location may be inadequate for full utilization of computer facilities since conditions within the firm are continually changing and what is appropriate under present circumstances may be totally inadequate for future applications.

[14] "Who Should Control Information Systems?" p. 138.
[15] James E. Ewell, "The Total Systems Concept and How to Organize for It," *Computers and Automation* (September, 1961), p. 10.

ORGANIZATIONAL LEVEL

Regardless of the locational preference of the EDP function, it is imperative that the individual in charge be afforded sufficient position in the organizational hierarchy to operate effectively. Many experts feel the responsibility for the EDP function should be at a high level in the organization;[16] in fact, some recommend that the level be no more than one step below the president or operating head of the company.[17]

Locating this function at lower organizational levels can create difficulties for the person in charge. Since it is necessary for the EDP function to cut across company lines, it could easily fail if buried under several layers of uninformed management.[18]

Locating data processing at the lower organizational levels can cause its share of problems. The manager of data processing cannot easily discuss proposed systems changes with other functional vice-presidents; he must do his talking through his superior. Proposals tend to be "watered down" in the course of such a process. Also, the other executives, busy with the problems of their own functions and perhaps not confident about their knowledge of data processing, tend to procrastinate on data processing problems.[19]

RESULTS OF THE STUDY

The sample used for this investigation comprised 200 firms selected at random from *Fortune* magazine's listing of the top 500 industrial firms in the United States during 1967. A questionnaire was mailed to the EDP managers in these companies. A total of 109 usable responses (54.5 per cent) were received and utilized in this study. The objectives of the study were:

[16] Lowell H. Hattery, "Organizing for Data Processing Systems," *Advanced Management* (March, 1961), p. 25.
[17] Marshall K. Evans, "Master Plan for Information Systems," *Harvard Business Review* (January-February, 1962), p. 101.
[18] W. C. Hume, "He Can Make the Difference Between Profit and Loss," *Iron Age* (Jan. 2, 1964), p. 178.
[19] Roger L. Sisson and Richard G. Canning, *A Manager's Guide to Computer Processing* (New York: John Wiley & Sons, Inc., 1967), p. 15.

To investigate the location of the electronic data processing function in the organization and to determine if this position is most advantageous.

To determine the organizational level of the EDP function in the management hierarchy.

To ascertain the actual and desired degree of management involvement in the purchase of new electronic equipment and in the implementation of computer applications.

To examine the current trends in computer applications.

ORGANIZATION UNIT RESPONSIBLE

The results of this study corroborate many of those reported in the literature. One of these findings is that the location of the computer activity in the organization is shifting away from the accounting department. Although 69.7 per cent of the companies responding indicated that the original position of EDP was within the accounting department, at the present time only 45.0 per cent have continued with this arrangement. A separate and independent electronic data processing function has been established in 49.5 per cent of the firms, and miscellaneous departments comprise the remaining 5.5 per cent. This information is summarized in Table 2.

A total of 45 companies (41.3 per cent) have altered the organizational placement of the computer system from the original setup. EDP was deemed important enough by 37 firms to give it a separate identity and organizational status, while in only five instances did the accounting department retain control; however, in these cases EDP was moved to a higher level within the department.

The reasons given for changing the location of the computer facility are listed in Table 3. As indicated, the main inducement for change was the increased importance of the EDP function as a company-wide service for all departments, and not for only one or two as was past practice.

One of the more significant findings of this study is that 95.4 per cent of the respondents believed that the EDP function should be independent of all operating departments. This weighty figure indicates that an independent activity is judged to be most advantageous and efficient for realizing the computer's potential. What makes this even more meaningful is that only 49.5 per cent of the businesses are pres-

Table 3. Reasons for Changing Original Location of EDP Function ($n=45$)

Reason	Number	Per Cent
Increased importance of EDP as an independent function	24	53.3
Need for better control	2	4.4
Organizational change	4	8.9
Increase efficiency	1	2.3
Need for more timely information	2	4.4
Other	12	26.7
	45	100.0

Table 2. Department Responsible for the EDP Function ($n=109$)

	Department Originally Responsible		Department Presently Responsible	
Department	Number	Per Cent	Number	Per Cent
Accounting	76	69.7	49	45.0
Data processing or systems	26	23.9	54	49.5
Administrative or management services	4	3.7	4	3.7
Information services	—	—	—	—
Functional department	2	1.8	1	0.9
Other	1	0.9	1	0.9
	109	100.0	109	100.0

ently organized in this manner. Even the companies with the computer located within the accounting department overwhelmingly favored functional independence.

The arguments advanced for this type of organizational design parallel those found in the literature. Most respondents (58.7 per cent) felt that the computer activity should serve all departments equally and that the best way to accomplish this was to remove it from the jurisdiction of all functional areas, particularly that of the accounting department. Such action would tend to eliminate biases occurring when data processing personnel report to an operating manager. Over 12 per cent concluded that independent status is also more conducive to management involvement while another 10.6 per cent believed this arrangement gives more economical and efficient service to all users.

Two of the respondents who were accounting managers considered the accounting department the most appropriate location for EDP. No reasons were given for their viewpoint. Three respondents were of the opinion that the organizational location was of little consequence. According to them an effective computer system depends more on the individual in charge than on the organization. A competent and aggressive executive is the key ingredient without which even a well-organized system would fail.

Further support for the independent position can be found in an examination of the problems associated with EDP organizational location (see Table 4). Most problematic situations are encountered in companies where the accounting department has responsibility for the computer; of the 49 firms (45.0 per cent) with this design, only ten encountered no significant problems. Accounting and financial bias was indicated by 17 companies as the main shortcoming. On the other hand, an independent EDP service created fewer problems. Of the 54 respondents granting autonomy to their computer departments, 35 (64.8 per cent) experienced no significant drawbacks related to the organizational design. The two main shortcomings that did occur were accounting bias and lack of management involvement. Although the weaknesses listed may not necessarily be a result of the structure of the data processing activity, there may be a relationship between computer location and the presence or lack of problems.

ORGANIZATIONAL LEVEL

The results of this study indicate that the level of the EDP function in the managerial hierarchy has been moving upward. The survey conducted by Ernest Dale in 1960 showed that most of the EDP managers queried were members of middle management.[20] However, in the companies sampled, only 51.8 per cent were originally in the middle management level or below, and the number presently at these levels has decreased even more (see Table 5). Now middle management comprises 28.7 per cent of the total, lower management 1.9 per cent, while the majority (53.7 per cent) are located at the upper management level.

Another indicator of the significance of EDP activity in the organization is the position of the executive in charge of the computer system (see Table 6). This study also bears witness to the loss by the financial officer of his control of computer operations. While he still directs half of the installations, at one time he was responsible for over three-fourths of them. More responsibility has accrued at the vice-presidential level (an increase from 7.9 per cent to 28.4 per cent). It is interesting to note that the president or chief executive still has not taken direct responsibility as was suggested might happen.

From Table 7 it can be seen that the higher the level of the computer location the more successful EDP appears to be. Of the 31 installations reporting to vice-presidents, 25 have experienced no significant problems. On the other hand, 45 of the 55 departments reporting to the financial executive encountered organizational problems. In general, EDP activity appears to be most efficient when placed at a high level in the organization.

MANAGEMENT INVOLVEMENT

The matter of management involvement in the computer function is the first of the last

[20] Ernest Dale, *The Decision-Making Powers in the Commercial Use of High Speed Computers* (Ithaca, N.Y.: Cornell Studies in Policy and Administration, Graduate School of Business and Public Administration, Cornell University, 1964), p. 20.

Table 4. Problems Occurring at Various Organizational Locations of EDP Functions[a] (n=109)

Department Responsible for EDP Function	No Significant Problems		Accounting Bias		No Management Involvement		Conflict Over Priorities		Poor Utilization		Poor Coordination		Other		Total	
	No.	%	No.	%	No.	%	No.	%	No.	%	No.	%	No.	%	No.	%
Accounting	10	9.2	17	15.6	8	7.3	4	3.7	4	3.7	4	3.7	2	1.8	49	45.0
Data processing	35	32.1	6	5.5	7	6.4	2	1.8	1	0.9	3	2.7	—	—	54	49.5
Administrative services	1	0.9	—	—	1	0.9	1	0.9	—	—	—	—	1	0.9	4	3.7
Information services	1	0.9	—	—	—	—	—	—	—	—	—	—	—	—	1	0.9
Other	1	0.9	—	—	—	—	—	—	—	—	—	—	—	—	1	0.9
	48	44.0	23	21.1	16	14.7	7	6.4	5	4.6	7	6.4	3	2.8	109	100.0

[a] Totals may not add up to the amount indicated because of rounding.

Table 5. Level of EDP Function in the Managerial Hierarchy* (n=108)

Level of Management	Previous Level of Management		Present Level of Management	
	No.	%	No.	%
President/vice-president	9	8.3	17	15.7
Upper management	43	39.8	58	53.7
Middle management	51	57.2	31	28.7
Lower management	5	4.6	2	1.9
	108	100.0	108	100.0

* Totals may not add up to the amount indicated because of rounding.

Table 6. Executive Responsible for EDP Activity (n=109)

	Executive Previously Responsible		Executive Presently Responsible	
Executive	No.	%	No.	%
President	3	2.8	2	1.8
Vice-president	8	7.3	31	28.4
Secretary/treasurer	3	2.8	4	3.7
Financial officer, controller	86	78.9	55	50.5
Director, management services	2	1.8	3	2.8
Director, data processing	4	3.7	10	9.2
Director, information	—	—	2	1.8
Functional department manager	2	1.8	—	—
No answer	1	0.9	2	1.8
	109	100.0	109	100.0

two objectives to be dealt with in this article.[21] The early and continuous participation of top management is one of the key factors in the development and successful operation of a sound EDP system.

THE CASE FOR INVOLVEMENT

In view of the capital outlay and the organizational implications involved, top management cannot afford to stay aloof.

If EDP is to be responsive to the total needs of top management, it demands total involvement on the part of that management. The executive look at EDP has got to be more than a glance through the plate glass window. They have to grasp the significance of a dynamic EDP operation, to see that EDP can give their organization a mighty weapon in the wars with competition, to understand that EDP is much more a profit maker than a cost cutter.[22]

EDP policies must be geared to the overall policies and objectives of the company. . . . Chief among the executive decisions to be made are those pertinent to setting the objectives for the computer installation, objectives within the company, may be changed from time to time, and establishment of priorities of objectives which are sought through effective use of the computer. Many times the priority value assigned to particular applications by the computer technicians are not at all similar to the values assigned by management in

[21] This section is from Peter P. Schoderbek and James D. Babcock, "At Last—Management More Active in EDP," *Business Horizons* (December, 1969), pp. 53–58.

[22] Arnold E. Keller, "EDP—Power in Search of Management," *Business Automation* (June, 1966), p. 51.

Table 7. Problem Occurrence and Organizational Location of EDP Function (n=109)

Executive to Whom Computer Activity Reports	No Significant Problems		Accounting Bias		No Management Involvement		Conflict Over Priorities		Poor Utilization		Poor Coordination		Other		Total	
	No.	%	No.	%	No.	%	No.	%	No.	%	No.	%	No.	%	No.	%
President	1	0.9	1	0.9	—	—	—	—	—	—	—	—	—	—	2	1.8
Vice-president	25	22.9	1	0.9	3	2.8	—	—	—	—	1	0.9	1	0.9	31	28.4
Secretary/treasurer	2	1.8	1	0.9	—	—	1	0.9	—	—	—	—	—	—	4	3.7
Financial officer, controller	10	9.2	19	17.4	11	10.1	6	5.5	4	3.7	3	2.8	2	1.8	55	50.5
Director of management services	—	—	—	—	1	0.9	—	—	—	—	—	—	2	1.8	3	2.8
Director of data processing	4	3.7	1	0.9	1	0.9	—	—	1	0.9	3	2.8	—	—	10	9.2
Director of information	2	1.8	—	—	—	—	—	—	—	—	—	—	—	—	2	1.8
No answer	1	0.9	—	—	—	—	—	—	—	—	—	—	1	0.9	2	1.8
	45	41.3	23	21.1	16	14.7	7	6.4	5	4.6	7	6.4	6	5.5	109	100.0

its broader understanding of the company's needs and requirements.[23]

A McKinsey & Company study in 1963 corroborated this concept of top management involvement, finding that firms with the most successful computer operations were precisely those in which top management participated actively in the function.[24] If top management has committed itself to the support of an effective computer system, it will expect equal support from its operating managers, each directly responsible for his own function. He must accept responsibility for adopting new improved information techniques and utilize these techniques on his own initiative. If he does not, top management may demand it of him, and if he fails to comply with these demands, he may be replaced by someone who will.[25] When operating management takes major responsibility for end results and participates in project selection and project manning, the computer systems have usually proved successful.[26]

It is also well known that people tend to resist changes that they have not helped to make; consequently, decisions made by computer personnel that affect the operating personnel, but which reduces their role to that of mere spectators, will not win general acceptance. The criticism frequently leveled at the computer staff—that they lack an awareness of operating realities—may carry considerable weight, thus further reducing their effectiveness for implementing changes.

In many instances, the lack of management involvement can be directly traced to apprehension about the computer. If the computer is viewed as an all-powerful device understandable only to computer specialists (and there is some evidence that this is indeed the case), then predictably the operating line personnel will avoid it at any cost. There are far too many known instances where operating personnel did not utilize the information presented to them simply because they lacked knowledge of how the information was derived or for what it was to be used.

However, the evidence mounts that line managers today are not nearly as mesmerized by the computer as they were five years ago, and in many instances the operating personnel are actually taking the initiative. The reason for this can be attributed to the increasing number of training programs offered by computer manufacturers, to the commercial training programs, and to the in-house training programs. Line personnel have come to realize that if they are to be held accountable for the results of their operations, they ought to have control of their information system, which in turn requires knowledge of the system. Also, it is almost impossible to evaluate an information system unless one has direct knowledge of the intricacies of the system itself.

ANALYSIS OF RESULTS

The findings of this study indicate that managers are taking a more active role. At one time almost all new computer applications were initiated by the EDP department; now, however, this department is responsible for less than 45 per cent of these new jobs in 72.4 per cent of the firms responding. Table 8 shows how computer applications are generated in all of the companies. Operating managers now originate over half of the new applications in 50.5 per cent of the companies surveyed. The increase in participation can in part be attributed to the education of these managers in computer concepts, and in part to the practical demands of the system itself.

Formal EDP training is given to functional managers in 74.3 per cent of the companies examined. The type of education naturally varies, but it usually takes the form of in-house training programs, computer manufacturers' schools, or some combination of the two. In-house instruction was offered in 75.3 per cent of those firms offering schooling and was the only instruction in 16.0 per cent of the cases. Computer manufacturers' facilities alone were utilized by 81.5 per cent or in combination with some other program. University or college courses were used only in conjunction

23 Raymond J. W. O'Toole and Edward F. O'Toole, "Top Executive Involvement in the EDP Function," *Management Controls* (June, 1966), pp. 125, 127.

24 John T. Garrity, "Top Management and Computer Profits," *Harvard Business Review* (July-August, 1963), p. 10.

25 John Dearden, "How to Organize Information Systems," *Harvard Business Review* (March-April, 1965), p. 69.

26 "Management's Role Spells Computer Success," *Steel* (April 22, 1963), p. 31.

Table 8. Initiation of New Computer Applications ($n=109$)

Percentage of New Computer Applications	Requested by Line Managers		Proposed by EDP Department		Directive of Top Management		Other	
	No.	%[a]	No.	%[a]	No.	%[a]	No.	%[a]
Not ascertained	4	3.7	4	3.7	4	3.7	4	3.7
None	4	3.7	14	12.8	19	17.4	85	78.0
1–15	8	7.3	20	18.4	40	36.8	15	13.8
16–30	29	26.5	30	27.5	22	20.2	1	0.9
31–45	9	8.3	15	13.8	7	6.4	1	0.9
46–60	27	24.8	12	11.0	13	11.9	—	—
61–75	13	11.9	10	9.2	2	1.8	—	—
76–90	12	11.0	2	1.8	1	0.9	1	0.9
91–100	3	2.8	2	1.8	1	0.9	2	1.8
	109	100.0	109	100.0	109	100.0	109	100.0

[a] Rounded off.

with other training and in those instances were used only 27.2 per cent of the time.

Although the top management level proposes fewer projects than other levels, a considerable number are introduced by this group (see Table 8). The applications initiated by these executives are usually company-wide projects with high priority, or concern areas where functional departments are not making the necessary innovations. In the latter case, once top management makes the initial move, the departmental manager usually steps in to accept responsibility for its successful operation. Increased management involvement in the selection of new applications is favorably regarded by the computer personnel. They feel that the operating managers are the individuals best suited to decide the needs of the functional areas and that the computer staffs' role is to provide guidance for implementation.

Once new applications have been considered, they must be evaluated. The EDP staff, which usually investigates their feasibility, presents its findings to top management for approval or disapproval. That top management makes this decision is true in 44 per cent of the cases; the manager of the user department in 23.8 per cent of the cases; and the financial officer in 16.5 per cent of the cases. Under present arrangements, the EDP staff makes the final decision only 13.8 per cent of the time. Correlation analysis shows a positive association of .55 between present procedures and what is considered the desirable method. This high value indicates that many firms are satisfied with their degree of management involvement in implementing new computer applications.

Top management takes an even more active role in the purchase of new electronic equipment, an action to be expected since a large capital outlay is usually involved. The final decision concerning purchase of new equipment is made by top management in eighty-two of the companies (75.2 per cent), although in a few cases this is just formal approval of the recommendations made by the data processing staff. The financial officer makes this decision 15.6 per cent of the time and the EDP department 7.3 per cent. A positive correlation of .64 exists between the present strategy and the ideal procedure.

It is important to note, however, that this decision is by no means arbitrary. Comprehensive feasibility studies are required, and several criteria must be met before approval is given. Economic consideration, the main factor, is involved in 88.1 per cent of the decisions and is the only factor 33.9 per cent of the time. More information is desired in 50.5 per cent of the firms and more timely information 51.5 per cent. All three are required 35.8 per cent of the time.

TRENDS IN APPLICATIONS

For the purpose of this study, computer applications can be broken down into six categories:

Financial and accounting—Financial reporting and analysis, accounting, payroll, invoicing, billing

Management planning and control—Capital investment analysis, resource allocations, mathematical model simulation

Marketing operations—Sales forecasting, sales analysis and control, market research, sales order processing

Distribution operations—Warehouse operations, shipment order processing, traffic, in-the-field inventory control

Factory operations—Materials control, production scheduling, quality control, in-the-field plant inventory control

Research, development, and engineering—Product test, engineering, research, product design and evaluation.[27]

This study indicates that the trend of computerization is away from financial and accounting applications (see Table 9). The percentage of applications in each of the above areas (44 per cent in accounting) corresponds very closely with the results of Neal J. Dean's study.[28] The greatest differences occurred in the areas of marketing operations (20 in contrast to 13 per cent in the Dean survey) and research, development, and engineering (7 in contrast to 11 per cent in the Dean study), but none of these differences are significant.

Table 9. Percentage Comparison of Major Computer Applications[a] in Two Studies

Computer Applications	Dean's Study, 1968	Authors' Study, 1969
Finance and accounting	44	44
Production	19	18
Marketing	13	20
Distribution	10	9
Research, development, and engineering	11	7
Planning and control	3	2
	100	100

[a] Multiple responses.

An inverse correlation of −.35 was noted between the percentage of accounting applications and the number of persons employed by the firm, and a correlation of −.48 between the number of EDP personnel and the percentage of accounting applications. This implies that, as the company and data processing activity grow, less emphasis is given to the accounting aspect of computer operations.

The figures in Table 9 reflect the average percentage of each application in the companies surveyed; the range of each of these applications is described in Table 10. While the accounting projects average 44 per cent, they account for 45 per cent or more of computer time in 40.9 per cent of the companies providing this information. Although 68 per cent of the respondents stated that all departments had equal access to the computer, special priorities are given to several departments or to special applications. The accounting department is given priority most of the time, as Table 11 indicates.

It was not too surprising to discover that twenty of the companies giving the financial area special priority have located their computer system within the accounting department. Although there may be other factors involved, this finding tends to support the suspicion that such a location gives preferential treatment to the department. There were some indications that, as the organizational level of the computed activity increase, special priorities decreased. A correlation of .44 exists between the level of EDP in the organization and the presence of accounting priorities.

SUMMARY

The findings of this study indicate that the location of computer activity in the organization is shifting away from the accounting department. An independent EDP department was found in half of the firms participating in the survey, and nearly all the respondents stated that this function ought to be independent. The main reason given was that EDP serves many different departments in the firm and should not be subservient to any one function. Fewer problems were found to occur in

[27] "Computer Usage in the Manufacturing Industry," *Business Automation* (October, 1966), p. 54.

[28] Neal J. Dean, "The Computer Comes of Age," *Harvard Business Review* (January-February, 1968), p. 89.

Table 10. Types of Computer Application ($n=109$)

Percentage of Total Computer Applications	Accounting or Financial		Management Planning and Control		Marketing		Distribution		Factory Operations		R&D or Engineering	
	No.	%	No.	%	No.	%	No.	%	No.	%	No.	%
Not ascertained	21	19.3	21	19.3	21	19.3	21	19.3	21	19.3	21	19.3
None	—	—	68	62.4	23	21.1	37	34.0	21	19.3	47	43.1
1–15	6	5.5	18	16.5	21	19.3	37	34.0	25	22.9	31	28.4
16–30	21	19.3	2	1.8	23	21.1	11	10.0	23	21.1	4	3.7
31–45	25	22.9	—	—	11	10.0	1	0.9	13	11.9	5	4.6
46–60	18	16.5	—	—	9	8.3	1	0.9	5	4.6	1	0.9
61–75	9	8.3	—	—	1	0.9	1	0.9	1	0.9	—	—
76–90	7	6.4	—	—	—	—	—	—	—	—	—	—
91–100	2	1.8	—	—	—	—	—	—	—	—	—	—
	109	100.0	109	100.0	109	100.0	109	100.0	109	100.0	109	100.0

Table 11. Computer Applications Receiving Special Priorities ($n = 109$)

Application	Number	Per Cent
Finance and accounting	22	20.2
Marketing	6	5.5
Factory operations	4	3.6
Research, development, and engineering	2	1.8
Other	1	0.9
None	74	68.0
	109	100.0

organizations with functional independence for the computer activity.

The level of the EDP activity has been moving up in the managerial hierarchy. At the present time almost three-fourths of the EDP departments are located at the upper management level, indicating that companies are recognizing the importance of this function. Computer systems positioned at the higher levels were found to experience fewer problems than those located at the lower levels.

The success of a computer installation is due in no small part to the degree of leadership and the continuous involvement of top management in the computer function. The findings of this study indicate that managers are indeed taking a more active part in the many areas affecting and affected by the computer. And as computer usage decreases in the area of finance and accounting and increases in the other functional areas of production, marketing, and so on, it can be expected that even more personnel will be involved with the computer, either by choice or by decree. In any event, it will be essential that all areas of the organization, both functional and staff, be considered in order to achieve a truly integrated information system.

27. ELECTRONIC POWER GRAB

ROBERT L. MCFARLAND *

Is it possible to "steal" a company in such a subtle way that few of the company officials and certainly none of the stockholders would be aware of it? "Stealing" here would mean actually making the key operating and policy decisions without the chief executive and top management being aware that they themselves were not truly in control of the overall operation. Could someone gain control over the relevant informational inputs of a centralized company computer facility, and specify the nature of the output of such an information gathering system without the awareness of top management? Could such an informational system be so manipulated that control could come to reside in one individual or several individuals working together? These questions imply, of course, that the theft would accrue to the great benefit of an individual or a given ingroup. In addition, it is assumed here that the individual's or ingroup's ability to remain hidden, but in complete control of the company, would be desirable for a considerable period of months or years.

Practically no discussion of these questions appears in the professional literature of operations research or of computer sciences. Nor have there been popular novels in the style of the famous "Executive Suite" referring to power plays centering around a company's computer. This lack of published scientific or fictional literature led the author to pull together his own observations and the observations of other people actively involved in the area of concern. Discussions were held with persons from top management groups of organizations possessing large central EDP facilities, from regional sales managers of several major computer manufacturing concerns, from members of the teaching staffs of certain commercial companies manufacturing computers who provide computer orientation and training for top management, and, finally, from a series of research consultants who function in the area of operations research and computer management. In general, the people interviewed maintained that they had not been involved in any power struggles revolving around a company computer, yet each seemed most anxious to discuss the issue.

As background to a discussion of this problem, we should recognize that as of 1964, over 21,000 computers were in use throughout the world and apparently over 7,000 additional computers are currently on order. These computer facilities vary in price from 12 thousand dollars to over seven million dollars. The United States Government alone spends close to one billion dollars per year on computer facilities and employs over 45,000 people in connection with its data processing activities. The Government, in the last decade, moved from possessing ten such facilities to over 1,200 in use today. Over half of the computer facilities in Government are employed in the Department of Defense.

Apparently over 500 different business and scientific usages of computers are now available for private industry. Among the industries with high computer budgets it is not infrequent that 10 to 12 percent of the *annual* capital expenditure is devoted to investing in additional new facilities in the EDP area. Such commitment of annual capital to computer expenditures represents the investment of huge sums of money by some of the shrewdest business minds in the world. Marshall K. Evans and Lou R. Hague in their article "Master Planning for Information Systems," which appeared in the *Harvard Business Review*, January–February 1962, provide a clue as to

SOURCE: *Business Automation* (February, 1965), pp. 30–39. Reprinted by permission of *Business Automation*,

* Northwestern University.

why these companies are engaged in such heavy capital expenditures. They say ". . . in U.S. industry today, the gathering, storing, manipulating and organizing of information for managing enterprises cost as much or more than does direct factory labor." The indications are that the relative proportion of company costs for information gathering, data processing and decision making in the years ahead will increase as automation further reduces manufacturing cost.

An article in the February 24, 1964, issue of *U.S. News and World Report,* entitled, "Is the Computer Running Wild?" expressed great concern over the possibility of EDP facilities and technology getting beyond the control of our society. A computer expert was quoted in that article as saying the "computer craze" could end as a nightmare for the modern executive. He envisions an office of the near future with computers grinding out a flood of statistics and draws this picture for a poorly planned system:

> There was a sales executive crushed under four tons of sales reports. There was a production engineer being strangled by punch tape. There was the president of the company, his office piled from floor to ceiling with reports, figures, indexes, computations, and permutations . . . his office stuffed, and he, emaciated and bug-eyed, reading his way through reports at a rate slower than reports were being produced.

ASK A STUPID QUESTION . . .

This nightmare would be the appropriate "living hell" for executives of any company who would permit themselves to operate under such impossible circumstances. Long before the advent of the computer, it was entirely possible for any executive to permit himself to be flooded by much irrelevant and extraneous material. Successful executives have long been aware of the necessity of guarding against such flooding or overloading.

Other experts were quoted in the same article as indicating much more appreciation for some of the truly perplexing problems confronting management and computer facilities supervisors. For example, Professor Elting E. Morrison of M.I.T. says that earlier machines developed by man—engines and generators—set clear limits as to how much misuse they would tolerate before resisting. He points out:

> Over-loaded, abused, they stopped working, stalled, broke down, blew up; and there was the end of it. Thus they set clear limits to men's ineptitudes.
>
> For the computer, I believe, the limits are not so obvious. Used with ignorance or stupidity, asked a foolish question, it does not collapse, it goes on to answer a fool according to his folly. And the questioner, being a fool, will go on to act upon the reply.

Thus one of the dangers of the computer technology is clearly indicated in Professor Morrison's remarks, insofar as man's intellect must determine what is to be put into a computer, how it is to be programed or processed, and how the information derived is going to be checked for its reliability, validity and usefulness.

As large companies with sizeable computer facilities have reached the point where the extremely heavy start-up costs and extremely long periods of writing and debugging the programs become relatively less pressing, certain new problems are beginning to emerge (in these companies). Philip Thurston, writing in the *Harvard Business Review,* January 1963, in an article entitled, "Who Should Control Information Systems?" says, "I consider that in the past decade a significant characteristic of information systems work has been to place a great degree of control in the hands of specialists. This situation has developed in part through the failure of top management to place controlling responsibility with operating managers."

STAYING ON THE TOP AT THE TOP

In personal interviews held in the Chicago area, nearly half of the people interviewed referred to the McKinsey report, which was authored by John Garrity and published in 1963 under the title "Getting the Most Out of Your Computer," as being the most pertinent single reference about appropriate top management control of computer facilities. In this widely distributed booklet, the McKinsey team provided certain bench marks for evaluating computer effectiveness. They felt that constructive, clear cut and positive answers to the following questions must be present if one is to predict a company's success in this area:

1. Is the computer systems effort, currently and cumulatively, on a self-sustaining basis?
2. Is the computer systems producing intangible benefits in the form of better operating information, reduced manufacturing cycles, improved customer service and the like?
3. Is the computer systems effort addressed to the key profit determinants of the business? Is it making itself felt in all major divisions and functions?

Here in brief summary is what these management consultants attempted to do. They studied 27 companies, nine of whom they indicated were highly successful in their computer applications. They then compared these nine companies with the remaining 18, whose computer applications seemed to be of average or inferior quality. Garrity, in summarizing the findings, pointed to the central issue involved in successful management of computer facilities when he said, "In the lead companies, as their actions indicated and the results show, each one of the top managements has correctly assessed the computer's potential and has given it the continuing management direction and guidance it so badly needs and so much deserves. . . . The computer's challenge to top management is that it (management) must direct, manage, and lead, if profits are to result."

The eleven major differences between the lead and average companies studied in the McKinsey evaluation which led to Garrity's remark can be stated precisely as follows: (1) Top management devotes time to the computer systems effort in proportion to its cost and potential; (2) Top management reviews, plans and follows up on computer systems results; (3) Computer applications are selected on the basis of careful feasibility studies; (4) Project plans are developed and progress reports planned; (5) Operating management participates in project selection and planning; (6) Operating management plays a significant role in project manning; (7) Operating management takes responsibility for progress and results; (8) The systems staff has a broad range and depth of technical skill; (9) Some management sciences people are located under the computer systems manager, although larger OR operations may be conducted in parallel to this operation; (10) The computer systems effort is organized on a divisional basis which conforms to the company's normal organizational pattern; (11) The corporate staff monitors progress and appraises results.

In general, conflict begins to develop in companies where real time computer capabilities become as badly needed as high speed batch processing. Such issues are very difficult problems for top management to solve, particularly when both types of applications are more than amply justified by each of the separate operating divisions.

ON THE COATTAILS OF THE COMPUTER

Another type of problem occurs as the result of simply increasing capitalization and size of the staff necessarily involved in operating the computer effectively. The middle management supervisor who had a hand in making the initial computer application to the first routine business problems, and who successfully carried through this application, tends to be promoted both salary-wise and echelon-wise. Thus the original "company parent" tends to rise in the company along with progressing sophistication of computer applications. This man typically tends to be a person with fiscal or accounting background, and his superiors in turn gain increasing say within the top management group as to what would be the appropriate use of the facilities. Quite naturally they tend to favor applications in areas in which they could depend upon "their boy" to deliver for them as he had quite obviously done in the past. This creates a situation in which many other worthwhile projects proposed by the other operating vice presidents get side-tracked or put on a very slow time scale.

When the time comes for either the direct computer facility supervisor or his immediate superiors to begin considering the purchase of the second generation or third generation computer facility, they quite naturally want to maintain their unilateral control over the new equipment. However, by that time, successful applications have been demonstrated in two or more additional divisions, and therefore the stage is set at the top management level for a showdown as to who should control the computer.

If the chief executive of the company has

not grown in this period of time in his own sophistication as to the computer applications, he very frequently will leave these kinds of arguments to be thrashed out two or three echelons below his direct perusal. Therefore, he avoids committing himself to one operating division or another of his company. However, those chief executives who stay with the developing computer facilities and who attempt to maintain direct managerial control over the process, soon delegate the direct operating responsibility for this facility to one of their immediate subordinates and place the computer facilities supervisor not more than two or three levels down below their own offices. A vice president of a steel company, in charge of the computer facilities, told me that such a decision is warranted if for no other reason than the fact that they were spending nine percent of their total annual capital in this area.

A NEED FOR LOYALTY

In many different companies effective use of the computer across several operating divisions becomes extremely difficult, if not impossible, if the computer facility and its staff are controlled primarily through lower echelon staff groups. In such instances, the technical staff may be highly competent, and attempt to initiate highly appropriate applications in a variety of divisions, but they are not in a position to secure sufficient loyalty and continuing attention to their program applications by the operating middle management group. Unless the top management group in each such division plays an active part in such activities, the operating middle management group will give such applications too low a priority for their monitoring and expediting.

Without firm, continuing direction by the chief executive, power struggles for control of these facilities then develop in the middle management area, or at a level approximately three steps down from the chief executive's office. In one printing industry, a fiscal accounting head found himself in a position where he really wanted a larger computer facility, but he also found that he would have to permit a drastic reorganization of this facility with a high probability that control of this larger facility would be placed considerably beyond his own control. He viewed himself as being not quite powerful enough, nor viewed favorably enough by top management, to insure that job assignment for himself, and consequently at this point he actually blocked further consideration of this larger facility, even though the original recommendation was his. Thus in the upper "never-never land" of middle management groups, computer control becomes quite involved and yet it tends to slow the computer program development and tends to insulate department by department. This is a situation in which the research group and the fiscal accounting group, in particular, often resolve the conflict by seeking geographical separation of their computer facilities. This resolution also occurs with fiscal groups and manufacturing groups, when the latter are attempting to use computer facilities for on-line control of automated equipment.

. . . AND A RELEVANT CONCEPT

Up to this point in the discussion, some of the relevant literature has been reviewed and some of the anecdotes which were collected in preparing this article have been presented. In general, these observations confirm what was found in the McKinsey report and urged by Thurston. But, the McKinsey report seems to suggest to the chief executive certain procedures which, while pointing to successful operations, are based largely on empirical day-to-day experience. These practical findings are not presented within an explicit theoretical framework. Looking at the systems and considering possible theoretical frameworks to be employed, the concept of the unified information flow system appears relevant. This concept is expressed by Joseph Redding in an unpublished manuscript, entitled "The Unified Information Flow Concept for the Organization of an Information Processing and Computing System," prepared for Standard Oil Company (Indiana) in February 1964. Redding bases this system on separating the output requirements from the information inputs by means of an information file or storage. He proposes that there should be only one file for all purposes, entering just a single recording of a given event and from which all reports are prepared. Separate programs would be used for updating of files, analysis of data, and preparation of reports.

ASK YOURSELF A QUESTION

Beyond Redding's concept, control systems theory applications seem to provide a method of synthesis which might be even more appropriate for consideration. For the present, however, I would like to discuss a theoretical matrix in which practical decisions must be made by top management, and point out some clues as to the nature of the concepts needed in this area. First, there are several questions which the McKinsey group recommended the chief executive ask of himself. Now, I am frank to say I do not know when the executive should ask these questions. Possibly he might do so while shaving in the morning. The McKinsey report lists them as follows:

1. Do I devote to the computer systems effort the time and attention that its cost and potential warrant, or have I backed away from my role by delegating the responsibility to the technical people three or four levels down?
2. Do I see that the computer is used for more than just routine record keeping, i.e., that we are also using this new resource to find new and better ways of running the business?
3. Have I insisted on carefully pricing out all proposed computer applications and do I follow up to insure that we have earned a significant tangible return?

Now, if the executive hasn't slit his throat in despair and utter frustration by this time, the McKinsey report continues by recommending further self-punishment by asking these final two questions:

4. Have I clearly indicated to operating managers that I hold them accountable for seeing that they get the most out of computer systems in running their divisions?
5. Have I provided the company with the kind of computer systems manager needed to get the job done; and have I given him the support, stature and staff he needs?

While I have been somewhat facetious in listing these remarks, I do think they reflect kinds of questions that imply control system ideology.

Control systems theory in a formal sense apparently has not been directly applied to the chief executive as he functions in his job world, and yet the critical elements for an effective control system are displayed quite consistently by the successful chief executive as portrayed in the McKinsey report. A successful executive must continually collect information from the subordinate parts of his over-all operation, and participate in the formulation of company policies, such as planning for future development, maintaining reasonable profit levels, and establishing good community and public relations. These considerations can be regarded as two separate types of input to his internal control system. Thus, the executive must acquire input information about the company internally as well as its relation to the larger environment. These data are regularly compared with the goals imbedded in the policies of the company which serve as the second form of input. His own activities in the formulation of lower-level policies are appropriately regarded as his means of attempting to reduce the discrepancies between the inputs from the environment external to himself and his internally perceived policy goals. His corrective actions (his output) consists of his own policy formulations which are intended to influence the lower echelon decision making of the company in a corrective manner.

What has impeded our looking at the executive himself as a feedback control system is the fact that such behavior occurs on an extremely slow time scale unlike the ultra-fast time scales found when we make control theory applications to electronic gear. The executive may have a conference on Monday regarding policy formulation, and he may take several days to compare the information that he has from additional company informational sources before he has arrived at a decision, say late Friday, to fire one of the operating managers. This slow time scale, however, should not be an impossible barrier to either behavioral sciences or physical sciences, because many phenomena studied in both scientific fields have similarly slow time scale characteristics. However, because of the time scale it is very, very easy to look at the chief executive and categorize his behavior as of a given hour or as of a given act. Such behavior then is viewed as separate autonomous units that might be related to his other activities in an empirical or a correlational sense. Thus, on a day by day basis it is extremely difficult to view the executive's behavior as a continuous control system. But all of his control system's inputs and outputs can be related simultaneously on the appropriately slowed time scale. Once this is done conceptually, one can see that the chief executive must direct his attention to a series of *identifiable controlled variables*. In this instance, I am using the concept of variable in the physical science sense, and I am further suggesting that the concept of

Ten Point Program For Success

Top management devotes time to the computer systems effort in proportion to its cost and potential.

Computer applications are selected on the basis of careful feasibility studies.

The corporate staff monitors progress and appraises results.

The systems staff has a broad range and depth of technical skill.

Operating management takes responsibility for progress and results.

Top management reviews and plans and follows up on computer systems results.

Operating management participates in project selection and planning.

Some management sciences people are located under the computer systems manager, although larger OR operations may be conducted in parallel to this operation.

The computer systems effort is organized on a divisional basis which conforms to the company's *normal* organization pattern.

Operating management plays a significant role in project manning.

controlled variable is an extremely useful one. We can distinguish between controllable variables and uncontrollable variables both in a physical system and a living system.

THE COMPLEX INDIVIDUAL

The research of the immediate years ahead lies in identifying which variables effective, successful managers actually do control. In our research in the mental health field, we have developed some paper and pencil test procedures, as well as some laboratory tests, in which it can be demonstrated that individuals do function as complex control systems monitoring clearly identifiable controlled variables. These methodologies developed in the mental health area seemed to warrant application to studies of the behavior of chief executives—not because the executives are mentally ill but rather because they are human! Our theoretical system then permits one to estimate the appropriate working procedures for the top executive and probably would enable him to move away from simply asking questions so artificially formulated in the five recommendations previously discussed. The top management group as a whole probably has arrived in its position of authority by identifying, more or less intuitively, the relevant controllable variables for their given company situation. Further research in a more rigorous control systems framework would permit a shift from the correlative approach to measuring these phenomena in a much more direct physical science type manner.

Finally, it is important to discuss briefly some of the strategies of conflict that would be involved in effective "computermanship." This section of this article is related to the concept of "How to steal a company without anyone ever catching on!" I would like to discuss this topic in terms of three problems. The first is (1) "How does one go about eliminating one's potential competition?" I will assume that the reader is bright, capable, aggressive and wishes to master sufficient computer technology, operations management and other human science activities to equip him to move ahead. However, one must eliminate competition by whatever means available if one is to "ever succeed in business by really trying!" So one should first consider those competitors who are 40 or more years of age. In general, one should repeatedly say to these men that the old ways are the best and these newfangled ideas are just costing the company a great deal of time and effort, and will certainly not be as effective as standard time-tested techniques. One should also slightly reinforce the competitor's fears in the direction that maybe this stuff is just too technical for him, that he would have to study too many months or years to try to catch up, and even if he did the field would have then taken another dramatic leap forward and he would still be left behind. If one is also sadistically inclined, one might well suggest that his learning capacities are being impaired by his increasing age.

A TIME FOR THE SHOWDOWN

For the successful budding executive to move ahead he must make some decisions as to when the showdown, or the confrontation, or the pure power play is to occur. Any good young Machiavellian knows that the time for the coup d'etat must be chosen with care. So consider for a moment (2) "How does one go about slowing down or delaying the showdown?" If one is in the computer facility proper, one should very seriously try to discourage many different divisions of the company from getting involved in using the computer facility. Of course, outright refusal to do such work is not a very wise strategy to follow. Rather, it would be much more desirable to slow down such applications by continually changing the program with *relevant* (not irrelevant) suggestions. In this way one can keep the other group in the writing and debugging stages for endless periods. In this situation, one should also encourage the development of small or medium size computer applications in different parts of the company, and one should pretend to have no awareness of Data Phone transmission or any technology which would suggest that the large computer installations could ever be a centralized phenomenon. One would also in this instance encourage great geographical separation between the various medium size computers.

SUPPORT BEGETS SUCCESS

Finally, then (3) "How does the young Machiavellian force a showdown?" If he feels he is ready for the showdown, there is a certain battle cry here which should facilitate it. Of course, the young man in question should be reasonably sure that he will end up either the technical director of the computer facility, or the executive who is charged with the operational responsibilities of this facility, before he starts the countdown. The battle cry for the showdown would be the insistence that he would demonstrate that the computer facility can produce tangible profits and maintain itself on a pay-as-you-go basis if he is given complete management responsibility. By now, this claim can undoubtedly be demonstrated in companies having had computer facilities for five years or longer, providing the management orientation McKinsey described exists in that company. The young man should bet that his management of the information flow systems could be carried out effectively by utilizing the systems approach and many of the operational research technologies.

Crucial to this ploy is the idea that his chief executive truly manages this part of the company's operations as he does other parts. The young Machiavellian would find himself out on his ear in eighteen months should he make such a battle cry his rallying point and should his chief executive fail to provide him with unqualified and continuing support. As in all power struggles, one takes a calculated risk in terms of either delaying or facilitating the showdown. But as our understanding of the empirical results in other companies grows, and we begin to articulate much more explicit management theory expressed particularly in a control systems framework, the chances of success and moving for the showdown will grow more favorable and this trend will continue into the future.

The ploys suggested thus far are more or less overt interpersonal actions. But such ploys, or similar ones, could be combined with sound operations research and programing competency. The young Machiavellian has now suddenly new dimensions in which to carry out the old power struggles. What if he organizes the informational flow of data so that actual decision making functions pass from the operating managers to the computer without their knowledge? This is often consciously and deliberately done by operating managers to facilitate administrative chores at the lowest management levels. But it can be done inadvertently.

For example, such an event nearly came to pass recently in a midwestern telephone company. Throughout most of the telephone system, the Traffic Management Division assigns telephone numbers to subscribers and assigns most equipment lines. These basic activities are crucial if economical and efficient use of telephone equipment is to be maintained. In this particular instance, a senior staff officer proposed in a meeting that number and line assignments are logically so simple that such items could be programed for continuous control by their computer (which is operated by another division). The staff immediately objected violently. They saw that these two activities, plus what is called "loading and balancing" procedures, constitute the basic operations that justify Traffic Management departments today. In former years their *raison d'être* was management of the large staff of local telephone operators, but this function has gradually been reduced as operators have been replaced by automatic dial equipment. Thus, a decision to program number and line assignments into a computer system would eliminate a major function of their entire division. Their few remaining functions, from a top management viewpoint, could be readily assigned to other divisions. Whether that fate will come to pass or not is not our concern here. Rather this incident illustrates how easy it is to "lose" control (power) by transferring forms of decision-making to the computer. In this instance, the senior staff man was proposing to serve as his own executioner. A less bright executive could be conned into a similar ploy by a clever "thief."

A second example, concerning the same company division, focuses on the second major functional area of "loading and balancing." Over 100 separate report forms were received by and processed in and through their basic data unit. A significant bulk of this mass of data was relevant to "loading and balancing," but very few men in this division could effectively read this data and take action to avert undesirable conditions from developing. One or two "pundits" high in the division had such skills and were accorded much honor, salary, etc., for their knowledge. However, these experts seemingly could not impart their skills to the younger men who would ultimately succeed them. In this instance, it did not appear that they were deliberately withholding their knowledge; they performed their activities in an intuitive manner. While they could logically justify their decisions after-the-fact, they simply could not specify the sequence of analysis they actually employed, and, consequently, they could not train their subordinates.

IT'S WHAT'S UP TOP THAT COUNTS

In contrast to this, technical or analytical skills are sometimes deliberately and consciously withheld as job insurance by a minority of older workers. The story is told of a Marine sergeant in charge of plumbing and sanitation at an East coast base who carefully memorized the blueprints of all water lines and hydrants and then burned them! Presumably he kept his job at that base until he retired because "the only set of blueprints left was in his head." This example can serve to remind us that the young Machiavellian might, by diligent effort, identify the company's relevant controllable variables as suggested by control system theory. Once he determined these variables he could program the data regarding them into the mass of other data typically associated with them. He need only check the key data occasionally to be able to prognosticate with amazing accuracy, should he wish rapid overt advancement. However, he or a group of associates might wish to use this information covertly. Such a circumstance could occur when that old dream (pre-SEC) of manipulating the company's public stock issue might appear to be "controllable." Here it would be assumed that neither the company officers nor the SEC could readily discern these manipulations. This then could be an instance where young Machiavellians would pass up a promotion to steal a company and thereby gain a fortune, and the manipulations might even prove to be legal.

THERE'S MORE TO COME

It should be clear now that from my viewpoint a company could be stolen without top management knowing it. Such a steal could be achieved through clever use of the company's centralized computer. The input information needed for effective predictions about the company's short term future operations could be buried among other traditional input information and could be easily overlooked by top management. It should be clear, too, that many more overt power struggles will occur in the years immediately ahead, and they will center around the control and use of computer facilities.

One can predict such struggles if for no other reason than that computer costs are approaching the ten percent level of available annual capital in many companies. Also, human nature being what it is, executive power struggles will continue even though the means to do so, and the objectives sought, are undergoing rapid technological change. "Who controls the computer controls the company," ceases to be a science fiction adage and becomes increasingly valid in the present industrial world.

Perhaps the most interesting in-fighting of the next five to ten years will occur when two highly effective executive vice presidents—each of whom has had considerable computer system training, operations research training, plus detailed knowledge of the operation of one or two of the company's major divisions—begin to struggle for ultimate control of computer facilities. That will truly be "a fight of the century."

BIBLIOGRAPHY

Baumes, Carl G., *Administration of Electronic Data Processing,* Studies in Business Policy, No. 98, The National Industrial Conference Board, 1961.

Bell, William D., *A Management Guide to Electronic Computers,* McGraw-Hill Book Company, 1957.

Brabb, George J., and Earl B. Hutchins, "Electronic Computers and Management Organization," *California Management Review,* **6**, No. 1, Fall, 1963, 33–43.

Buckingham, Walter, *Automation: Its Impact on Business and People,* Harper and Brothers, 1961.

Burck, Gilbert, and the Editors of *Fortune, The Computer Age,* Harper & Row, 1965.

Canning, Richard G., *Installing Electronic Data Processing Systems,* John Wiley and Sons, 1957.

Computer Systems—Their Contribution and Challenge to Management, McKinsey and Company, Inc., February, 1963.

Dale, Ernest, *Planning and Developing the Company Organization Structure,* Research Report, No. 20, American Management Association, 1952.

Evans, Marshall K., and Lou R. Hague, "Master Plan for Information Systems," *Harvard Business Review,* **40**, No. 1, January-February, 1962, 92–103.

Ewad, Elias M., *Business Data Processing,* 2d ed., Prentice-Hall, Inc., 1965.

Garrity, John T., *Getting the Most Out of Your Computer,* McKinsey and Company, Inc., 1963.

Guest, Leo C., Jr., "Centralized Data Processing for Decentralized Management," *Systems Magazine,* **20**, No. 5, September-October, 1956, 6–7.

Hattery, L. H., "Organizing for Data Processing Systems," *Advanced Management Journal,* **26**, No. 3, March, 1961, 23–25+.

Higginson, M. Valliant, *Managing with EDP,* AMA Research Study, No. 71, American Management Association, 1965.

Hoos, Ida Russakoff, "When the Computer Takes Over the Office," *Harvard Business Review,* **38**, No. 4, July-August, 1960, 102–14.

Lee, Hak Chong, *The Impact of Electronic Data Processing Upon Patterns of Business Organization and Administration,* School of Business, State University of New York at Albany, 1965.

McCarthy, E. Jerome, J. A. McCarthy, and Durward Humes, *Integrated Data Processing Systems,* John Wiley and Sons, 1966.

McNerney, John Peter, *Installing and Using an Automatic Data Processing System,* Division of Research, Harvard University, 1961.

Svec, Fred J., *Organizational Placement of the Computer Systems Designer,* U.S. Army Management Engineering Training Agency, 1968.

Wallace, Edward L., *Management Influence on the Design of Data Processing Systems,* Division of Research, Graduate School of Business Administration, Harvard University, 1961.

SECTION IV

TOTAL MANAGEMENT SYSTEMS

It has often been stated that we are in the "era of systems." There are behavioral systems, communication systems, data processing systems, transportation systems, information systems, records systems, and innumerable others. And to further befuddle the layman utilizing operational systems, these have been categorized as closed, open, structured, unstructured, controlled feedback, uncontrolled feedback, deterministic, oscillating, man-made, real time, reproducible, isomorphic, simple action, and by an ever-growing list of other euphonious labels.

The concept of system will not only mean different things to different people but it can even mean different things to the same individuals. Proponents of the systems viewpoint have themselves to blame for much of the unintelligible jargon currently associated with systems. It would not be difficult to pinpoint the many and diverse orientations to management systems now in vogue. This diversity of orientations is certainly nothing to be deplored: the growth of any discipline depends upon it. Also it is but natural that one views any concept from his own intellectual landscape with its own peculiar value judgments. However the confusion has reached such proportions that it is necessary to attempt some clarification—if possible!

In Part IV it was pointed out that one of the systems approaches holds that "systems" is a frame of mind, a way of thinking, a philosophy, rather than any certain body of knowledge or of techniques. According to this viewpoint the systems concept can be equally applied to all types of organizational structures irrespective of size or type of industry. It is therefore not limited by its inherent nature to only those companies with computer capabilities but is applicable to virtually all companies.

For others, "systems" brings to mind a configuration of costly complex equipment comprising electronic computers, input-output devices and the usual auxiliary equipment used in conjunction with data processing systems. What is liable to be ignored is the fact that all of this "hardware" represents but *tools* designed to aid the manager in applying the systems concept to his own specialized operations. The computer cannot make his decisions for him; it can however provide him with meaningful predictions of results obtained by pursuing alternative courses of action. But in any event, the collection and processing of information should not be made synonymous with the systems approach.

The total systems approach has recently appeared under many labels such as integrated management, unified operations management, total information systems, holistic systems, macro systems, interrelated systems and subsystems, and complete systems. In addition, articles have been appearing linking the total systems approach to personnel, production, inventory control, scientific decision making, and even to the management of managers.

In this present section will be found several articles in which the authors take a hard look at the total systems approach from a more or less pragmatic viewpoint. The theoretical approach which is fundamental is, however, not overlooked.

After listing the eight functional elements making up the management information system, Firmin and Linn devote their attention to the electronic data-processing system so often identified with it. Though the computer has given rise to the dream of a total management information system, the dream, they feel, may not merely be extremely difficult but in fact impossible to realize.

The remainder of the selection is concerned with the examination of the relationship of the management information system with managerial accounting and with managerial accounting education. As to the former, the hypothesis is formulated that the managerial accounting system is but a subset of the total information system: both share general objectives and can be described in the same general terms. Before the advent of the computer, the set and subset were often identified, but since its coming, the adequacy of the accounting system was soon felt. Other temporary systems were often created to fill the void.

Fundamental changes have since resulted. The computer accelerated organizational changes which in turn affected the managerial accounting system. On one hand, many lower-level clerical and middle-management jobs have been taken over by the computer; on the other hand, some lower-management positions have been enhanced by the allocation of planning and control functions, middle management has been upgraded, and top management has been liberated for almost exclusive attention to long-range planning.

Coincident with the changes in organizational structure was the new way of viewing the organization as a total entity, a set of interrelated subsystems. The increased awareness of the undesirable redundancies so frequently found in the discrete information systems in vogue focused attention on the vast capabilities of the computer for dealing with increasing and increasingly varied input and output characteristics, resulting in new conceptual models of the organization and of their data requirements.

The accounting model of the organization, with its emphasis on monetary measurement or historical orientation, good as it was, has since been found wanting. In its place have arisen other models reflecting behavioral features as well as scheduling, planning, decision, control, and evaluation measures.

The concept of a transaction was now made to include many properties not found in the traditional accounting concept. It necessitated the contributions of many different disciplines if a total management information system were to be achieved. Probability theory and statistics, behavioral science know-how, cybernetics, and information technology will have to be utilized.

The implications of the total management system on managerial accounting education are next spelled out. Educators in managerial accounting have the responsibility not only of conveying to their students the current state of the art but also of anticipating future changes. Management accountants will need to be trained to enlarge their vision beyond their own discipline and to encompass the entire organization within their grasp, to accept the newer techniques, and to participate actively in the processes of change.

A critical reexamination by accountants of the purpose and function of the information system is in order. Management needs must be recognized for what they are and all of the functional business areas must be better understood. The newer analytical methods must be learned, even if this entails more than a passing acquaintance with mathematics, statistics, information technology, and the principles of the behavioral sciences. Since managerial accounting is basically concerned with information—assessing information needs and designing appropriate systems for satisfying them—its future lies in its adaptability to the new direction imparted by the computer. Happily this direction is being realistically imparted by university programs currently in progress—an omen of better things to come in the accounting field.

In the selection by Asa Spaulding we have a theoretical as well as a practical approach to total systems. After underscoring the lack of clarity and consistency in the systems concepts, he prefaces his treatment of the conceptual approaches by a brief consideration of the evolution of the business enterprise. Historically, business progressed from the state where the owner was concerned with virtually all facets of the enterprise to the present state of the large complex organization where functional decentralization and delegation of authority are the universally recognized trademarks. The two basic problems of management, viz., communication and information, are continually under consideration in the remainder of the article.

The problem-oriented or the "piecemeal" approach to systems, though workable at times, has many inherent weaknesses, its chief defect being systems incompatibility. If practiced often enough, the piecemeal approach shows unmistakable evidence of being just "a thing of shreds and patches." After abandoning this approach as impractical, he defines the total systems concept and further elucidates some of the key words involved in this basic definition.

The dynamic processes of the business function are presented in three stages of increasing complexity, leading eventually to the total systems level. In the first, the simple straightforward procedural cycle is depicted from the initial decision to that of forecast, policy, design, action, results, evaluation, and back again to decision. The second stage employs in addition a somewhat unwieldy communication network that ties in all steps of the dynamic process with one another. The third stage is that of the total management information system with its automatic data-processing medium for communication and control of the various functions.

Spaulding definitely does believe that the total systems concept is practical. Without it "we can't do today's job with yesterday's tools and techniques and expect to stay in business tomorrow." However he views as one of the prime problems of the systems man that of selling the idea for a total management system to management itself.

When reading W. M. A. Brooker's selection, "The Total Systems Myth," it might be helpful for the purpose of making comparative evaluative judgments, to keep in mind what Kenneth Boulding had to say about general systems theories and the various levels that unfortunately have not yet been realized, Moravec's stand rejecting the total information system in favor of what he calls a fundamental information system, Harvey's down-to-earth appraisal of the limitations and advantages of what amounts to the total systems approach, and Young's indictment of systems managers for ignoring almost completely the behavioristic elements involved.

In his article Brooker examines the total systems concept as presented in various journals and textbooks and finds the exposition sadly inadequate. He finds the total systems approach overrated from the pragmatic viewpoint, though he does concede that it seems to be a very powerful motivational force for those concerned with the theoretical viewpoint. He believes that basically what is wrong is the underlying assumption that the total systems approach is of all possible approaches the most adequate and hence the most fruitful. His pointed darts are hurled not at an imaginary target of his own making but at the specific target fabricated from the utterances of some total systems advocates.

In his outline of a basic theory of business Brooker as a sociologist rightly lays stress upon the human elements. A business, he points out, is primarily a social group and as a social group it can and ought to be considered from the same perspective as other social groups. This sociological emphasis is necessary in view of the current misrepresentations of total systems and of the underestimations of the behavioristic elements. The total systems approach, he concludes, is a myth, and not a holistic or total approach.

Three distinct revolutions in management have taken place in the 20th century. The first was that of scientific management begun by Frederich W. Taylor, the efficiency expert. His management by exception lightened the burden of the manager by calling to his attention only those aspects of company operation that deviated from standards, and it did this in a kind of primitive real-time management information system. The second revolution occurred at the advent of office mechanization in the 1930s and 1940s, with the coming of the punched card and its related equipment. These wrought great changes in the composition of the labor force but did not ease the burden of management with respect to decision making. The third revolution took place with the coming of the computer. All of the gains predicted of the former revolutions were to be realized better and faster during the third. Top management, it was foretold, would need to rely less and less on middle management for decision making, and middle management would in turn shrink and eventually disappear.

The computer was hailed as the vehicle making possible at long last an *integrated system*. Westinghouse Electric and the dozen or so corporations studied by Vergin and Grimes were held up as examples of truly integrated systems. In his article, Crowley shows that this is not the case. After outlining the minimum qualications of a truly integrated system he states that there is to date no single system in operation that is truly integrated for complete management control. The reason is almost obvious: to remove the grave hazards associated with business decisions, management needs not only internally generated data but also all kinds of externally generated data (political, economic, social, legislative, and the like).

An *integrated management*, however, is one in which top management personnel is made one (integer) with the EDP system —that is, is brought closer to the operation of the EDP system—and in which the EDP control echelon is brought into the top management decision-making group. Integrated management is therefore not to be confused with or identified with total interated systems. The latter will, because of continual improvements and lower costs of EDP equipment, inevitably result regardless of whether management integration is ever realized.

While integrated management has not yet arrived, neither has integrated systems. This is so because the kind of information that top managers must have to answer the many perplexing and unsolved problems they daily face (such as information regarding labor conditions abroad, new tax laws, decisions by court systems, IRS, SEC, FEPC, patent courts, and the like) is still not available through EDP.

The EDP specialist, because of his privileged access to vital company data or his sophisticated computer know-how, is not *ipso facto* top-management material. Education, intelligence, and ability are also critical. Useful for evolving an integrated management is a broadening education of potential top level executives through job rotation, special assignments, and additional formal education (not necessarily in computer science).

The actual contributions of the computer and of EDP systems can best be grasped when one trichotomizes the levels of management decisions according to the type of control exercised. These three levels, in ascending order of complexity and authority-wielding power, are the operational, the tactical, and the strategic. The computer has been a great help in making data available for the simplest kind of decision making taking place on the lowest operational control level. For tactical control the computer has been of less help in decision making because of the large number of judgmental factors that need to be considered. At the strategic or highest level, the computer has been the least helpful. Here, unfortunately, speed is not always such a vital factor; here also qualitative factors predominate, and the predictive judgments to be made are not readily amenable to computer processing and outputing. However, the continuing progress being made in simulation techniques will someday render the computer more helpful at the higher management levels. Simulation enables executives to weigh the pros and cons of each alternative and to foresee the outcome of any particular decision before it is made. Heuristical programming that will enable the computer to take intellectual shortcuts and to use rules of thumb much as businessmen currently do has not yet evolved.

When one surveys the impact of the two previous revolutions on the decision-making process of top managers, one must agree with Crowley that the impact of the third revolution is still far less in effectiveness. One reason may be that the design and analysis involved in modelling and simulation take time, and to cut down on the time element, shortcuts have to be resorted to, thus casting some doubt on the accuracy of the results the decision makers must use.

EDP systems do not, and probably never will, replace the common-sense wisdom of the business manager. Real-time on-line systems are, interestingly enough, used for rapid processing of historical data on stock markets, commodity exchanges, race tracks, and the like. They have not yet been used to predict future commodity or stock prices, nor have they been used extensively to predict winners at the races. The day of push-button management decision making by Big Brother is, in Crowley's estimation, a long way off.

Konvalinka and Trentin's selection concludes this section on a predominantly pragmatic level. They expose some of the common fallacies associated with total systems, such as the identification of management information systems with electronic data processing and the inevitable computeritis. After treating briefly the concepts of information and decisions, they take up the nature, development, and the method of achieving management system. To provide the readers with a practical illustration of how a particular company might tackle the management information system problem, the authors have presented the case of the Able Manufacturing Company, a fictional corporation but one that represents a synthesis of actual cases experienced in their consulting capacities. They illustrate their treatment with well-designed charts and detailed tables.

28. INFORMATION SYSTEMS AND MANAGERIAL ACCOUNTING

Peter A. Firmin* and James J. Linn†

THE PERVASIVE CHARACTER OF MANAGEMENT INFORMATION SYSTEMS

Is Our Current Preoccupation with Systems Justified? Interdisciplinary literature in business administration, behavioral sciences, and computer sciences, as well as the literature of accounting and management science, abounds with discussions of and references to "management information systems," "total information systems," "the 'systems' approach," and other similar terms. Does this preoccupation presage revolutionary shifts in organizational structures and in our perception of organizational behavior? Are we on the threshold of unparalelled gains in managerial effectiveness? Or are we squandering our talents on fad and fetish? To answer these questions we must explore such fundamental problems as: "What is a 'management information system'?" "What do we mean by the 'systems' approach?" "What does all of this mean for [managerial] accounting?"

What is a Management Information System? The essence of *system* is interrelationship among elements. *Information* is purpose-oriented organized data and is a requisite for survival of *all* organizations. The interrelated networks (with their content) which transmute data into information throughout an organization constitute its information system.

All purposive organizations (even the "self-governed" ones) must be "managed"—directed towards a goal or purpose. The information system which enables the process of management is the management information system. The term "total information system" when applied to the management information system connotes *all* of the information needed by management and implies a "systems approach" to the study of management's information requirements and their satisfaction. The "systems approach" (in the context of the organization) connotes a perception of the organization as a set of interrelationships rather than as a set of independent elements or sub-systems.

A management information system is a system for accepting data as raw material and, through one or more transmutation processes, generating information as a product. It is composed of the following functional elements which relate the organization to its environments:[1]

1. Perception—initial entry of data, whether collected or generated, into the organization.
2. Recordation—physical capture of signs and symbols.
3. Storage—presupposes some expected future use, recordation, and a location.
4. Retrieval—search for recorded data.
5. Processing—transformation according to the *specific* needs of the organization.
6. Transmission—the flows which occur in an information system.
7. Presentation—reporting, communication.
8. Decision making—a controversial inclusion, except to the extent that the information system engages in decision making that pertains to itself.

What is the Relationship Between the Management Information System and the Electronic Data Processing System? Since

SOURCE: *Accounting Review* (January, 1968), pp. 75–82. Reprinted by permission of American Accounting Association.

* Tulane University.
† Tulane University.

[1] James J. Linn, *The Concept of the Information System of the Organization,* a paper presented at The Institute of Management Sciences 1966 American Meeting, College of Measurements in Management, Dallas, Texas, February 16, 1966, pp. 3–11 (multilithed), contains a comprehensive discussion of these elements.

management information systems inhere in organizations of all kinds, conceptually-oriented studies of them need not relate to implementation methodology. The existence of an electronic data processing system, for example, is not necessarily an essential part of a management information system. In any organization, the *management information system* may be a loosely joined set of sub-systems designed to serve the purpose of providing information for management. Such systems may be formal or informal, planned or *ad hoc,* integrated or separate. Their totality still could be called *a* management information system. Most systems analysts, however, would choose to call such disjoint subsystems several separate systems instead of one integrated management information system as the term is now used.

But it is exactly the computer-oriented revolution in information technology that has created the currently prevailing surge of interest in management information systems and which has kindled the hope that the "total" information systems dream might be realized. Electronic data processing systems have made practicable serious efforts to utilize the "systems approach" in the design and implementation of management information systems. Electronic data processing systems also have made feasible the radical changes in the nature of data input and information output required by management science models. As a consequence of this improvement in technology, management information systems both on drawing boards and in various stages of implementation usually include management science planning models as an integral part of the information generating process.[2]

Are Total Systems Feasible? Most systems analysts and corporate managers who talk about and aspire to "total" information systems realize that the ideal may be extremely difficult if not impossible to achieve. There has unquestionably been a great deal of overzealousness as well as extreme disillusion. As Anthony has remarked, "It is because of the varied and unpredictable nature of the data required for strategic planning that an attempt to design an all-purpose, internal information system is probably hopeless. For the same reason, the dream of some computer specialists of a gigantic data bank, from which planners can obtain all the information they wish by pressing some buttons, is probably no more than a dream."[3] Others have been less kind and have labeled the concept of the total information system as a myth or a chimera. At the very least we can agree with Churchill and Stedry, who pin the label of "awesome" on the concept of "total information."[4]

IMPLICATIONS OF THE INFORMATION SYSTEMS CONCEPT FOR MANAGERIAL ACCOUNTING

Managerial Accounting Systems are Subsets of Total Management Information Systems. The product of any managerial accounting system, like that of all other information systems, is information. The nature of accounting is that of an information system, as the American Accounting Association's 1965–66 Committee on Basic Accounting Theory has pointed out.[5]

As an information system, accounting deals selectively with problems of the same order as more general information systems. Managerial (and financial) accounting systems are comprised of the same eight functional elements which were listed earlier to describe the general class "management information system:" Perception, recordation, storage, retrieval, processing, transmission, presentation, and decision making. (Some would object to the last, "but the relationship between the processes of the information system and . . . decision making are close enough to raise the question of including decision making as part of the information system."[6])

Ideological support for this position has

[2] Neil C. Churchill and Andrew C. Stedry, "Some Developments in Management Science and Information Systems with Respect to Measurement in Accounting," in Robert K. Jaedicke, Yuji Ijiri and Oswald Nielsen (eds.), *Research in Accounting Measurement* (American Accounting Association 1965), p. 45.

[3] Robert N. Anthony, *Planning and Control Systems: A Framework for Analysis* (Graduate School of Business Administration, Harvard University 1965), p. 45.

[4] Neil C. Churchill and Andrew C. Stedry, *op. cit.,* p. 41.

[5] Norton M. Bedford, "The Nature of Future Accounting Theory," *The Accounting Review* (January 1967), p. 82.

[6] James J. Linn, *op. cit.,* p. 11.

been expressed by others. Managerial accounting has been tentatively defined by another committee of the American Accounting Association as a composite of data-gathering techniques embodied in a system whose focus is managerial planning, decision making, and control.[7] Anton has suggested that an effective accounting system, in addition to providing continuous data gathering and processing, must be integrated with the planning and control system.[8]

Finally, like general purpose information systems, the output of accounting systems purport to educate the recipients of that output.

Clearly, the hypothesis that the managerial accounting system is a subset—if not a *proper* subset—of the total information system is tenable. Both have the same purposes and can be described in the same general terms. How, then, has recent preoccupation with total information systems impinged upon conventional managerial accounting systems?

Fundamental Changes in Perspective Have Occurred. Until the advent of electronic data processing, integrated information systems in the large-scale enterprise were exceptional. Often, the managerial and financial accounting systems were (and still are!) the only formal information systems in the business organization. Such systems do not fulfill *all* the planning and decision-facilitating information needs of management. But they do represent viable models of the business organization. And management does use the output of these systems for decision making. In cases where management does not feel that the output of these systems is sufficient for its purposes, additional and often *ad hoc* systems are created.

One of the early effects of the "information systems syndrome" on managerial accounting was produced as a secondary result of computer-induced changes in the organizational structure of the enterprise. Many lower-level clerical and middle-management jobs have disappeared, and activities formerly performed at these levels have been "taken over" by the computer. In other organizations, middle-management positions have assumed even greater importance than before as planning and control functions have been moved to lower organizational levels. Concomitantly, top management has been able to devote more attention to understanding system interrelationships. In either case, fundamental changes in organizational structures (and hence in information systems) have occurred.

One of the obvious results of the introduction of computer technology has been a revision of reporting requirements, as well as, in some cases, a centralization of record-keeping activities and of information processing. These revisions of reporting requirements—in many cases involving more variety—have forced many to restructure their management information systems to take advantage of the ability of the computer to accept, store, rearrange, and process data with a great deal of flexibility.

And many organizations have begun to suspect that it may not make sense to support separate, disjoint, and uncoordinated functional area information systems for marketing, production, and personnel—and for management and financial accounting as well. This observation reflects one of the more subtle but perhaps even more important effects wrought by computer-induced information systems revisions. Even where the organization is some distance from a total information system, partial implementation of this concept through the use of electronic data processing equipment has changed the way we look at the organization. There is now a propensity to view the organization as a total entity and to attempt to analyze it as an interrelated system, not as a collection of subsystems.

These four factors—changes in organizational structure; perception of the organization as an interrelated set of subsystems; heightened sensitivity to possible undesirable redundancy of effort in separate information systems; and rapidly escalating capability of data processing equipment to deal simultaneously with varieties of input and output characteristics—have fostered an expanded concept of the transaction.

New Models of the Organization Exist. For many years the accounting model of the organization sufficed (however well or badly) as the major formal information system on

[7] Draft statement of the American Accounting Association Committee on Managerial Models, 1966–67.

[8] Hector R. Anton, "The Effect of Computers on the Reliability of Accounting Measurements," in Robert K. Jaedicke, *et al., op. cit.,* pp. 127–128.

which management decisions were based. The last two decades have witnessed the introduction of many newer and more sophisticated models of the organization and its subsystems. These models advance managerial effectiveness by furnishing new perspectives on organizational behavior and new approaches to decision-making. They require the use of varied data not limited to monetary measurement or historical orientation, and in some cases they mirror the fact that information flows needed by management are not always accompanied by resource flows. Such varieties of information do not always fit the traditional accounting mold.

These models include cost-effectiveness models reflecting the behavioral or modern theories of organization that business enterprises may have goals other than profit. They also include scheduling, planning, decision, control, and evaluation models which require data embodying non-monetary and non-historical measures.

New Organizational Models Have New Data Requirements. Different models may also require data of different degrees of accuracy and precision. Planning models may be extremely sensitive to certain parameters representing estimates of demand or production constraints, while some evaluation models need only consider broad ranges of performance. Planning models may require non-monetary statements of resources available and rates of resource consumption as well as requirements in dollar equivalents.

Some models which combine planning and decision functions require that decision rules be incorporated in the model so that certain types of decisions—usually routine—might be "made" automatically. Particularly in decision models, and to some extent in evaluation models, is it necessary to consider subjective factors which may defy quantification and which may not be expressible in monetary units.

Decision models should reflect the decision rules of the decision maker. But studies of decision making in the organizational setting have revealed that a vast amount of decision making is heuristic in nature and that the overwhelming number of uncertainties surrounding the decision frustrate optimization. In making decisions, the decision makers consider such difficult-to-quantify factors as the compatibility of intended decisions with existing operating constraints, optimum time for decisions, optimum amounts of information, conflicts of interest, the organizational scheme for rewarding successful decision making and penalizing failures, the relationship between payoff and risk, and degree of understanding of the decision which exists in the minds of subordinates.[9]

A New Concept of a Transaction is Needed —and is Feasible. The characteristic of electronic data processing systems which makes it possible to collect in one file various types and time-phases of data and to store this data separately for later interrelationship and analysis has supported mounting demand for integrated measures and data collection schemes. The potential ability to collect data on an integrated basis has eroded also the need for a common denominator of measurement, since we are now able to construct and utilize information vectors specifying an almost unlimited number of properties of the objects that we are attempting to measure.[10]

"Accounting [traditionally] has been concerned with communicating the effects of economic events. . . ."[11] Not all economic events are recognized by the conventional accounting model, however. Accounting theory defines a set of properties that an economic event must possess before it can be accepted as an input to the accounting system—before it can be recognized as a transaction. These properties include, for example, objectivity, quantifiability, verifiability, and freedom from bias.[12] Thus, many economic events relevant to decision making are not recognized by the accounting system. Price-level changes, increased employee skills, and intra-entity

[9] Samuel G. Trull, "Some Factors Involved in Determining Total Decision Success," *Management Science* (February 1966), B-271-B-280.

[10] Peter A. Firmin, "The Potential of Accounting as a Management Information System," *Management International Review* (February 1966), pp. 45–55.

[11] "[The] Institute of Management Science Committee Comments for Common Body of Knowledge Study," *Journal of Accountancy,* (December 1964), p. 80.

[12] Committee to Prepare a Statement of Basic Accounting Theory, *A Statement of Basic Accounting Theory* (American Accounting Association 1966), p. 8.

changes in asset values are but a few examples of such "non-transactions."

If multi-dimensional vectors are used to depict added (non-monetary) dimensions of the conventional accounting transaction, some progress toward data integration in the perception function of the information system will be made. But what is needed, in addition, is a concept of the transaction that will allow the point at which the system recognizes an entry to vary with the type of information flow. Some research has already been directed toward this objective.[13]

One of the most significant imports of the preceding discussion on data input requirements for various types of models and expanded transaction concepts is that the total information systems approach requires the design of data bases permitting and perhaps demanding the collection of data in the smallest whole unit which characterizes the most basic or elemental property of the object being measured.[14]

Implications of The Expanded Transaction Concept. The expanded transaction concept requires that the resources of the firm be reflected not only in monetary but also in other multi-dimensional forms as they move through the organization. Meaningful integration of such data in a total management information system involves the contribution of many different disciplines. Many types of models require operational facility in many aspects of mathematics. Planning, control, and evaluation models require a knowledge of probability theory and statistics. They also require an understanding of behavioral science as it relates to problems of motivation and goal perception; individual, organizational, or group conflicts; and responsiveness to controls. Above all, problems of measurement and communication as well as other aspects of information technology must be understood.

The expanded transaction concept has implications for preserving the reliability of information, and it has audit implications as well. When information is not accompanied by resource flows, the discipline enforced by the double-entry system of accounting is lacking. Lack of duality in the system requires that other forms of discipline be imposed. Problems of information reliability and system control, with their audit implications, also imply a need for new methods to evaluate system reliability and effectiveness.

WHAT ARE THE IMPLICATIONS OF THE INFORMATION SYSTEMS CONCEPT FOR (MANAGERIAL) ACCOUNTING

Educators Have Two Roles. To answer this question, we must first ask, "What role do we play?" One dimension of our role as educators is to convey the current state of the art to the student. We need to perceive the state of the art in contemporary managerial accounting, and we need to teach about this system. As a corollary, we need to sense changes in the state of the art and we need to evaluate and respond quickly to these changes.

In this dimension of our role, we have an obligation to "keep-up" with management. But this dimension of our role does not require us to pioneer or to lead management—we merely selectively transmit information about its state.

What does the state of the art reveal—and what are the portents for the future?

As we survey the state of the art, we note that in those organizations which have attempted to implement—even partially—broader concepts of management information systems, the impact on the traditional role of the management accountant has varied. The seriousness of this problem is reflected in the plethora of articles in our literature about "Who'll Be in Charge?" These articles discuss the importance of the role of the information system controller, and they issue repeated

[13] John Field has offered a view of the conventional accounting transaction based on the information patterns of technical information flows, operational planning information flows, contractual rights flows, credit flows, and property flows.

"The principle of this approach is that underlying the complexities of day to day phenomena are a relatively few elements or building blocks. The world of information revolves about transactions. All information, starting with research and ending with financial statements, is directed toward either activating a transaction or recording its occurrence. Particularly interesting is the fact that each transaction has a definite information pattern and that the patterns are remarkably similar to one another."

John Field, "Determining Information Patterns," *PMM&Co./Management Controls* (April 1967), pp. 77–82.

[14] James J. Linn, "A General Asset Model." Working paper No. 188–66 (Massachusetts Institute of Technology, 1966).

warnings that the controller or management accountant will lose ground unless he has the will and the capability to broaden his horizon. There are hints that management accountants are too involved in their own discipline and too restricted in their vision to appreciate the problems of the entire organization. Hence, they are not capable of operating in the richer world of the information specialists. Beyer and others urge that accountants change their attitudes—that they recognize accelerating change as a characteristic of our time and that they develop a total corporate viewpoint, accept new techniques and participate actively in the process of change.[15]

As teachers, we have a second and more important role—that of pioneer, developer, catalyst, innovator, leader. Not only do we have the obligation to register the current state of the art, but we must anticipate and foresee the future. For in a very real sense, we create today the accounting profession of tomorrow. The students of today will be the policy-making management accountants and partners in CPA firms of tomorrow, just as we and the management accountants and partner-level CPAs of today are the products of our educational system of yesterday. If we foresee that the accountant of 1980 will have to deal with expanded transaction concepts, and if we teach these concepts, he (and not someone else) *will* deal with them.

What Do We Need to Know? Accounting *is* concerned with the furnishing of information. It is an information system. The important question is, "To whom is the information being furnished, and for what purpose?" The answers, of course, are "To management," and, "To facilitate management decision making, planning, control, and evaluation." If new tools exist which can facilitate these functions, and if the utilization of these tools requires the construction of different kinds of data or the revision of information frameworks, and if these newer methods are effective—then we must recognize them and become proficient in their use.

We must focus—as always—on the requirements of the user. The implication here is that we must understand the user's job and his need for information. *Therefore, we need to understand management and all of the functional areas of business.* On top of this understanding we *then* superimpose our expertise in the design and control of information systems. This is not a new suggestion—this has always been our hallmark. In constructing traditional accounting models, we fashioned accounting reports along lines of classification which we believed would be useful. These classifications were predicated upon certain analytical methods. If these reports are no longer as useful as they once were because better methods of analysis and new uses exist, then we cannot ignore the new methods.

If understanding these newer methods requires that we become operational in mathematics, statistics, and other aspects of information technology, and if it requires that we comprehend fundamental concepts of behavioral science, then we must.

What is Managerial Accounting? The essence of [managerial] accounting—the thing which distinguishes accounting from other functional areas—is that our product is information. The "specialty" which we have is the ability to assess information needs and to design appropriate systems for satisfying them. We must construct reliable systems, borrowing as necessary from the bodies of knowledge in other disciplines. If the computer is to be a basic part of information processing, we must understand the computer. If the transformation process involves the application of a management science model, our accounting system must literally "wed" the model involved.

Some have raised questions as to whether this kind of activity—implementing a broadened concept of accounting or the information systems concept—is accounting or something else. Such inquiry is sterile. As Bedford has pointed out, accounting has always evolved, and the accountant of today might very well not be called an accountant by the accountant of yesterday.[16]

By whatever name, the accountant of the future is going to have to be a systems analyst. In the literature on systems, there is already evidence of a desire for better communication between systems and audit specialists. John Carey, in "The CPA Plans for the Future," foresees a whole new profession of information specialists.[17]

[15] Robert Beyer, "Management Information Systems: Who'll Be In Charge?", *Management Accounting* (June 1967), pp. 3–8.

[16] Bedford, *op. cit.*, p. 82.

[17] John L. Carey, *The CPA Plans for the Future*

It is abundantly clear that the fragmented information system of the past will not be optimal—if even useful—for the industrial enterprise for the future. It is also obvious that the information specialists who will design and implement tomorrow's accounting (information?) systems must have capabilities far beyond those now possessed by most accountants.

However, people do adapt to pressures of change. Ten years ago, it would have been hard to find a doctoral program producing the kind of accountants that we suggest will be typical of the future. Today, such programs exist and the output of such programs are already teaching in various universities in this country. Ten years ago, it would have been difficult to find a mathematical symbol in the literature of accounting. Today, our literature contains such articles. No longer can we say that management accountants must become part of the evolution of information systems —we *are* part of this evolution—a fact which is abundantly reflected in our literature and by such discussions as this.

(New York: American Institute of Certified Public Accountants, 1965), pp. 244–245.

29. IS THE TOTAL SYSTEM CONCEPT PRACTICAL?

A. T. Spaulding, Jr.*

Widespread attention is being given these days to the concept of a "total system" approach to the problem of information processing. At practically every conference and seminar held by the various management and data processing associations, considerable time is devoted to it. Almost every periodical that covers the systems and computer field includes numerous articles on the subject. And more and more talks and papers are being given on various aspects of it.

There seem to be differing opinions as to just what a total system concept really is. This fact is borne out by the lack of consistency in labeling it. A total system approach is often referred to as a "consolidated functions approach," or a "unified approach," or as an "integrated data processing system," and even as a "real-time system," as well as by a score of other presumably suitable names. The reason for this lack of consistency, perhaps, lies in the fact that the concept, as it has so far evolved, is very nebulous and has had meaning only in terms of its actual application to specific business information problems. Because it has been interpreted by so many people to mean so many different things, no clear-cut definition has yet been established or at least agreed upon.

Since this situation exists, it would be desirable for us to establish and agree upon a definition which will provide a basis for common understanding before an attempt is made to evaluate the practicality of the so-called total system concept. In this way, any evaluations we make or any conclusions we derive will be valid within the framework of our definition.

SOURCE: *Systems & Procedures Journal* (January–February, 1964), pp. 28–32. Reprinted by permission of *Systems & Procedures Journal*.

* President, Data Service Inc.

EVOLUTION OF THE BUSINESS ENTERPRISE

Before we consider our definition of a total system concept, let's look at the evolution of the business enterprise. It hasn't been very long since the modus operandi of almost every business enterprise was what might be considered a total systems approach. The owner of the enterprise, usually being the manager, salesman, and office clerk, as well as the janitor, conducted all or certainly most of the affairs of the business himself. Thus, every decision he made was based upon a complete knowledge of the overall business situation—from the community's economic and environmental conditions to his own firm's status of production and inventory.

As these organizations became larger and more complex, communication channels grew longer, slower and more difficult to maintain. Managers soon became aware of the fact that communication with and supervision of the various segments of the enterprise was almost impossible with the then existing organizational structures and systems. The outgrowth of this realization was the development of a new concept of organization, "functional decentralization." But even reorganizations and delegations of authority and responsibility which resulted didn't solve management's two basic problems:

1. Communication
2. Information

CONCEPTUAL APPROACHES TO SYSTEMS WORK

There have been a vast number of conceptual approaches to systems work down through the years. Unfortunately, these approaches have not kept pace with the tools and techniques developed for use in the field. There are, perhaps, a number of reasons for this: lack of recognition of systems as a profession, specialization and loss of perspective by the systems man, lack of interest and receptivity on the part of management and so on.

Considering the various approaches, we find that the traditional and most prevalently used has been the problem-oriented or "piecemeal" approach. The procedure usually followed here is to call in a systems man each time a problem of either an operating or routine nature arises. Information is collected, analyzed and evaluated. Recommendations are made. These recommendations usually require only the revision of an existing system, although sometimes they require that a new system be designed. If it's the latter, the systems man may end up developing procedures which are not consonant with company policy. In fact, since it is a new system he is designing, there may not even be policy covering the situation. In which case, he may, in essence, have to develop company policy himself. (Of course we know that every good systems man develops his systems within the framework of company policy.) However, this is certainly not the most enviable position for a systems man to be in constantly.

While there are certainly some attractive features of the problem-oriented approach, it has the major disadvantage of creating a "patchwork" situation. That is, it only patches up the weak spots in the overall system. When this approach is used long enough with no attempt at basic or total system design, systems incompatibility usually occurs. The various systems end up cutting across each other. This creates duplication of effort, decreased efficiency, in short, increased operating costs.

N. L. Senensieb, International Vice President of the Systems and Procedures Association, in his paper "Systems, Functions, Concepts, and Programs" suggests several other conceptual approaches to systems work. Following are the common ones: [1]

The Manual-Writing Approach tends to document the status quo, i.e., the existing system, and ignores the other creative phases of analysis and design which permit establishment of optimum systems.

The Forms Control Approach tends to overlook the fact that forms are a data transmission medium, and concentrates, instead, on the narrower paperwork cost control techniques.

The Accounting System Approach concentrates on perfecting the accounting system per se, forgetting this is only one major subsystem of the overall management information system.

The Mechanization Approach implies that mechanization is the only means by which office operations can be improved, and that a mechanized method is always an optimum one.

Because of the positive impact that many of the earlier office mechanization attempts had on office systems and procedures, the first electronic computers to be used as management tools were looked upon as a panacea for the continuing rise in clerical costs and information processing problems. Early applications were put on these so-called miracle-workers with the same traditional approach that was being used in general systems work. Little or no attempt was made to take advantage of the vast capabilities of this new medium. While recent approaches to computer utilization for processing business information have considered more fully the present state of the art in ADP machine development, relatively little has been accomplished in the area of total systems.

TOTAL SYSTEMS CONCEPT DEFINED

Having taken a look at the business enterprise as it has evolved over the years and having considered some of the conceptual approaches used in general systems work, we can now view our total systems concept as it applies to the management problems of communication and information. First, let's consider a definition for the total system concept:

Total System Concept: an approach to information systems design that conceives the business enterprise as an entity composed of interdependent systems and subsystems, which, with the use of automatic data processing systems, attempts to provide timely and

[1] N. L. Senensieb, "Systems Functions, Concepts, and Programs," draft of a college systems & procedures course outline, January, 1962, pp. 18–19.

accurate management information which will permit optimum management decision making.[2]

For the sake of clarity, let us digress for a moment to define several key words and phrases as they are to be interpreted within the context of our total system definition:

System: ". . . a set of related procedures (or equipment) which provide the plan of action (or vehicle) for carrying out the basic objectives of organization."

". . . directed orderly plan of interdependent and sequential functions, the execution of which enables an organization to fulfill its purpose." [3]

Automatic data processing system: a configuration of equipment comprised of some or all of the following:

1. electronic computer(s);
2. input and output devices, both local and remote;
3. auxiliary equipment which directly supports or services the computers (exclusive of communications equipment), i.e., tabulating equipment; and
4. communications, i.e., data transmission equipment used in support of the data processing equipment.[4]

Management information (system): a system which provides ". . . the right information for the right people at the right time at the lowest possible cost." [5]

DYNAMIC PROCESSES OF THE BUSINESS FUNCTION

Every action program or project executed by a business enterprise follows a dynamic process. This process begins with the board of directors, for example, stating in abstract terms the goals and objectives of the organization, i.e., the purposes for which the enterprise is being established. (We are excluding, for the moment, the profit motive which obviously is the underlying reason for the establishment of most business enterprises.)

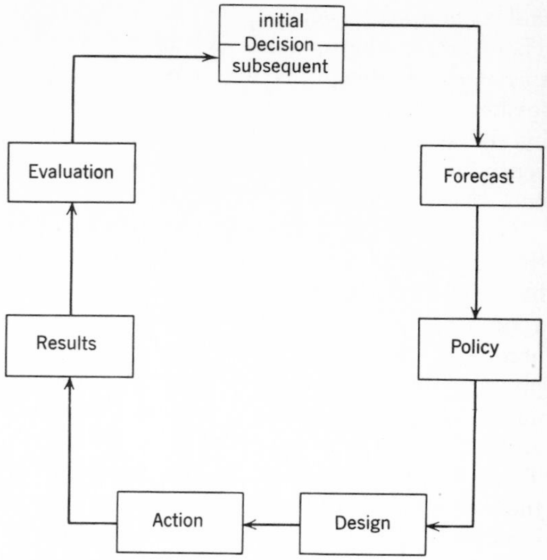

CHART I. Dynamic Processes of the Business Function. The dynamic process begins when management makes its initial decision and develops a forecast. Once policy is then established and a design effort is made, the action phase can be accomplished. Then come the results and evaluation steps.

Once these objectives have been established, they are communicated via the president, down through the executive and administrative officers, operating managers and supervisors, to the rank and file as management directives for accomplishing the specific programs and projects. This is where our dynamic process begins. (See Chart I.)

First, management makes its initial decision, i.e., it selects from among several alternatives what it wants to do; what type of program or project it wants to initiate. After this decision has been made, the next step is to develop a forecast. In other words, management determines the appropriate plans, i.e., what systems, etc., will be needed and their budgetary requirements. Not only financial budget requirements, but requirements for manpower, material, etc.

The next step in this dynamic process is the

[2] E. R. Dickey and N. L. Senensieb, "The Total System Concept," draft of entry for *The Encyclopedia for Management,* Reinhold Publishing Corp.

[3] *System and Procedures, Notebook for Systems Man,* rev. ed., Publication No. 460, U.S. Government Printing Office, 1963.

[4] *Preparation and Reporting Format of System Analysis Study on Potential Tactical Army ADPS Application,* USAEPG-SIG 940-25, U.S. Army Electronic Proving Ground, November, 1957.

[5] E. R. Dickey, "Total Systems," *Ideas for Management,* Systems and Procedures Association, 1963, pp. 331–345.

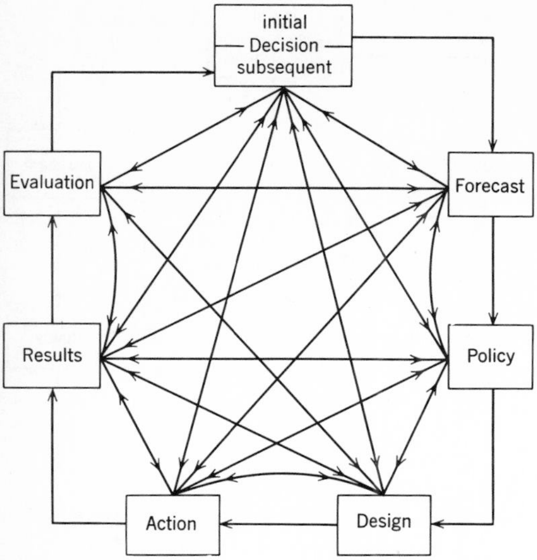

CHART II. Dynamic Processes of the Business Function. Command linkages among all steps of the dynamic process show an ideal network arrangement but no medium for transport of information back and forth nor a central control mechanism.

establishment of policy, i.e., the framework and guidelines for the accomplishment of the particular project. This is where specific individuals and activities are assigned their authority and responsibility for implementation, execution and follow through. Criteria which will serve as a basis for evaluating results are also established at this point.

The fourth step in our process may be referred to as the design step. This entails the actual detailed systems design effort; the development of the step-by-step procedures to be followed in carrying out the project; the selection of appropriate methods and techniques to be used; and the determination of rules to be followed within legal requirements.

Once the system has been designed, procedures developed, methods selected and rules actual implementation and execution of the determined, the action phase can be accomplished. This phase is nothing more than the project.

The next step in our model is the results step. This step is reflected by the information generated from the system in the form of records and reports.

The seventh step in our dynamic process is evaluation. Comparisons and analyses of the statistics compiled in the preceding step are made, based upon the approved criteria, and trends are established.

We are now back where we started—at the decision step. The only difference is that we are now concerned with subsequent decisions as opposed to initial decisions. These are the decisions that management makes as a result of evaluation of the entire process. The specific decisions obtained usually fall into one of three distinct categories:

1. Decision to continue with the present project with no modifications or changes;
2. Decision to make modifications and changes in the present project and continue; or
3. Decision to cancel the present project and initiate another.

Once this choice is made, the cycle is repeated. This, then, is our dynamic process for the business function.

Quite often the elements of this process are not individually identifiable. They are obscured by the interplay of each with the other in management decision making. Because these elements are so easily obscured, we recognize that there is something missing from our model. There is no communication linkage, i.e., no network which ties in, for example, forecast with action; results with policy; design with evaluation. And this is what is usually missing from most basic systems. There is, as a rule, no communications network which ties in each step of the dynamic process with the other.

The Chart II version of our model depicts communication linkages between all of the steps of the process. While this is an improvement over the original model, in that it shows the ideal network arrangement, there is no vehicle or medium for transporting information to and from the various steps, nor is there a central control mechanism which permits interpretation of information received and decision making.

Chart III of our dynamic process shows a total management information system and considers ADPS as the medium for controlling and communicating with the various functions of the process. While highly theoretical and idealistic from a conceptual standpoint, this idea can be developed into a practical, working system. Whether or not this actually occurs, however, depends upon several things.

First, there must exist on the part of management a desire to have a management information system. It doesn't matter whether the impetus for such comes from operating personnel, systems specialists, or from upper management itself. The main thing here is that there be a genuine desire to have such a system developed. Management's interest in this connection can usually be measured by its decisions on requests for the allocation of appropriate resources for accomplishing the task.

Second, management must be able to state in concrete terms, not in abstractions, what its objectives are and what the desired outputs from the system should be. If we consider this in the light of our management information system definition, management will have to decide what information it wants developed, for whom and when the information must be available. If this can be done in specific terms, development of the total system will be possible. Obtaining comprehensive information of this sort in a form which will permit basic systems design is by no means an easy task.

Third, the group selected to accomplish this task must have the ability, both in terms of its own technical competence as well as its knowledge of the overall situation, to take management's objectives and general systems requirements and convert them into related systems and subsystems which will comprise the total system.

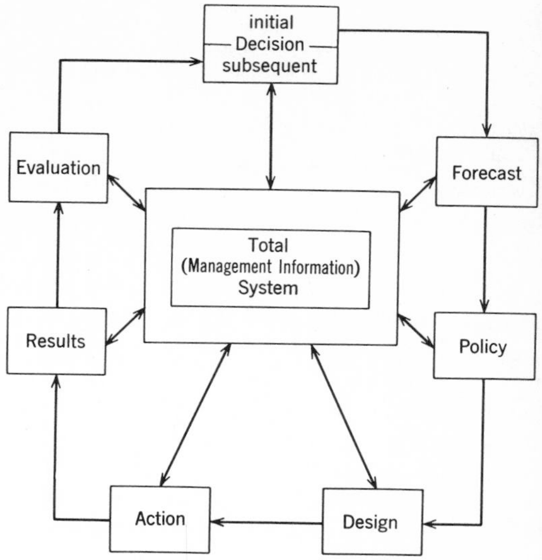

CHART III. Dynamic Processes of the Business Function. This highly theoretical information system can be developed into a practical arrangement if management has the desire for one and states what it desires from the system. Also, the group selected to accomplish such development must have ability.

ADVANTAGES OF A TOTAL SYSTEMS APPROACH

One might be justified in asking at this point, why go to all of the trouble of designing a total management information system? What are its advantages? Simply stated, the answer might be: to provide the right information for the right people at the right time at the lowest possible cost.

Some specific advantages that appeal to the writer from the standpoint of a life insurance company's operations are:

1. Permits the elimination of redundant files and duplications of clerical efforts;
2. Reduces the amount of manual handling of records, thereby minimizing the possibility of clerical errors;
3. Permits daily updating of records and files, providing current status information and identification of situations which may require individual attention and corrective action;
4. Relieves management and supervisory personnel of routine decision making through use of computer logic for the same; and
5. Permits better cost control and management of resources.

In answer to the question, "Is the total systems concept practical?", the author's personal opinion is that a total systems concept *is* practical. However, we as systems and data processing people need to have a clear understanding in our own minds of what we mean by a total systems concept, especially as far as it can be applied to our own organizations. After all, it's probably going to require a selling job in order to convey to management what the idea of a total systems approach is and what its advantages are. That is, selling the idea that we can't do today's job with yesterday's tools and techniques and expect to stay in business tomorrow.

30. THE TOTAL SYSTEMS MYTH

W. M. A. Brooker *

The purpose of this article is to examine critically the value of the total systems concept and to make predictions on the effects of its application. As is implied in the title, the author does not regard the concept itself as having the practical value claimed by its followers. On the other hand, the belief in this concept is a powerful motivating force among those who have accepted it as a frame of reference.

Why and what is untrue about the total systems concept? The basic error in the total systems concept is the assumption that the total systems approach is the most fruitful; that systems analysis in any situation is the most powerful kind of planning that can precede planned and profitable change for a company.

This article will discuss the foundations of the systems concept, the value of this concept and the limitations of its application. These limitations amount to an inadequacy as to the totality of pervasiveness of the approach, notwithstanding its value in an auxiliary role. We shall then discuss the requirements of an overall approach and outline an alternative in which systems theory occupies a significant but auxiliary role.

FOUNDATIONS OF THE SYSTEMS CONCEPT

The foundation of the systems concept seems to rest on the work of von Bertalanffy, who apparently coined the term "general systems theory." Hall, who is referred to by Bertalanffy, defines the system as . . . "a set of objects with relationships among the objects and among their attributes. Objects are simply the parts or components of a system." [1]

SOURCE: *Systems & Procedures Journal* (July–August, 1965), pp. 28–32. Reprinted by permission of *Systems & Procedures Journal*.

* B.A. M.Soc.Sc., University of Cape Town.

[1] Arthur D. Hall, *A Methodology for Systems Engineering*, Van Nostrand, Toronto, 1962, p. 60.

More specifically, systems are defined in terms of flows. According to Forrester: The business system is . . . "a system in which the flows of information, materials, manpower, capital equipment and money set up forces that determine the basic tendencies towards growth, fluctuation and decline." [2]

The flows of business system, according to Optner, are in the form of a closed system which . . . "can be defined as one which is free of variation or disturbance . . . the concept of the black box" [3] of which the basic model is thus:

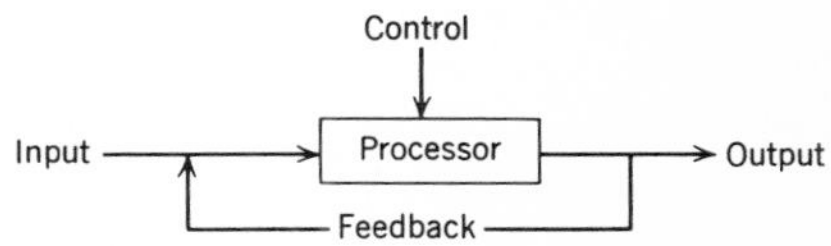

In its business form, this model becomes:

An advantage of the systems approach is that it focuses attention on broader issues than may be contained in a single department. This is because of the emphasis on inputs and outputs. What goes on *inside* the black box is of secondary importance. Naturally this has a healthy effect on any departmental narrowness of viewpoint.

The second advantage of the systems approach is that it aids in the formulation of purpose or objectives for a particular depart-

[2] J. W. Forrester, "Industrial Dynamics: A Major Breakthrough for Decision-Makers," *Harvard Business Review*, July–August, 1958, p. 52.

[3] Stanford L. Optner, *Systems Analysis for Business Management*, Prentice-Hall, Inc., 1960, pp. 3–15.

ment or operating area. The reason for the existence of any operating area can very neatly be expressed in the formula:

$$P = O - I$$

where P is purpose, O is output and I stands for input.

A third advantage of the systems approach is that it can sometimes be related to decision making. Forrester, for example, in his model for industrial dynamics, shows information flows controlling valves in material and money flows.*

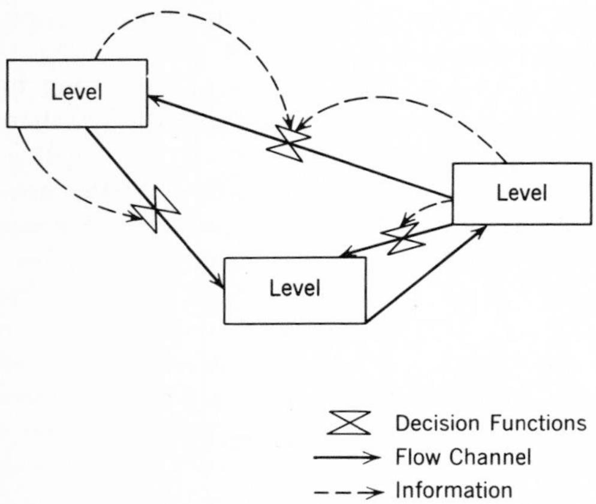

Forrester, incidentally, develops this theme very well in demonstrating the effect of varying sales volume on inventory levels.

DISADVANTAGE OF THE TOTAL SYSTEMS APPROACH

The author's main quarrel with the approach is that many of the followers of systems theory seem to have translated *general* systems into total systems; they give the impression that if systems are omnipresent they must somehow, like God, be omnipotent. General systems theory is a valid field of interdisciplinary study. Those who profess general systems theory realize its limitations, which are not recognized by those who take the *total* systems approach. As an example of an understanding of the limitations of the approach, let's refer again to Hall. Following his definition of a system quoted previously in this article he continues:

"Systems may consist of atoms, stars, switches, springs, wires, bones, gases, mathematical variables, equations, laws and processes." [4]

Nowhere in this list does he refer to businesses or people; nowhere in his book does he suggest the use of systems engineering models in business.

Bertalanffy remains conservative:

"General systems theory in its present form is one—and still very imperfect—model among others." Even then, this organismic picture would not claim to be a 'nothing but' philosophy: it would remain conscious that it only presents certain aspects of reality . . . but never exhaustive, exclusive or final." [5]

In contrast is the Forrester definition quoted above. Later, in his book, he says:

"Industrial dynamics models in their purpose and origin will be . . . similar to models of engineering systems . . . concentration must be on those factors that determine the characteristics of information feedback systems—structure, amplification and delays."

Even more ambitious is Wiener:

"It is the thesis of this book that society can only be understood through a study of the messages and the communication facilities which belong to it. . . ." [6]

THE ERROR IN THE "TOTAL" APPROACH

In a nutshell the objection to the "totality" of systems approach is that there is an assumption that this approach is the most important one.[7] This assumption is translated into practice by writers who define the role of change agents such as systems analysts in terms of the total systems concept.

In terms of this concept, the role of the change agents is to design the business system in terms of *flows* of information, materials, money and people, and to persuade members of the enterprise to adopt the system or subsystem so designed. The author has never come across a situation where this has actually been achieved nor has he read an account of where

* From J. W. Forrester, *Industrial Dynamics*, John Wiley & Sons, New York, 1961, p. 67.

[4] *Ibid.*, p. 60.

[5] Bertalanffy, *General System Theory—A Critical Review*, Yearbook of the Society for General Systems Research, Vol. VII, 1962, p. 10.

[6] Norbert Weiner, *The Human Use of Human Beings—Cybernetics and Society*, Doubleday-Anchor, New York, 1954, p. 16.

[7] The reason for the error lies in what the author calls the Magical Fallacy.

this has been done. This may be coincidental or it may be because of the following:

1. The total systems approach in business makes no attempt to explain, predict or understand why the human members of the business system act the way they do. It is concerned with components of a business system in the same way as communication theory is concerned with electronic components in a communications system, but it offers little or no understanding of those components either as individuals or as members of business organizations.

2. If it cannot explain the way things are, the total systems approach cannot be expected to explain the way things are going to be. Insofar as the total systems approach is weak analytically with regard to the most significant aspects of the business system (viz., the people), it must also be weak in predicting future developments with regard to people.

ILLUSTRATIONS OF THE MYTH

In order to demonstrate the points we have been making we are going to discuss two articles, both heavily influenced by the total systems concept.

The first is "Analyzing an Overall System" by Charles J. Berg.[8] Early in his article he defines a business system as a:

". . . set of policies, rules, and procedures which defines the actions, responsibilities, and authorities of all elements of a business organization in the day-by-day conduct of its normal activities."

This is all-encompassing, and justifies us as classifying it as being a holistic or total approach. How does Mr. Berg use it? The core of his article is concerned with the stepwise "analytical technique for defining our present position and for use as a systems reference point. Step One is the use of the conventional flow chart of the existing system, with each step analyzed and measured showing the amount of time, money and physical distance required in each processing component. It is not unusual to find at this stage that unnecessary transportation, time and money are incorporated into the system. Step Two relies on the information previously produced, but it is a modified form of the same information. This is the input-output analysis chart. This technique clearly depicts the multitudinous uses of various data. Generally it can be stated that where many inputs are used to devise many outputs, potential systems improvements are of a high order. Step Three is to relate the present system as described in steps one and two above into financial terminology. What lines on the statement are affected and what are the potential improvements available? Step Four is the allocation of people responsibility for the planned systems improvement, along with specific financial objectives to be attained. Step Five is to accomplish the improvements resulting from the analysis of the above information."

Diagramatically Berg expresses his approach as shown in Figure 1.

But the author does not fulfill his promise. In terms of his own definition of a business system his analytical technique is mainly concerned with "procedures and actions." He refers to policies, rules, responsibilities and authorities *of all elements of a business organization* in his definition of a business system quoted above, and says precious little about them in his analytical technique. Under which of his stepwise analytical techniques could one consider the following problems which have to be considered in any business organization?

What business should we be in? For example, should we diversify our operations, or consolidate? Should our business be divisionalized along product lines, customer grouping, or geographic areas? Should our engineering function be centralized or decentralized or along some combination of both?

In fact these problems cannot be subsumed under the techniques proposed because they are too narrow. The promise of total systems—evident in the definition—remains unfulfilled in the proposals for its creation.

Similar objections come to mind with a second article by Dr. R. L. Martino.[9] But in this case the gap between promise and proposal is even more blatant. The promise lies in the title: "The Development and Installation of a Total Management System."

Most business people are inclined to accept the simple notion that management is con-

[8] *Systems & Procedures Journal*, November–December, 1963.

[9] "The Development and Installation of a Total Management System," *Data Processing for Management*, April 1963, p. 31.

cerned with governing and controlling of the activities of a company, somewhat analogous to the executive branch of the government of a state. To enlarge "management" to "total management system" emphasizes the pervasiveness of the phenomena and also its completeness and orderliness. This promise is not borne out by the following:

". . . The primary objective in developing a total management system should be the production of detailed up-to-the-minute summaries of the past and the use of these summaries to project future activity. In essence the functions of a total management system are: (1) To predict; (2) To compare the prediction with actual results; and (3) To produce the deviations between the predicted and the actual."

In other words, the total system conceptualizers, when they really get down to it, talk of designing flows of information to enable management to do its job better. Martino represents this diagramatically in Figure 2.

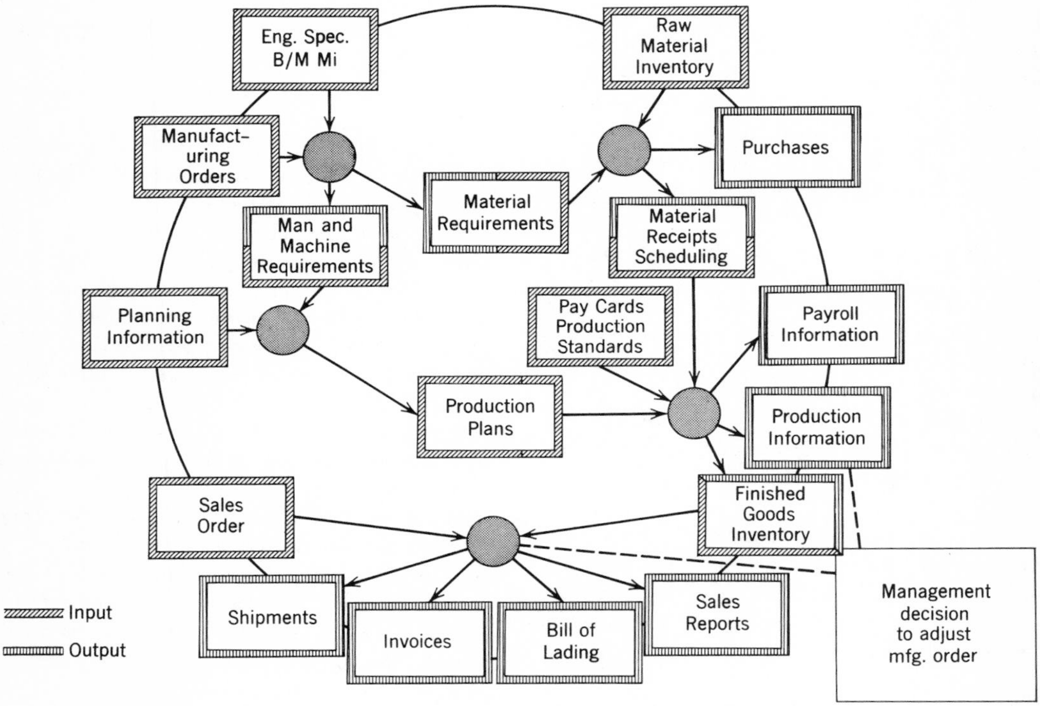

FIG. 1. The stepwise analytical techniques shown here are too narrow to fulfill the promise evident in the definition of total systems.

ONE: If you have a manufacturing order and this is combined with an engineering specification, bills of material and manufacturing information, these can be combined and materials information, manpower and the facilities required can be determined.
TWO: With material requirements being compared to raw material inventories, purchases and material receipts schedules can be derived.
THREE: Returning now to the manpower and facilities requirements, combining and comparing this with planning information, we can evolve specific production plans.
FOUR: Material receipts schedules and pay cards, along with production standards and the production plans, can be integrated to produce payrolls, production data and finished goods inventory.
FIVE: Coordinating the information of a sales order with that of the finished goods inventory, we can produce shipments, invoices, bills of lading and sales receipts.
SIX: Finally, we can build management decisions into the system which are necessary to operate it most effectively.

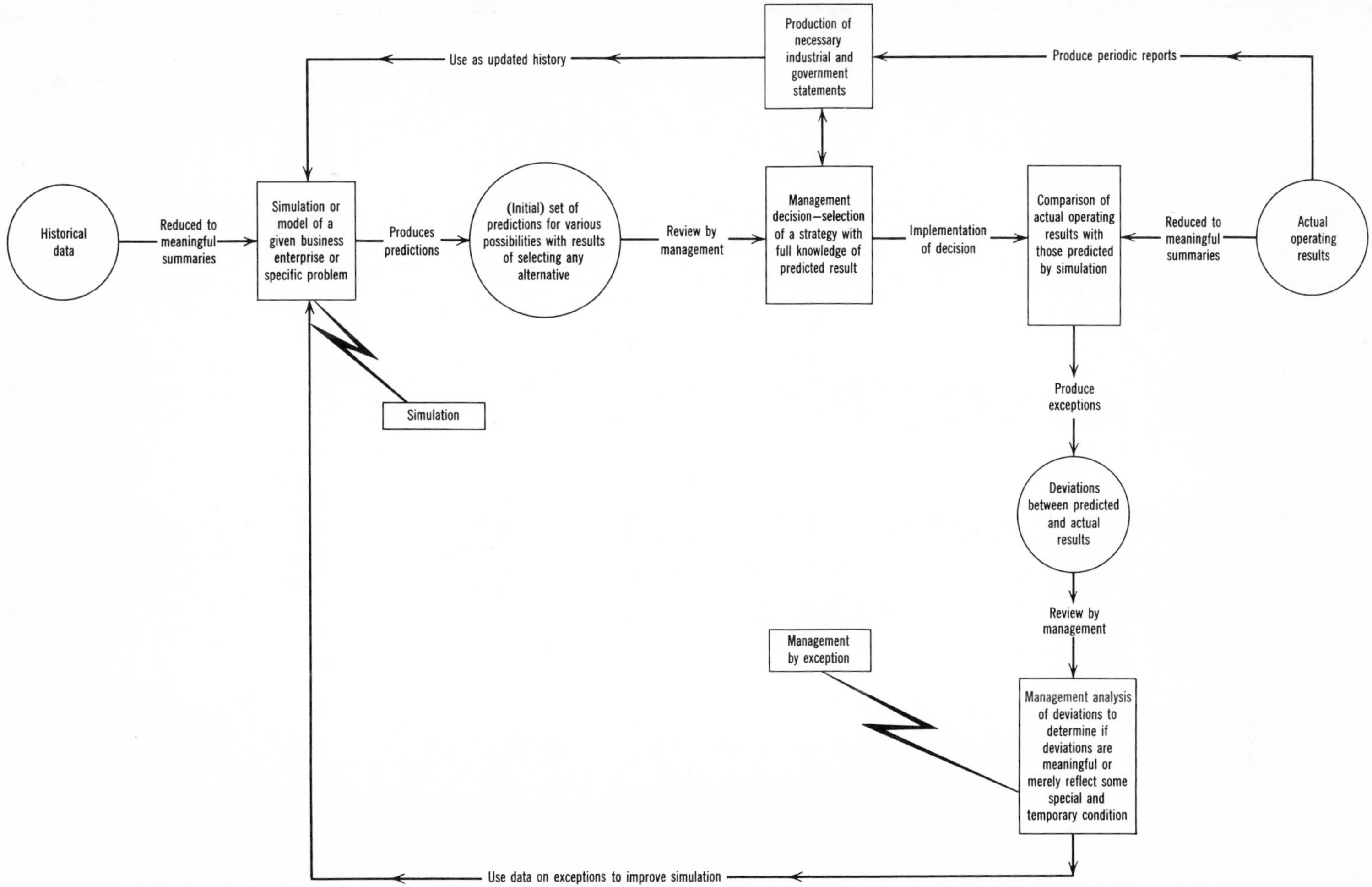

FIG. 2. This diagram shows what management does with various kinds of information. Management itself, however, is not part of the total management system, for nowhere is there any phase where management looks at itself or the organization of which it is a part.

The figure shows what management does with various kinds of information. In Martino's model, management *itself* is not part of the total management system, for nowhere is there any phase where management looks at itself or the organization of which it is a part. It is as though management were something like the driver of a car, detached; as though, like a car driver, management made the decisions, the "system" carried them out.

Factories, warehouses and saleshouses and other industries, services, utilities—whatever the business exists for—consist of much more than information handling systems glorified into some state of "totality." Just as a map of a country may cover the whole of it, it is not a "total" depiction of it, because in a country there are other dimensions and features that cannot be shown on a map. Similarly, in a business there are other dimensions and features which cannot be subsumed under the kinds of total systems we have been discussing.

REQUIREMENTS OF A GENERAL BUSINESS THEORY

What, then, are the theoretical requirements of change agents in business? The following thoughts are offered as criteria for basic theory:

A. Understanding for Action

1. It must be capable of understanding current problems of business. Therefore,
2. It should be capable of realistic predictions on consequences of proposed actions.
3. It should provide a basis for establishing direction for proposed change.

B. Basis for Theoretical Development

An acceptable basic theory should be broad enough to include other more specific theories. If, for example, we reject total systems theory as a basic tool, the basic tool we do adopt should be capable of covering the valuable aspects of such a theory.

OUTLINE OF A BASIC THEORY

What follows is a skeletal account of a theory which meets these requirements:

1. A business is primarily a social human group. The machines, however vast, are origi-

THE MAGICAL FALLACY

A danger in the development or use of symbols is due to the fact that they are selective; ". . . they do not express all that is given but only the aspects and relations considered important for the purpose at hand; hence there is always an aspect of hazard and adventure in the symbols from which the hypotheses are built . . .

"Symbols thus, by their selective nature, readily take on a normative role; being abstract, they tend to contain only that aspect of the referent which the selecting and symbolizing agent considers important or useful . . .

"The magical use of symbols is a natural but illogical development of this normative valuation function . . . magic imputes to the symbol itself an operative force . . . magic ignores the limitations imposed on symbols by their symbolic character."[1]

This error, which might well be called the magical fallacy, is present in the total systems concept. Battersby, in criticizing Forrester's *Industrial Dynamics,* says:

"Yet another source of disquiet on reading this book is the feeling that the author has fallen in love with his theory. The Galatean complex, like the deification of computers, is well known in the scientific world, its main symptom being the urge to conceal or excuse the loved one's blemishes and shortcomings."[2]

Geisler, in reviewing the *Theory and Management of Systems,* by Johnson, Kast & Rosenzweig (McGraw-Hill, New York, 1963), says:

"This is a disappointing book because it presents a glossy and superficial picture . . . the book seems to be a sales brochure trying to persuade the reader that the magical introduction of the systems approach opens the way to the wonders of modern management."[3]

[1] Leroy E. Noemker, *Symbol and Myth in Philosophy* in Altizer et al.: *Truth, Myth and Symbol,* Prentice-Hall Spectrum, 1962, Englewood Cliffs, N.J., p. 118.

[2] A. Battersby, "Book Reviews," *Operational Research Quarterly,* Vol. 14, No. 1, March 1963, p. 98.

[3] Murray A. Geisler, "Book Reviews," *Management Science,* Vol. 9, No. 4, July 1963, p. 702.

nated by and operated by human beings. Therefore, the theoretical basis should be human oriented.

2. There are three aspects of human groups which are important to the understanding of a business. They are objectives, or purpose; activities, or the actual work performed; and relationships which include cooperative and functional as well as the ever-present man/boss relationship. In addition, there are three corresponding concepts pertaining to the individual: values, status and activities.

3. The basis of the approach suggested is, first, that there are certain desirable or healthy conditions for these group and individual aspects, particularly in their relationship to one another. Second, it can be assumed that these conditions do not necessarily apply at all times. Third, it is suggested that the lack of desirable conditions applying will lead to the occurrence of certain effects or symptoms. Fourth, the approach envisages the use of various techniques to reveal these symptoms. Fifth, it is suggested that the symptoms can be used to identify the *causes* of malfunction, and sixth, that planning and executing projects which rectify causes are the proper work of systems analysts, or other change agents, in business.

4. The activities of business are only one of many aspects. Only when this aspect is viewed against its proper background of group purpose (or objectives) and structure, and individuals' values and status, should it be elaborated into a "totality" of system.

5. It is entirely possible to make use of the valuable aspects of systems theory (discussed in the early part of this article) within these other concepts, but then the systems aspect is no longer "total" but ancillary.

A PROPOSED ROLE FOR SYSTEMS ANALYSIS

How can the role of the systems analyst be met in view of these criticisms? The senior systems man in a company may be analogous to a cabinet minister in charge of communications (embracing, for instance, tele-postal-road-rail and air-communications). A minister of communications is concerned with the development of channels for the transmission of information in whatever form. Similarly, the VP of communications with a firm should be concerned with the development and maintenance of communication networks which best achieve company, and divisional if necessary, purpose(s).

This is far-reaching in that it would be extending throughout the whole but it is not holistic or "total" in the Wiener or Forrester sense. Systems departments, therefore, are not analogous to the management of a *real* whole (e.g., a company, a plant or a division).

Let us again take a geographic analogy. All the cities in North America are connected by a system of roads, but urban development—as in the case of corporate development—means working with the wholes in the situation.

City management and development undoubtedly requires auxiliary and parallel development and modification in the road system, and occasionally cities have to adjust to a road development program under the control of a wider authority which constitutes a natural whole,[10] such as a state government.

Roads in this way are analogous to the communications networks of business. Corporations as natural wholes are composed of other, smaller wholes (divisions, operating departments, staff functions, etc.), and the role of management is the continuous mutual adjustment of these parts to one another in order to achieve company goals. This process of continuous adjustment requires the continuous development of new communications transmittal, reception and storage, and it is the role of the systems analyst to carry out this development.

Sometimes, as in the case of a city having to adjust to the road development by a wider authority, the natural wholes (e.g., divisions, departments) within a company have to adjust to the communications system imposed upon them by the company as a whole.

The total systems concept implies—indeed some of its exponents, as we have seen, are quite explicit—that the communications system is the basis for understanding and changing society, or the micro-society that the corporation forms. This is not true; the systems concept is not that "total."

[10] J. C. Smuts, *Holism and Evolution,* Compass Books, New York, 1961.

31. CAN WE INTEGRATE SYSTEMS WITHOUT INTEGRATING MANAGEMENT?

WILLIAM J. CROWLEY*

It is now almost 50 years since the death of the world's pioneer efficiency expert, Frederich Winslow Taylor. During his relatively short life (he died at 59), Taylor developed and put into practice the basic principles of production efficiency and scientific management that contributed heavily to the success of American business in the 20th century. He developed and popularized the management tool that we recognize as the principle of *exception,* which is typified in the production and management accounting systems that we refer to as *standard cost* systems. His methods were tremendously successful with respect to the production of physical goods, and today his pioneering is fully recognized in efficiency engineering with respect to non-physical and productive service-type work, office and clerical work.

MANAGEMENT BY EXCEPTION

Taylor recognized the value of up-to-the-minute, accurate reporting. I recall, back in my student days, studying cost accounting. Modern then were the standard cost systems of Western Electric Company and the Link Belt Company. Under these systems early each morning the plant managers were given reports showing production for the previous day, with full action stimulating detail of *all variations* or *exceptions* from predetermined "standard" performance that had occurred with respect to men and material. These systems brought the manager valuable new management tools:

1. Only exceptions from expected optimum performance were brought to the attention of the manager, thus freeing him from the oppressive paper work burden to devote himself to problems that needed his attention.
2. Facts were brought to the attention of the manager immediately so that profit-making action could be taken when needed, or a primitive "real time" management information system.

Taylor's ideas stimulated a real production revolution. Many of the writers during his lifetime predicted tremendous savings in management time and effort and many other spectacular results.

Following World War I came the office mechanization—another revolution and the age of the NCR, Burroughs, McBee and IBM card systems. I can clearly remember the pitches of the machine salesmen, particularly during the 10 years from 1930 to 1940. The glowing sales talks about how the new systems and machines would give more data, more accurate data, and faster data. How management problems would be reduced. How the principle of "exception" reporting would come into general use. How decision making would be placed on a firmer basis. How managers' time would be saved and less effort would be spent ferreting out the necessary facts, and so on.

What has happened as a result of these two "great revolutions"? We have reduced physical work to its simplest possible components and replaced most of human labor with machine labor. We have reduced the work week of physical workers by half. We have increased the clerical, analytical, budget, audit and other white collar data-gathering and analyzing staffs immeasurably. But we have done very little to reduce the management decision-making tasks. In fact, we have increased the load on management as the result of tax, labor, anti-trust,

SOURCE: *Journal of Data Management* (August, 1966), pp. 14–18, 23–24. Reprinted by permission of Data Processing Association.

* Northern Illinois Gas Co.

wage, and many other laws passed by the state and the federal governments.

THE EDP REVOLUTION

Now we find ourselves in a new whirl of activity, the *electronic data processing revolution*. Before we've even reached the point where these new devices will take care of low level volume sorting and printing duties, the prognosticators are doing away with management, or at least, with that loosely defined group referred to as middle management.

The general idea, as we get into it now for the third time, is that:

1. More data will be processed.
2. Data will be processed faster.
3. The final synthesized results will be more accurate and more complete.
4. The principle of *exception reporting* will spring into full flower.
5. Final results will be delivered in such time that corrective management control, if needed, can be exercised.

As a result, top management can make more decisions without help from middle management, and finally middle management, for the third time since 1900, becomes obsolete.

To give you an up-to-date picture of top management operating in this new environment, let's turn to the *Fortune* magazine of April, 1964:

Members of Westinghouse Electric Corporation's executive committee recently filed into a small room in the company's new Tele-Computer Center near Pittsburgh and prepared to look at their business as no group of executives had ever looked at business before. In front of them was a large video screen, and to one side of the screen was a "remote inquiry" device that seemed a cross between a typewriter and a calculator. As the lights dimmed, the screen lit up with current reports from many of the company's important divisions—news of gross sales, orders, profitability, inventory levels, manufacturing costs, and various measures of performance based on such data. When the officers asked the remote inquiry device for additional information or calculations, distant computers *shot* back the answers in seconds.

TOTAL INTEGRATED SYSTEM

Here we have an example of an up-to-date, so-called *integrated system*, that is, one so designed that it provides timely collection, processing and reporting of all necessary management information. Now, if this system is a true *integrated system*, it will:

1. Supply historical data and analyses of that data.
2. Supply "on-line" data, that is, factual material picked right out of the system as fast as they are generated.
3. Supply data in "real time," fast enough so that management can exercise necessary management control instantly.

There is no doubt that the Westinghouse management information center does a remarkable job of work. But in my opinion, it has tackled only the easiest part of the total problem. It hasn't yet started to resolve the really tough management problems.

One factor that has set top business decision makers apart has been their drive to have the best possible knowledge of their business. These men have never failed to use all possible means to get accurate, timely data. That is why we have statistical departments, cost control departments, internal auditors and outside accountants, along with daily analyses of sales, purchases, inventories, and even customer complaints. That is why EDP systems have come into widespread use.

The business man uses *facts* as the basis for decisions—if he can possibly get facts. He insists on better and better information systems but, in most cases, only to the extent that they can be economically justified. I feel certain that as computer systems improve and their cost reduces, more and more computer-based equipment will be used for data assembling and processing tasks, and as a result we will develop to the point where we will approach integration so far as it relates to internally generated information needed for management control. I am certain that this progress will take place with increasing rapidity, even without deliberate integration of management.

However, there does not exist today a single system which is completely integrated for complete management control. In the past 10 years, there have been many dreams of attaining the goal of *total integration*, but up to this date it is still a dream. We hear of occasional claims that a "total integrated" system has been achieved, but on close investigation it is clear that the *goal* has been only partially achieved.

Recently, Dr. Roger Vergin (Assistant Professor of Business Administration at the University of California) and A. J. Grimes, as Ph.D. candidate at the University of Minnesota, made a thorough study of 11 firms that claimed to have successful "total integrated" systems. The study showed that not one of the 11 firms had a true integrated EDP system.[1] Byron K. Ledgerwood, editor of *Control Engineering*, wrote in *Input for Modern Management* (Summer, 1964):

> The public is being told the story that a significant portion of American business and productive operations are under the complete control of mechanical brains called computers. This conclusion is false.
>
> The truth is that after years of hard work by many engineers, we have barely scratched the surface. Their little scratches have been magnified into large crevices. Our successes have been primarily successes in mechanization, replacing manual manipulation, but not human intelligence. The next step, that of using controls and computers for decision making, is in its infancy.
>
> Every one of the present successful prototypes, in various stages of completion, is blown up to sound like a full scale, management-replacing "thinking machine." It only takes a quick tour around the plant floors and working offices of American industrty to show how false this is.

Even American Airlines' $30 million airline reservation system (known as SABRE) is not a "total integrated" system, even though it is the largest "real time" data processing system in operation. This system is essentially an "inventory" control type of operation. It affects day-to-day management decision making only at a very low level.

But this system does prove that even more sophisticated integrated systems are technically possible with presently available equipment, and with modern communication methods. Generally, today they are too expensive for the benefits sought.

At this point I'd like to interject one reservation. I do visualize *total integrated* systems that will collect, digest and deliver decision-inspiring data to management, but only that which can be generated from the flow of activities carried on by the firm's own employees, that is, data relating to inventory, availability and price; manpower availability and cost; sales and deliveries, and so on.

I do not visualize total integrated systems that will synthesize for management decision purposes all the facts relating to ambient political, economic and other factors that the management would like to have at its fingertips in order to remove all hazards from business projections and decisions.

But now, with "integrated systems" (related to internally generated facts) almost a certainty, why must we worry about "integrating" management?

TO INTEGRATE MANAGEMENT

Let me clarify the meaning of "integration." For our purposes, to "integrate management" means to bring top management personnel closer to development and operation of the EDP systems, and to incorporate the EDP control echelon into the top decision-making group of the enterprise.

We will get integrated systems even if we don't yet integrate management. The systems will come regardless of the attitude managements take with respect to integrating management. They will come because EDP equipment will be improved and made more economical. Our EDP staffs will become ingenious in the use of the equipment. It won't be absolutely necessary to integrate the procedures and system design staffs into top management to make broader use of EDP equipment and methods.

Management requires facts about the business. The responsibility for the operation of an integrated EDP system places the EDP staff in a strategic position, in that it has first access to timely, factual data. On first thought, this would seem to indicate that the computer operator or chief of EDP staff stands *ipso facto* in line to be Chairman of the Board of Directors.

But I don't happen to buy that idea, and here are my reasons. Let's go back to the West-

[1] The findings of Grimes and Vergin are presented in detail in "Management Myths & EDP," *California Management Review* 7 (Fall, 1964), pp. 59–70.

inghouse EDP system, where the executive committee sat before the large video screen, soaking up facts about their business. What kind of facts were they assimilating? Only internally generated facts made up the bases for the data they were viewing, facts relating to level and volume of orders, gross sales, inventory levels, their own manufacturing costs, and so on.

THE UNANSWERABLE QUESTIONS

Did these men make any decisions as they sat there? For example, did they telephone the Pittsburgh plant, and tell the superintendent, "You're pretty heavy on 1½″ brass flat head screws?" No, they did not—they merely sat there and absorbed some up-to-date internal information about their own operations. But the real problems were not collected, reported, analyzed and reported to them so as to simplify their tough management decisions. By the *real* problems, I mean the unanswerable, wait-out type of problems that are always hanging over the top manager's head, and which he must continually consider as he makes his day-to-day decisions. Here are some of the types of problems I mean:

—What effect will the new Labor government in Great Britain have on our sales there?

—Will there be any tariff changes?

—Will steel unions go out on strike this year, and if so, for how long?

—What new laws are likely to come out of Congress next year that will be either hurtful or helpful?

—What factors are causing the slowdown in our Pittsburgh plant, and what is the best way of taking care of them?

—What kind of a decision are we going to get out of the anti-trust case now pending in Appellate Court?

—Competitor "A" has taken certain steps which are hurting us. What counter measures should we employ?

—The IRS has just handed us a ruling that will increase our income taxes by several million dollars. What steps can we take?

—The SEC has just put out 68 new rulings. How do they affect us?

—The anti-trust division of the Department of Justice has just issued several decisions that make some of our operations appear to be contrary to the law as interpreted.

—The Fair Employment Practices Commission wants to send staff men to examine all our employment records. They claim we have knowingly violated the law.

—The Patent Court has ruled against us in a key case. What to do?

—Inflation.

—Business conditions.

And so on.

As one writer put it,

> The world has immemorially underestimated the order of talent required to run a complex business, particularly a highly competitive enterprise. Compared to the relatively formal problems normally encountered by engineers, physicists, and even medicos, the problems confronting the high corporate executives are gnarled and ill-structured. Wherever he looks deeply, he gazes into uncertainty.[2]

In short, the "total integrated" system as generally expected to develop is, even in its most modern concept, a limited system. It gives the top executive a clearer, more timely picture of what he already knows, better than anything else in the world, but it does *nothing* at all with respect to unsolved, unanswered problems that hang eternally over his head like a dense smog.[3]

So when we consider these so-called "total integrated" information systems, let's get away from the idea that they are going to make possible "push button problem solving."

If we consider the range of problems and uncertainties facing management, and the top man found that his chief of EDP staff could satisfactorily handle all of them, that EDP man would be moved up to Assistant to the Chairman at the earliest possible date, and I am sure he would be Chairman not too long thereafter. (This might be called "upstream integration.")

My point is that integration of the EDP specialist into top management will depend on his education, his intelligence, and his ability.

[2] Gilbert Burck, "Management Will Never Be The Same Again"—*Fortune,* August, 1964.

[3] But Westinghouse is experimenting with a plan to produce "Directive and Environmental Information" covering employees, stockholders, customers, government and the economy. The thought is to provide data that will help reduce uncertainty with respect to external environment.

It will not depend simply on the fact that his job has given him monopolistic access to valuable, timely, internal company business data.

Another point to be emphasized is that management must take advantage of all resources. It must train promising candidates for higher level jobs. It should try for all the advantages inherent in broadening men through job rotation, special assignments, and additional formal education. Also, the individual who aspires to a higher position must take a hand in the training. He must deliberately give up free time for additional education. And I will insist here, that a thorough education in EDP methods and equipment and nothing else, is *not* a key to an office in the Chairman's suite.

What about "downstream" integration of management? By this I mean the efforts of top management to learn more about the EDP system. My feeling is that this is not too important. The chief executive who has learned for years to rely on staff analysts, chemists, engineers, statisticians, cost control experts, budget experts, tax experts, legal experts, and other data analysis subgroups, can learn to rely on EDP staff experts. Top management, without necessarily becoming specialized in mathematics, statistics and electronics, will learn to use realistically the services of various staff specialists in these fields, as computer based techniques advance in the future.

In the future, however, I have no doubt that enlightened job rotation programs will ensure that promising candidates for top positions serve an apprenticeship on the EDP staff. The real advantage here is the fact that properly oriented managers will develop a greater feeling of security in using EDP based data and will also learn the limitations of that data, just as we learned years ago the limitations inherent in summarizations arrived at by applying statistical techniques to masses of raw data.

THREE KINDS OF MANAGEMENT DECISIONS

Management decision making falls into three rather broad levels,[4] which we might refer to as:

1. Operational Control—limited control of specific movements that are part of a tactical plan, without authority to change the basic framework or objective of the movement.
2. Tactical Control—the broader control required to manage forces and resources to carry out specific plans, generally including authority to vary the execution to reach the specified objectives.
3. Strategic Control—the science of planning, of both short and long ranges, setting policies and goals, making decisions relative to major commitments and resources, including the foreseeing of future problems and designing counter measures.

In many types of operational control, *i.e.*, the lowest level of management decision making, the computer has been of great help in making available the "decision-indicating" data. For example, this would cover activities such as inventory control or production scheduling, which in many plants is practically a phase of inventory control. In these areas, the variables are largely quantitative, and hence adaptable to EDP methodology.

When we move to tactical control, however, we find a great many judgment factors of qualitative nature that must be considered. Here the computer based system is of less help in decision making.

When we move up to the highest level, strategic planning, we find the computer of even less help. At this level of decision making, speed is not always vital. Also, high accuracy of data cannot be expected because of the nature of the problems, and decisions are based heavily on qualitative factors and on judgment in predicting future events.

Nevertheless, as time passes, the computer will be of additional help at the tactical and strategic levels. We will extend our problem-solving ability gradually through the use of *simulation* techniques. By simulation techniques, the analyst attempts to build an analog or pattern of the management system. He then utilizes all available information in attempts to quantify the results or outcome of different courses of action that might result from different management decisions, even to the extent of attempting to measure the odds of the possibility of each occurrence.

When an executive is trying to make up his mind about a problem, he weighs the *pros* and *cons* and tries to estimate the odds in his favor that would be obtained if he were to make a

[4] See John Dearden, "Can Management Information Be Automated?" *Harvard Business Review*, March-April, 1964, pp. 338–351.

particular decision. Simulation is a method of expanding and formalizing this process far beyond the capability of the human mind to do so. Here the speed of the computer enables us to quickly test the possible effects of different courses of action that might reasonably be projected.

HYPOTHETICAL MODELS

Another method that will be developed with respect to difficult business decisions will be the use of hypothetical models, which then can be varied and the results of changes tested rapidly on the computer. George M. Muschamp, in his article "The Emerging Philosophy of Systems Management," says: "Experimental model making has been steadily increasing in use for many years in its physical scale model form, in electrical analog form and in mathematical model form. Its use is accelerating."[5]

Still ahead of us, too, is the possibility of programming computers so that they will tend to simulate the processes of the human intellect in problem solving. It will take great ingenuity to design programs that will enable the computer to use intellectual shortcuts or rules of thumb that business men must use in difficult decisions. (The technicians refer to this as programming the computer "heuristically" so that it will use practical methods of problem solving, in terms of means *vs.* ends.)

But we have not yet arrived at the point where we can freely and profitably use these methods. The impact of technological change on the decision making process of the top managers of business and industry has not amounted to a revolution. Muschamp, in the article referred to above, points out an important factor limiting use of models in management decision making today. The time factor in model design and analyses is such that it forces short cuts that cause some doubts as to the accuracy of results. Thus our model analyses today tend to be hybrid art-science or hybrid empirical-mathematical systems. However, more progress will be made in this field. The success of our efforts will depend upon the quality and application of the specialists who learn the methods and how to apply them.

[5] George M. Muschamp, "The Emerging Philosophy of Systems Management," *Journal of Data Management,* October, 1964.

Top management will have to learn to utilize EDP staff men. But when they do, they must keep in mind that the results which these staff men produce *will not be the answers* to business problems. They will tend to be a series of possible answers, one for each of a number of different alternatives where variable patterns of action are possible; also that the answers submitted will be correct only if it can be assumed that the numerical values assigned to express the effect of various qualitative factors in the equation have been properly chosen.

Confronted with a series of possible answers furnished by the data processing staff, the top executive is faced with a decision-making burden. He must decide:

1. Have I chosen the right analyst?
2. Has he properly evaluated the various courses of action? *i.e.,* Are the various formulae correct?
3. Have reasonable numerical relationships been assigned to relate qualitative variables to the problem?

COMPUTER AND COMMON SENSE

After considering all this, one expert said, "To build all the variables and constraints that are involved here into an EDP program really seems to be a complex problem, and I am not at all sure at this point that the answer as developed on a computer will give as good a result as the common sense and experienced judgment that top management now provides."

At the present time, "real time—on line" systems are in use at financial exchanges and race tracks. They are used as reporting systems for commodity exchange, financial reporting system of the New York Stock Exchange, and totalizer boards at horse race tracks. Have you ever wondered why the computer isn't used to forecast results of horse races, or stock prices?

Investors and speculators have always recognized the need for timely information about the events in which they participate. But isn't it interesting that all these "real time" systems are "rapid but historical" systems? They list and evaluate only what the investors or bettors have done up to the particular moment. But when the investor or speculator needs *prediction* data based on the countless variables that exist, many of which are qualitative, he must depend on the human brain.

As another interesting speculation, I do not even care to cogitate about the Orwellian implications that are inherent in "push button management decision making." When that time comes, my mind shrinks from entertaining the likelihood that all private enterprise will vanish, and "Big Brother" will truly dominate all human decisions and actions.

I am sure that many EDP department heads and specialists will find fault with my conclusions. Just as in every line of endeavor that requires considerable study, we find a movement today toward a professionalization of the EDP work. This includes a striving towards greater recognition by the top management levels, based on far too many instances on the novel nature of the work and not on the value of the individual as a manager. We see considerable evidence of this in discussion and studies relating to the place of the EDP department in the enterprise.

CONCLUSIONS

First of all, we should recognize that in many cases integrated systems offer an economical and efficient means of gathering and synthesizing mass data of quantitative nature. We have no proof as yet that they are effective in extracting the inferences that a good manager could obtain. Collection and synthesis of mass quantitative data is only one aspect of problem solving. Another aspect is the extraction of meaningful conclusions from the data.

Secondly, these systems process only quantitative data which are chiefly internally generated. Except for some minor applications, they do not provide collection and analysis of external and qualitative data.

I would like to add that, if the EDP department functions as it should, as a true service department for the benefit of the total enterprise, it can operate from any point in the organization.

It doesn't make much difference how we answer the question: "Can we integrate systems without integrating management?" We are going to progress toward integrated systems. These systems, although fulfilling the definition of "total system" concept, will for a long time to come gather and analyze chiefly internally generated data. They will generate results that will lighten only the easiest part of top management's present decision-making burden.

Management will become integrated as a result of job rotation and promotion of capable EDP generalists. Top management, driven as it always is to know what's going on in the shop, will devote itself to learning what must be learned of computers and data systems in order to keep his job.

32. MANAGEMENT INFORMATION SYSTEMS

J. W. KONVALINKA * AND H. G. TRENTIN †

In a day when words are used with no real attempt to define them, it should be no surprise to find that some people are puzzled by the term "management information system." For one thing, people tend to confuse a management information system with an electronic data processing (or computer) system. Are they the same? If so, are all computers management information systems? If not, can you have a management information system without a computer?

Another series of questions surrounds the concept of the so-called "total" system. To what extent can all the managerial and decision making processes of a business be systematized? How necessary is it that all systems of the business be combined into one "total system"? In short, does a management information system (M.I.S.) have to be a total system? Finally, whether or not this is so, can an M.I.S. help you in planning and controlling your business?

All this confusion is blocking progress in the development and application of many of the newer management tools. This article is an attempt to put these questions into perspective and to suggest answers based on our experience in assisting clients to design and install management information systems. To do this we have divided the subject into four sections: (1) information and decisions, (2) development of M.I.S. concepts, (3) what an M.I.S. is, and (4) how you get an M.I.S. The emphasis is on the practical rather than the theoretical aspects of the question, and we have drawn examples from our experience to serve as illustrations wherever possible.

Information is vital to good decisions. The more pertinent and timely the information the better the decision—if the decision maker is equally capable in each case.

Military strategists will tell you that armies run as much on intelligence as they do on food. They will also tell you that no general ever has all the information he feels he needs before making a decision. An example: the decision General Eisenhower made to cross the English Channel in the face of an unexpected period of stormy weather and uncertainty about the disposition of the German forces in France. The winning general makes his decisions on a timely basis, using the best information available to him at the time and important intangible elements like experience, judgment, nerve, and an intuitive feel for people and situations.

Business managers operate in the same way. They continually make decisions regarding purchases, sales prices, products, people, acquisitions, and many other things which involve uncertainties of varying degrees about all of the pertinent facts and about all of the probable consequences of their decisions.

Let us not forget, though, that the amount and nature of the information desired by business managers vary with their personalities. Some are impatient with elaborate detail study and preparation and like to make quick decisions based on the information at hand as they begin their deliberations. These men get their best results when historical or environmental data are not the major influencing elements in the decision, for example, with a decision involving the introduction of a new product. Other managers delay decisions too long waiting for information that may be helpful but actually is not vital. Between the two extremes fall the vast majority of business managers, who generally achieve the right balance between waiting for more information and making quick decisions—but, like General Eisenhower, wish that more pertinent and timely information could somehow be made available on an economically feasible basis.

SOURCE: *Management Services* (September–October, 1965), pp. 27–39. Reprinted by permission of *Management Services*.

* Arthur Andersen & Co.
† Arthur Andersen & Co.

This important relationship between information and decisions has led to the great preoccupation with management information systems. The question has become an increasingly pertinent one in recent years. Tremendous information pressures have been exerted on every business by such external forces as rapid technological change, improved communications, and increased competition and by such internal stresses as interdepartmental rivalries, misdirected effort, and a general lack of control.

But if the pressures have grown, so have the means of coping with those pressures. The advent of high-speed data processing equipment and better communications (which also help to cause the pressure) offer an adequate solution to the problem. So do modern management techniques and scientific assistance such as operations research. The problem then becomes one of facing up to the information challenges and selecting the right combination of modern tools to respond effectively.

DEVELOPMENT OF M.I.S. CONCEPTS

Business literature in recent years has abounded with discussions of the need for and nature of management information systems.

The management scientists and operations researchers have made valuable contributions to better management decisions by the development of logical analytical approaches and specialized techniques. The operations researchers in particular have emphasized the importance of viewing the business as an integrated system and understanding the relationships among the various company functions. For instance, in tackling an inventory control problem, they have been more inclined than some of their predecessors to consider the impact on inventory decisions of forecasting methods, raw material purchasing strategies, production leveling requirements, and finished goods storage and distribution economics.

An example will illustrate. A highly fashion-oriented manufacturing company (whose M.I.S. will be described later), experienced heavy annual inventory losses because of markdowns of slow-moving styles at the end of the year. After various unsuccessful attempts to correct this condition, the problem was turned over to an operations researcher. The losses were traced to faulty forecasting based on salesmen's estimates, and a forecasting system was recommended which improved performance by a significant margin in its first full year of operation. Sales activity for several years was analyzed in complete detail to determine patterns of cumulative order build-up during the year. Based on the relation of early orders in the current year to the historical patterns, a system of projections of additional sales for the balance of the year was developed. A range of probabilities was determined at each reorder point which gave management an indication of its chances of selling various additional quantities of each style. This was expressed in dollars over the range of probabilities by applying unit profits anticipated if the additional goods were sold during the season and unit losses that would be realized if the additional styles had to be marked down at the end of the year.

After installation of this forecasting system, attention was turned to improving the system of buying raw material. Here the problem was one of reflecting the sensitivity in the demand for the finished product back into the purchasing commitments for material. This was done through an explosion of the material requirements for manufacturing and introduction into the final decision of such other factors as economic order quantity and the proper balance of inventory carrying costs.

With these two basic segments in place, the rest of the management planning and control structure was developed. Using similar approaches and enlisting the aid of specialists in data processing and production control where needed, the analysts made improvements in systems for deciding the desirable number of styles to be carried in the product line, scheduling and balancing operations, and developing data for short-range and long-range financial budgeting.

You can see from this example how logical it is to evolve an integrated information system to service all of the planning and control systems of a business. Sales and purchase figures, among others, are vital inputs to many of such systems and may readily be captured in suitable form in a well designed computer system and revised as required in the processing of data.

Management and research associations and electronic computer manufacturers have probably been more responsible for whetting the appetite of the businessman for an M.I.S. than any other source. We have all read the glowing promises in business literature and particularly in ads announcing new equipment. These seem to imply that computer systems are synonymous with management information systems and that management decisions can be automated.

Take the following excerpt from a recent newspaper ad of a computer manufacturer:

"The (blank computer) is a total management information system. It can give you a sure grasp of your business. The control of it. The understanding of it. That's what we mean by the best management control for your computer dollar.

"It can be analyst, planner, forecaster, designer, scheduler, controller, order processor, even customers' man. It can keep you informed, on line and in real time. It can free you to plan and work creatively. To focus on key decisions."

"COMPUTERITIS"

Computers have made possible the collection and dissemination of more information more quickly and economically. If used to process properly designed information flows, they will help achieve better management information systems—but they are not the automatic answer to the business manager's need for decision information. As a matter of fact, the cause of the computer has been unjustly hurt because it has too often been contracted for prematurely.

We have come to recognize the early signs of this condition. They involve undue preoccupation with how data will be processed and the characteristics of the hardware. We usually suggest at this point that hardware should be the last matter considered when thinking about an M.I.S. We tell the businessman who appears to be afflicted with "electronic computeritis" that he should first decide what kind of information he needs—how soon and often—and that what kind of equipment will do this best is a secondary, although an important, consideration. It is surprising to hear of the many early wrong notions that are dispelled by concentrating on the information requirements, with a consequent shrinkage to realistic size of the computer and communications plans.

Furthermore, large centralized data processing centers connected with areas of operation by wire communications facilities, sometimes called management information centers, are not necessarily a prerequisite to or concomitant of an M.I.S. The desirability of such large "figure factories" depends more on the size and nature of the business operation than on the nature of the M.I.S. Many excellent management information systems are serviced by local data processing centers, and the most common arrangement involves a combination of local and centralized centers.

Before leaving the role of computers as processors of integrated data for management information, we should emphasize their ability to use such data in specialized operations research techniques. For example, consider the use of linear programing, which is an analytical or computational technique for solving a general class of optimization problems involving many variables related in a complex way. The solution of these problems involves the attainment of a measure of effectiveness such as profits, costs, or quantities produced for a given set of restraining conditions, including material availability, production capacity, and government regulations. In a specific case, the linear programing technique may systematically search through unit cost and quantity tables of hundreds of alternatives for making products at various plants of a national company, shipping to and storing at various warehouses, and ultimately shipping to customers in order to arrive at an overall minimum cost solution. These many trial computations can be made by hand, but standardized computer programs are now available that reduce the time and cost and thereby extend the area of applicability of linear programing.

WHAT AN M.I.S. IS

In order to appreciate the significance of an M.I.S., we should explore the basic functions of management, namely, (1) planning, (2) execution, and (3) control.

The first function, which deals with company objectives and policies, covers the time period of, say, five or ten years forward. It is concerned with such things as total demand, share of market, new markets, new products, new plant sites, personnel sources and development, and capital requirements.

Execution, which involves carrying out the plans in the present, is what most of us in business do every day. We sell our products, manufacture more, build plants, hire people, pay our vendors and employees, and react to unplanned developments such as strikes and price cuts by competitors.

Control involves monitoring our execution by feedback techniques to determine that we are proceeding in accordance with plans and standards. The reports of our activities tell us how we are doing against sales quotas and expense budgets, whether we are in line on our capital appropriations expenditures, whether our manning tables conform to our standards, and so on through all phases of the business.

The management information system must provide the necessary intelligence on a timely basis to help management plan, execute, and control. Simply stated, an M.I.S. is a system of reports specially designed for this purpose, which means that they are position- or department-oriented to meet specific requirements. Incidentally, it was under the stress of this personal requirement that accounting and reporting of financial data were broadened over the years from a one-dimensional focus of "what did we spend our money for?" to a second dimension designed to show "who spent it and how does it correspond to budget?"—now referred to as "responsibility reporting."

Examples of some of the important elements which comprise an M.I.S. are the following:

1. Reports of historical company and environmental data for long- and short-range planning
2. Long- and short-range financial and operating budgets
3. Monthly financial and operating statements on a "responsibility" basis
4. Sales and order entry statistics, which provide input to many other systems such as sales quotas, salesmen's compensation, purchasing, manufacturing, shipping, and others
5. Reports to service the various control systems such as these:

   (a) Sales forecasting
   (b) Shipping and warehousing
   (c) Finished goods replenishment
   (d) Production control
   (e) Materials management
   (f) Manufacturing cost control
   (g) Personnel skills and manning control
   (h) Management incentives

6. Feedback which shows what should be done to the financial plan in view of actual results to date or what would happen to net income if hypothetical changes were made in the plan.

HOW DO YOU GET AN M.I.S.?

How to get an M.I.S. is the question many managers are grappling with today. And the question is a perplexing one for a number of reasons. For one thing, even though the basic concept of a "total" system is not difficult to understand, as a practical matter it poses a number of problems. How far should a company go in striving for a total system? Should it attempt to systematize and automate every possible function, stopping only at the highest policy and decision level? Or should it settle for something less, which might bring only an organized network of different systems sharing certain inputs and certain outputs? Then again, what effort is required to achieve a total system, and should the project be tackled in one phase or in several intermediate phases with the ultimate goal removed several years?

We are convinced that there is no easy answer to these questions. There is a finite limit to which systems development can be carried, and every company must decide for itself at what point that limit will be reached. You cannot simply transplant a system from one company to another. Not only are the systems requirements different from company to company but also the ability to perfect all management skills, including systematization, will not be the same in any two companies. Models from other companies, books, or computer manufacturer manuals may be helpful as checklists or guides, but the major portions of the system have to be especially designed to meet the needs of your business and its managers.

To provide an illustration of how a particular company might approach the M.I.S. problem, we have developed a hypothetical example that represents a synthesis of several of our assignments. The objective here is to portray graphically what types of systems can be combined to provide a "total" system and what the output of the system should be in terms of management control and information reports. In addition, we want to demonstrate how the M.I.S. project was organized. Our experience has led us to the conclusion that anything short of the approach outlined below will give inadequate results.

Able Manufacturing is a highly fashion-oriented company with manufacturing plants in various parts of the United States and nationwide sales and distribution facilities. A change in management prompted a critical new look at how the company had been faring.

Although the company was one of the leaders in its field, this position was the result of its pioneering effort. Competition from more vigorous young companies had leveled Able's rate of growth and reduced its rate of return to only tolerable percentages.

Typically, Able's new management embarked upon a profit improvement program which involved the introduction of many modern management techniques, including a management information system. After careful consideration of the alternative ways in which the project might be carried forward, Able's president accepted the recommendation that well organized interdepartmental teams be commissioned and given responsibility for the project, which was titled "Management Information System Development" (M.I.S.D.). This approach had the advantage of keeping the M.I.S. an entire company project, not just one organized by finance or administration. It also brought the right mixture of talents to bear on the problem, since Able felt that the basic information requirements should be set by the user of the information. Representation on the team from sales and production as well as the service departments helped assure that all information users would have a voice.

Organization of the effort was accomplished in the following way. A policy committee was appointed to plan and review M.I.S.D. activities on a broad basis. This committee met about once a month to authorize projects, hear progress reports, and make decisions. It consisted of the president, the executive vice president, the vice president of manufacturing, and the vice president of industrial relations and personnel. The selection of these men was made primarily on the basis of personal qualifications and characteristics rather than their functional responsibilities.

The policy committee selected an M.I.S.D. steering committee and approved its charter. This committee met as often as required, usually not less than once a week. The vice president of finance was appointed chairman, and with his participation a representative group of top and middle managers was selected from the various functional areas of the business, including the vice president of marketing, the comptroller, the newly appointed director of Management Information Systems, and others.

The charter of the steering committee (1) set forth the objectives in broad terms; (2) identified areas of special concern in developing an M.I.S. such as organization structure, management policies, and profit and cost center concepts; and (3) provided for the organization of task forces to conduct the required studies and make recommendations.

TASK FORCES

Personnel of the task forces were assigned, for the most part, on a full-time basis from the particular areas under study. Although the task force leader was usually a representative of middle or top management, most of the task force personnel were selected for their technical skills. To ensure that the data processing requirements of the M.I.S. would receive proper emphasis, members of the data processing staff were assigned to each task force. Technical representatives of our firm were attached to some of these task forces and were the means by which our consultants at the steering and policy committee levels helped plan and execute the M.I.S.D. effort. Each task force was charged with a specific task and timetable for reporting to the steering committee.

As the M.I.S.D. project developed it necessarily covered all areas of the business. It required approximately three years to complete. Its scope can be visualized from the following M.I.S.D. organization structure:

Policy Committee—
Steering Committee—
Task Forces
Company organization
Management and operating policies
Budgets
Monthly reporting
Expense management
Standard cost accounting
Data processing
Customer accounting and statistics
Long-range planning
Inventory management

As one of its early actions under this program the company placed orders for computing equipment of an advanced line announced by a manufacturer that had serviced the company's data processing needs in the past. This

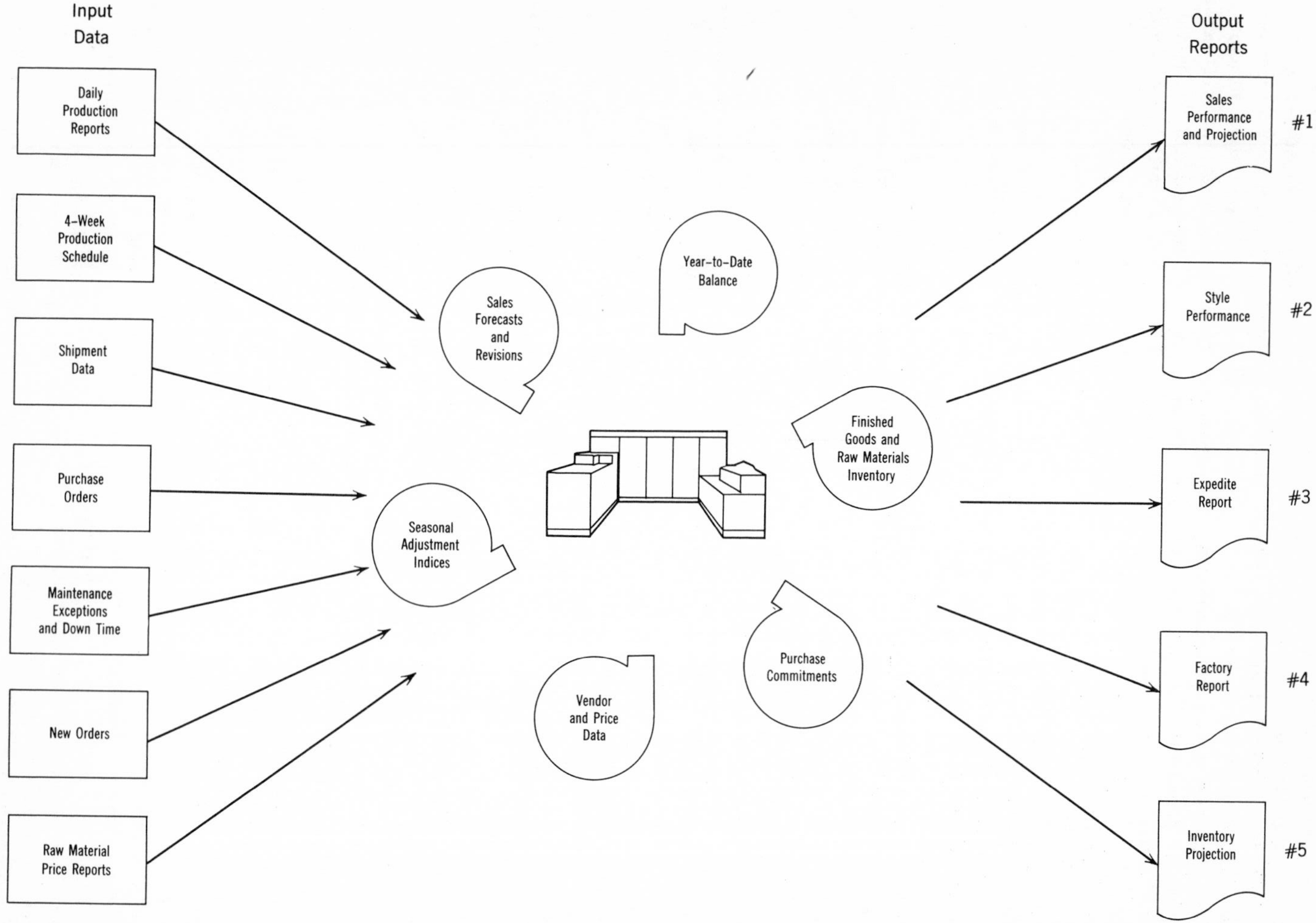

EXHIBIT 2. Able Manufacturing Company–Detail of Inventory Planning Information Flow Showing Selected High Level Reports.

was done on a generalized basis before the full requirements were known in order to reserve favorable delivery time, and the orders were particularized as the various task forces completed work in the assigned areas of the business.

In the exhibits you will see, in broad terms, the end product of the M.I.S.D. effort. Our objective is to show how the teams were able to organize virtually all of the company's procedural and information systems into one integrated M.I.S. utilizing common files or a "data bank." We also want to show how the reports generated by the new system brought many of the key variables in the business into a new focus to aid in prompt and decisive management action. Please bear in mind that not all of the subsystems were integrated at one time and that the ultimate usefulness of the reports was attributable to a strong management planning function as well as to a well organized information flow.

Exhibit 1 shows how the major business activities create data input to a central processing unit on a daily, weekly, and monthly basis. Such inputs of data in previous periods have resulted in master files of data relating to customers, employees, inventories, and all other phases of the business, accumulated from previous processing cycles. As current information is processed, the applicable master files are updated, and the prescribed control and information reports and documents are prepared automatically. The types and volumes of planning and control reports generated from the basic data are limited only by the needs of management and the creativity of the systems analysts assisting management in the definition of requirements.

In Exhibit 2 we have taken one segment—inventory planning—and illustrated in more detail how this process works. Exhibit 2 is followed by five typical reports that would be produced by the processing cycle in this area.

Able Manufacturing Company, Sales Performance vs. Plan
September 30, 196X, (000 omitted)

	Year to Date Sales			This Month Sales		
		Deviation from			Deviation from	
	Amount	Original Forecast	Latest Revision	Amount	Original Forecast	Latest Revision
Product Line A	$ 778	$ 58	$ 4 *	$ 86	$ 7 *	$ 2 *
B	907	21	5	98	6	1 *
C	829	19	2	90	3	3
D	786	9 *	2 *	85	4 *	2
E	800	15	6	86	6 *	3 *
F	691	11	1	75	9	6
G	850	12 *	3 *	92	3	1
H	1,123	17	4	122	11	4
I	878	9	1	95	2	6 *
J	987	25 *	7	107	5	4
Others	43,868	329	54	4,899	178	8
Total **	$52,497	$433	$71	$5,835	$200	$16

* Below plan

† Based on year to date sales after seasonal adjustment

Note: As well as reporting monthly sales by product line, this report shows the expected and actual results against the original forecast and all revisions. By the application of standard gross profit rates, the profit effect of all deviations can be measured, and revisions in the profit and production plans can be recognized and made on a timely basis.

** Total is arrived at by summing the positive deviations and subtracting the deviations below plan (the numbers with asterisks).

REPORT 1

CONCLUSIONS

In this hypothetical example we have digested the results of our experience in many management information systems consulting assignments. Some of you may be questioning the suggested scope of such an undertaking. You may have had the impression that such projects involved largely the installation of a computer with some peripheral activity concerned with determining needed statistical data and reports. It may be that some management information systems assignments stay confined to this relatively simple pattern, but the inevitable tendency to expand is easily explained.

The first expanding influence is the computer itself, which is identified with so many of the M.I.S. projects. Most observers dealing with the computer field have come to recognize that its scope and potential is such that the old compartmentalized notions of decision responsibilities and data processing interfere with efficient utilization of the new equipment and related techniques.

Secondly, the nature of a management information system leads naturally to a re-examination of many basic management approaches. The starting question, "What information do the various managers need to accomplish their missions?" evokes "What is their mission?" In most cases the answer to the second question is not readily forthcoming, for on probing you do not get articulate or unanimous answers to questions such as the following:

- Who has profit responsibility? Top management, marketing management, or manufacturing management?
- Who has responsibility for the size of inventories and obsolescence losses thereon?
- Should marketing management or manufacturing management make the final de-

Able Manufacturing Company, Sales Performance vs. Plan September 30, 196X, (000 omitted)

Projected Deviation of Future Sales †						Expected at Year End		
October		November		December			Deviation from	
Original Forecast	Latest Revision	Original Forecast	Latest Revision	Original Forecast	Latest Revision	Total Sales	Original Forecast	Latest Revision
$ 8*	$ 3	$ 5*	$ 2*	$ 15*	$ 2	$ 1,011	$ 30	$ 1*
3	1	7	2	10	6	1,180	41	14
5	2*	3*	1	12	4	1,078	33	5
9	3	15	3	8	4	1,022	23	8
7	4	6	1*	11	5	1,040	39	14
6	3	9	4	2*	3	898	24	11
2*	2	7	2	4	2*	1,105	3*	1*
5	4	12	2	9	5	1,460	43	15
1*	1	2*	2*	12	4	1,141	18	4
2	2	4	1	3	2*	1,283	16*	8
115	10	230	30	247	21	58,782	921	115
$141	$31	$280	$40	$299	$50	$70,000	$1,153	$192

REPORT 1 (*continued*)

Able Manufacturing Company Style Performance Report
September 30, 196X (week 39)

	Year to Date Deviations from Plan [1]			This Month Deviations from Plan [1]		
Style	Sales	Production	Ending Inventory	Sales	Production	Ending Inventory
XAGO	$ 300 *	$ 3,600	$ 3,900	$ 200 *	$ 500	$700
XDZG	600	—	600 *	350	—	350 *
YHQN	2,200	1,600	600 *	400	200	200 *
ZMVO	400	1,200	800	450	800	350
APET	1,900	4,000	2,100	200	400	200
DUFH	800 *	3,000	3,800	175 *	200	375
GBEN	1,100	—	1,100 *	250	—	250 *
JLMD	900	—	900 *	325	—	325 *
WBPN	100	2,400	2,300	190	680	490
PTSY	500 *	1,400	1,900	300 *	290	590
RVWB	1,000	2,700	1,700	510	470	40 *
Other styles	14,400	18,500	4,100	4,000	3,350	650 *
Total	$21,000	$38,400	$17,400	$6,000	$6,890	$890

* Below plan
[1] Based on year to date sales after seasonal adjustments
[2] And existing production plan

Note: This report expands on Report 1. It relates sales performance of a style to its production and inventory levels, to maintain maximum flexibility in production scheduling. Where a style is falling below its sales forecast, the basis is provided for curtailing production on that item and shifting the resulting available capacity to where it may be needed. (Total sales for the entire product line, Product Line B, are shown on Report 1.)

REPORT 2

cision on special product runs or unusual size of orders?

- Are the functions of staff and line management defined so that the responsibility for operating decisions is clear?
- Are the bases for measuring the performance of the various people in management specified?

Even in those cases where organizational responsibilities are clearly defined, the intense reappraisal of all activities occasioned by an M.I.S. project may result in changes in approach. For example, top management may well decide to change its approach on the assignment of responsibilities. Thus, we have heard it said that a company has been too manufacturing-oriented or too marketing-oriented or too research-oriented in the past and that the emphasis should be changed by giving more responsibility and authority to another functional group. You can appreciate how the nature and flow of information required would change if more emphasis were placed on marketing control of decisions regarding product lines, for instance, or on size of inventory, location of warehouses and plants, or order sizes.

MANUALS

Decisions relating to these matters should be reflected in organization and management policy manuals, and if these do not exist it is generally deemed desirable to prepare them as a prerequisite to, or concomitant of, the M.I.S. development.

Questioning of organizational responsibilities and management policies often stimulates a re-examination or revamping of control systems such as cost accounting and production

Able Manufacturing Company Style Performance Report
September 30, 196X (week 39)

Product Line B

Projected Inventory Level Using Latest Forecast[1,2]							
End of Week 40		41		42		43	
Units	Days' Sales	Units	Days' Sales	Units	Days' Sales	Units	Days' Sales
38	8	43	10	50	12	56	13
17	4	(6)	(1)	(2)	(1)	(6)	(2)
19	4	16	4	(20)	(4)	(24)	(5)
20	4	20	4	26	5	30	7
21	5	25	5	27	5	32	7
39	8	65	16	74	18	78	19
61	15	46	11	(53)	(13)	(60)	(15)
31	7	(8)	(1)	(2)	(1)	(5)	(1)
12	3	20	4	21	4	28	5
25	5	4	1	20	4	23	5
45	10	18	4	9	2	3	1
320	80	270	68	250	63	298	75
648	153	513	125	400	94	453	109

REPORT 2 (*continued*)

Able Manufacturing Company Weekly Expedite Report
September 30, 196X (week 39)

Style	Safety Stock (units)	Projected Stock-Out Next Six Weeks[1]: Week	Quantity Short	Item Now Running at Plants No.	Capacity to Cover Stock-Out Available at: Plant No.[2]	Line	Hours Needed to Restore to Safety
XDZG	25	41	31	1-6-3	4-6	1,7,15	192
YHQN	40	42	60	1-6-3	4-6	2,3,5	568
GBEN	100	42	153	2-7	—	—	791
JLMD	60	41	68	4-7	—	—	213

[1] Based on year to date sales (after seasonal adjustment) and existing production plan

[2] Based on existing production plan, subject to any prior special orders

Note: This report expands on expected stock-outs disclosed in Report 2, showing available plant capacity and amount of inventory and production hours needed to restore safety stock and cover planned requirements.

REPORT 3

Able Manufacturing Company Factory Report—September 30, 196X
(000 omitted)

	Year to Date				This Month	
	Earned Hours		Plant Utilization		Earned Hours	
	Number	Deviation from Plan	%	Deviation from Plan	Number	Deviation from Plan
Plant 1	98	3 *	78	2 *	11	.4 *
Plant 2	139	6 *	84	1 *	15	.7 *
Plant 3	117	5	86	6	13	.5
Plant 4	81	2	61	14 *	9	.2 *
Plant 5	108	9 *	84	3 *	12	1.1 *
Plant 6	144	4	82	2	16	.5
Plant 7	126	1	90	1 *	14	.2

* Below plan

Note: This report focuses on plant utilization and pinpoints variations from plan as well as the major reasons for those variations. The information here comes from the same source as the information on Report 3 relative to plant capacity for certain lines.

REPORT 4

Able Manufacturing Company Weekly Raw Material Inventory Projection
September 30, 196X (week 39)

Raw Material Code	End of Week		Lead Time	Safety Stock	On Order Due in Week						
	Material on Hand	Deviation from Plan			40	41	42	43	44	45	46
281	2,758	204	2	1		600		450			
282	204	816 *	3	2			1,400		1,400		1,800
284	421	286 *	2	1		100		400		400	
290	575	55	1	1	75		75		75		75
301	1,008	122 *	2	1		350		450		550	
350	900	500 *	3	2			1,500		1,500		1,500
423	847	47	2	1		500		400		300	
424	3,100	100	2	1							1,500
500	290	90	1	1	40	40	40	40	40	40	40
501	1,949	49	1	1	900			600		600	

* Below plan
1 Based on existing production plan
2 For quantity sufficient to restore safety stock

Note: This report helps ensure that the production plan and finished goods inventory levels can be met. Changes in either of these plans are reflected in this report, and attention is drawn to any exceptions in the planned level of raw materials inventory.

REPORT 5

Able Manufacturing Company Factory Report—September 30, 196X
(000 omitted)

This Month					
Plant Utilization		Lost Hours Due to			Available Hours Next Month
%	Deviation from Plan	Unplanned Down Time	Schedule Gaps	Production Balance	
78	2 *	.4	—	—	11.9
82	3 *	.2	.4	.1	16.4
82	2	—	—	—	14.2
65	10 *	.1	.1	—	9.6
88	1	.5	.6	—	13.7
87	2 *	—	—	—	17.3
90	5 *	—	—	—	14.3

REPORT 4 (*continued*)

Able Manufacturing Company Weekly Raw Material Inventory Projection
September 30, 196X (week 39)

Projected Usage in Week [1]							Projected Stock-Out [1]		Indicated Purchase Price [2] Variance
40	41	42	43	44	45	46	Week	Quantity	
45	45	40	42	45			—	—	—
400	400	400	400	400	400	400	40	996	5.5¢
150	150	150	150	150	150	150	43	79	14.7¢
80		80		80		80	—	—	—
	600		600		600		—	—	—
500	500	500	500	500	500	500	41	600	11.2¢
	90		210		660		—	—	—
375	375		375	375		375	—	—	—
90		90		90		90	—	—	—
300	300	300	300	300	300	300	—	—	—

REPORT 5 (*continued*)

and inventory management. For example, if manufacturing management were to be judged solely on cost performance and if this were carried to the point of introducing an incentive system based on actual performance against standard, the company would require a rather sophisticated standard cost accounting system and a set of performance reports to reflect results of operations. In a manufacturing company the cost consequences of manufacturing operations constitute a major segment of any M.I.S., which explains why cost accounting systems installations so often accompany M.I.S. development. In the same way, questions about inventory policy and responsibilities very often lead to much needed improvements in the production and inventory control systems.

In summary, the great current popularity being enjoyed by management information systems development is responsible for improvements in management skills and techniques in many companies which would not have accomplished them so soon otherwise. If your company has not had this experience yet, you should ask the door-opening question at your next staff or management meeting: "Do we have the information we need to run our business?"

BIBLIOGRAPHY

"A Total Management System," *Data Processing for Management,* April, 1963.

Carasso, Max, "Total Systems," *Systems and Procedures,* November, 1959.

Doherty, Philip A., and Justin G. F. Wollaston, "Effective Management of a Systems Project," *Management Services,* March-April, 1965.

Ewell, James M., "The Total System Concept and How to Organize for It," *Computers and Automation,* September, 1961.

Hoag, M., "What is a System?" *Operations Research,* June, 1957.

Hurni, Melvin L., "Decision Making in the Age of Automation," *Harvard Business Review,* September-October, 1955.

Lach, Edward L., "The Total Systems Concept," *Systems and Procedures,* November, 1960.

Lawson, C. L., *The Total Systems Concept—Its Application to Manufacturing Operations,* American Management Association, Report No. 60, 1961.

Milroy, Neil, "The Disintegration of an Information System," *The Canadian Chartered Accountant,* May, 1963.

Mockler, Robert J., "The Systems Approach to Business Organization and Decision Making," *California Management Review,* Winter, 1968.

Moravec, Adolf F., "Basic Concepts for Planning Advanced EDP Systems," *Management Services,* May-June, 1965.

Neuschel, Richard F., *Management by System,* McGraw-Hill Book Company, 1960.

McDonough, Adrian M., and L. J. Garrett, *Management Systems,* Richard D. Irwin, Inc., 1965.

Optner, Stanford L., *Systems Analysis for Business Management,* Prentice-Hall, Inc., 1968.

Prince, Thomas, *Information Systems for Management Planning and Control,* Richard D. Irwin, Inc., 1970.

Putman, A. O., et al., *Unified Operations Management,* McGraw-Hill Book Company, 1963.

Sethi, N. K., "Management by System," *Personnel Journal,* April, 1963.

Thrall, Robert M., C. H. Coombs, and R. L. Davis (eds.), *Decision Processes,* John Wiley and Sons, 1954.

Tilles, Seymour, "Manager's Job: A Systems Approach," *Harvard Business Review,* January, 1963.

Unlocking the Computer's Profit Potential, McKinsey and Co., Inc., 1968.

Woods, R. S., "Some Dimensions of Integrated Systems," *The Accounting Review,* July, 1964.

Young, Stanley, *Management: A Systems Analysis,* Scott, Foresman & Co., 1966.

———, "Organization as a Total System," *California Management Review,* September, 1968.

SECTION V

DESIGN, IMPLEMENTATION, AND CONTROL OF THE MANAGEMENT INFORMATION SYSTEM

Experience with any data-processing system will show that the success of any installation is dependent upon not only the design but also on the implementation and control of the system. Many an installation has failed because of inadequate consideration of each of these components of management information systems. It is axiomatic to state that design is related to control, since within any system documentation must be available in order for management to accurately assess results against the planned objectives. Control is necessary during the design stage, during programming, as well as during the computer-operation stage.

In the design of a system in which many of the components will be related to human endeavors, there is an obvious need to be aware of the human problems of systems. Fortunately some significant strides have been made in recent years in the interfacing of both man and machines into a compatible system. Firms have learned, often through costly experience, that people resist change. It would be modest to state that the area of systems can claim its rightful share of these discomforting and disabling experiences.

This final section is concerned with viewing systems as one continuous process—that is, a process of design, implementation, and control of systems. Although conceptually and temporally distinct, they still form interlocking links in the one ongoing process.

Recently many articles have appeared dealing with the design of total systems, a master plan for information systems,[1] and integrated system design,[2] all purporting to establish a structure by means of which the totality of business's information needs can be categorically processed. Granted that any workable program must be tailored to the particular type and size of business under consideration, the fact still remains that there are no standard specifications which one can follow to be assured of success. Typically, all systems designers start with the proposition that one must first establish long-range objectives, then analyze the existing system, develop immediate goals and target dates, and then begin to implement the plan. Such an approach appears highly superficial, being merely a reiteration of the traditional planning function which disregards current technological developments. What is needed is the application of common criteria in light of current equipment development. In this way, information needs will be ascertained more realistically and less idealistically.

Industry has in many cases approached systems design from a piecemeal standpoint, first wading into the automating of the payroll function, to be followed by customer billings, and then proceeding to the area of inventory control and scheduling. Perhaps this historical development was inevitable in view of the prevalent ignorance of computer potential. However, day-to-day observation of business procedures casts serious doubts on the sufficiency of this account. But no matter what the explanation, since business activities are increasing in both scope and complexity, the problems of integration and coordination are also on the increase, and the need for an integrated total systems approach is likely to assume greater urgency in the future.

When considering total systems design it is imperative that one keep in mind just what is and is not implied in such a holistic approach. There is definitely no *one* total information system which can indiscriminately serve all the needs of all of management. This conclusion can be logically derived as a corollary from the very concept of information as selected data for reducing the amount or range of uncertainty in decision-making. Because of the varying range of uncertainty, what may prove to be

[1] Marshall K. Evans and Lou R. Hague, "Master Plan for Information Systems," *Harvard Business Review,* January-February, 1962.

[2] Herman Limberg, "Blueprint for a Management Information System," *Data Processing for Management,* March, 1964.

useful information at one level may turn out to be useless at another.

Throughout the ages, down to our own space age, man has been ceaselessly searching for and achieving an ever greater degree of control over his environment. It is this control that has enabled him to create civilization as we know it, and it is this same control by which management hopes to implement ever more fully the short-range and long-range goals for the business enterprise. It is precisely for this purpose that the marvel of modern science, the electronic digital computer, is being increasingly utilized by enlightened, progressive management.

In nearly all previous sections of this part, control has figured as an important element in management systems. In Section I, Daniel rightly related information to both the planning and control functions of management. Elsewhere control was seen as one of the essential aspects of all systems. Tustin especially underlined the self-regulating feedback mechanism as paramount to the closed-loop control of the cybernetic system. PERT, real-time, and the whole field of computer science are oriented to management control. It is well nigh impossible to conceive of this area without touching on nearly all the other topics mentioned heretofore.

One of the several previously discussed constraints that systems designers must take into consideration is people. It is a sad fact that too often many of them ignore the human element in systems design. Indeed, the remark, "It would be a great system if it weren't for the people involved," is more than mere witticism or facetiousness. In the man-to-machine but especially in the man-to-man systems it is the human element that merits greater attention. Though systems do involve materials, energy, and information flow, it is the impact of these on the individuals that tends to be either overlooked or underestimated.

It is the behavioral scientist who has especially concerned himself with the problems involved in effecting change. The agent of change must therefore familiarize himself with the findings from the fields of cultural anthropology, sociology, psychology, and social psychology, for these have much to contribute to the solution of those problems plaguing management. Specialists at times tend to overconcentrate on their own tightly circumscribed arena of investigation and to act as if nothing of importance could possibly transpire elsewhere. Ackoff noted this tendency when he warned systems engineers:

> We must stop acting as though nature were organized into disciplines in the same way that universities are. The division of labor along disciplinary lines is no longer an efficient one. In fact, it has become so inefficient that even some academic institutions have begun to acknowledge the fact . . .
>
> No single individual can be educated so as to be expert in all the disciplinary approaches to systems. It is difficult enough to make him expert in one. We can, however, educate him to an awareness of what others know and can do in systems work and motivate him to desire to work collaboratively with them. Scientific snobbery must go.[1]

The one aspect of human problems that has been stressed over and over in the literature and for which there is by now a voluminous bibliography is resistance to change. Problems of resistance to change have been present throughout recorded history and their most recent manifestation has been occasioned by the introduction of electronic data processing and automation. The classic study dealing with this is the article written by Coch and French.[2] Though this somewhat lengthy article has

[1] Russell L. Ackoff, "Systems, Organizations, and Interdisciplinary Research," *General Systems*, **5**, 1960, pp. 1–8. Quotations are from pp. 6 and 8.

[2] Lester Coch and John French, Jr., "Overcoming Resistance to Change," *Human Relations*, 1948, pp. 512–532.

not been reprinted among the selections included in this reader, it is worth perusing. The shorter article by Lawrence Williams highlights this important problem area.

The selection by Johnson, Kast, and Rosenzweig places stress on the fact that the systems concept is essentially a frame of mind, that unless management responds to the systems approach by developing its own integrative philosophy, the total systems design will collapse under its own weight. To be successful, any systems engineering plan must include these three elements: identification of materials, of energy, and information flow. Raw materials are the wherewithal to be acquired, processed, and distributed. Energy includes not only physical energy in terms of electricity, gas, petroleum, etc., but also human energy in its physical and mental aspects. Information flow for routing of orders, production, accounting, and decision making is often the primary focus of attention for most systems engineers. But because it is people who can successfully resist the structural alignments called for in designing information decision systems, the human factors may at times be the crucial ones demanding special consideration.

The human factors involved in developing a system's design are treated *in extenso* by Bower and Sefert.[3] These factors must first be isolated if the systems analyst is to devise effective ways to minimize the human problems encountered in his role of bringing about change. For convenience in analyzing the effect of human factors on systems change three operational levels are examined in detail: top management (executives participating in companywide policy determination), middle management (middle and junior executives, operating supervisors, and foremen), and nonsupervisory employees (rank-and-file). Each of these three groups presents specific problems with their specialized fears, particular outlooks, appropriate motivation, etc. Also the techniques suitable for preliminary study, for implementation and follow-up are interestingly outlined and illustrated.

Modernization in the past has too often been almost exclusively identified with the installation of new facilities and the introduction of modern machinery, and not with innovation in the management function itself. The design and installation of total management systems, devices for forestalling the development of an unprofitable business situation within a corporation, involves a considerable number of technical problems. These problems are pinpointed in the second selection by R. L. Martino. Since these problems are quite formidable, involving a good deal of work, critical analysis, and far-reaching consequences for all concerned, it would be a sheer waste of time and of resources to undertake the installation of such a system unless the willingness to do the arduous work, to make the necessary decisions, and to commit the needed funds to the project were a foregone conclusion.

The functions of a total management system can be broken down for purposes of analysis into predictive, comparative, and ameliorative. It aims to predict the effect of choosing one or a set of alternatives from among many possible ones. This it does by a computer simulation process. The comparative function consists of relating the prediction to the actual results obtained, whereas the ameliorative function aims at reducing the deviations between the predicted and the actual results. However, to actually realize these functions the various stages of system development (definition of the problem, design of system, and evaluation and modification of the system) must be thoroughly understood and successfully implemented.

The article by Alan J. Rowe on the "Research Problems in Management Controls" certainly raises more questions than it answers. For him control includes such things as objectives, decision criteria for evalu-

[3] James B. Bower, and J. Bruce Sefert, "Human Factors in Systems Design," *Management Services*, November-December, 1965.

ating performance, decision rules for remedial action, and some measures of performance, while the control problem involves information on all of these, information so quantified as to be amenable to computer simulation.

Computer simulation Rowe views as a most fitting means of studying the dynamic response characteristics of business systems. For this end he describes business systems as a matrix of activities and responses with elements susceptible to computer simulation.

In shifting emphasis from computer simulation to feedback considerations, George Weinwurm both restricts and sharpens Rowe's field of view. He projects his brief discussion against the background of experience gained in military control systems (e.g., SAGE), for these are highly complex man-to-machine systems similar to those found in the world of business.

Since the most characteristic aspect of systems in general is feedback, Weinwurm distinguishes four distinct types of feedback in man-to-machine systems: feedback within the computer, between the computer and the system environment, between man and the machine, and between man and the system environment. Combinations of these may also occur. An interesting feature of these types is that they are characterized by time-cycle discriminants. While the first of these (intracomputer feedback) can be measured in fractions of a second (milliseconds, microseconds, and now nanoseconds), the other three, involving extracomputer interactions, consume much more valuable time. Where human decision making is involved, the use of faster and faster computers does little to solve the problem. The progress made in military applications has been due primarily to having more and more decisions programmed internally. However, before this can be done, decision rules will have to be more explicitly and more formally expressed. These rules must, moreover, cover every relevant situation and optimally every possible contingency. These rules must then be translated into a language that the computer can understand, another formidable task indeed. The most difficulty, however, will be encountered in the twilight area where no general rule suffices to cover a particular situation. It is in reducing this "circle of confusion" that the payoff for control systems takes place, but the price thereof is compromise.

In the final paragraphs some thought is given to the exciting idea of adaptive automata, of machines capable of learning from experience how to solve the problem with which they are dealing. The problem of having the machine adapt itself to increasingly complex environments under controlled conditions is, however, currently under consideration. The degree to which the machine simulates the real world will be only an approximate one, but the further question then arises: What approximation is reasonably sufficient? A test of the efficiency of the real-time man-to-machine SAGE system would be to have a war, an expensive and inhumane proposition. But even this would not suffice, for little of statistical significance could be derived from a sample of one.

The psychologist, Lawrence Williams, advances the hypothesis that much resistance to change is based on attitudes that are largely emotional. Consequently, the "logical" approach that the systems engineer is to employ in overcoming resistance is not that of sheer logic or of brute force. However, he can learn much of the real cause of the attitude from an examination of the statements proffered in opposition to the proposed change.

It may be something less than a compliment to learn that resistance to change is probably more prevalent on the level of middle managers than on that of the rank-and-file employees. This may be due to the fact that these individuals have more at stake.

The bulldozer method of attacking resistance to change is shown to be devoid of almost all merit. Even when short-run results are obtained, the costs must be carefully weighed. Often it retards subsequent change-adoption and dries up the pool of goodwill that may have existed in the past.

Possible loss of status and of existing informal relationships that have proved satisfying are singled out as human features to be considered when planning change. Differential motivation on the part of managers and employees, poor communication networks where top level managers learn of the resistance at lower levels only when it is too late, feasibility for change from both the technical and the human viewpoint, and the difficulty of translating the impersonal language of the technological system into the human language of the social system are succinctly but clearly discussed.

33. DESIGNING MANAGEMENT SYSTEMS

RICHARD A. JOHNSON,* FREMONT E. KAST,† AND
JAMES E. ROSENZWEIG ‡

The vast growth in size, complexity, and diversity of operations of the modern business organization has made the managerial function exceedingly difficult, but even more essential to the success of the enterprise.

During the past few years there have been many new concepts advanced for improving management; e.g., organization theory, decision theory, planning theory, and the behavioral theory of the firm. Each of these philosophies has helped to sharpen management skills; however, there is still a need for an operative theory of management—a theory which provides a conceptual framework of better business design and operation. It is our contention that today's large-scale business enterprise could apply the systems concepts to meet the growing complexities and proliferation of operations, for systems theory provides a conceptual framework within which the manager can integrate his operations effectively.

We are concerned here with design—the key activity in implementing the systems concept. This function is the means for establishing subsystems and larger systems into a composite, integrated whole. However, for completeness of presentation we will review general systems concepts briefly. Specifically, we will:

- Show the relationship between the systems concept and managing,
- Set forth a practical model using the systems concept,
- Discuss the scope of the design function,
- Introduce flow concepts in systems design,
- Discuss systems design as the implementation of the systems concept and
- Appraise some of the constraints on the design function.

SOURCE: *The Business Quarterly* (Summer, 1964), pp. 59–65. Reprinted by permission of *The Business Quarterly*.

* University of Washington.
† University of Washington.
‡ University of Washington.

SYSTEMS CONCEPTS AND MANAGEMENT

A system is "an organized or complex whole; an assemblage or combination of things or parts forming a complex or unitary whole." The term system covers an extremely broad spectrum of concepts. For example, we have mountain systems, river systems, and the solar system as part of our physical surroundings. The body itself is a complex organism including the skeletal system, the circulatory system, and the nervous system. We come into daily contact with such phenomena as transportation systems, communication systems (telephone, telegraph, etc.), and economic systems.

The systems concept is a useful way of thinking about the job of managing. It provides a framework for visualizing internal and external environmental factors as an integrated whole. It allows recognition of the proper place and function of subsystems. The systems within which businessmen must operate are necessarily complex. However, management via systems concepts fosters a way of thinking which, on the one hand, helps to dissolve some of the complexity and, on the other hand, helps the manager recognize the nature of the complex problems and thereby operate within the perceived environment. It

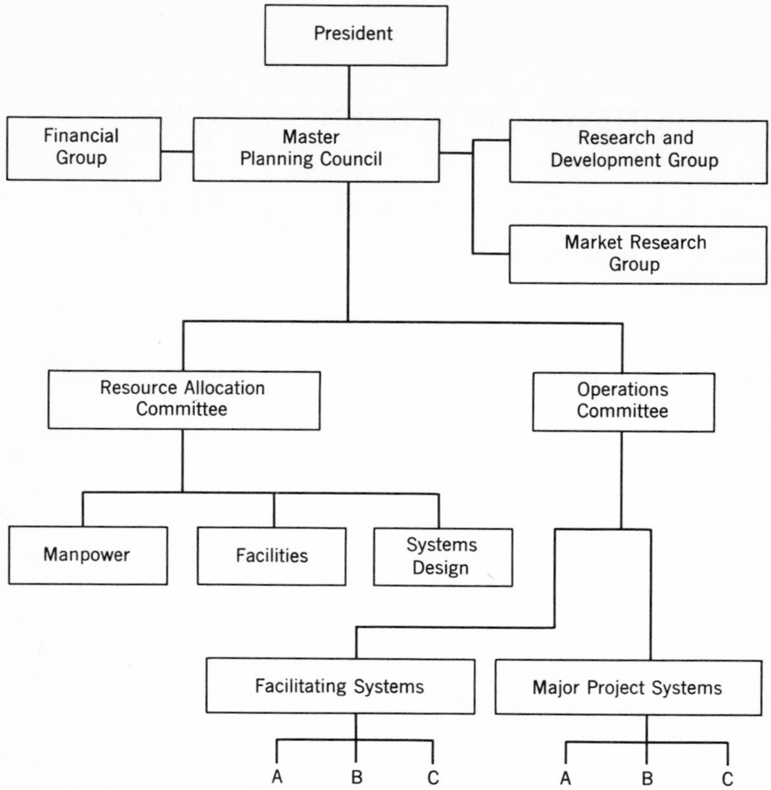

EXHIBIT 1. A Systems Model: Top Management.

is important to recognize the integrated nature of specific systems, including the fact that each system has both inputs and outputs and can be viewed as a self-contained unit. But it is also important to recognize that business systems are a part of larger systems—possibly industry-wide, or including several, perhaps many, companies and/or industries, or even society as a whole.[1]

The theory of systems is not new, for much of it has been developed and used in the natural sciences for many years. Further, it is being used to some degree in business. For example, systems theory is used in administering certain military programs where specification and time requirements are critical, and in some single-venture programs, e.g., construction projects. There is no reason, however, why this concept is not equally applicable to appliance manufacturing, retailing, or banking.

A MODEL OF THE SYSTEMS CONCEPT

Traditionally, business firms have not been structured to utilize the systems concept. In adjusting the typical business structure to fit within the framework of management by systems, certain organizational changes will be required. The following Model illustrates *one* arrangement which would implement the systems concept. We do not imply that this Model is the most effective arrangement, only that it illustrates the use of "systems thinking" in managing a business.

Referring to Exhibit 1, a master planning council engages in high-level design activity and establishes guidelines for the entire organization. This council would make decisions relative to the products or services the company supplied. Further, it would establish the

[1] For a more comprehensive discussion of these concepts see R. A. Johnson, F. E. Kast, and J. E. Rosenzweig, *The Theory and Management of Systems,* McGraw-Hill Book Company, Inc., New York, 1963.

limits of an operating program, decide on general policy matters relative to the design of operating systems and select the director for each new product. New-project decisions would be made with the assistance and advice of the product research and development, market research, and financial groups.

Within that framework, design activity is carried on by the resource-allocation planning group—a group which combines manpower and facilities to form working systems designed to accomplish given objectives. In both facilitating systems [2] and major project systems, additional design activity—systems review—is necessary to maintain working systems on a current basis.

The master planning council must have a definite approach to developing premises which serve as the basis for systems design. Meaningful information must be translated from environmental data on such questions as economic activity, political developments, and social trends. It is important that top management develop clear-cut systems of such information flow which will provide inputs for planning and decision making. In most companies such systems are left to chance, or at best, periodic review.

SCOPE OF THE DESIGN FUNCTION

Design means to "mark-out, designate, or indicate." It includes combining features or details and often calls for preparation of preliminary sketches or plans. The design function is important in establishing a relationship between the various stages or phases of a system, linking them together, and outlining the composite whole. For business systems the design function includes the arrangement of physical facilities for production and auxiliary activities. It also covers the arrangement of people and communication networks established to provide information concerning the process.

When establishing a new business operation, the design function seems fairly straightforward. However, the scope of systems design also covers the function of "redesign," assessing existing systems with an eye toward change. This activity has received considerable attention over the years under headings such as systems and procedures, work simplification, systems analysis, or systems engineering. Of these terms, *work simplification* seems to have the narrowest connotation in that it applies primarily to simple man-machine operations or clerical activity. However, as with most tools and techniques, its practitioners have proclaimed its applicability to a wide range of problems. In any case, it applies to existing systems rather than to the establishment of new systems.

Systems and procedures work has been pointed up as an all-encompassing activity, covering many facets of the business operation. However, implicitly it seems limited to the office, the flow of paper work, and the design of forms. Since the advent of electromechanical equipment, systems and procedures activity has included the designing and programming of data-processing systems. Unfortunately, EDP has been overemphasized in recent years to the exclusion of broader concepts of systems design. The specific aspects of programming, form design, and routing of paper work—as a part of the information-decision system—should be fitted into the overall systems design.

Another term used in describing this general sphere of activity is systems analysis. It also is focused on existing systems rather than on the design of new systems. Systems analysis often has a connotation of application primarily to information flow in the office and does not seem as applicable to a production or processing environment. This is not to say that it is not feasible; rather, most of the literature on the subject deals with information-processing problems.

Systems engineering implies the creation of systems as well as the analysis of existing systems. Systems engineering sometimes is assumed to deal only with physical components; that is, it deals with the integration of components and subcomponents into a total product such as a computer or missile. Using the definition of engineering as "the art and science by which the properties of matter and the sources of power in nature are made useful to man in structures, machines, and manufactured products," there is systems implication. Moreover, systems engineering can be defined as "making useful an array of components designed to accomplish a particular objective according to plan." This approach

[2] Facilitating systems are those designed to serve major project systems, e.g., a computer center.

implies the interaction of more than equipment. It suggests the development of a man-machine system which could function as a task-oriented assemblage. Systems engineering comes closest to implying design activity. In many cases the systems-engineering function involves "starting from scratch" to develop subsystems, larger systems, and a composite whole.

FLOW CONCEPTS IN DESIGN

One general approach to systems design involves identification of material, energy, and information flow. These three elements are part of every system and subsystem. Consideration of them plus the use of flow concepts facilitates thinking about systems of systems.

Material

The material aspects of any system include both the facilities involved and the raw material, if any, which flows through the process. A system must be designed to ensure the *acquisition* of raw materials and/or components necessary for processing into finished products. The systems design would include identification or transportation means required to move the raw material to the processing location.

The processing operation needs to be designed in terms of constructing new facilities or realigning existing facilities. Questions of plant layout and materials-handling equipment would be a vital part of the systems-design function for in-plant processing and in-plant material flows. Industrial engineers have considered problems of this nature for many years and have developed detailed methods and techniques for optimizing layout and material handling. The trend toward automation has been evident in many material-processing operations.

Much attention also has been focused on distribution of finished goods. Where items become raw material or components in additional processing operations, the distribution problem is often straightforward. In such cases the material flow would be considered part of the flow of raw materials for a subsequent processing operation. Physical-distribution management, for items moving from producer to ultimate consumer, can be a much more difficult problem. In this case, channels of distribution vary from direct producer to consumer to a myriad of combinations of middlemen. Inventory management, at various points along the distribution channel, must be considered, as well as modes of transportation. In many cases transportation costs have been isolated for analysis without reference to the impact of such decisions on stocks of material in the pipeline. Systems design, in this sphere, would concern itself with identifying the flow of materials and with the development of an explicit network of distribution, recognizing *all* the costs involved—handling, inventory, and transportation costs. Increased effort is being devoted to the design of explicit material-flow systems from a raw-material stage through the production process and to the final consumer.[3]

Whenever the operation in question involves the flow and processing of material, appropriate systems can be designed. For business operations such as insurance companies or other commercial institutions, there may be no flow of material per se. Rather, the material in these systems is represented by the facilities and equipment involved. Regardless of whether there is any material flow, all business operations, whether processing a product or service, contain elements of energy and information.

Energy

Some source of energy is present in any operating system. It may be electricity obtained from available sources or generated by a firm's own power plant. The process may require natural gas, petroleum, coal or other fuel for production. A business usually requires electrical energy for operating facilitating systems, if not for the main processing operation itself.

Another obvious source of energy is people. Both physical and mental energy are required to operate business systems. People represent a renewable source of energy, at least for the short run. As an energy source, people are quite variable as individuals. However, *in toto,* the group represents a reasonably stable source of energy for the system.

Electricity, natural gas, or petroleum can be

[3] See Stanley H. Brewer and J. Rosenzweig, "Rhochrematics and Organizational Adjustments," *California Management Review,* Spring, 1961, pp. 52–71.

described in terms of flow concepts. Energy flows are under continual inspection by systems designers. However, they are concerned primarily with the energy or power system itself, not the integration of the energy system with other subsystems and the whole. It is somewhat more difficult to visualize people, or the work force, in terms of flow concepts. However, in a very real sense, this is entirely appropriate. There may be a continual flow of workers in terms of shifts where 24-hour, 7-day weeks are scheduled. Even for 5-day, 40-hour weeks there is a systematic flow of worker energy into the operation. In a larger sense, a business operation maintains a flow of worker energy throughout its life—from the recruiting, hiring, and orientation stages, all the way to retirement. Thus all energy can be considered as a flow process both in and of itself and as a part of other systems.

Information

Another basic element in any system is information. It facilitates interrelationships among subsystems and provides the linkage necessary to develop systems of systems. Information flow may be developed to flow along with the routing of material. Requisitions, orders, bills of lading, packing slips, receiving information, inspection reports, accounts payable, and cheques might represent the information flow connected with the acquisition of raw material. The information flow appropriate to production control is another example. In this case production instructions, material requirements, processing information, inspection requirements, routing, and scheduling would be developed from engineering drawings and/or other specifications. The information would flow through the system along with the material necessary to accomplish the planned objectives.

The accounting system requires a flow of information toward the development of income statements and balance sheets for tax purposes or stockholder reports or both. While many data-processing systems have developed on the basis of periodic batch processing, more and more systems are being developed which call for flow concepts approximating real-time activity; that is, the action or activity to be considered is recorded at the time it happens and action is taken at that time.

Information flow is the primary focus of attention for systems designers in many cases. If manufacturing facilities are fixed and if layout requirements are rigid, then the only variables remaining are raw materials (which may be uniform), energy (in the form of power and/or people), and information (in the form of plans and instructions). Systems design in such cases must concentrate on the arrangement of people and the use of information flow to optimize decision making within the system under observation. For many other systems where manufacturing and material flow are not present—service, commercial, and many governmental organizations—the flow of information is the critical element. Information must flow to key decision points where action is taken with regard to a service to be performed by the organization in question. In such cases the system can be defined primarily on the basis of the flow of information to appropriate decision points. Subsystems can be identified on this basis, and they in turn can be interrelated to define the total system.

Unfortunately, most present-day systems of this nature have been established on the basis of people relationships and organization charts without regard for project systems or task-oriented groups. In many cases these organizations function primarily on the basis of informal relationships and informal communications systems. One of the main points in systems design is the necessity of recognizing the natural relationships of informal subsystems in developing a total system. It is by means of these flow concepts that the total system can be conceptualized as a system of systems. Particular emphasis will be placed on the design of information-decision systems. Such systems are integral parts of any operating system, whether it is designed to yield a product or service.

INTEGRATING FLOW CONCEPTS

Basic to the theory of systems is the premise that given certain inputs, the processor will give certain outputs or operate within established limits. However, the business firm, as a whole, is not a structured or predictable system. Its equilibrium cannot be determined by equation, and it will change, within limits, as the components of the system are rearranged or as the inputs are reallocated.

In more advanced form, a system will include some means of control, i.e., a sensor for measuring output or related characteristics, a means of comparing the measurement with a standard, and an activating group to adjust inputs to correct the indicated deficiencies. The objective is to control variables so the system will tend to stabilize near the ideal equilibrium point. This objective is possible only if the ideal standard can be determined and if the operating values can be measured. A complete system, including control, is illustrated in Exhibit 2.

It shows the flow of planning information as it releases resources of materials, energy, and processing information. A record of the plan is stored where it can be used as a standard for control purposes. The resources are released by an activating group. For example, detailed schedules are planned (processing information), workers are assigned to specific tasks (energy), and the necessary raw materials or purchased parts are provided (materials). The combination of these inputs into the system results in the performance of a task (processing), and output is produced.

Sensory devices are placed at strategic points in the system flow to measure performance or output. These measurements are fed back to a control group, and this information is compared with the standard. As significant deviations from plan are recognized, information to correct the situation is released to the activating group, which in turn will change the release of resources or information, energy, or materials.

DESIGNING OPERATING SYSTEMS

Operating systems have one thing in common: they should all use a common language for communicating among themselves and with higher levels. In addition, of course, each

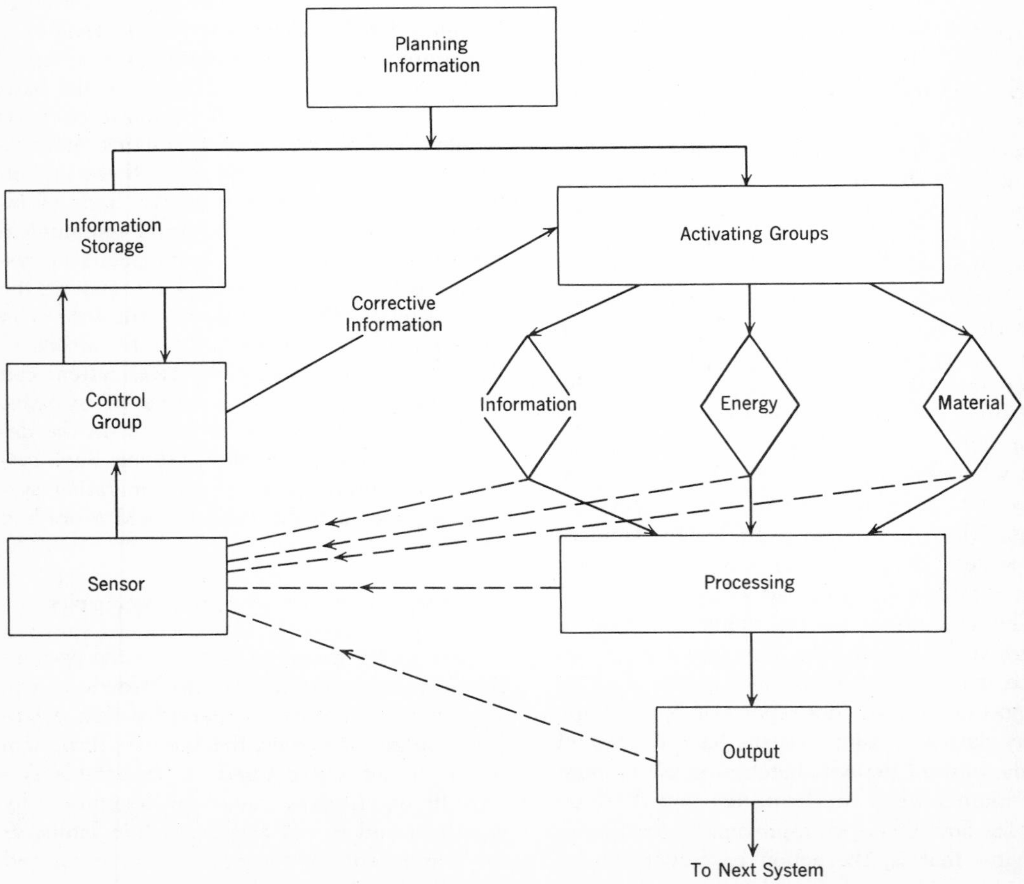

EXHIBIT 2. An Operating System.

system designed should be structured in consideration of company-wide policies. Other than these limits, each operating system can be created to meet the specific requirements of its own product or service.

The operating system is structured to (1) direct its own inputs, (2) control its own operation, and (3) review and revise its own system design as required. Input is furnished by three different groups: technical information is generated as input into the processing system, and in addition, technical information is the basis for originating processing information. Both technical and processing information are used by the material input system to determine and supply materials for processing. The operating system has its own control unit, which measures the inputs and outputs of system. However, corrective action, when necessary, would be activated by input allocation.

This model of an operating system can be related to any business situation. For example, if it represents a system to produce television sets, the technical information would refer to the design of the product, processing information would include the plan of manufacture and schedule, and the material input would pertain to the raw materials and purchased parts used in the processing. These inputs of information and material would be processed and become output. Process control would measure the output in comparison with the standard (information storage) obtained from input allocation and issue corrective information whenever the system failed to function according to plan. The design of the system would be reviewed continually, and the components rearranged or replaced when these changes would improve operating efficiency.

A systems-review function is an integral part of each project system. The system as a whole should be reviewed periodically by means of a thoroughgoing analysis and synthesis of the system and its components. The system should be broken down into its individual subsystems, and each of these should be evaluated in terms of the likelihood of continuing efficiency. Adjustments can be made on the basis of the results of such analysis. Then a process of synthesis must take place in order to restructure an integrated whole.

Why is it that subsystems and/or project systems must be reviewed and adjusted continually? One obvious reason was mentioned above; system requirements change over a period of time, and hence the system must be redesigned in the light of evolutionary trends. Static systems design goes out of date almost immediately. In fact, the battle cry of some systems analysts and designers is, "If it works, it must be obsolete!" As a particular project progresses through its life cycle, the product mission may change, as may other environmental or competitive conditions. Organizational adjustments may be required, or technological advancements may allow improvements in handling of either material or information flow.

Some systems are built around individuals within an organization. If identification of decision points is based on strong or dominant personalities, the information-decision system may be disrupted completely whenever key-personnel changes are made. Hence systems must be redesigned in order to accommodate the changes in managerial personnel.

The original allocation of resources may have been temporary in the sense of availability of necessary elements either internally or externally. Make-shift systems have a way of perpetuating themselves regardless of inefficiencies. It is important to reappraise the situation often enough to make sure that such temporary arrangements are revised when conditions allow.

Another typical problem is the tendency toward empire building, the accumulation of more than enough material, manpower, and facilities to accomplish given objectives. The project manager must resist the tendency towards bigness for the sake of prestige or status. A semi-detached, hopefully objective systems-review group can help nurture such a point of view.

Continuing attention must be devoted to systems review and the implementation of proposed changes. Follow-up is necessary because of the seemingly inherent resistance to change on the part of people involved in the system. Unless such resistance can be overcome, poor systems may be prolonged. Once the atmosphere is established for continual analysis and review, implementation of change becomes progressively easier.

CONSTRAINTS ON THE DESIGN FUNCTION

In order to place the systems-design function in proper perspective it is important to consider the various constraints on this activity. Policy decisions on the part of the master planning council not only provide guidelines for systems design at lower levels, they also provide boundaries. If top management does not embrace the systems concept as a managerial philosophy, systems design cannot be implemented. The proper atmosphere must be created at all levels in order for this approach to be utilized.

Other limiting factors include the amounts and kinds of facilities available as well as the work force and its skill mix. Elaborate and sophisticated systems designs might be forthcoming which could not be implemented because of lack of facilities and/or manpower. However, we suggest that the systems-design group start with designs for systems that are needed rather than those which obviously can be implemented. The organization will progress if it is forced to strain toward goals and objectives. If the design proves too much of a "cloud nine" approach, the system can always be scaled back to meet existing resources.

The resource-allocation council places constraints on the system-review function in terms of policy decisions with regard to allocation of the resources between major projects systems and facilitating systems. It may be that systems analysts within major project systems have designed optimal arrangements for their own operation without regard to other project systems. The resource-allocation planning group may decide that certain facilitating systems common to several or all project systems should be set up to serve the entire group. Thus policy decisions throughout the total system provide constraints within which systems designers must operate.

Along with policy decisions and equipment and facility limitations, another constraint which must be taken into consideration by systems designers is people. The remark "It would be a great system if it weren't for the people involved" is appropriate here. Problems of resistance to change or of out-and-out antagonism are evident throughout the literature describing impacts of automation and electronic data processing. Similar reaction is often evident when designing information decision systems which call for realignment of people and equipment according to the systems concept. These human factors are important variables in systems design and must be given consideration.

CONCLUSION

Systems design is the key activity in implementing the systems concept. This function provides an over-all framework by establishing subsystems, larger systems, and a composite, integrated whole.

We cannot overemphasize the fact that, first and foremost, the systems concept is a frame of mind. Management must be receptive to this approach and develop a philosophy in which planning, organizing, controlling, and communication are accomplished in terms of subsystems integrated into a composite whole. Once there is acceptance of the systems concept and the feasibility of organizing on the basis of a master planning council, a resource-allocation planning group, and an operations planning group (with facilitating and project systems reporting to it), the systems-design function can be carried out in a progressive atmosphere. The atmosphere created is all-important; it fosters creativity and innovation on the part of systems designers.

34. THE DEVELOPMENT AND INSTALLATION OF A TOTAL MANAGEMENT SYSTEM

R. L. Martino *

Modern business management is faced with a dilemma. At a time when profit margins are shrinking and both foreign and domestic competition are intensifying, heavy expenditures are required for modernization. Such expenditures are considered essential if a business is to remain competitive and if its profit margins are to improve.

In considering modernization, management usually thinks first in terms of facilities and machinery. Too often, however, that is as far as the improvements are carried. The need exists, and has long existed, for modernization of the management function itself. The need is especially acute today because of the great and growing complexity of both products and procedures. Management science has developed many new tools to modernize the management function; it is up to management to take full advantage of these developments.

Management systems in the past have been concerned mainly with the preparation and analysis of historical reports. While this kind of reporting is valuable, rarely is it timely enough to be truly useful. Production figures for January, for example, might not be available until mid-February (or later) when their usefulness will have diminished considerably.

OBJECTIVES

There is an urgent need in business to be able to look ahead as well as behind and to anticipate changes in markets and profit situations. Basically, *a system is required that will forestall the development of an unprofitable business situation.*

Therefore, the primary objective in developing a total management system should be the production of detailed, up-to-the-minute summaries of the past and the use of these summaries to project future activity. In essence, the functions of a total management system are:

1. To predict
2. To compare the prediction with actual results, and
3. To produce the deviations between the predicted and the actual.

Thereafter, the system should use these deviations to prepare a new, updated set of predictions which can be used as the basis for management decision. This concept is known as *management by exception.* While this term has been bandied about a good deal during the past few years, there are few instances where the concept has been applied in its fullest sense.

The predictive function, it should be understood, includes the determination and consideration of alternatives, and for each alternative, the effects of a decision. The method used in this process is called *simulation,* a technique wherein the various factors involved in a given situation are assembled into a model, usually of a mathematical nature. By varying the factors systematically, it is possible to weigh each alternative and its effects. Such information can be of great value to management in making decisions.

A total management system, then, produces basically two kinds of information for all levels of management:

SOURCE: *Data Processing for Management* (April, 1963), pp. 31–37. Reprinted by permission of Data Processing Magazine, The Publication of Computers and Information Technology.

* Special Editor, *Total Systems Letter.*

1. Predictions based on historical data and simulation.
2. Suggested changes of present procedures to make the selected predictions possible.

As indicated previously, the predictions are continually compared with actual results to determine deviations. These, in turn, are used to refine or revise the initial set of predictions and strategies. Then, the whole system recycles, producing new predictions, and so on.

The cycle of a total management system is summarized in the illustration in Figure 1. The upper portion of the cycle diagram, if followed in a counterclockwise manner, represents the regular path. That is, data are used to produce a model which in turn develops predictions for use by management. When decisions are reached by management as to the course of action to be followed, the program is implemented. Then, data obtained from operation of the program are used to produce required statements and reports, and are also used as updated history for the next cycle of the system. The lower half of the diagram represents management action required to analyze and correct deviations from the predicted results. The result of such action also becomes a factor in the next cycle of the system.

The value of exception reports drawn from these predictions and historical summaries will vary from function to function in the management system. For example, a daily comparison of predicted and actual sales might be quite useful to an order department, but a daily comparison of predicted with actual profits would not. Decisions as to the type and frequency of reports would be based on the function and on the degree of managed cost control involved.

SCIENTIFIC METHODS

In the development and installation of a total management system, scientific methods have played an increasingly important role. Management science involves the application of mathematics to management problems with the aid of the computer to prepare possible alternatives for management decisions. The computer is particularly valuable to management science because it can reduce vast quantities of data to meaningful trends.

When businesses were small and operations were relatively uncomplicated, management decision was often the responsibility of one man—the entrepreneur. Sufficient information was available so that the owner-operator could determine the best course of action by weighing all the alternatives and selecting the best. Whether he knew it or not, the entrepreneur simulated the operation of his business in his mind and, after weighing the various alternatives, made decisions based on the information available to him. And, because the operation was small and uncomplicated, the entrepreneur was in a position to know the consequences of his decisions.

As business volume increased and the organizational structures grew more complex, the lines of communication gradually became less direct and immediate. Without access to the most timely information, management could not know of every alternative course of action, let alone the result of each alternative.

The first attempt to ease the situation was mechanization of the accounting function. Unfortunately, the equipment available could not fully cope with the problem. While it is true that information became more readily available than previously, the voluminous reports in tabulating form were unwieldy and, by the time they reached operating management, they were often too dated to be of real value. To decision making top management, the reports were even less useful.

With the advent of the electronic computer and the introduction of mathematical techniques, management came a step nearer a solution. These new tools make it possible to simulate *all* the operations of an organization and thereby to reduce the overgrown and overly complex problems of business management to a workable form. The electronic computer can be introduced into any present corporate structure with little modification to the line and staff concept so that it is possible to simulate the function of the single entrepreneur without a return to that unrealistic organizational structure.

The emphasis upon computers, mathematics, and the scientific method does not diminish in the least the importance of common sense in distinguishing between what is wanted, what is possible, and what is currently being done. While it is true that methods and machines exist which will produce almost any desired report, economics and common sense must be applied to determine what

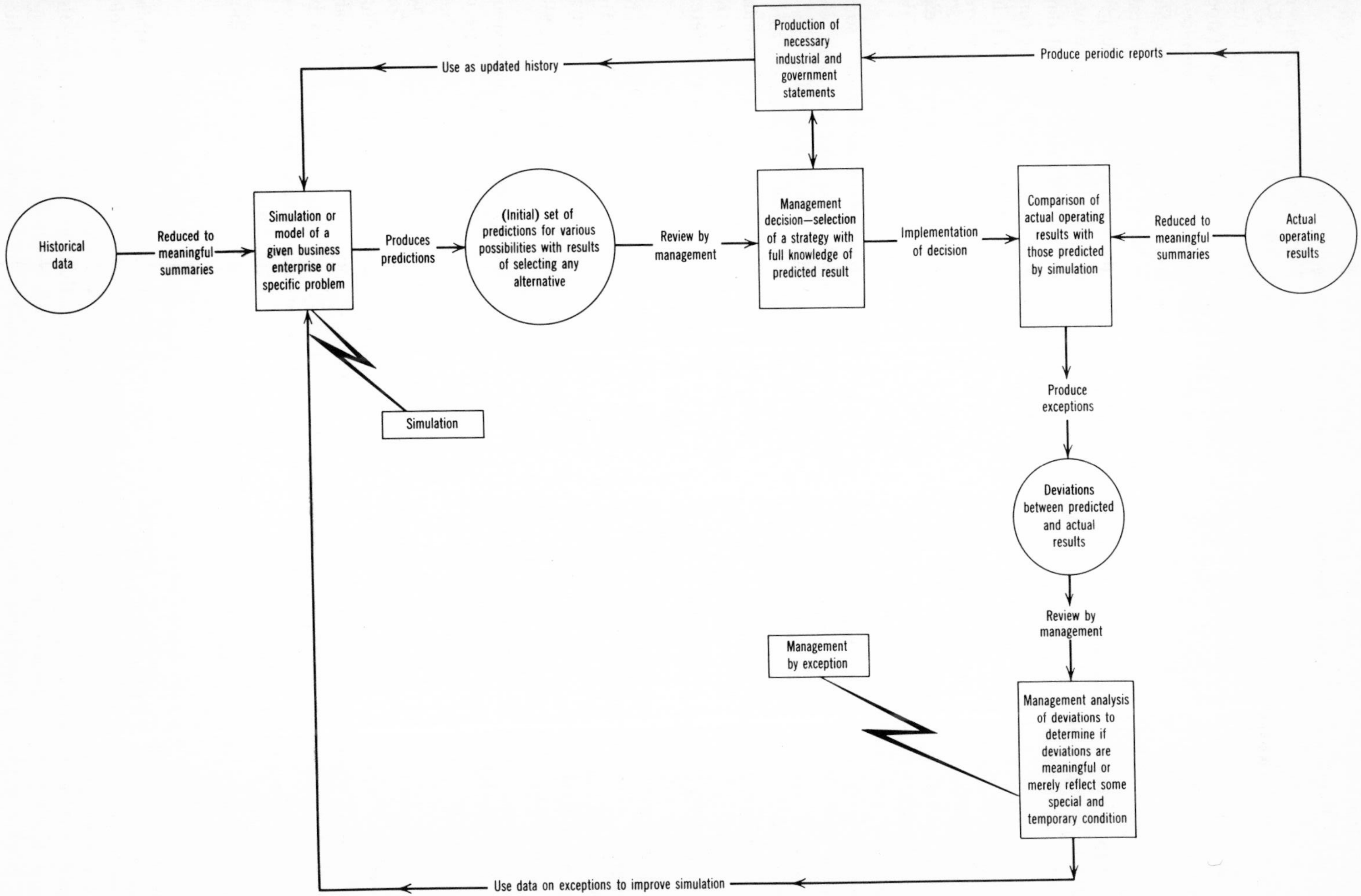

FIG. 1. Total management system cycle.

is realistic. In the development of any management system, too high an emphasis cannot be placed on basic, down-to-earth realism.

STAGES OF SYSTEM DEVELOPMENT

The development and installation of a total management system may be broken down into three major stages. These are:

1. Definition of the problem.
2. Design of the total management system.
3. Programming, cutover to the new system, and system evaluation and modification.

Within each of these areas there are a number of separate operations and activities which must be performed, many of which overlap one another. An arrow diagram [1] has been prepared which illustrates the interrelationship of these activities (see Figure 2). This diagram specifies the various tasks necessary to develop and install a total management system. Whereas the diagram is somewhat abbreviated, the exclusions would be of minor consequence to the overall logic of the plan.

PROBLEM DEFINITION

The first stage, problem definition, requires developing a realistic statement indicating the kind of system necessary to produce the reports needed for effective management. This phase must include establishing objectives of a total management system, personnel selection to develop and design such a system, and determining all requisite elements of the system.

Flow charting techniques have generally been used in the problem definition stage, but these charts are cumbersome, difficult to prepare, and difficult to read. Moreover, they often direct management's attention toward simply a mechanization of the old system rather than any bold new approach.

Problem definition for a total management system is based upon data handling procedures. The structure of any operating data system is based upon *data elements* (stock numbers, employee numbers, employee names) which are collected into *data files* (payroll register, stock inventory). Certain rules govern the use of data elements to produce new, or updated, data files. These new files are the *output* reports. The original data elements form the *input* reports to the system.

The rules governing the updating of information fall into three categories. These are:

1. Data movement—the transfer of an element of data from the old document to the new.
2. Arithmetic—the performance of some arithmetic operation upon one or more elements of data during the data transfer.
3. Logical decision—the examination of a data element in the input report to determine a course of action in preparing the output report. For example, the size of gross pay determines the income tax rate.

These three operations form the basis of any electronic computer program since all of the functions that any computer can perform may be reduced to data movement, arithmetic, and logical decision.

In his analysis of a data handling system, the systems engineer will isolate each type of data element and give it a name and number. Then he will determine the interrelationship of the various data elements, such as the format and type of documents in which the data will appear. At the same time, it is necessary to determine the logical selection rules to be used and the arithmetic calculations to be performed on the input data.

The steps in the analysis of a data handling system follow:

1. Determination of data elements.
2. Determination of the interrelationships of data elements and the location of data elements in the file.
3. Determination of rules governing the handling of data elements and data files.
4. Formulation of decision tables where logical choice would govern the selection of one of many possible paths.

[1] *How to read an arrow diagram.* Each job or activity in a project is represented by an arrow. Work flows from the tail of an arrow to the head, but the length of the arrow and the direction in which it points are immaterial. Dotted arrows do not represent real activities but are used to maintain logical relationships. The junction points of arrows are called events; they are numbered so that the tail of an arrow has a number smaller than the head. Events represent points in time as opposed to arrows which represent activities that consume time. The event also indicates the point in time when all preceding activities have been completed and succeeding activities can start.

5. Formulation of rules governing the production of specific reports required for specific management action.

Various techniques have been devised to assist in the collection of information required for problem definition. The best features of these techniques have been combined in a new system called START (systematic tabulation and analysis of requirements technique).

With this technique, the first step is to define the areas of decision (planning, controlling and operating) necessary to manage the enterprise. These areas of decision are determined from a study of the existing organization, operations and policies.

The problem definition phase, to this point, includes:

1. The establishment of operating objectives.
2. The selection and training of personnel to study the problem.
3. The use of START to analyze the present system and document the required system.

To complete the problem definition phase, management must establish the ultimate objectives of a new system so that parameters and response speeds can be determined. This procedure may lead to additions, deletions or revisions in the reports being produced which may, in turn, lead to the introduction of new data elements and the elimination of others.

Throughout problem definition and succeeding stages of the development and installation of a total management system, control should be maintained with the critical path method (CPM) and the multiple allocation procedure (MAP).

The critical path method is a management technique devised for the planning, scheduling and monitoring of large projects. The planning phase consists of drawing an arrow diagram of a project by assembling all of the project activities according to logical sequence and relationships. When time estimates are applied to each of the activities, it is possible to determine the longest (and therefore critical) path of activities. The arrow diagram thus provides easy visual assimilation of the plan and it functions as a working model which can be used to simulate project operations.

The multiple allocation procedure is used to allocate resources to the project and thereby place the plan on a calendar timetable. Resources are levelled to obtain the most economical schedule possible. MAP is applied after the logic of the arrow diagram has been thoroughly analyzed and refined. The allocation of resources automatically produces a schedule for the project. Then, when the project is in operation, data are collected and analyzed on a regular basis to be used in rescheduling or replanning when necessary.

Experience has shown that CPM and MAP used in combination enable management to determine the proper sequencing of activities and to allocate resources needed to perform these tasks in a coordinated fashion.

SYSTEM DESIGN

After the problem has been defined, the next step is to design the new system. This phase should include:

1. The continued examination of various scientific techniques, such as transportation models, simulation, and inventory models, and the final selection of those to be used in the new system.
2. The development of consolidated reports and report formats for historical record keeping to satisfy business and governmental requirements.
3. The testing of selected mathematical techniques which use recent and past experience as the basis for predictions. This would include the generation of management reports that compare the predicted with the actual and offer management various alternatives and the results of each alternative.
4. The selection of a judicious (economic) combination of telecommunications equipment to transmit data over large distances and the establishment of electronic data processing centers to meet present and projected (future) needs.
5. The development of an organization which will program and install the total management system, operate the equipment, and make full and effective use of the results of such a system.

The underlying objective in these considerations should be the most economical combination of equipment and people in an industrial complex in order to provide effective management.

While it is easy to speak of using equipment, especially electronic data processing equipment, one should never become so sophisticated as to overlook the use of pencil and paper. A real distinction between an expert and an amateur in the field of management systems and in the application of electronic data processing equipment and techniques is the ability to distinguish between the proper and improper use of machinery to solve a problem. Quite often the best and most adequate solution involves a simple technique applied with pencil and paper (and sometimes an eraser).

PROGRAMMING, CUTOVER, EVALUATION, AND MODIFICATION

Programming, which begins the third phase in formulating a total management system, has been greatly simplified by the great strides made with program compilers, especially COBOL (common business oriented language). With this automatic programming technique a single English language statement can be used to generate many computer instructions—fully checked and integrated in a running program. And looking ahead, it is conceivable that START will lead to the development of a system-type compiler that will eliminate even the block diagramming required with COBOL.

The cutover operation is so interrelated with programming and system design that it is best illustrated by the arrow diagram (Figure 2). Cutover entails such things as the design of forms, conversion of data, installation of new equipment, and the like.

No equipment should be ordered until the system design phase is virtually complete. Delivery should be specified for an appropriate time during the cutover phase. All too often equipment is ordered before the system is designed and then delivered before it is needed. Considering that rentals range between $10,000 and $50,000 per month, a poor decision or an ill-timed delivery can be extremely expensive. In addition, the cost of programming, which often exceeds equipment rental fees, can cause total costs to skyrocket if the programming effort is not phased in properly with the installation of the new system.

Once the new system is in operation, *system evaluation and modification* begin. This phase should be a continuing effort which seeks to take advantage of new developments as they occur. The ultimate evaluation of the system's effectiveness is, of course, the financial statement.

Throughout the period of development and installation of a total management system, a planned program of training must be conducted to ensure the support of middle management for the program. If this is not done, even the best engineered system may never be completely effective.

SUMMARY

This report is an outline of the basic steps, and an introduction to some of the problems, involved in creating a total management system. The task is not an easy one. It requires a great deal of work (particularly on the part of line personnel), considerable and searching analysis, and some far reaching decisions. The installation of such a system will have tremendous impact. Properly implemented, it will undoubtedly result in increased profits. Moreover, the total management system is designed to put managing back into the hands of management by producing the information needed to "really manage." The opportunity and challenge are here. But if there is any hesitancy—to do the work, to make the decisions, to commit the necessary funds—then there is no point in even starting.

35. RESEARCH PROBLEMS IN MANAGEMENT CONTROLS *

ALAN J. ROWE †

The purpose of this paper is to present a number of concepts pertaining to management controls and to discuss information requirements, decision rules and feedback mechanisms. The use of computer simulation as a means for studying the dynamic response characteristics of management controls in a business environment is also presented.

INTRODUCTION

The complex nature of modern day business gives rise to the need for effective means to study and design such systems. Since computer simulation has been applied to the problem of system design and study of management decision rules (1), it appears to be a suitable means for examining business system behavior and the associated management controls. In fact, the use of simulation to evaluate system designs has led to the term "policy laboratory" (2). Furthermore, the use of computer simulation will undoubtedly have profound effects on the design of real-time management control systems.

Managers are concerned with organizing the available resources subject to constraints such as capital structure, physical facilities and market position, to achieve purposeful objectives and assure survival of the business. In carrying out the control function, management uses an information and communication network which provides a direct link to persons concerned with utilization of the resources. Operating decisions, in turn, are based on information describing the status of the system as resources are used to produce goods and services. This information and the associated decision rules are seldom made explicit in an actual business; nonetheless, the informational aspects of the management control problem should be amenable to study via computer simulation.

SOURCE: *Management Technology* (December 1961), pp. 6–15. Reprinted by permission of the Institute of Management Science.

* A paper prepared in October 1960 at the Systems Development Corporation and received for publication in March 1961.

† University of Southern California.

DEFINING MANAGEMENT CONTROLS

In current business systems, measurement is often mistaken for management control. Although measurement is implied, control includes objectives, decision criteria for evaluation of performance, decision rules for corrective action and, of course, suitable measures of performance. To clarify the definition, we might consider the problem from the point of view of three separate systems: the data processing system, the management information system, and the management control system. These are shown in Figure 1.

Data processing is generally considered as carrying out the activities shown at the second level; whereas a management information system includes levels 1, 2 and 3. However, a management control system implies that all four levels are included. This manner of structuring the problem is similar to the familiar servomechanism feedback loop; however, in a business system we are dealing with a man-machine system, and, as yet, mathematical transfer functions have not been developed to describe human decision-making behavior. Thus, servo theory is not sufficient as the basis for the design of a complex man-machine system, although some progress has been made in dealing with specific physical responses (3).

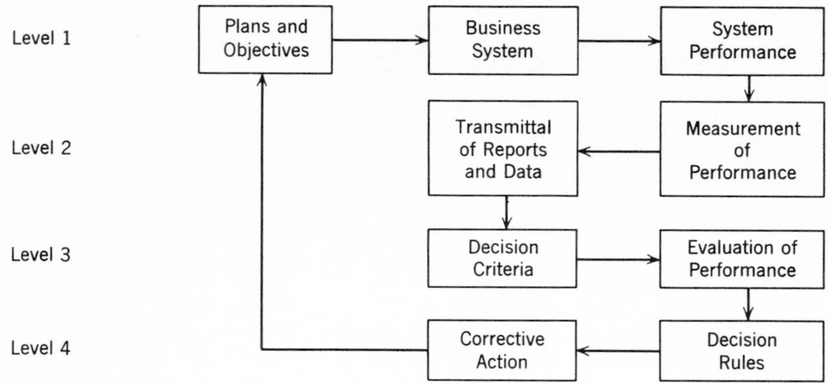

FIG. 1.

DESCRIBING A BUSINESS SYSTEM

A business consists of numerous activities such as sales, design, fabrication, etc., which, in effect, define its capabilities. However, the effectiveness with which these activities are executed depends to a considerable extent on the human organization charged with these responsibilities and their knowledge of the interactions among the system activities. A study of management controls should therefore explicitly consider these interactions.

One manner of characterizing a business system is as a matrix of activities and responses, as shown in Figure 2.

The elements of this matrix define the relationship between system activities and the decision rules which determine system responses. For example, element a_{11} is the budget allocation rule that determines the system response to sales requirements. The element a_{ij} refers to the delays incurred during the manufacturing process as a result of using priority decision rules to choose work from queues at machines. The element a_{mn} defines the manner in which information is used to achieve system control. Obviously, there would be many elements required for this latter activity in describing an actual business.

Activity	System Responses: Allocate Funds	Assign Personnel	Incur Delays	Generate Information
Sales	a_{11}	a_{12}		a_{lm}
Engineering	a_{21}			
Manufacturing			a_{ij}	
Planning				
Control				a_{mn}

FIG. 2.

INTERACTION OF CONTROL AND SYSTEM BEHAVIOR

The behavior of a complex business system can be described in terms of the basic business phenomena and the decisions made by managers. In order to simulate a business, however, it is necessary to formalize the decision rules used by management and to use transfer functions that describe the basic phenomena. The simulated system behavior is a combination of both factors and can be viewed as in Figure 3. Thus, changes in system behavior may be due to modification of the basic structure or simply to the interaction of the phenomena with control decision rules.

In a computer model, information is generated whenever the simulated physical system changes from one state or condition to another.

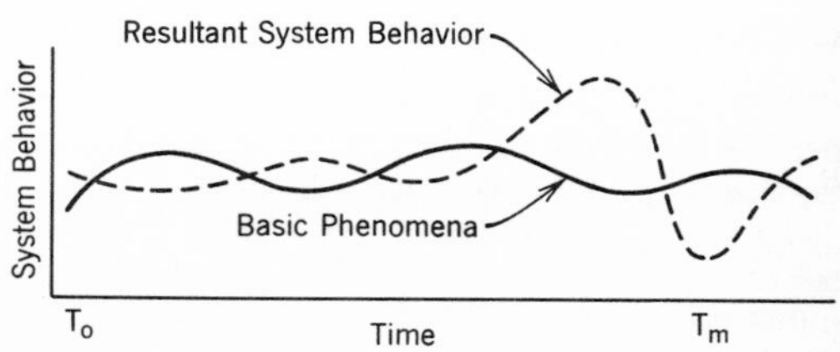

FIG. 3.

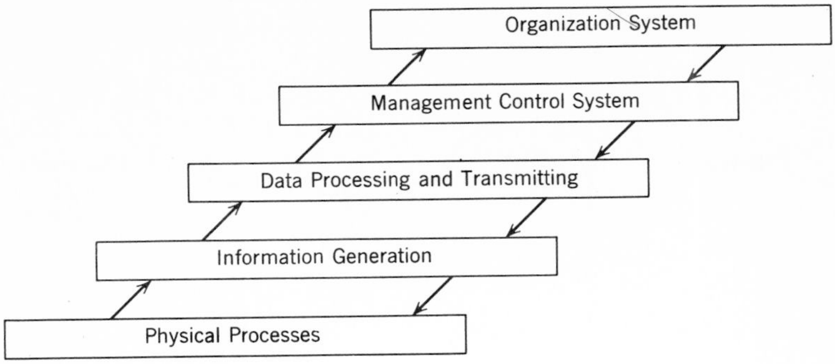

FIG. 4.

This is shown schematically[1] in Figure 4. This information is selectively updated and made available to the management control system which uses various decision criteria and decision rules to change or correct the state of the physical system. A number of these decisions may, however, be dependent upon the organizational level. Thus, tactical or operational decisions are made in the control system, whereas strategic or long-range decisions are generally made at the organizational system level (4).

THE CONTROL FUNCTION

For purposes of this paper, control is directly related to the decisions made in the system. If we examine the typical decisions made in a business, we find that there are decisions (such as budgeting) which affect the entire system; and other decisions that do not have an appreciable effect on the entire system. The former decisions are generally long range; whereas the latter tend to be operational in nature. However, the majority of decisions directly affect a number of other system activities. Because of interdependencies, these decisions are difficult to formulate explicitly. Thus, one of the major advantages of computer simulation is that the dependent relationships can be generated by continuous updating of interacting variables in the system.

Turning to the question of control itself, it should be capable of assuring the following system response characteristics.

- Adapting the system to changing conditions
- Stabilizing system response under variable demand
- Allowing maximum effectiveness of the system rather than imposing restrictive limits
- Providing a minimum time lag in correcting deviation in performance commensurate with the desired objective
- Implementing real-time control

The possibility of achieving real-time control appears very likely in view of the capability of computers to rapidly process data. However, the review frequency in real-time control systems should be matched with the response capability of the system. For example, if corrective action requires a minimum of one day, a review frequency of once a minute would be unreasonable. Since business systems often have long delays between measurement and corrective action, the significance of real-time control may differ radically from that used in military control systems.

In business, there are many interacting subsystems, and response depends on factors such as the status of subsystems, speed and amount of their changes and time dependencies. The time dependencies are important in the design of error correcting controls, as shown, for example, in Figure 5.

where t_0 = time that error of forecast is observed

t_r = time that error of forecast is reported

t_m = minimum time after t_r that the system can respond to a given correction

$p = t_m - t_r$ = minimum response period

The response period p is dependent both on the magnitude and the rate of change re-

[1] The manner of viewing the problem resulted from a discussion with Professor Daniel Teichroew of Stanford University.

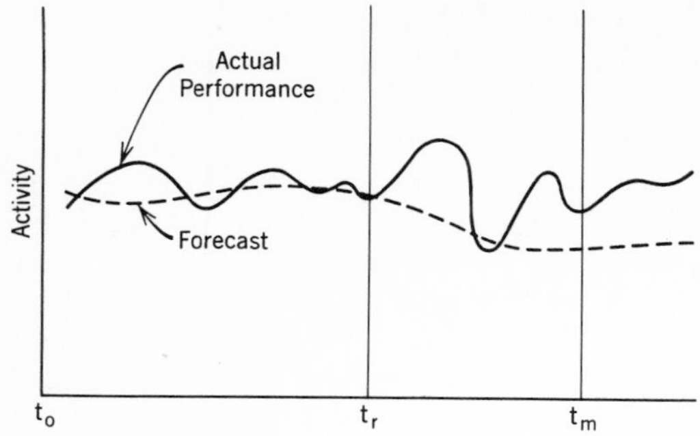

FIG. 5.

quired. Where the response period has to be made extremely short, as in military control systems, computer-based controls are often the only solution. Short response periods, however, are generally prohibitive for business systems due to cost and the design requirements. The cost of control is often overlooked; however, it is a significant factor and should be balanced with operating efficiency in the control system.

Another consideration in the design of control systems is the accuracy of error sensing techniques. Where there is loose coupling between system response and the forecast, extreme accuracy is unnecessary. However, where accuracy is required and the demand is a time series, the forecast can be improved by considering the current state of the system as the base point for predicting future demand. This is based on the assumption that the system is in a state of activity at time t and that the best estimate of the state at the time $t+1$ can be obtained by a form of exponential smoothing using both past history and anticipated events (see Figure 6).

A first attempt at explicit formulation is the following:

$$S_{i+1} = aS_{i-n} + (1-a)S_i + bE + (1-b)F,$$

where S_{i+1} = forecast state of the system for time $t+1$

S_i = present state of the system

S_{i-n} = past history of the system

a = a smoothing constant, which could be made a function of the variance of system activity

b = a smoothing constant such that the ratio a/b is made a function of time and error of forecast

E = environmental factors such as condition of the economy, etc.

F = forcing functions used by the business such as advertising, etc.

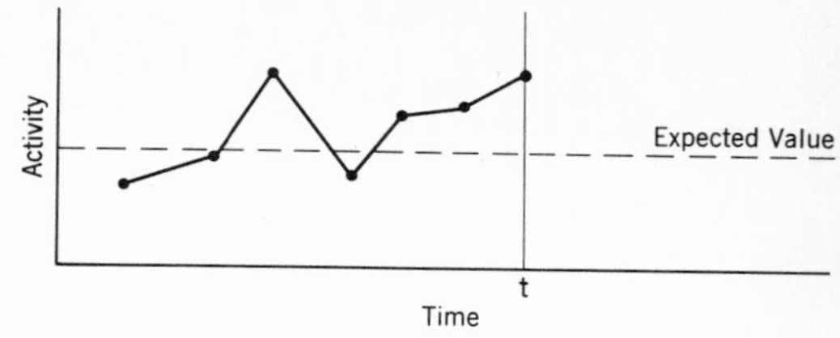

FIG. 6.

Although this formulation may lead to improved forecasts, the manner of responding to forecast is still not completely solved. A paper has been written which considers the problem of changing production and inventory levels in response to forecast demand (5). However, such decisions, like many in a business, interact with other system activities. Where there is a significant interaction, the decision rules controlling system response should take this into account.

Another consideration in the question of accuracy of forecast is the response mechanism. Since business is stochastic in nature, the error correction should hold performance within a specified band rather than directed toward an exact objective. In addition, the correction can be made as shown in Figure 7. First a large correction (from A to B) is made, and then only minor adjustments are made within the variance band, which is similar to the quality control technique.

Decision rules used as control mechanisms can affect performance by inducing fluctuations in an otherwise stable system. For example, consider a classical inventory problem, where the usage rate is constant and the replenish-

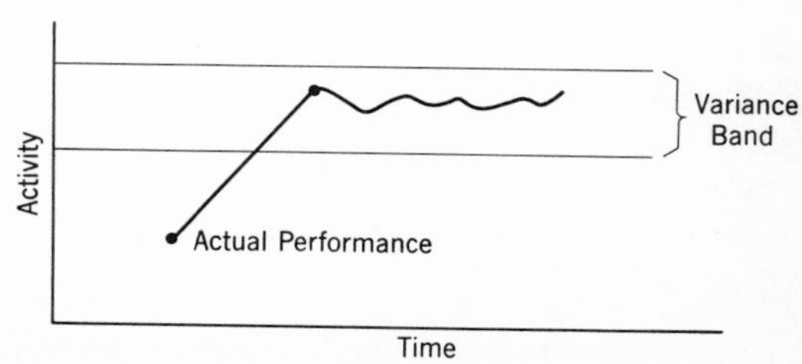

FIG. 7.

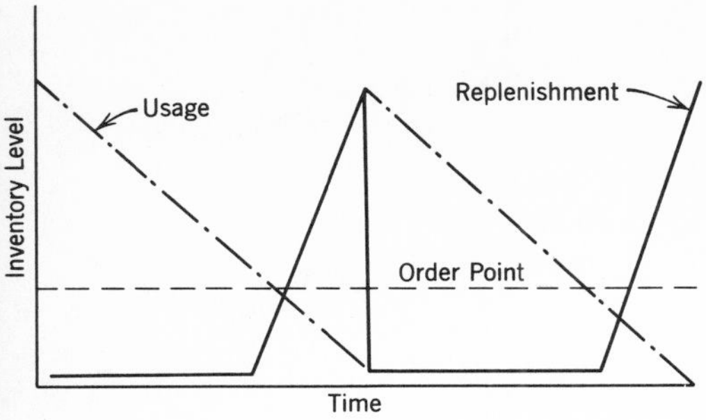

FIG. 8.

ment rate has a lag imposed by a reorder point rule as shown in Figure 8. The decision rule which leads to periodic replenishment will cause fluctuations in employment if the plant is producing a single product. Thus, labor productivity would follow the replenishment curve despite constant demand.

Often, due to considerations such as the physical processing, production cannot match consumption. A better understanding of the interaction of decision rules and physical processes is a prerequisite to the design of effective management control systems.

CONTROL SYSTEM DESIGN CONSIDERATIONS

The design of management control systems should take both variability of system performance and response characteristics into account. We can anticipate that the control would change radically for different types of business, if the variability of performance is assumed to increase as a function of the complexity of the business. Variability in the system is a measure of the error in predicting performance. Furthermore, it is assumed that the quantity of information required for control varies inversely with the stability of the system. Thus, a system which exhibits considerable variability would require a larger amount of information to maintain a given level of control. Of course, it is assumed that variability is caused by underlying phenomena rather than induced fluctuations resulting from the control system employed.

Since complex business systems will probably require large amounts of information for control purposes, the use of computer-based controls appears likely. However, the specific control system design is still subject to further research. An example of the use of computers for R&D control is the PERT (6) technique. This technique is used to schedule the vast interconnected number of components for the Polaris missile. Although the PERT system was initially designed for control of the many contractors working in the Polaris program, it is now being applied to the internal operations of a single business. This is but one of a class of computer-based control systems for use in business.

A significant design principle of real-time control through continuous monitoring has been demonstrated by computer-based control systems. Stated another way, the computer now provides the capability of continuously updating critical systems variables. In the PERT system, this would be the minimum slack path, while for other applications it can be extended to include a number of critical variables. If the variables are ranked in the order of their impact on the system, we can anticipate the curve shown in Figure 9.

Thus, a computer-based management control system could continuously monitor variables 1 through m which have the major impact on the system. The variables m through n could then be treated by exception reporting or other techniques. One means of determining which are the critical variables is by the use of computer simulation. Furthermore, since the variables which have a major impact could be continuously monitored in an actual business, this should lead to improved system control.

Another problem is that of local vs. total system control. Stated another way, the question is, what is the optimum combination of subsystem controls where there is interdependence? One approach to this problem which may be suitable is the joint optimization

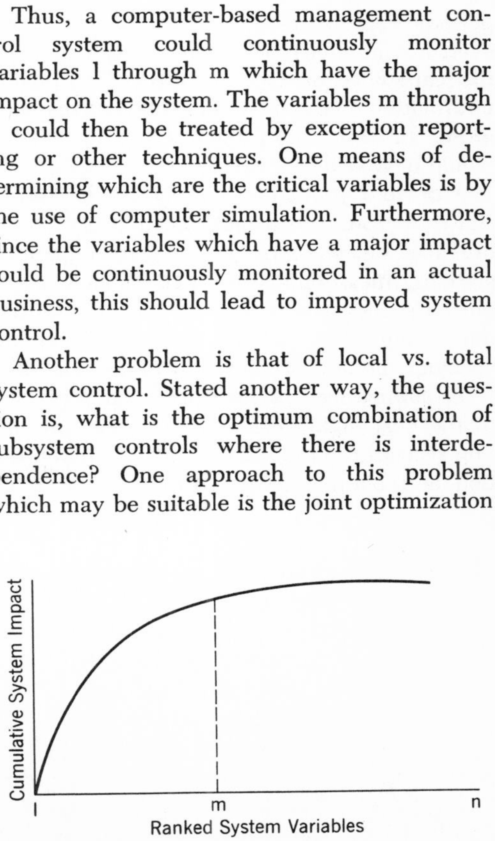

FIG. 9.

proposed by Markowitz in his book on portfolio selection (7). This approach uses quadratic programming to find the optimum which is defined in terms of expected values, variance and co-variance estimates.

Thus, the control system can be designed to achieve a given expected value with an associated risk. Since survival of the enterprise is an important management objective, this manner of formulating the problem of joint optimization should be useful in the control system design.

An integral part of any control system design is the measurement of performance. Not only must there be suitable measures, but these should be a function of the level of management. Since top management is primarily concerned with long-range decisions, there is loose coupling with the actual business processes. Thus, the amount of aggregation and frequency of information transmission should be appropriately designed into the measurement system. Rather than continuous reporting of system status to top management, periodic reports are generally sufficient. However, a computer-based system would provide the capability of random access to updated information on detail system status as the need arose. In this sense, then, top management would have real-time control.

A related problem to reporting of system status is the communication network in an organization. In current management control systems, measurement of performance is reported successively upward in an organization and is aggregated at each level. For example, consider the flow as shown in Figure 10. Each level summarizes performance and reports it to the next higher echelon, until the information reaches the top. At each level, summarization and biasing occurs. Although the levels act as filters in one sense, they can also introduce distortion in another sense. Furthermore, at no time does anyone but the top executive level have access to all of the information in the system. Contrast this with the concept of a system staff reporting to the top executive which acts as the summarizing medium using the computer for rapid, random access to detail system information. This would appear as in Figure 11.

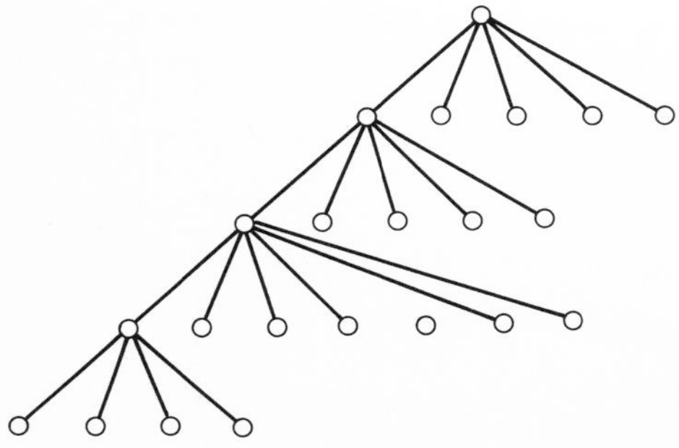

FIG. 10.

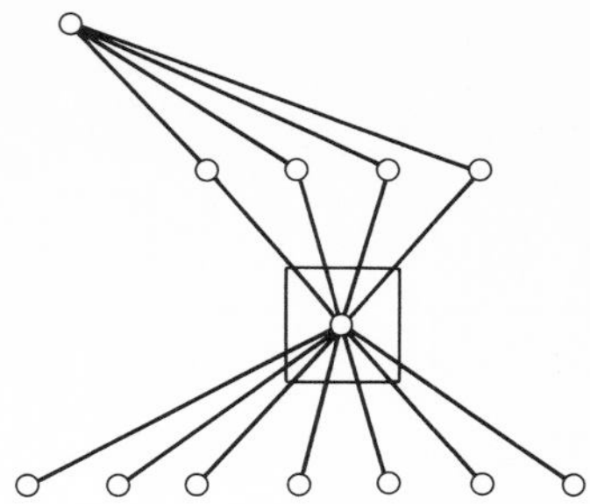

FIG. 11.

In this kind of application the computer would have direct access to all system information and have as much as 30% reported automatically. Not only is the information on system performance more timely and accurate, but the system staff as a team has an overview of the entire operation. Thus, we can anticipate that the organization design in computer-based control systems will be more closely matched with the information requirements of the system.

In a like manner, the design of the decision network poses a number of formidable problems. Current organizations lead to a cascading effect of decisions as a result of interpretation at each level and generally differing measures of performance. In addition to the cascade effect among levels, there are the conflicting objectives at any given level. Thus, there is a need for a design mechanism which treats the problem as a whole rather than the fragmented approach prevalent in industry today.

One attack on the problem which may prove worthwhile is the use of a decision matrix and mathematical operators to generate solutions. That is, rather than enumerate all possible combinations of a given set of decisions and system variables, heuristic rules can be used to select good solutions. Consider the following example:

There are four kinds of information, I_1 to

	D_1	D_2	D_3
I_1	e_{11}		
I_2	e_{12}		e_{23}
I_3		e_{32}	
I_4			e_{43}

FIG. 12.

I_4 which are used to make decisions D_1 *to* D_3 as shown in Figure 12. The number of possible combinations is $2^n - 1$, which equals 4095. If a particular combination of decisions and information is required to execute a given activity, then a rule can be used to choose from the twelve elements in the matrix to arrive at the solution. For instance, a rule might appear as follows:

Given conditions *XYZ*, use e_{11} and e_{12} for D_1, e_{32} for D_2 and e_{23} and e_{43} for D_3, where the *D*'s themselves may be complex functions.

Thus, the rule chooses a particular combination based on a set of conditions *XYZ*. This decision matrix approach is similar to the associative lists of Simon and Newell.

There are obviously many additional design problems which must be studied in management control systems. To experiment with these problems, however, it is necessary to have a suitable laboratory. Although there are some severe limitations to computer simulation, especially in regard to studying human behavior, nonetheless there are many facets of the control problem which can be profitably examined. Hopefully, as there is a better understanding of basic system phenomena, the design process itself will reach the point where management controls are no longer based on judgment alone.

CONCLUSION

Although this paper has undoubtedly raised many more questions than have been answered, the intent was to explore the problems associated with the study and design of management control. Since research is enhanced by experimentations, computer simulation has been proposed as the vehicle. A model of a business system (8) is now being programmed at the System Development Corporation (9) which should provide the means for studying many of the problems and questions raised in this paper. It is hoped that useful knowledge will be forthcoming from this effort in the attempt to design effective management controls.

REFERENCES

1. A. J. Rowe. "Application of Computer Simulation to Production System Design," *SP-85*. System Development Corporation, September 14, 1959.
2. D. G. Malcolm and A. J. Rowe. "An Approach to Computer-Based Management Control Systems," *SP-145*. System Development Corporation, August 3, 1960.
3. P. M. Fitts. "Engineering Psychology and Equipment Design," in S. S. Stevens (ed.), *Handbook of Experimental Psychology*, New York: John Wiley and Sons, 1951, Ch. 35.
4. A. J. Rowe. "Modeling Considerations in Computer Simulation of Management Control Systems," *SP-156*. System Development Corporation, March 3, 1960.
5. C. C. Holt, F. Modigliani, and H. A. Simon. "Lincar Decision Rule for Production and Employment Scheduling." *Management Science*, Vol. 2, No. 1, October 1955.
6. D. G. Malcolm, J. H. Roseboom, C. E. Clark, and W. Fazar. "Application of a Technique for Research and Development Program Evaluation," *SP-62*. System Development Corporation, March 1959.
7. H. M. Markowitz. *Portfolio Selection*. New York: John Wiley and Sons, 1959.
8. R. C. Crawford, et al. "Simulation of a Firm: The Mark I Model," *TM-528*. System Development Corporation.
9. J. B. Heyne. "Mark I Operational Specifications," *TM-536*. System Development Corporation, September 23, 1960.

36. COMPUTER MANAGEMENT CONTROL SYSTEMS THROUGH THE LOOKING GLASS

GEORGE F. WEINWURM *

A discussion of three aspects of the introduction of real time computer executive control systems into the world of business, using as a frame of reference the experience acquired through the design and operation of a similar military system, SAGE, over the past several years. In particular, consideration is given to the relative effectiveness with which the system communicates with its environment, the necessary compromises in the definition of the rules by which the system will function, and certain difficulties in the concept of executive control systems which are in some sense adaptive.

INTRODUCTION

The advent of electronic data processing equipment into the world of business has, as predicted, been followed by an increasing stream of practical applications. Perhaps the greatest challenge to the management scientist is presented by the concept of a *real time* man/machine system, of the type which would be involved in the actual decision processes essential to the everyday conduct of an industrial enterprise. This sentiment is not unreasonable, since developments in this area involve the deepest and most subtle considerations about the nature of automata and the practical business environment, as well as the men through whom the system must interact.

The diversity of endeavor which characterizes the world of business is a barrier to those seeking measures which remain significant from one field to another, or even within a single enterprise. Furthermore, the techniques of conducting a business, which historically have developed along lines peculiar to the needs of a specific organization, may be quite at odds with any effort at definition in terms of a machine-like program. The various considerations involved in balancing a system between the desires of a customer, however "non-optimum" they may be, as opposed to undertaking a revision of the customer's operating procedures, with the inherent risks implied, have been discussed and could easily fill many volumes (1).

Let us say that whatever experience has been acquired in the general area of executive man/machine systems is of real value, particularly since such systems are of comparatively recent vintage operationally. It is in this context that we will consider a widespread complex of computers, weapons, and men which since 1956 has been charged with the integrated defense of increasing portions of the continental United States against manned bomber attack, namely, the SAGE system. (The acronym represents the words Semi-Automatic Ground Environment.)

When compared to the multitude of computerized military command and control, or "L" systems now in various stages of development, SAGE appears as an earlier effort. Its significance lies in the fact that it represents the first occasion that an automatic man/machine system on the scale of conception of the cybernetic pioneers was actually built and operated in a live environment over an extended period of time. I am referring here to the work of men such as Wiener (2), von Neumann (3), and others.

It seems worthwhile to consider some general questions concerning the application of real time computerized executive control sys-

SOURCE: *Management Science* (July, 1961), pp. 411–418. Reprinted by permission of the Institute of Management Science.

* Systems Development Corporation.

tems to the problems of business, using the SAGE system, and some of the experiences acquired in its design and operation, as a frame of reference.

FEEDBACK

Perhaps the most characteristic aspect of systems in general is the notion of feedback, the measurement and comparison of output with some standard in order to affect future outputs. In the realm of real time man/machine complexes this concept appears in a number of ways:

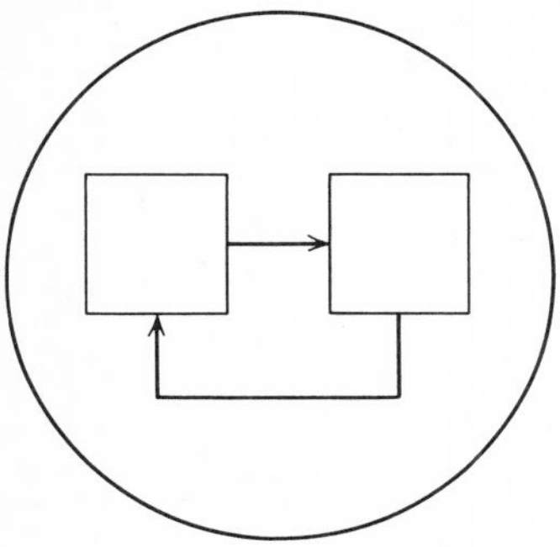

- Feedback within the computer—
  Checks on the progress and validity of certain calculations or events, etc.

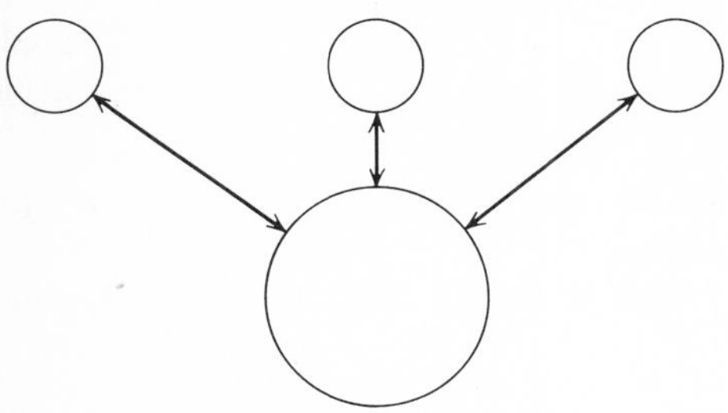

- Feedback between the computer and the system environment—
  Direct or circuitous automatic communication between the computer and other machinery in the system.

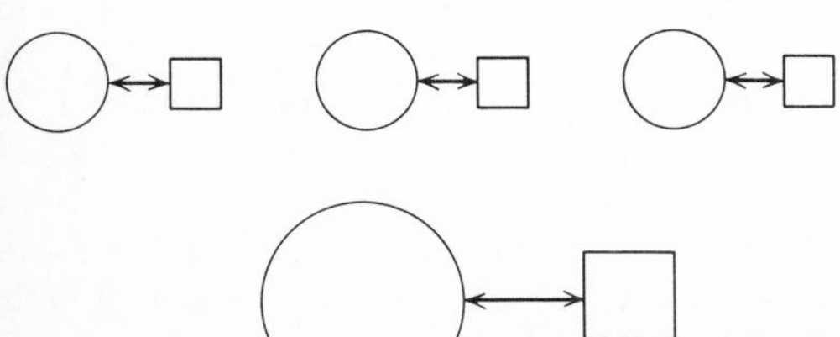

- Feedback between the man and the machine—
  Decision problems presented to an operator through some audible or visual indication, for his response through the means provided.

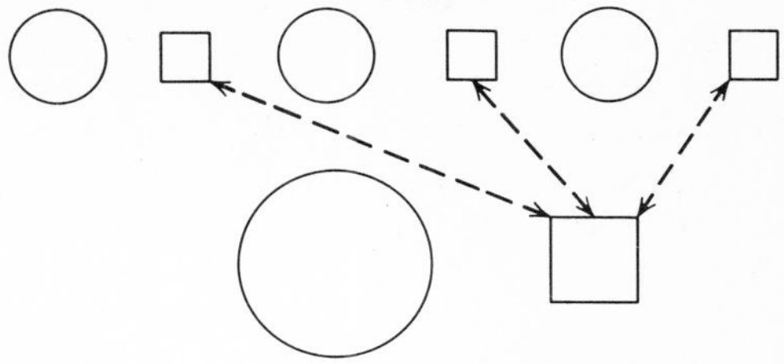

- Feedback directly between the man and the system environment—
  An operator may communicate directly with another operator by phone or radio, and subsequently insert information into the computer as desirable.

In all of the above cases we are seeking to minimize an error function of some kind, but the context of the communication involved greatly affects the way in which the problem is expressed, perhaps the fineness with which it may be considered, and certainly the approach to be taken toward its solution. Although all these feedbacks are in some sense discrete, many may, for all practical purposes, be considered as continuous or at least cyclic. In general, the more sophisticated problems will involve several types of feedback, even to the extent of using all four varieties many times over.

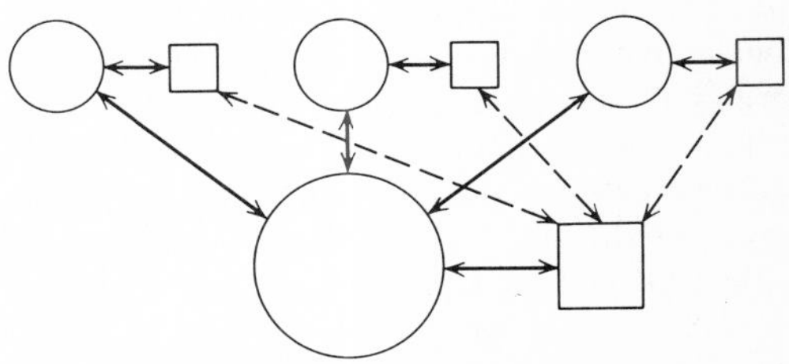

The most striking differentiation between these aspects of feedback is shown by considering the time required for one loop in the cycle. In general, checks within the computer will not exceed the order of a millisecond in SAGE. The three types of feedback necessitating interaction outside the computer will require 15 to 30 seconds, on the average: a ratio in time of at least 10^4. This has some rather interesting implications for real time systems. In the first place, a feedback loop which is discrete to the extent of the latter three varieties is difficult to analyze meaningfully within the existing tools of mathematical modeling, particularly in those areas involving human discretion (4). Secondly, a class of problems whose characteristics demand a relatively quicker feedback will not be within the capabilities of this system. Note that the situation will not necessarily improve with the introduction of a "faster" computer: in fact, the ratio will increase unless marked improvements are made in the general communication problem external to the machine.

In other words, we are emphasizing that the capabilities of a system, its "flexibility" in responding to various problems and environments, is dependent on more than the speed of the central computer. In terms of a present day complex such as SAGE, the hindrances which prevent the consideration of certain classes of problems probably have more to do with communicating with the environment than computing within the machine. Of course there have been significant advances in volume information transfer equipment in the past few years, and some of these devices will be available to improve the situation in future systems. In many cases, however, providing special equipment for a system of any magnitude may prove prohibitively expensive when compared to the use of existing telephone and teletype circuitry. In addition, for military applications, questions of security and survivability enter into the picture.

But the previous discussion has been rather mechanistic. A likely question is this: is not the communication problem described due largely to the need for human intervention; in other words, would not a greater degree of automaticity be the solution? The quick answer would be . . . in theory, yes; practically, not quite! The more complete answer involves a consideration of the way in which a real time program is prepared for operation in its environment.

RULES FOR DECISION

An early conception of an electronic digital data processor, as seen by Wiener (5), was described as follows:

> The ideal computing machine must then have all its data inserted at the beginning, and must be as free as possible from human interference to the very end. This means that not only must the numerical data be inserted at the beginning, but also rules for combining them, in the form of instructions covering every situation which may arise in the course of computation.

The difficulty in realizing this ideal is found in the reference of the ". . . rules . . . covering every situation which may arise. . . ." Certainly one of the characteristics of executive operation which the advent of computers has brought sharply into focus, if any further emphasis was needed, is the difficulty in establishing the ground rules in almost any situation, not to speak of all possible situations. Even in such a practical field as accounting, which one would think consisted of algorithms for counting value (what could be easier for a computer?), the incompatibilities which may arise between the rules used within an enterprise, or between several branches of the same company, are well known (6). The situation is no different in areas involving the operation of a business in a competitive environment, or in a war game, or in SAGE.

The evolution of a set of rules is, however, only a prelude to translating them into a language which may be manipulated by the machine. The supposition that all such expressions can be represented by a sufficiently lengthy string of yes/no propositions avoids two rather practical considerations:

- We must formulate exactly the right questions.
- We must ask them in exactly the right order.

Those who have attempted to evolve such a sequence of questions will verify that it is not as easy as one would assume. In fact, many of the "technical difficulties" exposed in checking out a program stem from a wrong question erroneously asked at a certain point in a sequence, or perhaps for some reason, by an inability to ask the proper question at the required moment. This latter situation is sometimes referred to as a "control problem."

Perhaps the greatest difficulty comes from dealing with the inescapable "maybe's"; those circumstances which fall outside the bounds of the rules which have been provided, either through some error or unforeseen circumstance, or because no general rule covering the situation could be agreed upon. For these cases, the real time program may follow one of a number of courses:

- Stop.
- Resort to some arbitrary solution which has nothing to do with the problem at hand, e.g., throw away the data and start somewhere else.
- Utilize a general problem solving routine, particularly in the case of a routine data error.
- Let an operator intervene.

The existence of "maybe's" in any but the most abstract or restrictive systems would not seem to require much substantiation, nor would the assumption that the first three alternatives to a situation falling outside the explicit rules for decision have a limited application. In other words, for any system approaching the complexity of an executive data processor, the kind of system we have been referring to, the intervention of an operator will certainly be required somewhere along the line.

But we have only approached the real problem. It is not overly difficult to provide a negative sort of logic by which problems are routed to an operator: in other words, anything other than the situations bounded by certain rules will be so referred. Now, we must define the ways in which we will permit the operator to respond to the machine, and furthermore, the ways in which the machine will consider the operator's response. Some extreme examples follow:

- We may require the operator to insert his responses into the computer via punched cards, using some machine language.
- We may provide a unique mechanical switch action to cover each response which the operator may desire to make.
- We may require the computer to stop until the operator's response has been received.
- We may permit the computer to continue with other problems, but wait for a response in the troublesome area.

Note that the answers in *these* areas, and the compromises which will necessarily be made in each case must be *specified in advance*. Even though we have been able to refer the "maybe's" to an operator with relative freedom, he will be restricted in his ability to respond by the equipment at his disposal, and by the computer program, both of which have been defined to some degree arbitrarily in advance.

In an operating system such as SAGE, experience has shown that the continual iterative process of defining the allowable boundaries of interaction between the operator and the machine, in terms of equipment, programming, training, and of course monetary restrictions, is of the greatest importance and is responsible for a major share of the effort required to keep the system running from the point of view of both the designer and the operating personnel.

Some mention should be made of the compromises which have proved useful in defining these man/machine interactions. A number of typical SAGE approaches would include the following:

- The operator is provided with a series of category selection switches by which he may discriminate between standard displays available at his console position.
- Certain displays are forced to an operator's position for his attention.
- The operator may respond through several general alphanumeric push-button modules which have been tailored to his individual task.
- Some processes are initiated solely by an operator.
- In other cases, the program will hold a problem for the operator's response although the computer continues to function in other areas.
- For certain critical situations where a delay may be significantly harmful, the program will wait a pre-set time for an operator's response, and failing to receive an indication, assume a pre-programmed case and proceed.

These types of man/machine interaction are clearly applicable to business situations. Consider, for example, a hypothetical *Air Freight* enterprise whose operations are controlled from a computer facility located at the home office, and tied by leased digital data lines to district offices throughout the service area. An operator at the central office would require a computer-driven visual display capability, and several general purpose push-button modules. Given this equipment, several types of interaction are possible:

- Displays indicating the present position of all company aircraft might be always present. By depressing the proper combination of buttons, an operator may request summary informational displays on a particular aircraft, freight order, or district office.

- Displays pertaining to an incoming request for freight routing would be forced to an operator's console.
- The computer will continue to display a forced request for freight routing until acknowledged by the proper button response, although continuing to function in other areas.
- An operator may choose to take button actions causing the computer to calculate and display several alternative routings for a specific freight order, based on combinations of least cost and time criteria.
- Confirmation of a selected routing must be initiated by an operator's button action, although the computer will transmit the appropriate messages to the requesting district office.
- If a position report indicates that an aircraft has landed at a location not specified on the flight plan, a special display will be forced to an operator. The absence of a proper button acknowledgement within a pre-set time will cause the computer to automatically transmit alert messages to all district offices having freight on the aircraft involved.

Although some rather complex decision hierarchies have been based on similar categorizations of interaction, the *technology* of computer systems has certainly outrun an appreciation of the broader aspects and subtleties of the man/machine relationship and the nature of the intercommunication which is desirable (7). The many rather arbitrary solutions which have been found to work for a multitude of specialized problems should not obscure the great need for a more general understanding, which is yet to come.

But a more visionary aspect of executive control systems remains to be considered, particularly with regard to the increasing number of references in recent years to so-called "adaptive" machinery, "general problem solvers," and the like. Is it not conceivable that a machine with a degree of "intelligence" and a broader view of the problems at hand could, in fact, circumvent many of the difficulties suggested earlier by "learning" its way to a solution, no matter what the problem? We will dwell upon this question somewhat further.

ADAPTIVE AUTOMATA

Certainly the present emphasis on parallel operation, which is found in many of the newer computer systems, begins to suggest the presence of a higher type of organization. The executive routines which evaluate tasks and assign priorities not only within a machine, but often for several machines, and the increasing amount of direct intercommunication between computers of various types suggest in some sense the theory of von Neumann mentioned earlier (8) which proposes that out of a "pool" of elementary machines, computers of certain special kinds could assemble automata of arbitrary complexity. Some of the work in pattern recognition (9) and general problem solving (10) is also of great interest.

But all this does not seem to be enough, at least in the foreseeable future. One reason is that although the theory of communication provides a measure for the information content of a message, in the sense of its degree of organization, or unexpectedness, it does not follow that this criterion necessarily provides an indication of the relative importance of a message. In other words, the information of greatest importance does not have to be contained in the message occurring with the lowest frequency. A system could be flooded with messages with the highest degree of organization, all containing information which was irrelevant to the problem at hand.

This situation casts some doubt on our ability to select a valid live environment to which our machine may adapt. There is a great deal of difference between training a machine to recognize the shapes of certain letters, and teaching it to separate more meaningful information from a flood of available literature than can the machine designers themselves—although this too has been postulated (11).

One approach is to simulate the real world to some degree of exactitude, and then permit the machine to adapt itself to increasingly complex environments under controlled conditions. The sufficiency of approximation, that is, a determination of the order of simulation which should be considered, may itself be a limiting factor for certain systems which cannot easily be made to "fail safe." Two examples which come to mind are a discussion of a computing machine with appropriate sensors which would perform the duties of a surgeon (12); and the control systems which function in a wartime environment, such as

SAGE. In spite of the best of simulated exercises, some say the only way to really evaluate a military system against the improbabilities of war is—to have one, at which point some one will surely complain that the sample was insufficient.

There is a diminishing requirement for "selling" the efficacy of simulation. In general, any environment can be simulated to some extent, and quite likely, the model can be improved over a period of time. An urgent need is for the development of a theory dealing with the order of simulation which is sufficient for a particular problem, whether the model is to provide a classroom for an adaptive man or machine. The question to be answered is not "why," or even "how," but "how much."

The potentials of adaptive automata are certainly impressive, and have been well documented in a number of fields. The general understanding of the manner in which these systems are to be brought to reality is, once again, a question which is largely unanswered.

SUMMARY

Charles Pierce has said that we do not want a logical machine to do its own business, but ours. The realization of this aim has been the topic of this discussion. In particular, we have tried to relate the overall capabilities of a computerized real time executive control complex to some of the compromises which must be made if the system is to function in a live environment, and to do this from the point of view of the experience which has been acquired through the operation of a similar system, SAGE, over the past few years.

The exciting future which awaits these systems is not altered by emphasizing the practical considerations involved in their design. On the contrary, herein lies the foundation for any subsequent realization of the hopes and plans of our day.

REFERENCES

1. C. West Churchman, "How Is Planning Possible," *Operations Research for Management,* edited by McCloskey and Coppinger, Baltimore: Johns Hopkins Press, 1956.
2. Norbert Wiener, *Cybernetics,* New York: John Wiley & Sons, 1958; and *The Human Use of Human Beings: Cybernetics and Society,* Garden City, New York: Doubleday & Co., 1950.
3. John von Neumann, "The General and Logical Theory of Automata," *The World of Mathematics,* edited by James R. Newman, New York: Simon & Schuster, 1956. Also, *The Computer and the Brain,* New Haven: Yale University Press, 1958.
4. Franklin V. Taylor, "Four Basic Ideas in Engineering Psychology," *The American Psychologist,* Vol. 15, No. 10, October 1960.
5. *Cybernetics,* p. 139.
6. See T. A. Wise, "The Auditors Have Arrived," *Fortune Magazine,* Vol. 62, Nos. 5 and 6, November and December 1960.
7. Taylor.
8. von Neumann, "The General and Logical Theory of Automata."
9. Frank Rosenblatt, *The Perceptron: A Theory of Statistical Separability in Cognitive Systems.* Cornell Aeronautical Laboratory Report VG-1196-G-1, January 1958; ASTIA Document No. 204-076.
10. Allen Newell, J. C. Shaw, and Herbert Simon, "Elements of a Theory of Human Problem Solving," *Psychological Review,* Vol. 65, No. 3, 1958.
11. W. Ross Ashby, "Design for an Intelligence Amplifier," in *Automata Studies,* edited by C. E. Shannon and J. McCarthy, Princeton University Annals of Mathematics Series, No. 34, 1956.
12. S. Gill, "Possibilities for the Practical Utilization of Learning Processes," *Proceedings of the Symposium on the Mechanization of Thought Processes,* National Physical Laboratory, Vol. II, 1958.

37. THE HUMAN SIDE OF A SYSTEMS CHANGE

LAWRENCE K. WILLIAMS *

The process of introducing complex systems into organizations is still part science and part art. The science includes the comprehension and design of the technical parts of the system, and the art involves the process of introduction primarily with regard to the human element.

The science has advanced to the point where nearly everyone describes procedural change in terms of its effect upon the total system rather than merely thinking of the introduction of another piece of "hardware." The large number of problems which grew out of early computer installations, when the computer was merely looked at as another piece of "hardware" rather than being looked at from the point of view of systems change, are now being anticipated to a much greater degree.

Most managements, for example, are now aware of the fact that the sponsoring agent for the computer in the organization will not be the only part called upon to make rearrangements. Rather, when the computer comes in the door, it usually affects a number of departments or units which are related to the sponsoring department and thus a total system is effected even though we may describe the change in terms of the piece of hardware or the technique that is being introduced.

There is still an art, however, to transferring a systems design into actuality. The process of making the new system acceptable to the human element and of modifying the human element so that it fits the requirements of the new system, if not an art, is certainly an inexact science. Perhaps one of the simplest ways of describing these problems in systems change is to note the fact that flow diagrams, new organizational charts and manuals of operation do not reflect the human element. They essentially describe an inanimate organization, and if everybody in the organization were merely a robot, most of the problems of systems change would be mitigated or disappear.

Fortunately or unfortunately, an organization is made up of people. The problems on the human side of a systems change involve the fact that there is considerable resistance to change, that downright acceptance of a change is quite often unique, and that the number of unanticipated consequences in terms of communication failures and road blocks thrown in the way from unexpected sources in the organization form a minimal list of problems. This leads the procedures specialist to the conclusion that individuals are highly irrational.

ATTITUDES: THE CORE OF RESISTANCE TO CHANGE

Even the most primitive analysis of the failures of a systems change usually results in the observation of attitudes and values which run counter to those required for accepting and endorsing the change. The whole concept of resistance to change, to a large degree, can be recoded as a problem of attitudes. Parenthetically, it should be noted that probably the poorest attitudes, if one wants to use this statement in terms of resistance to change, come from managers, not other employees. The middle level manager can and often does offer more resistance to systems change than all the employees reporting to him.

There is a complete literature on attitude formation and attitude change which suggests that attitudes are not formed in a logical manner nor are they changed in a logical manner. To a large degree, an attitude is a matter of emotion and not logic. While we

SOURCE: *Systems & Procedures Journal* (July–August, 1964), pp. 40–43. Reprinted by permission of *Systems & Procedures Journal*.

* Cornell University.

would all like to think that we have arrived at logical conclusions with regard to our political preference to people we like and dislike, the kinds of jobs we prefer, etc., there is every evidence that our most basic attitudes and values have not come about through logical deduction.

The impermeability of many attitudes to logic is amply demonstrated in such areas as prejudice and attempts to change styles of consumption in the area of marketing. It is here that the systems engineer is perhaps the most illogical. In an attempt to change attitudes, he uses logic. The systems engineer convinced of the logic of his plan and the logic of the system usually operates on this basis: if he can explain this highly rational and logical system to someone, they will automatically accept his point of view in terms of the merit and necessity of the new system.

The line manager who states that the new computer won't work is usually quite immune to new information. Attempts to give him more booklets and more short courses on how a computer works, for example, or showing him that the same system has worked in other companies, and finally, recourse to saying it slower and louder as if somehow the manager was an imperfect receiver, usually are all to no avail.

What this resistant manager is really "saying," even though he may not be conscious of the fact, is that "it is impossible to think that most of the decisions which I have thought important for 20 years can now be put over on the computer;" and "not only am I not superior but you are suggesting that I am inferior with regard to decisions that will come out of a *machine*." He may also be "saying" that "I am terribly afraid I will never be able to understand this new system, and no matter how much you talk or how much information you give me, I will never be on top of the new system the way I was with the old."

He may also be "saying" that "I have had 20 years of getting used to things the way they are, and any thought of changing the system is a violation of who I am and what I have been." This is perhaps what he is unconsciously saying and which we may get out of him if we have the time and the skill to explore fully the statement, "It won't work." If we engage in debate and counter argument with argument, we can go on for days, but we will probably never get close to the real cause of the attitude or the means of changing the attitude.

WHO WANTS TO LOSE STATUS?

The human side of the systems change also includes status. There is considerable status to being the oldest member of the work group who knows all the right answers. It is a considerable blow to have to start all over again and learn something new, and to be put perhaps at the same level or somewhat below the newcomers to the organization in terms of learning the language of the new technology or system.

It is also a blow when the responsibility of the unit that a person leads is transferred to another unit because it is logical from the point of view of the total organization. Get a person concerned enough about loss of status and he will commit himself to the antichange movement so strongly it is almost impossible to move him from this point of view. Again, the use of logic about the delights of the new system is to miss the point of the resistance.

THE UNSEEN ORGANIZATION CHART

The human side of the organization is also made up of a series of informal relationships. Many well-planned changes from the point of technology "go under" because of poor communications. Many organizational changes are based upon the belief that the organization works the way the organizational chart says it does. Very often, some of the best coordination and some of the best information in the system takes place in terms of informal connections that are not represented on the organizational chart. System changes which rearrange the relationships between units quite often assume that people communicate with each other and solve problems in keeping with the organizational chart. Operating under this assumption, systems practitioners make changes only to find that these changes are directly counter to a series of informal arrangements which have been making the organization work.

THE "LOGICAL" WAY TO HANDLE A CHANGE

The inability to cope with the resistance from the social system with regard to change often results in the "bulldozer approach." This school of thought advocates ramming the change through, for, after all, individuals can't resist completely as long as the company is paying the check. Many "successful" systems changes have been brought about in such a manner and, in fact, those who are concerned for the social side and for the minimizing of resistance are often viewed as missionaries who have somehow not seen what business and profits are all about. Before analyzing the results of the bulldozer approach, however, we should look at the causes.

Under the stress of production and time schedules, it is perhaps a natural consequence to resort to the use of formal authority and power in order to bring about change. Nearly every person responsible for change probably does become concerned with morale, resistance and the reaction of individuals; but under pressure, more often than not, the maxim is, "if logic won't do it, try force." Thus, one reason for the bulldozer approach is perhaps the fact that attempts to reduce resistance have failed.

This decision may also be coupled with the fact that those who are responsible for change often do not have complete communication with the top of the organization, which could be of assistance in countering resistance. If one looks at the cycle of major change in the organization, the usual observation is that once the top levels have made some major decisions about the nature of the change, cost and timing, the remainder of the work is delegated to lower levels in the organization. Very often, overt resistance does not come about until change is imminent. And even though the lower levels may be highly concerned, communication channels have been blocked with regard to communicating this to the top because the top is now unprepared to hear about these problems. Convinced that the system is logical and that the major decisions have been made, top management is often little interested and, until it is much too late, it does not hear about resistance at the bottom level where the change is being introduced.

Again, the inability to obtain attention from the top with regard to these problems results in an appeal for power and force which is usually forthcoming in order to protect the dollar investment, and again the bulldozer approach is in full swing.

Despite the fact that the adoption of the bulldozer approach can be readily explained, more investigation should be made into its implications. One of the more significant implications is the fact that after one change has been introduced, the system which has been subjected to the bulldozer approach is usually not ready for another significant change. Individuals who have not been forewarned, who have found their jobs done away with overnight, be they managers or nonsupervisory employees, are little inclined to accept. In fact, they go out of their way to reject any additional change.

While the bulldozer approach may work for one round of change, it increases the resistance for further rounds. Many system changes, particularly those which involve computer installations, involve a sequence of which the first round is only the forerunner of many changes. Even if additional changes are not contemplated, they are usually required as a function of making modifications in the first installation of change. It is highly questionable whether a systems change involving the bulldozer approach is really successful if it retards subsequent change and if it uses up any goodwill that may have been funded in the organization in terms of tolerance for change.

The bulldozer approach may also result in a resistance which spreads from the changed part of the system to that part of the organization seemingly unaffected by the change. If, for example, the managers in Sales feel that the managers in Accounting received a "raw deal," they tend to view any change coming into their own system with a great deal of suspicion and downright resistance.

In summary, the major disadvantage of the bulldozer approach is its effect upon subsequent changes. And it is still relatively easy for an outsider to predict the amount of resistance to change in an organization. He may merely use the following predictive hypothesis: *"The human element in an organization will react to change in terms of how the last one was handled."*

CAN ANYTHING BE DONE ABOUT IT?

While it may be all well and good to realize that much of the resistance to change is not necessarily logically based, or that it involves problems of status, or that we are dealing with informal systems not represented on the organizational chart, there is still a question as to whether anything can be done about it. Social science is of some assistance in this case, but its use is limited because the process of adjusting to change is probably still an art.

If we establish the premise that many of the individual fears are unfounded, then the notion of participation in the change can be of great assistance. Individuals are much more prone to adapt and actually work for changes when they have had a hand in the design of same. Moreover, they may be able to contribute to the overall design of a systems change at least with regard to the problems of introduction. Some forms of participation give individuals a chance to really understand the new system, and thus the fear of the unknown is mitigated; at least there is some feeling of control.

SELLING THE RIGHT PRODUCT

The system can also be sold in terms of objectives that are understandable and acceptable to those who must react to the change. The social system of the organization may not have any great degree of identity with the total organizational goals. People are interested in labor saving when it involves their labor, and they may be interested in their own efficiency. (For example, the sales department may be very much interested in a program that is going to lead to better relationships with customers.) Often, however, an attempt is made to sell the change in terms of the objectives that were used in getting the innovation accepted by the upper echelons of the organization. Yet there is no reason to believe that many of the lower levels can identify or indeed are necessarily interested in the phrasing of objectives of change in terms of how it appears to the total organization. They are interested in and are motivated primarily by terms of those objectives that are consistent with their own needs and activities.

While a certain procedural change may be one of the greatest things that has happened in terms of making the company important in the international market, this objective must be related to the objectives of some subpart of the system such as increased job security. Otherwise, it is doubtful whether anyone will really eagerly anticipate a change. It is primarily a matter of being receptive.

DON'T UNDERESTIMATE INFORMAL SYSTEMS

Those who are planning change cannot depend upon the organizational chart, but must become more conscious of informal communication and coordination systems. Much of this has to be a "seat of the pants" operation, and those responsible for the change must be sensitive to problems early in the introduction.

To assume that what is communicated is received and that if it goes through formal channels it will be received with the same reaction by everyone flies in the face of everything that nearly everyone knows about organizations but which too few take into account. Rumors should not be discarded because they are not consistent with fact; they should be analyzed in terms of what they indicate about the system. Assumptions about the formal organization must constantly be checked during a time of change much the way we would look at information loss in any other system.

Much more can be gained in understanding the nature of resistance if we do not assume that logic will effectively change attitudes and opinions. Challenging the resistant manager to debate may only be a greater way of entrenching rather than changing him. More adroitness in understanding the real causes of resistance by a fuller hearing and perhaps the offering of certain forms of assurances may be highly necessary in order to avoid certain forms of roadblocks.

MEETING FEARS HEAD-ON

All of the above assumes that change will be beneficial for the organization as a totality and also for the individual members. Often this is not the case; at least not to the degree people would like to think it is. Some individuals will have some of their authority stripped away from them; some will have to go through the strain of learning a totally new job. Assuming this as a cost of the change, and taking those steps necessary to find an alternative means of using the individuals or adjusting such problems on an individual basis may be far less costly in the long run than the amount of disruption, chaos and the resistances engendered by not anticipating and working with the problem.

It is just possible that some organizations are not prepared for change at the time it is suggested. Feasibility studies should look at not only the feasibility from the technical point of view but the feasibility from the human side. It is possible that some necessary arrangements and preconditioning are necessary prior to the introduction of the systems change. Most deadlines for introduction are based upon technical feasibility and not on any assumptions about the receptivity on the part of the organization's members.

Finally, much can be done by greater attention to predicting problems in the organization. The systems engineer who gives a complete hardware description to his change without suggesting or forecasting problems in the social system does a disservice to himself and to the organization. While it is true that even the most sophisticated technical descriptions do not necessarily lead to any predictions with regard to the impact on the social system, those in this position must find a language form and a means of describing their change that is closer to the problems of the social system with which they are dealing.

Instead of describing the computer in terms of its units of memory, one learns quite a bit more by describing the computer as an adjunct to decision making, and then asking about its impact on the organization in terms of those who have a role in the supporting decision-making structure. Describing the computer as a faster calculator also may raise more questions in advance about what will happen and what will be the consequences if we do away with those jobs where calculation is now being done by humans.

The language and variables of the technological system are quite unrelated in many instances to the language and variables of the social system, but more of us must become concerned with translating from one to the other if organizations are going to maintain the amount of receptivity required to continually introduce change into the existing establishment.

BIBLIOGRAPHY

Ansoff, H., and Richard C. Brandenburg, "A Program of Research in Business Planning," *Management Science,* February, 1967.

Blumenthal, Sherman S., *Management Information Systems: A Framework for Planning and Development,* Prentice-Hall, Inc., 1969.

Carzo, Rocco, and John Yanouzas, *Formal Organization: A Systems Approach,* Richard D. Irwin, Inc., 1967.

Cleland, David I., and William R. King, *Systems, Organizations, Analysis, Management: A Book of Readings,* McGraw-Hill Book Company, 1969.

Dearden, John, "Can Management Information Be Automated?" *Harvard Business Review,* March-April, 1964.

———, "How to Organize Information Systems," *Harvard Business Review,* March-April, 1965.

———, F. Warren McFarland, and William M. Zani, *Management Information Systems: Text and Cases,* Richard D. Irwin, Inc., 1970.

Elliott, C. Orville, and Robert S. Wasley, *Business Information Processing Systems,* Richard D. Irwin, Inc., 1968.

Evans, Marshall K., and Lou R. Hague, "Master Plan for Information Systems," *Harvard Business Review,* January-February, 1962.

Greenwood, Frank, Nicolai Siemens, and C. H. Marting, *Operations Research, Planning, Operating, and Information Systems,* The Macmillan Co., 1970.

Gregory, Robert H., and Richard L. Van Horn, *Automatic Data-Processing Systems,* 2nd ed., Wadsworth Publishing Co., Inc., 1963.

Heany, Donald F., *Development of Information Systems—What Management Needs to Know,* Ronald Press Co., 1968.

Jasinski, Frank J., "Adapting Organization to New Technology," *Harvard Business Review,* January-February, 1959.

Kast, Fremont E., and James E. Rosenzweig, *Organization and Management: A Systems Approach,* McGraw-Hill Book Company, 1970.

Kelley, Joseph F., *Computerized Management Information Systems,* The Macmillan Co., 1970.

Laden, H. N., and T. R. Gildersleeve, *Systems Design for Computer Applications,* John Wiley and Sons, 1963.

Livingstone, John Leslie, *Management Planning and Control: Mathematical Models,* McGraw-Hill Book Company, 1970.

March, James G., and Herbert A. Simon, *Organizations,* John Wiley and Sons, 1958.

Optner, Stanford L., *Systems Analysis for Business and Industrial Problem Solving,* 2nd ed., Prentice-Hall, Inc., 1968.

Pipkin, Ashmead P., "The Singularity of the Management Challenge of EDP," *Michigan Business Review,* July, 1969.

Prince, Thomas R., *Information Systems for Management Planning and Control,* Richard D. Irwin, Inc., 1966.

"Research Study Conclusions," *Computer Digest,* Diebold Group, Inc., August, 1967.

Richards, Max D., and Paul S. Greenlaw, *Management Decision Making,* Richard D. Irwin, Inc., 1966.

Ronken, Harriet O., and Paul R. Lawrence, *Administering Changes,* Harvard University, Graduate School of Business Administration, 1952.

Rowe, Alan J., "Management Decision Making and the Computer," *Management International,* **II**, No. 2, 1962.

Wilson, I. G., and M. E. Wilson, *Information, Computers and Systems Design,* John Wiley and Sons, 1965.

Wortman, Max S., and Fred Luthans (eds.), *Emerging Concepts in Management,* The Macmillan Co., 1969.

Yaffa, Earle, and Paul Hines, "Who Should Control the Computer?" *Management Review,* March, 1969.

Young, Stanley, "Designing a Behavioral System," *Proceedings of the 23rd Annual Meeting of the Academy of Management,* December, 1963.

Part Three

SYSTEMS APPLICATIONS

SECTION I

INDUSTRIAL DYNAMICS

INDUSTRIAL DYNAMICS

Born of the marriage of managerial art and the scientific approach, industrial dynamics has come upon the managerial scene and in its short life span it has succeeded in arousing considerable interest and acrimonious controversy in academia.

Over the years the Alfred P. Sloan School of Management at the Massachusetts Institute of Technology has been a bastion for the teaching of industrial dynamics, and the name most frequently associated with it has been that of Jay W. Forrester. In his article, "Industrial Dynamics—After the First Decade," Forrester reviews for the reader something of the exciting history of the movement, surveys the work currently in progress, discusses the status of feedback system theory and of industrial dynamics as a theory of structure, and outlines the task that lies ahead.

A perusal of this article can do no more than awaken in the reader an interest in and an urge to investigate and study more of this emerging science. As Forrester himself admits, the available literature is still somewhat inchoate and incomplete. Even his by now classic text *Industrial Dynamics* (1961) can mislead the reader into believing that he understands the subject when in fact the conceptual principles underlying feedback systems are only imperfectly apprehended. Consequently this brief article cannot bring about what major treatises have failed to accomplish.

Underpinning industrial dynamics is the notion that the feedback system concepts can supply the key to unlocking an understanding of the nature of the social structure and of its inherent relationships.

Industrial dynamics should not be regarded merely as a simulation technique (often incorrectly identified with the DYNAMO compiler, a computer program for simulating industrial-dynamics models) nor should it be looked on as the simulation process itself. Simulation is but a technique utilized by industrial dynamics, since the usual mathematical analytical solutions have been found inappropriate. Rather it should be viewed as the science of feedback behavior in social systems, as the interpretation and the extension of feedback system concepts to multiple-loop, nonlinear social systems.

The basic structure of any feedback system is the feedback loop. Within this loop the systemic conditions provide the input to a decision process that in its turn modifies the conditions of the system. This, then, is a continuously circulating process. Feedback systems are characterized by four quantifiable dimensions: order, direction, nonlinearity, and loop multiplicity.

Order, one measure of a system's complexity, represents the number of points at which information is integrated or accumulated. Unfortunately, little work has been done beyond the treatment of 2nd-order feedback systems in many of the sciences. Systems of interest to the manager generally begin wtih the 5th order and extend upwards almost indefinitely.

Direction, the measure of a feedback loop's polarity, is associated with the type of action produced. In a positive feedback loop, the action increases the system state to produce even more action, somewhat like the buildup in an atomic explosion. In a negative feedback loop, the action produced tends to return the system towards its equilibrium position. The negative feedback loop is therefore goal seeking. While positive feedback is an essential process in growth of all kinds (biological, crystallogical, sociological, demographical, and the like), most of the engineering literature deals with the negative-feedback loop. Only in the social and biological literature is attention appropriately concentrated on positive-feedback behavior, characteristic of the growth processes of greatest concern to the industrial manager.

Nonlinearity, the measure of a system's multiplication or division of variables, represents the degree of departure from linearity. Throughout the social system nonlinearity dominates behavior, yet linear systems are about all that have been examined. Nonlinear systems, of special interest to the manager, exhibit modes of behavior never found in linear ones.

Loop multiplicity is another measure of a feedback system's complexity that is of special concern to managers. Yet almost all of the available literature deals with single-loop feedback systems. In industrial and economic systems one would like to incorporate from two to twenty major loops in an effort to structure an adequate behavioral mode. Again, multiple-loop systems evidence types of behavior not found in simple-loop systems.

As one pushes forward into feedback systems of greater and greater complexity, dramatic qualitative changes in behavior modes become evident. The more complex systems manifest behavior that can in no way be viewed as merely an extension of the type of behavior found in simpler systems. Rather, entirely new phenomena appear. Thus, each additional order in system complexity up through the first several levels introduces entirely new dynamic phenomena. This observation applies to each dimension enumerated above.

The merit of industrial dynamics perhaps lies in its attempt to relate structure to behavior. For this purpose four hierarchies of structure are distinguished.

At the first hierarchy, industrial dynamics deals with systems that are closed, systems in which what crosses the boundary is not a function of the activity being investigated within the boundary. What is outside the system is essentially independent of anything on the inside. At the second hierarchy, industrial dynamics deals with the identification of the multiple interacting feedback loops producing the system's characteristic behavior. It is within the context of the feedback loops that all decisions are posited.

It is only at the third hierarchy that the substructure of the loops is detailed. Two classes of basic variables are to be noted. One class is called the *level* variables, the other, the *rate* variables. The level variables are the accumulations within the system that are necessary for describing the present status of the system. Even in a system without any activity, one should still be able to observe these level variables. The rate variables, which represent activity, define the rates at which the level variables are changing. These are the policy statements or decision functions causing the system to evolve, and consequently they have several components: the goal of the decision-making process, the apparent states of the system (the informational inputs underlying the decision process), the determination or assessment of the discrepancy between the state of the system and its goal, and the remedial action to be taken. The level and rate variables constitute both a necessary and a sufficient substructure within the feedback loop.

At the fourth hierarchy, the DYNAMO compiler enables the investigator to generate the level variables by a process of integrations (accumulating the effects of all the rates).

The task that lies ahead is still formidable, and consists chiefly of developing the many insights afforded by industrial dynamics into the principles, theory, and behavioral modes of feedback structures; of developing a mathematics of feedback systems; and of inculcating this viewpoint in the managers of tomorrow.

In his reading, Edward Roberts takes up for consideration industrial dynamics and its interrelationship to management control systems.

Every organization is itself a kind of control system. There are the inevitable objectives to be reached, the decision-making processes that mediate the idealized goals and the apparent progress of the company toward these goals, and the implementation of the policy-making decisions that translate the objectives from the realm of the potential to that of the actual—all of these in one continuous, complex, and interrelated feedback system.

As a philosophy industrial dynamics views organizations from this control system type of perspective, and as a methodology it aims to redesign organizational structures and policies consonant with this viewpoint. If a company's likelihood to succeed depends on such features as the flow of information, men, money, materials, orders, and capital equipment, then in insisting that each of these be viewed as an essential part of a total system and not in isolation, industrial dynamics reveals its own total systems approach to the problems of management control.

The traditional approaches to management control systems have too often proved inadequate. Many fail to solve the problems for which they were designed, and the least successful even manage to create other insoluble problems of their own. This unfortunate situation, by no means an archaic phenomenon, is illustrated by telling examples from the field of R & D projects, production-inventory-employment control, logistics, and quality control systems. Both facets of the situation are convincingly portrayed: that in which management control systems proved inadequate for the task for which they were designed and that in which they compounded an already perplexing situation by giving rise to additional problems.

Three general principles are inferred from the examples: the boundaries of a management control system design study must not be drawn to conform with organizational structure merely because of that structure since key factors may lie outside the conventional structure; management control system design must be viewed as a form of man-machine system design; and an effective total systems approach to management control will necessarily be one involving many departments and levels beyond that of middle management.

Industrial dynamics has not been without its share of critics. It is difficult to say whether the opposition voiced is due to the inherent limitations of the technique or to the overstated claims of its proponents. Ansoff and Slevin in "An Appreciation of Industrial Dynamics" seem to subscribe to both views. Forrester, they claim, has tried to prove his case by showing that all who disagree with him are either wrong, unsuccessful, or both. Greater humility in searching for the truth, the whole truth, and nothing but the truth, could not but have advanced his cause. Instead, his pontications have aroused irritation, if not outright resentment, in many quarters.

The other point is treated extensively in the reading by Ansoff and Slevin, who as outsiders attempt to analyze the merits and limitations of industrial dynamics.

One distinctive feature is the insistence that the simulation employed be completely quantitative not only for the statistical data gathered but also for the decision rules explicated by the managers. The possible disparity between the rules verbalized and those actually used and the need to adjust for this discrepancy seem to have escaped the attention of the industrial dynamicists. Also the possibility that the decision rules will vary from one circumstance to the other suffers a similar neglect.

The various sets of equations used to portray levels and flows of elements include level, rate, supplementary, auxiliary, and initial value equations. Some feel that all this is necessary, not by the nature of the case, but because of the special ID compiler, DYNAMO.

The end result of simulation in Forrester's view is the reproduction of the real world, not a forecasting of future system conditions. Thus industrial dynamics is concerned with the dynamic processes of the model, with stability, oscillation, growth, general time relationships between changing variables, etc., not with correspondence between predicted and observed time-phased behavior.

In model validation two aspects must be noted: the model's capability of describing (and predicting) the behavior of the system with reasonable accuracy, and the production of improvements in the real world system similar to those produced in the model. The proof of the pudding is in the eating.

Unless tried in the real system, the changes brought about in the model will remain but mere exercises.

The determination of the sensitive parameters for the ID model seems to be more a matter of individual judgment than one based on scientific criteria. Yet the need to validate the model by the use of historical data of the company still remains. Unless the model is faithful to reality, the degree of sophistication, no matter how large, is irrelevant.

The desire to quantify is indeed admirable, and one that burns in the heart of many a scientist. What is less admirable, however, is the requirement that in simulation all relevant variables and phenomena be quantified. The reduction of all descriptive knowledge to quantitative measures, effected by the table function in the DYNAMO compiler, may be a convenience, but its validity is not to be presumed. The behavioral sciences are beset with the same frustrating problem.

To sum up, the arguments of the industrial dynamics for complete quantification are neither very explicit nor persuasive. They expose the quantifier to the same pitfalls so deplorable in the work of other scientists—the use of models that do not convey a sense of close correspondence to reality. The technique of quantification, unformalized and untested, thus renders the process more an art than a science.

As with other managerial techniques, industrial dynamics has been found to be most useful in dealing with price-quantity problems, less useful in organizational design, and least useful in the product-market strategy. Although industrial systems are inherently information-feedback systems, it does not necessarily follow that all aspects of a company can best be and should be studied by means of an information-feedback model. Again, production and distribution are probably those aspects of a company's operations most amenable to such treatment.

Industrial dynamics is not easy to apply. The reasons for this are that not too many people at present are well versed in the complex technique, and that a considerable volume of data must be amassed if the hundreds of equations are to be set up. The amassing of this company data can create a problem because of its psychological and sociological overtones.

One of the decided benefits of industrial dynamics lies in its forcing the managers to crystallize their decision-making processes. Anything that makes one formalize his mental processes cannot but lead to greater insights.

Whether industrial dynamics is better than other techniques still remains to be demonstrated. Its superiority can be established only by a demonstration that the improvement in the firm's operations brought about by its use is greater than that achievable by other means.

As for the critical question, "Can industrial dynamics qualify as a theory?", the answer depends on what one understands by a "theory." Generally, a theory is constituted of a definitive body of theorems, but it also enjoys predictive capability. By means of the theorems the analyst can make predictions about the relationships of variables not previously observed. When these predictions are validated with the observed relationships in the real world, the theory is considered to be upheld. Industrial dynamics can hardly lay claim to being a theory in this sense.

38. INDUSTRIAL DYNAMICS—AFTER THE FIRST DECADE

JAY W. FORRESTER*

Industrial dynamics, described as the application of feedback concepts to social systems, is evolving toward a theory of structure in systems as well as being an approach to corporate policy design. In high-order, nonlinear systems, with multiple loops and both positive and negative feedback, are found the modes of behavior which have been so puzzling in management and economics. The time is at hand when more sharply defined concepts and principles can form a core through management education to interrelate the functional areas and to move from static to dynamic understanding of systems. To do so should help close the gap between what the management school can now teach and what the manager must understand if he is to successfully cope with the increasing complexity of our society.

HISTORY

A decade has passed since the first work on organizing system concepts into the form which has come to be called "industrial dynamics."[1] Four years before 1956, the Alfred P. Sloan School of Management at MIT had been started with the generous support of Mr. Sloan, who believed that a management school in a technical environment would develop in new and important directions that would be different from management schools in other kinds of academic settings. When the author came to the School from his background in feedback control systems, computers, and practicing management, it was for the planned purpose of searching for and developing the linkages which might exist between engineering and management education. It was the expectation that these lay in the areas of operations research and the application of computers to processing management information.

The year 1956–57 was devoted to examining the national activity in operations research which was aimed at bringing mathematics and scientific method to bear on problems in industry. The study indicated that operations research was not dealing effectively with the broader, top-management problems. Most of the work was concentrated on individual decisions structured as open-loop processes, meaning that the inputs to the decision process were considered as unaffected by the decisions themselves. But decisions are made for the purpose of influencing the environment and thereby generating different inputs to succeeding decisions. Although the open-loop assumption simplified analysis, the assumptions underlying the analysis could be invalidated by the closed-loop structure surrounding the actual decision process.

Furthermore, the mathematical orientation of management science, the concentration on analytical solutions, and the optimization objectives could cope only with rather simple situations. They excluded treatment of the more complex management relationships and also forced neglect of most nonlinear phenomena. It appeared that management science as it then existed did pay its way by working on significant problems. However, there was no substantial body of opinion either inside or outside management science that believed that the problems being attacked were the major ones that made the difference between the companies that succeed and those that stagnate or fail.

The manager's task is to interrelate the separate functions of the company, to create the flows that cause the company and market mutually to support one another, and to interweave the tangible economic variables with the intangible variables of psychology and power structure. None of these was being adequately reached by the management science

SOURCE: *Management Science* (March, 1968) pp. 398–415. Reprinted by permission of Institute of Management Science.

* Massachusetts Institute of Technology.

[1] This article assumes some familiarity with the basic material in [3].

activities which remained focused on the separate corporate functions and were thus being applied within sharply restricted areas of decision-making. Furthermore, the methods did not seem amenable to much broadening of scope. The manager's principal problems seemed not to lie in decisions taken as isolated events, but rather in policies that deal with streams of decisions and in the structure of the managerial system that interrelates information sources, policy, and action.

The first year of exploration pointed toward the concepts of feedback systems as being much more general, more significant, and more applicable to social systems than had been commonly realized. Feedback system analysis had been extensively applied by engineers in the design of technical devices. Cybernetics as another name for feedback processes was becoming a common word in the biological sciences. The elementary idea of feedback as a circular cause-effect phenomena could be traced back through centuries of economic literature. But even so, the implications, the importance, and the principles of feedback processes were only beginning to be understood. Rather than its having been exhaustively studied, it became increasingly clear that the systems frontier had only begun to open. Feedback processes emerged as universal in social systems and seemed to hold the key to structuring and clarifying relationships that had remained baffling and contradictory.

Aided by a grant from the Ford Foundation, a research program began to relate the elementary concepts of feedback systems, previously developed in the engineering fields, to the processes in social systems. Compatible with the overriding determination to avoid restriction to simple linear systems, analytical treatment was subordinated. One could for the first time turn away from mathematical solutions as the principal means of analysis because computers had reached the point where convenient low-cost system simulation was possible. With simulation available as a procedure for determining the behavior of a model system, it became fruitful to concentrate not on mathematical methods but on the fundamental nature of structure in systems. This work led to a simple and general structure that seemed capable of representing the interactions within any type of system. This generalized structure serves, not only as a framework for organizing observations and experience, but also expedites the simulation stage of system studies. The structure is discussed in a later section.

The past and immediate future of industrial dynamics divides into three periods:

Period One, 1956–1961, Structural Concepts and Steady-State Dynamics. The structure of systems was identified in terms of feedback loops and their component substructures. Examples of system formulation were developed. Applications of the concepts were made to "steady-state" dynamics which concentrate on the fluctuation about equilibrium conditions and which do not involve the processes of growth and decline. This was a period when "enterprise engineering," meaning corporate policy redesign, formed the focus of industrial dynamics. The first period ended with the publication of *Industrial Dynamics* [3].

Phase Two, 1962–1966, Growth Dynamics and General Systems Theory. This has been a period of consolidation and of clarifying the concepts about systems in the social sciences. Experimental educational programs have been tried for the teaching of system principles. It has been a time for reaching a better understanding of the educational materials and methods that will be required to make the concepts of dynamic systems accessible to the average student of management. During this period, examples of industrial dynamics modeling were extended into situations where nonlinearity was of dominant importance. The positive feedback processes of growth in products, companies, and economies have been explored. During this period the view of industrial dynamics was enlarged not only to include the application to enterprise design but also to become a general systems theory to serve as a unifying framework capable of organizing behavior and relationships in areas as diverse as engineering, medicine, management, psychology, and economics. The literature as yet only inadequately conveys the industrial dynamics work of this period in growth and life cycle dynamics [4, 12, 13, 14], education [5, 6, 9], and systems theory [5, 7].

Phase Three, 1967–1975, Foundations and Bridges. The forthcoming period must provide the literature and educational materials necessary to make the theory and the art of dealing with systems more generally accessible. At the present time systems concepts are scattered and incomplete, feedback theory exists in an unnecessarily forbidding mathematical context, and the field lacks interpretation into the specifics of social systems. There needs to be developed a simplified interpretation of the mathematics of feedback processes. The principles of dynamic behavior in systems need to be identified and illustrated with practice exercises for the student. Bridging articles and applications from system theory to a variety of fields need to be presented both to demonstrate generality and to provide guides to the art of system identification and interpretation.

THE PRESENT

Industrial dynamics, described as the science of feedback behavior in social systems, is still in a very early stage of development. Many people have been exposed to an introduction to the subject, but, except by serving an apprenticeship in the development of the field, there as yet exists almost no educational opportunity for developing professional competence.

Industrial dynamics is seen very differently by different people. Some observers see it merely as a simulation technique, apparently thinking of industrial dynamics as synonymous with the DYNAMO compiler. The DYNAMO compiler is a computer program for simulating industrial dynamics models but certainly is not the only possible method for such simulation. Simulation, in turn, is not the essence of industrial dynamics; simulation is merely the technique, used because mathematical analytical solutions are impossible, for exposing the nature of system models. To those at the center of industrial dynamics activity, the subject is the interpretation and the extension of feedback system concepts to apply in the multiple-loop, nonlinear systems to which the social processes belong. Although still very incomplete, industrial dynamics is a body of theory dealing with feedback dynamics. It is an identifiable set of principles governing interactions within systems. It is a view of the nature of structure in purposeful systems.

At MIT the first-term subject in industrial dynamics is a popular management elective. Some 120 undergraduate and graduate students take the subject each year. A substantial fraction come from other departments. The subject is also presented to the hundred men in the Sloan Fellow and the Senior Executive Development Programs. But any single-term treatment is incomplete and somewhat superficial. It conveys the importance of structure in determining the behavior of systems. It opens to the student the hope of a better understanding of managerial systems. But it does not prepare the student to proceed by himself. The student exposure in a one-term subject succeeds and fails in much the same way as the book *Industrial Dynamics* [3]. It is probably fair to say that this book seems readable without any specialized training. However, it can be misleading. Many readers can read the book without being aware of the extensive background in feedback systems underlying the presentation. The book does not attempt to convey the principles of feedback systems. The reader without a foundation in feedback dynamics can read the book without realizing that he does not have the conceptual and theoretical background necessary to carry on the work discussed in the book. After reading the book, and apparently understanding it, such a reader turns to the world around him and finds himself unable, without guidance, to apply successfully the industrial dynamics approach to systems. This difficulty reflects the inadequacy of the present literature and educational materials.

Because the literature is dominated by industrial dynamics applications to production and distribution processes, many people see only a usefulness to such areas and fail to see the generality and the extensions to such areas as marketing, finance, and competition. This deficiency in the literature can now be remedied. Time and effort should yield results.

The very widespread but shallow exposure to industrial dynamics has created acceptance beyond the availability of skilled practitioners to deliver on its hope and promise. Thirty or more universities are teaching industrial dynamics to some extent; in most places this is as part of another course, usually one in production emphasizing simulation methods and the dynamics of production processes. Many industrial organizations have some industrial dynamics activity, but most are in the early phases of self-education. There is widespread international interest in industrial dynamics. The Japanese are active and have translated parts of the American literature and have written a number of original articles. A German translation of *Industrial Dynamics* [3] is in process. Interest in Scandinavia, the United Kingdom, and France seems substantial.

Inquiries in a steady stream come from companies ready to establish industrial dynamics systems groups when competent personnel are available. However, it has become increasingly clear that management schools and social science departments are not training men with adequate depth in system dynamics to fill such openings successfully. The only class of person now having a high probability of success is the one who has studied the dynamics of feedback processes in an engineering curriculum and who then extends and generalizes these ideas in applying them to social systems. The supply of men with such training is much too small to create any significant impression on the demand. The present imbalance between opportunity on the one hand and supply on the other points clearly to the need for much more adequate literature and new and more intensive educational programs.

STATUS OF FEEDBACK SYSTEM THEORY

Because industrial dynamics is a feedback system view of social behavior, it is well to have some perspective on the status of feedback theory. The basic structure of a feedback system is a loop within which the system condition provides the input to a decision process that generates action which modifies the system condition. It is a continuously circulating process. Every decision—personal, corporate, national, international, or in nature—occurs within such a context.

Such an assertion of total generality sometimes generates the response that such a broad concept could have no usefulness because it would not divide the decision-making field into categories—that something which is all-encompassing is empty of meaning. But we do not consider physics meaningless because all its phenomena are based on the atom, nor is biology without interest because of the pervasive presence of the cell. The word "decision" is used here to mean the control of an action stream. Such an action stream may be the time devoted to sleeping in response to one's physical state, the effort to improve products in response to market information about product acceptance, the change in interest rates in response to money supply, the change of prices in response to a world-wide commodity shortage, or the rate of consumption of rabbits as a response to the size of the coyote population. As in these and all other decision streams, the action resulting from the decision stream affects the state of the system to which the decision stream itself is responding.

The feedback concept is found throughout the professional and also the public literature. However, only in the engineering fields is there a well-organized body of theory dealing directly with the processes of feedback dynamics. Most of this material is written in the field of electrical engineering. One could probably assemble a forty-foot shelf of books devoted to the subject. Consider what such a library would contain. To measure the scope of the existing literature, we might examine four dimensions or characteristics of feedback systems—order, direction of feedback, nonlinearity, and loop multiplicity.

System Order

The order of a system can be expressed in a variety of ways. In physical systems the order is often defined in terms of the number of energy storage elements. In a system expressed as a differential equation the order is equal to the highest derivative. In a system expressed as a series of integrations the order is equal to the number of integrations. In a system expressed in first-order difference equations (which are integrations), the order is equal to the number of difference equations. The number of "levels" (which are first-order difference equations, i.e., integrations) in the industrial dynamics terminology is equal to the system order. In more practical terms, the order of the system is equal to the number of accumulations. In a managerial system one will increase the order of the system for each bank balance, each pool of machine tools, each group of employees, each information variable which measures *average* system activity, and each attitude or psychological state necessary to describe the system.

An examination of the feedback literature will show that most of the material deals with first and second-order systems. A small percent of the literature presses into the region of third and fourth-order systems and beyond. Yet even elementary managerial phenomena usually require a minimum of fifth to twentieth order for adequate representation. Any effort to represent realistically a comprehensive industrial system may carry one well up toward hundredth order. A ratio of ten or more exists between the solidly established literature and the models needed to exhibit the modes of behavior that dominate industrial and economic systems.

Polarity of Feedback

A feedback loop is described as being positive or negative in its action. This refers to the polarity or algebraic sense of influence around the loop.

A positive feedback loop has a polarity around the loop such that action increases a system state to produce still more action. Positive feedback takes place in the build-up phase of an atomic explosion. It occurs in management where salesmen produce revenue to support still more salesmen. Positive feedback in the system description of the process in the multiplication of rabbits. The positive feedback loop produces exponential departure from some reference or neutral condition, often that of zero activity. Positive feedback is an essential process in the growth of products, companies, or countries.

By contrast, the negative feedback loop is goal seeking. A departure from the reference point produces action tending to return the system toward the equilibrium position, that is, the goal. A negative feedback loop may approach its equilibrium position in a smooth, exponential, non-oscillatory manner; or it may approach equilibrium through a decaying series of oscillations; or it can be unstable and produce ever wider swings around the "equilibrium" position which is crossed but to which the system never settles.

Probably 99% of the literature on feedback systems deals with the negative feedback loop. The negative loop is more difficult and subtle than the positive loop. But all processes of growth are manifestations of positive feedback behavior. Positive feedback in the engineering literature is almost entirely omitted because the emphasis has been on steady-state control for maintaining equilibrium conditions. The same is mostly true in the mathematical literature of economics. Positive feedback must usually be omitted from analytical mathematical treatment of linear systems because, in linear systems, a positive feedback loop leads to infinite excursion and destructive consequences. It is in the social and biological systems that so much practical attention is focused on positive feedback behavior. Models of positive feedback processes are feasible when the nonlinearity of natural systems is included to limit the growth phase, or when simulation is used for system study and the time span is short enough that the normal growth phase is not exceeded.

Degree of Nonlinearity

Without attempting a rigorous definition, we can say that a system is nonlinear if it contains a multiplication or division of variables or if it has a coefficient which is a function of a variable. For example, the rate of sale in a market might be expressed as the product of the number of salesmen multiplied by the sales effectiveness, where the sales effectiveness may depend on such things as the price, quality, and delivery delay of the product. But if these latter are variables, the sales rate is a nonlinear function of the variables representing the number of salesmen and the sales effectiveness. Likewise, throughout our social systems, nonlinearity dominates behavior.

In a general sense we can speak of the degree of nonlinearity of a system. The degree of nonlinearity implies the number of policies in the system that are nonlinear and the extent to which the system modes of behavior arise only because of the existence of nonlinearity. The degree of nonlinearity, although not a well-defined concept, might be thought of as a scale extending to the right from an origin, which point of origin represents linear systems. Almost all of mathematical analysis lies within the end point at the beginning of the line. Most of the processes of life and society lie along the scale to the right. Probably not more than two per cent of the literature of feedback systems deals with nonlinear behavior, and that which does is limited to very special cases of nonlinearity.

The importance of nonlinearity is well put by Kovach [10]:

> We have broken through the sonic barrier, we are well on our way to conquering the thermal barrier and we are now at the threshhold of the nonlinear barrier. Of all three, this last seems the most insurmountable. Strange

that these nonlinear phenomena that abound so widely in nature should be so intractable. It is almost as if Man is to be denied a complete knowledge of the universe unless he makes a superhuman effort to solve its nonlinearities. . . . In a way we have been lulled into the belief that everything is ideal, homogeneous, uniform, isotropic, perfect as well as frictionless, weightless, but withal infinitely rigid. . . . We have, so to speak, located a few nonlinear zippers in the blanket of nonlinearity that covers us. Opening these zippers has allowed us to put our hand through and try to fathom the vast unknown in this way. . . . It seems entirely plausible that the qualitative habit of thought will eventually supersede the present quantitative one in mathematics. There are certain indications in science and many in mathematics which point to the analysis of structure as the mathematics of the future. In simple language, it is not things that matter, but the relations between them.

Multiplicity of Loops

The literature of feedback systems is mostly devoted to the single feedback loop. Only a small fraction of the literature deals with systems of two or more interconnected loops. Yet, to represent adequately managerial systems one must incorporate from two to twenty major loops, each of which may contain many minor loops. For example, a simple structure describing the growth in sales of a new product might contain three nonlinear loops—a positive sales-department loop of salesmen producing orders, leading to revenue to hire more salesmen; a negative market loop in which orders alter backlog to change delivery delay to modify the attractiveness of the product to change order rate; and a negative capital-investment loop where order backlog leads to expanding production to reduce the backlog.

Models of Increased Complexity

As one moves toward systems of greater complexity in any one of the preceding dimensions—order, inclusion of positive feedback, nonlinearity, and multiple loops—he finds that system behavior changes in major qualitative ways. The more complex systems do not merely show extensions of behavior seen in the simpler systems. For example, the way in which system behavior can change as the order of a negative feedback loop is increased is well known. A first-order, negative feedback loop can show only exponential approach to its equilibrium position. A second-order loop introduces the possibility of an entirely new mode of operation—it can show fluctuation either as a damped oscillation or as a growing instability. A third-order system is the simplest one that is capable of showing fluctuations superimposed on exponential growth. More comprehensive models can represent important modes of behavior that are recognized in actual systems but which have previously resisted analysis.

Nonlinearity can introduce unexpected behavior in a system. A nonlinear system can be unstable for small disturbances but stable with sustained oscillation for larger disturbances. Nonlinearity can cause a feedback loop to shift its fundamental character between positive feedback and negative feedback. Nonlinearity can cause dominance to shift from one loop in a system to another. For example, the positive feedback characteristic of growth of a new product can be suppressed and dominance shifted to a negative feedback loop which produces stagnation in product growth.

Multiple feedback loops produce system behavior not seen in the simpler systems. For example, in a multiple loop system containing nonlinearities, the system behavior becomes surprisingly insensitive to change in values of a majority of the system parameters. In some system models, 90% of the parameters can be changed individually by factors of as much as five without substantially affecting the system behavior. Partly this is due to the dilution caused by a single parameter being immersed in a large number of others. But even more importantly, it arises from the intrinsic propensity of a multiple-loop nonlinear system to defeat changes in the system policy statements. A substantial change can be made in a particular policy. However, the system warps in such a way that the incoming information to that decision point shifts to new values which, when processed through the new policy statement, yield approximately the old result. Time after time the manager encounters this in actual practice where a major policy change aimed at correcting a corporate problem seems to produce almost no result. Within a model of a complex system one discovers orderly processes to explain how the system defeats attempts to change its behavior. But there are exceptions, and some of the most useful insights to come from industrial dynamics show which policies in a system have enough leverage so that by changing them one can hope to alter system behavior.

INDUSTRIAL DYNAMICS AS A THEORY OF STRUCTURE

It may be helpful to distinguish two aspects of a system investigation—that relating to structure, and that relating to dynamic behavior. The two are intimately interwoven because it is the structure which produces the behavior. However, one's interest in the two aspects is sequential. There must be structure before there is a system that can have behavior. It is in the absence of a unifying structure that management education and practice have been particularly weak. Bruner, in his perceptive book on the educational process [1], discusses with great clarity in the first several chapters the importance of structure for expediting learning.

Industrial dynamics is a philosophy of structure in systems. It is also gradually becoming a body of principles that relate structure to behavior. The structure which is codified in industrial dynamics has its counterpart in other fields and other bodies of literature. It is in industrial dynamics, however, that the structure has probably been given its sharpest definition and its most rigorous application.

Structure is seen as having four significant hierarchies:

- The Closed Boundary
  - The Feedback Loop as the Basic System Component
    - Levels (the integrations, or accumulations, or states of a system)
    - Rates (the policy statements, or activity variables, or flows)
      - Goal
      - Observed Conditions
      - Discrepancy between Goal and Observed Conditions
      - Desired Action

At the first hierarchy, industrial dynamics deals with closed systems. This means that the behavior modes of interest are generated within the boundaries of the defined system. It does not mean that one believes that nothing crosses the boundary in the actual system between the part inside the boundary and that outside. Instead, it means that what crosses the boundary is not essential in creating the causes and symptoms of the particular behavior being explored.

Within the boundary, the system is seen as one composed of feedback loops. Every decision exists within one or more such loops. The loops interact to produce the system behavior. A model of a system is formulated by starting with the loop structure, not by starting with components of loops.

At the third hierarchy, loops are themselves composed of two classes of variables, called "levels" and "rates" in the industrial dynamics terminology. Levels are the variables, generated by integration, which at any moment define the state of the system. Rates are the flow variables that depend on the levels and which are integrated to produce the levels. This concept of the level and rate variables appears with different terminology in other fields. The level and rate variables are a necessary and sufficient substructure within the feedback loop.

At the fourth hierarchy, the level variables are generated by the process of integration and have no significant subsubstructure except for the rates flowing into them. The rate variables do have an identifiable subsubstructure. The rate variables are the policy statements of the system and within each there is explicitly or implicitly a statement of the goal of that decision-making point in the system, the observed condition, a discrepancy based on the relationship of goal and observed condition, and the desired action that results from the discrepancy.

The Closed Boundary

The feedback loop is fundamentally a closed process in which a decision, acting through time delay and distortion, influences the state of the system which, after further time delay and distortion, is detected as the observed state of the system. The focus of attention is on how this loop operates. Forces may impinge on the loop from the outside, but our interest is in how the characteristics of the loop itself cause it to amplify or attenuate disturbances or produce growth. The boundary encloses those elements necessary to give the system its intrinsic character. The boundary implies dynamic independence in the sense that any variable crossing the boundary from the outside is not itself a function of the activity within the boundary. Anything on the outside is essentially random or independent of anything on the inside. There are no closed loops of significance to the particular study going from inside the system to outside of the boundary and returning.

Where to draw the boundary depends intimately on the specific system behavior being studied. If one's interest is restricted to a particular mode of behavior, the boundary must necessarily include those elements which generate the mode. Focusing attention on a different behavior mode may well produce substantial changes in the boundary. For an industrial system model, the boundary should include those aspects of the company, the market, the competitors, and the environment which are just sufficient to produce the behavior being investigated. Anything not essential to producing the mode of behavior under study should be left outside the system boundary. Perhaps the point can be illustrated by a recurring example in our Industrial Dynamics Summer Session Programs. The participants go through all of the stages of defining a system, building a model of that system, and examining the dynamic behavior through computer simulation. The price and supply instability in a commodity market is often taken as a vehicle. The problem starts at the simplest level of showing how the supply and consumption responses to price can cause a recurring imbalance between supply and demand. Because government price support programs play a conspicuous part in many commodities, Summer Session participants often feel compelled to incorporate such government activity in the first model. But such a step should be guided by answering this question: "Is the government activity *essential* to *creating* the fluctuation of price and supply, the fundamental cause of which is being explored?" Of course it is not. Commodity prices have been unstable long before there were government price support programs. Price support programs may be helpful or harmful, but they are not necessary in demonstrating the classic and fundamental processes of price and supply instability.

The concept of the closed boundary seems elementary yet it is apparently hard to grasp. It asserts that exogenous variables are not the key to the character of the system. Test inputs to a system may be used for study, but they are for the purpose of causing the system to divulge its inherent nature.

The Feedback Loop

The feedback loop is seen as the basic structural element of systems. It is the context within which every decision is made. Every decision is responsive to the existing condition of the system and influences that condition. This is a statement equally true for the forces that control the flow of electricity into a capacitor, for the conscious decisions of the individual or the manager, and for the selective decisions of nature that fit species to the environment by the processes of evolution. The skilled industrial dynamics analyst operates through an iterative process that cycles through the four hierarchies of structure. Yet the focus is always on the higher levels, until these have been satisfactorily established, before devoting much attention to the lower levels. In other words, establishing the system boundary comes first. The second stage is the identification of feedback loops and should come before the detailing of the level and rate substructure. It is here that the man without a solid background in the dynamic nature of feedback systems is at his greatest disadvantage. He is not able to correlate observed symptoms and behavior with probable loop structures. He does not see in the history of a real life situation the evidence that points toward the significance of the different positive and negative feedback loops and their interactions.

Levels and Rates

The industrial dynamics structure recognizes two classes of fundamental system variables as being necessary and sufficient. (The auxiliary equations are algebraically part of the rate equations. The first-order smoothing equations can be decomposed into a simple level equation and two rate equations.) The level equations at any moment in time describe the condition or state of the system. The level variables carry the continuity of the system from the present toward the future and provide the information on which rates of flow are based. The rate variables are the activity or flow variables. The rates change the values of the levels. The level equations are integrations which accumulate the effects of the rates. The rate equations are algebraic expressions without reference to time.

The rate and level concepts are found in the literature of many fields. In economics, the levels are often referred to as stocks and the rates as flows or activity. In engineering feedback systems the "state variable approach" shows increasing prominence. Some quotations from engineering convey the same ideas that are associated with the industrial dynamics level variables. "The state variable approach aids conceptual thinking about these problems, and nonlinear system problems as well. Furthermore, it provides a unifying basis for thinking about linear and nonlinear problems . . . the state of the network is related to the memory of the network . . . heuristically, the state of a system separates the future from the past, so that the state contains all the relevant information concerning the past history of the system required to determine the response for any input . . . the manner in which a system reaches a present state does not affect the future output. The present state of a system and the present and future inputs to a system uniquely determine the present and future outputs . . . the outputs of the integrators in the simulation diagram are used as the components of the state vector . . . although the outputs of the integrators in the simulation diagram form a natural state vector, these variables may not be physically measurable in a system," [2, Chapter 5].

In business, the financial accounting statement implicitly recognizes level and rate variables by separating these onto the balance sheet and the profit and loss statement. The balance sheet gives the present financial condition or state of the system as it has been created by accumulating or integrating the past rates of flow. The profit and loss variables (if one overlooks the fact that they do not represent instantaneous values but are instead averages over some period of time) are the rates of flow which cause the level variables in the balance sheet to change.

The same concept of level and rate variables, cast in a different terminology, can be found in the field of psychology where we might quote from the foreword by Cartwright to a book of papers by Lewin. "The most fundamental construct for Lewin is, of course, that of 'field.' All behavior (including action, thinking, wishing, striving, valuing, achieving, *etc.*) is conceived of as a change of some state of a field in a given unit of time . . . in treating individual psychology, the field with which the scientist must deal is the 'life space' of the individual . . . it is the task of the scientist to develop constructs and techniques of observation and measurement adequate to characterize the properties of any given life space at any given time and to state the laws governing changes of these properties . . . Lewin's assertion that the only determinants of behavior at a given time are the properties of the field at the same time has caused more controversy than any of his other systematic principles. This principle asserts that the life space endures through time, is modified by events, and is a product of history, *but only the contemporaneous system can have effects at any time,*" [11, Foreword]. The field or life space of Lewin seems clearly to correspond to the level variables which we here use. The "behavior" and the "laws governing changes of these properties" correspond to the rate variables.

Policy Substructure

The rate equations are the policy statements in a system. They are the rules whereby the state of the system determines action. A policy statement is seen as having four components. The first is the goal of the decision-making process. It is the objective toward which this part of the system is striving. In the very broad sense used here, physical processes have goals just as do individuals in their decision making.[2] Second, the policy specifies certain information inputs on which the decision-making process is based. These are the apparent states of the system. Apparent state must be distinguished from true state. It is only the *available* information which governs a decision. A true system state may be delayed, distorted, biased, depreciated, and contaminated before making its appearance at the decision point as an apparent state. Both true and apparent states are system levels. Third, the policy describes a process for determining the discrepancy between goal and observed condition. Fourth, the policy defines a desired action which will result from the

[2] The float and valve in a toilet tank have the goal of keeping the tank full. An identical conceptual structure describes a pail of water with a hole—the outflow (action) depends on the difference (discrepancy) between the water level (apparent condition) and the water level at the hole (the goal).

discrepancy. The preceding structure of a policy has been discussed in more detail elsewhere, [3, Chapter 10].

Comments on Structure

Some persons have criticized the industrial dynamics structure as being stylized or naive or oversimplified. Some seem to feel that the system concepts have been adjusted to fit the DYNAMO compiler rather than *vice versa*. We believe that the structure will come to be recognized as having simple elegance, universality, and a fundamental character common to a very broad range of systems running from physical devices through medicine and psychology to social and ecological systems.

Once one has come to have confidence in the generality of a system structure, that structure is a tremendous aid to organizing knowledge in a particular situation. One organizes knowledge for a purpose. The purpose may be to explain and perhaps to alter some specific mode of behavior. Without a purpose or objective there is no basis for defining a system. But once this objective is clear, he can then deal in terms of the closed boundary concept. Attempting to define the boundary focuses attention on what must be included to generate the symptoms and behavior mode of the system. Definition of the boundary is no doubt done while perceiving the next level of structure dealing with feedback loops. As the loops are defined, these become the paths through the real-life system which are to be represented in the specific model of that system. The loops represent the cross-sections out of reality which are to be recognized as important for the purposes of the particular study.

After establishing the boundary and the feedback loops, one begins to sort system variables into levels and rates. All variables that define the state of the system are levels and will be represented as integrations (first-order difference equations). All variables that define activity will be algebraic and belong to the class of rate equations. Levels determine rates, and rates generate levels. Any path through a system structure will necessarily encounter alternating level and rate variables. The subsubstructure within a rate or policy statement focuses attention on the concepts which must be incorporated.

After one has practice in its use, a formal, dependable, and general structure reduces by as much as two orders of magnitude the time necessary to establish the significant relationships that are buried within the conflicting, inadequate, and irrelevant information found in an actual situation.

It is perhaps unnecessary to point out that an industrial dynamics structuring has almost no relationship to the normal corporate organization chart. The dynamic system structure deals with information flows and decision points that control specific action streams. The decision stream at one particular policy point in the system may represent contributions from a number of persons or levels in the actual organization. Conversely, any particular person is likely to be a part of several different decision points controlling quite different flow rates.

The levels in an industrial dynamics model are cast in terms of first-order difference equations. Because the solution interval is made sufficiently short, this is entirely equivalent to a system of integrations. One might comment then on the choice between a system of equations cast in the form of integrations versus a system of differential equations. Engineering systems are almost universally defined in terms of differential equations. But this seems artificial. It tends to focus attention on the wrong direction of causality. For example, if one is filling a tank from a garden hose, our perception of reality suggests thinking of the water in the tank as the integral (accumulation) of the stream from the hose. The alternate statement, built around differentiation rather than integration, would define the water flow rate from the hose in terms of the derivative of water level in the tank. This derivative formulation comes close to implying that the water flows from the hose *because of* the change in water level. The differential equation formulation tends to obscure the direction of causality in systems.

One can go a step further in questioning the differential equation description of a system and call attention to the fact that nowhere in nature does the process of differentiation take place. No instrument measures derivatives. Devices which nominally measure rates of flow in fact measure average rates over some time span and operate on principles that involve integration. When a physical solution to a differential equation in engineering is to be obtained, as on a differential analyzer, the equation is first integrated enough times to eliminate derivatives. "Differential analyzer" is a misnomer; the machine is assembled from integrators.

In teaching system dynamics we have found it much easier and much more natural to the student to deal exclusively with the processes of integration and to make no reference to differentiation. Differentiation is seen as a mathematical artificiality which does not have a real life counterpart in the systems being represented.

THE TASK AHEAD

The reader is, of course, correct if he observes that the available literature and educational materials do very little to help him achieve the understanding of systems implied by the preceding sections. The industrial dynamics literature suggests the promise of advantages which may accrue from a better understanding of systems, but it does not adequately convey the essential mathematics of the field, nor expose the principles which should guide judgment in modeling of systems, nor does it provide an adequate number of examples to be used as guides in system structuring.

If system structure and dynamic behavior are to form a thread that runs through a management education and integrates the functional areas into a cohesive whole, several gaps must be filled. There must be an appropriate treatment of the mathematics of system dynamics. There should be examples of the system structures that generate some of the principal modes of behavior seen in corporate and economic systems. There should be bridging articles to show how system concepts can be applied in the functional areas and to management policy.

Mathematics of Feedback Systems

There are now numerous books on the mathematics of feedback systems, but most of these concentrate on obtaining analytical solutions. For this reason the mathematical techniques are pressed to the absolute limit. Even so, the systems dealt with are too simple to be of much managerial interest. While concentrating on the mathematical frontier, the existing treatments do not adequately stress the simple concepts of dynamic behavior with a primary aim of improving the individual's intuitive sense of how feedback systems function. At MIT we are now embarking on an interpretation of the existing mathematics to simplify, to expose more clearly the concepts, and to make the material a base from which intuitive judgments and simulation studies can be extended.

Principles of Feedback Behavior

Besides a mathematical treatment of systems, there seems to be a need for a descriptive treatment which verbally identifies principles and illustrates these by examples. Such a treatment would depend heavily on simple problems and exercises aimed at making the concepts and the techniques part of the working skills of the student. The author is now writing such a book with an accompanying workbook of exercises.

System Examples

A person applying the industrial dynamics approach to actual corporate problems seems to do so by drawing heavily on his mental library of the systems which he has previously studied. If others are to be able to do the same, such libraries of examples must be put in orderly written form. Such a series of structures would identify those relationships which are found repeatedly in industry. [References 8, 12, and 13 suggest the nature of this approach.] Such a treatment of systems should concentrate on the minimum structure necessary to create a particular mode of behavior. Along with such an identified structure would be presented the ensemble of data which in the actual situation indicates that the particular subsystem is apt to be dominant. Historical data are often decisive in distinguishing between the possible subsystems that might be causing a corporate difficulty.

Bridging Articles

A series of articles is necessary to show how system structuring can be brought to bear on the problems that manifest themselves in various functional areas of management. Difficulties that appear in one functional area are apt to be caused by a system that cuts through several functional areas. Such articles would create ties between different fields which now are too highly compartmentalized.

Management Education

Management education has been without a foundation of theory to serve the function that physics provides to the technological professions. Although many academic programs in management treat economics as a discipline underlying management, we might better see both management and economics as systems having the same conceptual structure and exhibiting similar kinds of dynamic behavior. They differ in scale but not necessarily in nature or essential complexity. The physical size or scope of a system has but little to do with the complexity of the model necessary to represent that system adequately. The bigger the system, the greater can be the degree of aggregation. A model of an economy need not contain all component companies. A model of a company does not represent each person. A model of human behavior would not reach to the individual cell. A model of dynamics of a cell would aggregate to a much higher level than individual atoms and most molecules. In fact, the models needed in each of these systems would probably be of about the same complexity.

The nonlinear, multiple, feedback loop structuring of systems with associated dynamic principles should grow into a foundation and central core to unify management education. The same approach to organizing relationships should serve in each functional area, in economics, and in psychology. Linking between the areas would then become easy if they were cast in a common underlying structure.

As management education moves toward a greater emphasis on systems, the mathematical threads running through the academic material will change. The future will show less concentration on statistics and matrix algebra and more on the continuous variables of causal systems. There is a common foundation beneath statistics and the mathematics of continuous processes, but the two branches of mathematics seem to produce very different attitudes in students (or the paths are followed by students who previously had developed different attitudes). The branch of mathematics dealing with random events seems to be associated with a view of the world as being capricious and beyond control. The mathematical branch through differential equations (or the preferred integral formulation) emphasizes the cause-and-effect relationships and supports the attitude of an environment that can be altered and controlled. Statistics seems to concentrate on the deviation of processes from the mean, with insufficient attention to the ways of changing the mean. The approach through continuous variables lays first emphasis on the causal structure that controls the mean and, when this is understood, adds randomness to determine the influence of uncertainty on the system.

Industrial dynamics has more in common with the case study approach than with most other methods in management education. But it goes further than discussion of a case. Building a model of a process enforces more disciplined thought than does mere discussion, just as a written description usually leads to more careful thought than does a conversation. So model building leads to a better considered and more precise statement of the system description. After a model has been formulated, model simulation shows whether or not the agreed component assumptions can lead to the expected behavior. The simulation result is often not as expected. The degree to which the model behaves like the actual system that is being modelled is one measure of model validity. This check is never achieved in a mere case discussion of a management system problem.

Industrial dynamics should help fill in the management part of management education. Now much of management education serves the interests of the staff advisor but not of the line manager. The manager's viewpoint has traditionally been reserved for a policy course taken usually at the end as a capstone to a management education. But systems thinking and the ability to deal with dynamic interactions takes much longer to learn than the facts of the functional areas. In response to the systems challenge, we should expect to see a core being developed through the entire management curriculum. This core will be a new ensemble of subjects that deal with the mathematics of systems, the dynamic principles of systems, the conversion of experience and descriptive knowledge to a precise structured form, policy design through simulation experiments, coordination of model systems and case discussions, and a policy course that builds descriptively and intuitively beyond a foundation of policy studies in the form of dynamic models.

Exploration of system dynamics by way of more comprehensive models is opening the door to a new understanding of feedback processes in social systems. The future will no doubt show that we now know only a fragment of what we need to learn about the principles, theory, and behavior modes of feedback structures.

REFERENCES

1. Bruner, Jerome S., *The Process of Education,* Harvard University Press, 1960.
2. DeRusso, Paul M., Rob J. Roy, and Charles M. Close, *State Variables for Engineers,* John Wiley & Sons, Inc., 1965.
3. Forrester, Jay W., *Industrial Dynamics,* The M.I.T. Press, 1961.
4. ———, "Modeling the Dynamic Processes of Corporate Growth," *Proceedings of the IBM Scientific Computing Symposium,* December 7–9, 1964, pp. 23–42.
5. ———, "The Structure Underlying Management Processes," *Proceedings of the 24th Annual Meeting of the Academy of Management,* December 28–30, 1964, pp. 58–68.
6. ———, "A New Avenue to Management," *Technology Review, Vol.* **LXVI**, Number 3, January, 1964.
7. ———, "Common Foundations Underlying Engineering and Management," IEEE *Spectrum,* September 1964, pp. 66–77.
8. ———, "Modeling of Market and Company Interactions," *Proceedings of the American Marketing Association,* August 31-September 3, 1965.
9. Jarmain, W. Edwin, editor, *Problems in Industrial Dynamics,* Cambridge, The M.I.T. Press, 1963.
10. Kovach, Ladis, D., "Life Can Be So Nonlinear," *American Scientist,* vol. **48**, No. 2, pp. 218–225 (June 1960), published by the Society of the Sigma Xi.
11. Lewin, Kurt, edited by Cartwright, Dorwin, *Field Theory in Social Science,* Harper, 1951.
12. Nord, Ole C., *Growth of a Product: Effects of Capacity-Acquisition Policies,* Cambridge, The M.I.T. Press, 1963.
13. Packer, David W., *Resource Acquisition in Corporate Growth,* Cambridge, The M.I.T. Press, 1964.
14. Roberts, Edward B., *The Dynamics of Research and Development,* New York, Harper and Row, Publishers, Inc., 1964.

    For a bibliography on industrial dynamics see the following:

15. ———, "New Directions in Industrial Dynamics," *Industrial Management Review,* Vol. **6**, No. 1, Fall 1964, Alfred P. Sloan School of Management, M.I.T.

39. INDUSTRIAL DYNAMICS AND THE DESIGN OF MANAGEMENT CONTROL SYSTEMS

EDWARD B. ROBERTS *

The usual approaches to management control system design often fail to be effective, sometimes creating problems more significant than those they resolve. Such failures result from lack of total system understanding, from use of subsystem constraints, and from inadequate or improper treatment of the human decision-making elements of the system. Examples drawn from Industrial Dynamics research studies illustrate these problems and provide some pointers for remedying the difficulties.

THE ORGANIZATION AS A CONTROL SYSTEM

Every organization is a control system. Each has direction and objectives, whether explicit or implied. Each has beliefs as to its current status. Each has policies and procedures whereby it reaches decisions and takes actions to attain its goals more closely. Every organization actually contains a myriad of smaller control systems, each characterized by the same goal-striving, but not necessarily goal-attaining, behavior.

The organization as a whole or any one of its component subsystems can be represented by the feedback process shown in Figure 1. Four characteristics of this diagram are noteworthy. First, the transformation of decisions into results takes place through a complex process which includes a basic structure of organizational, human, and market relationships; this structure is sometimes not apparent because of its numerous sources of noise or random behavior and due to its often lengthy time delays between cause and effect.

The second aspect to be noted is the distinction between the achievements that are apparent in the organization and those which are real. The real situation is translated into the apparent through information and communication channels which contain delays, noise, and bias. These sources of error may be the inadvertent features of an organization's communication system, or they may result from the chosen characteristics of a data-processing system which sacrifices accuracy for compactness. In any event, however, the bases of actual decisions in an organization may be assumptions which bear but little relation to fact.

The third feature of the diagram is that the decision-making process is viewed as a response to the gap between objectives of the organization and its apparent progress toward those objectives. Although both the objectives and achievements may be difficult to define precisely and measure accurately, such a goal-seeking behavior is nonetheless present in all organizations and in every subsystem of the organizations. At any level of an organization, many similar decisions are being made. The real problem of the management control sys-

SOURCE:

This article is based on studies supported by grants of the Ford Foundation and the National Aeronautics and Space Administration. The computer simulations were carried out at the M.I.T. Computation Center. The paper was presented at the Stanford University Seminar on Basic Research in Management Controls, February 20, 1963. The writer is grateful to Professors Donald C. Carroll, Jay W. Forrester, and Donald G. Marquis for their many helpful comments.

* Massachusetts Institute of Technology.

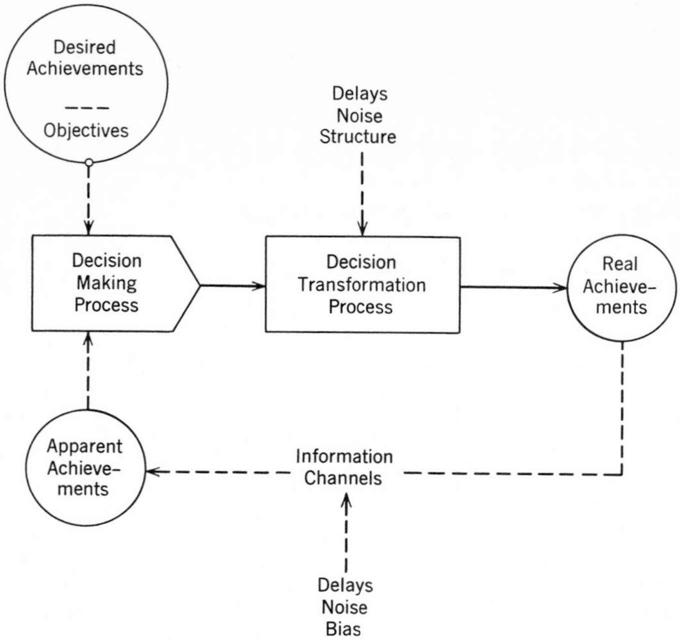

FIG. 1. Control system structure of organization.

tem designer is to recognize these multiple decision loops and their interrelationships, and to develop policies and an organizational structure that will tie these activities into progress toward total organization objectives.

The fourth characteristic of Figure 1 is the continuous feedback path of decision-results-measurement-evaluation-decision. It is vital to effective system design that each element of this feedback path be properly treated and that its continuous nature be recognized. Whether the decision in the system is made by the irrational actions or logical deductions of a manager or by the programmed response of a computer, the system consequences will eventually have further effects on the decision itself.

INDUSTRIAL DYNAMICS—PHILOSOPHY AND METHODOLOGY FOR CONTROL SYSTEM DESIGN

Industrial Dynamics is a philosophy which asserts that organizations are most effectively viewed (and managed) from this control system perspective. It is also a methodology for designing organizational policy. This two-pronged approach is the result of a research program that was initiated and directed at the M.I.T. School of Industrial Management by Professor Jay W. Forrester. The results of the first five years of this program are described in Professor Forrester's book, *Industrial Dynamics,* which also discusses a variety of potential applications to key management problems.[1]

Industrial Dynamics recognizes a common systems base in the flow structure of all social-economic-industrial-political organizations. This perspective ties the segmented functional aspects of formal organizations into an integrated structure of varying rates of flow and responsively changing levels of accumulation. The flow paths involve all facets of organizational resources—men, money, materials, orders, and capital equipment—and the information and decision-making network that links the other flows.

Industrial Dynamics views decisions as the controllers of these organization flows. Such decisions regulate the rate of change of levels from which the flows originate and to which they are sent. In the flow diagrams drawn as part of an Industrial Dynamics study, decisions are even represented by the traditional con-

[1] Jay W. Forrester, *Industrial Dynamics* (Cambridge: The M.I.T. Press, 1961).

trol valve symbol of the engineer. Figure 2 shows such a decision, based in part on information about the contents of the source level, controlling the rate of flow to the destination level.

The system structures and behavioral phenomena that are studied by the Industrial Dynamics methodology are present at all levels of the corporation. The top management of the firm is involved in a system that can be studied and aided in the same manner as the middle management of the organization, and again in the same fashion as the physical operating system of the plant. The potential payoff from changes derived from system studies increases greatly, however, as the study is focused higher up in the organization. For all studies the pattern of forming a dynamic verbal theory, developing mathematical equations, computer simulation of the model, and derivation of improved policies is followed. The problems encountered in these phases do not significantly change as we move from the bottom to the top of an organization. Only during the final stage of implementation of system change does the problem complexity get significantly greater the higher the level of organization involved. But the impact of improved corporate-level policy on company growth, stability, and profitability can readily justify this added effort to renovate top management policy making.

PROBLEMS OF MANAGEMENT CONTROL SYSTEMS

The preceding discussion has focused on the nature of organizational problems as management control system problems, and on the intended applicability of Industrial Dynamics to these problems. Observation of several different types of management control systems and a survey of the literature in this field lead to a belief that a new attack on control system design is needed. The traditional approaches to management control systems have mushroomed in number and sophistication of applications as operations research and electronic data processing have developed during the post-war era. Although these systems have made significant and successful inroads, many fail to cure the problems for which they were designed; other management control systems even amplify the initial difficulties or create more significant new problems. All this is tak-

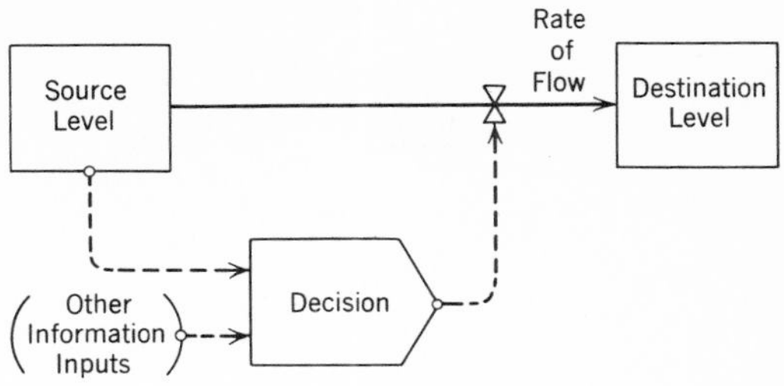

FIG. 2. The decision as a controller.

ing place even as we derive enhanced but misplaced confidence in the systems.

Several examples will help to illustrate these problems and lead us to some findings about the design of management control systems.

Systems Inadequate for Their Problems

Sometimes the management control system is inadequately designed for the problem situation. In such a case the control system may improve performance in the trouble area, but be far short of the potential gains. At times the limited effectiveness may transform a potentially major benefit to the company into but a marginal application.

The Control of Research and Development Projects

One example of an area in which the traditional approach to control system design has proven inadequate is the management of research and development projects. The intangibility, lack of precise measurements, and uncertain character of R and D results are partly responsible for this failure. But a more basic lack of system understanding has implications of even greater significance. All systems of schedule and/or budget controls that have been tried till now have failed to achieve success in R and D usage. These techniques have included Gantt charts, milestone schedules, and computerized systems of budgetary and manpower control.

The latest approaches to control of research and development projects are based on PERT (Program Evaluation Review Technique) or PERT/COST. The management control systems implied by the methods used can be represented by the diagram of Figure 3. As shown here, the basis of the current sophisticated methods is a single-loop system in which

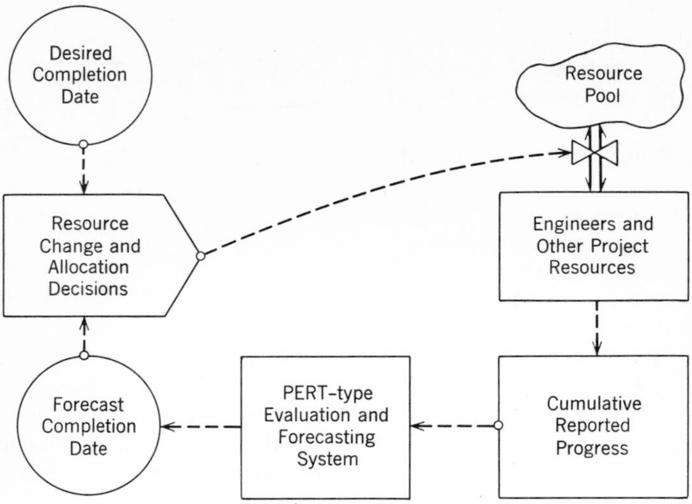

FIG. 3. Assumed basis of current R and D project controls.

the difference between desired completion date and forecast completion date causes decisions to change the magnitude or allocation of project resources (manpower, facilities, equipment, priorities). As these resources are employed, they are assumed to produce the progress that is reported during the project. These reports are processed through a PERT-type evaluation and forecasting system to create the forecast completion time.

But the design of a management control system based on such a set of assumptions is doomed to failure, since some of the most vital aspects of the real system have been excluded from the underlying analysis. For example, the lack of tangible, precise measurement sources is entirely ignored. Yet these factors contribute much of the error between the *real* situation in the project (its true scope and actual progress to date) and that which is *apparent* to those doing the engineering work.

Another part of the real system which appears to be ignored by current R and D control system designers is the human element in the project actions and decisions. The attitudes and motivations of the engineers and managers, their knowledge of the schedules and current estimates in the project, the believed penalty-reward structure of the organization—all affect the progress and problems that are reported upward in the organization. Furthermore, these same factors even affect the rate of real progress toward project objectives. All systems of measurement and evaluation (in R and D, manufacturing, government, universities, or what-have-you) create incentives and pressures for certain actions. These interact with the goals and character of individuals and institutions to produce decisions, actions, and their results. For example, a system which compares "actual to budgeted expenditures" creates an incentive to increase budgets, regardless of progress; one which checks "proportion of budget spent" creates pressures on the manager or engineer to be sure he spends the money, whether or not on something useful. The presence of such factors in research and development ought to be recognized in the design of systems for R and D control.

Adding these two additional sources of system behavior to the earlier diagram produces the more complete representation of a research and development system that is pictured in Figure 4. But even this is an incomplete representation of the complex system which interrelates the characteristics of the product, the customer, and the R and D organization. A proper characterization of research and development projects must take into account the continuous dynamic system of activities that creates project life cycles. Such a system will include not just the schedule and accumulated effort, costs, and accomplishments. Rather, it will encompass the full range of policies and parameters that carry a research and development project from initial perception of potential need for the product to final

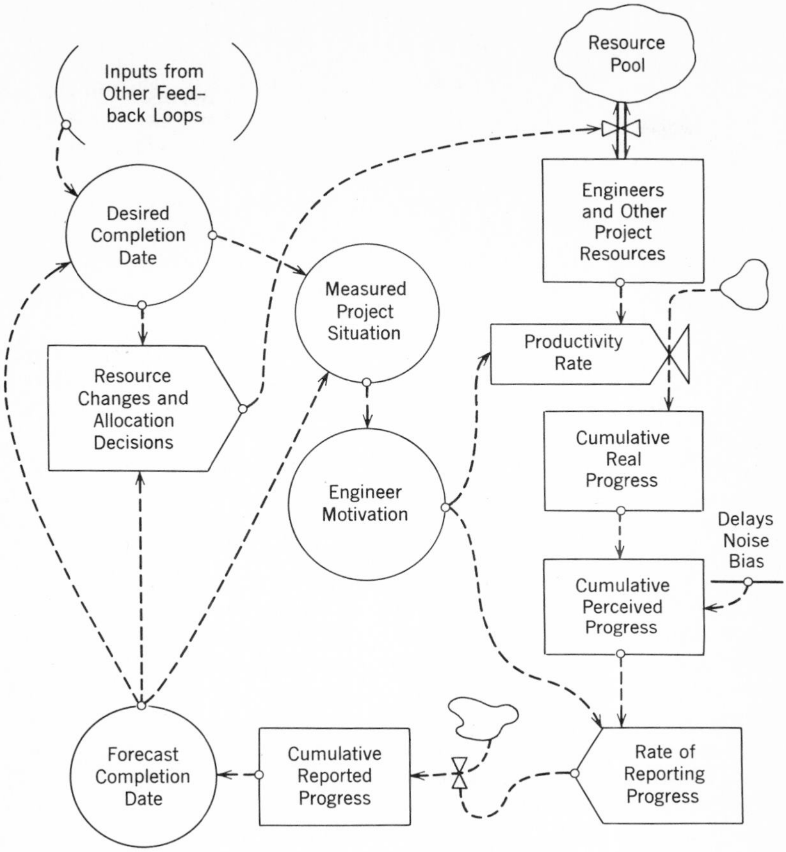

FIG. 4. More complete representation of R and D system.

completion of the development program. The fundamental R and D project system is shown in Figure 5, from which we have developed an Industrial Dynamics model of research and development project dynamics.

Some of the results of simulation studies of this model are of particular interest to designers of management control systems. They demonstrate the importance of taking cognizance of the complete system structure in at-

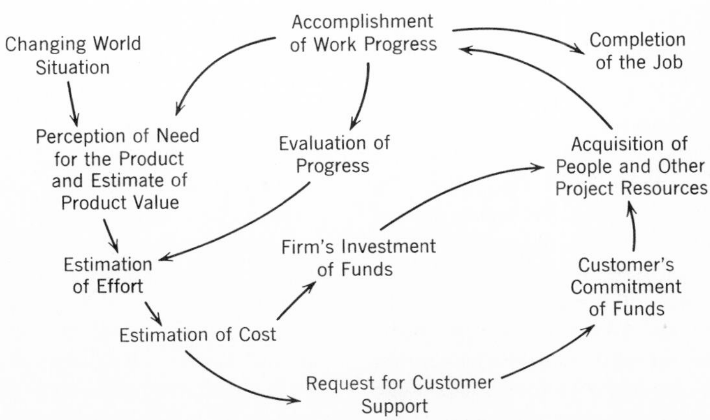

FIG. 5. Dynamic system underlying R and D projects.

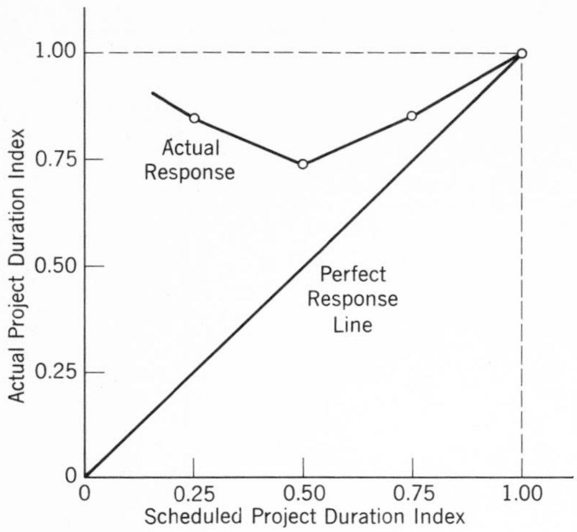

FIG. 6. Scheduled versus actual project durations.

tempting to create and implement methods of system control. For example, one series of simulations of the general project model was conducted in which only the scheduled project duration was changed in the various runs. Within the model the effort allocation process *attempts* to complete the project during this scheduled period. However, the actual completion dates of the projects seem only remotely responsive to the changes in desired completion time.

Figure 6 demonstrates the nature of this response, using the outputs of four model simulations. The horizontal axis is an index of the scheduled project duration as a percentage of the maximum schedule used; the vertical axis shows actual completion time in a similar percentile manner. If changes in schedule produced corresponding changes in actual completion dates, the curve of results would have followed the diagonal "perfect response" line; that is, a 50 percent reduction in scheduled duration should produce a 50 percent reduction in actual duration, if control is *perfect.* But the actual response is far from perfect; a 50 percent schedule change effects only a 25 percent actual change. And at the extreme, the actual change is even in the opposite direction, taking longer to complete the urgent crash project because of the resulting organizational confusion and inefficiencies. Of course, this response curve does not present the simulation data on the manpower instability, total project cost, and customer satisfaction changes that also accompany shifts in the project schedule.

Some of the implications of Figure 6 are more clearly presented in the next curve. Here the slippage in project schedule is plotted as a function of the scheduled duration, the points on the curve coming from the project model simulations. A completion time slippage of 242 percent of schedule was incurred in the crash project, with a rapid decrease in this percentage completion date overrun as the schedule is dragged out. When the project is slowed too much, the slippage increases again as lack of enthusiasm induces further stretch-out during the project life.

The principal point made by these two illustrations is that many factors other than desired schedule determine the resultant actual schedule of research and development projects. *Control systems for R and D which resort to schedule and effort rate control without full understanding of the system structure of projects are bound to be ineffective.* The current PERT-based project control systems seem guilty of this error in design philosophy. In fact, many aspects of our government contracting program suffer similar faults of inadequate system understanding, producing ill-conceived policies with attendant poor results. For example, increased risk-taking (i.e., greater willingness to invest company funds prior to contract receipt) and higher bidding integrity by R and D companies would act in the best interest of the government customer of research and development. However, our simulation studies show that neither policy is in the short-term best interests of the R and D companies, under existing government regulations and practices. Thus the contracting policies, a

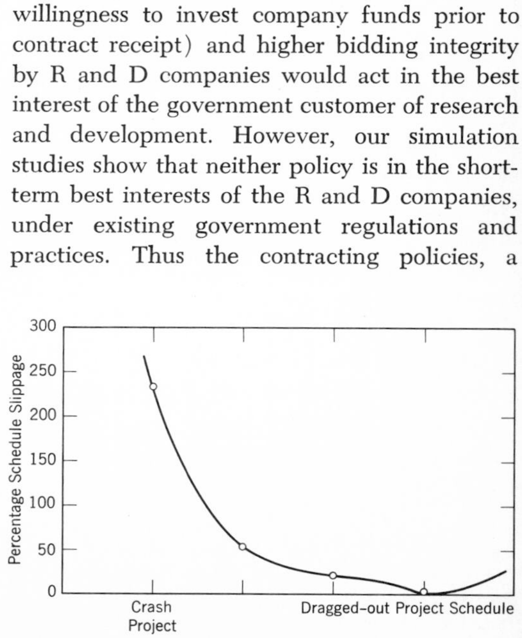

FIG. 7. Schedule slippage as a function of schedule.

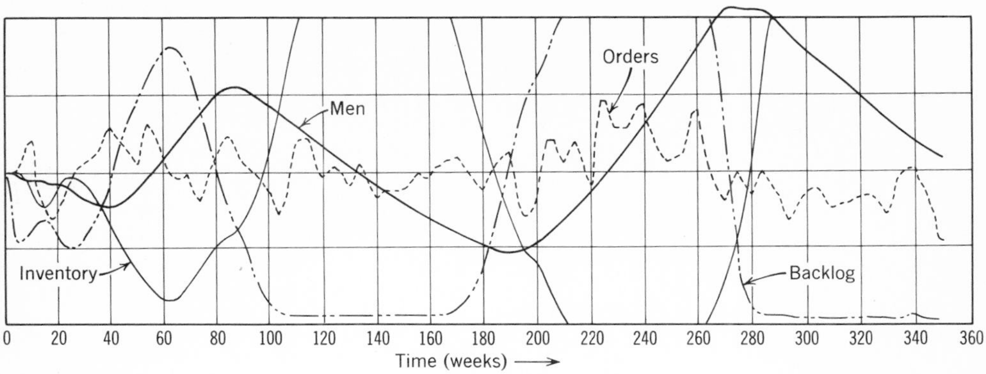

FIG. 8. Management by crisis.

government control system for R and D procurement, act to the detriment of national objectives by inducing company behavior which produces unsatisfactory project outcomes.[2]

The proper design of research and development control systems, for both company and customer, should take into account three things: (1) the source of internal action, information, and control in a project is the individual engineer; measurement and evaluation schemes and the internal penalty-reward structure must be designed with him in mind; (2) the total results of research and development projects are created by a complex dynamic system of activities, which interrelates the characteristics of the product, the customer, and the R and D firm; control systems which ignore vital aspects of these flows cannot succeed; (3) institutional objectives of R and D companies (profits, growth, stability) can be aligned with the objectives of government customers; procurement policies constitute the system of control which can effect or destroy this alignment.

A Production-Inventory-Employment Control System

As another example, let us take the case of an industrial components manufacturer who initially has no formal production-inventory-employment control systems. Such a firm operates by its response to current problems. It follows the example of the firemen trying to use a leaky hose—as soon as one hole is patched up, another leak occurs elsewhere. A company operating in this manner does not keep sufficiently close tabs on changes in sales, inventories, backlogs, delivery delays, etc. Rather, when customer complaints build up on company delivery performance, people will be hired to increase production rate and repair the inventory position. Similarly, when a periodic financial report (or the warehouse manager's difficulties) shows a great excess in inventory, workers will be laid off to reduce the inventory position. Despite the obvious faults, the majority of our manufacturing firms have these problems. The dynamic behavior of such a firm (as here illustrated by simulation results of an Industrial Dynamics model) has the appearance of Figure 8, with wide swings in sales, inventories, employment, order backlog, and correspondingly in profitability. The potential for a well-designed management control system in such a firm is enormous.

The traditional approach (some may prefer calling it the "modern approach") to the design of a control system for such an organization will recognize that: (1) better information on sales is necessary; (2) such information should properly be smoothed to eliminate possibilities of factory response to chance order-rate variations; (3) inventories should be periodically (perhaps even continuously) checked, and reorders generated when needed to bring stocks into line with target inventories; (4) order backlogs should not be allowed to drift

[2] A general theory of research and development project behavior, a model of the theory, and extensive simulation studies of parameters and policies influencing R and D outcomes are reported in the author's book, *The Dynamics of Research and Development* (New York: Harper and Row, 1964).

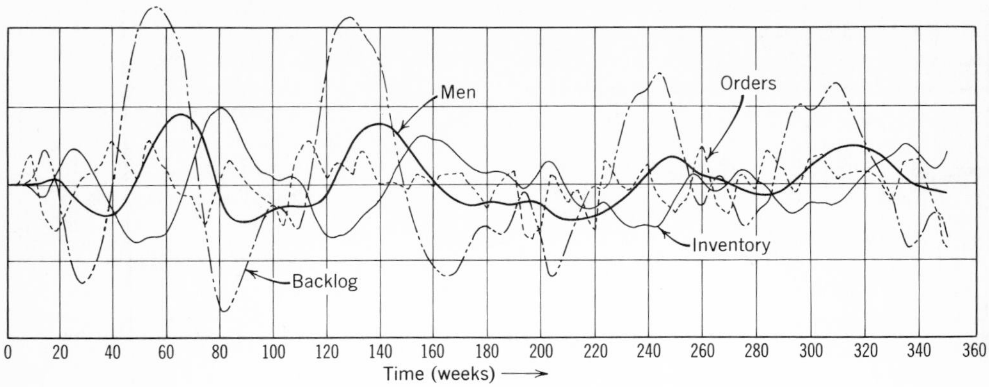

FIG. 9. Effects of management control systems.

too far from the normal levels; and (5) work force should be adjusted to meet the desired production rate that stems from consideration of current sales volume and the manufacturing backlog situation. Using our earlier company model, we can readily build into the model a management control system that incorporates all these features. The modeled company would then be a leader in its use of management control techniques. And, as Figure 9 illustrates, the company would have benefited by this approach. With the new control systems installed, fluctuations in the business have in general been reduced in magnitude as well as periodicity. Yet the basic dynamic pattern observed in the earlier diagram is still present—periodic fluctuations in sales, larger ones in inventories, and corresponding variations in production rate and work force. The latter situation is similar in character to that which we encountered at the Sprague Electric Company, at the beginning of our Industrial Dynamics study program with them several years ago.

Let us briefly review their case. The Sprague Electric Company is a major producer of electrical components, with an annual sales volume of approximately 75 million dollars. The particular product line which was selected for Industrial Dynamics research is a relatively mature industrial component, developed by Sprague several years ago and now past its market introduction and major growth phases. The principal customers of the product are manufacturers of military and high-grade consumer electronic systems. The industry competition is not price-based, but is rather dependent on product reliability and delivery time.

The work structure of the company, including its inventory and manufacturing control aspects, is diagrammed in Figure 10. Orders arrive from the customers, and a determination is made as to whether or not they can be filled from existing inventories. Orders for those catalogue items not ordinarily stocked, or for those which are currently out of stock, enter into the backlog of manufacturing orders. The customer orders for which inventory is in stock are processed and shipped from inventory.

The inventory control system of the company attempts to maintain a proper inventory position for the product line. Target inventories are adjusted to take into account average sales, and inventory reorders are generated to reflect the shipping rate from inventory and the desired inventory corrections. The orders for inventory replacements enter into the manufacturing backlog.

Production rate in the company is determined by the level of employment, with manufacturing output being sent to the customers or to inventory in reflection of the relative production order backlogs. Control of both backlog size and employment level is attempted by means of the employment change decision of the company.

As the curves of Figure 9 demonstrated, inventory, backlog, and employment all had sizable fluctuations, despite the existing controls in these areas. They seem to reflect, with some amplification, the variability in incoming orders. Given this situation of fluctuating sales, the traditional management control designer would either express satisfaction with the system performance or perhaps seek additional improvement by parameter adjustment. Neither approach would get at the source of the difficulties, and this source is not the fluctuations in incoming customer orders.

To determine the real system problem, let us examine our next diagram (Figure 11). Here we have duplicated the manufacturer's organization of Figure 10 and added a representation of the customer sector of the industry. The customers receive orders for military and commercial electronic systems. These are processed through the engineering departments, resulting in requirements for components. Customer orders for components are prepared and released as demanded by the delivery lead time of the component manufacturers. Delivered components enter into the system manufacturers' component inventories and are used up during production of the systems.

Having added this sector to our diagram, we now discover the presence of another feedback loop in the total company-customer system: changes in the company delivery delay will affect the customer release rate of new orders, which in turn will influence the company delivery delay. This loop amplifies the system problems of the company, being able to transform slight variations in system orders into sustained oscillations in company order rate, producing related fluctuations in company inventories, backlog, employment, and profits.

Let us follow through a possible dynamic sequence that will illustrate the full system interactions. If, for any reason, system orders received by the customers temporarily increase, the customers will soon pass this along to the component supplier as an order increase. Since, even under ordinary circumstances, weekly fluctuations in order rate to the component manufacturer are sizable, some time will elapse before this order rate change is noticed. In the meantime, the component manufacturer's inventory will be somewhat reduced, and the order backlog will be increased. Both of these changes tend to increase the delivery delay. The smaller inventory allows fewer incoming orders to be filled immediately; the larger backlog causes a longer delay for the now increased fraction of orders that must await manufacture. As the customers become aware of the longer lead time, they begin to order

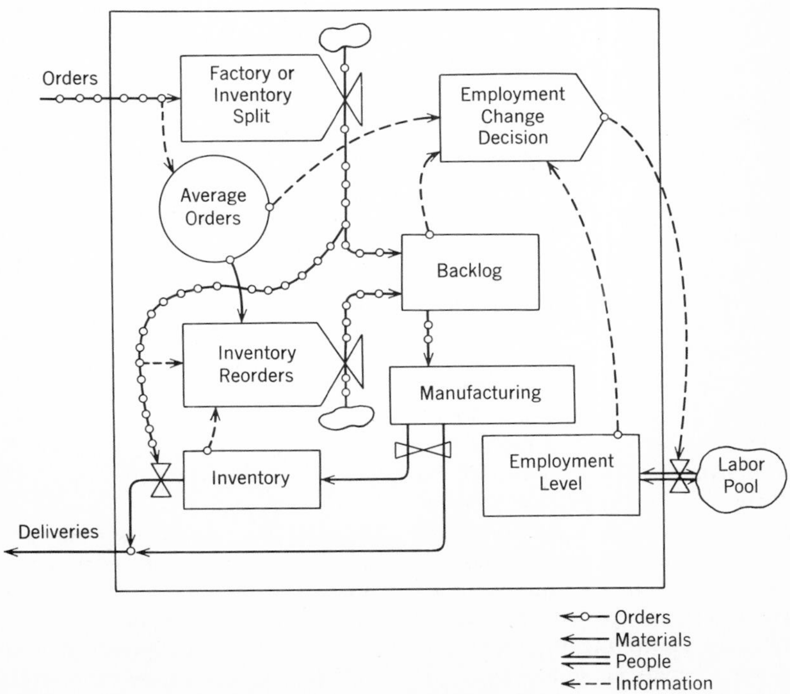

FIG. 10. The manufacturer's organization structure.

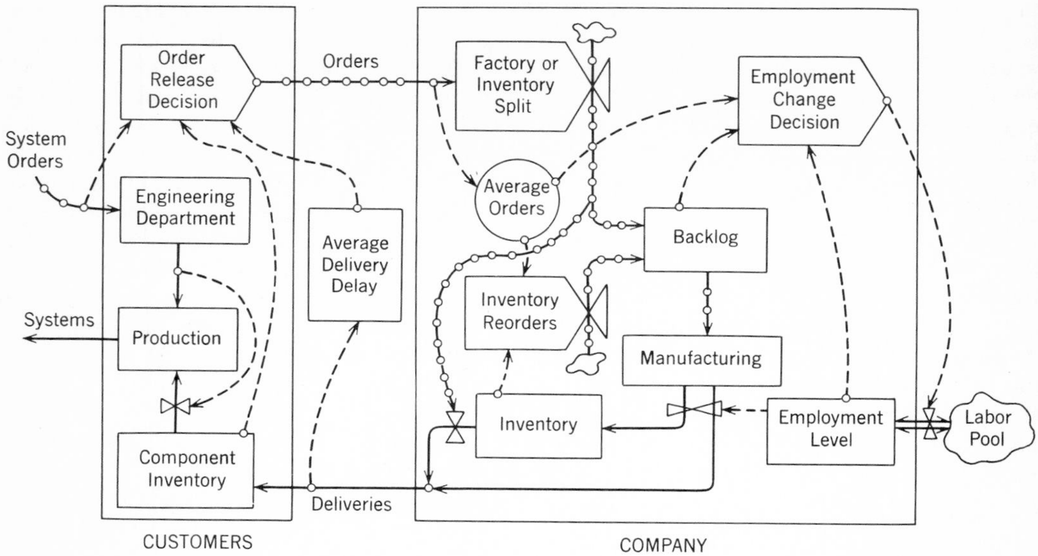

FIG. 11. Company-customers systems.

further ahead, thus maintaining a higher order rate and accentuating the previous trend in sales.

Eventually, the component manufacturer notes the higher sales, larger backlog, and lower inventory, and begins hiring to increase his factory employment. The employment level is set higher than that needed to handle the current customer order rate, so that backlog and inventory can be brought into line. As the increased work force has its gradual effect on inventory and backlog, the changes tend to reduce the delivery time. The information is gradually fed back to the customers, lowering the order rate even below the initial value. This set of system interactions can produce order rate fluctuations unrelated to the basic demand pattern for the customer products.

To dampen the fluctuations in customer order rate, the component manufacturer must control not inventory or backlog or employment, but rather he must stabilize the factory lead time for deliveries. This can readily be accomplished once the nature of the need is recognized. System behavior can also be improved to a great extent when the component manufacturer becomes aware that his inventory control system does not really control inventory, but it does contribute to production overshoots of any change in orders received.

The details of the Sprague case, the model for its study, and the new policies now being implemented at Sprague are discussed fully in Chapters 17 and 18 of *Industrial Dynamics.* It is sufficient for our purposes to show the effects of the new policies applied to the same situation shown earlier in Figure 9. The curves shown on the next graph (Figure 12) demonstrate a higher degree of stability achieved in all variables except inventory, which is now being used to absorb random changes in sales. In particular, the enployment swings have been dampened significantly. The simulation results forecast significant benefits to the company deriving from the application of this new approach to management policy design. Our experiences during the past year of system usage at Sprague seem to support the initial hypotheses, and the product line is currently benefiting from higher productivity, improved employment stability, higher and smoother sales, and lower inventories.

SYSTEMS CREATING NEW MANAGEMENT PROBLEMS

The two control system areas discussed above were intended to demonstrate that many management control systems are designed in a manner that makes them inadequate to cope with the underlying problems. In each example, however, certain aspects of the systems were described which actually aggravated the existing problems. Our discussion of research and

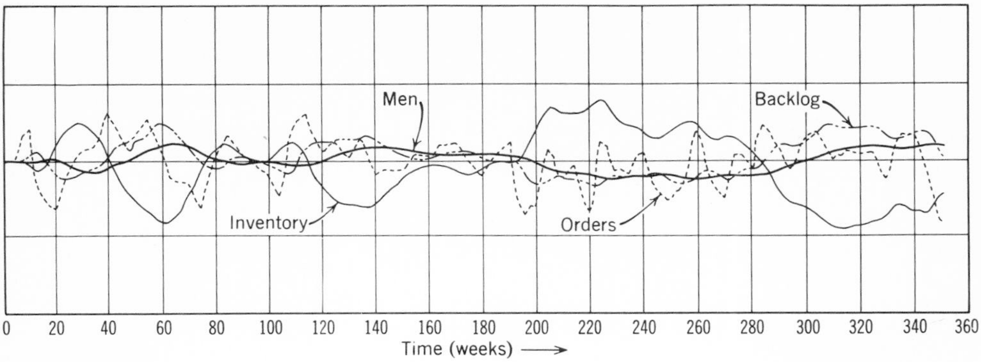

FIG. 12. Effects of industrial dynamics policies.

development project control indicated that government contracting policies often create resulting behavior that is contrary to the government's own interests. In the Sprague case, the inventory control system amplified sales changes to create wider swings in production and employment than actually existed in orders received from the customers. Other examples can be presented which have similar effects: the attempt to achieve management control leads to situations in which initial difficulties are amplified or significant new problems are created.

Problems of Logistics Control

One apparent instance of this type occurs in the Air Force Hi-Value Logistic System. This inventory control system was developed over a long period of time at great government expense by some of the nation's most sophisticated control system designers. The Hi-Value System is intended to provide conservative initial procurement and meticulous individual item management during the complete logistic cycle of all high-cost Air Force material. Yet an Industrial Dynamics study of this system by a member of the M.I.T. Executive Development Program concluded that the system behavior can result in periodic overstatement of requirements, excess procurement and/or unnecessary repair of material, followed by reactions at the opposite extreme.[3] These fluctuations produce undesirable oscillations in the repair and procurement work loads and in the required manpower at Air Force installations, supply and repair depots. The study recommended changes in policy and information usage that tend to stabilize the procurement system behavior.

Quality Control Systems

A commonly utilized management control system has as its purpose the control of manufacturing output quality. The feedback system apparent to the designers of such quality control systems is pictured in Figure 13. Component parts are produced by a process that has a certain expected quality or reliability characteristic. The parts are inspected for flaws and rejects discarded or reworked. Statistically designed control charts determine when the production process is out of control, and reports are fed back to production to correct the problem sources.

The effectiveness of such quality control systems becomes questionable when we view the performance curves generated by a typical system. Figure 14 plots component production rate and inspection reject rate over a period of two years. Wide periodic swings in reject

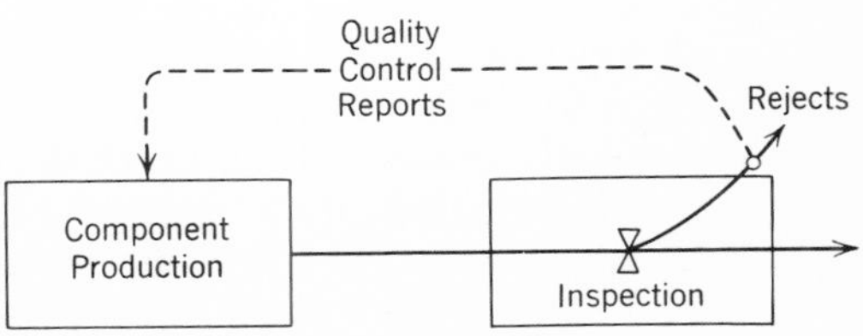

FIG. 13. Theoretical quality control system.

[3] Max K. Kennedy, "An Analysis of the Air Force Hi-Value Logistic System; An Industrial Dynamics Study" (unpublished S.M. thesis, M.I.T. School of Industrial Management, 1962).

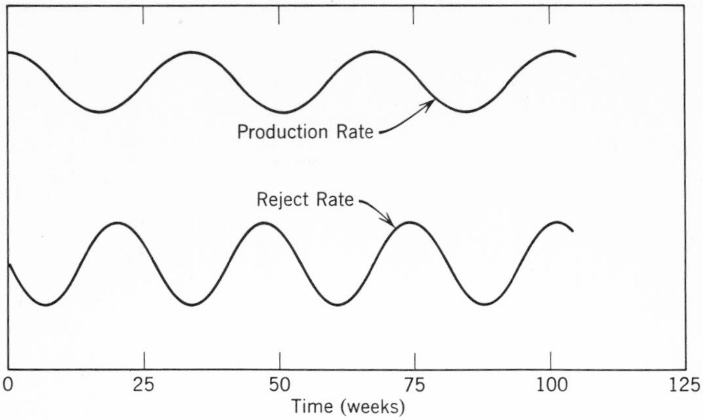

FIG. 14. Quality control system performance.

rate produce violations of the control system tolerance limits which cause machine adjustments in production and temporarily lower production rates. But what causes the oscillations in the reject rate? Its periodic nature suggests seasonal fluctuations in production quality, often strangely encountered in many manufacturing plants. The manager has almost no way of checking the validity of such an assumption. Therefore, since the explanation seems reasonable, it would probably be accepted under most circumstances.

This situation illustrates one of the key problems in quality control—the lack of an objective confirming source of information. We are in a more favorable position to understand the phenomenon, however, since the results were produced by a computer simulation. The surprising fact is that the actual production quality was held constant, without even random variations, throughout the two years of the run. This means that the oscillations of reject rate and production shown in Figure 14 are not responses to outside changes, but rather are internally created by the behavioral system.

Let us examine a more complete picture of the total factory system, as shown in the next diagram. Components are produced, then inspected, rejects being discarded. The accepted components are forwarded to an assembly operation, where they enter into the manufacture of complete units. In an electronics plant, for example, the component production and inspection might correspond to a grid manufacturing operation, with the assembly operation putting together complete electronic tubes. When the tube is put through a life test, tube

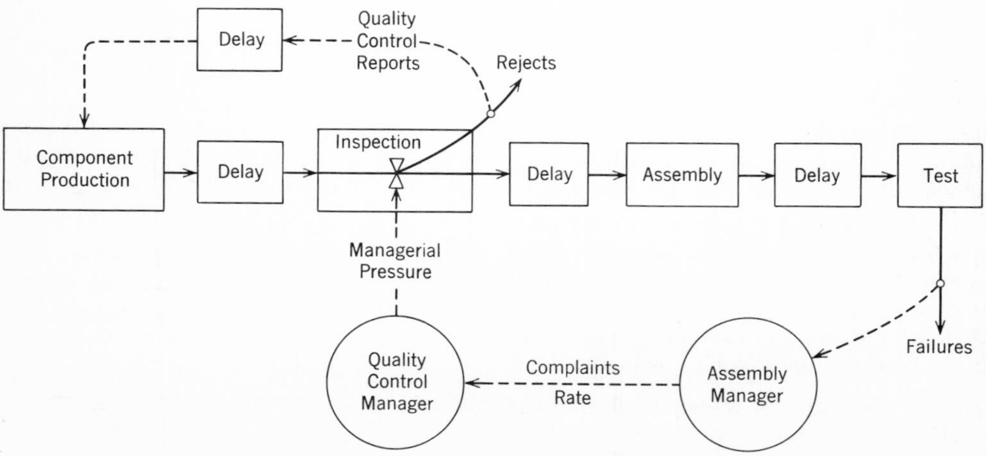

FIG. 15. More complete representation of quality control system.

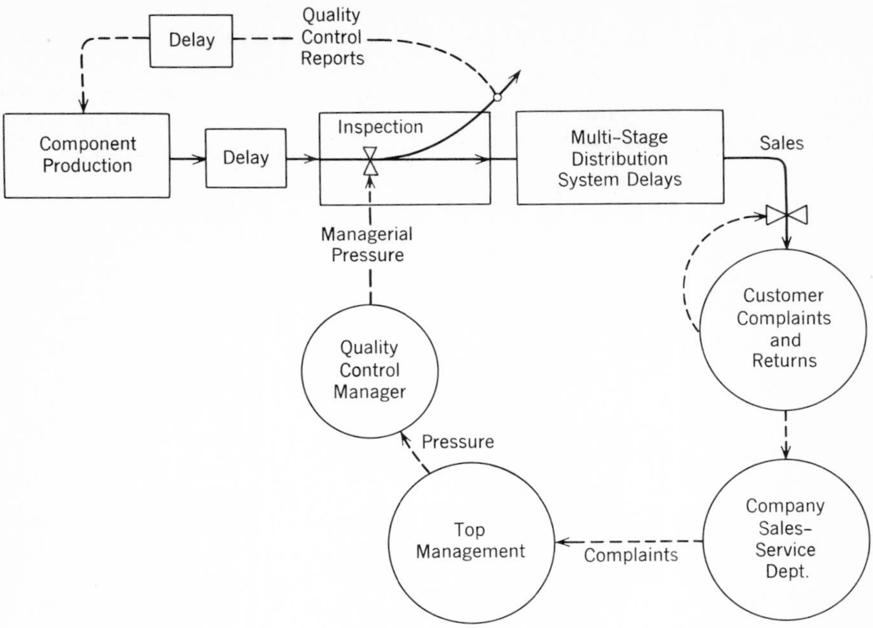

FIG. 16. Total quality control system.

failure and the source of failure are far more obvious than are the grid imperfections during the component inspection. Should too many imperfections get through component inspection, eventual tube failure rate will produce complaints by the assembly manager to the quality control manager. As these complaints continue to build, the quality control manager puts pressure on his inspectors to be more careful and detect more of the poor grids. In response to this pressure, the inspectors reject far more grids. Without an objective measure of grid quality, the reject rate tends to be a function of subjective standards and inspection care. Under pressure from the manager, the inspectors will reject any grid which seems at all dubious, including many which are actually of acceptable quality. As the rejects rise, fewer poor grids enter the assembly process, thus causing fewer tube failures in test. The assembly manager's complaints drop off and, in fact, soon switch to a concern for getting more grids for his assembly operation. Without pressure from the quality control manager and with counterpressure to get more grids to the assembly operation, the grid inspectors tend to slacken gradually their care and their reject standards. Eventually, the number of rejectable grids getting into the tube assembly creates the problem of tube failures again, and the cycle repeats. Given normal delays in such a process, the entire cycle takes on a seasonal appearance. Thus, a system intended to assure control of product quality actually creates serious fluctuations of rejects, component production, and tube failures, all attributed to unknown factors "out of our control."

The consequences of such a situation are even more serious when the inspection output is distributed to eventual customers through the normal multi-stage distribution system. In this case the customer complaints and store returns also affect sales. These influences combine after a long delay to produce significant top management pressure on the quality control manager in reflection of a situation which existed many months before. In both Figures 15 and 16, the quality control manager's response is a key to system behavior. Here the manager of the formal quality control system is himself the most important aspect of the total system of quality and production control.

SOME PRINCIPLES OF MANAGEMENT CONTROL SYSTEM DESIGN

The examples discussed represent a wide range of management control systems. Study of these applications produces some general principles of management control system design.

A. The key to effective control often lies outside the boundaries of *conventional* operational control systems; in fact, it is sometimes outside the *formal* boundaries of the company organization.

Too many organizations give up altogether too soon the battle for mastering a management problem caused by factors apparently "out of our control." Government changes in project funding of research and development, the cyclic swings in customer orders in the production-inventory case, seasonal variations of product reject rate in the quality control problem are all examples of such factors. Yet in each case successful control system management rests within the access of company policy.

Project success in R and D is strongly influenced by company integrity and risk-taking. Yet the customer can affect these results by redesigning his own policies to achieve more desirable company behavior. Again, in the Sprague case the system requiring control included the ordering decisions of the customer, certainly not part of Sprague's formal organization. But the basis for system control exists in the stabilization of the input to the customer decision, the component delivery delay. And the key to quality control involves recognition of the total system of product flow to assembly (or to customers) and the resulting feedback of complaints and pressures.

The boundaries of a management control system design study must not be drawn to conform with organizational structure merely because of that structure. System boundaries cannot ignore vital feedback channels for information and action if the system is to be effective.

B. The proper design of management control systems often requires inclusion of the effects of intangibles; in particular, the role of decision makers who are part of the total system of control must be treated carefully.

Control system designers who are working with computers often have as their end product a computer model for calculating (or searching for) an optimal control decision. Yet while being willing to model a decision for a machine, they seem unwilling to include in their studies any models of man—of human decision making within the control loops. Our initial example emphasized that a properly designed R and D control system should be based on models of engineer and manager decision making in both the company and customer organizations. In the production-inventory control case, the modeling of aggregate customer decision makers is a vital part of the system. Finally, we observed that the decision making and responses of both managers and inspectors are crucial aspects of the quality control case.

These illustrations emphasize the usual failure to recognize and cope with the nature of human response in organizations. The decision makers, single or aggregated—their motivations, attitudes, pressures, and models of response—must be included in management control system design. *The man (and manager) is part of the system of control, and management control system design must be viewed as a form of man-machine system design.*

C. A true understanding of total system basis and system behavior can permit effective design of both operational control systems and top management policy, without differences in philosophy or methodology of approach. In fact, most significant control system applications inherently require supra-functional or multi-departmental organization.

In the Sprague case, for example, successful control involved consideration of such aspects as customer service (marketing), inventory and production rate (manufacturing), and employment policies (personnel). Thus what often gets treated as a middle-management problem becomes resolvable only at the top policy-making level of the firm. The important elements in research and development tend not to be middle-management concerns for schedules, but rather top management policy affecting investment planning, customer relations, and company-wide attitudes. Management control systems can therefore seek to achieve the major goals of the organization as a whole, and not just the sub-optimizing aims of individual segments. A great present hazard, in fact, is the common planning and programming of control systems at the wrong level of the company, by people who lack total system perspectives and the authority to achieve broad system integration.

The Industrial Dynamics program has demonstrated the possibilities of examining and treating system problems of great variety and scope of complexity. We have dealt with many situations in which stabilization was needed and more recently with other cases in which balanced growth was the objective of the policy design efforts. The potential advantages to companies who pioneer in this work are significant and may become the basis of our future industrial competition. In this regard, it seems fitting to close with the implied advice of the Japanese scholar who said: "When your opponent is at the point of striking you, let your mind be fixed on his sword and you are no longer free to master your own movements, for you are then controlled by him." [4]

[4] Takawan, as quoted by Charles H. Townes, "Useful Knowledge," *Technology Review*, January, 1963, p. 36.

40. AN APPRECIATION OF INDUSTRIAL DYNAMICS

H. IGOR ANSOFF* AND DENNIS P. SLEVIN†

Industrial Dynamics is a recently developed and fast-moving area of management analysis. Since its inception it has gained both staunch opponents and severe critics. This paper is an attempt at an impartial appreciation of Industrial Dynamics. The model-building process employed in ID is briefly described. The ID is discussed as a simulation approach to problem solving. The strengths, the apparent shortcomings and areas of applicability are discussed. Next a question is raised regarding ID's claim to the status of a "general systems theory." It is suggested that little evidence to date qualifies ID to be viewed as a distinctive body of theory about behavior of firms.

INTRODUCTION

This paper was undertaken on the suggestion of Professor Thrall and Dr. M. Geisler who felt that a non-partisan evaluation would contribute to a greater understanding of Industrial Dynamics. It should be stated at the outset that the authors are not accomplished practitioners of Industrial Dynamics (although one of the authors has worked extensively with feedback control theory). The views expressed were gleaned largely from published literature and to a smaller extent from conversations with practitioners. One of the reviewers of this paper has suggested that no one who has not practiced Industrial Dynamics can hope to understand it. While we disagree with this dogma, we grant the point that as outsiders we have a limited view of some of the intricacies of this approach and its application.

We are grateful to Professor Forrester for a fruitful exchange of letters and an extensive critique of this paper. He has urged us to retain as much of our position as we feel justified to do since it does represent an outsider's perception. We have tried to accept his criticisms where matters of fact were involved, but we largely retained our views where matters of interpretation and evaluation were involved.

SOURCE: *Management Science* (March, 1968), pp. 383–397. Reprinted by permission of Institute of Management Science.

* Carnegie-Mellon University.
† Carnegie-Mellon University.

WHAT IS INDUSTRIAL DYNAMICS?

Jay W. Forrester in his definitive book, as well as many of his followers, claims great generality for the applicability of Industrial Dynamics to the problems of industrial organizations. Since as we shall see below, ID is not a well-circumscribed body of theory, it is possible to define it through a series of stages of increasing specificity. Therefore, the range of its applicability is dependent on the definition one adopts.

At the very broadest level is Forrester's own definition:

> Industrial Dynamics is the study of the information-feedback characteristics of industrial activity to show how organizational structure, amplification (in policies), and time delays (in decisions and interactions) interact to influence the success of the enterprise. It treats the interaction between flows of information, money, orders, materials, personnel, and capital equipment in a company, an industry, or a national economy [11, p. 13].

Forrester further states that the approach is "experimental," by which he means that models constructed in ID are a mathematical replication of the structure of the real firm, including the flows of money, men, materials, and information, as well as location of the decision foci.

The specific steps to be used in constructing and running a simulation are as follows:

1. Identify a problem.
2. Isolate the factors that appear to interact to create the observed symptoms.
3. Trace the cause-and-effect information-feedback loops that link decisions to action to resulting information changes and to new decisions.
4. Formulate acceptable formal decision policies that describe how decisions result from the available information streams.
5. Construct a mathematical model of the decision policies, information sources, and interactions of the system components.
6. Generate the behavior through time of the system as described by the model (usually with a digital computer to execute the lengthy calculations).
7. Compare results against all pertinent available knowledge about the actual system.
8. Revise the model until it is acceptable as a representation of the actual system.
9. Redesign, within the model, the organizational relationships and policies which can be altered in the actual system to find the changes which improve system behavior.
10. Alter the real system in the directions that model experimentation has shown will lead to improved performance.

Forrester insists that, to be useful, the above steps be constructed in the language of the practicing manager: ". . . mathematical notation can be kept close to the vocabulary of business; . . . (so that) each variable and constant in an equation has the individual meaning to the practicing manager" [11, p. 55].

To this point the approach would raise few objections from a great majority of practicing management scientists interested in simulation. They would cheerfully admit to being "industrial dynamicists," although a few would give Forrester credit for discovering the central ideas. However, as one examines Forrester's particular interpretation of the respective steps shown above, his viewpoint becomes increasingly distinctive.

One distinctive feature is an insistence that the simulation be completely quantitative. There is, for example, no allowance for rank ordering of alternatives, nor for any form of human participation in the simulation runs. Forrester justifies this position, first, on the basis of his conviction that managers in the real world apply rather simple decision rules which lend themselves to quantification. Secondly, he points out that "a formal quantitative statement carries with it no implications one way or the other regarding absolute accuracy" [11, p. 50].

The process of abstracting the model from the real organization consists, on one hand, of gathering empirical performance data, and, on the other, of using interview techniques to elicit from managers the rules which they apply in making decisions. Of the two sources the latter is more important: "Models will be based primarily on our descriptive information . . . , not on statistical data alone" [11, p. 130]. Forrester does not appear to see any need to make allowances for the possibility that the rules which the managers verbalize may not be the ones they actually use, nor the possibility that they will vary the rules from one set of circumstances to another.[1]

In developing the model, our "concentration must be on those factors that determine the characteristics of information-feedback systems-structure, amplification, and delays" [11, p. 130]. Verbal description and observations are interpreted in flow charts which portray levels and flows of elements: information, money, orders, materials, personnel, and capital equipment. The "exercise" aspect is important. The verbal description of the firm is translated into a logical framework, and the feedback characteristics become graphically evident via the closed loops on the flow charts.

Equations showing these functional relationships are then formed. This is done in terms of levels and flows. The former are described by means of level equations:

$$\text{New Level} = \text{Old Level} + (\text{Rate of inflow} - \text{Rate of outflow}) \times \text{time increment}$$

The only assumption needed to make this relation generally valid is that the above six flows are "incompressible."

The second basic type of equation is a rate equation. It serves two purposes. First, as a description of decision functions. In this role, rate equations are made to depend only on the value of levels in the time interval under consideration. As Forrester points out, this is

[1] For a simulation of the firm which made such allowances, see Bonini's thesis, "Accounting Information Systems in the Firm," Carnegie Institute of Technology, 1962.

equivalent to basing decisions on only the information available about past performance of the system.

In the second role, rate equations are used to determine system dynamics, such as delay in transit of a particular flow between two levels. The rate equation for a delay takes the form:

$$\text{OUT. KL} = \text{STORE. } K/\text{DELAY}$$

where:

OUT. KL = Outflow rate during the time period K to L

STORE. K = The amount stored in the delay at time K

DELAY = A constant, the average length of time to traverse the delay

This equation, used in conjunction with an appropriate level equation, introduces a "first-order exponential delay." Such delay exhibits an exponentially decaying rate of outflow in response to an impulse input. A step function input produces a gradually rising output to a new level.

The dynamic properties of the first order delay may not be adequate to describe slower responding systems such as, say, shipment in transit. To accommodate for these, Forrester constructs higher order delays by feeding the flow through two or more first-order delays.

The level and the rate equations are the basic building blocks of the simulation model. Supporting these are "auxiliary equations," "supplementary equations," and "initial value equations." The latter are self-explanatory. Supplementary equations are used in coupling the model to the printed or plotted results, and auxiliary equations are component statements of rate equations.

One purpose of this highly stylized structure and of a comparably stylized system of notation is to make the model compatible with a special compiler called DYNAMO which was developed at MIT for solution of problems in ID. Given the data and model in the specified form, the DYNAMO compiler checks these equations for logical consistency, solves the system of equations, and tabulates data and graphically plots the variables specified. This compiler is quite a convenience, and greatly reduces the amount of effort required in simulation runs.

Forrester has a distinctive philosophy regarding the *end purpose* of industrial simulation. "Mathematical models should serve as tools for "enterprise engineering," that is, for the design of an industrial organization to meet better the desired objectives" [11, p. 56]. He interprets this to imply that while a useful system should be able to reproduce the "nature" of the system, it need not forecast the specific condition of the system at some future time. He concludes that this is fortunate "because there is ample reason to believe that such prediction will not be achieved in the foreseeable future" [11, p. 56].

Many workers in management simulation may be left at this point with an uncomfortable feeling that failure to predict outcomes places the model in a status of doubtful validity. Forrester feels otherwise. Validation is to be obtained by observing whether the model reproduces or predicts the "behavior characteristics" of the system such as stability, oscillation, growth, average period between peaks, general time relationships between changing variables, and tendency to attenuate externally imposed disturbances.

Thus, both the purpose and the validation of the model are addressed to what may be called dynamic or process characteristics of the model, rather than to correspondence between predicted and observed time-phased behavior.

This has a strong resemblance to the typological techniques used in servomechanism design and also in analysis of behavior of certain types of nonlinear differential equations.

While the approach to validation is clear, Forrester's view to its implementation shows a curious paradox. While insisting on reduction of model *content* to fully quantitative terms, he argues that model *validation* need not meet this requirement since "a preponderant amount of human knowledge is in nonquantitative form" [11, p. 128].

INDUSTRIAL DYNAMICS AS A SIMULATION APPROACH

For a relatively new management science technique, Industrial Dynamics has generated a considerable amount of critical comment. One of the reasons for this appears to stem from the fact that Forrester and his followers have not been particularly modest about claims for the breadth and superiority of his discovery. In order to sort out valid from apparently exaggerated claims, we shall start by discussing Industrial Dynamics as a simulation approach within the limits of the definition quoted in the last section.

In a later section we shall deal with wider claims of Industrial Dynamics as a pervasive and superior technique for dealing with a majority of problems of industrial organizations.

Industrial Dynamics shares with other simulation approaches some difficult problems of model validation. In this discussion we shall take validation to mean a test which establishes, first, that a model is capable of describing (and predicting) the behavior of the system with satisfactory accuracy; second, and more important for a management scientist, that changes in the model which produce desired improvements will produce closely similar improvements when applied to the real world system.

In defense of its validity, Industrial Dynamics simulation has been likened to wind tunnel tests in aerodynamics and to pilot plant test in chemical process design. This comparison has been aptly questioned by Charles C. Holt:

I should like to question Professor Forrester's going back and forth so facilely between a chemical pilot plant, a wind tunnel, and a simulation model for a computer. As we all know, one of the beauties of a computer is its flexibility. You can program on it practically any process involving information handling. Now, the wind tunnel and the pilot plant are governed by the same laws of nature that govern, respectively, the airplane and the full-scale pilot plant. We don't have to ask whether Mother Nature is really applying the same rules or physical laws to the model phenomena. On the other hand, when we go into a business organization and observe its structure and come home and build a model with our bare hands, there is a very real question as to whether we have brought home the baby. I think the problem of validating the model here is extremely critical in the effective use of this sort of approach [20, pp. 82–83].

It needs to be added that the presence of "Mother Nature" in both the wind tunnel and the power plant is not sufficient to permit successful translation of tests to full size design. In both cases the designer needs knowledge of *scaling laws* which permit comparison about the two regimes; these laws, in turn, are derived from general theories appropriate to the respective areas of phenomenology.

Perhaps the most charitable thing which can be said about the "wind tunnel analogy" is that it helps to explain the simulation concept to the uninitiated businessman. As an approach to validations it raises more questions than it answers.

A somewhat different criticism has been voiced by Harvey M. Wagner. He asks:

Does Industrial Dynamics represent a truly scientific approach? Or does it represent the judgmental approach of a particular scientist? Are there principles for applying industrial dynamics as a diagnostic tool which are not tied to the personality traits of a particular practitioner? What is the likelihood of two industrial dynamicists coming to the same recommendations when faced with the same strategic problem? [43, pp. 185–186].

While the question is valid, it should not be pointed at ID in particular, but rather to the field of *prescriptive* management science in general. What is the likelihood of any two other management scientists who are not professed industrial dynamicists, coming to the same recommendation? Two men approaching a production scheduling problem may perceive it in very different terms: one as a linear programming model and another as a quadratic decision rule. Both will be "right" to the extent that each, with different tests of validity, can probably show that his model describes an aspect of the real universe. But will their recommendations be the same, or even addressed to similar changes in organizational performance?

To go even further, much of management science problem solving, *outside* ID, dispenses with a descriptive validity test. The proof of the pudding is in the eating! Each of our analysts may reap glory and promotion if the changes suggested through his analysis produce improvements when applied to the real world system. Thus, it seems unfair to level the charge of *non-repeatability* of an analysis against ID any more than against general management science practice.

However, the issue of validation remains. The prescriptions offered by the analyst are not accepted as valid until they have been tried on the real system[2] and produced a desired kind of change in performance. The attitudes of management scientists to this issue appear to be polarized to two extremes. Some, whose backgrounds are frequently in mathematics and/or econometrics, view the problem to be akin to predictive validation. They are not overly concerned with being right the first time: a "reasonable" model can be tested on the real system then reconstituted and tested again until satisfactory correspondence between test and prediction result.

Another view, sometimes regarded as old-fashioned, is frequently held by scientists whose background is in traditional physical sciences or engineering. Here considerable emphasis is placed on making models "true to life" the first time, on observing carefully, on testing boundaries, on testing internal logic of the model, on obtaining parameters from real life situations.

Forrester belongs to this latter school and justifiably so! He is concerned with the fact that "an actual test is possible only after the change has been made and there is some measurement . . . in the real system! [11, p. 117]. Behind this is an apparent concern with the costs of being wrong (both to the system and to the career of the analyst) if the recommended change produces no improvement when applied to the firm.

As a result, Forrester exhibits much concern with the care which should be exercised in the course of an Industrial Dynamics study. What he has to say on this point will not be new to many trained model builders. He advises special concern with choice of system boundaries (old-fashioned engineers will recognize this as the choice of the "free body"), selection and interconnection of variables and the choice of values of parameters. With respect to parameters, he feels that the "system dynamics will be found insensitive to many of them" and the "few sensitive (ones) will be identified in model test" [11, p. 119]. Just how this is to be done in a multiparameter system, short of laborious sensitivity studies, he does not say.[3] One of Forrester's co-workers, Kenneth J. Schlager, appears to feel somewhat differently about the issue of parameters:

> To achieve such validity—these constants to which the model operation is sensitive—must be determined accurately with meaningful data from company operations. During early phases of the projects in two of the companies, data collection and analysis were hurriedly performed; but difficulties were encountered in demonstrating validity, and the data-collection phase had to be redone. I believe these validity tests of the model, using historical data, are an absolute necessity [38, p. 22].

This far our discussion was concerned with the process of assuring faithfulness of model to reality *in the process of its construction.* To borrow a term from industry, we might call this "quality assurance." There is little "science" in this part of management scientist's job, and Forrester properly acknowledges this fact and offers common and useful guidelines for the process.

In dealing with "quality control"—tests of a completed model—Forrester, like a majority of other workers in simulation of complete organizations, bases it on historical data [cf. 11, p. 120]. However, his view of this process is distinctive in several respects.

As discussed in a preceding section, he requires that tests be performed not on outcomes of a time-phased series of events, but rather on the "dynamic" characteristics of these series such as time intervals between peaks, natural periods, time-phased relationships between variables, and characteristics of transient response. He justifies this choice by pointing out that "the economic system contains large "noise" forces that are not explained by the behavior laws that we are justified in hypothesizing" [11, p. 124]. Therefore, comparison of the model states with historical states of the system will not produce useful prediction about future comparisons.[4]

[2] Or a carefully controlled experiment which can be shown to be related to the real world system in the sense described by Holt's remarks above.

[3] We would not be concerned with finding some sensitive ones. It is the undiscovered ones that present some new problems.

[4] The same conclusion has been reached by other workers who were concerned either with military problems in which end-states could not be satisfactorily defined (for example, the state of "victory" in limited war, or with problems of the firm in which reliablility of the prediction of future states fell rapidly in the very time region in which the performance of the system is of greatest interest.) (See, for example, H. I. Ansoff, *Corporate*

Having established a "dynamic validity" principle to be obtained through historical comparisons, Forrester remains vague on several points. Beyond examples of properties stated above, the specific criteria to be applied in the analysis are not specified and, are presumably left to individual judgment. Nor is the degree of correspondence to be sought between these properties in the model and in history. Thus, the validation process is not only qualitative, but it is also largely subjective.

Turning to the problem of prescriptive manipulation of the model, Forrester states that the model should, at all costs, be addressed to questions that are of consequence to the success of the organization, "The value of the objective transcends all other considerations in determining the utility of the model," [11, p. 116]. There is, however, the question of how changes in dynamic properties of the model will relate to this objective. Without such relationship it is not clear in which direction useful changes in the system should be made. It is not, for example, *a priori* evident that the most stable system is the best, nor the most responsive one. On this Forrester has little to say. Presumably the relationship will become evident in the particular simulation, perceived subjectively, and system variables would be manipulated in the right direction.

By way of a summary, it is useful to return to the comment by Wagner quoted earlier. The preceding discussion would suggest that "the likelihood of two industrial dynamicists coming to the same recommendation when faced with the same strategic problem," [9, p. 186], would be even less than the likelihood for two average management scientists. The latter would be similarly subjective in their model building activity but would make an effort to establish an explicit test of descriptive validity. They would also establish an explicit objective function and measure their manipulation of the model against it (regardless of whether it is process or outcome oriented). To paraphrase a previously quoted paragraph by Forrester in which he argues for complete quantification of the model,[5] they would very likely feel that a formal objective statement or a formal validity test carries with it no implication one way or the other regarding absolute accuracy.

QUANTITATIVE MODELLING

A desire to make one's models fully quantitative is natural and common to a majority of workers in management science. Reduced to quantitative terms, a model acquires visibility, flexibility, as well as potential generality of application. The language of both inputs and outputs becomes unambiguous (even if not necessarily meaningful). Therefore, Forrester is not unique, nor to be criticized for quantitative models. What is open to question, however, is the requirement that in a simulation approach *all* variables and phenomena which are relevant to the real world problem be quantified:

In formulating a quantitative model, we must have the courage to include *all the facets*[6] that we should consider essential to a verbal description of the phenomena under study. In the past, so long as mathematical models were restricted to those which could be solved analytically, the models could not accept the wealth of concepts that exist in descriptive knowledge. Simulation models and electronic computers change this picture, [11, p. 61].

Evidences of this "courage" are present throughout the literature. Edward Roberts speaks of the "% Quality of a firm" (0–100%), [30, p. 55]. David W. Packer talks of "Pressure for Expansion" in the firm, measured on a scale from −5 to +5 pressure units, [28, p. 76]. And Ole C. Nord presents a plot of the "Quality of a firm" (0–10 quality units) vs. time, [26, p. 13]. It is not clear that understanding of very difficult concepts like "pressure for expansion" or "quality of the firm" is enhanced by drawing simple graphs, nor is it made clear by the authors how empirical data for such graphs is to be collected and verified.

Relationships of this kind are accommodated in the model through the means of the *table function* provided in the Dynamo compiler. This characteristic of the compiler enables the dynamicist to include any arbitrary functiton of one variable by merely alternately typing in the respective values of the ordinates separated by slashes. This device is very convenient and enables the swift incorporation

Strategy, McGraw-Hill Book Company, Chapter 4.)

[5] See paragraph 5 of this paper.

[6] Italics supplied by the authors.

of arbitrary functions in the simulation. It is also perhaps very dangerous, for it encourages the inclusion of hidden arbitrary assumptions which are, at best, validated by plausibility arguments. In a study by Packer [28], for instance, there are included a total of 11 assumed table functions along with about 24 assumed constants. This is in a model totaling about 115 equations.

Attempts at complete quantification run into some special problems in the area of behavioral interactions. The manager is interrogated by a dynamicist and is made to verbalize the basis on which he makes particular decisions. He may, to please the analyst, focus on the "hard facts" which he manipulates in making production scheduling decisions; *e.g.*, inventory levels, his anticipation about lead times, volume of orders, *etc.* But "soft facts" may be equally influential: the pressures on him from the production manager on one side and the sales manager on the other, his perception of the kind of performance (conservative or aggressive) desired by his immediate superior, the amount of personal exposure to criticism which will result from a particular decision. It is not clear that converting these facts into quantitative single independent variable table functions will enhance understanding of the complex power and social variables which influence decision making, nor that this will lead to desirable recommendations for systems redesign. For example, it is possible that instead of modifying the quantitative decision rules at a particular level of responsibility, one should change the motivation of the manager by changing the level of responsibility which is assigned to him, [for a discussion of goal versus performance, see 41].

Problems similar to the above are encountered by all analysis of industrial behavior. However, there are several reasons for underlining them in a critique of Industrial Dynamics. First, Forrester's arguments in favor of complete quantification of all relevant phenomena are neither very explicit nor persuasive. One gets the suspicion of a man being driven by a computer. Behind the protestation of validity of quantification one senses the spectre of Dynamo, the investment it represents, and its appetite for data in a very particular data format.

Secondly, having committed himself to the path of full quantification, Forrester in his book is not as careful as he could be in facing up to the difficulties and limitations that this path implies. For example, he is not explicit about the likelihood that this path will produce the very kind of models he finds objectionable in the work of other scientists—models that fail to convey a sense of close correspondence to reality.

Thirdly, and perhaps most importantly, Forrester fails to formalize the process of abstraction of data from managers and to provide tests of validity of the information obtained. Thus, to the point of definition of the decision function the process remains an art of model building.

The problems raised by the format of the Dynamo compiler and the quantification requirement can be handled more constructively. Instead of dealing with limitations, one can address himself to identifying those problems of the firm and of other industrial organizations which are most likely to fit the model format. One would expect that better structured functional areas would be the most likely candidates for simulation, and among these, the descending order of fit would range from production and distribution, to marketing and down to research and development. On the general management level one would expect Industrial Dynamics to be the most useful in operating problems dealing with price-quantity problems, less useful in organizational design, and least useful in studies of the firm's product-market strategy. This ranking is indirectly confirmed by published applications of Industrial Dynamics. The Sprague Electric Study [1] was apparently most successful in production and inventory control and disappointing in marketing (see quotation below).

The three studies done by Schlager [38] concerned three types of production problems and offer little evidence one way or the other; although, Schlager's third study approached some *R & D* problems with apparent success. Roberts' book on *R & D* management offers inconclusive evidence, since the simulation performed apparently used a considerable amount of synthetic data. Readers of the book are forced to judge the application on the apparent plausibility of Roberts' reasoning rather than specific successful organizational redesign which resulted from his work.

Another major characteristic to be considered in determining areas of applicability of

Industrial Dynamics is the specific model structure incorporating concepts of levels and flows and built around the concept of tight loop information feedback. Forrester, in his book, makes a point that industrial systems are inherently information feedback systems. Granting the point, it does not necessarily follow that *all* aspects of the firm are best studied by means of information feedback systems.

This suggests that the appropriateness of the information feedback viewpoint should be determined on the basis of the relative influence of the feedback information on the decision in any given situation. Again this suggests production and distribution systems as the best candidates and others as poorer ones. This seems to have been borne out by the Sprague Electric Study.

In one major respect, however, the Sprague Industrial Dynamics project has not had the predicted effect. This is in the area of long term fluctuations in demand and the interactions between Sprague's own actions and those of its customers in a closed loop feedback system.
. . . . . The importance of the closed feedback concept in virtually all socioeconomic systems is one of the corner-stones of the Industrial Dynamics approach. The Sprague project does not, to date, support that part of this concept which implies that a relatively few easily discernible factors interact to form feedback loops which dominate the given system, [1, p. 18].

By way of summary, we can quote Charles C. Holt who has put the problem of model selection in a very clear way:

The notion of circular causality that is incorporated in Forrester's "information-feedback system" is an important analytical model which in any particular situation is capable of being either true or false. There is no denying that certain situations involve simultaneous determination (rather than unidirectional causality): for example, a manager with a budget constraint governing several different types of expenditure. It will not *always* be wise to limit ourselves to models based on circular causality in spite of the computational simplicity that may be obtainable by this approach, [20, p. 71].

A question intimately related to the applicability of a management science technique concerns its cost-benefits. How difficult is it to apply and what benefits does it bring?

In answer to the first part of this question, Construction Industrial Dynamic models involves considerable effort. This is due to a variety of reasons. There are not many people well versed in the techniques used in this sort of analysis. Acceptance by a firm is not easily won, and an Industrial Dynamics model calls for a significant amount of information collection. One of Schlager's most significant difficulties appeared to be the collection of meaningful operating data for the model.

But this is not surprising. One would expect any model, consisting of 200 equations and attempting to model an aggregate system by interrelating its micro-components, to require a sizable data collection effort.

However, this condition is not fixed. As more people become competent in Industrial Dynamics and as more firms rely on EDP systems, we would expect the costs of application of this technique to be reduced.

On the benefits side we find a phenomenon not untypical of many quantitative techniques. Both dynamists and managers profess that a significant benefit comes before the simulation during the flow chart modeling of the firm. This appears to have a therapeutic effect on the managers, forcing them to crystallize decision making processes and to order their thoughts according to a systematic, information feedback model. The benefits of this step are significant, and the costs are clearly an order of magnitude less than those involved in a full-fledged simulation.

Although this suggestion might be objectionable to the purists, perhaps an Industrial Dynamics application which stops at the flow charting stage would be preferable for some firms from the cost-benefits standpoint.

This "exercise" aspect, taken along with the dynamist's insistence on qualitative validation, leads to an interesting question: how do we evaluate Industrial Dynamics as being more beneficial than another quantitative method? Since the results are assessed on a qualitative basis, how do we determine that this system is any better than an "art of management" technique. On this point, we should have to agree with Professor R. A. Howard in saying that "the dynamicist should be judged not on his ability to make an absolute improvement in a firm's control but rather on his ability to improve the firm's operations beyond the improvement that could be achieved by having the operations subjected to the review of any careful observer."

AN OVERVIEW

In trying to arrive at an impartial evaluation of Industrial Dynamics a noninitiate is confronted with a perplexing problem. Forrester and his followers, having defined their approach as "*a* way of looking at the business firm," proceed to create the impression that it is also *the* way which should supersede and unify previous (according to them) unsuccessful approaches. No effort is evident to establish limitations (alongside with strengths) of the technique. A reviewer is thus forced to attempt to separate claims from substance.

Having attempted this in the preceding pages, we emerge with a view of Industrial Dynamics as a simulation approach based on a view of the firm as a feedback system. It appears that many management problems of the firm can be successfully described through feedback representation. Many others can be found in which other types of representation lead to more immediately useful results. Thus, while a feedback representation is indeed conceptionally descriptive of all modes of behavior of the firm (just as it is of all human activity, according to Wiener), the usefulness of feedback model should depend on the particular circumstances. This is synonymous with saying that a management scientist must fit his models to the real world and not *vice versa*.

It needs to be added that perception of the feedback nature of organizations is not original with Forrester. Others (among them Tustin, Simon and Cooper) have applied servomechanism theory to economic problems. The distinctive nature of Forrester's work lies in the fact that he boldly treated behavior of the firm as a whole and that he made the management decision process the center of his concern.

Beyond a simulation approach what else is Industrial Dynamics? Is it a predictive or a normative theory of the firm or of management behavior? The answer of course depends on what one means by a "theory." For many management scientists a theory would have to meet conditions similar to the following:

1. It should embrace a well-defined body of observable variables.
2. It should have an explicitly stated set of hypotheses about these variables.
3. It should present a calculus, a method which, relying on the hypotheses, permits construction of statements about the variables.
4. Finally, in the very nature of the above definition, a theory is a statement of its own limitations, an implicit definiton of areas of experence to which the theory does not apply.

This definition, when satisfied, permits an analyst to make *predictions* about the relations of variables which have not been previously observed. It also permits a *verification of validity* of theory through comparison of relations established in theory with observable relations in the real world. When the above conditions are satisfied, a theory possesses an invaluable property of transferability of insights and predictions from one observable situation to another. In perusing ID literature one searches in vain for statements which even begin to describe ID as a theory in the sense described above. The very fact that feedback representation is used does, in principle, make it possible to translate mathematical feedback control theory into theorems and generalizations applicable to the firm. Such translation, for example, was successfully made by Simon in 1952 when he applied Laplace transform theory to inventory problems of the firm, [39]. What one gets instead are prescriptions of how to construct models for individual situations; but no unifying insights are apparent.

In his comments to the authors of these pages Forrester remarked that he views ID as a beginning of a "systems theory" of the firm in much the same way in which Cybernetics is a theory of social behavior. Two interpretations are possible to his comments. One is that this is indeed a very early beginning since no semblance of a body of theory has emerged to date. The other interpretation is that Forrester's ideas of what constitutes a theory are very different from ours.

Some of Forrester's comments support the first interpretation. Thus, he says, "I feel we are not ready to attempt this last level of abstraction[7] until we have achieved acknowledged success in applying art and judgment

[7] At which, if one interprets him correctly, general theory is formulated.

and intuition to the extraction of the decision policies themselves! [11, p. 101]. In other words, thorough empirical descriptive work must precede efforts at generalization.

The question remains open as to whether the "empirical descriptive work" done to date will lead to unifying theoretical insights or whether it will remain a type of model building technique. Another question can be raised regarding our current state of readiness to generalize, as well as regarding an incremental approach to development of theory which is implicit in Forrester's remains. Some would argue that typical progress in an area of knowledge is through a confusing and frequently overlapping pattern punctuated by flashes of speculative generalizations and that such generalizations are the real lever to progress of a theory, rather than painstaking empirical descriptive work. However, regardless of which path is optimum, the burden of proof at this point in time rests with Industrial Dynamics.

If Forrester had been more willing to focus on the specific merits of his approach, one can speculate that full recognition of his contribution to management science would have been more unanimous and would have come sooner. Instead, he has preferred to establish his case by trying to prove that those who believed differently from him are either wrong or unsuccessful or both. This "proof by denial" permeates much of his definitive book. To quote at random:

> Economic models have enjoyed a long history of research but little general acceptance as a tool to aid top management. . .
>
> Many of the past failures . . . can be traced to unsound methods and attempts to reach unachievable objectives, [p. 53].

and again:

> The communications barrier has been nearly impenetrable between the mathematical models in the social sciences and the industrial and government executives, [p. 54].

and again:

> University research in management has the same opportunity to assume aggressive, innovative leadership that we have seen in the great schools of medicine, science and engineering, [p. 360].

This was written in 1961 after a fifteen-year period which many people, disagreeing with Forrester, would describe as a period of revolutionary advances in management science.[8]

[8] In his critique of our paper, Professor Forrester suggests that if *Top Management* is emphasized as the recipient of the work, then his remarks are *indeed* true.

REFERENCES

1. Carlson, Bruce R., "An Industrialist Views Industrial Dynamics," *Industrial Management Review,* Fall 1964, pp. 21–29.
2. ———, "Industrial Dynamics," *Management Services,* May-June, 1964, pp. 32–39.
3. Drucker, Peter F., "Thinking Ahead: Potentials of Management Science," *Harvard Business Review,* January-February 1959, pp. 25–30, 146–150.
4. Fey, Willard R., "An Industrial Dynamics Case Study," *Industrial Management Review,* Fall 1962, pp. 79–99.
5. ———, "An Industrial Dynamics Study of an Electronic Components Manufacturer," *Transactions of the Fifth Annual Conference of the American Production and Inventory Control Society,* September 1962.
6. Forrester, Jay W., "Advertising: A Problem in Industrial Dynamics," *Harvard Business Review,* March-April 1959, pp. 100–110.
7. ———, "A New Avenue to Management," *Technology Review,* January 1964, pp. 1–11.
8. ———, "Common Foundations Underlying Engineering and Management," *I.E.E.E. Spectrum,* September 1964, pp. 66–77.
9. ———, "Dynamics of Corporate Growth," *Proceedings of M.I.T. Conference*

on Management Strategy for Corporate Growth in New England, November 1963.

10. ———, "The Impact of Feedback Control Concepts on the Management Sciences," *1960 F.I.E.R. Distinguished Lecture,* Foundation for Instrumentation Education and Research, October 1960.
11. ———, *Industrial Dynamics,* M.I.T. Press, 1961.
12. ———, "Industrial Dynamics," in Carl Heyel (ed.) *The Encyclopedia of Management,* New York, Reinhold Publishing Company, 1963, pp. 313–319.
13. ———, "Industrial Dynamics: A Major Breakthrough for Decision Makers," *Harvard Business Review,* July-August 1958, pp. 37–66.
14. ———, "Management Science—Its Impact," *Technology Review,* January 1962, pp. 27–38.
15. ———, "New Frontiers," *Proceedings of the Eastern Joint Computer Conference,* December 1958.
16. ———, "New Opportunities for Instrumentation and Control in Management Systems," *Journal of Engineering Education,* June 1963, pp. 766–771.
17. ———, "The Relationship of Advertising to Corporate Management," *Proceedings of the Fourth Annual Conference of the Advertising Research Foundation,* October 1958.
18. ———, "Simulative Approaches for Improving Knowledge of Business Processes and Environments," *Proceedings of the 13th CIOS Conference,* 1963, pp. 5–9.
19. ———, "Systems Technology and Industrial Dynamics," *Technology Review,* June 1957, pp. 417–422, 428–432.
20. Greenberger, Martin (ed.), *Computers and the World of the Future,* M.I.T. Press, 1962.
21. Hanika, F. DeP., "Industrial Dynamics at M.I.T.," *The Manager: Journal of the British Institute of Management,* August 1962, pp. 46–47.
22. Jarmain, W. Edwin (ed.), *Problems in Industrial Dynamics,* Cambridge, The M.I.T. Press, 1963.
23. Johnson, R. A., F. E. Kast, and J. S. Rosenzweig, *The Theory and Management of Systems,* New York, McGraw-Hill Book Company, 1963, pp. 31, 147, 236–239, 308–309.
24. Katz, Abraham, "An Industrial Dynamics Approach to the Management of Research and Development," *I.R.E. Transactions on Engineering Management,* September 1959.
25. "New Ways to Spot Company Troubles," *Business Week,* November 4, 1961, pp. 158–160.
26. Nord, Ole C., *Growth of a New Product—Effects of Capacity Acquisition Policies,* M.I.T. Press, 1963.
27. Orr, Daniel, "Two Books on Simulation in Economics and Business," *Journal of Business,* January 1963, pp. 69–76.
28. Packer, D. W., *Resource Acquisition in Corporate Growth,* M.I.T. Press, 1964.
29. Pugh, Alexander L., III, *DYNAMO User's Manual,* Second Edition, Cambridge, M.I.T. Press, 1963.
30. Roberts, Edward B., *The Dynamics of Research and Development,* New York, Harper & Row, 1964.
31. ———, "Industrial Dynamics and the Design of Management Control Systems," *Management Technology,* December 1963, pp. 100–118, and a chapter in C. Bonini, R. Jaedicke, & H. Wagner (eds.), *Management Controls: New Directions in Basic Research,* New York, McGraw-Hill Book Company, 1964, pp. 102–126.
32. ———, "New Directions in Industrial Dynamics," *Industrial Management Review,* Fall 1964, pp. 5–20.

33. ———, "Research and Development Policy-Making," *Technology Review,* June 1964, pp. 32–36.

34. ———, "Simulation Techniques for Understanding R & D Management," *1959 I.R.E. National Convention Record, Part 10,* March 1959, pp. 38–43.

35. ———, "Toward a New Theory for Research and Development," *Industrial Management Review,* Fall 1962, pp. 29–40.

36. Sakakura, Shogo, and Kazuo Watanobe, *Industrial Dynamics,* Tokyo, Toyo Keizai Shinpo Sha, 1963 (available in Japanese only).

37. Schall, W. C., "Industrial Dynamics Proves Out for One Firm," *Instrument Society of America Journal,* September 1962.

38. Schlager, Kenneth J., "How Managers Use Industrial Dynamics," *Industrial Management Review,* Fall 1964, pp. 21–29.

39. Simon, H. A., *Models of Man,* John Wiley & Sons, 1957.

40. Sprague, Robert C., "Industrial Dynamics: Case Example," in Carl Heyel (ed.), *The Encyclopedia of Management,* New York, The Reinhold Publishing Company, 1963, pp. 319–322.

41. Swinth, Robert, *Certain Effects of Training Goals on Subsequent Task Performance,* Jones Publishing Company, 1963.

42. "Utilities Launch Susquehanna River Basin Study," *Electrical World,* July 20, 1964, pp. 20–21.

43. Wagner, Harvey M., "Industrial Dynamics" (book review), *Management Science,* October 1963, pp. 184–186.

44. Weymar, F. Helmut, "Industrial Dynamics: Interaction Between the Firm and Its Markets," in Wroe Alderson and Stanley Shapiro, (eds.), *Marketing and the Computer,* Englewood Cliffs, New Jersey, Prentice-Hall, Inc., 1963, pp. 260–276.

BIBLIOGRAPHY

Carlson, Bruce, "An Industrialist Views Industrial Dynamics," *Industrial Management Review,* VI, Fall, 1964.

Forrester, Jay W., *Industrial Dynamics,* John Wiley and Sons, 1961.

———, "Common Foundations Underlying Engineering and Management," *IEEE Spectrum,* September, 1964, pp. 66–77.

———, "The Structure Underlying Management Processes," *Proceedings of the 24th Annual Meeting of the Academy of Management,* December, 28–30, pp. 58–68.

———, "Market Growth as Influenced by Capital Investment," *Industrial Management Review,* Winter, 1968.

———, "A Deeper Knowledge of Social Systems," *Technological Review,* April, 1969.

———, "Systems Analysis as a Tool for Urban Planning, *National Academy of Engineering Symposium,* October 22–23, 1969.

Schlager, Kenneth J., "How Managers Use Industrial Dynamics," *Industrial Management Review,* Fall, 1964.

Swanson, Carl V., "Design of Resource Control and Marketing Policies Using Industrial Dynamics," *Industrial Management Review,* Spring, 1969.

———, "Resource Control in Growth Dynamics," Unpublished Ph.D. dissertation, MIT, Cambridge, Mass., 1969.

———, "Designing Information and Control Systems for Effective Response to Demand Changes," *Proceedings of the 1970 Summer Computer Simulation Conference,* Denver, Colorado, June 10, 1970.

Wright, Richard D., "Scannell Transportation: An Industrial Dynamics Application," Unpublished M.S. thesis, MIT, Cambridge, Mass., 1969.

———, "An Industrial Dynamics Design for Improved Profitable Growth," *Proceedings of the 1970 Summer Computer Simulation Conference,* Denver, Colorado, June 10, 1970.

SECTION II

PERT AND PERT/COST

In the history of science and technology, the innovations that predominate are those involving minor adaptations and rearrangements of items from the cultural inventory. It is only rarely that something approaching a "revolution" appears on the scene. Yet when these drastic changes are carefully scrutinized, one generally finds that they too have had their roots sunk deep in the past achievements of many great minds. One would not be too rash to say that the remarkable discoveries and advances made in the field of atomic science have revolutionized the state of physics in the present century. Some do not hesitate to assert as much for PERT in the area of managerial science.

PERT is an acronym for Program Evaluation and Review Technique, a planning and control technique devised for large complex projects. Like other great "revolutionary" techniques it too had its predecessors. It is generally admitted that PERT owes much to the Critical Path Method and to the now famous Gantt Chart Method. However, as a refinement of previous methods it has effected significant changes in planning and control, so much so that some enthusiastic advocates look upon PERT as a panacea for all that ails management. A more sobering exposition would undoubtedly reveal that PERT was originally conceived not as a nostrum for management fevers but as a rationally based total system approach to the planning and control aspects of research and development projects currently in vogue.

PERT had its origins in the United States and developed in the wake of the rapid technological advances made after World War II. Weapon and support systems had by then reached such complex proportions that new techniques for managing their development, production, and installation were definitely needed. Because of the threatening aspect of international politics, the Cold War, etc., it was imperative that these systems be made operational in the shortest possible time.

Existing techniques proved unsuitable. Because of the interdependency of so many complex systems and subsystems, all surrounded by a great deal of uncertainty due to the unique nature of these never-before-attempted tasks, something new had to be developed consonant with the magnitude of the projects. That it was the Navy's Fleet Ballistic Missile program that occasioned the emergence of PERT in 1958 is a matter of historical record. Since then the proliferation of similar modified techniques has been truly phenomenal. From its original use in an astonishing Space Age project PERT has spread to many less exotic and more mundane tasks as book publishing, house building, theatrical production, marketing, and even making organizational changes.

Basically PERT is a managerial tool employing networks. The networks used are but "flow diagrams consisting of the activities and events which must be accomplished to reach the program objectives, showing their logical and planned sequences of accomplishment, interdependencies, and interrelationships." [1] The idea to be underscored is that the PERT net-

[1] PERT FUNDAMENTALS (Washington: PERT Orientation and Training Center, 1963), Vol. III, p. 16.

work depicts not only the many and varied components making up a system or subsystem, but also the all-important, intricate interrelationships that prevail among these. (The actual fundamentals of PERT network construction are outlined in one of the following selections.)

No doubt, the computer has had a hand in making PERT the success that it is. Although a PERT network with a hundred or so activities can be handled manually, it would be rather cumbersome and time-consuming to do so. A computer performs the same task with much greater speed and with a saving of human energy (and patience). Computers though are not essential in the use of PERT.

As this technique matures and as further experimentation and refinements occur, PERT will bring management an even more useful tool for planning and control of projects both large and small.

In the first selection David Boulanger presents a quick overall view of PERT with its network construction and network analysis. For illustrative purposes a hypothetical program, the Vehicle Armament System, is presented with its appropriate PERT network. Since the mechanics of PERT calculations are being stressed, each of the ingredients needed for network analysis, e.g., the determination of t_e, T_E, σ^2, slack time, etc., is explained briefly, its formula given, and then calculated. The real value of PERT for reevaluation and optimizing of resources is just barely touched on in the concluding section of the article.

That PERT/TIME has proved its usefulness as a planning and control device with respect to the time resource has been unmistakably shown in recent years. PERT/COST is presented by DeCoster in the second selection as a challenging new addition to management's repository of tools for optimizing project costs.

PERT/TIME was initially devised as a planning and control tool for the construction of complex weapons systems where time was of the essence. Its detailed network with the flow of activities and events all carefully mapped and with appropriate time schedules indicated represented a real breakthrough in management planning and control. With this technique various time-options can be selected for system simulation to ascertain which of the alternative options is best from the standpoint of time.

Of late a further refinement has been added to PERT/TIME. This is PERT/COST. When the optimum mix of time and cost is added to the alternative time-options, the manager can obtain time-cost totals for a realistic appraisal of the entire complex project. PERT/COST differs from conventional expense budgeting in several ways: (1) PERT/COST being activity-oriented cuts across organizational structures and accounting periods and focuses on the project work package. (2) PERT/COST uses activity time in place of volume as the variability factor.

DeCoster goes into much detail to show how a PERT/COST network can be constructed on the basic PERT/TIME framework. The project is broken down into successively smaller units, into subdivisions, work packages, tasks and subtasks, each with its dollar value, activity time, machine and personnel requirements. In all of this it is of paramount importance that the cost estimates be sound and consistent with company policy. To insure that the best cost estimates will be assigned, various approaches have been developed for this purpose: the single expected cost estimate, the combined expected cost estimate, the optimum time-cost curve, and the three separate cost estimates—each approach having its own advantages and limitations.

PERT/COST's merit lies not only in planning but also in control. Feedback data can be generated that will enable the project manager and others to compare continuously the actual cost expenditures with those previously estimated during the planning stage. And finally, though the basic problems of PERT/COST are many and formidable, still there is in it great potential to be exploited.

The reluctance to adjust to the requirements of PERT/Cost by contractors is no less today than when PERT/Cost was originally devised and mandated by the Department of Defense. It was perhaps because of this overt resistance to the imposition of PERT/Cost on government-contracted projects that the Department has lifted its mandate and expressed satisfaction with any comparable substitute. This is likewise true for PERT/Time.

While PERT/Cost is not required *per se*, the costing of work packages, which constitutes the essence of PERT/Cost, is ascertained in some other way. Yet the basic work breakdown structure that gave such visibility to PERT/Cost still serves admirably for both configuration management and engineering control. Thus, while few contractors would admittedly subscribe to the basic tenets of the PERT/Cost system as originally formulated, they are actually realizing them under an assumed name, with some minor modifications of their own.

PERT and PERT/Cost have recently been replaced in terminology by other systems. One such system is Cost Schedule Control Systems Criteria (CSCSC). Contracts no longer call out specific control systems, but rather call out the criteria that each specific project must meet. Some of these criteria are networks, work packages at certain levels, interrelationships of time and cost data, and the like, all of which are familiar to PERT and PERT/Cost users.

In the reading "Is PERT/Cost Dead?", Peter Schoderbek provides some insights into the reasons why the technique has not lived up to its potential. It comes as no great surprise to find that many of the problems center about factors extrinsic to the system rather than focusing on its intrinsic deficiencies. Probably the single greatest barrier to the full deployment of the PERT/Cost system is the reluctance of contractors and subcontractors to divulge cost data to both government personnel and other contractors. Cost information is often the only measure of a firm's efficiency or inefficiency, and to make known this confidential information runs counter to all sound business principles. Prime contractors are especially sympathetic with this viewpoint, since in most cases they in turn are subcontractors on other projects in which they would be required to reveal their own cost structures.

The limited experience with PERT/Cost has raised problems that have not been satisfactorily resolved—the overreporting of data and the redundancies of inputs and outputs. While contributing to the "information explosion," they have not provided more meaningful information upon which to base decisions, but have merely required additional data collection and reporting. Likewise, as noted in earlier readings, cost information basically reflects historical data and does not serve to pinpoint causes but merely indicates that problems exist.

There is little question that a firm's accounting structures evolved over a span of time, developed for the firm's individual needs, type of business, talents, and the like, may not be compatible with the collection of costs as advocated by PERT procedures. In fact, it would be unusual to find an accounting system that could naturally integrate with some other system. It would also be foolhardy to expect firms to hop to attention and adopt a system that has not stood the test of time. In this regard the author notes the importance of accepting variations within individual firms in order to make PERT/Cost compatible with internal controls.

At the present time there is sufficient evidence to support the contention that PERT/Cost updating has not provided for more rapid and more timely reporting. It is still true that many guess estimates are still used. Other factors—such as the frequency of updating, invalid estimating, improper allocation of resources, the padding of estimates in order to "play it safe," and budget manipulation—all present obstacles to the full deployment of PERT/Cost.

It is also suggested by Peter Schoderbek that the impetus found in many government-imposed PERT/Cost systems is often provided by a single individual or office. As the political winds shift, a corresponding shifting of attention to the programs, projects, and methods initiated by prior appointees also follows. There is, understandably, a natural reluctance to change in the short run when changes in the long run appear in the offing.

The author believes that PERT/Cost can "make it" on its own merits. With more experimentation, suitable adaptions will follow, allowing the system to claim its rightful place in the arsenal of management planning and control techniques.

It was noted previously that PERT has found many applications beyond those initial ones of construction, and research and development projects. Recently it has merged with an older managerial tool—Line of Balance (LOB)—to provide for the total management and control of items from their initial conception on the drawing boards to their final delivery site.

Just as PERT serves to highlight the critical areas in the research and development phase of one-time projects, so LOB serves a similar function in the production status of items. Both PERT and LOB admirably serve their specific purposes in their restricted areas, but at present there is no technique for the critical transition period from the production of the first item until steady production is initiated. Thus, with PERT/LOB, management can plan and control the entire cycle of a project from its early planning stage through initial development with final or intermittent production.

Guy Black's article, "Systems Analysis in Government Operations," outlines the various steps in systems analysis, discriminates between systems analysis, engineering, and management, and highlights the pitfalls that need to be avoided. The author, Guy Black, although a member of the staff of the Council of Economic Advisers at the time of his writing, does not clutter the article with econometric illustrations but handles the subject with clarity and directness.

The current scene is first surveyed. The drive to make program packaging and budgeting methods operative throughout government is noted, and the prospects for applying systems to nondefense government projects are judged to be quite favorable.

The systems approach is seen to be a rather complex one, consisting of systems analysis, systems engineering, and systems management. Analysis, the touchstone of the systems approach, is all pervasive, beginning with program design and continuing throughout the life cycle of the project. It is used for continuous reevaluation and rescheduling of the ongoing program, since its function is to identify the one best system and the most efficient way of operating that system. Systems engineering is called upon to divide the overall tasks into manageable subtasks and to allocate these to various engineering groups. It must also watch over the interfacing problems likely to arise when various groups operate in their own restricted spheres with minimal concern for the work of others. Systems management is responsible not only for ordering and phasing the two previous elements—analysis and engineering—but also for interpreting to the analysts the customer's objectives and for following the completed design from engineering, to production, to testing, to training of suitable operating personnel, and to final use.

One should perhaps distinguish the process of systems analysis from its structure. The process may and often does look messy, confused, and disordered, dealing as it often does with ill-defined problem assignments but the structure that emerges in phases, fed by input-output contributions, may be a thing of beauty.

Six distinct phases of systems analysis include the following: (1) understanding and translation into analytically meaningful terms the objectives sought by the complex program; (2) construction of the model;

(3) quantification of the relationships between the model variables and the systems output; (4) quantification of the relationships between the model variables and the systems inputs; (5) determination of the overall input-output relation of the intermediate relationships with the structure of the model; and (6) determination of an optimum systems design and optimum systems operation.

Each of these phases is then treated in detail. Before one can even begin to understand the problem, one must first identify the objects and activities that are to constitute the system. This in itself can be a highly creative act. Only then can objectives be stated. These must be carefully thought out and expressed not just in high-sounding words but in operational terms. This can result in a critical examination of the reasons for the project's very existence. Some of these objectives may be found to be rather complex; some may be mutually inconsistent. These must then be assessed, ranked, and traded off, one against the other. This problem-definition phase is indeed quite critical. The temptation is always there to make the problem simple enough to be easily manageable. However, the resulting analysis may be irrelevant for real-world application. Here, therefore, exists a great need for communication and cooperation between systems analysts and top management if false starts (always expensive) are to be avoided. The story of King Midas well illustrates the problem that can arise when one, in conceptualizing his objectives, fails to follow through with a consideration of their implications (latent functions).

The model subsequently constructed attempts to relate the relevant variables that are presumed to interact. These are typically expressed in mathematical form and are related to one another by equations capable of mathematical manipulation. The model need not consider *all* variables, since some will have but minor effects on the system. Lack of proper data and the presence of important factors making for an unmanageable analysis may force simplification of the model. The model, however, must be subsequently checked in order to assess the possible effects of whatever was left out.

Treating system characteristics as variables is one thing; determining their range is another. This latter step calls for technical know-how and creative thinking, especially when systems configurations not previously in existence, are what is really needed. Here the outsider has something constructive to offer.

Any working model must relate both inputs (expressible in costs) and outputs (expressible in benefits) to the operation of the system. The reason for this is that inputs do not directly produce outputs: they must be transformed into outputs by the system's technology.

The model must then combine the separate input and output expressions into an overall input-output expression in which the systems technology is the connecting link.

The final phase of analysis concerns optimization of both design and operation. Here the benefits—the quantity and type of system outputs—must be carefully considered. These benefits can be complex and elusive, since various systems configurations often produce several benefits in differing proportions. A number of different techniques are serviceable. One is to agree on several combinations of outputs producing seemingly equal total benefits, although the proportion of individual benefits may differ. Another is to specify several combinations of equal cost and to select the one considered to yield the greatest benefit. Other methods must be resorted to where it is impossible to measure the benefits accruing from certain technical results. Typically ill-suited for optimization studies are statistical-cost data, since they deal with average relationships. Even when the formally provable optimum configuration cannot be ascertained, the best of these can be chosen and considered the optimum.

In all realistic analysis the quantification of the parameters is a prime requisite. But this demands real data, and often the type of data needed is not readily available. Demonstration projects and pilot projects are often undertaken, at least in part, for the purpose of generating data for parameter quantification. But this can be very expensive. Before doing so, the analyst should be able to justify such a costly experiment with the overall project cost.

In the final section of his article, Black deals exclusively with the relationship of the systems approach to Program Packaging and Budgeting Systems (PPBS). The latter is but a method of financial planning and control of government operations by breaking down the program tasks into suitable work packages. These work packages can logically be traded off on a cost-benefit basis against other work packages. The internal contents of a work package need be of no major concern. Program packaging thus tends to relate activities with similar objectives. Much of what follows is similar to or analogous with what has already been said of PERT/Cost. Black takes pains to demonstrate that PPBS is a system in the sense that he intends ("composed of a number of semi-autonomous parts which interact with each other to achieve movement toward common objectives").

The question of suboptimization is touched on in passing. Here a group in the organization is responsible for less than the whole of an organization's performance. Although the term has acquired something of a pejorative connotation, still the process is absolutely necessary if systems analysts are ever to bring the project down to manageable proportions. Suboptimization need not lead to deleterious results; it only will if the problems have been poorly defined at the lower levels.

To sum up, systems analysis is a meaningful integration of a body of analyses directed to the design and implementation of real systems. And PPBS, a systems approach, has many interesting possibilities that can only be realized in the future.

41. PROGRAM EVALUATION AND REVIEW TECHNIQUE [1]

DAVID G. BOULANGER [2]

Since the first management "principles" were introduced, most planning and control methods have been predicated on using historical data. Early shop practitioners sought the most efficient utilization of time by employing timestudy and task-setting methods based on stopwatch measurement of "past" processes that were physical and finite in character. Few useful techniques have been offered facilitating forward planning of management activities for which empirical information was not available.

Current industrial activities, however, can be summarized as heavily oriented toward research and development. A "one best way" of planning and pursuing R&D projects in terms of most efficient use of time presents some intangibles that cannot conveniently be measured. This growing condition, particularly in defense industries, has prompted the development of a prognostic management planning control method called Program Evaluation and Review Technique, or PERT.[3] This article intends to briefly present the idea of the PERT method in a manner permitting the reader to ascertain its potential usefulness. . . .

The PERT technique was developed as a method of planning and controlling the complex Polaris Fleet Ballistic Missile Program for Special Projects Office (SP) of Bureau of Ordnance, U.S. Navy. The team consisted of members from SP, the contractor organization, and Booz, Allen and Hamilton, Chicago.[4]

[1] From *Advanced Management* (July–August, 1961), pp. 8–12. Reprinted by permission of *Advanced Management Journal.*

[2] General Electric Company.

[3] Various acronyms are coined (*e.g.,* PEP, PET, etc.) to describe modifications from the PERT method described here.

[4] See Malcolm, D. G., J. H. Roseboom, C. E. Clark, and W. Fazar. "Application of a Technique for Research and Development Program Evaluation," *Journal of Operations Research,* Vol. 7, No. 5 (September–October, 1959), pp. 646–669.

Over-all, PERT appears to be a manifestation of the program concept of management with emphasis on "management by exception," in that potentially troublesome areas in R&D programs can be spotted and action taken to prevent their occurrence.

PERT, as a dynamic program tool, uses linear programming and statistical probability concepts to plan and control series and parallel tasks which appear only remotely interrelated. Many tasks involve extensive research and development which itself is difficult to schedule, least of all to find a "one best way" of doing it. PERT's objective is to determine the optimum way by which to maximize the attainment, in time, of some predetermined objective that is preceded by a number of constraints—hence its linear programming feature. A measure of the degree of risk is predicted in probabilistic terms to foretell the reasonableness of accomplishment on scheduled time—hence its statistical probability feature.

PROGRAM NETWORK DEVELOPMENT

The bar chart, presumably derived from Gantt and still widely used, serves to plan the occurrence of entire phases of tasks in series and parallel groups over a time period. Figure 1 illustrates a sample.

An outgrowth of the simple bar chart, called a "milestone chart," indicates significant event accomplishments as illustrated in Figure 2.

Neither technique ties together interdependencies between tasks and significant events. Series and parallel paths should indicate the interrelationship constraints between events and tasks as shown by the arrows in Figure 3.

A network *event* describes a milestone, or checkpoint. An event does not symbolize the performance of work, but represents the point in time in which the event is accomplished. Each event is numbered for identification.

Arrows connecting events are *activities,* and represent performance of work necessary to accomplish an event. No event is considered accomplished until all work represented by arrows leading to it has been completed. Further, no work can commence on a succeeding event until the preceding event is completed.

If we include in Figure 3 the estimated weeks to accomplish each activity, *e.g.,* $\xrightarrow{3}$, the earliest time objective Event 11 above can be accomplished is the sum of the longest path leading to it. This is the *critical path,* and is identified by the heavy lines connecting Events 2, 6, 10, and 11 totaling 17 weeks. The critical path contains the

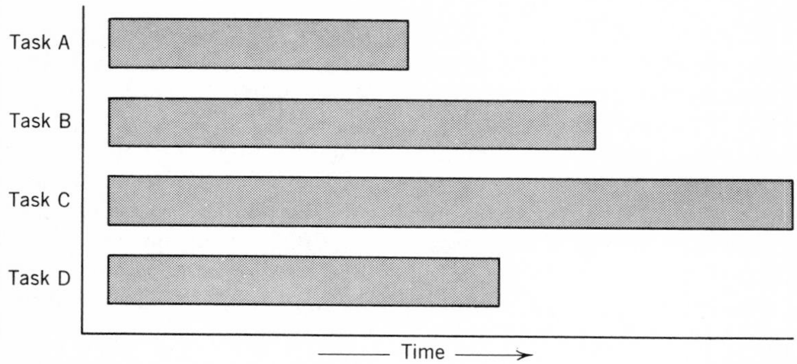

FIG. 1. Program bar chart.

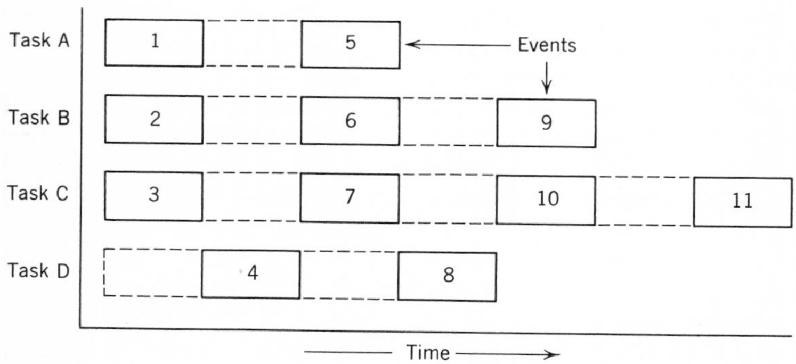

FIG. 2. Program milestone chart.

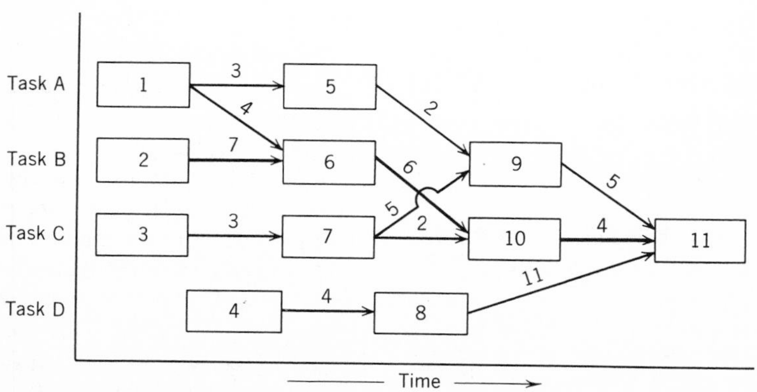

FIG. 3. PERT network.

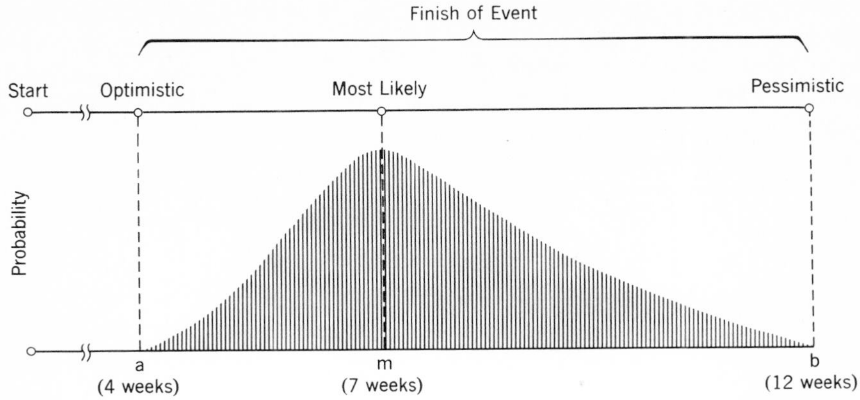

FIG. 4.

most significant *and* limiting events retarding program completion in less than 17 weeks.

But the time required to complete a future task is more realistically stated in terms of a likelihood rather than a positive assurance. To apply this likelihood in a probabilistic sense, three time estimates are stated as a future *range of time* in which an activity may be accomplished. The three time estimates are called *optimistic, most likely,* and *pessimistic.* They serve as points on a distribution curve whose mode is the most likely, and the extremes (optimistic and pessimistic) whose spread corresponds to the probability distribution of time involved to perform the activity. It is assumed there would be relatively little chance (*e.g.,* 1 out of 100) the activity would be accomplished *outside* the optimistic or pessimistic time estimate range. Figure 4 illustrates the estimating time distribution for completing an activity some time in the future.

From the three estimates (a, m, b above), a statistical elapsed time (t_e) can be derived by solving $t_e = \frac{a + 4(m) + b}{6}$ for each activity.[5] Following this, a statistical variance (σ^2) can be derived by solving $\sigma^2 = \left(\frac{b - a}{6}\right)^2$ for each activity.[6] Variance may be descriptive of uncertainty associated with the three time estimate interval. A large variance implies greater uncertainty in an event's accomplishment and *vice versa,* depending on whether the optimistic and pessimistic estimates are wide or close together. This facilitates evaluating risks in a program network, and using trade-offs in time and resources to minimize risk and maximize more efficient use of "factors of production."

[5] The elapsed time formula is based on the assumption that the probability density of the beta distribution $f(t) = K(t - a)\alpha(b - t)\gamma$ is an adequate model of the distribution of an activity time.

[6] The statistical variance formula assumes the standard deviation as $\frac{1}{6}(b - a)$.

PROGRAM NETWORK ANALYSES

The analytical value derived from any PERT network depends on the configuration and content of the network. Every network should contain events which, to the program team's best knowledge, serve to significantly constrain the achievement of the end objective event. Next, events are interconnected with "activities" to illustrate their flow and interdependencies. After the network of events and activities is defined, three time estimates for each activity are made.

To illustrate network development and analyses, a hypothetical R&D program is assumed specifying contract completion 11 months (47 weeks) after order. Fixed resources are allocated to the program: *e.g.,* 40-hour work week, given personnel, budgeted money, *etc.* Management now is interested in:

1. What's the one best way of conducting effort toward completion?
2. What's the earliest expected time we can complete the program?
3. What are our chances of completing within the contract limitations of 47 weeks?

The network in Figure 5 is a simplified analogue of our plan to develop a "vehicle

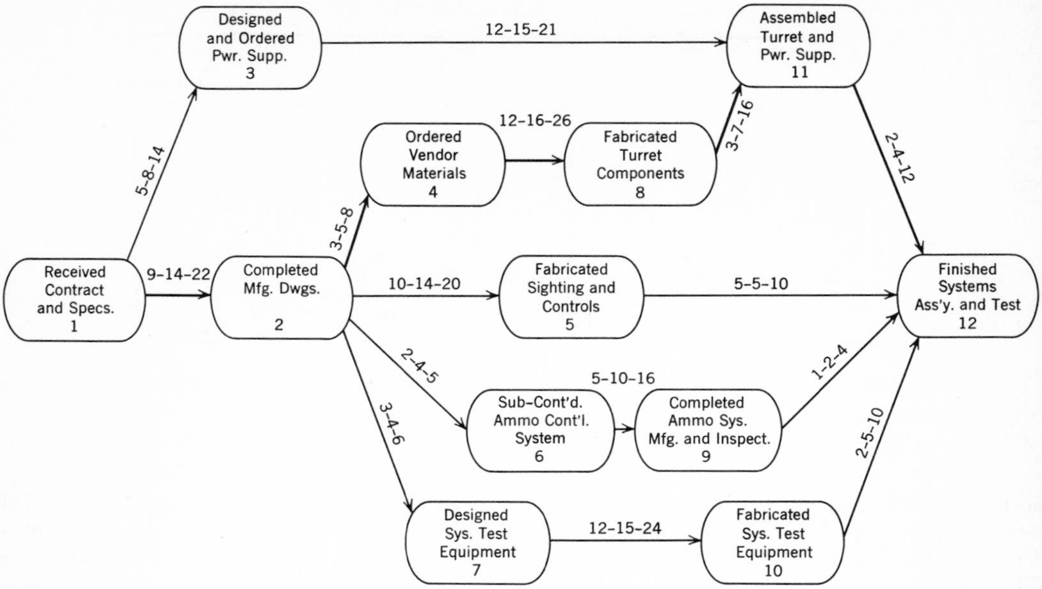

FIG. 5. PERT network vehicle armament system.

armament system." Events are described with a verb in the past tense to indicate their end accomplishment at a fixed point in time.

The analysis of the network is next performed and explained below.

Column A. Each event is listed beginning with objective event back to the start event.

Column B. The preceding event(s) is (are) listed beside each event. Hence, there is a succeeding and preceding event for each activity.

Column C. Statistical elapsed time (t_e) for each activity is found by substituting optimistic, most likely, pessimistic estimates for a, m, b and solving $t_e = \dfrac{a + 4(m) + b}{6}$.

Column D. Variance (σ^2) for each activity is found by substituting optimistic and pessimistic estimates for a and b and solving

$$\sigma^2 = \left(\frac{b - a}{6}\right)^2.$$

PERT Analyses

A Event	B Pre. Ev.	C t_e	D σ^2	E T_E	F T_L	G $T_L - T_E$	H T_S	I P_R	J $T_L - T_E$	K Event
12	11	5.0	2.78	49.5	49.5	0.0	47.0	.28	0.0	2
	5	5.8	.69						0.0	4
	9	2.2	.25						0.0	8
	10	5.3	1.78						0.0	11
11	8	7.8	4.70	44.5	44.5	0.0			0.0	12
	3	15.5	2.25							
8	4	17.0	5.44	36.7	36.7	0.0			9.5	7
4	2	5.2	.69	19.7	19.7	0.0			9.5	10
5	2	14.3	2.78	28.8	43.7	14.9			14.9	5
9	6	10.2	3.36	28.5	47.3	18.8			18.8	6
6	2	3.8	.25	18.3	37.1	18.8			18.8	9
10	7	16.0	4.00	34.7	44.2	9.5			20.5	3
7	2	4.2	.25	18.7	28.2	9.5				
3	1	8.5	2.25	8.5	29.0	20.5				
2	1	14.5	4.70	14.5	14.5	0.0				
1	—	—	—	—	—	—				

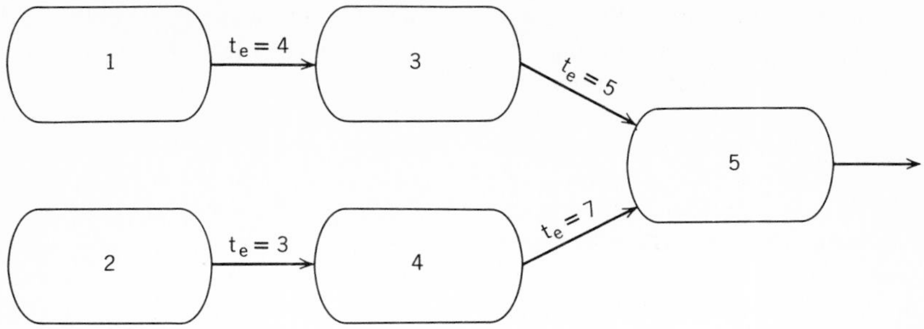

FIG. 6.

Column E. Earliest expected time (T_E) of accomplishment for each *event* is found by adding the elapsed time (t_e) of each activity to cumulative total elapsed times through the preceding event, staying within a single path working from "start to finish." When more than one activity leads to an event, that activity whose elapsed time (t_e) gives the greatest sum up to that event is chosen as the expected time for that event. For example, the earliest expected time to *accomplish* Event 5 below is 10 weeks. (See Figure 6.)

Column F. Latest Time (T_L) for each event is found by first fixing the earliest time of the objective event as its latest time. Next, the sum of the elapsed times (t_e) in Column C (*i.e.*, 5.0 weeks) for the activities lying between the given event and the objective event is subtracted from the earliest time of the objective event. When more than one activity leads from an event, the activity which gives the *least* sum through that event is selected.

Some events may be completed later than the expected time and have no effect on meeting the objective event. Knowledge of "slack" time in a network (*i.e.*, how much and where located) is of interest in determining program effects of "trade-offs" in resources from high-slack to low-slack areas.

Since linear programming theory says "negative slack" is not admissible (*i.e.*, not technically feasible at the objective event assuming fixed resources), we commence from an objective viewpoint to compute "positive" (or non-negative) slack. In spite of theory, a latest time derived from a fixed contractual date *less* than earliest expected time must be recognized to determine how much network "compression" is necessary to meet a scheduled date with reasonable assurance. The theory simply recognizes time is not reversible; therefore, to alleviate "negative" slack one must either extend contractual dates or employ added resources like overtime, more funds, personnel, *etc.* We assume in our analyses that resources are fixed at inception of program to maintain profit potentials.

Column G. Slack time for each event is found by subtracting Expected Time from Latest Time ($T_L - T_E$). The purpose is 1) to locate the critical path in the network designated here by events having zero slack and 2) to determine next-most-critical paths, as well as those events having substantial slack.

The critical path contains events most apt to be troublesome technically or administratively, and are danger points causing potential over-all schedule slippage. Next-most-critical path(s) is (are) found by substituting next higher slack event(s) into a second single path from start to finish. For example, the second-most-critical path is found by including Events 7 and 10 (whose slacks of 9.5 weeks are the next-higher slack event over the critical path events) to give a new critical path described as Events 1, 2, 7, 10, 12. Next-most-critical paths should be observed because their criticalness may be nearly as severe as the original critical path.

By locating events having substantial slack time, it becomes possible to effect trade-offs in resources to those events having little or zero slack. For example, Events 6 and 9 each have 18.8 weeks slack, meaning their expected time of completion could be intentionally delayed 18.8 weeks without causing slippage in over-all program schedule. A point of optimization in network development is approached when the greatest possible number of events have the smallest possible range in slack from the lowest to highest slack value.

Column H. Schedule Time (T_S) is the contractual date of completion. A scheduled time may also exist for major events within a network, which later facilitates evaluating the range of risks throughout a program plan.

Column I. Probability (P_R) of meeting a scheduled time is calculated to determine feasibility of program accomplishment under the constraints in the network. Generally, probability values between .25 and .60 indicate an acceptable range to proceed with a program as depicted in the network. Probability values less than .25 assume the schedule time, T_S, cannot reasonably be met with the given resources. Values higher than .60 may indicate excess resources "built in" the network, and may warrant consideration for their use elsewhere. Probabilities need not be computed where schedule time (T_S) and expected time (T_E) are equal, as this assumes .5 or 50 per cent probability of completing on schedule.

Probability of events is computed as follows:

1. Solve for each event which has a schedule time (in our example, the objective event):

$$\frac{T_S - T_E}{\sigma_{\Sigma\sigma^2}*} = \frac{47.0 - 49.5}{\sqrt{18.31}} = \frac{-2.5}{4.279} = -.584$$

2. Refer answer to Area Under the Normal Curve Table and compute probability P_R.

The value −.584 refers to −.584 standard deviations from the mean under a normal curve. Referring to a normal curve table, we find its corresponding per cent of area under the normal curve to be about −.21904. Thinking of area under the normal curve and probability as synonymous, we subtract −.21904 from .50000 (the mean of a normal curve) to derive a probability of .28096, or 28 per cent. Explained, there is a 28 per cent chance of meeting the schedule time of 47.0 weeks; hence it may be "acceptable" to proceed with the program under plans and resources factored in the network. Any standard of "acceptability" in probability terms should be flexible according to the importance of a program and the consequences if schedule time should not be met. Therefore, any probability value attached to a program plan should be viewed and used cautiously.

* Read as "standard deviation of the sum of the variances." In our example, this is solved by: 1) finding the sum of variances ($\Sigma\sigma^2$) for the events in the Critical Path, that is, 4.70 + .69 + 5.44 + 4.70 + 2.78 = 18.31; 2) finding the square root of 18.31 = 4.279. Probability for *any* event in a network can be computed if a T_S and T_E value is known, and by finding that event within a single network path.

Diagrammatically, 28 per cent probability is roughly represented by the shaded area under the normal curve below (Figure 7).

Columns J and K. Under Column J is the ascending order of slack, and under Column K their corresponding event numbers. This brings out the Critical Path as 0.0 slack events, next-most critical path(s), and those events or paths with high slack from which resources and time may be deployed to events having zero or low slack. This facilitates locating the "one best way" of reaching the objective event in relation to time.

REEVALUATION AND OPTIMIZATION

A potential value from PERT at inception of an R&D program is the opportunity it affords to introduce revised constraints into the plan and then simulate its outcome. If repeated, the optimum network can be sought, its troublesome areas located, and various tasks set under optimum conditions before time, cost, and performance were expended. Computer programs are available to expedite this, but manual methods are economical for networks up to 200 events depending on complexity of event interrelationships. Various schedules and performance reporting formats can be developed from the analyses for team use and management analysis.

Two advantages from PERT are 1) the exacting communications it offers to participants in a program and 2) its use as a planning foundation to support bid proposals. Each participant can see his relative position and understand the timing and relationship of his responsibilities to other participants on the program team. Often the intangibles and assumptions that plague accurate bid proposals are brought out when supported with a PERT network and analyses.

USING PERT FOR RESOURCES PLANNING, COST ANALYSES [7]

Considerable study is reported with PERT applied to resources (manpower and facilities) planning. Introducing a second variable to

[7] Notes from American Management Association Meeting, Saranac Lake, New York, March 27–29, 1961.

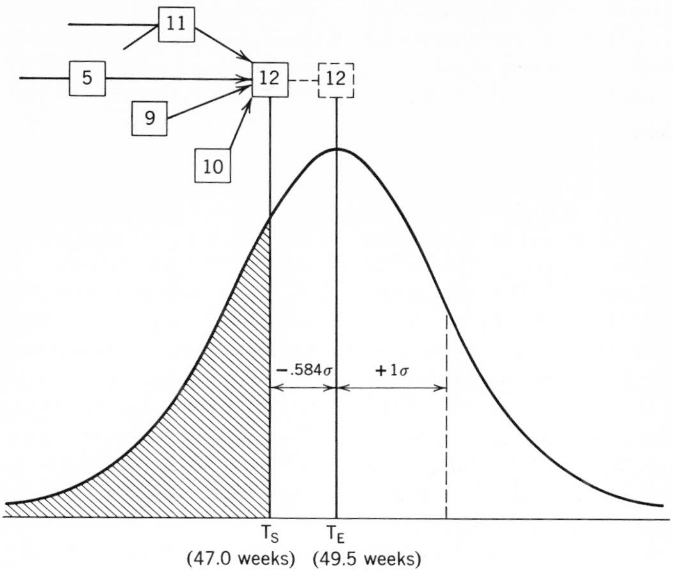

FIG. 7.

create a simultaneous two-dimensional model whose objective functions are to be optimized —while their preceding constraints are being manipulated (at the same time satisfying various restrictions placed on potential solution)— will be more difficult to perform, and probably involve more elaborate procedures.

Some work is reported with PERT applied to cost analyses of a program (presumably assuming a three- or N-dimensional model with variables of time, resources, cost, *et al.*). It appears the object would be something analogous to predetermining that point on an average total cost curve where marginal cost intersects marginal revenue—hence, maximization of profits. Some suggestions have been offered relative to the "assumed" linearity between time and cost, in the duration of a program, but this needs clarifying before concrete methods of planning costs by PERT can be formulated.

42. PERT/COST—THE CHALLENGE

DON T. DECOSTER *

Each day that passes sees the growth of new management planning and control tools. Many of these new tools leave the accountant with the unhappy feeling that he should be participating in their use but that he lacks the orientation for active involvement. The desire of the accountant to become involved with these tools is evident from the growth of "management planning and control" chapters in textbooks and the numerous articles dealing with the managerial aspects of accounting output.

One of the newest tools, if evidenced by current publications, is Program Evaluation and Review Technique (PERT). Recently, there have been many discussions, publications, and applications of this technique. PERT's acceptance has been widespread. The accountant must become involved with PERT if he accepts the challenge of Norton Bedford that "the accounting profession has the potential to become one of the great professions if it will accept all phases of measurement and communication of economic data as within its province." [1]

The principal motivating factor in PERT development has been the growth of the concept of systems management within the military services. With programs of unprecedented size, complexity, and breadth, an integrating device has become mandatory. In addition, time is of the essence in weapons system design and development. PERT/Time has been a powerful tool in the kit of managers for planning, coordinating, and integrating these weapon systems.

The culmination of PERT/Time is the network. This network is a pictorial representation of the events and activities that lead to completion of the end objectives. The events represent the beginning and/or ending of activities. An *event* is a specific accomplishment, or milestone. The *activities* represent things that must be done in going from one event to another. The activity is the time-consuming task. The activities are related to their order of precedence in accomplishing the events. The end result is a network depicting a well-thought-out plan. After the flow of activities and events is mapped, schedule timing can be superimposed. When completion times are included on the activities, the critical path (longest time path) can be determined.

At this point the manager has a tool which needs no further justification. The network presents a clear picture of all the activities and events that must be accomplished before the end objective can be attained. The individuals with responsibility for accomplishment will have discussed all of the relationships, potential drawbacks, and completeness of the plan. When times are imposed upon the plan, the problems of a timely completion are apparent. The activities affecting a timely completion and the schedule's effect on workloads are laid bare for scrutiny. When actual times become available, the updated estimates provide a dynamic control tool to anticipate adverse results. There can be little question that PERT/Time is a tool which, when applied with common sense and vigor, represents a "breakthrough" in management planning and control of the valuable resource of time.

TIME-COST MIX

PERT/Cost is, in reality, an expansion of PERT/Time. With times indicated on the network, it becomes possible to consider alternative plans of action. As the network is being developed, time-options are presented which can be considered. Techniques of system simulation can be employed to ensure that the

SOURCE: *Management Services* (July–August, 1965), pp. 13–18. Reprinted by permission of *Management Services*.

* University of Washington.

[1] John L. Carey, *The Accounting Profession: Where Is It Headed?* (New York, American Institute of CPAs, 1962), p. 94.

activities and events will lead to the best climax. The next logical step, with time-options available, is to obtain the optimum mix of time and cost. This has led to the attempt to assign costs to the activities on the network. An additional advantage when costs have been assigned to the network for time-cost options is that they can be summed for total cost planning and control.

The development of a system for cost accumulation synchronized with the PERT/Time network must be founded upon objectives consistent with the responsibility of management. In program management, the manager is faced with a twofold job. He is charged with the financial planning and control of his firm's resources, while at the same time he is committed to delivery of the end items with a minimum of cost incurrence to the customer.

This was recognized by the developers of PERT/Cost, NASA and the Department of Defense, when they visualized it as a three-part system.[2] Basic PERT/Cost is intended to assist the project managers by assigning costs to the working levels in the detail needed for planning schedules and costs, evaluating schedule and cost performance, and predicting and controlling costs during the operating phase of the program. In addition, there are two supplemental procedures. The Time-Cost Option Procedure displays alternative Time-Cost plans for accomplishing project objectives. The Resource Allocation Procedure determines the lowest cost allocation of resources among individual project tasks to meet the specified project duration. The basic system is to provide total financial planning and control by functional responsibility, while the two supplements are to achieve minimum cost incurrence.

The concept of cost predetermination for planning and control is not new to the accountant. The entire function of budgeting is predicated upon predetermination. Comprehensive budgeting relates income budgets, covering revenues and expenses, to the financial goals of the firm. The expense budgets lead to financial planning and control via projected income, while at the same time the flexible budget and the expense forecasts serve as tools for decision making by relating costs to volume.

[2] *DOD and NASA Guide: PERT/Cost.* Published by the Office of the Secretary of Defense and the National Aeronautics and Space Administration, June 1962.

PERT/Cost estimates are a new way of looking at the expense budgets. If properly conceived, they can become an integral part of the comprehensive budget program. Yet they differ from conventional expense budgeting in certain respects. From the financial planning and control viewpoint, the PERT/Cost estimates are not concerned with accounting periods. PERT/Cost is activity oriented. There is a cutting across of organizational structures and time periods to define "things to be accomplished." The focal point of cost accumulation shifts from the department to the project work package. The annual budget is bypassed to encompass an end item accomplishment. From the detailed decision-making viewpoint, where the flexible budget normally uses volume as the factor of variability, PERT/Cost attempts to use activity time. These two differences will now be examined in more detail.

COST FRAMEWORK

The establishment of a PERT/Cost system begins by developing a framework for gathering cost data and preparing the schedule for all activity levels. The project is defined, then broken down into end item subdivisions, and then into work packages which are assignable to front-line supervision. The integration of the work packages is accomplished through the conventional PERT/Time network. When the interrelationships and time paths have been plotted, the responsible operating and managerial personnel develop cost estimates for each work package.

It is important that both cost and time be planned and controlled from a common framework. From such a framework, the managers can obtain an accurate picture of progress and at the same time appraise realistically the consequences of alternative courses of action. The PERT/Time network is this common framework. This imposes upon the network developers the responsibility of carefully defining the activities so that they can represent cost centers as well as the areas of work effort.

The identification of the project objectives in terms of end items is the starting point for network design to be used with PERT/Cost. By using a top-down approach in the development of the network, the total project is fully planned and all components of the plan are included. Standard units for the breakdown of

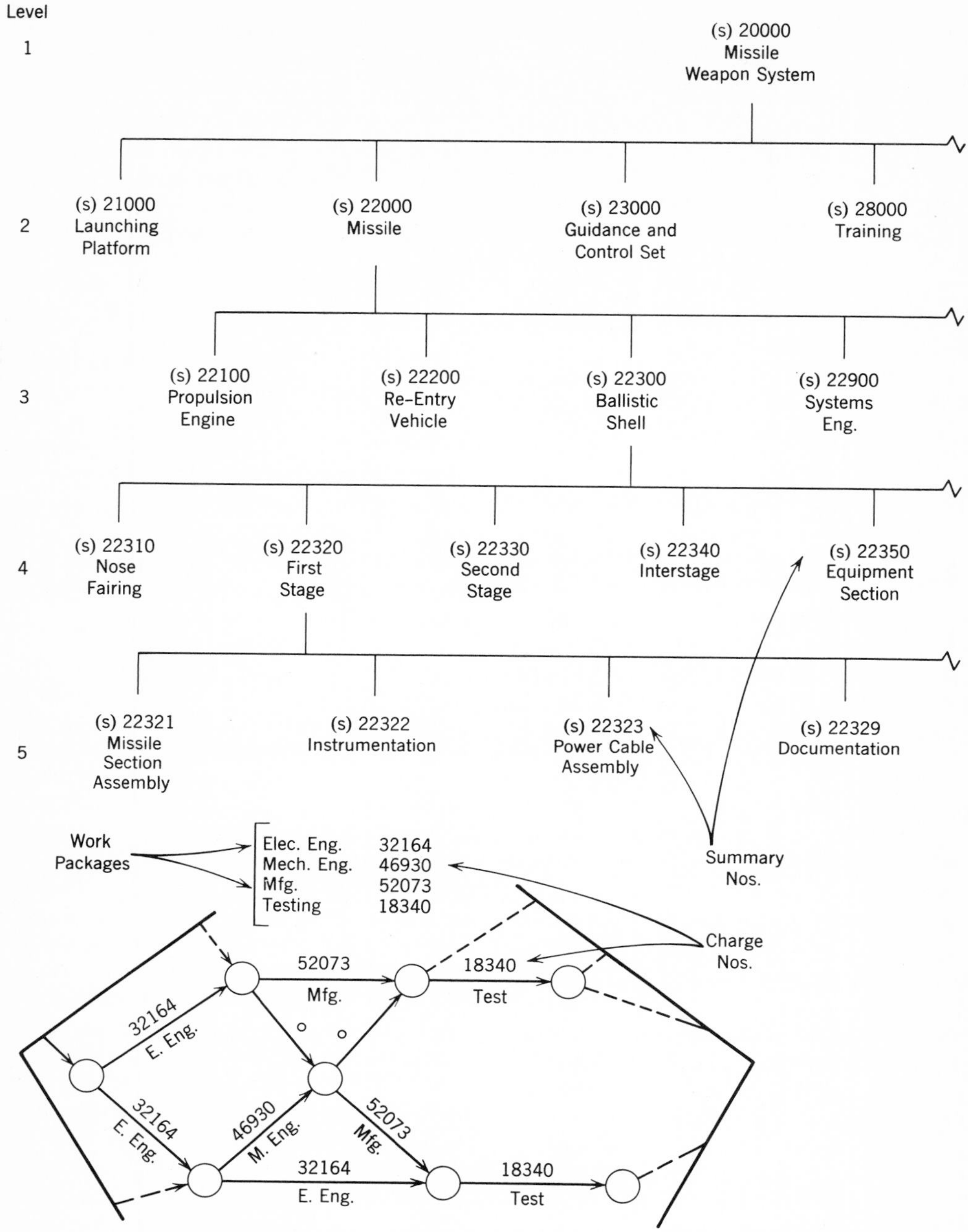

Simplified Example of a Work Breakdown Structure and Account Code Structure

work below the project level are system, subsystem, task, and subtasks. The work breakdown continues to successively lower levels until the size, complexity, and dollar value of each level is a workable planning and control unit. These subdivisions are end item subdivisions representing horizontal segments of the total project. The final step would be to divide each of these end item subdivisions into the tasks that must be done to complete them; i.e., design, manufacturing, testing, and so forth. This concept is demonstrated in the illustration [3] on this page. It is this project work breakdown that serves as the input data to the network.

[3] *Ibid.*, p. 28.

The theoretical optimum level of cost accumulation would be the functional level of each of the end item subdivisions. For example, a cost account would be established for mechanical engineering of the instrumentation, one for manufacturing, and one for testing. The PERT/Cost estimates would then be made for manpower, material, and overhead charges for each of these work packages. It is obvious that a cost accounting system broken down into such intricate detail would comprise numerous accounts. The pragmatic number of account subdivisions will naturally depend upon the detail needed for planning and control, the dollar value of the subdivisions, the activity time on the network, and the machine and personnel capacity available. A practical compromise is often necessary.

PERT/COST COST DEVELOPMENT

Once the network has been established, based upon the project work breakdown, costs can be estimated. If the breakdown has been made satisfactorily, it will serve as both an estimating and actual cost accumulation vehicle. The proper implementation of PERT/Cost, like budgeting, must rest upon active participation by the responsible executives. This was recognized by the NASA/DOD PERT/Cost Guide when it was recommended that the operating and management personnel develop the cost estimates for each work package.[4] As with budgeting, any accounting work during the estimation period would be of coordinating nature.

The development of the cost estimates must rest upon a sound philosophical basis consistent with management needs. Presently there are four approaches to developing the cost estimates:

1. A single cost estimate of expected actual cost
2. Three cost estimates combined by formula into expected cost
3. Optimum time-cost curves (used in construction industries and by NASA/DOD Resource Allocation Procedure Supplement)
4. Three separate cost estimates (used in the NASA/DOD Time-Cost Option Procedure Supplement)

Each of these theories of PERT/Cost estimating has as its goal the assigning of the best cost estimates possible to the network. Yet each offers the manager separate, distinct planning capabilities.

A single cost estimate of expected actual cost is based upon the summation of the cost elements. These estimates are first made by determining the manpower, material, and other resources required to complete each work package. The estimates for the direct costs applicable to the network activities are expressed in terms of expected dollar expenditures. Indirect costs may then be allocated to the individual work package or added to the total cost of the project.

The three-cost-estimate approach has as its goal the determination of the "expected cost." The advantage of the three cost estimate over the single cost estimate is that the result is subject to probability analysis. The formula combines an optimistic, most likely, and pessimistic cost estimate. The mean cost for each activity is calculated by the formula:

$$C_e = \frac{C_P + 4C_L + C_O}{6}$$

where C_P is the pessimistic estimate, C_L is the most likely cost, and C_O the optimistic estimate. The standard deviation of the cost distribution can insert probability into the analysis. With this expected cost, the manager cannot necessarily assume that he has the optimum cost-time mix. However, if the cost estimates are realistic, the probabilities of achieving the expected cost can be used for project negotiations.

A third approach to cost estimates is the optimum time-cost curve concept. This is differential costing with time as the factor of variability. The intention of this approach is to optimize time and costs by using optimum estimated costs. It assumes there is a direct relationship between time and costs on any activity. This relationship can be expressed by a continuous curve. If a cost curve can be developed similar to Figure A, many insights can be gained. Network schedules can be modified to obtain the lowest cost commensurate with the customer's delivery desires. Other questions can also be anticipated—questions such as: How long will completion take with a fixed budget? What will the costs be to complete the project within a given time period? In theory this concept is undoubtedly superior to either the one or three formula estimates, but without complete his-

[4] *Ibid.*, pp. 109–113.

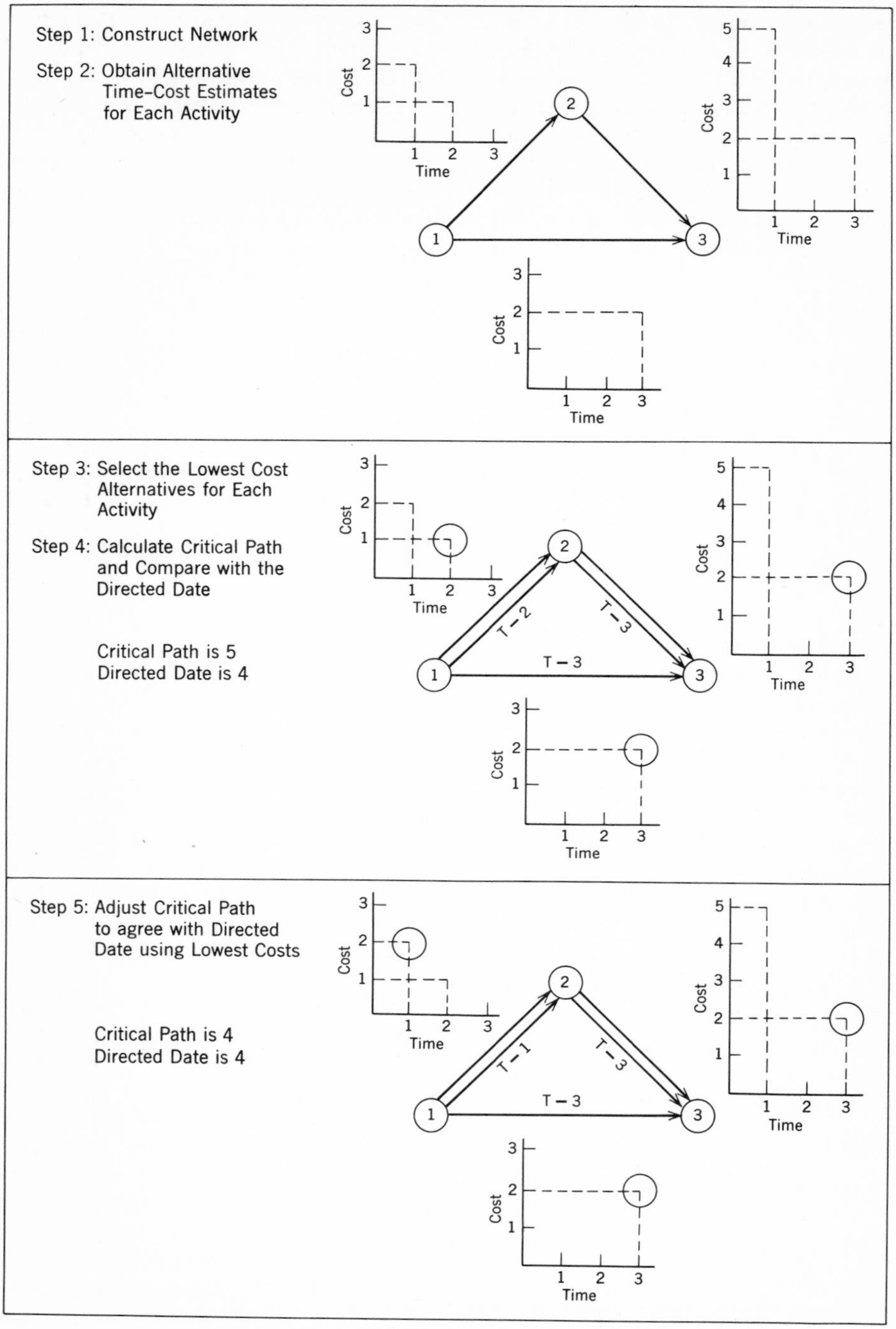

A Summary of the Resource Allocation Procedure. In the Resource Allocation Procedure, we can determine how to accomplish a project by a specified date at minimum cost. The critical path here is the path from Event 1 to Event 2, and from Event 2 to Event 3 since this will require five days at absolute minimum costs. But the Directed Data for completing the project is four days from its beginning. Thus, from the time-cost chart, we find that we can cut the time between Events 1 and 2 to one day, but we double the cost of this activity. Since shortening the time of the second step in the critical path would cost more, however, we choose to reduce time of the first step to one day.

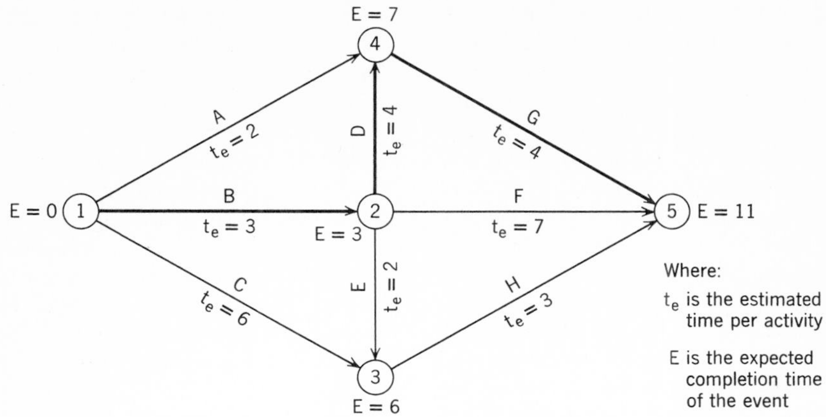

An Illustration of Normal-Crash Procedure. The critical path of this network is eleven days. To accelerate the program one day, activities B, G or D must be condensed one day. Based upon cost curves computed on a normal-crash basis, the table of costs on page 397 is available.

torical cost data the development of this curve is impractical.

Because the development of continuous time-cost curves for all activities is extremely difficult, if not practically impossible, the Resource Allocation Supplement to PERT/Cost was developed. This supplement is a variation of continuous time-cost curves which can be used in planning a small group of *significant* activities representing only a minor portion of the over-all project. This method is also based upon the concept that activities are subject to time-cost tradeoffs. The steps of this procedure are shown in the diagrams: "A Summary of the Resource Allocation Procedure."

Another alternate to overcome the practical problem of the continuous cost curve is a linear function based upon two time-cost relationships. The cost and time expenditures are forecast for two conditions: normal and crash.

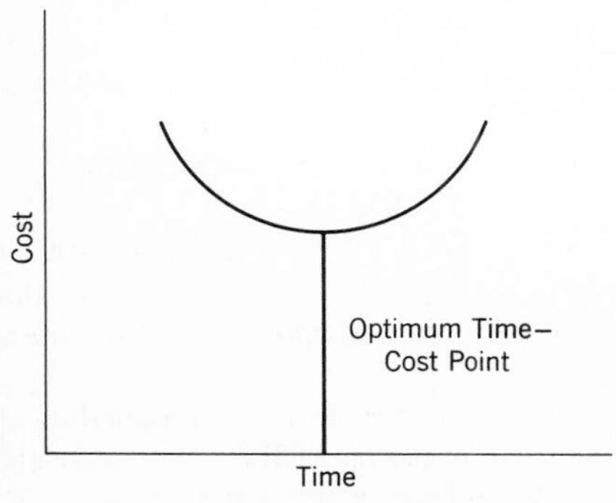

FIG. A.

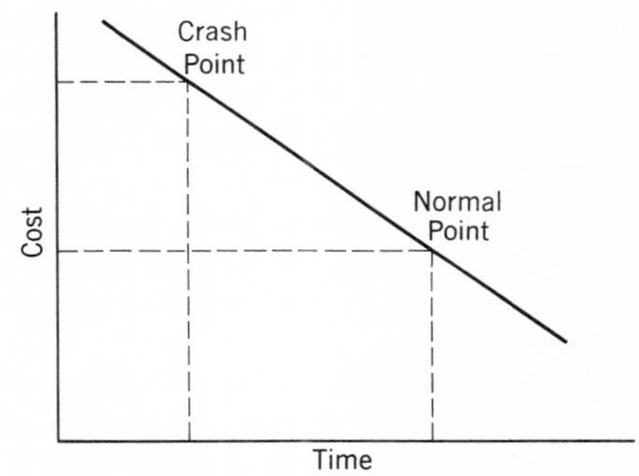

FIG. B.

The normal point is the minimum activity cost and the corresponding time. The crash point is defined as the minimum possible time to perform the activity and the related cost. A linear function is assumed to exist between these points. Figure B shows this graphically. This method is similar to the high-low point method of fixed and variable cost determination and suffers from the same type of criticism.[5] The problems of realistic estimates, discretionary costs, stair-stepped cost functions, incorrect correlation between time and cost, and external factors are continually present. It is justifiable due to its relative simplicity when the element of nonpredictable error can be permitted. A simplified, but typical usage is shown in the illustration of normal-crash procedure.

[5] Glenn Welsch, *Budgeting: Profit Planning and Control* (Englewood Cliffs, N.J., Prentice-Hall, Inc., 1957), pp. 173–174.

The NASA/DOD PERT/Cost Guide presents a time-cost option (called the Time-Cost Option Procedure Supplement) based upon three time estimates. The single estimate of expected cost and the three-cost-estimate formula methods do not indicate whether there may be a substantially more efficient alternative plan. The continuous cost curve concept provides these data,[6] but requires considerable sophistication in cost analysis, or else, considerable supposition. The time-cost supplement recognizes that a single estimate will normally be used for contract proposals and that additional data are needed to provide information as to the amount of time that might be saved by spending more money or the amount of money that could be saved by extending the contract time. The three time estimates used are:

The Most Efficient Plan. This is the network plan that will meet the technical requirements of the project utilizing the most efficient use of present resources. This is the plan that would be chosen without budget and time constraints.

The Directed Date Plan. This is the network plan developed to meet the technical requirements of the project by the specified completion date.

The Shortest Time Plan. This is the network plan that will meet the technical requirements of the project in the shortest possible time.

Since the desired plan is the most efficient plan, any study should begin there. This most efficient plan must then be modified to achieve the project's objectives by the specified date. The most efficient plan when altered to attain the desired delivery date becomes the directed date plan. The directed date plan is then revised to obtain the shortest time plan. The work packages that have not changed in evolving the alternate plans will utilize cost estimates for the most efficient plan. New cost estimates will be necessary only on those work packages that are expected to increase or decrease because of the modifications. With three estimates on these work packages, the customer is apprised of the impact of his decisions during negotiations. Once the customer has made his decision, the appropriate cost estimate can be assigned to the network.

These cost estimating techniques represent the current approaches to computing forecasted costs. When coupled with a sound approach to determining the project work breakdown, forward planning is definitely facilitated. To this point PERT/Cost is a planning tool, but the loop between planning and control is not closed. For control there must be comparisons of actual cost expenditures with those estimated during the planning stage. The accountant must play an active role when the loop is closed between the planning and control phases. The generation of feedback data consistent with the planning stage calls for a chart of accounts correlated to the PERT network.

[6] See Figure A.

THE PERT/COST CHALLENGE

The accountant is charged by management and society with providing financial information for all levels of decision making. If the accountant is to serve the managers effectively, he will have to broaden his influence beyond the confines of historical data to include all areas of the firm and the future. PERT/Cost offers him one challenge in this direction. It can be seen that if PERT/Cost can be coordinated with PERT/Time, the manager has an excellent tool for project planning and control. In addition to financial reporting both on the total cost level and the individual manager's level, it offers distinct opportunities for decision making during both the planning and control phases.

The discussions here might lead one to believe that PERT/Cost offers no problems. Unfortunately, this is not the case. Despite the potential there are basic problems. An enumeration of some of these problems would include:

1. PERT/Cost for decision making in optimizing costs requires a sophistication of cost analysis that is not possessed by some firms.
2. There is a lack of historical information for assigning costs to networks since the concept is new.
3. There is difficulty in making project costs compatible with fiscal practices.
4. The problems of overhead charges, joint costs, and incompatibility of the organizational cost flow with the functional flow are numerous.
5. There is a problem of reconciling the "jobs" that are using PERT/Cost with those that aren't for fiscal reporting.

Activity	Normal		Crash		Acceleration Cost per Day
	Days	Cost	Days	Cost	
A	2	80	1	130	50
B	3	70	1	190	60
C	6	110	5	135	25
D	4	60	3	100	40
E	2	90	1	100	10
F	7	85	6	115	30
G	4	105	3	175	70
H	3	50	2	70	20
Totals		650		1015	

Since Activity D costs $40 to accelerate whereas Activity G costs $70 and Activity B, $120, accelerating Activity D is least expensive. The total cost of completing the program in ten days is $690 ($650 + $40). By compressing the project one day, Activity F enters the critical path. To accelerate the program to nine days the following activities could be reduced: G and F at a total cost of $100 or B at a cost of $60. Therefore, for the reduction to nine days the cost would be $750 ($650 + $40 + $60).

6. The personnel and machine capabilities are not always available.

7. Cost accumulation for financial stewardship reports can conflict with the cost centers for PERT/Cost and can therefore create redundant systems.

8. The conversion of project oriented costs to mesh with annual budget concepts requires additional analysis.

If the problems associated with PERT/Cost can be resolved, PERT with COST could be considered a major breakthrough as was PERT with TIME. The majority of the potential problem areas with PERT/Cost lie in the controller's department. These difficulties present a very real challenge to the controller. PERT/Cost is putting the adaptability of the accountant to the test.

43. IS PERT/COST DEAD?

PETER P. SCHODERBEK*

On June 1, 1962, Secretary of Defense Robert S. McNamara and Robert C. Seamans, Jr., associate director of the National Aeronautics and Space Administration (NASA), adopted the PERT/Cost system as a standard tool for planning and controlling costs and schedules in major weapons and space programs. Thus, a second useful dimension was added to the already time-tested basic PERT system.

ACCEPTANCE LUKEWARM

The Army, Navy, Air Force, and NASA are now applying PERT/Cost to several multi-million-dollar research and development programs. Yet the acceptance of this technique has been relatively lukewarm, even among defense contractors, and the rest of industry has shown little interest in it.

Will PERT/Cost survive? This article attempts to throw some light on that question by means of an analysis of the system's pros and cons, with emphasis on some aspects of its implementation. It is assumed that the reader is generally familiar with PERT/Cost concepts and principles.[1] However, its key features will be reviewed briefly.

WHAT PERT/COST IS

PERT/Cost is a technique for planning, monitoring, and controlling the cost of and progress in attaining technical performance objectives. Its basic elements include the following:

Work Breakdown Structure—This is the backbone of the PERT/Cost system. The work breakdown structure, defined in terms of "end items" (performance, schedule, cost), serves as the framework for integrating cost and schedule planning and as the basis for construction of the PERT network depicting the overall project; it defines the tasks to be performed and the interrelationships; and it provides for the summarization of cost and schedule status of the total project.

Work Packages—A package is simply a specific task to be performed, e.g., engineering, manufacturing, testing. End items in the work breakdown structure are divided and subdivided into progressively smaller units until a manageable working level for planning and control purposes is achieved. The end item subdivisions appearing at the last level in the work breakdown structure are work packages. The work package is the basic unit for the assignment of schedule and cost responsibility to first-level supervision.

Account Code Structure—An account code structure allocates number of codes for work packages and summary items to permit the summation of schedule and cost information by

SOURCE: *Management Services* (November-December, 1968), pp. 43–50. Reprinted by permission of Management Service.

* University of Iowa.

[1] PERT (Program Evaluation and Review Technique) was explained in an earlier issue of MANAGEMENT SERVICES (January-February '66, p. 30). Its extension, PERT/Cost, was described in detail in an article by Don T. DeCoster ("PERT/Cost—The Challenge, May-June '64, p. 13) and evaluated in an article by this author ("PERT/Cost: Its Values and Limitations" by Peter P. Schoderbek, January-February '66, p. 29). Other helpful references include the following: *The Control of Schedules and Costs in Major Weapon and Space Programs,* U.S. Army Management Engineering Training Agency, Rock Island, Illinois; *PERT/Cost Manual,* General Dynamics Corporation, Pomona, California, June 15, 1963; *PERT, PERT/Cost and Line of Balance,* National Security Industrial Association, Washington, D.C., April 1, 1964; *Network-Based Management Systems by* Russell D. Archibald and Richard L. Villoria, John Wiley and Sons, Inc., New York, 1967; and *Implementation of PERT/Cost* by Richard E. Matthews, Management Systems Corporation, Cambridge, Massachusetts.

product item, responsible organizational unit, manpower skill, and time period. In this way costs can be identified and accumulated both horizontally and vertically.

Networks—The PERT/Cost networks, as in basic PERT, portray the activities and events necessary to achieve the project objectives. All activities on the network are related to specific work packages.

Reports—Standard reports are provided for as well as ones tailored to meet the specific needs of the entire management spectrum ranging from first-line supervision to top management. These reports are problem-oriented in that they highlight deviations from the plan.

BENEFITS

Unquestionably, PERT/Cost has many benefits. It greatly facilitates the assessment of project status with respect to financial planning; it highlights time-cost interrelationships and the financial effects on the project of alternative allocations of resources and possible changes in scheduling; it permits evaluation of progress from multiple information sources; it provides a unitary set of reports for appraising both the financial and the physical status of a project.

PERT/Cost also contributes to better conceptual planning by financially quantifying the project tasks to be performed and by assessing the adequacy of funding requirements for meeting total project costs. It provides a framework for comparing time schedules and resource estimates of various contractors.

By integrating PERT/Time with PERT/Cost, one can determine whether the various-level managers are meeting their schedule commitments, the cost estimates, and the technical performance standards and, if not, decide how resources can be best recombined so as to minimize costs.

In measuring the progress of a specific project, the sum of actual costs to date can be compared directly with the funds authorized and the estimated cost of completion of the project. Such comparisons will reveal potential cost over-runs and under-runs and will pinpoint those work segments requiring cost control action.

PROBLEMS

In spite of these impressive advantages of PERT/Cost, the technique has generally had rough going in defense companies. Some of the problems that have arisen are, no doubt, inherent in the system itself, but others have been created by factors peculiar to the defense companies. At any rate, they jeopardize the technique's effectiveness and erect barriers to the realization of its full potential.

LACK OF CONTRACTOR SUPPORT

PERT/Cost was met with less than enthusiastic acceptance on the part of major contractors as well as small subcontractors. Principally the reasons are twofold: (1) a reluctance by contractors to divulge internal cost data, and (2) the lack of a profit incentive to use PERT/Cost.

There is great reluctance on the part of contractors and subcontractors to reveal internal cost data to outsiders, not because the data are sacred in themselves but because they may provide a measure of efficiency as compared to competitors. Traditionally only top management was endowed with the privilege or responsibility of managing this information. To disclose such information to government officials or to prime contractors is alien to hallowed business principals. Subcontractors are especially reluctant to divulge cost information to prime contractors, falling back on the "confidential" company policy label. Prime contractors, on the other hand, sympathize with this attitude, knowing full well that these subcontractors may be and often are prime contractors on other projects. The situation may be reversed, and the primes will be in the same position, i.e., subcontractors that will have to reveal their own cost structure.

One of the present areas of disagreement about the revealing of cost data is the required level of disclosure. The government, to ensure efficient use of its funds, desires detailed information down to the work package level; industry, on the other hand, feels that cost summarizations down to the fifth floor level should be sufficient and that any details beyond this would represent an unnecessary expenditure of effort with but marginal utility. Both positions are understandable, legitimate, and incompatible.

In a way, industry has asked for much of its troubles by operating under cost-plus contracts where the rule rather than the exception was to understate proposal costs. In cost-plus contracts there is no penalty for underestimation of costs. Thus, contractors tended to understate costs in order to win contracts and then exerted little effort to control costs, knowing full well that they would later have the opportunity to increase the dollar value of the contract at renegotiation time. R & D contracts are typically written for a year at a time, and the work to be performed is defined in a general tasks form extending over a several-year effort. When new one-year contracts are written, tasks not completed in the previous year are included among the new tasks. Thus, it is rarely easy to relate costs incurred to progress achieved. The project manager is frequently not in a position to see the difference between the actual costs and the original estimates until the project is well under way or near completion. Then it is too late to do anything other than find the money to complete the project at the higher cost or cancel the project.

Contractors have little incentive to make the PERT/Cost system effective since it means fewer dollars in their pockets in addition to extensive government control over their financing. The fulfillment of the stated objectives of PERT/Cost makes it more difficult for contractors to conceal anticipated cost over-runs and schedule slippages; previously these over-runs could be masked until the government was so deeply committed that the only realistic alternative was to grant the money.

OVER-REPORTING

One of the most common weaknesses of PERT/Cost is the over-reporting of data. The PERT/Cost system is capable of producing reports at any desired level of detail, from the activity report at the detailed network level to the management summary report for the entire system. Although the DOD PERT Coordinating Group (now defunct) had specified the requisite formal reports, the particular level of detail varies with each of the project management levels.

Because of the computer's capabilities, there is a strong temptation to generate a vast number of reports that management neither needs nor utilizes. This increase in the quantity of data generated does not necessarily lead to better-informed decisions. The very redundancy of inputs, and more often of outputs, can in fact reduce the manager's effectiveness. A great deal of the useless information flowing across the manager's desk reaches him only because it is standard practice or because of a misinformed directive. It is not uncommon for some managers to operate under the erroneous assumption that the more data available the better must be the decision reached. But even the continuous updating of information will not of itself lead to better decisions. What is needed is a clear understanding of the type of information actually required by the decision maker at his own level. It should be fairly obvious that even now information must still be carefully filtered at the various levels just as was the case a decade ago when computers were first coming into use in the business world.

DATA PROBLEM

It is a common misconception that in the PERT/Cost system summarization of data is all that is required to manage the many parts of the program. While this summarization may be adequate for the collection of cost figures, it is often inadequate in terms of relevance for decision making, for evaluating alternative strategies, and for assessing future changes in the entire system. Too often PERT/Cost is expected to replace internal control systems or, for that matter, the accounting system. It does neither; it is not an accounting system in the true sense of the word, nor does it replace conventional control systems. Its chief effect is to supplement the firm's internal operating practices.

The information needed by managers at the various levels of a project is not a simple summarization of costs but a penetrating analysis of the technological state of an element of the program or a functional grouping of relevant data. Because summarization reduces or eliminates data, it does not of itself provide the intensive visibility for micromanagement.

SUITABILITY OF REPORTS

Much has been written about how easy it is to adapt PERT/Cost to a firm's accounting structure. This simply is not generally true.

Although many large contractors have an accounting system which allow for the collection of costs by contracts, end items, functional cost categories, etc., most systems do not fit PERT's data needs. Current accounting systems for the estimation of manpower costs, skill classifications, time/cost tradeoffs, and optimum schedules are still generally inadequate for compliance with the requisite PERT/Cost reports. Most current accounting systems were developed to accommodate the needs of contractors and are related to the firm's particular products, methods of production, internal structure, and the like. In fact, it has been strongly recommended by the accounting profession that different treatments be mandatory in different business situations.

Thus, any attempt to apply uniform regulations in regard to PERT/Cost reporting is inimical to sound project management. This is not to imply that industry would or should be given free rein in its reporting procedures but rather that the PERT/Cost system should provide for flexibility by taking account of the notable differences between organizations with various product mixes and organizational structures.

VARIATIONS MUST BE ACCEPTED

Firms should not be coerced to adapt their internal accounting systems simply to comply with regulations. Rather, the variations in company practice should be accepted in the initial stages of involvement. The attempt to apply uniform procedures to all firms would vitiate the PERT/Cost concept. Entirely new thinking is required to adapt PERT/Cost into operating reality in terms of budgeting, scheduling, reporting, valuing, and controlling. Only the passage of time and accumulation of more experience will permit the development of a truly compatible system.

One widely touted advantage of PERT/Cost is its timely and accurate reporting. However, careful scrutiny leads one to question whether it is fast enough to be useful or accurate enough to be reliable.

TIMELINESS OF REPORTS

It is relatively easy to gather historical costs; it is much more difficult to estimate the costs of physical progress for work packages in various stages of completion. The rule of thumb—that the value of work performed to date is to be measured by the actual costs, divided by the latest estimate to complete, times the budget to date—is not an accurate guide for evaluation, especially when progress is not on target or when the "approved interim changes" that have been made are not reflected in a new contract value. In the latter case, the value of work performed would be much less than the actual amount spent. The fact that this formula has already been subjected to much adverse criticism in the literature indicates that a complete re-evaluation of its usefulness ought to be undertaken.

For the sake of timeliness, contractors and subcontractors are often required to submit "estimated actuals" for the preceding month's work. This procedure could conceivably be worthwhile if the prime contractors and their subcontractors used the same accounting cut-off dates. Seldom is this the case, and the result is a proliferation of dates on which information becomes available. This practice coerces the use of "estimated actuals" by subcontractors, which typically provide less accurate data. Realistically, most contractors can only supply their cost information to the next tier in about fifteen working days after the cut-off date. Consolidation, analysis, and evaluation by management may take another seven or eight working days. When several tiers of major subcontractors are involved, it may take up to a month to present the desired information. By requiring early monthly reporting of estimates to complete just for the sake of timeliness, PERT/Cost may be responsible for the accumulation of data that are close to two months old and, more important, have little accuracy and even less timeliness.

Under the PERT/Cost system, work packages in progress are required to be updated at least once a month, at which time new time and cost estimates to complete are made. The summarization of cost data at the various levels is supposed to provide top management with the needed visibility to control the project. In practice, this updating works fairly well, although a few problems do occur. One not unusual difficulty experienced is the revision of estimates to complete for tasks extending far into the future. Obviously, estimates to complete for tasks with a time duration of only one, two, or three months are much more meaningful than ones involving nine or ten months. Actually, submission of estimates to complete work of a long duration should not occur too frequently. The DOD and NASA Guides to PERT/Cost clearly specify that the lowest work package should not exceed $100,000 in cost and three months in elapsed time. However, many work packages require more than 90 days simply because the activity involved does not have a recognizable event within that time span.

FREQUENCY OF UPDATING

Another complication experienced in the updating of estimates is their frequency. Little is to be gained by continually re-estimating work packages on a monthly basis unless trouble is being experienced or it is desired to manage a program element by exception. Re-estimation done in a mechanical fashion is neither economical nor practical, especially when carried out in areas where costs are not currently affecting overall performance. In fact, the adulteration of critical data with routine data tends to diminish the effectiveness of the "management by exception" reporting capability inherent in the PERT/Cost system.

INVALID ESTIMATING AND ALLOCATION

An earlier article by this writer[2] pointed out that the effectiveness of the PERT/Cost system (and for that matter any scheduling and budgeting system) depends upon the validity of the information fed into the system. Too frequently time estimating is done by personnel who are not thoroughly familiar with or responsible for the tasks to be accomplished. Even when the estimator is experienced, he is often unable to apply this experience if there is not a clear item definition in the work breakdown stage or clear identification of work packages. Consequently, time estimates and estimated dates of completion can often be less than realistic.

'PLAYING IT SAFE'

Frequently there is also a desire on the part of estimators to "play it safe." More than one engineer has confided to this writer that he attempts to deviate very little from his ("padded") estimates because of fear of reprisal. One engineer put it this way, "I got chewed out something terrible when I missed my estimate by 40 per cent, and I can guarantee you that I won't miss another one." Many department heads are aware of the resulting duplicity and try to take appropriate remedial action. In one instance, the department head cut down an estimate that he considered out of line. When the engineer was asked in confidence what he thought of the fact that his estimate had been cut from 27 weeks to 20 weeks, he replied, "I kinda expected that, so I built up my estimate in the first place. This job should actually only take about 18 weeks, which still gives me about two weeks to play around with."

So long as the above attitude prevails, PERT and PERT/Cost will definitely not realize their full potential. It is unfortunate that this posture is still present in many companies today.

DEPARTMENT HEADS GUILTY, TOO

In the same vein, department heads do not want to incur cost over-runs that reflect adversely on their performance, and, as a result, they too are tempted to pad estimates in an effort to compensate for possible errors in time estimates.

BUDGET MANIPULATIONS

In many work packages that are of long duration there is frequent budget adjustment to eliminate over-runs or under-runs although the scope of the work to be performed has not changed. In an effort to stay within allotted budgets, the reporting of labor classifications for work packages is likely to be manipulated. For example, suppose that a manager in an engineering department has one work package in which he expects to have an under-run and another in which he will experience an over-run. One can be reasonably sure that a trade-off of resources will occur that will not show up in any reporting system. After all, the department head is often indifferent as to which accounts these costs are charged to so long as he stays within his own overall budget.

MISLEADING ASSUMPTIONS

Similarly, there may exist budget pools from which allocations are made to conform with the work effort regardless of the precalculated costs. Too often PERT/Cost reports are constructed simply by taking the elapsed time that an activity consumes and multiplying this by the number of personnel in the department to arrive at a payroll cost. Too often this does not reflect the true man-hours required to perform the work packages. In some instances there may even be use of a composite rate that does not differentiate skill or salary ranges. Obviously such reporting based on misleading or at best dubious premises is likely to prove misleading—and often highly erroneous.

[2] See Schoderbek, *op. cit.*

Because of the complexity of internal structures of firms, especially in the R and D field, it is extremely difficult, if not impossible, to assess on a uniform basis the cost of installing and operating PERT/Cost. Much of the present effort in this respect has resulted in duplicative measures, and the substantial cost of the system is primarily an additive cost for most firms, i.e., firms operate with their traditional reporting systems and then adapt the data for PERT/Cost reporting. This is not too dissimilar to what occurred in the early days of PERT, where in a few instances PERT was actually applied *post factum*.

HISTORY IN ACTION

Some progress, however, has been made. The cost of PERT/Cost can be broken down into two segments: (1) the initial cost of installation, which would be a one-time cost, and (2) the operating cost, which would be the cost of maintaining the PERT/Cost system less the cost of the traditional accounting system of the firm.

In principle, this sounds quite convincing; in practice, PERT/Cost has been rather expensive. Actual data from test cases have not provided the necessary spectrum of costs at various levels of contractor responsibility. It is highly doubtful whether an accurate cost differential between the firm's conventional accounting system and PERT/Cost can ever be obtained. Other sensitive questions can also be raised, e.g., are implementation costs to be charged only to the project in question; are they to be treated as a fixed overhead; or are they to be pro-rated and applied to later projects also?

EXPERIENCE WITH PERT/COST

Although PERT/Cost has been operational for about five years, actual experience with it has been somewhat limited. In the three major test cases it has been a qualified success.

The Mauler Weapon System can be cited as one of the most successful applications of the concept (although the project was terminated after expenditures of $300 million because of technical problems). In this case the Army controlled the time and cost elements of the project but could not adequately control the technical performance aspect. In fact, the application of the PERT/Cost technique did highlight the technical difficulties. The cost of using PERT/Cost on the Mauler project was not insignificant although the actual figures are still unavailable.

The controversial F-111 (TFX) also employs PERT/Cost. However, this project exhibits many of the problems often encountered in the operational aspects of the system. Although from a technical standpoint this project cannot fail by edict of the Secretary of Defense, cost over-runs in the magnitude of two billion dollars are currently expected. It would be a truism to state that adequate cost control measures are lacking in this instance. The Navy is also testing the PERT/Cost concept with its missile SUBROC (W 30-A), but little external information is available about the results.

It is well known that many available management techniques are accepted only because of some dictate or sheer expediency rather than because of their true value. Such was the case with PERT, which has taken close to a decade to become fully accepted on its own merits. DOD obviously hastened its acceptance in the defense industry.

Much of the impetus for the acceptance of PERT/Cost was provided by Thomas Morris, who several years ago was the Assistant Secretary of Defense for Installations and Logistics. When he resigned to accept a position in industry, his replacement, Paul Ignatius, allowed PERT/Cost to remain offstage, and little was done to prove or sell this technique to defense companies. With the death of the Secretary of the Navy, John McNaughton, Mr. Ignatius was appointed to fill this position. Mr. Morris, who meanwhile had accepted the position of Assistant Secretary of Defense for Manpower, was reappointed to his old position. Thus, while PERT/Cost has lain somewhat dormant for several years, its revival can soon be reasonably expected.

THE FUTURE

Is PERT/Cost dead? Hardly! Even without the impetus supplied by the government it has sufficient momentum to go it alone. Despite its limitations, there is little reason to doubt that PERT/Cost has added a new and worthwhile dimension to the field of operational control. As the technique matures through more imaginative use and guided experimentation, the refinements that are bound to result will bring management within close range of its desired goal.

44. THIRD GENERATION, PERT/LOB

PETER P. SCHODERBEK* AND LESTER A. DIGMAN†

The new technique described in this article, PERT/LOB, is significant to management because it extends the potentials of PERT (Program Evaluation and Review Technique) and LOB (Line of Balance) for planning and control. Whereas PERT is useful mainly in the initial development of a new product, construction, or item of military hardware, and whereas LOB is useful mainly in the production stage, PERT/LOB is valuable in the many activities between R&D and quantity production. In this article the authors describe the basic principles of LOB and PERT/LOB and show how the new technique would be used in a specific case to help executives plan and control work on a project.

After a rather inauspicious beginning in 1958, PERT has won acceptance by an ever-increasing segment of industry. Though born and reared in the United States, it has been adopted by Canada, has crossed over to Great Britain and the European continent, and has penetrated even behind the Iron Curtain. It is now an accepted fact that PERT has revolutionized the planning and control functions of management; and in its short life span it has undergone much experimentation and seen many a modification.

The "first generation" of PERT is referred to as PERT/Time. The "second generation" is the PERT/Cost system, which was developed in 1962 for the specific purpose of integrating time data with the associated financial data of physical accomplishment. Though current effort is devoted primarily to improving the PERT/Cost system, PERT/Time itself is not being neglected. Indeed, it is taking on a new look.

PERT's historical antecedents can be found in the Gantt bar charts, which have been around for many years. It is, therefore, not much of a surprise to learn that the latest adaptation of PERT concerns another charting technique—LOB. The LOB technique has been used as a tool in the control of production activities for some 25 years. Although PERT/Time and PERT/Cost (or, collectively, PERT) may have recently gained the limelight, LOB has been developing quietly in the wings. While PERT has proved most successful in the development stages of large, complex projects of a nonrepetitive nature, such as R&D and construction, LOB has proved itself as an effective management tool for *steady-state* production activities. Actually, many companies employ both techniques on large projects, PERT in the development phase and LOB in the production phase.

With the recent government emphasis on so-called project life cycle management—i.e., the centralized management of a project through the concept, definition, development, production, operational, and disposal phases—there is an obvious need for a single management tool to control complex projects from inception to completion. While both PERT and LOB admirably serve their specific purposes in development and production, until recently there was no effective management technique to employ during the *transition* from development to prototype production and add-on production. In spite of the closer control being increasingly exercised in the development and production phases, some of the effectiveness of the entire system is generally lost during the transition phase. This has caused much concern. In government projects the transition phase is often critical because of schedule commitments to other countries, the need for early operations, and the need for better utilization of facilities. In industry the transition phase is crucial because of commitments to industrial customers and marketing deadlines.

PERT/LOB is designed to provide better

SOURCE: *Harvard Business Review* (September-October, 1967), pp. 100–110.

* University of Iowa.
† Army Management Engineering Training Agency.

control during the critical transition phase, though its application is not limited to that period. Because the approach is a combination of PERT and LOB, it is applicable wherever and whenever PERT or LOB can be of service. In situations where nonrepetitive activities occur, PERT/LOB is equivalent to basic PERT; in situations where repetitive activities occur, PERT/LOB is equivalent to basic LOB. And in the transition phase, where one-time and repetitive activities are intermingled and pose difficulties which neither PERT nor LOB alone can handle effectively, PERT/LOB enables the manager to plan and control effectively using tools with which he is already familiar. Thus management can plan and control the *entire* development-production life cycle using a single technique (see Fig. 1).

PERT/LOB is of greatest value in relatively low volume, new product situations. An ideal application is where development of a new item *and* production of a limited quantity of that item are critical. This is the rule rather than the exception not only in the defense industry but also in the space program, the computer industry, and special-purpose equipment programs. Tomorrow's executive will be more and more concerned with such situations. Because PERT/LOB is ideally suited to the needs of the project manager and the new product manager, it is a tool truly deserving of more study and wider application.

The advantages of PERT/LOB to the defense industry have become more impressive since the Pentagon began emphasizing project life cycle planning and contracting (in contrast to the conventional phase-by-phase practice). The technique enables the contractor to bid more realistically and to estimate costs more accurately on a life-cycle basis, providing greater assurance to the government that thorough and comprehensive planning has taken place.

Before delving into the specifics of PERT/LOB, let us review briefly some of the fundamentals of the LOB technique. In light of the voluminous literature that has appeared in recent years, we shall assume that the executives we address are passably familiar with the PERT technique.

THE ABCs OF LOB

LOB is a management-oriented charting tool for collecting, measuring, and presenting information relating to time and accomplishment during production. It shows the progress, status, timing, and phasing of the interrelated activities of a project; these data provide management with a means of comparing actual with planned performance. In addition, management receives timely information concerning the critical areas where the project is, or will be, behind schedule. LOB differs from other control techniques in that it is utilized mainly in the production process, from the point when incoming or raw materials arrive to the shipment of the end product. It is basically a means of integrating and monitoring the flow of materials, components, and sub-

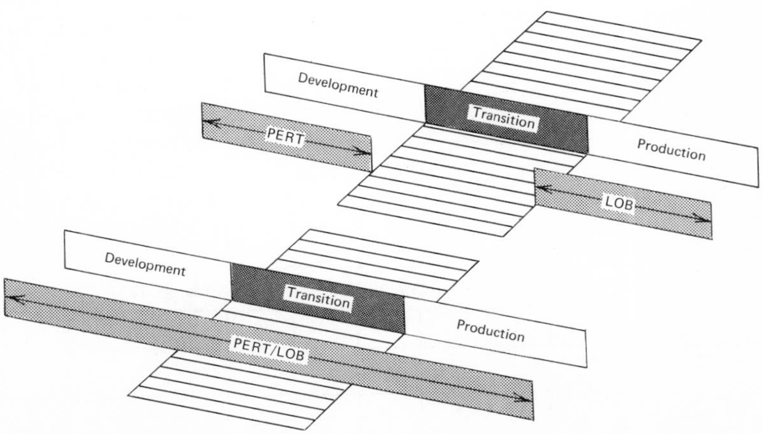

FIG. 1. Role of PERT/LOB. PERT and LOB do not cover the critical transition phase, but PERT/LOB does.

components into manufacturing in accordance with phased delivery requirements.

There are four elements or phases comprising the LOB technique. Let us look at each of them in turn.

1. The Objective

For a production process where a quantity of the end item is being made under contract, the objective is the required delivery schedule. The delivery information used is of two kinds: (a) the *planned* schedule, representing the contractual requirement; and (b) the *actual* schedule, showing the calendar date of delivery.

To illustrate this and other aspects of LOB, let us turn to a fictional case. XYZ Corporation has a contract to manufacture and deliver 36 test prototypes of a mobile missile system. The required delivery schedule is shown in Fig. 2. As can be seen from the chart, the delivery of the 36 missiles is to take place over a time span of 11 weeks, with the first scheduled for delivery in January 1967 and the last scheduled for delivery in early April 1967. It is assumed that "today" is March 28, 1967. (As we describe this case in more detail, the information will be arranged in such a way that we can then go on to apply the newly developed computer program offered by Control Data Corporation.)

2. The Program

Once the objective is determined, the next task is to define the program. The program is simply the production plan with a graphic flow chart plotted against the lead time required before shipment. The monitoring of progress is done against key plant operations or assembly points in the manufacturing cycle, known as control points. Table 1 depicts the control points for XYZ Corporation's missile production plan from the first tasks of purchasing and fabrication to the shipping of the missile assemblies to the test site. Figure 3 depicts the production plan in its graphic form, indicating manufacturing interrelationships, how each major component fits into the

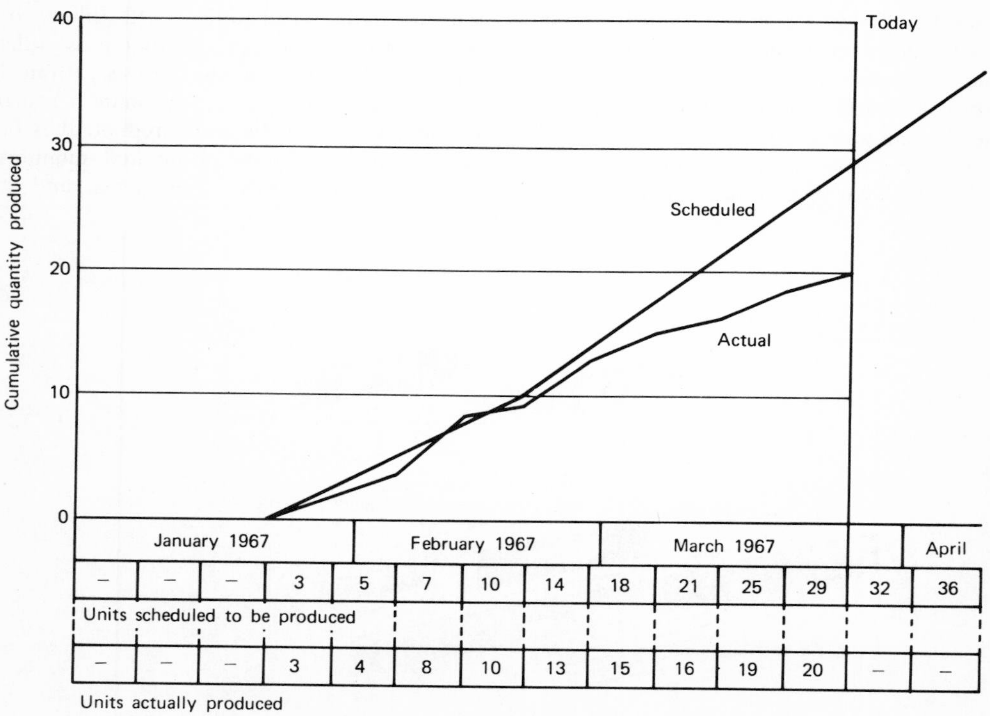

FIG. 2. XYZ Corporation: mobile missile system schedule objective.

Table 1. XYZ Corporation: Production Control Points

Description	Control Point Number
Begin ballistic shell fabrication	1
Begin motor fabrication	2
Complete shell fabrication	3
Begin chassis casting	4
Complete chassis casting	5
Receive ground vehicle engine components	6
Receive guidance components from subcontractor	7
Complete shell assembly	8
Complete assembly of ground vehicle engine	9
Complete air vehicle/guidance assembly	10
Complete ground vehicle assembly	11
Ship assemblies to test site	12

assembly process, the necessary lead times, and the exact point in the cycle where each component must be available.

In the coding of the control points, standard symbols are employed (see the key in Fig. 3). The lead-time scale represents the number of working periods (in this case, weeks), counting backwards from total completion, that are needed to complete each major action.

The development of the production plan requires the determination of the various operations to be performed and sequence of operations, and the determination of the processing times and assembly lead times of materials and components. The production plan is then constructed by plotting the selected events and operations in their proper sequence, beginning at the point of delivery and moving consecutively from left to right across the schematic diagram (Fig. 3), and from top to bottom wherever two or more points have a common position along the horizontal scale. As will be shown later, each of these 12 control points or milestones is keyed by corresponding number to a bar graph in the progress position of the LOB chart.

As Fig. 3 indicates, the production cycle for each unit or missile is five weeks.

In order to manage such a program effectively, the number of control points generally should not exceed 50. In the event that there are more than that number, the situation can best be handled by charting "families"; that is, each control point can represent a grouping of related items. It is also possible to develop a chart for each category of parts, such as government-produced, customer-furnished, purchased, and so forth. If separate charts are utilized, a summary chart is necessary to indicate the overall state of the project. This summary chart can easily be made by selecting key control points from each of the supporting charts.

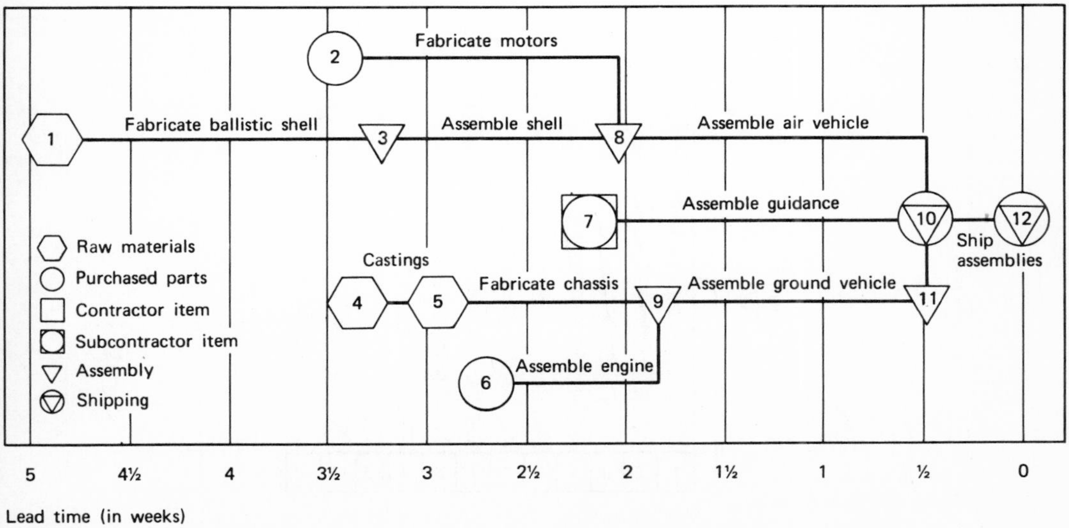

FIG. 3. XYZ Corporation: activity interrelationships and time schedules. (Numbers denote control points.)

3. *Program Progress*

The program progress (sometimes called production progress) diagram is shown in Fig. 4. It quantitatively represents the least available part associated with a given control point. It is a bar chart which shows the cumulative quantities of materials, parts, and subassemblies processed at the control points as of a given time. This information is accumulated by physical inventory for each control point.

The progress chart uses the same vertical quantity scale as the schedule objective chart (Fig. 2). By utilizing the same numbers, the horizontal scale corresponds to the numbered control points in the production plan.

4. *Deriving the LOB*

The LOB depicts the cumulative parts or components in terms of end-item sets for each control point which must have been completed as of the progress review date—March 28, 1967, in this case. (The progress review date becomes the "today" line for all reference purposes. The end-item delivery requirement is found by simply drawing a vertical line at the progress review date and extending it to intersect the production objective chart, as is done in Fig. 2.) The LOB is shown in Fig. 4. Let us look at the information that is summarized here for management.

Control Point 1, we have seen, is concerned with ballistic missile shell fabrication, which requires approximately two weeks for each missile, ending with Control Point 3. Control Point 1 must occur five weeks prior to delivery of the completed missile (see Fig. 3).

By the review date of March 28, 1967, not only must 29 end items have been readied, but an additional quantity must be on hand to meet the shipping schedule 1½ weeks later. The exact number required is found by erecting a perpendicular at the calendar date which is 5 work weeks after March 28—or at the final delivery date, if that comes sooner (as it does in this case). The cumulative delivery curve at that point calls for 36 units. (In Fig. 2, the perpendicular would meet the end of the "Scheduled" line, which is opposite 36 on the vertical scale.) Accordingly, for Control Point 1, 36 units should be available on March 28. The LOB is projected at this level to the progress chart (Fig. 4).

Similarly, Control Points 2 and 3, which are scheduled about 3½ weeks prior to delivery date, must provide requirements for March 28,

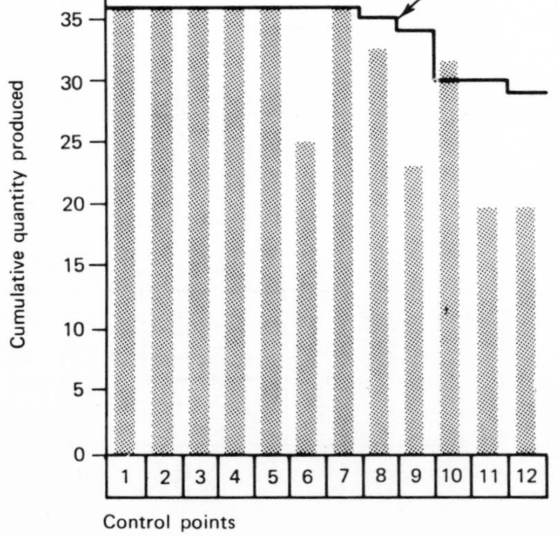

FIG. 4. Program progress chart as of March 28, 1967.

namely 36 units. As for Control Points 10 and 11, which are required a half week prior to shipment, one notices that the ordinate at these points corresponds to 30 units.

By following the same procedure, levels for each control point can be constructed. The end result is the characteristic step-down contour of a Line of Balance. By comparing the LOB with the actual performance of each item, a graphical portrayal of program status is afforded. (In our example, actual performance is represented by the heights of the bars in Fig. 4.)

As mentioned earlier, each milestone in the plan is keyed to the bar chart by an identifying number. The length of the bar represents the number of items that have been used or are available for use. All of the control points that are behind schedule are shown by bars which fail to meet the LOB. The first of these in our example is Control Point 6 (Fig. 4). Inasmuch as Control Points 9, 11, and 12 are also behind schedule, it is evident that Control Point 6 is the "culprit" causing these "downstream" problem areas.

Let us now turn our attention to the integrated PERT/LOB technique with which the remainder of this article will be concerned.

HOW PERT/LOB WORKS

PERT/LOB is a technique which integrates the planning elements of PERT with the control elements of LOB. It represents an attempt to provide close project control during the transition from the development phase to the production phase or during production start-up. It brings together the major benefits of both techniques, integrating PERT's planning discipline with LOB's ease of control.

More specifically, PERT/LOB broadens PERT by allowing inclusion of repetitive activities in the network. In addition, it:

- Highlights critical activities that may deter the completion of the project or task.
- Points to problem areas as well as the present status of repetitive activities.
- Helps management to provide for effective scheduling of production outputs.
- Helps executives to predict schedule and cost requirements at any point in time and to relate their current efforts to future schedules.
- Permits trade-off analyses of both time and cost considerations.

In general, PERT/LOB provides the wherewithal for measuring actual against planned performance in a manner permitting compliance with contractual commitments.

As with PERT, PERT/LOB utilizes a time-oriented network with activities representing the flow of work to be performed. The planning is similar to that in PERT; in fact, all of the steps occurring in both the planning and control cycles of PERT apply as well to the PERT/LOB system.

Work Breakdown

The first step in the PERT/LOB system involves the identification of the objectives of the program. As the objectives are divided and subdivided with ever-greater detail, they form the work breakdown structure which establishes a common framework for the program.

The lowest breakdown items (end items) are further subdivided into work packages. These form the basic planning and control tool, as in the PERT/Cost system. Work package determination and size follow the same criteria utilized in PERT.

Repetitive Time Estimates

Time estimates must be established for the various activities. The single time estimate is used both for nonrepetitive activities and for repetitive ones. However, for the repetitive activities, a time estimate should be made for each batch or lot size. The estimate should take into account machine capability, size of production run, machine loading, and learning considerations. Seldom is the estimated time constant for all batches. It may, however, stabilize at a certain point, that point being determined by the learning time involved on the job. Learning considerations can easily be included in the PERT/LOB system.

Since the size of the batch may range from a single unit to the entire production quantity, the time estimate must reflect this lot size. For example, if a part is to be cast, then it might be feasible to do the entire quantity at one time; therefore, the one-batch time is the activity time. The batch-size quantity involves a consideration of the required number of items, cost data, inventory data, processing times, line balancing, resource availability, and other pertinent factors.

In repetitive activities, it is sometimes possible to overlap batches, i.e., to start production on the second batch before the first batch is completed. A plan can be developed which consists of the estimated elapsed time for each batch, the minimum time between successive batches, the batch size, and the production rate plotted against the time needed for the planned production quantity. Figure 5 shows

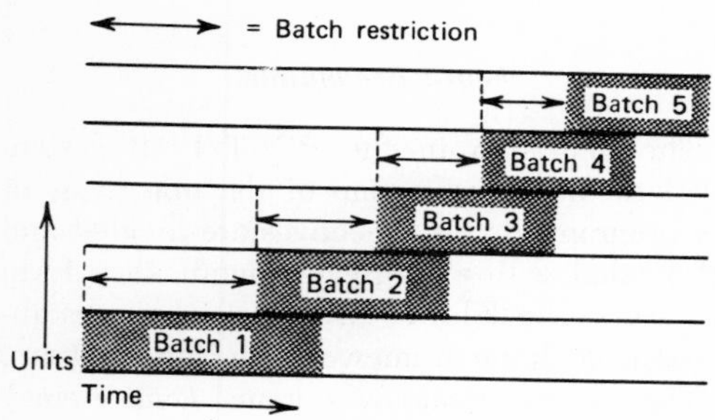

FIG. 5. Repetitive activity production plan.

a repetitive activity production plan. The time between batches is called *batch restriction*, since this time obviously restricts the start of successive batches. This time restriction is determined by such things as the available storage space, capacity limitations, and setup considerations.

Network Construction

The work breakdown structure provides the basis for the construction of networks at any desired level of detail by identifying the end items to be accomplished at that level. The PERT/LOB technique can accommodate both the development network, which deals primarily with one-time activities, and the production network, which is concerned with the repetitive production sequence. It follows that PERT/LOB can portray both types of activities which typically occur in the transition phase between development and production. A repetitive *activity* is represented on the network by an open box on an activity arrow (see, for example, the "manufacture missiles" arrow in Fig. 6). A repetitive *event* is shown by an X in a circle (see the nodes at each end of the "manufacture missiles" arrow). The repetitive events of the network become the LOB control points.

Just as more detailed networks are utilized at the lower levels with PERT, so too are they with PERT/LOB. Also, as with PERT, the nature of an activity sometimes depends on the management level from which it is viewed. For instance, Figure 6 shows the manufacture and assembly of 20 missiles as a one-time activity for top management. It is, however, a "repetitive" activity to the next level of management; this is because of the repetition of

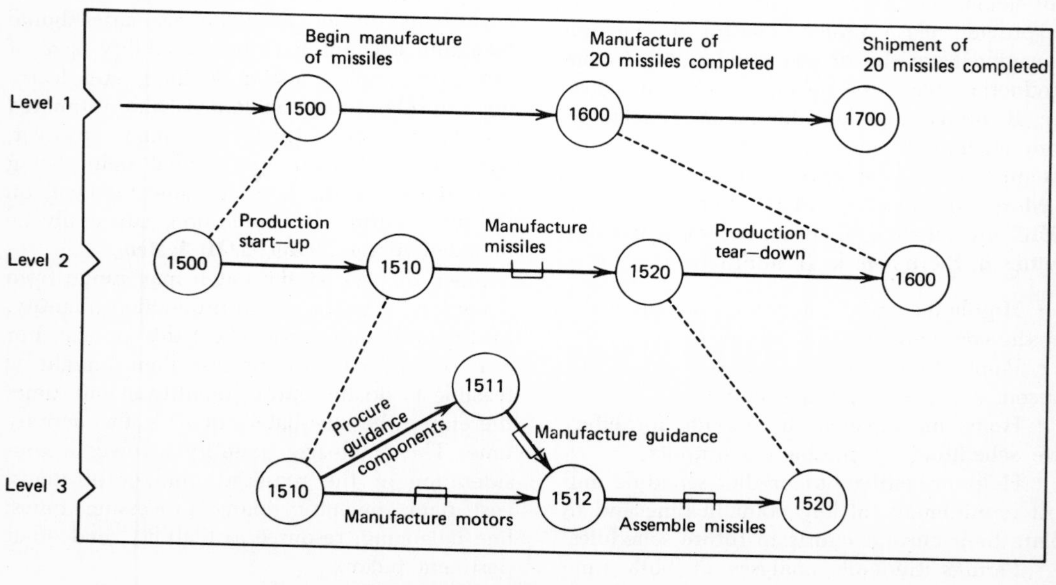

FIG. 6. Three-level network plan.

the events "start manufacture" and "complete manufacture" for each unit or each batch.

Thus Fig. 6 shows the repetitive activities and events required to complete each unit or batch, as they would be seen at three different managerial levels. The dotted lines indicate additional detail for an event or activity. For instance, the second-level activities are an amplification of the job of getting missile manufacture under way with the production of batches; again, the third-level activities amplify further the job of manufacturing 20 missiles.

All units or batches must be numbered consecutively beginning with 1. As with LOB, production quantities must be considered in terms of equivalent units (EU). The number of identical items that go into the final end item must be determined. This number equals one EU; for instance, two tracks per tank equals one EU, and 50 logic modules, type 5A6W, per missile equals one EU.

Included in the PERT/LOB system is a stability point. This is the batch number at which the decrease in elapsed batch time between successive batches due to learning is no longer considered significant.[1] In practice, it is the point where no further learning is considered necessary for the job and the point at which the batch time becomes constant. Referring to Fig. 5 again, if the elapsed time for Batch 5 is the same as for Batch 4, no further learning is expected after Batch 4. Therefore, completion of Batch 4 becomes the stability point.

In PERT/LOB, network coding and integration are done as in PERT.

Figure 7 shows a prototype production network and the related activity data for the XYZ Corporation's project. The network has been expanded to include production start-up, batches, and learning, which conventional LOB cannot satisfactorily accommodate. The network is comprised of regular activities and repetitive activities. (Several dummy activities are also created in order to give the computer complete instructions when the program is run off.) Figure 7 also shows the interrelationships of the milestones portrayed in Fig. 3.

[1] For an analysis of learning curve concepts, see W. B. Hirschmann, "Profit From the Learning Curve," *Harvard Business Review,* January-February 1964, p. 125.

Time Calculations

Network calculations are basically similar to those in the PERT system. The earliest expected completion date (T_E) and the latest allowable date (T_L) are computed, as are the critical path and activity slack times. The only notable difference is that in PERT/LOB repetitive activities have multiple contact points rather than a single point as in the PERT system. T_E, T_L, and slack time figures are calculated for each batch of repetitive activities; since this becomes quite burdensome if done manually, it is desirable to utilize a computer to perform the calculations. We performed the calculations for the XYZ Corporation using a new computer program developed by Control Data Corporation.

Reports for Management

Although management can have as many output reports as it would receive in the PERT system, it probably will not want them. PERT/LOB utilizes primarily the milestone report, the production status report, and the activity report:

- The *milestone* report, which has a PERT-like format, deals with the events that represent major milestones of accomplishment in completing the program. Figure 8 shows top executives of XYZ Corporation whether or not work on the milestone jobs of the missile project is on schedule.
- The *production status* report, illustrated in Fig. 9, portrays essential production information at each of the control points corresponding to those on the PERT/LOB network (Fig. 7), and adds the projected completion dates for the control point activities. Like the milestone report, it is of especial interest to top management.
- The *activity* report, unlike the preceding ones, is for the middle management specialist. It is very similar to the PERT activity report, as Fig. 10 indicates. Only those columns labeled "RATE" (rate of production activity beyond the stability point), "UNIT NR" (unit number for time data shown), and "BATCH NR" (batch number for time data shown) are different from those displayed for PERT. The data show managers of the XYZ Corporation how different jobs in the missile project stand in relation to the schedule.

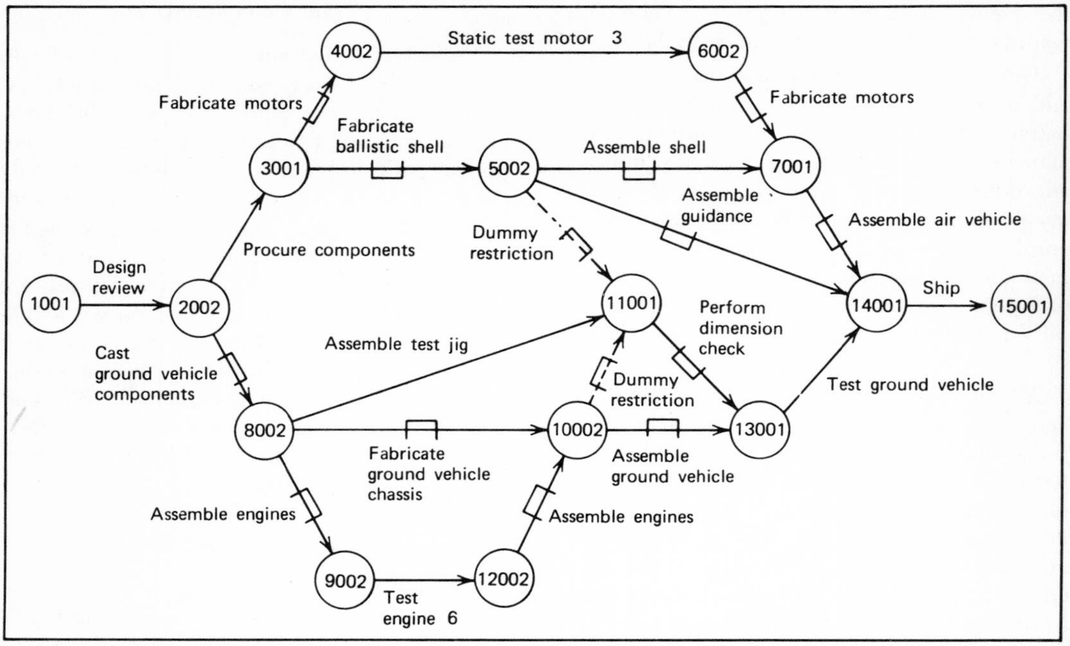

FIG. 7. Prototype production network: activity interrelationships and supporting data.

Designation	Description	Type	How batched
1001–2002	Perform design review	One-time	
2002–3001	Procure missile components	One-time	
2002–8002	Cast ground vehicle components	Repetitive	2 batches; each has 18 units
3001–4002	Fabricate motors	Repetitive	2 batches; the first has 3 units, the second has 33 units[a]
3001–5002	Fabricate ballistic shell	Repetitive	6 batches; each has 6 units
4002–6002	Static test motor no. 3	One-time[b]	
5002–7001	Assemble shell	Repetitive	4 batches; each has 9 units
5002–11001	Dummy restriction	Repetitive	36 batches; each has 1 unit
5002–14001	Assemble guidance	Repetitive	9 batches; each has 4 units
6002–7001	Fabricate motors	Repetitive	12 batches; the first has 3 units, the others have 12 units each[a]
7001–14001	Assemble air vehicle	Repetitive	6 batches; each has 6 units
8002–9002	Assemble engines	Repetitive	2 batches; the first has 6 units, the second has 30 units[a]
8002–10002	Fabricate ground vehicle chassis	Repetitive	6 batches; each has 6 units
8002–11001	Assemble test jig	One-time	
9002–12002	Test engine no. 6	One-time[b]	
10002–11001	Dummy restriction	Repetitive	36 batches; each has 1 unit
10002–13001	Assemble ground vehicle	Repetitive	9 batches; each has 4 units
11001–13001	Perform dimensional check	Repetitive	36 batches; each has 1 unit
12002–10002	Assemble engines	Repetitive	6 batches; the first has 6 units, the others have 6 units each[a]
13001–14001	Test ground vehicle	One-time	
14001–15001	Ship system to test site	One-time	

[a] Dummy batch has zero time.
[b] With unit designator.

THE REPORT IS SORTED BY
1ST KEY= SUCC.
2ND KEY= TE.

PROJECT PERT LOB TEST CASE	REPORTING ORGN.	CONTRACT NO.	REPORT DATES
			TERMS (SPAN)ENTIRE PROJ
NETWORK NUMBER -0	TECH APPT	42605	CUT-OFF DATE 28MAR67
SUB-NET NUMBER -0			RELEASE DATE 28MAR67

MILESTONE NUMBER	LEVEL NR.	MILESTONE DESCRIPTION	ACTUAL DATE	EXPECTED DATE	LATEST DATE	SCHEDULED DATE
2002	2	PERFORM DESIGN REVIEW	21OCT66	21OCT66	16NOV66	
3001	1	PROCURE MISSLE COMPONENT	18NOV66	18NOV66	15DEC66	
4002	2	FABRICATE 4 MOTORS	1DEC66	1DEC66	27DEC66	
5002	2	FABR. BALLISTIC SHELL	18FEB67	18FEB67	18FEB67	
6002	2	STATIC TEST MOTOR 3	1DEC66	7DEC66	31DEC66	
7001	1	FABRICATE 32 MOTORS		11FEB67	9MAR67	
7001	1	ASSEMBLE SHELL		2MAR67	2MAR67	
8002	2	CAST GND VEHL COMPONENTS	4NOV66	4NOV66	13JAN67	
9002	2	ASSEMBLE ENGINES		4NOV66	5JAN67	
10002	2	ASSEMBLE ENGINES		8DEC66	28FEB67	
10002	2	FAB GND VEHL CHASSIS		22DEC66	28FEB67	
11001	1	ASSEMBLE TEST JIG		12NOV66	17FEB67	
11001	1	DUMMY		22DEC66	14MAR67	
11001	1	DUMMY		18FEB67	14MAR67	
12002	2	TEST ENGINE 6		8NOV66	7JAN67	
13001	1	ASSEMBLE GROUND VEHICLE		17JAN67	15MAR67	23MAR67
13001	1	PERFORM DIMENSION CK		23FEB67	15MAR67	
14001	1	ASSEMBLE GUIDANCE		4MAR67	28MAR67	
14001	1	TEST GROUND VEHICLE		8MAR67	28MAR67	
14001	1	ASSEMBLE AIR VEHICLE		28MAR67	28MAR67	8APR67
15001	1	SHIP SYSTEM TO TEST SITE		4APR67	4APR67	

FIG. 8. Milestone report.

THE REPORT IS SORTED BY
1ST KEY= SUCC.
2ND KEY= TE.

PROJECT PERT LOB TEST CASE	REPORTING ORGN.	CONTRACT NO.	REPORT DATES
			TERMS (SPAN)ENTIRE PROJ
NETWORK NUMBER -0	TECH APPT	42605	CUT-OFF DATE 28MAR67
SUB-NET NUMBER -0			RELEASE DATE 28MAR67

CONTROL POINT	DESCRIPTION	TOTAL UNITS TO BE PRODUCED	SCHEDULED OUTPUT TO DATE	ACTUAL OUTPUT TO DATE	VARIANCE UNITS	(O/O)	SCHEDULED COMPLETION DATE	PROJECTED COMPLETION DATE(OR TE)	VARIANCE (WEEKS)
2002	PERFORM DESIGN REVIEW	36	36	36		0.0	21OCT66	21OCT66	0.0
5002	FABR. BALLISTIC SHELL	32	32	32		0.0	18FEB67	18FEB67	0.0
7001	FABRICATE 32 MOTORS	36	36	33		0.0	11FEB67	11FEB67	0.0
7001	ASSEMBLE SHELL	36	36	25	-3	-8.0	2MAR67	2MAR67	0.0
8002	CAST GND VEHL COMPONENTS	30	30	23	-11	-30.0	4NOV66	4NOV66	0.0
10002	ASSEMBLE ENGINES	36	36	36	-7	-23.0	8DEC66	8DEC66	0.0
10002	FAB GND VEHL CHASSIS					0.0	22DEC66	22DEC66	0.0
11001	ASSEMBLE TEST JIG					0.0	12NOV66	12NOV66	0.0
11001	DUMMY					0.0	22DEC66	22DEC66	0.0
11001	DUMMY					0.0	18FEB67	18FEB67	0.0
13001	ASSEMBLE GROUND VEHICLE	36	36	20	-16	-44.0	23MAR67	17JAN67	9.5
13001	PERFORM DIMENSION CK	36	36	29	-7	-19.0	23FEB67	23FEB67	0.0
14001	ASSEMBLE GUIDANCE	36	36	36		0.0	4MAR67	4MAR67	0.0
14001	TEST GROUND VEHICLE					0.0	8MAR67	8MAR67	0.0
14001	ASSEMBLE AIR VEHICLE	36	30	32	+2	+7.0	8APR67	28MAR67	1.9

FIG. 9. Production status report.

THE REPORT IS SORTED BY
1ST KEY= PRED.
2ND KEY= SUCC.

PROJECT PERT LOB TEST CASE	REPORTING ORGN.	CONTRACT NO.	REPORT DATES
			TERMS (SPAN)ENTIRE PROJ
NETWORK NUMBER -0	TECH APPT	42605	CUT-OFF DATE 28MAR67
SUB-NET NUMBER -0			RELEASE DATE 28MAR67

PRED EVENT	SUCC EVENT	ACTIVITY DESCRIPTION	RATE	UNIT NR.	BATCH NR.	ELPSD TIME	EXPECTED DATE	LATEST DATE	SCHED DATE	ACTUAL DATE	PRIM SLACK	SECD SLACK	DEPT.	TL*
1001	2002	PERFORM DESIGN REVIEW				3.0	21OCT66	16NOV66		21OCT66	3.6	3.0		11NOV66
2002	3001	PROCURE MISSLE COMPONENT				4.0	18NOV66	15DEC66		18NOV66	3.6	3.0		10DEC66
2002	8002	CAST GND VEHL COMPONENTS		18	1	1.0	28OCT66	27DEC66		28OCT66	8.2	7.6		22DEC66
			18.0	18	2	1.0	4NOV66	13JAN67		4NOV66	9.7	9.3		11JAN67
3001	4002	FABRICATE 4 MOTORS		4	1	1.6	1DEC66	27DEC66		1DEC66	3.6	3.4		24DEC66
				32	2	0.0	18NOV66	31DEC66		18NOV66	6.0	5.8		30DEC66
3001	5002	FABR. BALLISTIC SHELL		6	1	3.4	14DEC66	17JAN67		14DEC66	4.7	3.0		4JAN67
				6	2	2.0	28DEC66	17JAN67		28DEC66	2.7	1.0		4JAN67
				6	3	2.0	11JAN67	26JAN67		11JAN67	2.2	0.5		14JAN67
				6	4	1.8	24JAN67	9FEB67		24JAN67	2.4	2.1		8FEB67
				6	5	2.0	7FEB67	10FEB67		7FEB67	0.6	0.3		9FEB67
			3.3	6	6	1.8	18FEB67	18FEB67		18FEB67	0.0	0.7		24FEB67
4002	6002	STATIC TEST MOTOR 3		3		0.8	7DEC66	31DEC66		7DEC66	3.6	3.4		30DEC66
5002	7001	ASSEMBLE SHELL		9	1	2.4	13JAN67	2FEB67			2.7	1.0		20JAN67
				9	2	1.9	25JAN67	9FEB67			2.2	0.5		27JAN67
				9	3	1.7	18FEB67	23FEB67			0.6	0.3		21FEB67
			10.0	9	4	1.5	2MAR67	2MAR67			0.0	0.7		7MAR67
5002	11001	DUMMY		1	1	0.0	14DEC66	17FEB67			9.3	0.0		
				1	2	0.0	14DEC66	17FEB67			9.4	0.0		
				1	3	0.0	14DEC66	18FEB67			9.5	0.0		
				1	4	0.0	14DEC66	18FEB67			9.6	0.0		
				1	5	0.0	14DEC66	21FEB67			9.7	0.0		
				1	6	0.0	14DEC66	21FEB67			9.8	0.0		
				1	7	0.0	28DEC66	22FEB67			7.9	0.0		
				1	8	0.0	28DEC66	22FEB67			8.0	0.0		
				1	9	0.0	28DEC66	23FEB67			8.1	0.0		
				1	10	0.0	28DEC66	23FEB67			8.2	0.0		
				1	11	0.0	28DEC66	24FEB67			8.3	0.0		
				1	12	0.0	28DEC66	24FEB67			8.4	0.0		
				1	13	0.0	11JAN67	25FEB67			6.5	0.0		
				1	14	0.0	11JAN67	25FEB67			6.6	0.0		
				1	15	0.0	11JAN67	28FEB67			6.7	0.0		
				1	16	0.0	11JAN67	28FEB67			6.8	0.0		
				1	17	0.0	11JAN67	1MAR67			6.9	0.0		
				1	18	0.0	11JAN67	1MAR67			7.0	0.0		
				1	19	0.0	24JAN67	2MAR67			5.3	0.0		
				1	20	0.0	24JAN67	2MAR67			5.4	0.0		
				1	21	0.0	24JAN67	3MAR67			5.5	0.0		
				1	22	0.0	24JAN67	3MAR67			5.6	0.0		
				1	23	0.0	24JAN67	4MAR67			5.7	0.0		
				1	24	0.0	24JAN67	4MAR67			5.8	0.0		

FIG. 10. Activity report.

CONCLUSION

To recapitulate, PERT/LOB greatly broadens the useful area of application of both PERT and LOB by combining the most desirable features of each—the planning of PERT and the control of LOB. Inclusion of the capability to handle learning enables management to carry out still broader and more realistic planning and control.

PERT/LOB is usable in any situation in which PERT or LOB has application. If no repetitive activities are present, the result will essentially be PERT; if no one-time activities are present, the result will essentially be LOB. Most situations, as we know, represent some midpoint between these two extremes. It is for these situations that PERT/LOB is specifically designed.

The availability of a computer program makes it easier to manage the operation of a PERT/LOB system. A suitable computer program also makes it practical to include cost data, as is done in the PERT/Cost approach. In fact, if a computer program could be developed that would integrate the key cost data of both PERT/Cost and PERT/LOB, we might well see the fourth generation in PERT systems—what might be called PERT/LOB/Cost. Such a system would enable integrated time and cost planning and control from the early stages of product development through to quantity production.

45. SYSTEMS ANALYSIS IN GOVERNMENT OPERATIONS

GUY BLACK*

Non-defense Federal government departments and agencies are in the second year of program development and budgetary review in the context of a program packaging structure, in which activities with related objectives are grouped in common packages for analytical and budgetary purposes. One advantage in this approach is that activities can then be cost-benefit traded relative to a simplified objective structure. Where activities are complex and interrelated, it is particularly useful to develop a system concept as the framework for analysis.

This paper seeks to introduce the concepts and methodology of systems analysis as applied to non-defense government operations. It places systems analysis in the context of an overall systems approach intended to develop and implement the best possible system configuration. A broad overview is presented of the problems of objectives, model building, quantification of system parameters, ambiguities in concepts of benefit, cost, and optimization. The organizational problem of integrating system analysis and program packaging concepts is discussed, particularly for an agency characterized by bottom up planning, extensive and detailed routine budgeting, including comments on control of suboptimization of systems analytical capability directly supporting top management and supporting analytical capability throughout the organization.

THE CURRENT SCENE

The term "Systems Approach," which suggests a meaningful integration of activities, is closely associated with spectacular programs of large size. The systems approach is often described in a manner endemic to many professions, that profession X is what X-ists do. Others describe the bricks and mortar of a systems structure, without describing the structure itself. It is inherent in systems work that relatively few of those whose efforts are integrated by systems management need understand the overall system or the manner in which their particular efforts are integrated with those of others. (Misunderstanding is common even among those who legitimately claim experience with the systems approach.)

In recent years the Federal government has sought to cope more successfully with large, complex and interacting problems, and to obtain suitable analytical and managerial machinery for this purpose. Part of this process is the current drive to make use of program packaging and budgeting methods throughout government. The need for an accurate and deep understanding of what these new approaches entail is very great. The systems approach must supplement existing skills within the framework of an existing bureaucratic structure. Administrators have need to communicate successfully with systems practitioners. A principal purpose of this paper is, therefore, to give some insight into the purposes which systems analysis can serve in government, its methods, pitfalls and problems.

The conditions for more frequent application of systems capability to nondefense government are currently very favorable. The support for such methods is strong at high levels in government. The enactment of new legislation has given new missions to many agencies. Established programs are being reexamined. A government-wide planning, programming and budgeting system implemented by Budget Bureau Bulletin No. 66-3, requires department and agency heads to establish an adequate central staff for analysis, planning, programming and budgeting, to structure their activities by broad categories or "packages"

SOURCE: *Management Science* (October, 1967), pp. 41–58. Reprinted by permission of Institute of Management Science.

* The George Washington University.

and to evolve comprehensive multi-year plans within the framework of the program structure [20]. It is quite apparent that the Bulletin envisages a considerable increase in the analytical content that Federal agencies will use in developing their programs.

A BRIEF DESCRIPTION OF THE SYSTEMS APPROACH

The systems approach is operational in the sense that it seeks to bring to fruition a complex result in which the interactions between major elements have been carefully worked out. The approach itself is complex: if "approach" is taken to mean the overall process, a number of system-oriented specializations may be identified. Systems management itself is overall in concept, facing different tasks as a program of systems development moves from system conceptualization to system analysis to system engineering to ultimate fruition in a functioning and hopefully optimized system. In the large, the managerial technique for organizing and managing the implementation of a new system may be the most important result of military systems experience.

It would be misleading to offer a definition of the systems approach with any pretense that it would be universally understood. First of all, it is not useful to use the term to describe what may be produced by a small team. Second, for the term to serve any useful purpose, it must not encompass all management of complex and large scale activity, but must serve to distinguish some types from some others.

The most useful distinctions are in the manner in which analysis is used in support of management and the manner in which responsibility for design and implementation is concentrated. Analysis is pervasive. Analytical support does not stop with the design of a system, but continues until the design is brought to fruition. Continuing analysis provides the means for continuous re-evaluation and re-scheduling of an on-going program, as exemplified by program evaluation and review techniques (PERT).

Another important attribute of the systems approach, its approach to organizational control, comes to a head in the concept of a systems manager who has responsibility for cutting across traditional lines of responsibility. In manipulating the design and implementation of system attributes, he can avoid many of the conflicts which would be typical when a system is worked on by many groups for which some part of the system is only one of many responsibilities. Authority of such scope makes it meaningful to take into account broader-based trade-offs between system design, system operation, and system support, because the power exists to implement the results.

The system approach thereby opens the door for a tremendous expansion of analytical activity. And analysts have responded to the opportunities. A body of tools including means for integrating many small analyses has been developed. Techniques common in operations research and management science have been widely used. The resulting cross-fertilization has given impetus both to management science generally, and to systems analysis [12].

Systems Analysis

Systems analysis, in many ways the touchstone of the systems approach, is undertaken with a view to making possible rational decisions as to the design, selection or operation of a system. Ideally, analysis seeks clear identification jointly of one best system and the most efficient way of operating it.

Systems analysis has been notoriously hard to describe. One source of confusion is the distinction between the process of systems analysis and the *structure* of systems analysis. The process often displays the disorder and confusion which are common with ill-defined problem assignments. However, a completed system analysis will generally be found to be structured by phases, some of which supply inputs to other phases, and receive the outputs of others in turn. In retrospect, it may be a thing of beauty, but one should not look at the mess on the studio floor.

The first phase of a systems analysis is understanding and translating into analytically meaningful terms objectives that may be sought by some complex of equipment and/or activity, given the environment in which it is to operate. With this in hand, one can proceed in turn to (2) state in an analytically manageable way the general interrelations between variables—this amounts to construction of a model; (3) quantify the functional relationships between those variables and system output; (4) quantify the functional relationships between those variables and system inputs; (5) combine (3) and (4) into an overall input-output relationship that submerges intermediate relationships within the structure of the model; and (6) determine from the input-output relationships of optimum system design and the level of inputs and outputs that corresponds to an optimum operation of that system.

A systems analysis in the full sense is feasible only when each of the above steps is feasible. Even where one or more is not, system analytical *techniques* may greatly reduce the need for intuitive approaches and provide highly useful information on a system problem.

Systems Engineering

The above analysis seeks to create a broad framework of the system, taking account of what can be designed without actually undertaking that design. System analysis generates specifications that are design goals. There will be far too many design goals for any one engineering team to manage. Tasks must be subdivided and assigned to various groups. Systems engineering first becomes the major effort after the evolution of broadly stated system specifications from systems analysis. Following this, systems engineering undertakes to divide the overall task into sub-tasks. It makes assignments to various engineering groups so that each can operate in a restricted sphere with minimal concern for the manner in which other groups fulfill their tasks, except as their work affects the interaction between sub-systems being designed by various groups. Systems engineering has been well done if after every task is completed according to specifications, the results can then be smoothly integrated into a working over-all system.

In the interests of time, many parts of a system will be under design concurrently by different design groups. The solutions of the various groups must be watched as they interface each other. System engineering performs this overall coordinating role. It may also take principal responsibility for some aspects of design such as system weight, commonality of parts, reliability. It must, most of all, continually evaluate the evolving system vis-à-vis the objectives originally set for the system and the preceding systems analysis. During this phase, there may be some redoing of systems analysis, in support of system engineering.

That most of the design groups engaged in the detailed design of elements of a system can be directed at well-defined problems of limited scope is a powerful advantage which flows from systems engineering. A division of intellectual labor is achieved.

Systems Management

Systems management has the responsibility for ordering and phasing not only systems analysis and systems engineering, but the early step of interpreting the customer's objectives to system analysts and the later steps of moving the completed design from engineering to production, to testing, to the development of supportive systems (e.g., trained personnel) and to final use. It must schedule, control, and press the system forward, locating the requisite resources. How systems management differs from other management is most simply explained in the context of the modern industrial organization. Consider for the moment the flow of information and decision making in a hypothetical extremely centralized functionally structured organization. Although information may be exchanged horizontally between functions, power to make interfunctional decisions is restricted to the upper ends of each hierarchy. Coordination between functions must flow up to the top and back down.

The unworkability of such an extreme is obvious. Management is typically decentralized to some degree—often by the creation of a hierarchy of general managers who exercise authority over some multi-functional part of the organization at a lower level than the chief executive. When a *task* that has the scope of a system is the focal point for such an assignment, systems management has been created —and we are faced with the essence of the systems management approach. Systems management is a special application of decentralized management.[1]

Only in exposition are the phases of the systems approach separate. Systems analysis is continually a tool of systems engineering and systems management. Some of the inputs in the initial as well as follow-on systems analysis are obtained from systems engineering or specialized engineering groups. As the sys-

[1] See [19]. This simple statement does not do justice to the bulk and complexity of the literature on systems management.

tems evolve, systems analysis is further refined, with feedback effects perhaps on the very engineering groups that supplied the new information. And not uncommonly the customer changes his concept of what he wants in the light of information developed.

The Tools of Systems Analysis

One reason that systems analysis has been so hospitable to, and has borrowed extensively from, other disciplines, including economics, engineering, and operations research, is that systems analysts are usually transplants from one of these disciplines. A most interesting example is the way in which the engineering theory of servo-mechanisms has been adapted to describing the dynamic character of highly complex socio-economic relationships. Of great potential value, but not so fully exploited, are the extensive modeling activities of econometrics, with techniques for the simplification of functional relationships by treating a host of uninteresting minor variables as random elements. Developments in decision theory have been substituted for techniques which limited analysis to over-simplified statements of objectives. Linear programming has been widely used in problems where an optimum is sought within constraints.[2]

Setting aside important elaborations of method for the purpose of exposition, the concept of systems analysis can be communicated in simpler terms. One particular merit in emphasizing simple models is that in fact, for many socioeconomic activities of government, there is no tradition of analysis of system-wide scope. Much of value can be accomplished without the more difficult techniques.

THE PHASES OF SYSTEMS ANALYSIS

General

At the start of systems analysis there is a need to identify some group of objects and activities as a system, e.g., a ground transportation system, or alternatively, a system including air, sea, pipeline, and other means of transporting both passengers and freight. The proper system concept is not initially obvious. Typically, the first statement of the problem gives only a most general clue. Systems are not necessarily known as such in advance; indeed, delineating in an analytical manner a complexity of activity traditionally only known to be somehow related may be a highly creative act. Also, choosing the bounds of the system judiciously may go a long way toward making analysis efficient and to the point. Boundaries to limit a problem and simplification are essential, both to highlight what is relevant, and to reduce the complexity of reality to the scope of existing analytic methodology.

Stating Objectives

The first step in an analysis is stating objectives in the context of the applicable constraints, i.e., a definition of the problem which is rigorous enough for analysis to proceed. It is surprising how many programs do not have well-thought-out objectives, or have objectives that are available only as high-sounding but nonoperational concepts. To cast objectives in rigorous terms may bring about a deep searching examination of the reasons for an activity's very existence. In many activities, interaction with the environment is critical, either to exploit the environment, or to cope with it, and it is not unusual to discover that the interaction is very little understood.[3]

The complexity of objectives becomes obvious in this process. Multiple objectives are more common than not, and some inconsistency among them is so common as to be assumed. It is in such contexts that objectives must be stated. Some may be upper or lower limits that cannot be exceeded, while others may be traded off against each other.

The difficulty of handling objectives may lead the analyst to choose simplifications that, while reducing real-life problems to analytic feasibility, make the resulting analysis irrelevant for those charged with real-life responsibility. The closest possible contact between systems analysts and "top management" should be maintained during the problem definition phases of systems analysis. False starts resulting from wrong definition of problems are frequent. Because of the difficulty humans

[2] Chestnut [5] and Hall [8] present a sampling of the tools as seen by hardware-oriented systems analysts.

[3] Schelling [14] [16] develops these points further. Wherever opponent behavior reflects the characteristics of the system, employed system choice may usefully rely on game theory.

have in conceptualizing objectives until they become aware of their implications, i.e., the story of Midas, some iteration of problem definition is desirable—even efficient. New information may also lead to a recasting of the whole system concept.

A Jamming Model

The term "model" usually refers to a partially closed system of interrelated functions which thereby constitute a simplified representation of an existing or projected reality. It is often useful to present the model of a system as a block diagram. Such a presentation highlights interactions internal to the model and flows that connect the model with the outside world. It identifies the various inputs to a particular sub-system, which may be traded off against each other, and the division of outputs among several recipients. Circular flows of inputs and outputs in feedback loops may be developed. And alternative system concepts may have quite different internal "block box" structures. Typically, these flows are expressed in mathematical form in order to make use of the power of mathematical methods.

Manipulation of mathematically expressed relationships may be illustrated by a model of a hypothetical electronic jammer on a battlefield [2]. The objective of this system was to maintain a jamming electrical field of a certain level at a point in enemy territory. Solutions were wanted for system design; that is, what system can produce the field at minimum cost, including operating costs.

Some part of the model is derived directly from the laws of physics, such as jammer power required to produce a given field (proportional to the square of the distance), an output relationship. Others are empirical or engineering in nature, such as input relationships describing cost of the materials used to construct the jammer, approximated as a linear function of the power output; and the rate at which, due to attrition from enemy action, jammers must be replaced, which is taken as inversely proportional to the distance of the jammer from enemy lines. By combining several interconnected relationships, inputs and outputs for the system as a whole can be directly related.

Several questions pertinent to system design and operation can be stated more precisely. The design problem is:

(*a*) What output power should the jammer have?

and the operating problems are:

(*b*) How far should the jammer be placed from enemy lines?

(*c*) At what rate will jammers be destroyed by enemy action?

(*d*) What will be the cost of providing jamming continuously?

The essential relationships can be stated in the following form:

$$(1) \qquad P = aD^2$$

$$(2) \qquad C = b + cP$$

$$(3) \qquad R = d(D - t)^{-1} \quad D > t$$

$$(4) \qquad S = RC$$

where P is power of the jammer in watts;
D is distance from jammer to what is jammed in yards;
C is unit cost of jammers in dollars;
R is replacement rate of jammers in units per month; and
S is cost of maintaining jamming continuously in the face of attrition, in dollars per month.

The factors a, b, c, d, t are parameters of the particular relationships. For example, "t" represents the distance of the target of jamming behind the enemy lines.

The model can be solved by elementary calculus to indicate system cost per month equal to:

$$(5) \qquad S = (d/D - t)\,(b + caD^2)$$

and the distance D which is least cost is determined by $dS/dD = 0$, viz.,

$$(6) \qquad D_{\text{opt}} = t(1 + (1 + b(act^2))^{1/2})$$

This expression yields an additional unexpected result. Since zero is the minimum possible value of the parameters a, b, c and t, the minimum possible value of D_{opt} is $2t$ (t^2 goes to zero faster than t). Since "t" represents the distance behind enemy lines of whatever is jammed, the jammer should never be located closer to the enemy line than the "victim" of jamming is behind it.

This is an example of how a useful result

may sometimes be obtained from a model without any data at all. However, real-life coefficients and numbers must usually be substituted for abstract parameters. In practice, the systems analyst must rely on persons expert in technology or operations for these numbers. If engineers can specify that $a = 10^{-4}$ watts per square yard:

$$(1a) \qquad P = 10^{-4}D^2$$

This expression states, for example, that a 100-watt jammer could produce the specified electric field at 1,000 yards. Likewise, if cost analysts can specify that:

$b = \$10{,}000$, and $c = \$10$ per watt; the expression

$$(2a) \qquad C = \$10{,}000 + 10P$$

states that jammers cost a minimum of $10,000 each, the cost increasing by ten dollars for every watt of jammer output. Where d is 10,000 unit-yards per month and t is 100 yards,

$$(3a) \qquad R = 10{,}000\,(D - 100)^{-1}$$

These parameters mean that at a distance 10,000 yards from the enemy lines, the attrition rate would be one per month; at a distance of 1,000 yards, attrition would be 11, and so on.

The least operating cost occurs when jammers are placed 3,300 yards from the enemy lines, operating with a power of 1156 watts. Jammers would cost $21,560, and would have to be replaced at an approximate rate of three per month.

Models as a Means for System Design

A systems analyst's model does not primarily explain or predict the operation of an existing system, although it does take account of the operation as affected by system design. On the other hand, models are often constructed in economics for the analysis of an economy which exists, and will not be easily changed. The economist is in the position of a field commander who is given a jammer with a 1,156 watt transmitter, and has to locate it in the most effective spot. He would discover from an analysis of system operation that it should be operated at 3,300 yards.

A systems analysis is usually concerned, however, with selecting the characteristics of a system not yet built. The analyst will concern himself with the characteristics of a system—operated in a certain way—which would produce the best result. Systems analysis is especially useful where some fundamental change in existing arrangements, such as high speed ground transportation or an SST, is under consideration, even though analysis of existing systems to determine the optimum mode of operation can also be highly useful. The day-to-day analysis of optimum modes of operating refineries or electric power grids is akin to this type of analysis.

A useful model will always leave out minor effects that complicate the analysis and are believed a priori not to materially affect system design. The model builder may, however, be forced to simplify the model structure even more, where data are lacking or where factors that may well be important would result in an unmanageable analytic problem. Delayed feedback, in which system output affects the inputs, is frequently represented in over-simplified form for such reasons. It will seldom be entirely clear a priori what can be safely omitted, so it is always important, on the conclusion of a systems analysis, to examine the possible effects of whatever was left out.

As a practical matter, whether or not dynamic considerations or secondary factors should be taken into account depends on the depth of the a priori knowledge on which systems analysis seeks improvement. Where it is quite limited, the greater speed with which results can be obtained from relatively simple nondynamic models may be a strong argument for simplicity.

In a very real sense, an ability to treat system characteristics as variables is fundamental in systems design through systems analysis. To determine the range over which system characteristics can be varied is therefore a very important early step, and it may call for unusual breadth of exploration of technical possibilities. For example, available technical experts whose experience is with existing equipment may be familiar only with the input-output relationships for familiar equipment. The alternatives known to them may not include systems that are technically feasible, although not yet in existence. The practical question confronting the system analyst is, then, where to find an insight into the full range of systems, particularly configurations which deviate markedly from those with which the established experts are familiar. Some of the more successful systems analysts have been particularly adept at ferreting out possible system configurations outside the range of existing experience. Doing so usually means flying in the face of established practice, with the usual human problems.

There is considerable experience to demonstrate the inability of either technological experts or management groups to appreciate the technical potentialities for new system configurations. Burton Klein has commented on how far from the mark was the consensus on the feasibility of the jet aircraft engine. Starting in the 1920's, successive panels of experts reached increasingly gloomy conclusions right up to World War II, when a British company developed an experimental engine at a cost of about $25 thousand—about the amount that committees had spent arguing over the problem in ten years [11]. Klein must be correct in maintaining that the door should be left open to many technologies during the preliminary stages of analysis, and that a substantial portion of initial efforts should be directed broadly at fundamental research.

That systems analysts should take the initiative in seeking new technological solutions is very much in tune with current thinking on innovation and technological change. The outsider who invades an area of activity of previously established experts, bringing to bear information and technologies not previously considered, has been shown to be one of the powerful forces for change and innovation.[4] But frequently, when all is said and done, only a limited number of major systems types are possible. System characteristics may not be continuous variables, as transmitter power was in the example. If a road is to be built, it may have to be on one side of the river or the other.

Input-Output Relationships

Particular requirements must be met if mathematical models are to be solvable. The complexity of mathematical requirements, important to the practicing analyst, are only mentioned by way of warning.

Another often-overlooked requirement of model building is that two basic types of functional relationships are needed in system models, e.g., inputs and outputs. The reason deserves some emphasis. Inputs do not produce outputs directly: they are transformed into outputs by the technology of the system, as labor, leather and capital equipment would be transformed in a shoe factory. Thus, a model must contain functional relationships that relate:

- input requirements to the operation of a system, which may be expressed as costs;
- output from the operation of a system, which may be expressed as benefits or results.

The model finally combines separate input and output expressions into an over-all input-output expression in which the internal functioning of the system is the common link. The transformation process depends on the technology of the system. The system "machine" absorbs inputs according to its rate of operation, and ejects output according to that rate. An input function is, therefore, a statement of quantity of inputs as a function of rate, and an output statement is similarly a statement of output as a function of rate.

In order to use systems analysis for public policy purposes, a great deal must be known about such functional relationships in areas of social concern. For example, we have no workable function relating the level of juvenile delinquency to any particular quality of housing, although we know a great deal about how quality of housing is related to labor and material inputs.[5] But to seek an expression for a relationship between labor and materials and juvenile delinquency is less easy and less useful than seeking separate input and output relationships, each tied to system characteristics rather than directly to each other. No matter how well we can estimate the dollar cost of that housing, until the benefit function gap is filled, a system analysis of juvenile delinquency will be on a shaky footing.

Benefit Functions

The output of a system results in benefits, the amount of which depends on the quantity

[4] See [15]. This book reviews and consolidates much of current thought on innovation and diffusion of ideas.

[5] There are ways of using models or solving system models where functional relationships cannot be specified. A simulation exercise involving real people may be employed, for example.

and type of output. Where one type of benefit, easily measurable, is appropriate, the analyst is lucky; the assumption traditional to microeconomics that profit, measured in dollars, is the only result sought by business has this advantage. But increasingly, attention has been given to the complexity of the structure of benefits really sought. Particularly with government activities, the structure of benefits is complex and elusive.

A benefit function is the embodiment of the structure of benefits, and the manner in which one can be substituted for another without changing the combined benefit from all system outputs. Great care must be exercised that various benefits are incorporated into the function in order to obtain a true measure of the extent to which the complex of objectives is achieved. For example, benefit per unit of cost is not usually satisfactory in a typical analysis. Such a ratio is entirely different from net benefit (the difference between total benefit and total cost). Maximizing the ratio seldom maximizes net benefit. A common difficulty is that various system configurations quite commonly produce several benefits in different proportions.[6]

A number of techniques at least help. One is to agree on several combinations of outputs that are considered to produce equal total benefits, although the proportion of individual benefits may differ. Perhaps 10 apples and 12 oranges are considered to be as beneficial as 8 apples and 15 oranges. However, having agreed on this does not make it possible to compare the benefit of 10–12 with the benefit from 20 apples and 24 oranges, as benefits are subject to diminishing returns—and not necessarily at the same rate for apples and oranges. While the least cost of achieving either of two benefit levels can be determined with relative ease, unless we can legitimately reduce benefits to a common measure, it will not be possible to compute the *extra* benefit of the 20–24 combination as compared to a 10–12 combination. Unless we can compare benefits and costs, we will have difficulty saying whether 10–12 or 20–24 gives the greater *net* benefit.

A variation of the above approach is to specify several combinations of equal cost and select from them the one considered to yield the greatest benefit.[7]

Where the best way of achieving certain technical results can be established, without knowing how to measure the benefits from those results, another technique is useful. This halfway house can be illustrated by the problem of selecting enough spares for a new electronic system to keep it operating without shutdowns. Failure of electronic parts is a random event, such that there is always some finite probability that any number of spare parts may be exhausted. But this probability can be reduced by buying more spares; the point is to make the proper trade-off between reducing the risk of not having spares for whatever part needs replacement and spending money on spare parts. If the solution to the question of how far to go to avoid shutdowns is a value judgment, the analyst, as a technician, cannot objectively identify an optimum.[8]

However, for a given expenditure on spares, the less chance of running out the better. And the analyst can determine how the least likelihood of shutdown can be achieved by taking account of the failure rate of different parts relative to their cost. He can repeat this for many levels of expenditure and can combine all these determinations into a functional relationship in which the probability of adequacy of spares increases as a function of expenditure at a decreasing rate. Here his analysis reaches an end. The final value judgment on expenditure versus probability of adequacy properly belongs to someone else. But whoever makes that judgment has been relieved of any concern over the internal design of spare parts kits. By providing an uncluttered view of the way in which risk of shortage declines as a function of optimally allocated expenditure, the analyst has simplified the exercise of value judgment by eliminating purely technical considerations. It is implicit in this approach that

[6] See [7]. Another of the difficulties with multiple criteria of benefit is that various members of the organization will not have the same structure of values.

[7] The theory of benefit functions is closely related to welfare economics. In practice, the type of model used in a system analysis may be much influenced by the extent to which benefit levels can be compared. The survey in [8, Chapter 6] is useful. In [6, pp. 138–152] there is a useful suggestion as to how several criteria of benefit can be ranked and weighted.

[8] For a theoretical development and a numerical example, see [3].

the administrator does not care which part happens to fail—his objective is operation of the overall system.

Cost Functions

Statistical cost data, while descriptive of existing systems, are not really suitable for optimization studies. For example, if a cost analyst were to develop a regression from data on the number of nurses and the number of beds from 100 hospitals, he would obtain a description of an average relationship. However, about half of the hospitals would—by the inherent nature of the statistical technique—be found to have fewer nurses than would be predicted by the regression from the number of beds. The analysis tells nothing about nurse requirements in the efficient hospitals which are the concern in an optimizing problem. An envelope curve, falling along the lower boundary of a graphical representation of such data, would present a better picture of efficient hospitals.

A more suitable but more expensive approach would be to develop optimum staffing plans for a range of hospital sizes, the result to be summarized as a functional relationship. This kind of synthesis is usually the only way to obtain data on systems not found in real life, and it is often the best way to obtain optimized designs and associated costs even for real life systems.[9]

Optimization

In non-probablistic cost-effectiveness formulations, the configuration yielding the maximum net benefit (that is, gross benefit minus cost—on the assumption that the system will be operated as efficiently as possible) is typically the optimum system configuration.[10] For practical purposes, the optimum may be a configuration which apparently cannot be significantly improved upon, although it cannot be formally proved to be optimum. Frequently, the number of system configurations that can be fully explored is limited, and the "best" of these may be taken as the optimum, though strictly speaking, it is not. The term "satisficing" has been used to describe the cessation of optimizing efforts when further searching does not seem worth the effort. In short, the analytical effort of seeking a precise optimum often displays diminishing returns.

Sometimes the effects of arbitrary assumptions can be explored by sensitivity analysis. Not uncommonly, net benefits do not change markedly with small changes in system characteristics. Sometimes they are not sensitive even to drastic changes. There is always a danger that a so-called optimum merely follows from assumptions whose arbitrariness is concealed by analytical camouflage. The structure of a systems analysis will, for this reason, always be of concern to the decision-maker.

Quantification of Parameters

The data requirements of systems analysis can be very large. A systems model is a powerful aid in the design of data gathering programs in support of systems analysis, since it is the variables in the model for which data are needed; other data are mostly superfluous. The functional relationships in a model also indicate what data are relevant to decision-making.

The "marginal" characteristic of many systems choices further serves to reduce data needs. This happy result is likely where incremental changes from pre-existing systems, i.e., modifications of an existing system, are under consideration. Unfortunately, organizations with volumes of average cost data often have nearly no incremental cost data. It may sometimes be extracted from existing records, but often not. Much of the effort that goes into arbitrary allocations of fixed costs not only has no significance for systems analysis, but even substantially reduces the usefulness of data as published.

Systems analysts must sometimes face the need for expensive procedures for data generation. It has, of course, always been common in engineering to run multiple experiments to establish empirical relationships for the purpose of engineering design. Experiments for the sake of data are expensive. It is up to the analyst to show that experiments will contribute to system design commensurately with their cost. Even in non-systems-oriented Fed-

[9] See [1] and [4]. Also, [14, pp. 264–299] is quite informative on costing methods.

[10] Hall [8, Chapter II, pp. 297–320] and the lengthier works he references at the end of the chapter discuss probabilistic optimization in more detail.

eral programs, "demonstration projects" and "pilot projects" undertaken partly for the purpose of data generation are common. Too often, however, insufficient attention is paid to the "instrumentation" of such projects, and good data are not obtained.

Sensitivity analysis permits insights to be obtained concerning the required extent of data collection efforts to meet specified needs of statistical accuracy. This is accomplished by determining how sensitive the solution of the model is to errors in data. Models can be constructed which minimize data problems. Where many data are unavailable, the argument for a complete systems analysis may not be strong.

THE RELATION OF THE SYSTEMS APPROACH TO PROGRAM BUDGETING

PPBS and the Systems Approach

Program Packaging and Budgeting (PPBS) is a method of financial planning and control of government operations. It refers to the structuring of governmental activities into packages, composed of elements which can rationally be traded against each other on a cost-benefit basis. The packages themselves, with equal logic, can be cost-benefit traded off against other packages. If the elements of packages are consistent in objectives and in some sense are meaningfully associated, this packaging contributes to rational decision making. Within a package, it is presumed possible to trade-off the mix of contents with reduced need for concern over the internal content of other major packages. It is permissible also to trade-off package against package without undue concern over the internal content of any package.

It will be seen that the philosophy of PPBS and systems analysis have much in common. PPBS is properly called a system because it is composed of a number of semi-autonomous parts which interact with each other to achieve movement toward common objectives. In the most formal sense, the design objective of PPBS is the Federal Budget, with funds allocated among major programs, and within the structure of each program, in such a way as to provide an optimum result for a given overall expenditure. PPBS is properly called a planning system because it is designed to plan and control over time, a flow of costs and benefits that result from decisions at a point in time.

Program packaging tends to display in juxtaposition activities with similar objectives that in practice may be separately administered and subject to inconsistent program decisions. This was well illustrated by John Meyer's proposal to consider the interstate highway program, domestic navigation aids, FAA activities, and NASA's aircraft technology program as part of a common program package for intercity transportation [12, p. 108]. As Smithies points out [12, pp. 2–32], the manner in which budgets are structured does make a difference in the extent to which budgets can be reviewed and appraised rationally and appropriate trade-offs can be made. Meyer's arrangement immediately suggests questions of relative balance: Why, for example, should $3.8 billion be expended on general intercity transportation and only $0.8 billion on urban commuters?

Equally important is the change in the time perspective of the budget process. One-year budgeting of programs which include delayed benefits and future costs is not likely to make rational decision making easy. Program packaging also highlights the need and enhances the possibilities for deeper analysis. In the words of Smithies, program budgeting starts with the structuring of the problem and ends with the analysis of the data. The central objective of PPBS is to achieve an allocation of resources by rational means. These means employ marginal comparisons of incremental benefits from the expansion of particular programs with attendant incremental costs, and produce comparisons of the net change in benefit from shifting funds from one program to another.

Systems analysis can make its most effective contribution to PPBS below the program package level because of the manner in which governmental planning is conducted. The structure of government contains many activities legitimately but not easily defined as systems: public health, education, transportation, defense, and internal revenue. Program elements, which may be submerged as parts of program packages, can often be effectively treated as self-contained systems.

Whether systems analysis can often be used for the analysis of major program packages has been questioned by D. K. Price, who seems to doubt whether systems analysis and operations research are effective in the evaluation of broad aggregative program packages conceived in a political context.[11] The fundamental difficulty should be clear from previous comments. All steps—criteria, models, benefit and cost functions, data collection and optimization—become increasingly complex as packages encompass greater universes. Even in the Department of Defense, a small proportion of elements had been system-analyzed when the program package budget was first installed. The program-packaging framework will, in fact, absorb whatever intensity of analysis can be applied, but is sufficiently flexible not to demand any particular level.

Suboptimization and the Locus of Analysis

Historically, planning and budgeting have shown a continuing development. In consequence, the concepts of PPBS bear a meaningful relationship to other systems of planning and control. The end result of any planning carried to completion is a detailed guide to implementation. For practical purposes this is usually structured as subplans groups for various functions. Each group has its marching orders.[12]

The source of the details of a plan are, generally, quite close to the elements of an organization whose operations most effect or depend on those details. The germinal point for the initial development of an element (of an over-all plan) is likely to be fairly low in the hierarchy of the organization. The over-all plan emerges with the consolidation of the products of a bottom-up process. There are a number of reasons for this. One is that actually, in an on-going organization, most decisions as to the scope and nature of activities are highly similar to decisions that have been made routinely or, in the language of Herbert Simon, are programmed [17]. The needed technical information for unprogrammed decisions may exist only within the subordinate parts of an organization, remote from top management. Quite likely, if an organization is to use systems analytical techniques in support of its planning, it is there that the effort must be undertaken.

A great deal might be said about various organizational positions for a systems analytical capability. There are, in fact, arguments for close liaison with top management (so that it will be aware of the most vital objectives of the organization) and with lower echelons (where it will have the greatest impact on the choices made in the first round of planning). Placing systems analytical capabilities at several levels—as has been done to some extent in the Department of Defense—may be a better solution than having a single systems analysis group.[13]

However, even in the milieu of bottom-up planning, some central guidance as to objectives and goals is necessary. In the words of Bureau of the Budget Circular 66-3, "The entire system must operate within the framework of over-all policy guidance."

A systems analytical group associated with a managerial group whose responsibility is for less than the whole of an organization will tend to accept as its own the restricted objectives of that managerial group. This has been given the name "suboptimization," and it should not be surprising if the resulting analysis overlooks some effects for which it feels no responsibility.

In the context of systems management, this means that a headquarters systems analytical group, with the over-all objective firmly in mind, must work with groups which have been assigned more limited objectives. It must make sure that unhappy suboptimizations are avoided in systems analyses conducted at lower echelons.[14]

The term suboptimization has unfairly ac-

[11] See Price [13]. Alain Enthoven has commented that systems analysis has not been particularly useful in determining the allocation of funds among defense program packages. See also A. Wohlstetter's comments in [14, pp. 103–148].

[12] See Stedry [18]. Stedry has demonstrated experimentally the point that one function of budgets is to raise the level of aspiration. In short, a high degree of success in adhering to a plan may indicate that the plan was not sufficiently demanding.

[13] It is interesting, in retrospect, to read the comments in Hitch and McKean [10] on "excessive centralization of decision-making." Although the remarks are made with particular reference to research and development, they have perhaps a wider applicability.

[14] Hitch [9] has discussed the suboptimization problem. In an appendix to Hitch and McKean [10, pp. 396–402], Enthoven has discussed (in a rather mathematical way) the conditions under which decentralization and suboptimization are likely to work well.

quired a bad connotation. Indeed, suboptimization is essential to bring systems analysis to manageable proportions. Suboptimization will lead to faulty results only if systems analysts at lower echelons have their problems defined improperly. A headquarters management systems analysis group must take responsibility that the sum of suboptimizations adds to an over-all optimum by advising a lower echelon systems analytical group on the framing of its objectives, but it must do this in such a way that the lower echelons can concentrate on its subsystems without having to take into account the detail of other subsystems, or the system as a whole. How a major system is broken into subsystems will affect how well an optimum system design is achieved. Yet, specific performance criteria usually cannot be established until subsystem groups have given the headquarters systems analysis group the means for a systemwide optimization.

CONCLUSION

Casual readers of the literature on the systems approach are likely to confuse its principal elements; their close interrelationship makes this easy to do. *Systems Analysis,* particularly appropriate to cost-effectiveness analysis, has been recommended as a tool in PPBS. Yet other elements of the systems approach, including scheduling and control procedures (i.e., PERT), clearly have potential applicability to the management of multi-year programs of nondefense government.

Program budgeting and the systems approach are not the same, but they have an affinity for each other. Program packaging simplifies the comparisons of efforts with similar objectives and means. "Bottom-up" is the common rule; this is full of implications for systems analytical support for planning. Spillovers of costs or benefits—outside the scope chosen for the systems analysis—are an expected result of any less than global systems analysis.

The concept of a program budget, as outlined in the 1949 budgeting and accounting report by the Hoover Commission [21], pointed out that program budgets would expedite executive and legislative reviews on two principal counts:

First, on the desirable magnitude of any major government program or function in terms of need, relation to other programs and proportion of total government expenditures; second, by identifying the most efficient and economical of possible arrangements of the work.

Perhaps these recommendations were premature given the complexity of Federal government functions and the status of systems capability at the time. Experience with broad system concepts was then rare.

It is legitimate to inquire whether the experience presently available can not now be applied widely, and particularly to the newer programs. For this to happen, it will be necessary to treat as systems many related operations for which administrative responsibility is fragmented. The program packaging concept is significant pressure in that direction.

It is insufficient to consider systems analysis to be merely a generic name for a collection of techniques. A meaningful integration of a body of analyses directed to the design and implementation of a system is essential in any real systems analysis. While the quality of a systems analysis cannot be judged entirely from the quality of sub-analyses, it is certainly correct that a systems analysis cannot be meaningful if sub-analyses are not of high quality.

It would seem to be inherent in the whole concept of PPBS that the function of controllership is central in the managerial control of operations. A budget, while only a reflection of actual operations, is a powerful control device. One of the interesting possibilities in the PPBS approach is that it may require more rigorous justification of proposed activities and choke off many that cannot be justified because of the intractability of analysis, inadequacy of basic data, or unavailability of competent analysts. It can be argued that PPBS, by strengthening the hand of the financial end of management, is a force for caution and conservatism. The impact in the Federal government remains to be seen.

REFERENCES

1. Black, G., "Synthetic Method of Cost Analysis of Agricultural Firms," *Journal of Farm Economics,* Vol. 38 (May 1955), pp. 270–279.
2. ———, *Cost Considerations in the Evaluation of Electronic Countermeasure*

Systems, Report EDL-M109, Electronic Defense Laboratory, Mountain View, California, April 1957.

3. ———, and Proschan, F., "On Optimal Redundancy," *Operations Research,* Vol. 7 (1959), pp. 581–588.
4. Chenery, H. B., "Engineering Production Functions," *Quarterly Journal of Economics,* Vol. 63 (Nov. 1949), pp. 507–31.
5. Chestnut, H., *System Engineering Tools,* Wiley, New York, 1965.
6. Churchman, C. W., Ackoff, R. L., and Arnoff, F. L., *Introduction to Operations Research,* Wiley, New York, 1957.
7. Cyert, R. M., and March, J. F., *A Behavioral Theory of the Firm,* Prentice-Hall, Englewood Cliffs, N.J., 1963, pp. 26–36.
8. Hall, A. D., *A Methodology for Systems Engineering,* Van Nostrand, New York, 1962.
9. Hitch, Charles J., "Economics and Military Operations Research," *Review of Economics and Statistics,* Vol. XL, No. 3 (Aug. 1958), pp. 199–200.
10. ———, and McKean, R. N., *The Economics of Defense in the Nuclear Age,* Harvard University Press, Cambridge, Mass., 1960, p. 254.
11. Klein, B. N., in Tybout, R. A. (ed.), *Economics of Research and Development,* Ohio State University Press, Columbus, Ohio, 1965, p. 320.
12. Novick, D., ed., *Program Budgeting: Program Analysis and The Federal Budget,* Government Printing Office, Washington, D.C., 1965.
13. Price, Don K., *The Scientific Estate,* Harvard University Press, Cambridge, Mass., 1965, p. 126.
14. Quade, E. S., ed., *Analysis for Military Decisions,* Report R-387-PR, RAND Corporation, Santa Monica, California, 1964.
15. Roger, E. M., *The Diffusion of Innovations,* Free Press of Glencoe, New York, 1962.
16. Schelling, T. C., *The Strategy of Conflict,* Harvard University Press, Cambridge, Mass., 1960.
17. Simon, H. A., *The New Science of Management Decision,* Harper and Row, New York, 1960.
18. Stedry, A. C., *Budgetary Control and Cost Behavior,* Prentice-Hall, 1960, pp. 19–26.
19. U.S. Air Force, Systems Command, the 375 series of manuals.
20. U.S. Bureau of the Budget, "Planning-Programming-Budgeting," Bulletin 66–3, Oct. 12, 1965.
21. U.S. Commission on Organization of the Executive Branch of the Government, *Budgeting and Accounting: A Report to the Congress,* Government Printing Office, Washington, D.C., Feb. 1949, pp. 8–12.

BIBLIOGRAPHY

Archibald, Russell D., and R. L. Villoria, *Network-Based Management Systems,* John Wiley and Sons, 1967.

Cleland, David I., and William R. King, *Systems Analysis and Project Management,* McGraw-Hill Book Company, 1968.

Concepts Associated with Systems Effectiveness, Bureau of Naval Weapons, Navweps Report 8461, June, 1963.

Dooley, A. R., "Interpretations of PERT," *Harvard Business Review,* March-April, 1964.

Fazar, W., "Progress Reporting in the Special Projects Office," *Navy Management Review,* April, 1959.

Hill, Lawrence S., "Some Accounting Problems in PERT/Cost," *Journal of Industrial Engineering,* February, 1966.

Levy, F. K., G. L. Thompson, and J. D. Wiest, "The ABCs of the Critical Path Method," *Harvard Business Review,* September, 1963.

Miller, Robert W., "How to Plan and Control with PERT," *Harvard Business Review,* March, 1962.

Miller, Robert W., *Schedule, Cost, and Profit Control with PERT: A Comprehensive Guide for Program Management,* McGraw-Hill Book Company, 1963.

Neuwirth, S. I., "An Introduction to PERT," *The Journal of Accountancy,* May, 1963.

"New Tool for Job Management," *Engineering News-Record,* January, 1962.

PERT Summary Report, Phase I, Department of the Navy, Bureau of Naval Weapons, Special Projects Office, 1958.

PERT Fundamentals, Washington: PERT Orientation and Training Center, 1963.

Phelps, H. S., "What Your Key People Should Know About PERT," *Management Review,* October, 1962.

Ramo, Simon, "Weapons Systems Management," *California Management Review,* Fall, 1958.

Roman, D. D., "The PERT System: An Appraisal of Program Evaluation Review Technique," *The Journal of the Academy of Management,* April, 1962.

Rosenweig, James, "The Weapons Systems Management and Electronic Data Processing," *Management Science,* January, 1960.

Ross, W. R., "Accounting Aspects of PERT/Cost," *Management Accounting,* April, 1967.

———, "Evaluating the Cost of PERT/Cost," *Management Services,* September-October, 1966.

Schoderbek, Peter P., "PERT/Cost: Its Values and Limitations," *Management Services,* January-February, 1966.

———, "The Sociological Problems of PERT," in Peter P. Schoderbek (ed.), *Management Systems, A Book of Readings,* John Wiley and Sons, 1967.

Schoderbek, Peter P., "PERT: Its Promise and Performance," *Michigan Business Review,* **17**, January, 1965, pp. 25–32.

———, and Lester A. Digman, "Third Generation in PERT Systems," *Academy of Management, Proceedings of the 27th Annual Meeting,* State College, Pennsylvania, 1968, pp. 195–200.

Thompson, V., "PERT: Pro and Con About This Technique," *Data Processing*, October, 1961.

U.S. Air Force Systems Command, *USAF PERT/Cost System Description Manual*, AFSC PERT Control Board, March-December, 1963.

U.S. Air Force Systems Command, *USAF PERT/Time System Description Manual*, Government Printing Office, 1963.

SECTION III

REAL-TIME SYSTEMS

In a previous section concerned with the design of information systems it was pointed out that one of the important elements of such a system was the feedback component. There it was stated that for information to be useful it must decrease the degree of uncertainty surrounding decision making. Such information, if timely, concise, and meaningful, could provide managers with nearly all the decision-making tools necessary to run the company. While present-day computer systems cannot quite live up to these expectations, such a goal may not be unrealistic within a decade. For with computer science feeling at ease in its seven-league boots, the ideal process of converting available business data into timely, concise, and meaningful information may be near at hand.

We have already seen that the new breed of manager is a systems man who is more of a problem-solver and less of a specialist than his former counterpart. Whereas his predecessor relied heavily on intuition and the "feel of the market" for correlating and integrating the many facets of the business concern, the manager of today utilizes the electronic computer to assess the ever-changing relationships of the variables involved. Besides supplying him with the historical accounting and financial data, it can also provide him with "real time" information—instantaneous information.

A real-time system can be defined as one in which the results of the system are available in sufficient time to effect the decision-making process. It does this by being tied in to "live" operations. In some cases this will mean supplying the decision maker with data that truly reflects conditions as they are developing. In other situations the information generated need not be instantaneous; it suffices that the information be timely enough to be useful for decision making. A real-time system thus classifies and integrates data from several different sources, and when called upon, can divert to managers the necessary information in a concise and meaningful form.

With computerized real-time systems it is now possible to utilize simulation models to ascertain the impact of various alternative decisions before actually committing oneself (sometimes irrevocably) to a specific course of action. Dozens of possible situations or combinations of such can be simulated when management is provided with a continuous flow of real-time information. With such computerized business operations at his disposal, the manager of today will surely become a manager of "situations."

While most of the some 15,000 computer installations are still oriented to the processing of routine data and clerical operations, there is a growing realization among the new breed of managers of the vast potential available with real-time systems. The demonstrated success of the widely heralded SAGE and SABRE programs has caused many an organization to strike out in new directions the better to get the advantage over its competitors.

Against the background of information technology, with all its attendant perplexities, Donald Malcolm outlines some of the problems that faced the designers of the SAGE system and the solutions now incorporated in it. In doing so he offers business managers concerned with the issues of design, implementation, and control, valuable parallels taken from military systems. Before doing so, however, he details the four major uses of electronic computers in the management process. He does this to offset the situation, both unfortunate and unfortunately too common, in which computers are used improperly, tapping at most one-tenth of their potential.

Computers can be used as a data-processing tool in the routine automation of existing information, in communication, and in reporting and control systems; as a design tool in problem solving in the research and design of management control systems, in policy determination, and in planning studies; as a training tool in presenting educational and simulation exercises; and finally, as an on-line controlling device for effective decision making.

It is in real-time control, communication, and information systems that computers come into their own. In real-time *control,* information is instantaneously transmitted to a centralized computer that processes it, compares it with predetermined decision criteria, and issues instructions for corrective action if necessary. In real-time *communication,* the output informs the affected parties as it is developed by the computer, and in real-time *management information,* suitable summarizations of the information are prepared, transmitted, and displayed to high-level management. These are all *real-time* systems, since their elements are controlled instantaneously and not after the fact. The best known examples of real-time systems are to be found in the military.

Two such systems are indicated: SACCS (Strategic Air Command Control System) and SAGE (Semi-Automatic Ground Environment). Only the latter, a continental air command and warning system, is detailed in the remainder of the article.

The SAGE system functions as a vast network of air-defense centers. It not only receives information from multiple sources and processes and displays this information rapidly, but it also issues battle orders to jet interceptors and to other air-defense weapon systems. All aircraft flights in and near the continental United States are monitored on the "exception principle." This is indeed a big order, and to carry it out, six general requirements for air defense control are explicated: provide positive recognition of an air attack; be operable as a man-machine system immediately upon installation and at high efficiency; be operable with high reliability on a continuous basis; provide up-to-the-minute status of defense capability; be capable of issuing immediate and appropriate defense instructions; and be adaptable to an ever increasing air-defense weapons capability.

How these diversified requirements were met is then interestingly unfolded. Of course, automation or semiautomation was the key to these operations.

Twenty-six SAGE sectors are organized into seven SAGE divisions. In each sector there is a direction center for receiving information from many sources in the area. The direction center also outputs data to certain weapons, to adjacent direction centers, to radar sites, to teletype circuits, and the like. At each divisional level there is a combat center with about the same functions and equipment as in the direction centers. However, it is the direction center that is the smallest self-sufficient component in the SAGE system. Here the man-machine interfacing takes place in four principal areas: manual data input room, air-surveillance section, identification section, and weapons-direction section.

To insure maximum reliability and maintainability, two computers are provided. About 100,000 individual instructions are programmed for defense, but when one considers those involved in system training and in the production of the programs themselves, the number comes to something like one half million. The SAGE computers have on-line control features, decision-making features, display features, provision for simulation, error-correction features, and data-processing features.

The heart of the article is in the application of the SAGE experience to the design of management control systems. First of all, a systems-engineering approach was used. Designing the SAGE system took several years. Here the primary focus was on system requirements. These were carefully and precisely ascertained. Steps to follow are outlined in order: establish criteria for management-information needs, make a preliminary system design, evaluate, and test the design. Once the system is installed, debugging, modification, and extension of the system round out the process.

Perhaps what is unique about the SAGE system is its systems-training approach. Training in SAGE involves elaborate computer simulations of a predicted attack environment. Proficiency is judged not on an individual basis but by measures in the total system context. Here is where management could learn a lesson. If simulation exercises, along with appropriate criteria for evaluating individual performance in relation to the total system performance, were incorporated in management control systems, their acceptance would be greater and their ultimate efficiency considerably enhanced.

The SAGE system does represent a high degree of centralization of activities. This was brought about by the creation of a system manager's office invested with managing the efforts of the systems analysts, designers, manufacturers, programmers, and trainers. Business managers could well look on the possible effects of such centralization on the organization. To achieve such recentralization, they would have to permit the systems designer to eliminate certain functions.

On-line integrated computer operation is indeed possible, as witnessed by SAGE, but whether this feature is always feasible for routine management functions only a systems analysis can reveal. Management by exception, another SAGE characteristic, could and should find greater applicability in the managerial world. Fast simulation of possible alternative courses of action can help sharpen managerial decisions. As pointed out elsewhere, all of this requires precise formulation of objectives, translation of these into operational terms that are programmable on the computer, and the like. What seems to be needed is a team of many skilled specialists not only in systems design and management but also in such fields as mathematics, statistics, and psychology.

In R. W. Parker's reading, the SABRE system is discussed in some detail. This is American Airlines' real-time passenger-reservation system. Besides giving some general idea of what the system does, Parker details the three major elements of the system: the input/output devices used at reservation and ticket sales desks, the electronic reservations center with its two IBM 7090 computers, and the communication network consisting of more than 31,000 miles of leased facilities and about 50 terminal interchanges. The development and implementation of this very complex system with regard to the hardware, software, and personnel involved is interestingly depicted and the discussion of the practical difficulties encountered that follows is both frank and illuminating.

In his selection, "The Myth of Real-Time Management Information," John Dearden not only seriously questions the utility of a real-time *information* system for top management and the practicality of a real-time management *control* system but he raises grave doubts about the worth of a real-time system in other areas of concern for top managers. His estimate of the real-time system is succinctly expressed in the concluding sentence of his introduction, ". . . of all the ridiculous things . . . foisted on the long-suffering executive in the name of science and progress, the real-time management information system is the silliest."

Dearden launches into the battle by first attacking the semantic confusion and vagueness that too often appears in the literature when real-time information systems are cursorily defined. That this is not something unique to real-time information systems is nowhere intimated. He fails to mention that the same situation holds for the very concept of systems as such or, for that matter, for the concept and definition of cybernetics, automation, etc., and for some of the behavioral sciences themselves, like sociology, social psychology, and perhaps for business management too.

He then proceeds to identify the "real-time system" with a computer system possessing certain definite characteristics: a computer that can be interrogated from remote terminals and with "on-line" data that will be updated as events occur. What these "events" are he does not specify. He further limits the application of the concept to data stored either in the computer memory itself or at least in random access files, thus specifically excluding all data stored on magnetic tapes. The reason for this is not any intrinsic characteristic of real-time systems but the increasingly less expensive new generation of computers now available, together with the latest advances made in data transmission equipment and techniques.

He further limits the subject under discussion by restricting "top management" to the "president and executive vice president in centralized companies, plus divisional managers in decentralized companies." The entire discussion that follows is thus predicated upon these initial definitions and delimitations of "real-time systems for top management." One must keep these definitions in mind when perusing the article.

One cannot, of course, question Dearden's right to define these terms the way he does. Definitions, after all, are but the basic assumptions from which one wishes to begin a discussion. But to be optimally meaningful and useful to others, a definition should be neither too broadly nor too narrowly conceived. This is but in keeping with the cardinal rules of logic pertinent to definitions. One can therefore level the same indictment against him that he leveled at the authors of the definitions that he himself deplored. Theirs were too broad; his are too narrow!

In the subsequent sections Dearden considers the general functional categories of top management and their applicability to real-time systems. Six categories are singled out: management control, strategic planning, personnel planning, coordination, operating control, and personal appearances. The last of these could well be equated with *social functioning,* since it involves such things as entertaining visiting dignitaries, giving out 25-year watches, etc. Only the first five categories are assumed to have any bearing on real-time management information systems, and each is in turn measured against the yardstick of real-time practicality and found wanting.

As for management control involving, as it must, an objective, a system of evaluating performance, and an "early warning" system, Dearden not only cannot see how a real-time information system can be used but also rejects the belief that any attempted use would enhance control. Strategic long-range planning fares no better. A real-time information system will not appreciably help matters. The much-proclaimed use of models, of computer simulation, of interaction with the computer are all dismissed. Personnel planning, it is true, can be facilitated by the use of timely computer-spewed information, but whether it should be so employed, especially when visual displays are involved, is the big economic question. A real-time system, according to Dearden, is neither necessary nor useful for the solution of the coordination problems typically facing top management. Because most top executives spend only a modicum of their time on operating functions, it seems apparent that a real-time information system operating from their offices would be difficult to justify monetarily.

One must admit, that given the narrowly circumscribed definitions that Dearden outlines, these conclusions can logically be deduced. However, the wisdom of thus proceeding is questioned when one realizes that there is nothing in the nature of real-time systems that demands that expensive computer facilities be employed solely and directly for the president, vice president, and divisional managers. If one admits, as Dearden seems to, that staff specialists can well be entrusted with the task of developing models, of computer simulation, etc., not continuously but at particular moments in time, and of reporting the results back to top executives, then decisions reached on the basis of these results must be considered related in a meaningful, albeit expensive way to model building, computer simulation, and the rest.

After carefully weighing the pros and cons of replacing the traditional published reports for management by console and display device manipulation by top executives to obtain desired information, Dearden discusses what he considers the three major fallacies upon which the desirability of real-time information systems rests: improved control, scientific management, and logistics similarity. The myth of improved control is grounded partly on the feeling of insecurity that managers often experience with regard to the imperfect type of control that they exert and partly on the glittering promise that knowing everything that happens when it is happening will help ameliorate the situation. Real-time systems will not eliminate this feeling of insecurity. The myth of scientific management is based upon the assumption that the only scientific way to manage is by using a computer. The fallacy of logistics similarity is founded on the belief that management control systems are but higher manifestations of logistics systems. Any real-time system is a logistics system in which rapidity in handling and transmitting a vast amount of data is an essential prerequisite. Such rapid processing and transmitting of voluminous amounts of data are not, in Dearden's view, a critical factor in management control systems.

With an eye to the near future, five to seven years distant, Dearden predicts that real-time information systems will be of little use in improving management control. As for the more distant future, some fifteen to twenty years hence, the question is quite different. Some experts believe that the new breed of manager will function in a peopleless, paperless office, with only his thoughts and his computer terminal and visual display devices. But since God alone can know with certainty what the next two decades will bring, one cannot say that these dreams of experts will not become a reality or that they will not remain what they now are—pipe dreams. Dearden rightly urges executives to use caution, to be open-minded to suggestions for improving management information systems but at the same time not to precipitously discard the tried and proven methods now in use. Over two centuries ago the famous poet and critic, Alexander Pope, gave somewhat similar sensible advice:

Be not the first by whom the new are tried,
Nor yet the last to lay the old aside.

After Dearden's searing condemnation of real-time systems, it should come as no great surprise to find disciples of real time rise to its defense. Mr. Head, who is himself a champion and noted writer of real-time systems, wastes little time in shadow boxing, but immediately sheds his robe and commences sparring with his opponent. His first blows land on the initial premises that Dearden says constitutes a real-time system. The attack is well planned and executed and obviously accomplishes its purpose. He then exchanges verbal blows with Dearden with respect to the managerial functions outlined by his opponent. These are taken up one by one and shown to be wanting. One need not be a ring official to pass verdict on the outcome. Some good arguments, to be sure, were voiced by both men, but the gambling type of individual has long since collected his bet.

46. EXPLORING THE MILITARY ANALOGY—REAL-TIME MANAGEMENT CONTROL

DONALD G. MALCOLM*

Many writers have described the era of "information technology" our society is now entering as one wherein the capability to formulate decision criteria precisely and to process information electronically will create markedly new patterns in management. Prognostications include a trend toward recentralization of many management functions, toward semiautomated management, and toward an organizational philosophy formed around the precise information and communication needs of the activity.

This chapter explores how far we have come in learning to "design" optimum management controls, and presents the thesis that the prototypes of integrated and automated management functions are perhaps first being experienced in the current development of such real-time military control systems as SAGE and SACCS. A study of approaches and solutions to the design problems of these military systems offers some valuable parallels to the design problems in business management controls. In the following pages, some of the problems that faced the designers of the SAGE system will be examined, along with some of the solutions now embodied in the system. Finally, a plan to bring experience in military control systems to bear on research at SDC in business management control systems will be discussed.

However, before turning to this task, it is necessary to establish some points of reference in regard to current uses of electronic computers in the management domain.

SOURCE: *Management Control Systems,* John Wiley and Sons, 1960, pp. 187–207. Reprinted by permission of John Wiley and Sons.

* Systems Development Corp.

USES OF ELECTRONIC COMPUTERS

In the rush to apply computers to the automation of existing information systems, the task of redesigning a given system so as to be consistent with an integrated total company information-communication need is generally not undertaken. Rather, an application is made in one component of the organization with little attention given to the total company system beyond a compatibility check. While this approach may be justified on grounds that improvements of this size and scope must start modestly and build gradually and surely, there is a growing recognition of some of the suboptimal results that can occur. Thus, electronic computers are not being used in ways that tap even one-tenth of their ultimate potential in the management process—particularly in industry. The situation will become a matter of greater concern to the users of computers as the nature of this potential and the means of achieving it become better recognized. In short, the situation will appear to get worse before effective long-range programs are designed and under way.

An examination of the four major uses of computers in the management process will help to elaborate on the above statement. The major uses of computers are:

- As *a data-processing* tool in the automation of the information, in communication, and in reporting and control systems.
- As *a design tool* in problem solving in the research and design of management control systems, in policy determination, and in planning studies.
- As *a training tool* in presenting training exercises.
- As *a controlling device* in decision making—an "on-line" controlling device.

For the purpose of this discussion, a management control system is defined as a set of policies, procedures, and information processing which is designed to give direction to activities by clearly establishing goals, by measuring progress toward these goals, and by indicating or initiating corrective action. Over the years, management has developed several approaches for providing control. Typical methods have included organization, planning, scheduling, inventory, quality, cost, and manpower controls. It is significant to note that each of these is a component or function of the establishment and that the concept of integrated total system control still remains virtually unexploited.

A Data-Processing Tool

Since the first installation of a large-scale electronic computer strictly for business use in 1954, at General Electric in Louisville, there has been a mushroom-like growth in the application of computers to the routine automation of existing information, communication, personnel, and data reporting systems, such as payroll, inventory position and control, production release, and invoicing systems. Of the over 650 million dollars worth of computers installed by mid-1959 and the 600 million dollars worth of equipment on order, it has been estimated that up to 90 per cent of machine time will be used for applications in these areas.

It should be pointed out that most of the systems being automated are not evaluated for the purpose of determining whether or not they best perform the function for which they were initially designed. The majority of such computer installations are undertaken for the purpose of reducing time in report preparation or in an attempt to effect clerical savings.

A Design Tool

The computer is being used increasingly as the vehicle for research in the design of management control systems and for policy determination. Another important use is in operations research studies, where complex analyses can only be performed efficiently and in a timely manner on the computer. These studies can, therefore, be categorized into two broad approaches—complete analytical formulation of a complex problem, and computer simulations to solve problems experimentally.

Analytical formulations of problems using approaches such as linear programming have in many cases been built into the on-going control of operations. In a like manner, the simulation approach has been useful as indicated by the considerable number of projects undertaken in systems design and evaluation, systems research, and planning and training.[1] The use of analyses of this type will be necessary for on-line management controls to provide the predictive capabilities desired by management.

A Training Tool

There is a growing utilization of computers in the area of education and training. Simulation exercises are proving to be a most effective way of posing realistic, fast reacting system problems to business studies, managers, and executives. The "automated case history" approach provides the immediacy and realism needed to obtain real involvement and the motivation on the part of the trainee. It is evident that system training in large, new systems will necessitate appropriate computer simulation training exercises in order to assure effective introduction of these systems.

A Controlling Device

At present, only exploratory work is underway in using the computer directly in management decision making. In this category of usage the computer may be viewed as an "on-line" or "in-line" controller—operating on the information received concerning sales, production, changes in environment, etc. to make decisions on personnel requirements, schedules for production, inventory pricing, etc. on an up-to-date basis. Such usage, to be effective, involves having adequate decision-making criteria in a computer model of the company. The challenge facing the would-be designer of a truly integrated on-line control system is:

- To utilize the computer and associated input-output equipment as an on-line device.
- To make the computer an effective instrument for experimenting with and evaluating the effectiveness of proposed changes in policies, procedures, and plans.

The only significant strides currently being

made are in some of the components and subfunctions of the business.

REAL-TIME CONTROL, REAL-TIME COMMUNICATION, AND REAL-TIME INFORMATION SYSTEMS

In using a computer as an integral on-line controlling device, the "real-time control, communication, and information system" has evolved as a system design concept. By this is meant that the information is transmitted instantaneously, without conversion, into a centralized computer which processes it, compares it with predetermined decision criteria, and issues instructions to men and/or machines for corrective or purposeful action. This may be thought of as "real-time control." Further, the computer by means of direct out-puts informs affected parties of this information as it is developed. This is "real-time communication." Lastly, suitable condensations of the above information are prepared, transmitted, and displayed to higher levels of management for broader system decisions. This is "real-time management information."

The meaning of the word "real-time" lies in the fact that information is used as it develops and that elements in the system are controlled by the processed information immediately, not after the fact or by making periodic forecasts of the expected future state of the system. The best-known examples of systems of this type are currently to be found in the military. It is in these applications that we may find some guidance in the way of design approaches that may be useful in evolving better on-line management control systems.

MILITARY OPERATING AND COMMAND CONTROL SYSTEMS

In recent years the application of electronic computers to military operating and command control systems has proceeded at an increasing rate. In the Air Force these are referred to as electronic support systems. As an indication of the extent of interest in such systems, the Air Force is currently spending more than a billion dollars per year on them. However, this expenditure includes equipment in addition to the computers. In many of these systems, the computer complex is the central nervous system which processes, integrates, and analyzes the various information inputs, makes and communicates appropriate decisions, and develops the display information required by the ultimate human decision makers. A few examples of such centralized, real-time, computer-controlled systems are:

- SACCS (Strategic Air Command Control System)—a system which is designed to keep the SAC Commander continuously posted on the up-to-the-minute status of every SAC bomber and missile. There are several echelons of management control to be tied together in this system, involving a network of computers for information and control purposes.
- SAGE (Semi-Automatic Ground Environment)—a continental air command and warning system. SAGE is a system designed to maintain a complete, up-to-date picture of the air and ground situation in the continental United States and other parts of North America, to control modern air defense weapons rapidly and accurately, and to present appropriately filtered pictures of the air and weapons situation to Air Force personnel who conduct the air battle.

Several similar control systems such as one for processing intelligence information and one for weather information are under development.

SAGE—A DESCRIPTION OF ITS FUNCTION[2]

From the preceding discussion it is evident that real-time control systems differ significantly from current business and logistic management control systems. To better illustrate the nature and scope of such real-time activity, a brief description of the SAGE system may prove useful.

The Semi-Automatic Ground Environment (SAGE) system is a vast interconnected network of air defense direction centers which receive information from many sources, process the information rapidly on AN/FSQ-7 Military Computers, display pertinent information to human decision makers, and generate battle orders to jet interceptors and other weapons in the air defense system. SAGE centralizes the air defense system for the handling of information and direction of weapons.

The air defense system requires monitoring of all aircraft flights in the United States and around its perimeter to determine whether the aircraft are friendly or hostile. Since there are close to 50,000 scheduled flights in the United States every day (and many more that are not scheduled), it is necessary that SAGE operate on the "exception principle." The approach is to keep track of flights until they can be identified by several means, then reject further consideration.

Air Defense Requirements

What are the management-like system requirements for integrated control of weapons defending a country from airborne attack? The various weapons and input sources involved are operated by the three military services; they are developed and improved by many different companies. As a result, control information requirements are diverse and non-standardized. The general requirements for an air defense control system may be stated approximately as follows:

- Provide positive recognition of an air attack.
- Provide up-to-the-minute status of defense capability.
- Be capable of issuing immediate defense instructions.
- Be operable immediately upon installation, at high efficiency.
- Operate on a continuous basis with high reliability.
- Be adaptable to a growing air defense capability.

A brief discussion of each of these points will bring out some of the problems faced by the system designers and implementers.

Provide Positive Recognition of an Air Attack. In order to recognize an air attack and its changing character during a battle, the following system capabilities are required:

1. Disseminate decisions and orders without delay to those who will take the necessary action.
2. Direct, using rapid communication media, the various weapons to specific targets and control each to the degree required by the weapon design.
3. Display the defense-in-action on suitable consoles for management decision making.
4. Coordinate among all operating personnel, the various echelons, the military services, and civilian agencies involved.
5. Human factors must be taken into account in the entire operation.

Be Operable, as a Man-Machine System, at High Efficiency, Immediately. The system must function effectively the first time an attack occurs and under conditions of high turnover of diversely skilled personnel. A means for the following must be provided:

1. Continual training of personnel in individual and team skills.
2. Operate the system with simulated inputs to obtain experience in operation during an attack. A high degree of realism is necessary to properly exercise the system and bring it to a high level of preparedness.

Be Operable with High Reliability on a Continuous Basis. To operate continuously, a high order of reliability and maintainability is required. This involves a set of duplicate computers as well as duplicates of other equipment and alternate communication lines. This factor accounts for a large portion of the expense of the system.

The following functions must be performed:

1. *Surveillance* of the airspace in which air flights of hostile intent may occur. Detection of all aircraft movement.
2. *Monitoring* of all flights which enter, or could enter, the airspace. This means most of the flights in the country.
3. *Identification* of all flights monitored by matching and correlating with flight plans or other identifying information. When necessary, initiate direct means of identification by Air Force aircraft.
4. *Communicate* and *coordinate* information on a country-wide basis, with emphasis on adjoining areas and the next-higher headquarters. This description of the air situation is necessary to determine whether an attack is present or imminent.

Provide Up-to-the-Minute Status of Defense Capability. To perform this function, the system must:

1. Keep all echelons informed as to the status of all the various weapons available.
2. Provide all echelons information on the immediate situation, both as to individual weapons and as to the air and battle situation. This information must be suitably filtered, summarized, and communicated for higher echelons.

3. Provide display and/or built-in decision-making means to permit rapid and accurate evaluation of alternatives in allocation, assignment, and commitment of weapons.

Issue Immediate and Appropriate Defense Instructions. In order to provide immediate response and to effect control, the system must:

Be Adaptable to Growing Air Defense Weapons Capability. In order for the system to grow and adapt to ever-changing weapons technology, the system must have the following attributes:

1. The computer program must be modified to integrate new weapons that are continually being added to the defense. This necessitates the use of a general purpose, internally programmed, large storage capacity computer.
2. Changes in existing weapons, their control apparatus, etc. must be handled without undue delay and rearrangement of the whole system.
3. As a corollary to this, new characterization of attack configurations must be able to be added to the system.

The SAGE System

How were the complex and diverse requirements for an integrated air defense control system met? As one might expect from his experience in the automation of a portion of a business enterprise, the techniques and procedures in use which were developed over a long period of experience were not scrapped, but rather consideration of their automation was used as a starting point in the design of the new system. In all, development of the system involved the cooperation of thousands of individuals and the combined efforts of a large number of scientific, business, and military organizations.

In order to meet the requirements listed above, provision had to be made for the automation or semi-automation of the following:

- Collection of information and data and elimination of noise therefrom.
- Sorting, correlating, and further processing of the information.
- Generation of displays to permit human monitoring, decision making, and intervention.
- Displays must include a presentation of the air situation and be kept current.
- Means for identifying individual aircraft in the air situation.
- Filtered and summarized displays to permit high echelons to make general decisions about the situation.
- Transmission of information and data to all points where it is needed.
- Means for deciding about the use of weapons and for directing them against the attack.
- Means for computing control information and transmitting it to the various weapons.
- Means for system training.

These many functions point up the size of the task and the need for a uniform description of the system design. SAGE was therefore designed as a network of interconnected direction centers as shown in Figure 1. Here are shown twenty-six SAGE Sectors organized into seven SAGE Divisions. There is a direction center in each sector which receives information and data from many sources in its area—from radars about present positions of aircraft, from air traffic control centers about flight plans, from weapons bases about weapons status, etc. The direction center's data and information sources are shown in Figure 2. At each division level there is a combat center which has essentially the same functions and equipment as the direction center.

At each direction center, the man-machine operation is conducted in four principal places. These are: the Manual Data Input Room, where information arriving by telephone or teletype is entered into the computer; an Air Surveillance Section, where the machine make-up of the air situation is monitored and assisted; an Identification Section, where the aircraft "tracks" shown in the air situation are identified by matching them with known flight plans and other known or requested information; and a Weapons Direction Section, where the individual interceptions of hostile aircraft are directed and monitored. In all, over one hundred display consoles and some sixty-five military and civilian contractor personnel work in a SAGE Direction Center.

The network of long-range and gap-filling radars which formed the basis of our air defense system before and during the development of SAGE are now connected to their direction center by means of automated digital data links. Similar links connect adjacent direction centers for the "cross-telling" of pertinent

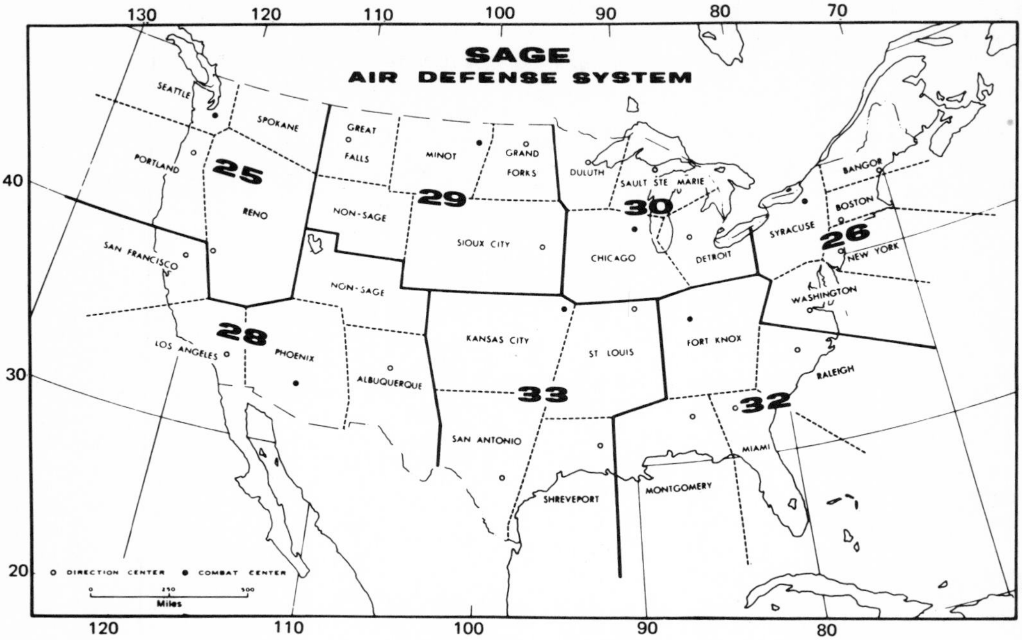

FIG. 1. Map showing air defense sectors.

radar and other data. Real-time data on present aircraft positions are also relayed from "manual" direction centers (areas where SAGE is not operational) and from extensions to the radar net on ships and aircraft which range outward from our perimeter, by telephone and teletype. This information is inserted into the computer by card punch entry equipment in the manual data room. Other items of information, entered in a like manner, are civil and military flight plans, weather information, and weapons status, although some of the last is by automatic data link direct to the computer input system, as are the radar and cross-tell data. Extensive voice communications are also available.

The direction center transmits output data by an automatic digital data link directly from the computer output system to certain weapons, to adjacent direction centers, to combat centers (higher headquarters), and to radar sites for requesting height information. Information is also fed automatically from the computer to teletype circuits, to certain weapons systems, to adjacent manual direction centers, to higher headquarters, etc. Associated with one of the direction centers in each SAGE Division is a Combat Center, where the next-higher echelon or organization operates with filtered and summarized data from the direction centers under its command.

A Review of SAGE Design Features

The Direction Center is the smallest self-sufficient component in the SAGE system. The Direction Center is a man-machine data-processing and on-line control complex, at the heart of which is a pair of large, high-speed, general-purpose digital computers generally referred to as the Q-7 Military Computer. Associated with the computers are the necessary input and output systems and other auxiliary equipment. Two computers are "duplex" to provide the necessary reliability and maintainability. If one computer should fail, the second can take over immediately. The magnitude of the SAGE task may be best realized perhaps by the fact that the operating computer program, which has to be designed to include every function of air defense in which the computer is involved, consists of approximately 100,000 individual instructions and that these programs, together with programs involved in system training and in the production of the programs themselves, involve on the order of a half-million instructions.

In Figure 3 the system design of SAGE is

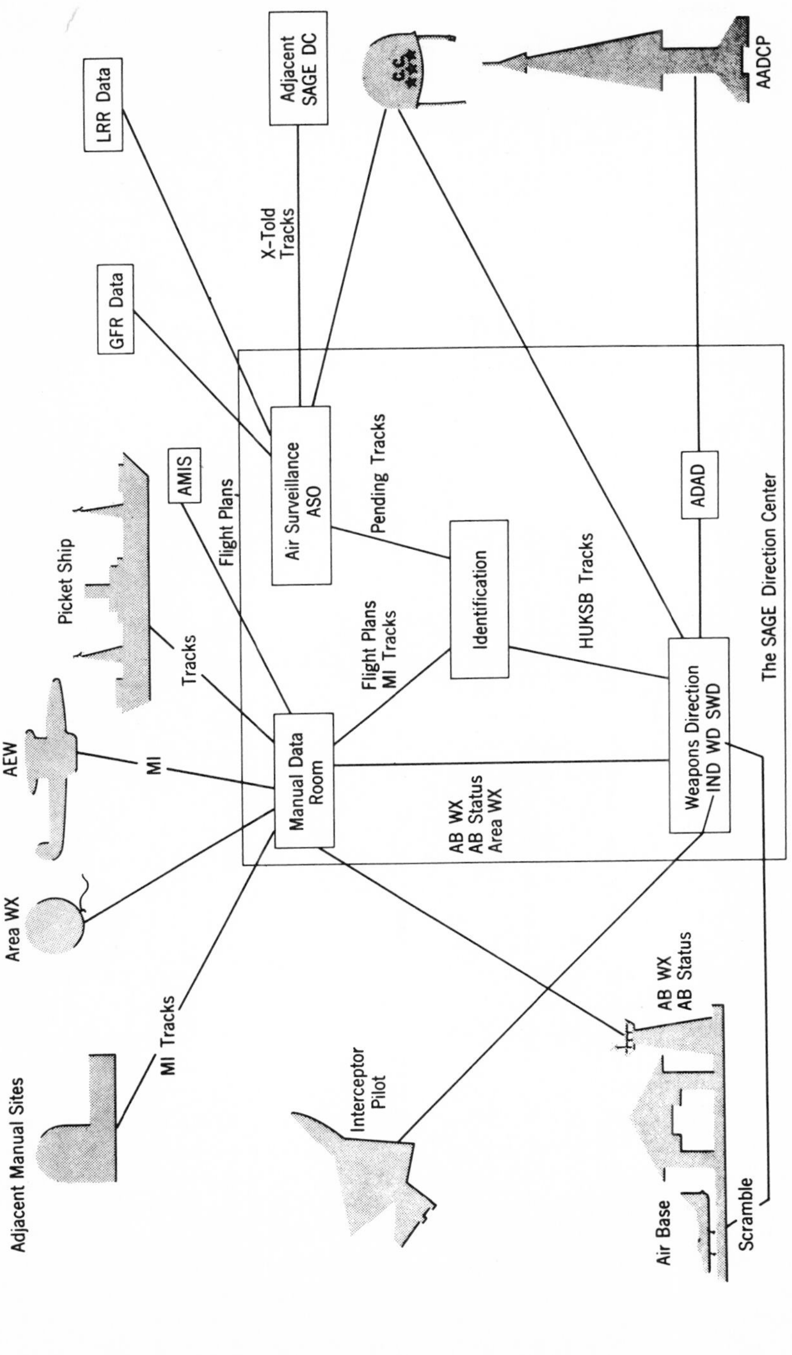

FIG. 2. SAGE operations inputs.

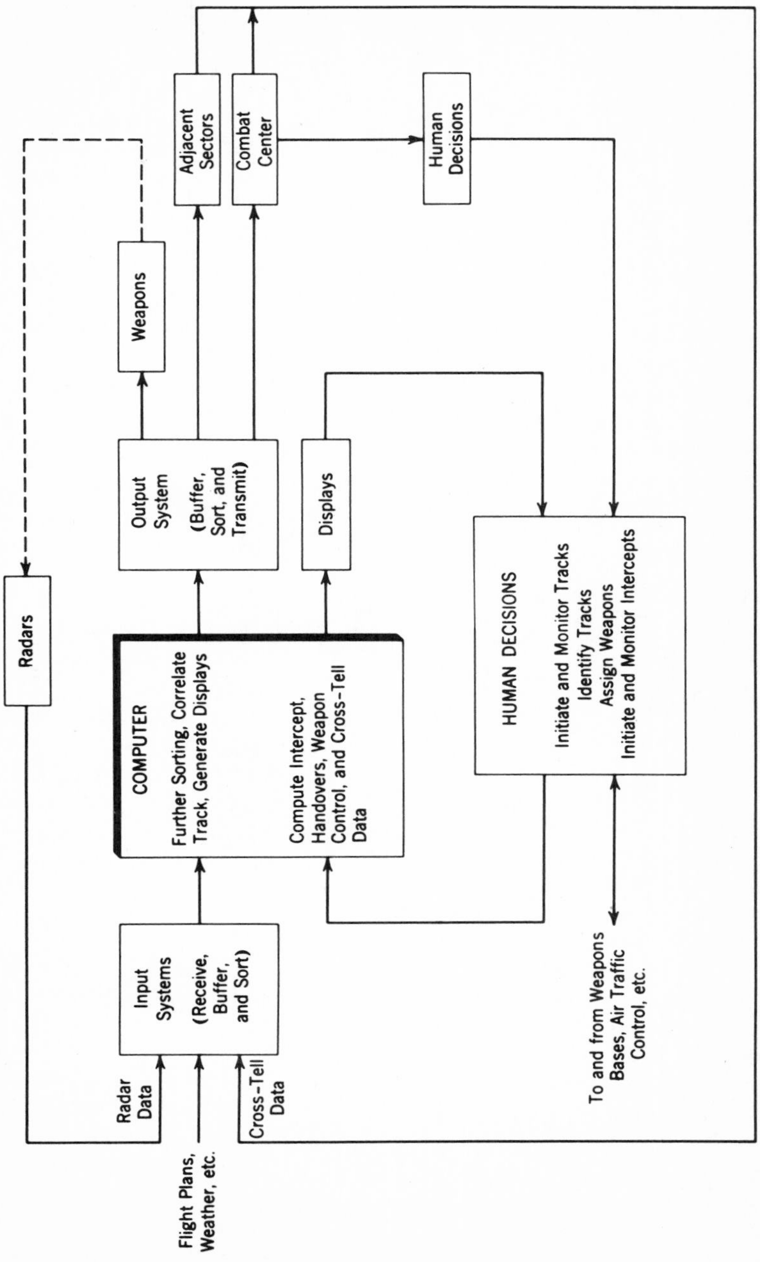

FIG. 3. Conceptual system design of SAGE.

depicted in block form. Here the manner in which the human and automated decision-making activities are made, the closed loop feedback of control and monitoring information, and the central role of the computer are illustrated. Features of the SAGE system design include:

On-Line Control Features

1. Automated and semi-automated real-time assemblage of information from many sources.
2. High-speed communication of assembled information to the computer through input systems that provide for some monitoring and noise elimination, for sorting, temporary storage, and buffering between real-time and computer processing cycles.
3. Use of the above-mentioned automatic transmittal features for communication with many and various types of agencies and equipments including weapons systems, individual weapons, other computers, higher headquarters, height finders (requests for inputs), etc.

Decision-Making Features

1. Use of an on-line, man-computer, sample-data system for control purposes.
2. Use of an extensive, multi-informational, dynamic display system to permit human monitoring, intervention, and decision making.
3. Use of on-line, low-level decision making by the computer.
4. Automatic display in real time of decision alternatives by the computer.
5. Man assistance of and intervention in machine information processing by real-time monitoring.

Display Features

1. Use of approximately 4000 data selection buttons, 130 action buttons, and 64 light guns for direct communication between the operators and the computer.

Provision for Simulation

1. Built-in simulation and recording equipment and programming for system training.

Error Correction Features

1. Use of duplicate equipments and self-diagnostic and self-error-detecting maintenance procedures to achieve very high reliability in operation.

Data-Processing Features

1. Use of a general-purpose information processing and computing device with large and readily available information storage capacity and with very-high-speed computing capability.
2. Automatic real-time transmittal of control and other operational information in digital form through a versatile output system that sorts information according to destination and acts as a buffer between computing cycles and transmitting equipment.
3. Use of a large integrated computer program of some 100,000 instructions which includes and ties together 100 subprograms and handles thousands of types and varieties of information, controls the sequence of operations of all subsystems, performs all information handling and computing tasks, and assists in evaluation of alternatives and in decision making.

A comparison of the SAGE computer itself with some of the modern scientific commercially available computers may be of interest. The SAGE computer was designed in the period 1951 to 1954. Since the computer is produced by the International Business Machines Company, who, together with Massachusetts Institute of Technology's Lincoln Laboratory, also created the design, it is most appropriate to make a few simple comparisons with the latest of IBM's computers. Table 1 compares the SAGE computer (two of which are in each direction center) with the IBM 704, 709, 7090, and the Q-7A employed in the combat center.

APPLICATION OF SAGE EXPERIENCE TO THE DESIGN OF MANAGEMENT CONTROL SYSTEMS

The SAGE experiences can be appraised from several standpoints: the hardware, the air defense characteristics, and the computer programming are a few. The purpose here is to explore the experience from the point of view of the manager who must initiate effective programs, provide sufficient resources, and develop a proper organization for the system. The following may offer guidance to managers who desire to develop a real-time management control system.

Table 1. Comparison of Computer Characteristics

Characteristics	AN/FSQ-7 (SAGE Computer)	IBM 704	IBM 709	IBM 7090	AN/FSQ-7A (Improved SAGE)
Word length (bits)	32	36	36	36	48
Minimum computation cycle (μsecs)	12	24	24	4.8	2.5
Maximum random access storage capacity (bits)	2,228,224	1,179,648	1,179,648	1,179,648	3,932,160
Random access storage time (μsecs)	6	12	12	2.4	<2.5
Maximum drum storage capacity (bits)	4,765,592	294,912	294,912	None	13,369,344
Total maximum internal storage (bits)	6,993,816	1,474,560	1,474,560	1,179,648	17,301,504
Maximum number of tape units	6	10	48	64	16
Card readers or entry punches	4	1	3	8 each	1
Output printers	1	1	3	8	1
Live input-output features	Yes	Not included in design			Yes
Tubes (approximate)	58,000	5,000	10,000	(Transistorized)	(Transistorized)

Systems Analysis Approach

In reviewing the development of SAGE one is impressed, first, with the fact that several years were taken in its design. Further, as has been pointed out, in designing a system of this magnitude the primary focus was on determining precise system requirements. Thus, in many respects SAGE has evolved from answering the question "What must we have in the way of a system?" to asking "What can we do to improve or automate existing practices?" As we look over the current process of creating new management control systems in either the military or in industry, it becomes obvious that the latter approach is often the easiest to justify and has therefore been the traditional route.

The design process stemming from asking the former question, which in essence becomes "What is the best system?", is often called the systems analysis or systems engineering approach to the problem. Thus, one principle in creating a new system involves a careful look at the requirements of the system via the systems engineering approach. A list of steps involved in this approach follows:

1. Establish criteria for management information needs.
   - Determine current information, decision, display, and report practices, using a graphical flow form.
2. Make preliminary system design.
   - Develop a preliminary statement of system requirements; i.e., specify reporting frequencies, types and routings of reports, type of equipments, displays, etc.
   - Determine what to automate or computer program and what to leave as currently performed.
3. Evaluate preliminary design.
   - Determine hardware cost, training implications.
   - Assess the nature of the improvement to be gained.
4. Develop a revised model of the proposed system.

- Test the design, using the systems analysis approach.
- Use an approach involving simulation or gaming to obtain the participation of the ultimate users.

5. Develop system specifications.
6. Install, debug, modify, extend the system.

Systems Training Approach

In providing a major resynthesis such as the SAGE system, it has been found necessary to train people in the new methodology. Training in SAGE involves elaborate computer simulations of a predicted attack environment. This requirement represents a new concept to the management world. Basically, the justification for elaborate training stems from the fact that there is no other way to adequately prepare people for the acts that they would have to perform under a real attack situation.

An important additional value in this approach is the proficiency obtained by operating the system as a whole, involving the communications and interrelations of many people and machines. The proficiency of individuals, then, is properly judged by measures in the total system context. One would not want, for example, to emphasize performance in one part of the system that would act to the detriment of the total system. To adequately demonstrate proper performance in such a broad system, a comprehensive means of training using simulated exercises has been provided. In short, one wants to train each person to act in an optimal way from the total system point of view. Thus, whether the environment is real or hypothetical (as in SAGE) is not the only factor in determining the need for simulation in training.

Thus, if a drastically new concept of management control is to be developed, it appears quite likely that the installation time, the acceptance, and therefore even the ultimate efficiency attainable by the system will be considerably enhanced by appropriately designed simulation exercises along with proper criteria for measuring individual performance in relation to total system performance.

Organizational Dynamics

In the design and implementation of SAGE, the ability to centralize many activities has been made possible. As the Air Force perceived the comprehensive changes in the Air Defense Command structure required to support these concepts, it organized the air defense function more centrally, using the control system as the guiding structure. Further, in developing the over-all SAGE system itself, it was found necessary to create a proper management organization to guide the process of design and implementation. The concept of a system manager, or ESSPO (Electronic Support Systems Project Office), has come into being with the mission to properly manage the joint efforts of system analysis, system design, computer manufacturer, computer programming, and system training activities.

While the following is a very broad generalization, it would appear that the quickest route to effective development of a truly integrated management control system involves proper points of view on the part of management in regard to the possible effects on organization; that is, the possibility of recentralization and elimination of certain functions must be within the system designer's scope. In addition, it appears necessary that the organization to perform the system analysis have proper organizational status itself and that top management plan for the necessary lead time for this activity. While quite evident, the thought should be emphasized that top management support and participation is vital in order to obtain results.

Advances in Management Techniques

On-Line Control—A Technical Achievement. The SAGE system has proven that an on-line, direct read-in-read-out, integrated computer operation is possible. This is an important technical achievement that can have significant implications in the management controls area. The feasibility of utilizing this feature can best be determined by a systems analysis bringing out the cost and effectiveness of the application.

Management-by-Exception.[3] The large data-processing capacity available in SAGE made possible a centralized operation with large masses of data carefully sorted by built-in criteria. The outputs presented to the decision maker are only the exceptions requiring attention. This feature could be extended in current management control systems on a centralized basis.

Interrogation, or Fast-Simulation, Possibilities. The ability for the human monitor to ask the computer certain questions like "What would happen if I issued this order?" has been also demonstrated on SAGE. This interrogation feature, utilizing "fast simulation," requires the building of analytic models for desired predictive purposes. Using appropriate models, this capability can be applied on an on-line basis in management control systems.

Precise Formulation of Objectives for Computer Programming

In utilizing computer based systems it has become quite evident that there is need for precise formulation of what is to be done by the computer program and precise, as well as concise, computer programming languages. In this regard considerable activity is required: first, to develop precise statements of objectives, translate them into appropriate analytic models of the problem and thence into operational instructions, for the computer programming task; secondly, to recognize and participate in the development of appropriate computer languages to facilitate the large labor involved in computer programming; and thirdly, to develop and test adequate decision-making criteria required in the formulation of those functions to be automated. This field of computer programming development requires considerable augmenting in building total system management controls.

To perform the computer programming task—perhaps the most complex, difficult, and time-consuming task—has been the increasing refinement and coverage expected of SAGE as new weapons are added. The computer program must be comprehensive enough to handle a wide variety of possible situations and must include precise rules (or formulas) for handling these situations. Specifying these rules—making certain they are the right ones, are efficient, etc.—is a task referred to as formulation. Once the situation to be controlled is recognized and the rules are determined, the task of designing the program can be done.

The point of these remarks is to stress the need for continued research in the area of computer programming techniques in view of the fact that it is a very rapidly changing technology. It appears likely that any approach to systems design will involve a team of many skilled people, including engineers, mathematicians, psychologists, statisticians, computer specialists, management, and system specialists.

BUSINESS MANAGEMENT CONTROL SYSTEMS RESEARCH

The remarks of Leavitt and Whisler in their provocative article "Management in the 1980's" are appropriate at this point.[4] Perhaps the way of Management Control Evolution may be epitomized by their observation concerning the growing "information technology":

> . . . the upshot of Taylorism (Scientific Management, Industrial Engineering Approaches) seems to have been the separating of the hourly worker from the rest of the organization, and the acceptance by both management and the worker of the idea that the worker need not plan and create. Whether it is psychologically or socially justifiable or not, his creativity and ingenuity are left largely to be acted out off the job in his home or his community. One reason, then, that we can expect top acceptance of information technology (automatic decision making in effect) is its implicit promise to allow the top to control the middle just as Taylorism allowed the middle to control the bottom.

It has not been the purpose of this discussion to assert positively that the approach in military real-time control systems, which has been quite effective in the military application, is either necessary or practical cost-wise in the management control domain. While the concept appears quite promising, these are questions that can only be resolved by further study. The possibility of developing a comprehensive, integrated, total company on-line controlling concept is worth serious study. If the lead time can be reduced in arriving at the desiderata of truly designed information-communication systems, a significant contribution to the management field would be made.

To explore the nature of the research, a project in Business Management Control Systems Research has been established. This research project is aimed at developing a generalized computer model of a business, one which will permit experimentation with certain policies, procedures, and organization. Hopefully, this research will lead to some answers to questions concerning cost and effectiveness of various management control system approaches. The results may some day permit us to truly design management control systems that are more nearly optimum from all points of view.

REFERENCES

1. D. G. Malcolm, "The Use of Simulation in Management Analysis—A Survey and Bibliography," *Operations Research,* Vol. 8, No. 2 (1960).
2. Acknowledgment is made to R. C. Hopkins for his assistance in preparation of this material. A more detailed discussion of many points contained herein is included in his paper *Significance of SAGE to the Feasibility of Semi-Automated Management,* SP-87, System Development Corporation, 1959.
3. Examples of this feature are found in certain military management controls. For example, the PERT system in the Navy Polaris program permits all of the planned activities in that program to be monitored centrally by the exception principle. See: D. G. Malcolm, "Application of a Technique for R and D Program Evaluation," *Operations Research,* Vol. 7, No. 5 (September-October, 1959).
4. H. J. Leavitt and T. L. Whisler, "Management in the 1980's," *Harvard Business Review,* November-December, 1958.

47. THE SABRE SYSTEM

R. W. Parker *

American Airlines' SABRE system is a large, real-time teleprocessing system designed to perform all the data collection and processing functions associated with the sale, confirmation and control of an airline reservation. Controlled through a computing center at Briarcliff Manor, N.Y., 30 miles north of New York City, it provides each American reservation sales agent with direct access to every available seat on any of the airline's flights. In addition, complete information on any passenger's reservation including name, itinerary, telephone number and related data is recorded on disc at Briarcliff and is, therefore, available to every agent in the system.

Access to the passenger name record makes it possible for any of American's sales agents immediately to confirm, alter or cancel all or part of a passenger's itinerary—no matter where or when the original reservation was made. Access in less than 3 seconds to the name record also provides authorization to the ticket agent to confirm the space and issue the passenger's ticket at an airport or city ticket office.

In addition to controlling seat inventory and maintaining passenger records, SABRE automatically:

—notifies agents when special action is required, such as calling a passenger to inform him of a change in flight status;

—maintains and quickly processes waiting lists of passengers desiring space on fully booked flights;

—sends Teletype messages to other airlines requesting space, follows up if no reply is received, and answers requests for space from other airlines;

—provides arrival and departure times for all the day's flights.

SOURCE: *Datamation* (September, 1965), pp. 49–52. Reprinted by permission of *Datamation*.

* Director of SABRE Data Processing, American Airlines.

The system is made up of three major elements:

1. *Input/Output Devices.* At 1,008 reservations and ticket sales desks of American Airlines at 60 separate locations, these sets enable agents to communicate *directly* with the Briarcliff center. Teletype interface equipment, consisting of input communications adapters and output communications adapters, facilitates the handling of reservations traffic with other airlines.

2. *The Electronic Reservations Center.* At the heart of the system in Briarcliff Manor are two IBM 7090 computers, one of which is always on-line. The other 7090 acts as a standby and is used for other applications until it is required to take over the real-time job. Connected to the 7090's are six high-speed drums and 16 1301 disc files with a total capacity of over 700 million characters.

Information arriving at Briarcliff passes first through a duplex console which functions primarily as a switch to indicate which of the 7090's is on-line. From the duplex console, it passes to the real-time channel which formats serially transmitted messages into computer words and performs validity checks before passing data on to the 7090. The 90 is, of course, the logical controller and processor of the system. The most frequently used programs stay in the 90's core. Other programs, temporary storage and frequently accessed records reside on drums which have an access time of 11.25 milliseconds. Passenger name records and other records with a lower frequency of access are stored on discs which have an average access time of 115 msec.

3. *The Communications Network.* Agent sets are linked to the computer center by more than 31,000 miles of leased communications facilities. Also included in the network are 43 Terminal Interchanges which act as an interface between the I/O devices and the high-speed lines; one TI can handle 30 I/O devices.

In the field, agent sets and communications adapters are connected to a terminal interchange. The agent sets transmit pieces of customer transactions; the various parts of a customer's transaction with an agent are transmitted individually to the computer. The customer's name is transmitted as a message, his telephone number is a message, the flight number is a message. The communications adapters, on the other hand, transmit complete Teletype messages with longer messages broken into convenient "buffer loads."

Every input message will cause some kind of a response to be sent back to the input device which generated the message, and no device can transmit a second message until it has received a response relative to the first message.

The information entered into the terminal interchange from the I/O devices does not automatically pass out onto the high-speed line. The transmission of information from the TI is computer controlled from Briarcliff by a polling procedure. We have nine high-speed input/output line pairs; four or five TIs are attached to each of these pairs, and polling is carried out independently and simultaneously for each pair.

The situation with outputs from the computer is a little simpler. Output messages travel from the computer via a high-speed line to the terminal interchange and then without delay to the appropriate I/O device.

DEVELOPMENT AND IMPLEMENTATION

The development and implementation of a system as vast and complex as SABRE was not, needless to say, a simple undertaking. With our 20-20 hindsight, we can see many instances in which we could have saved ourselves some trouble by traveling an alternate path. Nonetheless if we had to do it all over again, we would do exactly what we did the first time in a vast majority of cases.

The decision to embark on the SABRE system was an outgrowth of several years of study and was American Airlines' answer to the growing complexity of our business. As air travel increased, it became more and more difficult for us to maintain records of all our passengers on all our flights with the accuracy and timeliness required to provide good service. Visualize, if you will, the difficulty of controlling manually the passenger name records and the inventory for 76,000 seats a day. The communications problems became horrendous, particularly when a passenger was involved in a multi-segment itinerary and each boardpoint had to be notified.

An agreement with IBM to produce SABRE came a year after the formulation of objectives by American in 1958. During the intervening year economic analysis satisfied American that a fully mechanized reservations system would, as traffic grew, increase in cost at a lesser rate

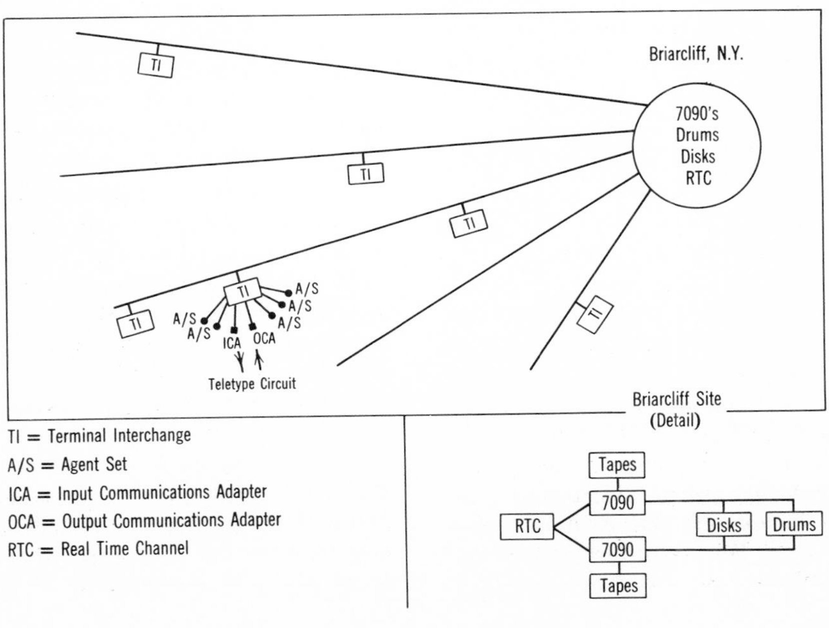

than the growth in business. On the other hand, it became apparent that the manual system when projected into the future, increased in cost at a rate equal to and, in some areas, greater than the growth of passenger volume. During this period, we also conducted the analysis necessary to make our choice of vendor. Perhaps the most significant factor in arriving at a vendor is the amount of backing and support we could expect.

THE AGENT SET

The design of the agent set was a joint IBM/American Airlines undertaking. Several man-years of experimentation went into the development of a device that was easy to learn, operate, and maintain. The most frequently performed actions are automated so the number of buttons to be depressed for a single action is minimized. Infrequent actions and variable data such as name, phone number, etc., are input through a typewriter keyboard.

The number of agent sets for the initial installation was determined by an application of queueing theory. American Airlines has a standard time within which incoming telephone calls must be answered. It was determined to provide enough sets so that this standard would be met in the peak hour of the average business day of a peak month when each set is manned. We had an accurate forecast of incoming telephone call volumes arrived at by applying statistical techniques to historical data and growth forecasts. The equation we used provided the number of manned positions (agent sets) when given the average number of phone calls and the average servicing time per call.

The determination of the number of terminal interchanges and the high-speed line configuration was performed on a somewhat more subjective basis. The number of TI's was determined by the maximum foreseeable number of input/output devices predicted during the life of the system. The placement of the TI's and, therefore, the lines was influenced by our desire to have the reservation offices protected against total lack of communication resulting from a failure on a single line. Therefore most major AA cities are serviced by more than one of our nine high-speed line pairs. A location serviced by two TI's, for example, has each TI hooked up to a different line. A further objective of the line configuration was line balance to achieve equal traffic over all lines and TI's. This was deemed necessary in order that we achieve a response time—from input to answer back—of under 3 seconds.

The size of the file system was determined by forecasts of passenger transactions in number and size and by analysis of the "booking curve." A booking curve is essentially a table which tells what fraction of today's bookings applies to flights *n* days in the future. The curve varies with seasonal peaks in our business. Thus we determine how many records we would create, how long they would be in the files and hence what our maximum requirement would be for file space assuming that the files would be duplexed. We began operation with 24 disc modules and now are up to 32.

The original assumption on main frame hardware was that 7090's with a 32K memory would be adequate to handle all foreseeable volumes. However, in 1963 we discovered, after we had a number of cities already on the system, that we were saturating the computer with only 30% of our volume on the air. Therefore, we modified the 7090's to 65K to provide more core space for programs and thus eliminate the loss of computer time experienced by the necessity of waiting for programs. The system currently is capable of handling approximately 2,100 inputs per minute, and some 40,000 passenger name records in a day. The average passenger name record consists of 10 separate inputs to the computer.

DEVELOPING SOFTWARE

The general process by which the functional requirements of American Airlines were translated into operating computer programs has consisted of seven major steps.

1. Functional requirements were prepared by American Airlines people selected because of their thorough knowledge of reservations and sent to programming school to acquaint them with the capabilities and limitations (for as we all recognize, there are limitations) of data processors and, specifically, the 7090.

2. The functional requirements were translated by the programming staff into preliminary program specifications outlining in general and quite broadly how the programs would be designed to carry out these functions. This step revealed that in most instances what the airline-oriented people conceived of as a function re-

quired more than one program and, in a few instances, that one program could readily be used to carry out parts of several functions.

3. The preliminary program specifications were reviewed and discussed by the functional design group with the programming people and final program specifications were prepared.

4. From the final specifications, functional descriptions were written, translating the programs back into procedural language and describing, therefore, the manner in which the system would operate to carry out the reservations functions. The functional descriptions were then submitted to the people in the regular general office staff organization who were responsible for the operation of these functions in American Airlines. They were asked to sign off on these to indicate they were satisfied that the functions in which they were concerned would be carried out properly by the system.

5. We were faced with the problem of training some 1,500 people in 100 locations in the use of SABRE, so we developed a training section which was responsible for the maintenance of training materials and for the instruction of instructors. We had a small training facility at the SABRE processing site to which we brought from each of our 37 cities those people who were responsible for training all of the others. We gave them a thorough two-week course which encompassed the 35 hours of training which they would later give the agent personnel in their cities, as well as an equal amount of background information and practice in teaching techniques.

Training in the field stations presented no real problem. A program was developed in the computer which allowed trainees to practice all possible inputs to the system without endangering the permanent records on disc or drum. Our personnel policy guaranteed that no permanent employee would lose his job as a result of SABRE. Thus morale was good and conversion to the new system easy. The checking features in the SABRE programs actually add to the confidence of the reservations agents.

6. Close to a half million lines of code were written to convert the program specifications into machine language. We tapped almost all types of sources of programming manpower. The control (executive) program was written by IBM in accordance with our contract with them. We used some contract programmers from service organizations; we used our own experienced data processing people; we tested, trained and developed programmers from within American Airlines, and hired experienced programmers on the open market. Line-for-line programming was used in the real-time system for computer efficiency.

7. Testing of our real-time programs involved several steps. The first program checkout work was done without a control program or special equipment on a standard 7090 at the Time-Life Data Center. The method of testing employed a special hardware/software simulation routine called the SABRE Debugging Package (SDP). This package allowed program testing on a 7090 without the use of the special SABRE hardware, such as discs, drums, or the real-time channel. It simulates the existence of all the special hardware of the SABRE system as well as all control program functions previously noted.

TESTING THE SOFTWARE

With the arrival of the system at Briarcliff, individual programs could be combined into functional packages and, for the first time, run in conjunction with the actual control program. The method of testing these packages involved the programmer employing actual agent sets, constructing test cases, and testing the logic of his programs and the validity of the results utilizing the real system.

While this was an excellent way to test the logic of a single path through the system, this method of testing proved lacking for a number of reasons:

a. Only one programmer could adequately test his work at one time.

b. It was very time-consuming to construct the cases and get the system to test the desired paths.

c. It was difficult to tell what caused discrepancies when they did occur.

In order to solve these problems and maintain an adequate testing schedule, another simulation package was evolved. This package (as opposed to SDP) used all the special SABRE hardware, the control program and debugged operational programs. It simulated only the remote agent sets. Input messages were punched into cards and read by the simulator just as though they came from agent sets. They were then turned over to the actual program to operate on in a real-time environment.

In conjunction with the development of the

agent set simulator, we developed a set of preset system records called the pilot system. These records constituted all the records for a very small airline. They included several flights for a number of days, with different configurations of inventory pre-sold. The use of this system obviated the need for each programmer having to put in his test input deck the necessary inputs to get the system to a desired point, thus speeding up the running time of each test.

The agent set simulation package has since gone through many modifications and refinements; however, the basic logic of the package has remained unchanged. Today it is our main test tool and debugging aid prior to actually introducing any change into the system for live test.

The final thing to be done before the first city was cutover to SABRE was to run all individual packages together, operating on common data. The phase was called laboratory system testing. In it, 40,000 typical SABRE inputs on selected flights for a 36-day period encompassing two schedule changes were acted upon in a real life environment. Inventory and availability on these flights were compared to predetermined results. Many new discoveries were made running under this system. Several programming and operating problems were uncovered and corrections made to the system. Upon the successful completion of lab system, AA and IBM management felt that we had a working system, and in early 1963 we began processing reservations with the SABRE system. The last city was mechanized in December 1964.

Implementation of the checked-out system was performed on a location by location basis rather than function by function. This shortened the learning period in each city and enabled us to operate the airline with only a small percentage of our reservation function undergoing a major change at any one time.

No matter how careful you try to be in the planning, programming and testing phases, errors slip into a system, particularly when the system is as involved as SABRE. By using location by location implementation, we were able to work most of the major "bugs" out of our system during the cutover of our first few cities. By the time we had a large portion of our revenue dependent on SABRE, we had a rather smooth-running operation.

The chronology of SABRE ran as follows:

Preliminary study	1954–1958
Precontractual analysis	1958–1959
Contract	1959
Functional requirements	1960–1962
Program specifications	1960–1962
Coding	1961–1964
Single path testing	1961 on
Equipment arrival	January 1962
Package testing	1961–1962
Final checkout	Oct.–Dec. 1962
Test city parallel operation	Dec. 1962–Mar. 1963
First firm cutover	April 1963
Several more cities cutover	May 1963
Further cutover delayed pending addition of memory to 7090	June–Nov. 1963
Remainder of American cities added to system	Nov. 1963–Dec. 1964

THE VALUE OF HINDSIGHT

In retrospect there are some things which we would do a little differently if we were going to start over.

In the first place, we would start concentrating earlier on how to operate and control the implemented system. The control of the operation of the computer room has to be far more rigid in a real-time system than in a batch processing shop. Minor operating errors can cost major dollars. We are still working on programs to reduce our exposure to human error, and, of course, the best way to reduce this exposure is to eliminate operator intervention.

The second area we would now emphasize earlier is that of utility routines. Among the types of utilities required in a real-time system are those which analyze error conditions upon a stop of the real-time system and which permit a quick restart of the system with a minimum risk of violation of the vital records in storage. We have such utilities now but had we anticipated less than ideal operating conditions earlier in the game, we could have shortened our total implementation period.

Another type of utility required in a real-time system is real-time file fallback. A duplex system becomes simplex in a hurry when a file fails because of hardware problems. It is desirable in order to minimize risk when one file of a pair fails to copy the contents of the surviving file onto a spare and thus to re-establish the protection of a duplex mode. Our fallback utility was not ready when we went on the air and we, therefore, lost some operating time until it was completed.

Another factor which must be emphasized during our development phase is system measurement. It is extremely important to know how much computer time is being expended by each type of transaction in order to establish the capacity and useful life span of a given system. It is also desirable to develop means to measure the quality of input being performed in the field. Inefficient use of remote input devices can overload a real-time system and, in effect, shorten its life span. Thus the software must monitor the user and isolate those individuals or locations where improved supervision or training is required.

The introduction of communication into a data processing system results in a new management problem. There are new interfaces established within the user company and among the vendors of computer and communications equipment. Procedures must be established which quickly trace a source of trouble, whether the difficulty lies with the user, the computer vendor or the communication carriers. What is of prime importance is the development of an attitude among all concerned to expend effort to fight a problem to solution first and worry about jurisdictional or company loyalties after the line has been restored to service. We have been able to solve most of our "interface" problems due to excellent joint participation among American Airlines, IBM, AT&T and the local telephone companies. Without the establishment of collectively agreed-upon procedures and reporting techniques, the solution for each problem would, I am sure, be much longer.

48. MYTH OF REAL-TIME MANAGEMENT INFORMATION

John Dearden *

The latest vogue in computer information systems is the so-called real-time management information system. The general idea is to have in each executive's office a remote computer terminal which is connected to a large-scale computer with a data bank containing all of the relevant information in the company. The data bank updated continuously can be "interrogated" by the manager at any time. Answers to questions are immediately flashed on a screen in his office. Allegedly, a real-time management information system enables the manager to obtain complete and up-to-the-minute information about everything that is happening within the company.

The purpose of this article—aimed at a time span of the next five to seven years—is to raise some serious questions concerning the utility of a real-time information system for top management. I will try to show that it would not be practicable to operate a real-time *management control* system and, moreover, that such a system would not help to solve any of the critical problems even if it could be implemented. I will also try to show that in other areas of top management concern a real-time system is, at best, of marginal value. It is my personal opinion that, of all the ridiculous things that have been foisted on the long-suffering executive in the name of science and progress, the real-time management information system is the silliest.

MEANING OF REAL-TIME

One of the problems in any new field of endeavor is that there is frequently no universally accepted definition for many of the terms. It therefore becomes nearly impossible to question the validity of the concepts underlying the terms because their meanings are different to different people. The term "real-time" is no exception. In fact, in a single issue of one computer magazine, back-to-back articles defined real-time differently; and one example, cited in the first article as an illustration of what real-time is *not*, appeared in the second article as an illustration of what a real-time system *is*.

Semantic Confusion

One concept of real-time is demonstrated by these two quotations:

- "A real-time management information system—i.e., one that delivers information in time to do something about it." [1]
- "A real-time computer system may be defined as one that controls an environment by receiving data, processing them and returning results sufficiently quickly to affect the functioning of the environment at that time." [2]

The problem with both of these definitions is that they are too broad. *All* management control systems must be real-time systems under this concept. It would be a little silly to plan to provide management with budget performance reports, for instance, if they were received too late for management to take any action.

The following is a description of real-time that comes closer to the concept of real-time as it is used by most systems and computer people:

SOURCE: *Harvard Business Review* (May–June, 1966), pp. 123–132. Reprinted by permission of *Harvard Business Review*.

* Harvard University.

[1] Gilbert Burck and the Editors of *Fortune, The Computer Age* (New York, Harper & Row, Publishers, 1965), p. 106.

[2] James Martin, *Programming Real-Time Computer Systems* (Englewood Cliffs, New Jersey, Prentice-Hall, Inc., 1965), p. 378.

The delays involved in batch processing are often natural delays, and little advantage can be obtained by reducing them. But elimination of the *necessity* for such delays opens new and relatively unexplored possibilities for changing the entire nature of the data processing system —from a passive recorder of history (which, of course, is valuable for many decisions) to an active participant in the minute-to-minute operations of the organization. It becomes possible to process data in *real-time*—so that the output may be fed back immediately to control current operations. Thus the computer can interact with people on a dynamic basis, obtaining and providing information, recording the decisions of humans, or even making some of these decisions.[3]

System Characteristics

To expand somewhat on this description, the term "real-time system" as used in this article will mean a computer system with the following characteristics.

1. *Data will be maintained "on-line."* In other words, all data used in the system will be directly available to the computer—that is, they will be stored in the computer memory or in random access files attached to the computer. (This is in contrast to data maintained on magnetic tapes, which must be mounted and searched before information is available to the computer.)
2. *Data will be updated as events occur.* (In contrast to the "batch" process, where changes are accumulated and periodically updated.)
3. *The computer can be interrogated from remote terminals.* This means that the information stored in the computer can be obtained on request from a number of locations at a distance from the place where the data are processed and stored.

Perhaps the most widely known example of a real-time system currently in operation is the American Airlines SABRE system for making plane reservations.

POTENTIAL APPLICATIONS

With the new generation of computers, random access memories have become much less expensive than has been true until now. This fact, coupled with the advances made in data transmission equipment and techniques, will make many real-time applications economically feasible.

Real-time methods will improve those systems where the lack of up-to-the-minute information has in the past resulted in increased costs or loss of revenue. I believe that many companies will employ real-time methods to control all or part of their logistics (the flow of goods through the company) systems. For example:

> A manufacturer of major household appliances might have raw material and work-in-process inventories in his manufacturing plants, and finished goods inventories both in company and distributor warehouses and in dealer showrooms. There is a more or less continuous logistics flow all along the route from raw material to retail customer. If all of the data on inventory levels and flows could be maintained centrally and updated and analyzed continuously, this would not only solve many of the problems now faced by such a manufacturer, but would make it possible to provide better all-around service with lower inventory levels and lower costs (particularly in transportation and obsolescence).

There are, of course, many other potential applications for real-time management information systems, and I believe that they will be used extensively in the next few years. However, these applications will take place almost exclusively in logistics, and, as I shall explain later on, techniques that may improve a logistics system will not necessarily improve a management control system. I want to make it clear at this point that I am not opposed to real-time systems per se. I believe they have valuable applications in operating situations. I am only opposed to using real-time information systems where they do not apply. The balance of this article will consider top management's use of real-time systems.

MANAGEMENT FUNCTIONS

As used here, the term "top management" will apply to the president and executive vice president in centralized companies, plus divisional managers in decentralized companies. In other words, I am considering as top management those people responsible for the full range

[3] E. Wainright Martin, Jr., *Electronic Data Processing* (Homewood, Illinois, Richard D. Irwin, Inc., 1965), p. 381.

of a business activity—marketing, production, research, and so forth. I am also assuming that the company or division is sufficiently large and complex so that the executive makes only a limited number of operating decisions, if any. I believe that this is a reasonable assumption in considering real-time management information systems. A company where the president makes most of the operating decisions could scarcely be considering a sophisticated and expensive computer installation.

Six Categories

This part of the discussion considers, in general terms, the functions of top management. The purpose here is to establish how a typical executive might spend his time so that we may later evaluate the extent to which his decision making can or cannot be helped by real-time computer systems. I have divided top management's functions into six general categories —management control, strategic planning, personnel planning, coordination, operating control, and personal appearances. Each is discussed below.

1. *Management Control.* One of the principal tasks of a manager is to exercise control over the people to whom he has delegated responsibility. Ideally, this control consists of coordinating, directing, and motivating subordinates by reviewing and approving an operating plan; by comparing periodically the actual performance against this plan; by evaluating the performance of subordinates; and by taking action with respect to subordinates where and when it becomes necessary.

The formal management control system will, of course, vary with the type and size of business as well as with the type and amount of responsibility delegated to the subordinate. Nevertheless, all effective formal management control systems need three things:

(a) A good plan, objective, or standard. The manager and the subordinate must agree as to what will constitute satisfactory performance.

(b) A system for evaluating actual performance periodically against the plan. This would include both a clear explanation of why variances have occurred and a forecast of future performance.

(c) An "early warning" system to notify management in the event that conditions warrant attention between reporting periods.

2. *Strategic Planning.* This consists of determining long-range objectives and making the necessary decisions to implement these objectives. Much of top management's strategic planning activity involves reviewing studies made by staff groups. Capital expenditure programs, acquisition proposals, and new product programs are examples of studies that fall into this area.

Another phase of strategic planning consists of developing ideas for subordinates to study—that is, instead of waiting for staff or line groups to recommend courses of action, the executive develops ideas of his own as to what the company should be doing.

3. *Personnel Planning.* This important function of management deals with making decisions on hiring, discharging, promoting, demoting, compensating, or changing key personnel. In the broadest sense, this consists of organizational planning. Personnel planning is, of course, related both to management control and strategic planning. Nevertheless, there are so many unique problems associated with personnel planning that I believe it is reasonable to consider it as a separate function.

4. *Coordination.* Here management's function is to harmonize the activities of subordinates, especially where it is necessary to solve a problem that cuts across organizational lines. For example, a quality control problem might affect several operating executives, and the solution to this problem might require top management's active participation. In general, this activity tends to be more important at the lower organization levels. The president of a large, decentralized company would perform less of this coordination function than his divisional managers because interdepartmental problems are more common at the divisional level.

5. *Operating Control.* Almost all top executives perform some operating functions. For example, I know a company president who buys certain major raw materials used by his company. Usually, the operating decisions made by top management are those which are so important to the welfare of the company that the executive believes the responsibility for making them cannot be properly delegated.

6. *Personal Appearances.* Many top executives spend much time in performing functions that require their making a personal appearance. This can vary from entertaining visiting

dignitaries to giving out 25-year watches. (I shall assume the activities involving such personal appearances will not be affected by a real-time management information system.)

REAL-TIME PRACTICALITY?

The purpose of this part of the article is to examine, in turn, each of the management functions described above (except No. 6) to see whether or not it can be improved by a real-time information system.

Management Control

I do not see how a real-time system can be *used* in management control. In fact, I believe that any attempt to use real-time will considerably weaken even a good management control system. (In setting objectives or budgets, it may be useful to have a computer available at the time of the budget review to calculate the effects of various alternatives suggested by management. This, however, is not a real-time system, since a computer console need be installed only for the review sessions.)

Calculating Performance. In the area of performance evaluation, real-time management information systems are particularly ridiculous. When a division manager agrees to earn, say, $360,000 in 1966, he does not agree to earn $1,000 a day or $1,000/24 per hour. The only way actual performance can be compared with a budget is to break down the budget into the time periods against which performance is to be measured. If the smallest period is a month (as it usually is), nothing short of a month's actual performance is significant (with the exception of the events picked up by the early warning system to be described below). Why, then, have a computer system that allows the manager to interrogate a memory bank to show him the hour-to-hour or even day-to-day status of performance against plan?

Even assuming objectives could logically be calendarized by day or hour, we run into worse problems in calculating actual performance, and worse still in making the comparison of actual to standard meaningful. If the performance measures involve accounting data (and they most frequently do), the data will never be up-to-date until they are normalized (adjusted) at the end of the accounting period. I will not bore you with the details. Suffice it to say only that a real-time accounting system which yields meaningful results on even a daily basis would be a horrendous and expensive undertaking.

Let us go one step further. Performance reports, to be meaningful, must include an explanation of the variances. This frequently involves considerable effort and often requires the analyst to spend time at the source of the variance in order to determine the cause. Would this be done every day or oftener? Ridiculous! There is one more thing about performance reports. The important message in many reports is the action being taken and the estimated effect of this action. In other words, the projection of future events is the important top management consideration. Will this be built into the real-time system? Since this involves the considered judgment of the subordinate and his staff, I do not see how this could possibly be done even on a daily basis.

Early Warning. How about real-time for providing an early warning? Here, also, I do not see how it could be of help. Early warning has not been a problem in any top management control system with which I have been acquainted. In most instances, when situations deteriorate to the point where immediate action is required, top management knows about it. As the manager of a division ($100 million a year in sales) said to me, when I asked him how he knew when things might be out of hand in one of his plants, "That's what the telephone is for."

In any case, it is possible to prescribe the situations which management should be apprised of immediately, without even relying on a computer. Furthermore, the important thing is to bring the situation to top management's attention *before* something happens. For example, it is important to inform management of a threatened strike. Yet a real-time management information system would pick it up only *after* the strike had occurred.

In summary, then, early warning systems have been put into operation and have worked satisfactorily without a real-time system. I see nothing in a real-time management information system that would improve the means of early warning, and such a system would certainly be more expensive. (Note that here I am talking about management control systems. The early warning techniques of many logistical control systems, in contrast, could be greatly improved by real-time systems.)

My conclusion on management control is that real-time information cannot be made meaningful—even at an extremely high cost—and that any attempt to do so cannot help but result in a waste of money and management time. Improvements in most management control systems must come from sources other than real-time information systems.

Strategic Planning

Since strategic planning largely involves predicting the long-run future, I fail to see how a real-time management information system will be of appreciable use here. It *is* true that past data are required to forecast future events, but these need hardly be continuously updated and immediately available. Furthermore, much of the preparation of detailed strategic plans is done by staff groups. While these groups may on occasion work with computer models, the models would certainly be stored away, not maintained on line between uses.

Perhaps the most persistent concept of a real-time management information system is the picture of the manager sitting down at his console and interacting with the computer. For example, as a strategic planning idea comes to him, he calls in a simulation model to test it out, or a regression analysis to help him forecast some event; or, again, he asks for all of the information about a certain subject on which he is required to make a decision.

It seems to me that the typical manager would have neither the time nor the inclination to interact with the computer on a day-to-day basis about strategic planning. Problems requiring computer models are likely to be extremely complex. In most instances, the formulation of these problems can be turned over to staff specialists. Furthermore, I think it would be quite expensive to build a series of models to anticipate the manager's needs.

Under any conditions, strategic planning either by the manager alone or by staff groups does not appear to be improved by a real-time system. Models can be fed into the computer and coefficients can be updated as they are used. Between uses, it seems to me, these models would be most economically stored on magnetic tape.

Personnel Planning

A real-time management information system does not help the top manager to solve his problems of personnel planning, although the computer can be useful in certain types of personnel data analysis. About the only advantage to the manager is that information becomes available somewhat more quickly. Instead of calling for the history of a particular individual and waiting for personnel to deliver it, the manager can request this information directly from the computer. Therefore, while a remote console device with a visual display unit *could* be used for retrieving personnel information, the question of whether it *should* be used is one of simple economics. Is the additional cost of storing and maintaining the information, plus the cost of the retrieval devices, worth the convenience?

Coordination

The coordination function is very similar to the management control function with respect to potential real-time applicability. A manager wants to know right away when there is an interdepartmental problem that will require his attention. As is the case with early warning systems developed for management control, a real-time system is not necessary (or even useful, in most cases) to convey this information. Further, I cannot see how a real-time management information system could be used in the solution of these coordination problems, except in unusual cases.

Operating Control

There is no question that real-time methods are useful in certain types of operating systems, particularly in logistics systems.[4] To the extent that a top executive retains certain operating control functions, there is a possibility that he may be able to use a real-time information system. Because of the necessity of doing other things, however, most executives will be able to spend only a limited amount of time on operating functions. This means generally that they must work on the "exception" principle. Under most conditions, therefore, it would seem much more economi-

[4] See Robert E. McGarrah, "Logistics for the International Manufacturer," *HBR*, March–April 1966, p. 157.

cal for a subordinate to monitor the real-time information and inform the top executives when a decision has to be made.

It is very difficult to generalize about this situation. Here, again, it appears to be one of simple economics. How much is a real-time system worth to the manager in relation to what it is costing? I cannot believe that there would be many instances where a manager would be concerned with operating problems to the extent that a real-time information system operating from his office would be justified.

REPORTING BY COMPUTER

In recent months, there have been experiments to replace traditional published reports by utilizing consoles and display devices to report information directly to management. Although these techniques, strictly speaking, are not real-time, they bear such a close relationship to real-time systems that it will be useful to consider them here.

Modus Operandi

The general idea is that the information contained in the management reports would be stored in the computer memory so that the manager could ask for only the information he needed. This request would be made from the computer console, and the information would be flashed on a screen in his office. For example, a manager could ask for a report on how sales compared with quota. After looking at this, he could then ask for data on the sales of the particular regions that were below quota and, subsequently, for detail of the districts that were out of line.

The benefits claimed for this type of reporting are as follows:

- The manager will receive only the information he wants.
- Each manager can obtain the information in the format in which he wants it. In other words, each manager can design his own reports. One manager may use graphs almost exclusively, while another may use tabulation.
- The information can be assembled in whatever way the manager wants it—that is, one manager may want sales by areas, and another may want it by product line. Furthermore, the manager can have the data processed in any way that he wants.
- The information will be received more quickly.

Important Considerations

Before installing such a system, it seems to me, a number of things should be taken into account.

First, what advantage, if any, does this system have over a well-designed reporting system? Since the storage and retrieval of data in a computer do not add anything that could not be obtained in a traditional reporting system, the benefits must be related to convenience. Is there enough additional convenience to justify the additional cost?

Second, is it possible that for many executives such a system will be more of a nuisance than a convenience? It may be much easier for them to open a notebook and read the information needed, since in a well-designed system the information is reported in levels of details so that only data of interest need be examined.

Finally, will the saving in time be of any value?

It seems to me that the two main considerations in installing such a system are the economics and the desires of the particular executive. There is one further possibility, however, that should be carefully considered. What will be the impact on the lower level executives? If these people do not know the kind of information their superiors are using to measure their performance, will this not create human relations problems?

Without going into the details, I can see many problems being created if this is not handled correctly. With a regular reporting system, the subordinate knows exactly what information his superior is receiving—and when he receives it—concerning his performance. Furthermore, the subordinate receives the information *first*. Any deviations in this relationship can cause problems, and the use of a computer to retrieve varying kinds of information from a data base is a deviation from this relationship.

THREE FALLACIES

If management information on a real-time basis is so impractical and uneconomic, why are so many people evidently enamored with this concept? I believe that the alleged benefits of real-time management information systems are based on three major fallacies.

Improved Control

Just about every manager feels, at some time, that he does not really have control of his company. Many managers feel this way frequently. This is natural, since complete control is just about impossible even with the best management control system. Since most companies have management control systems that are far from optimum, there is little wonder that a feeling of insecurity exists. In the face of this feeling of insecurity, the promise of "knowing everything that is happening as soon as it happens" has an overpowering appeal.

As explained previously, real-time will not improve management control and, consequently, will not help to eliminate the insecurity that exists. What is usually needed is a combination of improved management control systems and better selection and training of personnel. Even at best, however, the executive will have to accept responsibility for what other people do, without having full control over their actions.

"Scientific Management"

There appears to be considerable sentiment to the effect that the scientific way to manage is to use a computer. This fallacy implies that the executive with a computer console in his office is a scientific manager who uses man-machine communication to extend his ability into new, heretofore unavailable, realms of decision making.

I believe that it is nonsense to expect most managers to communicate directly with a computer. Every manager and every business is different. If a manager has the necessary training and wishes to do so, it may be helpful for him to use a computer to test out some of his ideas. To say, however, that *all* managers should do this, or that this is "scientific management," is ridiculous. A manager has to allocate his time so that he spends it on those areas where his contribution is greatest. If a computer is useful for testing out his ideas in a given situation, there is no reason why he should have to do it personally. The assignment can just as easily be turned over to a staff group. In other words, where a computer is helpful in solving some management problems, there is no reason for the manager to have any direct contact with the machine.

In most instances, the computer is of best use where there are complex problems to be solved. The formulation of a solution to these complex problems can generally be done best by a staff group. Not only are staff personnel better qualified (they are selected for these qualifications), but they have the uninterrupted time to do it. It seems to me that there is nothing wrong with a manager spending his time managing and letting others play "Liberace at the console."

Logistics Similarity

This fallacy is the belief that management control systems are merely higher manifestations of logistics systems.

The fact is that the typical real-time system, either in operation or being planned, is a *logistics* system. In such a system, for example, a production plan is developed and the degree of allowable variances established in a centralized computer installation. The actual production is constantly compared to plan; and when a deviation exceeds the established norm, this fact is communicated to the appropriate source. On receiving this information, action is always taken. Either the schedules are changed or the deficiency is somehow made up.

Notice that speed in handling and transmitting vast amounts of information is essential. This is the critical problem that limits many manual logistics systems; and the computer, particularly with real-time applications, goes a long way toward solving the speed problem.

In contrast, speed in processing and transmitting large amounts of data is *not* a critical problem in *management control* systems. Consequently, the improvements that real-time techniques may effect in logistics systems cannot be extrapolated into management control systems.

The critical problems in management control are (a) determining the level of objectives, (b) determining when a deviation from the objective requires action, and (c) deciding what particular action should be taken. The higher in the organizational hierarchy the manager is positioned, the more critical these three problems tend to become. For example, they are usually much more difficult in planning divisional profit budgets than plant expense budgets. In some instances the computer can help the manager with these problems, but I do not see how it can solve them for him. Furthermore, the use of computers in solving these problems has nothing to do with real-time.

SHORT-TERM VIEW

While real-time management information systems may be very useful in improving certain kinds of operating systems, particularly complex logistics systems, they will be of little use in improving management control. This is particularly true in the short-range time span of the next five to seven years.

The following is a checklist of questions that I believe the manager should have answers to before letting anyone install a remote computer terminal and a visual display screen in his office:

1. What will the total incremental cost of the equipment and programming be? (Be sure to consider the cost of continuing systems and programming work that the real-time systems will involve.)
2. Exactly how will this equipment be used? (Be sure to obtain a complete description of the proposed uses and the date when each application will become operational.)
3. Exactly how will each of these uses improve the ability to make decisions? In particular, how will the management control system be improved?

With precise answers to these three questions, it seems to me that a manager can decide whether or not a remote terminal and visual display device should be installed. Do not be surprised, however, if the answer is negative.

LONG-RANGE OUTLOOK

What are the prospects of real-time systems, say, 15 or 20 years from now? Some experts believe that, by that time, staff assistance to top management will have largely disappeared. Not only will the staff have disappeared, but so will most of the paper that flows through present organizations. A manager in the year 1985 or so will sit in his paperless, peopleless office with his computer terminal and make decisions based on information and analyses displayed on a screen in his office.

Caution Urged

It seems to me that, at the present time, the long-term potential of real-time management information systems is completely unknown. No one can say with any degree of certainty that the prediction cited above is incorrect. After all, 15 or 20 years is a long time away, and the concept of a manager using a computer to replace his staff is not beyond the realm of theoretical possibility. On the other hand, this concept could be a complete pipedream.

Under any circumstances, many significant changes in technology, organization, and managerial personnel will be required before this prediction could be a reality for business in general. As a result, if such changes do occur, they will come slowly, and there will be ample opportunity for business executives to adjust to them. For example, I believe there is little danger of a company president waking up some morning to find his chief competitor has installed a computer-based, decision-making system so effective that it will run him out of business.

I believe all executives should be open-minded to suggestions for any improvements in management information systems, but they should require evidence that any proposed real-time management information system will actually increase their effectiveness. Above all, no one should rush into this now because of its future potential.

The present state of real-time management information systems has been compared to that of the transportation field at the beginning of the Model-T era. At that time, only visionaries had any idea of how transportation would be revolutionized by the automobile. It would have been foolish, however, for a businessman to get rid of his horse-drawn vehicles just because some visionaries said that trucks would take over completely in 20 years.

It seems to me that this is the identical situation now. Even if the most revolutionary changes will eventually take place in management information systems 20 years hence, it would be silly for business executives to scrap present methods until they are positive the new methods are better.

49. REAL-TIME MANAGEMENT INFORMATION? LET'S NOT BE SILLY

ROBERT V. HEAD*

Inevitably, as real-time systems assume an increasingly important role in many industries, the general business publications must come to venture into the real-time world. Last year, for instance, there was Fortune's excellent series on "The Computer Age." And now we find the Harvard Business Review, the prestigious elder statesman of these journals, providing commentary on the subject in its pages. The May-June issue of HBR harbors not the genteel and judicious overview that one might have expected, but rather a crude frontal assault by John Dearden on the "Myth of Real-time Management Information."

Professor Dearden, who is a sort of house oracle on information systems at the B School, thinks that real-time management information systems are silly. He says so plainly at the beginning of his polemic and at the end. He even says so in the middle.

Things get off to an interesting start with an assertion that "allegedly, a real-time management information system enables the manager to obtain complete and up-to-the-minute information about everything that is happening within the company." The reader is left to puzzle out for himself who, besides Mr. Dearden, would make such a sweeping allegation. Certainly no responsible real-time system designer, who has learned to be wary of words like "complete" and "everything." Up-to-the-minute information about *everything?*

With this for openers, the author proceeds to identify three characteristics of a real-time system, all irrelevant to an evaluation of management's need for timely information. He says first that "data will be maintained 'on-line.' In other words, all data used in the system will be directly available to the computer—that is, they will be stored in the computer memory or in random access files attached to the computer." This statement, of course, blithely ignores the fact that one can provide real-time management information without maintaining all data on line. To the contrary, most system designers contemplate a hierarchy of storage, with only the most critical data stored in main memory or direct access storage and the less critical and more voluminous files maintained on magnetic tape and other less expensive media.

Next, Mr. Dearden asserts that, according to his view of a real-time system, "data will be updated as events occur." He does not perceive that one can do a splendid job of providing real-time management information from a data base which is maintained by off-line techniques. This is, in fact, exactly the method by which the central information files of several real-time commercial banking systems are updated.

Thirdly, Professor Dearden says that real-time systems are characterized by computer-stored information which "can be obtained on request from a number of locations at a distance from the place where the data are processed and stored." He thus singles out one of the most expensive features of certain real-time systems, such as SABRE, but neglects to note that a real-time management information system need not necessarily have remote terminals at all. There are perfectly respectable systems housed entirely under one roof and possessing no more than one or two terminals to provide real-time management information.

The body of Mr. Dearden's paper is devoted to a discussion of several basic managerial functions and to a consideration of the appropriateness of real-time systems in supporting these functions. The first is Management Con-

SOURCE: *Datamation* (August, 1966), pp. 124–125. Reprinted by permission of *Datamation.*

* Consolidated Software, Inc.

trol. Here, Mr. Dearden somewhat grumpily concedes that "it may be useful to have a computer available at the time of the budget review to calculate the effects of various alternatives suggested by management" but his previously defined view of real-time systems leads him to conclude that usage of the computer in this fashion "is not a real-time system, since a computer console need be installed only for the review sessions." Seemingly, Mr. Dearden feels that a system cannot qualify as real-time unless it makes information available when it is *not needed*. Actually, the hallmark of a real-time information system is its responsiveness to managerial needs, not how many consoles it drives or how frequently these consoles are connected on line.

Another management function which Mr. Dearden analyzes is that of Early Warning about potentially troublesome managerial problems. Here he expresses the somewhat startling opinion that "early warning has not been a problem in any top management control system with which I have been acquainted." One wonders how many of Mr. Dearden's executive readers would concur in this curious judgment.

In considering the management function of Strategic Planning, the author concedes "that past data are required to forecast future events," but goes on to complain that "these need hardly be continuously updated and immediately available." Absolutely correct, but the information is nonetheless needed in real-time *during* the planning session.

Personnel Planning is another management function identified by Mr. Dearden. In solving problems of personnel planning, "about the only advantage" that he can see to a real-time system "is that information becomes available somewhat more quickly." Perhaps the professor is making progress after all, for one must agree that, while this may not be the *only* advantage to any real-time system, it is an advantage which is oftentimes of critical importance in personnel or any other kind of planning.

Mr. Dearden concludes his survey of top management functions by discussing the applicability of real-time systems to Operational Control. He says that "it is very difficult to generalize about this situation" before going on to generalize later in the same paragraph that "I cannot believe that there would be many instances where a manager would be concerned with operating problems to the extent that a real-time information system operating from his office would be justified."

Are you beginning to get the idea? Set up some straw men in the form of assertions that no self-respecting system designer would utter, then proceed to demolish them. The notion of the console in the office is perhaps the author's favorite straw man. Either that or he is genuinely unaware that it is a matter of the utmost indifference whether a manager prefers to obtain his real-time information directly or through staff assistants who operate the consoles.

If you stay with him to the end, Professor Dearden offers some fascinating conclusions. He believes that "there is little danger of a company president waking up some morning to find his chief competitor has installed a computer-based, decision-making system so effective that it will run him out of business." There are many systems professionals who hold the opinion that this is a clear and present danger, particularly in the case of company presidents who heed the type of counsel provided by Mr. Dearden.

The author winds things up with what could very well go down as one of the most inappropriately chosen analogies in contemporary business literature when he compares the development of real-time systems to that of the automobile. He says "It would have been foolish for a businessman to get rid of his horse-drawn vehicles just because some visionaries said that trucks would take over completely in 20 years."

BIBLIOGRAPHY

Barrett, E. F., *Memory Considerations for an On-Line Processor,* Proceedings On-Line Data Processing Applications Conference, January, 1963.

Blumenthal, S. C., "Management in Real-Time," *Data Processing Magazine,* August, 1965.

Coyle, R. J., and J. K. Stewart, "Design of a Real-Time Programming System," *Computers and Automation,* September, 1963.

"Data Transmission and the Real-Time System," *Dun's Review,* September, 1965.

Desmonde, W. H., *Real-Time Data Processing Systems: Introductory Concepts,* Prentice-Hall, Inc., 1964.

Douglas, R. M., "Digital Computer Achieves Real-Time Flight Simulation,"

Dowse, R. G., "The Systems Approach to Data Transmission," *Computer Journal,* October, 1963.

Hartmann, H. C., "Management Control in Real Time Is the Objective," *Systems,* September, 1965.

Head, R. V., *Real-Time Business Systems,* Holt, Rinehart and Winston, 1964.

Head, R. V., "The Programming Gap in Real-Time Systems," *Datamation,* February, 1963.

Head, R. V., "Real-Time Systems Configurations," IBM Systems Research Institute Paper, April, 1963.

Head, R. V., "Real-Time Programming Specifications," *Communications ACM,* July, 1963.

Holdiman, T. A., "Management Techniques for Real-Time Computer Programming," *Journal of the ACM,* July, 1962.

Hosier, W. A., "Pitfalls and Safeguards in Real-Time Digital Systems with Emphasis on Programming," *IRE Transactions on Engineering Management,* June, 1961.

Mapletoft, J. T., "Satisfying the Need to Know in Real-Time," *Systems and Procedures Journal,* March-April, 1965.

Margartis, P., "A Real-Time Management Information Retrieval System," *Data Processing,* July, 1965.

Martin, J., *Programming Real-Time Computer Systems,* Prentice-Hall, Inc., 1965.

———, *Design of Real-Time Computer Systems,* Prentice-Hall, Inc., 1967.

Ream, N. J., "On-Line Management Information," *Datamation,* March, 1964.

Shays, E. M., "The Feasibility of Real-Time Data Processing," *Management Services,* July-August, 1965.

Spitler, R. H., and B. K. Kersey, "A Research Laboratory for Processing and Displaying Satellite Data in Real-Time," *Data Processing,* January, 1965.

Sprague, Richard E., *Electronic Business Systems,* the Ronald Press, Inc., 1962.

———, "Electronic Business Systems—Nineteen Eighty Four," *Business Automation,* February, 1966.

———, "On Line-Real Time Systems as a Long-Range Planning Goal," *Total Systems Letter,* April, 1966.

"Time-Shared Programming," *Business Management,* January, 1965.

SECTION IV

PROLOGUE TO THE FUTURE

The Roman seers read the entrails of animals, the Greeks consulted oracles, while the American? Well, the common man looks up his horoscope in the daily paper while the sophisticate will program a computer to predict the future course of events.

Since this book has dealt with management systems as currently used in the business world, it seems appropriate to survey here the future applications of systems and to depict the future state of the arts. It is an easy enough task to formulate sweeping generalizations that are sufficiently ambiguous to encompass all possible contingencies and then to proclaim one's personal infallibility when all events fall neatly under the blanket statement. No one would be unduly aroused by the pronouncement that it is anticipated that business organizations will in the future utilize the systems approach even more than at present. Such an encyclopedic prediction is reminiscent of the thinking evidenced by J. P. Morgan who, when asked to predict the future course of the stock market, blandly replied, "I predict that it will continue to fluctuate."

While it is indeed difficult to make precise, exact, and unambiguous predictions, nevertheless, projection of present trends can serve as a starting point. It is, no doubt, a truism to assert that the systems concept will be integrated to a much greater extent in the near future both because of the availability of the new tools facilitating this approach and because of the obvious need to ensure corporate survival in a dynamic, competitive economy. The current need for continually improving upon the managerial processes has been amply demonstrated by both educators and businessmen. Forrester, in discussing the managerial process, enjoins the business organization to view itself as a system of interrelated and interfunctioning parts. He states:

> Management has been practiced, so far, as a skilled "art," lacking a foundation on a "science" of *integrated* underlying principles. The science of industrial systems is now rapidly evolving and should provide to management of the future a basis similar to that which physics provides to engineering. This does not imply "automatic management" but the reverse—a new managerial opportunity and challenge. The demands on the manager will become greater rather than less. In addition to experience, judgment and intuition, the manager will need a professional understanding of the dynamics of business growth and fluctuation. Adequate theory and technical methods now exist for "designing" more successful organizations. Lacking is the counterpart of an "applied science" and "practical engineering" for interpreting theory into results. As theory and methods are extended and the gap between them and practicing management is closed, we can expect management education to take on the characteristics of a profession wherein skilled art is superimposed on a foundation structure of basic principles of economic growth and corporate evolution.[1]

Much of what the future holds in store is simply more of what we have today, with perhaps an overlay of more sophistication. In fact, many of the forces that will shape the future have already been at work for a number of years. Recent developments in the area of information technology (discussed in Parts II and III) are beginning to make inroads in the organizational structure. Several companies have already reorganized around information centers. With the widespread adoption of digital computers which store, transmit, and report data, the information available to managers has increased to such a degree that decisions are typically being made more efficiently. The ability to immediately retrieve information from memory files has already proven to be a valuable asset in decision making. The very near large-scale adoption of on-line computers will further facilitate management control. While the use of automated management control de-

[1] Jay W. Forrester, *Management and Management Science,* M.I.T., School of Industrial Management, Memorandum D-48, June 1, 1959, p. 1.

vices has, it is true, been largely confined to the military, the potential for the business firm remains highly promising. Within the next five years real-time systems will no longer command the awe that now envelopes the onlooker; the mystique will have disappeared and it will be regarded as another matter-of-fact piece of hardware in the computer complex. Remote computing and time-shared systems will also have become commonplace.

The use of simulation, characteristically embedded in the industrial dynamics model, will be the subject of ever more costly research. More routinizable managerial functions will be assigned to computer decision making. The whole texture of managerial decision making will be so altered that the manager of the future would regard today's decision-making apparel as one belonging to the equivalent of management's Stone Age.

Operations research will come of age as business firms become better acquainted with this scientific technique. The various tools generally associated with operations research, such as queuing theory, inventory theory, linear programming, and search theory will daily find more practical applications to the problems of the business world. The successful applications, well-publicized, will contribute much to breaking down the skepticism and overcoming the resistance of businessmen reluctant to try the new approach. The potential areas of application are indeed numerous, and while current efforts have been largely expended in the sphere of production, possible extensions to marketing and finance will soon become common. Attempts have already been made to relate operations research to sales effort, to promotional effort, etc.; the use of game theory in capital budgeting and the application of scientific techniques to mergers and acquisitions have already taken place. While operations research is basically quantitative, it nevertheless neither avoids nor overlooks the behavioral aspects of management problems.

Within the past few years there have been dramatic changes regarding the traditional functions of planning, organizing, and controlling. An earlier selection by Emery foretold the centralization of the planning function and the routinization of many day-to-day operations. The organizing function has already seen many changes and the success achieved by the military in establishing project control managers with authority cutting across traditional organizational lines presages future industrial acceptance.

The control function will also assume new dimensions with the rapid response made possible by on-line computers. The cybernetic approach to control discussed earlier is only now beginning to make a dent in the business world. The development of new planning and control techniques and the refinement of presently existing ones, such as PERT and PERT/COST, will continue to assist the busy and harassed manager in making timely and responsible decisions wherever and whenever necessary.

The systems manager of the future may be a new breed, distinctly different from the one on the contemporary scene. One of the prime requirements of the new breed of manager will be that he understand the entire business, not as so many isolated elements but as a "going concern," as a *system*. He must be capable, above all, of bringing together the many individual segments, frequently diverse and sometimes strongly self-oriented, into an integrated dynamic system, thus blending individual objectives into a common organizational goal.

Unlike the traditional specialist, the new systems manager will be a super-generalist. As a systems man he will be concerned with the optimization of overall organizational objectives. He will be a problem-solver instead of a technically oriented machine-man or specialist. Whether or not the systems manager of the future will be an updated experienced manager of today or a distinctly new breed is immaterial; in any case an almost radical orientation toward the job will be required, for the successful manager of the future must utilize the systems approach to the management problems that will face him in an ever growing complex business world. The systems approach is not something like a suit of clothes that can be donned at will; it is rather a way of life itself, a way of thinking, a conceptual frame of reference that must permeate one's every decision and outlook.

* * *

George Kozmetsky's manager, idling in his rocker, could pleasantly reminisce about the many changes that had transpired since launching his business career in the late 1960s.

The 1970s saw the emergence of the nonroutine industries. These were faced with problems whose solutions constituted a new order; their base was technology, their product output not very large, and they often required the cooperation and coordination of government, industry, and education. The dissemination of these nonroutine industries altered the nature of the manager's tasks from that of a supervisor and motivator to that of one capable of managing the diverse intellectual resources needed to solve the interdisciplinary problems of the decade.

By the 1980s this ability was in very great demand. Universities were engaged full time in turning out the new breed of managers who alternated between campus, business, and government. Of prime importance was their ability to tap intellectual resources, their interest in solving complex problems, and their creative potential. These were truly interdisciplinary scientists.

The chief problem facing these managers revolved around their intellectual resources —the scientists and technicians. The latter were especially mobile, since their specialized knowledge was often serviceable for one project only. This created a type of occupational unemployment, job switching, and "brain drain." Another of their problems was motivating people engaged in short-term projects; however, the great strides made in psychological research enabled managers to be almost-expert motivators.

In the 1980s and 1990s organizations were almost completely identified with social objectives. Profit-making and personality enrichment were the twin tracks on which the organization ran.

By the year 2001 the fears occasioned by automation had been generally dissipated. Most of the old mass-production workers (now a third of the labor force) had been upgraded to supervisors or middle managers; the 40-hour work week had long since been scrapped and a work load of four hours a day, five days a week had become typical.

Middle managers, with the help of the computer, handled the day-to-day factory operations. Top managers with tremendous authority for decision making occupied their time in strategic planning, since committee meetings and routine briefings had long since been eliminated. Study formed part of the daily routine—the natural sciences, social sciences, and the arts.

As a result, the tailor-made solutions to problems were no longer as messy as they were in the 1960s. Government, industry, and education, by working hand in hand, had brought about noticeable improvements in the quality of living.

The knowledge explosion was never capped. Managers finally had to resign themselves to knowing that they would never know all that they needed to know. But at least they had the keen satisfaction of knowing that social life was better for all, thanks to the key role they played in society.

Neither the 30-year projections of Kozmetsky nor the 10-year projections of Joseph hurl us into the nightmarish world of "1984" or the "Brave New World" of Aldous Huxley. Earl Joseph, in his reading, focuses on the changes in the management information system that will come about as a result of the advances in computer technology. Specifically, he zeroes in on the following points.

In the 1970s computers will be larger, faster, more reliable, and longer lived. They will have greater memory capabilities and faster and more varied random access; they will make far fewer errors; and they will be in operation for more years than at present. Future systems will also be more modular, allowing both hardware and software to be pieced together and tailored for management information systems.

Computer memories will have greater capacity and will be more economical. Since the 1950s, memory capacity has been increasing by a factor of 10 every decade. By mid-1970, computer memories will have a billion bits or more. Memory units have also sped up and are reducing in cost by a factor of more than 10 every decade. Billions of bits will be accessible in fractions of a microsecond and the cost per bit will be down to about 1/10 of a cent instead of the $1-per-bit cost in the mid-1950s.

Time sharing in real time will allow many managers to have access to the computer all at the same time. For the manager of the 1970s this will be a *must*. By the end of the decade, graphic terminals will be inexpensive enough to be on every manager's desk. Picture phones, of which there will be over a million in use, are ideally suited for presenting graphic real-time data to tomorrow's managers.

The reliability of tomorrow's computers will be noticeably enhanced. The mean time between failures in the early to mid-1950s was measured in a few hours. At present, for the central processing unit (CPU), the mean time between failures is measured in thousands to ten thousands of hours. In the late 1970s, the mean time between failures will be measured in years. This greater reliability will result from computers capable of switching automatically from a failing component to a good built-in spare component.

Instead of the present three to five years of usable life, a ten-year lifespan is contemplated for the computer of the future. Increased longevity will allow us to evolve new applications rather than to revolutionize them.

The one major problem that will continue to haunt the manager of the 1970s will be that of computer language. Languages must be developed to a point at which the basic words (instructions) can be made more complete. Instead of handling a few hundred instructions with many thousands of variations, computers will be designed to be readily adaptable to various languages and to allow the user to specify the instructions that he needs. Unfortunately programming will continue to remain the biggest expense. At the beginning of the decade, programming accounts for more than 75 percent of the total systems cost. As a result, present software can no longer be economically discarded, but must be and will be adapted to the next generation of computers.

Multiprogramming systems will appear. Special packaged programs for management information systems will be developed, with packages of application programs and packages of systems programs. The computer itself will decide which programs will be needed for the job. Simulation will be a normal operational procedure and management by exception at long last a reality.

These predictions by Joseph, himself a researcher in advanced computer-systems design, seem to be based on realistic foundations. It is to be hoped that these management-information-system predictions will also take into account the types and sources of information needed by middle and top management as specified by Johnson and Derman in their article, "How Intelligent Is Your 'MIS?'"

50. REFLECTIONS OF A 21ST CENTURY MANAGER

GEORGE KOZMETSKY*

The end of the 20th century was duly marked by global celebrations. But for a relatively small group of Americans there were special satisfactions in entering the year 2001. They were the managers of various enterprises —in business, government and industry— whose careers extended all the way back to the late 1960s. Now in their fifties, they could look back on a period of extraordinary change. The manager's responsibilities had changed drastically while the composition of industry itself was marked by numerous stages of transformation.

Back in the early 1970s, they recalled, managers began to recognize new kinds of organizations. For convenience, these developing organizations were known as *nonroutine industries.*

Those nonroutine industries were made up of units of government, industry and education engaged in nonrepetitive or "nonroutine" pursuits. The education industry itself was a leading nonroutine industry. The defense and space industries were certainly nonroutine industries, and so were large segments of the medical, electronics, oceanography and "urban problem" industries. So were many areas of government.

The new industries had certain common characteristics. Often, for example, they were working on problems that required new orders of solutions. No textbooks held the answers to questions that arose in planning and building livable megalopolies, exploring the reaches of space or controlling the environment. Frequently, answers had to be improvised. The temporary solution to the problem of air pollution in Los Angeles, for example, was typically makeshift and typically "messy." When the pollution index struck a certain level, motorists were required to pull over to the curb and turn off the engine. As pollution grew worse, power plants were required to switch from diesel fuel to natural gas. Solutions to many such problems, ranging from garbage disposal to land pollution, were frequently patchwork and "messy," offensive to anyone who liked solutions to be "clean" and permanent.

Nonroutine industries were also technologically based; their products were the end result of much labor and thought by scientists, engineers and other technical and professional talents. Even as early as 1969, 70 percent of the available scientists and engineers were hired by the "nonroutine" industries.

Another characteristic of the new industries was that the number of units they produced was not very large. Sometimes, in fact, the "unit" consisted only of a program or a plan. If the "units" were products, they ranged from one-of-a-kind to small production runs. The computer industry, for example, produced only 14,300 units in 1968, after 20 years of existence as an "industry." In contrast, the old mass-production auto industry turned out 10 million units.

Still another characteristic of the emerging industries was that their new products or proposals often required the cooperation and coordination of segments of government, education and industry. Problems associated with urbanization, for example, involved a large amount of interaction among public and private organizations. So did problems related to transportation, space exploration and health.

The rise and spread of such new industries gradually changed the nature of the manager's tasks.

In the old, mass-production industries, the manager was principally a supervisor of specialists. To his office came the experts in his company, the professionals in such fields as accounting, personnel, marketing, finance and production. But in the nonroutine industries,

SOURCE: *Bell Telephone Magazine* (March-April, 1969). Reprinted by permission of Bell Telephone Magazine.

* University of Texas.

the manager had a different set of appointments. His office visitors were men in government, university professors, the many scientists and engineers within his own company, and numerous outside consultants.

More and more, it appeared, the manager of a nonroutine industry was not merely the supervisor and motivator of an assortment of talents; he was also a man with the ability to break across the artificial barriers among disciplines and professions. His experiences in education and government, as well as in business, enabled him to locate and tap expertise on short notice. He was, in fact, a manager of *intellectual resources.*

The ability to manage intellectual resources assumed overwhelming importance in the decades of the 1970s and 1980s. By then, education had unquestionably become America's leading industry, requiring a vast number of skilled managers. In 1980, college enrollments were three times higher than in 1970, and they advanced even faster in later decades. (In the year 2000, for example, the University of California had 275,000 students, compared with 99,000 in 1969, and that was fairly typical of the larger educational units. Education was a life-long process for virtually all of America's 400 million people.)

Even as early as the 1970s, it had become quite common for a manager to leave The Company after five or six years in the demanding top echelons. Sometimes he went off to serve in government; often he joined a university. But in any kind of organization he was marked by his ability to tap intellectual resources, in the interest of solving problems and creating new knowledge.

The university was the ideal place for honing his abilities as a manager. The campus was obviously rich in intellectual resources. It offered him the chance to bring together different disciplines in an informal atmosphere and get them to work on a particular problem. The solutions they found—often unusual—could perhaps be applied in a few years to some industry, just as space technology and techniques had been adopted by industry in the 1960s.

Of course, the manager who could shuttle easily among government, industry and educational organizations was not particularly new. Such managers appeared noticeably in the 1960s. People like John Gardner, Robert McNamara, George Romney, Daniel Moynihan, Sol Linowitz, Dean Rusk, Orville Freeman and McGeorge Bundy were merely a few of the managers who could move gracefully—and successfully—from campus to a foundation, from business to government. Behind them were hundreds of lesser-known managers with similar adaptability. Increasingly, the business manager in most demand was one who could skillfully bring together experts of government and education into the planning stages of a project, drawing on *their* intellectual resources. But as the one-of-a-kind projects so typical of the nonroutine industries became more common in the 1970s and 1980s, the manager's tenure with a particular organization was significantly shorter than it was in the 1960s.

The need for managers of intellectual resources was intense, even in the 1960s. The shortage of such managers would have been worse, however, if the nation had not embarked on the era of manned space flight. With that era came the rise to prominence of the interdisciplinary scientists.

What America needed and got in that period was an increasing number of Leonardo da Vincis—people who could work across the sciences; people who could comprehend the subtleties of cellular biology and at the same time design the mechanical apparatus needed to keep living organisms alive and normally adjusted to the hostile environment of space. In addition, these same individuals were expected to manage and integrate their portion of the operation with the longer range objectives.

At the same time, a number of corporations—particularly those in the mass-production or routine industries—were themselves busily training future managers, even if they sometimes failed to realize the fact. It was occasionally noted, even in the 1960s, that systems experts quickly learned many of the essential details of running a company in the process of analyzing systems and structuring problems. As problem-solving by computer became more general in the 1970s, the systems experts were logical candidates for top management. It was they, after all, who could superbly perform what was to become the manager's chief function—the structuring of problems. And so, between the space programs and management training by computer, America had developed at least a stopgap supply of managers for the 1970s and 1980s. By this time, too, the leading university business schools had modernized their programs and were training many managers for the new-style enterprises.

One of the particularly vexing problems for nonroutine industry managers in this period involved an essential segment of their intellectual resources—the scientists and technicians. In the 1970s, most technically trained people had become even more mobile than managers.

The tenure of technically trained people on a project often lasted for just a few years. As soon as their specialized knowledge was exhausted, they found it necessary to acquire some other specialty—for their specialties were often usable for one project only.

For all the talk about shortages of engineers and scientists in the 1960s, for example, there began to appear a kind of occupational unemployment; like actors, scientists found themselves "at liberty." When England found it couldn't compete in atomic energy and in the aircraft industries, the requirements for technical people were cut back 50 percent. Job switches and "brain drains" became common.

Motivating people to do their best in short-term projects was particularly trying for managers in the 1970s. In those years, however, enormous strides were made in understanding how people store and process information internally—in other words, how they think. The psychology developed from research in that area also was applied to problems of human behavior; and by the 1980s, knowledge of learning and motivation was as advanced as were chemistry and biology in the 1960s. By the end of the century managers in both routine and nonroutine industries were superior motivators.

The motivation question affected entire organizations, of course. Back in the 1960s, corporations were becoming aware of what was popularly called "social responsibility." Many companies quickly laid claim to the virtue; others said they had it all along. In any case the question became increasingly academic as corporate policies and activities seemed increasingly to involve the public interest. By the 1980s and 1990s the largest corporations squarely identified their goals with social objectives, and the manager became concerned with developing industrial strategies that would mesh with the goals of raising the quality of life. The motivating force behind his company, as he saw it, was the need to furnish people with the things that gave full meaning to life. Philosophical questions found a permanent place on the agenda of board meetings, and the chairman was as concerned about them as about return on investment.

On the eve of year 2001, a manager could take some satisfactions in the ways that some of the fears of the 1960s and 1970s had disappeared.

In those years, he recalled, there had been widespread concern that automation would create disastrous problems of chronic unemployment. When it developed that computers could not only think but could also frame questions better than most humans, there was further alarm. And when automated equipment began to produce automated equipment—in effect, a machine with the human power of reproduction—there was something akin to terror. Was man becoming obsolete?

In retrospect, the fears were groundless. The machines were actually helping to open up new opportunities and force the continuous upgrading of tasks.

Some of the biggest changes of all had occurred within the old mass-production industries. A third of all working people were in these industries by the year 2000, and virtually all could be considered supervisors or middle-managers. The 40- and 35-hour work week had disappeared many years before; supervisors and maintenance workers were in the automated factory only four hours each day. A typical factory had six shifts, five days weekly.

The managers at middle levels handled actual operations of the factory. They turned their tactical problems over to self-organizing computers, which in turn put the solutions into automatic operation—subject, of course, to the middle-manager's veto.

The top manager had an enormous amount of authority, compared with the top manager of the 1960s. All lines on the organization chart led to his office. The trend really started in the 1960s with the centralization of certain operations, like payroll and billing, that was made possible by computers. As computer applications spread during the 1970s, companies recentralized authority and control. By the year 2000, the top manager and the machines were directly responsible for virtually all decision making. The authority of middle managers was severely limited.

A high percentage of the top manager's time

was devoted to strategic planning. He was concerned with the day-to-day operations of the company only to the extent of monitoring performance—to make certain that decisions were in line with his company's goals and policies.

Top managers had ample time for such strategic planning. Committee meetings and routine briefings had long been eliminated. The chief executive carried out communications with a voice-writer, color TV-telephone and computer display board. In strategic planning, he concentrated on formulating specialized management principles which would eventually be built into the computer; the computer could then offer solutions to specific problems in line with management principles and company goals.

When he wasn't planning, the manager was studying. His administrative aide (upgraded from secretary) helped assemble research and study sources.

His study efforts were considered an essential part of his daily chores. For in the nonroutine industries, a manager needed a deep knowledge of the natural sciences, the arts, the social sciences and the physical sciences. All in all, he needed to keep abreast of 10 different fields in detail, and he needed a good conceptual knowledge of 90 others.

Other things had changed for the manager too. Communications had removed the necessity for most face-to-face meetings, and communicating itself was much briefer. And the proliferation of governmental authorities, with their overlapping jurisdictions, finally gave way in the late 1970s to a balance of federal and regional authorities, making communicating with government easier.

Solutions to problems were still tailor-made, but they were no longer "messy." With government, industry and education working toward the common goals of improving the quality of life, conflict of interest—that had made for patchwork solutions in the 1960s—had been largely eliminated.

Not all problems had been ironed out in the last third of the 20th Century, of course. The knowledge explosion, for instance, was never really tamed. Despite the compression and fast transmission of data in forms other than the old printed word, managers had still to find some way to keep completely current, because knowledge kept doubling at ever faster rates. The typical manager in the year 2000 was more or less resigned to the idea that he would never know all he needed to know.

But, on the whole, for the manager, the satisfactions in reaching the 21st Century far outweighed any yearnings for simpler times. His skills had played no small part in easing burdens so that people had more meaningful control over their lives, enabling them to manage their own destinies.

51. THE COMING AGE OF MANAGEMENT INFORMATION SYSTEMS

EARL C. JOSEPH*

By the mid-1970s, unless managers use management information systems in their daily conduct of business, they will find themselves incapable of performing management tasks.

Tomorrow's managers at all levels and for all functions will be deeply involved in the use of computers. They will make daily use of computers in carrying out their management responsibilities. This involvement will be the result partially of the greater knowledge of the computer's power possessed by the young men entering corporate financial management and partially of the many programs that will become available to help executives.

Today's educational institutions have a special need to prepare their students for the age when the computer will serve as a partner in the management of any business. Industry must also educate its managers and professionals to use computers. The opportunities to use computers effectively, with their tremendous capabilities for assisting management, represent a real challenge to managers and computer system designers alike. Here, in the implementation of the computer for management use, is the future promise for curing the problems and ills now facing the professional manager.

The computer's role is to help management executives organize and manage as they desire. There is little doubt that computers will become increasingly important in helping executives achieve their goals. This trend is clearly visible today by the greatly expanding range of computer applications currently being implemented and used. It is especially encouraging to see these management aids evolve into systems that are really being used.

SOURCE: *Financial Executive* (August, 1969), pp. 45–52. Reprinted by permission of *Financial Executive*.

* Univac Company.

Indicative of the expanding role of computers is the placement of computer operations and decisions at higher levels in the organization. The trend is to move EDP management away from its traditional assignment under the controller or financial officer and to give it executive status of its own. This movement is an assertion that the computer can help all areas of management rather than just the traditional areas. The shift upward clearly points to management's awareness of the computer's importance. Such movement merges computerized information systems, placing financial and operational levels closer together.

A question that has been often asked in the last year or so is, "Is MIS practical today?" The answer is yes, because:

- Computers are now large enough and fast enough.
- Memories have sufficient capacity and have become economical;
- Time sharing, which permits multiple access computing, allows many users (managers) to use the computer at the same time;
- Multiprogramming and multiprocessing systems have been developed;
- A basic set of computer programs to support the needs of MIS are now available.

Today, terminals connected to a remote computer can be used by a number of managers at a cost of $10 to $20 an hour. It's not very much, is it? In fact, in many cases, it is less than it would cost to add a man to your staff. We also have large computers that have been around a few years and which we have learned how to use. They are fast enough to accommodate many managers on line at the same time. And we now have the economical mass storage that makes management information systems feasible.

What about the future? What will happen

in the 1970s that will make it even easier to use the computer for management information systems? First let's look at programs. We are going to have total operating systems to support the computer system operation. One of the most important types of programs we are going to have is the packaged program—packages of application programs and packages of systems programs, where the manager requesting information can piece together his management information systems when he needs them. We can't do that very easily today, because today's computers do not adapt to our language. The next generation of computers will adapt to man's language.

Another thing holding management information systems back is the cost of the terminal. Computer graphic terminals are somewhat costly, but their cost will come down drastically in the near future. In fact, in the late 1970s we can expect to be able to afford the graphic terminal on just about every manager's desk. Bell Telephone Laboratories expects to have 100,000 picture phones in use before 1975, and over a million in use between 1975 and 1980. That's a powerful lot of picture phones! And picture phones make nice computer terminals for presenting graphic real-time data of what is going on in the company.

We can also expect some breakthrough in the mass memory area from about 1972 to 1974. These breakthroughs will lead to extremely large memories of 100 billion bits or more at very low cost. The storage will be random access—we will be able to get at the data in microseconds.

All of this taken together is going to make it almost impossible *not* to use management information systems. Today, if your company were to implement MIS for your business from scratch by piecing together parts of programs, designing and programming other parts, it would be very costly—sometimes millions of dollars.

REAL-TIME ASSISTANT

By 1975, to do the same thing will cost tens of thousands. The cost to the on-line user, to you as the manager, for having a computer assist in making decisions, will be measured in pennies.

This is why we won't be able to get along without the computer in business. The computer will have such an effect on business that we will not be doing business as we are today. Managers will not be making decisions as they are today. It will bring about a tremendous revolution in business, perhaps one of the largest.

Not only is equipment changing, but the concept of management information systems itself is changing. Another word is being added —"control." Management information and control systems. In this type of system, management is going to have an assistant to control the business in real-time and provide a service on-line to its people and its customers.

In the past, management information systems meant programs to handle the administrative details. Most management information systems are like that today. There are other types, however. MIS aid is needed for planning and scheduling; for assisting managers in the decision-making process; and for management control—the current awareness function. If the manager has to dig out the information manually, he usually cannot dig it out in time to make use of it. So what we need is a system, a type of exception reporting system, that makes the manager aware of information at the time he needs to know it.

In this type of system there is the environmental feedback on how the total business is operating—the total company including the customer. It will operate in a closed-loop fashion, where the computer decides what to run as a result of the information it is getting. Today, practically all of our computer operations are triggered by specific commands for specific tasks. In the type of system we are looking for in the future (it is projected by 1975), the computer will decide what program should be run.

I am not talking about a type of system where the computer is going to take over, but strictly a type of system that is an aid to the people in the system—an aid to the managers and professionals. I am talking about a system that will tie in all the people in an organization, on-line. It will keep in its files updated profiles of the information needs of each person in the system. Each has changing needs (changes from day to day, month to month, year to year) and, therefore, each profile of information requirements needs to be kept up to date. The computer itself will keep track of these changes for each individual as they occur.

The system will allow the user to question

the system by asking, "What happens if I do this?" The "what if" question requires a powerful programming system to back it up. The computer needs to run a simulation of the total operation of the company, including the customers. That is a pretty big order.

But these types of simulations are now becoming available. When the manager is allowed to ask the computer, "What happens if I do this?" the computer runs a simulation which will give him a tested answer or a tested set of alternatives. Thus, a manager can test out a decision before he implements it by getting from the computer the probable outcome. Imagine how important it would be for managers to be able to ask that type of question.

We have a few such systems in the research stage already. Such systems will call managers —dial them up on the telephone and speak to them—to pass on high priority information and to trigger managers into action. These elaborate systems will make management by exception a reality. I think from this you can see how powerful management information systems will be in the coming decade.

To illustrate how these systems work, I would like to set up a hypothetical example. Suppose I am the manager and put into the computer my PERT updating information. (PERT is a planning tool that allows the computer to determine whether I will meet my schedule. The information I put in is my best guess of where I am and of how long it will take me to do certain items.) If I put in my current input this week and the computer runs the analysis program and determines I am going to have 13 weeks negative slack, I am going to miss my schedule by almost three months! If I am working on a six-month project, three months late is pretty bad. What does the computer do? It calls me up on the telephone and makes me painfully aware of this fact.

Next week I put in my PERT input (if I try to beat the system by not putting it in, the computer is going to run the PERT assuming that there is no change), and supposing I don't do a very good job of improving my situation, I will still have a negative slack. Instead of calling me up and telling me that I am going to be late, the computer also calls my boss. You can see how the computer is starting to control its environment!

Let's say the following week I put in my input and I still didn't improve enough. Instead of calling up just me and my boss, it calls up my bosses' boss. 1984? No; it is the opposite. It allows the manager to do the job of management in real time; it tells him when he must do something to help the situation —like how to keep me from getting fired.

Another example: A foreman comes in in the morning—quite a bit earlier than the people working for him. What does he do? He goes to the stockroom to see what stocks are available; he goes around to each machine to see which ones are operating; he goes to the time clock to see who has punched in; and then he assigns the jobs. In the meantime, he has to look at the planning chart to see what he has planned out and what things have to be done that day rather than the next or next week. He has to do these things over and over again each day. It is a lot of leg work. He does not have a lot of time to do the things that any foreman or any manager should do—to interface with people. He shouldn't have to do the same thing over and over again.

DAILY ROUTINE CHANGES

With the aid of an MIS, the foreman's day would start differently. The computer would have printed out the itinerary for the day when the foreman arrives at work; it would keep track of what is in the stockroom; it would keep track of what machines are operable; it would keep track of people as they punch in. And so the computer has all the information it needs to print out the itinerary after looking over the planning chart to see what the foreman previously planned. The foreman is left with the details of interfacing with the people—the thing he should be doing.

But the day isn't over yet. At 10:00 machine "B" breaks down, and Mary Jo goes home because she has a toothache. What does the foreman have to do? He has to re-do completely the morning cycle. He must go back to the crib to see what materials are there, what machines are available, whom he can reassign, and so forth.

With an on-line management information system, what would he have to do? The computer would already know that Mary Jo went home because she punched out. The computer, depending upon the type of system you have, may or may not know that the machine broke down. If it doesn't, the foreman puts that information in. The computer then types out or calls up on the telephone, depending on the type of system you have, what the alternatives are for the foreman, thereby saving him considerable time.

For still another example, let us suppose I am a computer designer and I get a new assignment: I have to design a new, medium-scale computer, and I have to design the program address counter. Program address counters have been designed thousands of times. Why should I have to design it over again?

If I had a system such as an on-line MIS where I could retrieve the information, the system would know even ahead of me that I am going to get this assignment. It could then send through the mail, instead of calling me up on the telephone, the possible designs that I might use. Then I make a selection from the possibilities described by the computer rather than run to various other designers and the libraries, ending up not finding anything I can use and redesigning the counter. The computer would then tell me what part needs to be changed or optimized.

So I can save a lot of time by using management information systems. They do the leg work that I am currently required to do today.

Computers designed specifically for management information systems are non-existent today. We are using computers designed for application to general purposes. What about the future? We are starting to design for MIS. Future systems will be more modular, allowing both hardware and software to be pieced together and tailored for MIS.

What specifically do we need for MIS? We need lots of memory capacity. We need hardware in our computer systems that assists with the task of file protection and security—many levels of locks and keys. We need a fast mass memory.

What is happening in the area of fast mass memory is rather dramatic. Memory units are speeding up and coming down in cost by a factor of more than 10 every 10 years. This trend is still continuing. The cost of memory in the mid-1950s was about $1 per bit; in the mid-1960s it was about 10 cents per bit; and by the mid-1970s, if this progression continues, we can expect it to be about one tenth of a cent.

THINGS WILL BE DONE DIFFERENTLY

There is going to be an even bigger cost reduction for random-access high-speed memory. The cost for such memory is going to come down to considerably less than one cent per bit. The improvement in costs for this type of memory will be a factor of 10 or 100. You can't imagine what this is going to do for the computer field. We just won't do things the way we used to.

In the mid-1950s the average speed of the main memory was about 10 microseconds; by the mid-1960s, about one microsecond; and by the mid-1970s a tenth to a hundredth of a microsecond is predicted. Capacity of memories? Here again we see a breakthrough—one of the reasons why the cost is coming down. Memory capacity has been increasing by a factor of 10 per 10 years. In the mid-1950s the central memory capacity of the computer was about 100 thousand bits; in the mid-1960s, one million to 10 million bits. By the mid-1970s the capacity of the central memory will be close to a billion bits of memory. This is exactly what we need to make management information systems economically feasible. The cost of the memory and the speed at which information can be processed are the main things holding back MIS. But this will soon change.

Before 1960, the cost of a single logic gate was $2.00. Today, with the advent of integrated circuits and MSI (medium scale integration of circuits), a gate cost about 10 cents. In the early 1970s, between 1970 and 1971, we can expect that the cost will be about a penny or so per gate. Soon thereafter they will be considerably less costly, and programs with built-in logic will be feasible.

Another trend is occurring in the input-output areas: the use of computers via remote computer terminals. Terminals, especially the cathode-ray tube terminal, need to become less expensive—and they will. Storage near to the terminal will be necessary. In fact we are approaching the era of the "intelligent terminal"—terminals that will do a number of things that computers now do. These terminals can be located at the source of the data and at data dissemination points. It is at these points that we need some of the computer's capabilities, and the future "intelligent terminals" will provide us with these capabilities.

COMPUTERS STILL MAKE MISTAKES

The main thing that has held up the time-sharing portion of the MIS system, and time sharing in general, has been the low reliability of systems. Computers are considerably more reliable than they were in the past, but they still make mistakes. The mean-time between failures in the early to mid-1950s was measured in a few hours; in other words, one error every hour or two. In the mid-1960s the mean-time is considerably longer. For the central processing unit, the computer, mean-time between failures is measured in thousands to ten thousands of hours. In the total system —the peripherals, the memory, and the CPU —it is again down to a few hours. A few tens of hours in most cases. This is not reliable enough when you have hundreds or thousands of people on-line using the computer.

Univac is making a breakthrough in this area. We have improved the reliability of our total system so that the mean-time between failures is measured in years. Greater reliability has been accomplished by implementations of such things as self-repair—the capability of switching from a failing component to a good component. In other words, the system has built-in spare parts.

The biggest problem in the computer field is programming. The problem arises because computers do not use the language that you and I would like to use.

Language—computer language and the language with which we communicate with one another—has developed along similar lines. Languages start out with a few number of words. For example, early computers had from 15 to 60 instructions.

The next stage in development of any language is to make the basic words more complete. Latin is a very good example. Latin words have a lot of beginnings and endings and sentences have complex structures. Today's computers are like that. We have maybe 100 to 200 instructions in the repertoire with many thousands of variations on those instructions. In fact, we built one computer which had 64 instructions with a total of 30,000 variations.

What would happen if writers were restricted to 100 different words? You can imagine how long it would take them to express their ideas. This is part of the problem we have in communicating with computers: it takes a long time to program them.

Thus, the next step—one that we are beginning now with our software—is to get rid of some of the complexity and add words as they are needed. Computers will be designed to allow the user to specify the words or the instructions that he needs.

Such systems are called extensible or enhanceable language systems. They give the computer the ability to adapt to language, whether it is English or Russian, the language of a manager, a chemist, a manufacturing foreman, or the top executive. Many different languages can be conditioned in at the same time.

PROGRAMMING—THE BIGGEST COST

The primary purpose of such systems is to avoid the expense of lengthy programming. At present we spend more than 75 per cent of our total system cost for programming. In the early 1950s we spent only about 5 per cent. In the 1965 era we hit the half-way mark; 50 per cent of our cost was in the hardware and 50 per cent was in the software. But today, only four years later, we are up to 75 per cent, and we are projecting that by 1970 about 80 to 85 per cent of the total cost of the system will be attributable to programming. This makes it mandatory that we use our old or current programs on our next generation system.

With language enhanceable systems, we can capitalize on past software investments. Specifically, we can tell our new computer to imitate the languages of the old computers that the programs we want to use were written for. This will save billions of dollars of software (currently in the neighborhood of $3 to $5 billion of software is in use). In the past, we threw away our software investment when we went to the next generation system. There was no way of capitalizing on it. We can't afford that any longer, and our next generation's systems must be able to capitalize on this software investment—and they will.

In spite of the many changes coming in the field, computers are going to stay in the field a lot longer. The average life of a computer in the 1950s and 1960s was about three to five years. In the 1970s we are predicting up to 10 years for the life of the computer system. This is both good and bad: we can evolve into the system we are using, and thus make the programs more useful and less costly. It allows us to get our applications working so that we will not have to re-do them as the next piece of hardware comes out, as we did in the past. But, if our computers are going to stay out in the field longer, it is going to take longer for new innovations to get into the hardware. In other words, we will sort of batch the new "goodies" before we put them into our computers.

The longer life predicted for future computer systems is especially nice for the management information system. It will allow us to evolve these applications rather than to revolutionize them, and more managers will evolve into using MIS. But, as a company starts to use management information systems, it soon learns it never really had any problems before. Why is this? The answer is simply that you don't really know your problems until you see them in real-time. With management information systems, however, we have one big difference: we have the tool to do something about the problems that are newly made visible.

We can also expect that in the 1970s we are going to have some new communication systems. In fact, the technology might allow us to get out of the Gutenberg rut that we have been in for many hundreds of years. Some people, myself included, are predicting that sometime in the late 1970s we will be going to "paperless books." In some senses, we are almost there now. A lot of people don't read newspapers any longer. Most of our young people do not rely upon the newspapers or magazines or journals for news. They rely on TV. We can expect that because of the cost and problems of getting technical information, we are going to go on-line with the computer to disseminate such information.

The number of steps which an author must tread to get an idea to the reader is tremendous today. In my experience, which I think is typical, I go through maybe three or four drafts, with my secretary typing each. Maybe two or three editors go through it in a hurry a number of times.

THE COMPUTER—JACK-OF-ALL-TRADE

Just think how the process would be speeded up if I had a computer that would take over these secretarial and editing functions, in real-time, with my input to the computer. Suppose I have an interactive system where I can get a dialogue going with the computer, in real-time, where the computer helps the total process. It corrects the spelling, edits, takes out or tells me about redundant information, tells me that I should reorder the information to connect up this thought with that thought, etc. Can you imagine how easy it would be to be an author when we have such an aid? It would considerably speed up the way we get thoughts down so other people can use them.

Instead of printing out the edited manuscript, the computer can send it on-line to some publisher. Which publisher? It is not somebody who is going to produce a book or a journal. It is somebody who is going to distribute the information completely by electronic means to the user. So, the main purpose of the publisher here is to decide whether this piece of material is worth publishing. Once that decision is made, it goes out in real-time.

Suppose major cities have computers that are communicating with many users—an information utility. The users' first look at the author's information would not be the total material but an abstract of the material (located by title or key words or something like that). For some users there would be kept profile files of the material they want or are interested in. So the system would be set up to make these individuals aware of the new information that is available. And when information of interest is generated, the utility makes them aware of it. However, most users would query the system. They would actually see something that they like or think they can use, then they would look at the textual material.

Future picture phones and the current CRT terminals are good enough to do some browsing in this type of information utility system. In fact, we can envision even flat types of display devices that can be carried just like a book and probably weigh no more. These devices allow us to be on-line with the computer/communications systems in the 1970 decade. Can you imagine how much quicker ideas would be passed out. Can you imagine how the business of transmitting information and the publishing business would change? Can you imagine how much cheaper it would be to the user to get information if he did not have to go through all the steps that we go through now, of printing the material and distributing it?

PROGRAM CHANGES COMING

Programs are going to change quite a bit in the next generation. They are going to be modular, first of all. With the third generation computer system, we have quite a bit of modular hardware with which the user pieces together the system. The fourth generation computer will have modular programs—both system and applications programs. But most importantly, we are going to have application packages, such as MIS.

In summary, MIS systems and the computers to run them will be bigger, more economical, and easier to use. Future computer systems will contain many new features, commonly called "bells and whistles." And as always, some will prove to be useless and others will lead to new problems as time marches on. Hopefully, most of them will be found to be useful. They will also be more reliable, less costly, and have more built-in features, there will be more application programs for management use, more memory capacity, and greater efficiency.

No fact of contemporary life is more challenging to society than the present rapidly advancing technology and continual managerial change. These changes are speeded by the computer and communications industries. We could never go back to the pre-computer era—our dependence on computers is now far too great. Not only are the material and economic conditions of life enhanced and affected by this advanced tool of the cybernated age; it has and will continue to effect far-reaching changes in the way we manage.

Those of us working in the computerized management information system field are predicting that such systems certainly will evolve and come into mass use by executives. We further predict that those managers, companies, politicians, and governments who do not use such systems by 1975 to 1980 will simply not be able to compete in a society which does.

WHERE ARE WE GOING?

I have tried to put on tomorrow's glasses in order to see where we can go, rather than wear yesterday's glasses and see only how bad it was. I have fixed primarily on the period five to ten years hence. Because of the high cost of programming and the need to capitalize on the costly investment in programs, new advances and ideas will tend in the future to rest on the shelf much longer than advances have in the past. The state of the economy that surrounds programming will govern our actions more than we would like; it will inhibit our ability to advance into the future as promptly as we know we could. Thus, there should, of course, be some skepticism concerning the certainty of these predictions. The era that we thought we had entered when yesterday's advances sparked heated controversy, only to drop in importance as even more revolutionary hardware changes were thrust upon us, now appears to have been altered into an era where today's problems could be with us for a long time to come.

Author Index

Subject Index